COMMENTARIES

ON THE

Laws of England

IN FOUR BOOKS

BY

SIR WILLIAM BLACKSTONE, Knight

One of the Justices of His Majesty's Court of Common Pleas

WITH

NOTES SELECTED FROM THE EDITIONS OF ARCHBOLD, CHRISTIAN, COLE-
RIDGE, CHITTY, STEWART, KERR, AND OTHERS; AND IN ADDITION,
NOTES AND REFERENCES TO ALL TEXT BOOKS AND
DECISIONS WHEREIN THE COMMENTARIES HAVE
BEEN CITED, AND ALL STATUTES
MODIFYING THE TEXT

BY

WILLIAM DRAPER LEWIS, Ph. D.

Dean of the Department of Law of the University of Pennsylvania

BOOK 3

PHILADELPHIA
REES WELSH & COMPANY
1900

CONTENTS OF THE ANALYSIS OF BOOK III.

PRIVATE WRONGS.

CONTENTS OF THE ANALYSIS OF BOOK IV.

PUBLIC WRONGS.

ANALYSIS.

BOOK IV.*—OF PUBLIC WRONGS.

CHAPTER XVIII.

CHAPTER XIX.

CHAPTER XX.

COMMENTARIES

ON

THE LAWS OF ENGLAND

BOOK III

OF PRIVATE WRONGS

COMMENTARIES

ON

THE LAWS OF ENGLAND.

BOOK THE THIRD.

Of Private Wrongs.

CHAPTER I.

OF THE REDRESS OF PRIVATE WRONGS BY THE MERE ACT OF THE PARTIES.

At the opening of these commentaries,(*a*) municipal law was in general defined to be, "a rule of civil conduct, prescribed by the supreme power in a state, commanding what is right, and prohibiting what is wrong."(*b*)(1) From hence therefore it followed, that the primary objects of the law are the establishment of rights, and the prohibition of wrongs. And this occasioned(*c*) the distribution of these collections into two general heads; under the former of which we have already considered the *rights* that were defined and established, and under the latter are now to consider the wrongs that are forbidden and redressed, by the laws of England.

*2]   *In the prosecution of the first of these inquiries, we distinguished rights into two sorts: first, such as concern, or are annexed to, the persons of men, and are then called *jura personarum*, or *the rights of persons;* which, together with the means of acquiring and losing them, composed the first book of these commentaries: and secondly, such as a man may acquire over external objects, or things unconnected with his person, which are called *jura rerum*, or *the rights of things:* and these, with the means of transferring them from man to man, were the subject of the second book. I am now therefore to proceed to the consideration of *wrongs;* which for the most part convey to us an idea merely negative, as being nothing else but a privation of right. For which reason it was necessary, that before we entered at all into the discussion of wrongs, we should entertain a clear and distinct notion of rights: the contemplation of what is *jus*(2) being necessarily prior to what

---

(*a*) Introd. § 2.
(*b*) *Sanctio justa, jubens honesta, et prohibens con-*

traria. Cic. 11. *Philipp.* 12. Bract. *l.* 1, c. 3.
(*c*) Book i. ch. 1.

---

(1) I imagine this to be a misquotation of the following passage:—" Est enim lex nihil aliud, nisi recta et a numine Deorum tracta ratio, imperans honesta, prohibens contraria." Phil. xi. 12.—Coleridge. ["Law is nothing else than right reason drawn from the will of the gods, commanding what is right and prohibiting the contrary."]
(2) [Right.]

may be termed *injuria*,(3) and the definition of *fas*(4) precedent to that of *nefas*.(5)

Wrongs are divisible into two sorts or species: *private wrongs* and *public wrongs*. The former are an infringement or privation of the private or civil rights belonging to individuals, considered as individuals; and are thereupon frequently termed *civil injuries:*(6) the latter are a breach and violation of public rights and duties, which affect the whole community, considered as a community; and are distinguished by the harsher appellation of *crimes* and *misdemeanors*. To investigate the first of these species of wrongs, with their legal remedies, will be our employment in the present book; and the other species will be reserved till the next or concluding one.

The more effectually to accomplish the redress of private injuries, courts of justice are instituted in every civilized society, in order to protect the weak from the insults of the stronger, by expounding and enforcing those laws, by which rights are defined and wrongs prohibited. This remedy is there-
*3] fore *principally* to be sought by application to these *courts of justice; that is, by civil suit or action. For which reason our chief employment in this book will be to consider the redress of private wrongs by *suit* or *action* in courts. But as there are certain injuries of such a nature that some of them furnish and others require a more speedy remedy than can be had in the ordinary forms of justice, there is allowed in those cases an extrajudicial or eccentrical kind of remedy; of which I shall first of all treat, before I consider the several remedies by suit: and, to that end, shall distribute the redress of private wrongs into three several species: first, that which is obtained by the *mere act* of the *parties* themselves; secondly, that which is effected by the *mere act* and operation of *law;* and, thirdly, that which arises from *suit* or *action* in courts, which consists in a conjunction of the other two, the act of the parties co-operating with the act of law.(7)

And *first* of that redress of *private* injuries which is obtained by the *mere* act of the *parties*. This is of two sorts: first, that which arises from the act of the injured party only; and, secondly, that which arises from the joint act of all the parties together: both which I shall consider in their order.

Of the first sort, or that which arises from the sole act of the injured party, is

I. The *defence* of one's self, or the mutual and reciprocal defence of such as stand in the relations of husband and wife, parent and child, master and servant. In these cases, if the party himself, or *any* of these his relations,(8)

---

(3) [Injury.]
(4) [Lawful.]
(5) [Unlawful.]
(6) For further definition of wrongs see Ayers *et al. v.* Lawrence *et al.*, 59 N. Y. 198 (1874). Dow *v.* Norris, 4 N. H. 20 (1827). Huntington *v.* Attrill, 146 U. S. 669 (1892). State *v.* Rickey *et al.*, 9 Halstead's Rep. (N. J.) 293 (1827).
(7) Territory *v.* Flowers. 2 Mon. 531; 534 (1877).
(8) It is said that, according to 1 Salk. 407, 1 Ld. Raym. 62, and Bul. N. P. 18, a master cannot justify an assault in defence of his servant, because he might have an action *per quod servitium amisit* [By which he lost his service] (see Book 1, p. 429). But, according to 2 Rol. Abr. 546, D. pl. 2, Owen, 151, Bac. Abr. Master and Servant, P., such an interference by the master is lawful; and lord Hale (1 vol. 484) says, "That the law had been for a master killing in the necessary defence of his servant, the husband in defence of his wife, the wife of the husband, the child of the parent, or the parent of the child, for the act of the assistant shall have the same construction in such cases as the act of the party assisted should have had if it had been done by himself; for they are in a mutual relation to one another." But though, as observed by the learned commentator, the law respects the passions of the human mind, yet it does not allow this interference as an indulgence of revenge, but merely to *prevent* the injury, or a repetition of it; and therefore, in a plea by a father, master, etc., founded on this ground, it is necessary to state that the plaintiff *would* have *beat* the son, servant, etc., if the defendant had not interfered; and if it be merely alleged that the plaintiff *had* assaulted or beat, etc., it will be demurrable, for if the assault on

be forcibly attacked in his person or property, it is lawful for him to repel force by force; and the breach of the peace which happens is chargeable upon him only who began the affray.(d) For the law in this case respects the passions of the human mind, and (when external violence is offered to a man himself, or those to whom he bears a near connection) makes it lawful in him to do himself that immediate justice to which he *is prompted   [*4 by nature, and which no prudential motives are strong enough to restrain.

It considers that the future process of law is by no means an adequate remedy for injuries accompanied with force; since it is impossible to say to what wanton lengths of rapine or cruelty outrages of this sort might be carried unless it were permitted a man immediately to oppose one violence with another.(9) Self-defence, therefore, as it is justly called the primary law of nature, so it is not, neither can it be in fact, taken away by the law of society.(10) In the English law particularly it is held an excuse for breaches of the peace, nay, even for homicide itself: but care must be taken that the resistance does not exceed the bounds of mere defence and prevention: for then the defender would himself become an aggressor.(11)

II. Recaption or *reprisal* is another species of remedy by the mere act of the party injured. This happens when any one hath deprived another of his property in goods or chattels personal, or wrongfully detains one's wife, child, or servant: in which case the owner of the goods, and the husband, parent, or master, may lawfully claim and retake them wherever he happens to find them, so it be not in a riotous manner, or attended with a breach of the peace.(e) The reason for this is obvious; since it may frequently happen that the owner may have this only opportunity of doing himself justice: his goods may be afterwards conveyed away or destroyed; and his wife, children, or servants concealed or carried out of his reach; if he had no speedier remedy than the ordinary process of law. If therefore he can so contrive it as to gain possession of his property again without force or terror, the law favors and will justify his proceeding. But as the public peace is a superior consideration to any one man's private property; and as, if individuals were once allowed to use private force as a remedy for private injuries, all social

(d) 2 Roll. Abr. 546. 1 Hawk. P. C. 131.   (e) 3 Inst. 134. Hal. Anal. § 46.

---

the master, etc. be over, the servant cannot strike by way of revenge, but merely in order to prevent an injury. 2 Stra. 953. When a person does not stand in either of these relations, he cannot justify an interference *on behalf* of the party injured, but merely as an indifferent person, to preserve the peace. 2 Stra. 954.—CHITTY. See Webb's Pollock on Torts, 201. A son is justified in using the same means to protect his mother, who is seriously ill, against danger to her life by the noise of rioters, as though such danger resulted from an attack upon her person. Patten v. The People, 18 Mich. 314. The defence of a servant will be excused or justified by the same means used to justify or excuse the defence of one's self. Pond v. The People, 4 Cooley (Mich.) 205.

(9) A man may justify an assault and battery in defence of his land or goods or the goods of another delivered to him to be kept. Hawks, P. C. b. 1, c. 60, § 23. Seaman v. Compledick Owen's R. 150. But one is not justified in assaulting a trespasser without first requesting him to depart or desist and upon his refusal sufficient force may be used to compel him. Weaver v. Bush, 8 Term R. 78. Butler's N. P. 19, 1 East, P. C. 406. But where notice to desist or depart cannot be given from the nature of the case, it may be dispensed with. Pond v. The People, 4 Cooley (Mich.) 150. As to the amount of force one may use, see Scribner v. Beach, 4 Denio, 450 (1847). 2 Barb. Rights of Persons and Property, 774. Pond v. The People, 4 Cooley (Mich.) 150 (1860). Logue v. The Commonwealth, 38 Pa. 265 (1869).

(10) Law of Self Defense, Anthony, 3.

(11) The force should be no more than is sufficient to ward off the injury. Malone's Criminal Briefs, 291 (1886). People v. McLeod, 1 Hill (N. Y.) 420 (1841). The quality, quantity and time of justifiable defence depend upon the reasonable necessity of each case and the reasonable necessity, depending upon the particular circumstances of the case, is a question of fact. Aldrich v. Wright, 53 New Hampshire, 419 (1873).

justice must cease, the strong would give law to the weak, and every man
        would revert to a state of nature; for these reasons it is provided that
*5]   this natural right of recaption *shall never be exerted where such exer-
        tion must occasion strife and bodily contention, or endanger the peace
of society. If, for instance, my horse is taken away, and I find him in a
common, a fair, or a public inn, I may lawfully seize him to my own use; but
I cannot justify breaking open a private stable, or entering on the grounds
of a third person, to take him, except he be feloniously stolen;(*f*) but must
have recourse to an action at law.(12)

III. As recaption is a remedy given to the party himself for an injury to
his *personal* property, so, thirdly, a remedy of the same kind for injuries to
real property is by *entry* on lands and tenements when another person without any right has taken possession thereof.(13) This depends in some
measure on like reasons with the former; and like that, too, must be peaceable and without force. There is some nicety required to define and distinguish the cases in which such entry is lawful or otherwise; it will therefore
be more fully considered in a subsequent chapter; being only mentioned in
this place for the sake of regularity and order.

(*f*) 2 Roll. Rep. 55, 56, 208. 2 Roll. Abr. 565, 566.

(12) In the case of personal property improperly detained or taken away, it may be
retaken from the house and custody of the wrong-doer, even without a previous request.
Bowler *v.* Eldridge, 18 Conn. 1, 17 (1846). Where one's property is wrongfully taken, the
owner may retake it wherever he may find it. He may enter upon the lands of another
to do so providing he gives notice of his intent. But he is not justified in breaking the
peace. Richardson *v.* Bartley, 2 Monroe (Ky.) 328 (1842). And, unless it was seized or
attempted to be seized forcibly, the owner cannot justify doing any thing more than
gently laying his hands on the wrong-doer in order to recover it, (8 T. R. 78. 2 Roll.
Abr. 56, 208. 2 Roll. Abr. 565, pl. 50. 2 Leonard, 302. Selw. N. P. tit. Assault and Battery;)
nor can he without leave enter the door of a *third* person, not privy to the wrongful
detainer, to take his goods therefrom. 2 Roll. Abr. 55, 56, 308. 2 Roll. Abr. 565, I. pl.
2. Bac. Abr. Trespass, F.
    If the possession of one's property be held by another, the owner may take possession
if he can do so without tumult and riot or breach of the peace; but he has no right to
use unreasonable violence. Davis *v.* Whitridge, 2 Strobh. 232.
    The owner of personal property left in the possession of a third person may, by his
own act, repossess himself of such property, though it be taken from the possession of
such third person by virtue of a writ of replevin; and the plaintiff in the replevin cannot
maintain trespass against him. Spencer *v.* McGowen, 13 Wend. 256. One whose chattel
has been wrongfully taken from him may enter upon the land of the taker for the purpose of retaking it, without subjecting himself even to nominal damages. Chambers *v.*
Bedell, 2 Watts & Serg. 225.—Sharswood.
    But where one lawfully acquires possession of the property the owner is not justified in
entering upon his land to retake the goods. The Law of Torts, Clark and Lindsell, 270
(1889). Hilliard's Law of Torts, 139 (3 ed.). Marvell *v.* Gray's Lessee, 1 Swan's 104 (1851).
Moore *v.* Shenk, 3 Pa. 19 (1846). Anthony *v.* Haney, 1 Moore and Scott's Reports, 307–8.
Bingham's, 193 (1832). Shireman *v.* Jackson, 14 Ind. 460 (1860). Yet, where one makes
a forcible entry in order to gain possession of land wrongfully detained, an action for
trespass will not lie, although an indictment for breach of the peace may be had. Jackson *v.* Stansbury, 9 Wend. 201 (1832). Bowler *v.* Eldridge, 18 Conn. 1 (1846).
    Where one sells goods which are in his possession the vendee has an implied license to
take them. Lawson's Personal and Property Rights, 1764 (1890).
    (13) With respect to *land* and houses also, resumption of possession by the mere act of
the party is frequently allowed. Thus, if a tenant omit at the expiration of his tenancy
to deliver up possession, the landlord may legally, in his absence, break open the outer
door and resume possession, though some articles of furniture remain therein; and, if
the landlord put his cattle on the land, and the tenant distrain them as damage-feasant,
he may be sued. 1 Bing. R. 158. 7 T. R. 431, 432. 1 Price R. 53. And. 109. 6 Taunt.
202. If the landlord, in resuming possession, be guilty of a forcible entry with strong
hand, or other illegal breach of the peace, he will be liable to an indictment. 7 T. R.
432. 3 T. R. 295. 6 Taunt. 202. 8 T. R. 364, 403. But the circumstance of the owner

IV. A fourth species of remedy by the mere act of the party injured is the *abatement* or removal of *nuisances*. (14)(15) What nuisances are, and their several species, we shall find a more proper place to inquire under some of the

of property using too much force in regaining possession, but taking care to avoid personal injury to the party resisting, will not enable the latter to sue him. See cases in last two notes. But if any unnecessary violence to the person be used in rescuing or defending possession of real or personal property, the party guilty of it is liable to be sued. 8 T. R. 299. Id. 78. 1 Saund. 296, n. 1. So, as the law allows retaking of the possession of land, it also sanctions the due defence of the possession thereof; and therefore, though if one enter into my ground I must request him to depart before I can lay hands on him to turn him out, yet if he refuse I may then push him out, and if he enter with actual force I need not first request him to be gone, but may lay hands on him immediately. 8 T. R. 78. 1 Salk. 641. See 1 Bing. 158. See also, Newkirk *v*. Sabler, 9 N. Y. 652, 657 (1851). See also Washburn's Easements and Servitudes (4 ed.) 715, 758. Jackson & Gross' Landlord and Tenant in Pennsylvania (2 ed.) 743.

(14) As to the right of an individual to abate a public nuisance there is some conflict of opinion, but it is generally conceded that any one, irrespective of the personal injury done, may do so. Hart *v*. Mayor, etc., of Albany, 9 Wend. (N. Y.) 609 (1832). Little *v*. Ince., 2 Upper Canada, C. P. 545 (1854). Griffith *v*. McCullum, 46 Barb. (N. Y.) 561 (1853–4). Harrower *v*. Petson, 37 N. Y. 301 (1862). There is no absolute general rule on the subject. Each particular case depends upon its own circumstances. Watts *v*. Norfolk and W. R. R. Co., 39 W. Virginia, 211 (1895). But a civil action will not lie for a public nuisance unless special injury has been done thereby. Justices etc. *v*. Griffin and West Point Plank Road Co., 15 Georgia, 62 (1804).

Private nuisances may be abated by any one injured, thereby, providing that he does not create a riot or disturb the peace in the removal of it. 2 Barbour's Rights of Persons and Property, 779. Weimer *v*. Bunbury, 30 Michigan, 211 (1874). Brill *v*. Flagler, 23 Wendell (N. Y.) 357 (1840). But the abater of a nuisance is not justified in destroying anything other than that which constitutes or causes the nuisance. Thus, if a house is built too high, only that part which renders it a nuisance may be pulled down. Hoyt *v*. Kimball, 49 New Hampshire, 328 (1870). 9 Rep. 53. God. 221. 2 Stra. 686. A public nuisance may be abated without notice; likewise, a private nuisance arising by an act of commission and where the security of life or property requires such speedy remedy as would not allow time to give notice, one is justified in abating without notice, a private nuisance arising from an omission. Harvey *v*. DeWoody *et al.*, 18 Arkansas, 258 (1856).

(15) If a house be built across a highway, any person may pull it down; and it is said he need not observe particular care in abating it, so as to prevent injury to the materials. And though a gate, illegally fastened, might have been opened without cutting it down, yet the cutting would be lawful. However, it is a general rule that the abatement must be limited by its necessity, and no wanton or unnecessary injury must be committed. 2 Salk. 458. As to private nuisances, they also may be abated; and, therefore, it was recently held, that if a man in his own soil erect a thing which is a nuisance to another, as by stopping a rivulet and so diminishing the water used by the latter for his cattle, the party injured may enter on the soil of the other and abate the nuisance, and justify the trespass; and this right of abatement is not confined merely to a house, mill, or land. 2 Smith's Rep. 9. 2 Rol. Abr. 565. 2 Leon. 202. Com. Dig. Pleader, 3 M. 42. 3 Lev. 92. So it seems that a libellous print or paper, affecting a private individual, may be destroyed, or (which is the safer course) taken and delivered to a magistrate. 5 Coke, 125, b. 2 Camp. 511. Per Best, J., in the Earl Lonsdale *v*. Nelson, 2 Bar. & Cres. 311, "nuisances, by an act of *commission*, are committed in defiance of those whom such nuisances injure, and the injured party may abate them without notice to the person who committed them; but there is no decided case which sanctions the abatement by an individual of nuisances from *omission*, except that of cutting the branches of trees which overhang a public road or the private property of the person who cuts them. The permitting these branches to extend so far beyond the soil of the owner of the trees is an unequivocal act of negligence, which distinguishes this case from most of the other cases that have occurred. The security of lives and property may sometimes require so speedy a remedy as not to allow time to call on the person on whose property the mischief has arisen to remedy it: in such cases an individual would be justified in abating a nuisance from omission without notice. In all other cases of such nuisances, persons should not take the law into their own hands, but follow the advice of lord Hale, and appeal to a court of justice;" and see, further, 3 Dowl. & R. 556. And it was held in the same case, that where a person is bound to repair works connected with a port, and neglects to do so, another person cannot justify an entry to repair without averring and proving that immediate repairs were necessary, and the party's right to use the port. As to cutting trees, "if the boughs of your trees grow out into my land, I may cut them." Per

subsequent divisions. At present I shall only observe, that whatsoever unlawfully annoys or doth damage to another is a nuisance; and such nuisance may be abated, that is, taken away or removed, by the party aggrieved thereby, so as he commits no riot in the doing of it.(*g*) If a house or wall is erected so near to mine that it stops my ancient lights, which is a *private* nuisance, I may enter my neighbor's land and peaceably pull it down.(*h*) Or if a new gate be erected across the public highway, which is a *common* nuisance, any of the king's subjects passing that way may
*6]   cut it down and destroy it.(*i*)   *And the reason why the law allows this private and summary method of doing one's self justice, is because injuries of this kind, which obstruct or annoy such things as are of daily convenience and use, require an immediate remedy, and cannot wait for the slow progress of the ordinary forms of justice.

V. A fifth case in which the law allows a man to be his own avenger, or to minister redress to himself, is that of *distraining* cattle or goods for the non-payment of rent, or other duties;(16) or distraining another's cattle

---

(*g*) Rep. 101. 9 Rep. 55.
(*h*) Salk. 459.   (*i*) Cro. Car. 184.

Croke, J., Rol. Rep. 394. 3 Buls. 198. Vin. Abr. Trees, F. & tit. Nuisance, W. 2, pl. 3. —CHITTY.

(16) As to distresses in general, see Gilbert on Distresses, by Hunt; Bradley on Dist.; Com. Dig. Distress; Bac. Abr. Distress; Vin. Abr. Distress; 2 Saunders, index, Distress; Wilkinson on Replevin. Owen *v.* Boyle, 9 Maine 47. As the law allows a creditor to arrest the person of his debtor as a security for his being forthcoming at the determination of the suit, so in certain cases it permits a landlord to distrain for arrears of rent, in order to compel the payment of it. It is laid down that the remedy for recovery of rent by way of distress was derived from the civil law; for anciently, in the feudal law, the neglect to attend at the lord's courts, or not doing feudal service, was a forfeiture of the estate; but these feudal forfeitures were afterwards turned into distresses according to the pignotary method of the civil law; that is, the land let out to the tenant is hypothecated, or as a pledge in his hands, to answer the rent agreed to be paid to the landlord; and the whole profits arising from the land are liable to the lord's seizure for the payment and satisfaction of it. Gilb. Dist. 2. Gilb. Rents, 3. Bacon on Govt. 77. Vigilius, 257, 271, 326. Cromp. Int. 9. 2 New R. 224. The distress could not at common law, before the stat. 2 W. and M. c. 5, be sold, but could only be impounded and detained, in order to induce the tenant to perform the feudal service. Distresses, therefore, were at common law only allowed when the relation of landlord and tenant subsisted, and when, consequently, there remained feudal service to be performed; and hence the necessity at the present day that the landlord distraining should, at time of the distress, be entitled to the legal reversion; and hence the consequence that if a landlord, after rent has become due, and before payment, conveys his legal estate to another, he cannot distrain, (Gilb. Action Debt, 411. Bro. Debt, pl. 93. Vaughan, 40. Bac. Abr. Distress, A.;) and, for the same reason, it is necessary to aver in an avowry and cognizance that at the time of the distress the tenancy subsisted. The common law was altered, as far as regards tenants holding over, by the 8 Anne, c. 14, which provided that if a person retain possession of the estate after the expiration of his tenancy, the landlord, if his interest continue, may distrain within six months. Before this statute it was usual, and still may be expedient, to provide that the last half-year's rent shall be paid at a day prior to the determination of the lease, so as to enable the landlord to distrain before the removal of the tenant. Co. Litt. 47, b. If by agreement or custom the tenant has an away-going crop, and right to hold over to clear the same, the landlord may, during such excrescence of the term, distrain at common law. 1 Hen. Bla. 8. So the 11 Geo. II. c. 19, s. 8 enables a landlord to distrain for double rent if a tenant do not deliver up possession after the expiration of his own notice to quit, by which he incurs double rent so long as he holds over. When the lessor has not the legal estate or reversion, he should reserve a power to distrain, which will entitle him to do so. Co. Litt. 47, a. 5 Co. 3. But though the principal object of a distress was to compel the performance of feudal services, and, consequently, if rent be reserved on a letting merely of personal property, no distress can be taken, (5 Co. 17. 3 Wils. 27,) yet a distress may be made for rent of a readyfurnished house or lodging, because it is then considered that the rent issues out of the principal,—the real property demised. 2 New Rep. 224.

damage-feasant, that is, doing damage or trespassing upon his land. The former intended for the benefit of landlords, to prevent tenants from secreting or withdrawing their effects to his prejudice; the latter arising from the necessity of the thing itself, as it might otherwise be impossible at a future time to ascertain whose cattle they were that committed the trespass or damage. (17)

As the law of distresses is a point of great use and consequence, I shall consider it with some minuteness: by inquiring, first, for what injuries a distress may be taken; secondly, what thing may be distrained; and thirdly, the manner of taking, disposing of, and avoiding distresses.

1. And first it is necessary to premise that a distress,(*j*) *districtio*, is the taking a personal chattel out of the possession of the wrong-doer into the custody of the party injured, to procure a satisfaction for the wrong committed.(18) 1. The most usual injury for which a distress may be taken is that of non-payment of rent. It was observed in the former book,(*k*) that distresses were incident by the common law to every *rent-service*, and by particular reservation to *rent-charges* also; but not to *rent seck* till the statute 4 Geo. II. c. 28 extended the same remedy to all rents alike, and thereby in effect abolished all material distinction between them.

So that now we may lay it down as a universal principle, *that a [*7 distress may be taken for any kind of rent in arrear; the detaining whereof beyond the day of payment is an injury to him that is entitled to receive it.(19) 2. For neglecting to do suit at the lord's court,(*l*) or other

---

(*j*) The thing itself taken by this process, as well as the process itself, is in our law-books very frequently called a distress.

(*k*) Book ii. ch. 3.
(*l*) Bro. Abr. tit. *distress*, 15.

Accepting a note of hand and giving a receipt for the rent does not, till payment, preclude the landlord from distraining; and so if the landlord accept a bond; but a judgment obtained on either of such instruments would preclude the right of distress. See Bull. N. P. 182. An agreement to take interest on rent in arrear does not take away the right of distress. 2 Chit. R. 245. Where there are rents for which the party cannot distrain, although he may have an assize, yet remedy may be had in equity. Per Comyns, B., Exch. Trin. 5 & 6 Geo. II. 1 Selw. N. P. 6 ed. 673.

To entitle a person to distrain for non-payment of money, it must be due under a *demise*, Weis *v.* Jahn, 8 N. J. 93, 94 (1874), and for rent *fixed* and certain in its nature; and therefore, if a person be let into possession under an agreement for a lease which does not contain words of immediate demise, no distress can be made, unless from a previous payment of rent or other circumstance a tenancy from year to year can be inferred; and the only remedy is by action for use and occupation. 2 Taunt. 148. 5 B. & A. 322. 13 East, 19. Scruggs *v.* Gibson *et al.*, 40 Georgia 511, 522 (1869). So, as lord Coke quaintly says, (Co. Litt. 96, a.,) it is a maxim in law that no distress can be taken for any services that are not put into certainty nor can be reduced to any certainty, for *id certum est quod certum reddi potest*, [That is certain which can be made certain,] but yet in some cases there may be a certainty in uncertainty. Therefore, if a man hold land, paying so much per acre, although in the terms of the demise the number of acres be not fixed, the lord may distrain. (Vin. Abr. Distress, E. Form of avowry, 3 Chitty on Pl. 4th edit. 1051;) but where an estate has been let without in any way fixing the amount of rent, the only remedy is by action. Boone's Law of Real Property, § 109. The law of distress has been abolished in New York, Wisconsin, Minnesota, and Utah. It is absolute in the New England states, North Carolina, and Missouri. There are statutory provisions concerning it in Alabama, Tennessee, and Ohio. For the places where it exists and where it does not, and the substitutes in the respective states, see 1 Woodfall's L. & F., 412.

(17) Hard *v.* Nearing, 44 N. Y. 472, 488 (1865). Shouffler *v.* Cooper, 1 Watts and Sergeants (Pa.) 400 (1841). Richardson *v.* Williamson, 24 Cal. 289, 302 (1864). The term cattle was formerly used so generally as to include horses and chattels. Cobbey on Replevin, § 37. The right to distrain has been materially changed by statute in the United States; and while much curtailed, it is still true that the right to distrain cattle damage-feasant is generally recognized.

(18) Hard *v.* Nearing, 44 N. Y. 472, 488 (1865). Cobbey on Replevin, § 37. Binn's Justice (Brightly, 10 ed.) 336.

(19) The right to distress can be exercised only when a particular relation exists

certain personal service,(*m*) the lord may distrain of common right.(20)   3. For amercements in a court-leet a distress may be had of common right; but not for amercements in a court-baron, without a special prescription to warrant it.(*n*)   4. Another injury for which distresses may be taken is where a man finds beasts of a stranger wandering in his grounds *damage-feasant;* that is, doing him hurt or damage by treading down his grass or the like; in which case the owner of the soil may distrain them till satisfaction be made him for the injury he has thereby sustained.   5. Lastly, for several duties and penalties inflicted by special acts of parliament, (as for assessments made by commissioners of sewers,(*o*) or for the relief of the poor,)(*p*) remedy by distress and sale is given; for the particulars of which we must have recourse to the statutes themselves: remarking only that such distresses(*q*) are partly analogous to the ancient distress at common law, as being repleviable and the like; but more resembling the common law process of execution, by seizing and selling the goods of the debtor under a writ of *fieri facias,*(21) of which hereafter.

2. Secondly, as to the things which may be distrained, or taken in distress,(22) we may lay it down as a general rule, that all chattels personal

---

(*m*) Co. Litt. 47.
(*n*) Brownl. 36.
(*o*) Stat. 7 Anne, c. 10.

(*p*) Stat. 43 Eliz. c. 2.
(*q*) 1 Burr. 589.

---

between the parties, and the party vested with such rights cannot transfer them, without transferring with them, the interest to which they are incident; and the party who is liable to pay rent and to be distrained on account of his situation cannot divest himself of the situation by assignment of his interest in the land charged with the rent, and at the same time secure to himself the right to distrain his assignee. Shouffler *v.* Cooper, 1 Watts & Sergeant (Pa.) 400 (1841). Distress is incident to every such demise or lease independent of any stipulation in the lease. But, to entitle the party to distrain, there must be rent due in the legal sense of that word. One man may be in possession of another's house or land with his consent, and may be bound to render him such a sum for the use and occupation of it as a jury shall deem a proper equivalent for the rent: but if there be no actual demise, nor any contract for a demise amounting to as much, and no fixed rent has been agreed on or paid, the owner cannot distrain; for in his avowry to an action of replevin for such distress he would be bound to state an actual tenancy and the definite terms of it, which it would be impossible to do under such a relation as above supposed. Kegan *v.* Johnson, 2 Taunt. 148. Dunk *v.* Hunter, 5 B. & A. 322.—COLERIDGE.

(20) Scruggs *v.* Gibson *et al.*, 40 Ga. 511, 522 (1869).

(21) [That you cause to be made.]

(22) Besides the rules in the text, it is a maxim of law that *goods in the custody of the law* cannot be distrained: thus, goods distrained, damage-feasant, cannot be distrained, (Co. Litt. 47, a.;) so goods taken in execution, (Willes, 131;) but the goods so taken must be removed from the premises within a reasonable time, or they will not be protected. 1 Price, 277. 1 M. & S. 711. However, growing corn sold under a writ of fi. fa. cannot be distrained unless the purchaser allow it to remain uncut an unreasonable time after it is ripe, (2 B. & B. 362. 5 Moore, 97, S. C.;) but goods taken under a void outlawry are liable to distress. 7 T. R. 259. For the protection of landlords, by the 8 Anne, c. 14, s. 1, no goods taken in execution upon any premises demised can be removed until rent, not exceeding one year's arrear, be paid. Under this act the sheriff is bound to satisfy the rent in the first instance. 4 Moore, 473. In cases to which the statute applies, the landlord is entitled to be paid his whole rent without deducting poundage. 1 Stra. 643. Rent only due at the time of the levy can be obtained under the act, (1 M. & S. 245. 1 Price, 274;) but forehand-rent, or rent stipulated to be paid in advance, may be obtained, (7 Price, 690;) so rent that falls due on the day of the levy. Tidd, Prac. 8 edit. 1054. After the landlord has had one year's rent paid him, he is not entitled to another upon a second execution, (2 Stra. 1024. 2 B. & B. 362. 5 Moore, 97, S. C.,) unless, as we have just seen, the goods be not removed within a reasonable time. The ground landlord is not within the act where there is an execution against the under-lessee. 2 Stra. 787. If the sheriff remove the goods without payment of the rent, and after notice and a formal demand of the rent, an action on the case lies against him. Vin. Abr. Dist. c. 3. Stra. 97. 3 B. & A. 440. But no specific and formal notice is necessary. 3 B. & A. 645. 4 Moore, 473. 2 B. & B. 67, S. C. The action lies though part only of

are liable to be distrained, unless particularly protected or exempted. Instead therefore of mentioning what things are distrainable, it will be easier to recount those which are not so, with the reason of their particular exemptions.(r) And, 1. As every thing which is distrained is presumed to be the property of the wrong-doer, it will follow that such things wherein no man can have an absolute and valuable property (as dogs, cats, rabbits, and *all animals *feræ naturæ*,)(23) cannot be distrained. Yet if deer [*8 (which are *feræ naturæ*) are kept in a private enclosure for the purpose of sale or profit, this so far changes their nature, by reducing them to a kind of stock or merchandise, that they may be distrained for rent.(s) 2. Whatever is in the personal use or occupation of any man is for the time privileged and protected from any distress; as an axe with which a man is cutting wood, or a horse while a man is riding him.(24) But horses drawing a cart may (cart and all) be distrained for rent-arrere; and also if a horse, though a man be riding him, be taken *damage-feasant*, or trespassing in another's grounds, the horse (notwithstanding his rider) may be distrained and led away to the pound.(t)(25) Valuable things in the way of trade shall not be liable to distress; as a horse standing in a smith-shop to be shoed, or in a common inn; or cloth at a tailor's house; or corn sent to a mill or a market. For all these are protected and privileged for the benefit of trade, and are supposed in common presumption not to belong to the owner of the house, but to his customer.(26) But, generally speaking, whatever goods and chattels the

---

(r) Co. Litt. 47.
(s) Davis v. Powl, C. B. Hil. 11 Geo. II.

(t) 1 Sid. 440.

---

the goods be removed, (4 Moore, 473. 2 B. & B. 67, S. C.;) but the landlord's consenting to the removal waives the remedy. 3 Camp. 24. An executor or administrator, (1 Stra. 212,) or a trustee of an outstanding satisfied term to attend the inheritance, may sue. 4 Moore, 473. 2 B. & B. 67, S. C. Instead of an action, the landlord may move the court out of which the execution issued that he may be paid what is due to him out of the money levied and in the sheriff's hands, (Ca. *temp*. Hardw. 255. 2 Wils. 140,) and the court will grant the motion, though the sheriff had no notice of the rent due till after the removal. 3 B. & A. 440; and see further, on this point, Tidd's Prac. 8 edit. 1053–1055.

The recent bankrupt act provides that, in case of bankruptcy, no distress made after act of bankruptcy shall be available for more than a year's rent, but the landlord may prove for the excess. 1 Geo. IV. c. 16, § 74; and see *ante*, 2 book, 473.

For the protection of landlords, by the 56 Geo. III. c. 50, no sheriff or other officer shall carry off, or sell, or dispose of, for the purpose of being carried off from any lands, any straw, chaff, turnips, in any case, nor any hay or other produce which, according to any covenant or written agreement, ought not to be so carried off, provided notice be given to the sheriff of the existence of such covenant; but, by third section, the sheriff may sell on condition of such crops being consumed on the land. The sixth section provides that landlords shall not distrain for rent on the purchaser of any such crops sold according to third section, nor on articles or cattle, etc. employed for the purpose of consuming such crops.—CHITTY. See also, Ward v. Fagan, 28 Mo. 117 (1887). Reeves v. McKenzie, 1 Bailey (S. C.) 503 (1830). The C. R. R. & B. Co. v. Davis, 19 Ga. 437, 438 (1856). Binn's Justice (Brightly, 10 ed.) 337.

(23) [Of a wild nature.] *Ex parte* Cooper, 3 Tex. 489, 494 (1878).

(24) Jackson & Gross' Landlord and Tenant in Pennsylvania (2 ed.) 144. Binn's Justice (Brightly, 10 ed.) 338.

(25) But this doctrine is contrary to Sayer Rep. 139. 2 Keb. 596. Cro. Eliz. 596. Co. Litt. 47, a. Roll. Abr. Distress, A. pl. 4; and was expressly overruled in 6 Term R. 138, on the ground that the distraining a horse as damage-feasant whilst any person is riding him would perpetually lead to a breach of the peace. And it has been held that nets or ferrets cannot be taken damage-feasant in a warren if they are in the hands of the person using them. Harg. Co. Litt. note 13. Cro. Eliz. 550. So a loom cannot be distrained while in the hands of the weaver, (Willes, 517,) nor wearing-apparel if in actual use; but if put off, though only for the purpose of repose, it is liable to be distrained. 1 Esp. Rep. 206. Peake's Rep. 36, S. C.—CHITTY. See Binn's Justice (Brightly, 10 ed.) 338. Lawson's Rights Remedies and Practice (ed. 1890) vol. 3, 2479.

(26) As to this exception in favor of trade, see Gilb. Dist. by Hunt, 39, so cattle and

landlord finds upon the premises, whether they in fact belong to the tenant or a stranger, are distrainable by him for rent: for otherwise a door would be open to infinite frauds upon the landlord; and the stranger has *his* remedy over by action on the case against the tenant, if by the tenant's default the chattels are distrained so that he cannot render them when called upon.(27)

---

goods of a guest at an inn are not distrainable for rent, but a chariot or horses standing at livery are not exempt. 2 Burr. 1498. Mr. Sergt. Williams, in 2 Saund. 290, n. 7, suggests that it should seem that at this day a court of law would be of opinion that cattle belonging to a drover being put into ground, with the consent of the occupier, to graze only one night on their way to a fair or market, are not liable to the distress of the landlord for rent; and lord Nottingham intimated the same opinion in 2 Vern. 130; and Mr. Christian, in his edition, has the following note of a decision to the same effect:—"Cattle driven to a distant market, and put into land to rest for one night, cannot be distrained for rent by the owner of the land, such protection being absolutely for the public interest." Tate *v.* Gleed, C. P. Hil. 24 Geo. III. Gilb. Dist. by Hunt, 47. It was before held that cattle going to London, and put into a close, with the consent of the landlord and leave of the tenant, to graze for a night, might be distrained by the landlord for rent, (3 Lev. 260. 2 Vent. 50. 2 Lutw. 1161;) but the owner of the cattle was afterwards relieved *in equity* on the ground of fraudulent connivance and concealment of the demand for rent by the landlord, and he was decreed to pay all costs both of law and equity. 2 Vern. 129. Prec. Ch. 7. Gilb. Dist. by Hunt, 47. As courts of law now take notice of fraud, as well as courts of equity, when it can be fully proved, there would now be the same result at law.

Goods of a principal in the hands of a factor are privileged from distress for rent due from such factor to his landlord, on the ground that the rule of public convenience, out of which the privilege arises, is within the exception of a landlord's general right to distrain, and therefore that such goods are protected for the benefit of trade. 6 Moore Rep. 243. 3 B. & B. 75, S. C. So goods landed at a wharf and consigned to a broker, as agent of the consignor, for sale, and placed by the broker in the wharfinger's warehouse for safe custody until an opportunity for selling them should occur, are not distrainable for rent due in respect of the wharf and warehouse, as they were brought to the wharf in the course of trade. 1 Bing. 283. So goods carried to be weighed, even at a private beam, if in the way of trade, are exempt; so is a horse that has carried corn to a mill to be ground, and during the grinding of the corn is tied to the mill-door. Cro. Eliz. 549, 596. Goods in a public fair are exempt from distress, unless for toll due from the owner. 2 Lutw. 1380. Goods in possession of a carrier are also exempt, and this though the carrier be not a public one. 1 Salk. 249.—CHITTY. So also are goods deposited in a warehouse by one other than the occupant and in the ordinary course of trade. Owen *v.* Boyle, 9 Shepley (Maine) 47 (1842). Walker *v.* Johnson *et al.*, 4 McCord (S. Carolina) 552 (1828). And goods which have been sent to an auctioneer to be sold on the premises cannot be distrained for rent. Adams *v.* Grane & Osborne, 1 Exche'r (C. & M.) 380 (1833).

The American courts have adopted the principle stated in the text, and carried it out in application with great liberality. Thus, goods in an auctioneer's room, or in the store of one who takes merchandise on storage or on commission to sell, have been held to be exempt. Hinely *v.* Wyatt, 1 Bay, 102. Brown *v.* Simms, 17 Serg. & Rawle, 138. Walker *v.* Johnson, 4 McCord, 552. Bevan *v.* Crooks, 7 Watts & Serg. 452. So it has been held that the goods of a boarder are not liable to be distrained for rent due by the keeper of the boarding-house. Riddle *v.* Welden, 5 Wharton, 9. Stone *v.* Matthews, 7 Hill, 428.—SHARSWOOD.

(27) As if horses or cattle are sent to agist, they may be immediately distrained by the landlord for rent in arrear, and the owner must seek his remedy by action against the farmer. The principle of this rule extends to public livery-stables, to which if horses and carriages are sent to stand, it is determined that they are distrainable by the landlord as if they were in any public place, (3 Burr. 1498;) so upon the same principle the goods of lodgers or any other person on the premises are liable to be distrained; and to exempt goods from distress on the ground of their being in an inn, they must be within the very precincts of the inn, and not on other premises at a distance belonging to it (Barnes, 472;) and even within the inn itself the exemption does not extend to a person dwelling therein as a tenant rather than a guest. 1 Bla. Rep. 484.

As to the remedy over by an under tenant or lodger, see the cases cited in 3 Bar. & Cres. 789, in which it was held that where the tenant of premises had underlet a part by deed, and the original landlord distrained for rent upon the under-tenant, the latter could not support assumpsit against his immediate lessor upon an implied promise to indemnify him against the rent payable to the superior landlord.—CHITTY. Goods of a

With regard to a stranger's beasts which are found on the tenant's land, the following distinctions are, however, taken. If they are put in by consent of the owner of the beasts, they are distrainable immediately afterwards for rent-arrere by the landlord.(*u*) So also if the stranger's cattle break the fences and commit a trespass by coming on the land, they are distrainable immediately by the lessor for the tenant's rent, as a punishment to the owner of the beasts for the wrong committed through his negligence.(*v*) But if the lands were not *sufficiently fenced so as to keep out cattle, [*9 the landlord cannot distrain them till they have been *levant* and *couchant* (*levantes et cubantes*) on the land; that is, have been long enough there to have lain down and rose up to feed; which in general is held to be one night at least:(28) and then the law presumes that the owner may have notice whether his cattle have strayed, and it is his own negligence not to have taken them away. Yet, if the lessor or his tenant were bound to repair the fences and did not, and thereby the cattle escaped into their grounds without the negligence or default of the owner; in this case, though the cattle may have been *levant* and *couchant*, yet they are not distrainable for rent till actual notice is given to the owner that they are there, and he neglects to remove them:(*w*) for the law will not suffer the landlord to take advantage of his own or his tenant's wrong.(29) 3. There are also other things privileged by the ancient common law; as a man's tools and utensils of his trade, the axe of a carpenter, the books of a scholar, and the like: which are said to be privileged for the sake of the public, because the taking them away would disable the owner from serving the commonwealth in his station.(30) So, beasts of the plough, 4, *averia carucæ*,(31) and sheep, are

(*u*) Cro. Eliz. 549.
(*v*) Co. Litt. 47.
(*w*) Lutw. 1580.

---

stranger on the premises of a delinquent taxable are not exempt. Sears *v.* Cotterell, 6 Mich. 251, 266 (1858).

(28) Levant and couchant in this sense means that the cattle must be lying down and rising up on the premises *for a night and a day*, without pursuit made by the owner of them. Gilb. Dist. by Hunt, 3 edit. 47.—CHITTY.

(29) In the case of Poole *v.* Longuevill, 2 Saund. 289, the contrary was determined; but that case was overruled in 2 Lutw. 1580; and the result of the cases seems to be, that if a stranger's beasts escape into another's land, by default of the owner of the beasts, as by breaking the fences, otherwise sufficient, they may be distrained for rent immediately, without being *levant* and *couchant;* but that if they escape there by default of the tenant of the land, or for want of his keeping a sufficient fence, then they cannot be distrained for rent or service of any kind till they have been *levant* and *couchant*, nor afterwards by a landlord for rent on a lease, unless the owner of the beasts neglect or refuse, after *actual notice*, to remove them within a reasonable time; but it is said that such notice is not necessary where the distress is by the lord of the fee or by the grantee of a rent-charge. 2 Lutw. 1573. Co. Litt, b., n. 3. Gilb. Dist. by Hunt. 3d edit. 45. 2 Saund. 290, n. 7, 285, n. 4. See further, Vin. Abr. Fences.—CHITTY.

(30) A stocking-frame (Willes, 512) or a loom, (4 T. R. 565,) being implements of trade, cannot be distrained; but it must be observed that utensils and implements of trade may be distrained where they are not in actual use and no other sufficient distress can be found on the premises. Co. Litt. 47, a. 4 T. R. 565. And it should seem that if there be reasonable ground for presuming there are not sufficient other goods, the party may distrain implements of trade, and is not bound to sell the other goods first, (6 Price's Rep. 3. 2 Chitty's R. 167;) and this rule of exemption does not extend to cases where a distress is given in the nature of an execution by any particular statute, as for poor-rates and the like, (3 Salk. 136. 1 Burr. 579. Lord Raym. 384. 1 Salk. 249, S. C.,) nor where the distress is for damage-feasant. Com. Dig. Distress, B. 4.—CHITTY. Materials delivered by a manufacturer to a weaver cannot be distrained for rent due by the weaver. Wood *v.* Clark, 1 C. & J. 483, 497 (1831). Neither can goods left for sale at a store, Conah *v.* Hale, 23 Wend. 462, 478 (1840), nor pianos hired by tenants be taken by the landlord, Lazarus *v.* Dose, 3 Cape Good Hope, 42, 43 (1884–5); but things which are on a person's property to be manufactured, but which were not sent or delivered to such person by the owner, can be distrained for rent due by the tenant of the premises. Clark *v.* Millwall Dock Co., Law Rep. of Q. B. Div. 494, 500 (1886). Owen *v.* Boyle, 22 Me. 47, 76 (1842).

(31) In actual use, but not otherwise. 4 T. R. 566. Also see 2 Inst. 132, where other

privileged from distresses at common law;(*x*) while dead goods, or other sort of beasts, which Bracton calls *catalla otiosa*,(32) may be distrained. But as beasts of the plough may be taken in execution for debt, so they may be for distress by statute, which partake of the nature of executions.(*y*) And perhaps the true reason why these and the tools of a man's trade were privileged at the common law, was because the distress was then merely intended to compel the payment of the rent, and not as a satisfaction for its non-payment:(33) and therefore to deprive the party of the instruments and means of paying it would counteract the very end of the distress.(*z*) 5. Nothing shall be distrained for rent which may not be rendered again in as good plight as when it was distrained: for which reason milk, fruit,

*10] and the like cannot be distrained, a distress at *common law being only in the nature of pledge or security, to be restored in the same plight when the debt is paid.(34) So, anciently, sheaves or shocks of corn could not be distrained, because some damage must needs accrue in their removal; but a cart loaded with corn might, as that could be safely restored. But now, by statute 2 W. and M. c. 5, corn in sheaves or cocks, or loose in the straw, or hay in barns or ricks, or otherwise, may be distrained, as well as other chattels.(35) 6. Lastly, things fixed to the freehold may not be distrained; and caldrons, windows, doors, and chimney-pieces; for they savor of the realty.(36) For this reason also corn growing could not be distrained, till the statute 11 Geo. II. c. 19 empowered landlords to distrain corn, grass, or other products of the earth, and to cut and gather them when ripe.(37)

(*x*). Stat. 51 Hen. III. st. 4, *de districtiones caccania*, [Of exchequer distraint].

(*y*) 1 Burr. 589.

(*z*) Ibid. 588.

---

authorities are collected. The modern case just cited contains much learning upon what is, and what is not with reference to the freehold, distrainable.—CHITTY.

(32) [Chattels not privileged from distraint.]

(33) Cook *v.* Wise, and Newton *v.* Wilson, 3 H. & M. (Va.) 483, 495 (1809).

(34) Binn's Justice (10 ed.) 338 (1895).

(35) This provision extends to corn in whatever state it may be, whether threshed or unthreshed, (1 Lutw. 214;) and, as observed by Mr. Bradby, inasmuch as this statute directs the distress to be sold unless replevied within five days, perhaps the rule of the ancient common law with respect to the perishable nature of the distress no longer extends in the case of a distress for rent to any thing which is not liable to deterioration within the five days. Bradby on Dist. 213. A sale by a landlord of standing corn, taken as a distress before it is ripe, is void, and the tenant need not replevy, neither can he sue the seller, in an action on the case, for selling such corn before the expiration of five days. 3 B. & A. 470.—CHITTY. Given *v.* Blann, 3 Blackford (Ind.) 64 (1832).

(36) Co. Litt. 47, b. This rule extends to such things as are essentially part of the household, although for a time removed therefrom,—as a millstone, removed to be picked. Bro. Abr. Distress, pl. 23. 4 T. R. 567. As to what are fixtures, see 2 Chit. Com. Law, 268. Com. Dig. Biens. H. Chitty's Law of Descents, 256, 257. 4 Moore, 281, 440. 2 D. & R. 1. 5 B & A. 826. 2 Stark. 403. 2 B. & C. 608. 4 D. & R. 62, S. C. 1 M'Clelan Rep. Ex. 216.—CHITTY. The landlord cannot pursue and seize the goods of the tenant till the rent is due. If the tenant removed the goods when rent was due, the landlord may pursue and seize the goods within thirty days, and if no rent was due at the time of the removal, he may seize the goods within thirty days after the rent became due. Reynolds *v.* Shuler, 5 Cowen (N. Y.) 323, 329 (1826). Gilb. Dist. 56, etc. Hargrave's Co. Litt. 47, b. n. 6.

(37) The act applies only to corn and other produce of the land which may become ripe, and are capable of being cut and laid up: therefore trees, shrubs and plants growing on land which the defendant had demised to the plaintiffs for a term, and which they had converted into a nursery-ground, and planted subsequently to the demise, were held not distrainable by the former for rent. 2 Moore, 491. 8 Taunt. 431. S. C. 3 Moore, 114, S. P. 3 B. & A. 470.—CHITTY.

To these heads of things not distrainable may be added all goods in the custody of the law, whether as being already distrained damage-feasant, or taken in execution. In this

Let us next consider, thirdly, how distresses may be taken, disposed of, or avoided. And first I must premise that the law of distresses is greatly altered within a few years last past. Formerly they were looked upon in no other light than as a mere pledge or security for payment of rent or other duties, or satisfaction for damage done. And so the law still continues with regard to distresses of beasts taken *damage-feasant*, and for other causes, not altered by act of parliament; over which the distrainor has no other power than to retain them till satisfaction is made.(38) But, distresses for rent-arrere being found by the legislature to be the shortest and most effectual method of compelling the payment of such rent, many beneficial laws for this purpose have been made in the present century, which have much altered the common law as laid down in our ancient writers.

In pointing out therefore the methods of distraining, I shall in general suppose the distress to be made for rent, and remark, where necessary, the differences between such distress and one taken for other causes.

*In the first place then, all distresses must be made *by day*,(39) [*11 unless in the case of *damage-feasant;* an exception being there allowed, lest the beasts should escape before they are taken.(*a*) And, when a person intends to make a distress, he must, by himself or his bailiff, enter on the demised premises; formerly during the continuance of the lease, but now,(*b*) if the tenant holds over, the landlord may distrain within six months after the determination of the lease; provided his own title or interest as well as the tenant's possession, continue at the time of the distress.(40) If the lessor does not find sufficient distress on the premises, formerly he could resort nowhere else; and therefore tenants who were knavish made a practice to convey away their goods and stocks fraudulently from the house or lands demised, in order to cheat their landlords. But now(*c*) the landlord may distrain any goods of his tenant carried off the premises clandestinely, wherever he finds them within thirty days after, unless they have been *bona fide* sold for valuable consideration; and all persons privy to or assisting in such

(*a*) Co. Litt. 142.   (*c*) Stat. 8 Anne, c. 14.   11 Geo. II. c. 19.
(*b*) Stat. 8 Anne, c. 14.

last case, however, so long as they remain on the premises, the statute 8 Anne, c. 14 gives the landlord a beneficial lien on them, for which see *post*, p. 417.

The words of the statute 11 Geo. II. c. 19 are, "corn, grass, hops, roots, fruits, or other product growing on the estate demised." The court of Common Pleas has determined that the general word "product" does not extend beyond things of a similar nature with those before specified, to all of which the process of becoming ripe, and of being cut, gathered, made and laid up when ripe, was incidental. It was held therefore that nursery trees and shrubs could not be distrained. Clark *v.* Gaskarth, 8 Taunt. 431. —COLERIDGE.

(38) The distress must not be made after *tender* of payment of the entire rent due. According to 8 Co. 147, a., Gilb. Dist. by Hunt, 76, etc., 3 Stark. 171, 1 Taunt. 261, tender upon the land before the distress makes the distress tortious; tender after the distress, and before the impounding, makes the detainer, and not the taking, wrongful; tender after impounding makes neither the one nor the other wrongful; but in the case of a distress for rent, upon the equity of the 2 W. & M. c. 5, a sale of the distress after tender of the rent and costs would be illegal.—CHITTY. Brantley's Personal Property, § 82. 1 Lomax's Digest, 550.

(39) Pulling *v.* The People, 8 N. Y. 384, 388 (1850).

(40) Although this proviso is in terms confined to the possession of the tenant, yet it has been holden that where the tenant dies before the term expires, and his personal representative continues in possession during the remainder and after the expiration of the term, the landlord may distrain within six calendar months after the end of the term for rent due for the whole term. 1 H. Bla. 465. And in 1 H. Bla. 7, n. a. it was holden that the term was continued by the custom of the country for the purpose of giving a right to the landlord to distrain on the premises in which the way-going crop remained. See 1 Selw. N. P. 6 ed. 681.—CHITTY. But a landlord cannot distrain goods belonging to the tenant which never have been upon the premises. Bradley *v.* Piggott, 1 Miss. 348, 349 (1829).

fraudulent conveyance forfeit double the value to the landlord.(41) The landlord may also distrain the beasts of his tenant feeding upon any commons or wastes appendant or appurtenant to the demised premises.(42) The landlord might not formerly break open a house to make a distress; for that is a breach of the peace. But when he was in the house, it was held that he might break open an inner door;(d) and now(e) he may, by the assistance of the peace-officer of the parish, break open in the daytime any place whither the goods have been fraudulently removed and locked up to prevent a distress; oath being first made, in case it be a dwelling-house, of a reasonable ground to suspect that such goods are concealed therein.

Where a man is entitled to distrain for an entire duty, he ought to distrain for the whole at once, and not for part at one time and part at another.(f)(43)

*12] But if he distrains for the whole, and there is not sufficient on the premises, or he happens *to mistake in the value of the thing distrained, and so takes an insufficient distress, he may take a second distress to complete his remedy.(g)(44)

Distresses must be proportioned to the thing distrained for. By the statute of Marlbridge, 52 Hen. III. c. 4, if any man takes a great or unreasonable distress for rent-arrere, he shall be heavily amerced for the same. As if(h) the landlord distrains two oxen for twelve pence rent; the taking of *both* is an unreasonable distress; but if there were no other distress nearer the value to be found, he might reasonably have distrained *one* of them; but for homage, fealty, or suit and service, as also for parliamentary wages, it is said that no distress can be excessive.(i) For, as these distresses cannot be sold, the owner upon making satisfaction, may have his chattels again. The remedy for excessive distresses is by a special action on the statute of Marlbridge; for an action of trespass is not maintainable upon this account, it being no injury at the common law.(j)

When the distress is thus taken, the next consideration is the disposal of it. For which purpose the things distrained must in the first place be carried to some pound, and there impounded by the taker. But in their way thither they may be *rescued* by the owner, in case the distress was taken without cause or contrary to law: as if no rent be due, if they were taken upon the highway, or the like; in these cases the tenant may lawfully make rescue.(k) But if they be once impounded, even though taken without any cause, the owner may not break the pound and take them out; for they are then in the custody of the law.(l)

(d) Co. Litt. 161. Comberb. 17.
(e) Stat. 11 Geo. II. c. 19.
(f) 2 Lutw. 1532.
(g) Cro. Eliz. 13. Stat. 17 Car. II. c. 7. 1 Burr. 590.
(h) 2 Inst. 107.

(i) Bro. Abr. tit. *assize*, 291; *prerogative*, 98.
(j) 1 Ventr. 104. Fitzgibb. 85. 4 Burr. 590.
(k) Co. Litt. 160, 161.
(l) Co. Litt. 47.

---

(41) See 11 Geo. II. c. 19, sects. 1, 2, 3. The act is remedial, not penal. 9 Price, 30. It applies to the goods of the *tenant* only which are fraudulently removed, and not those of a stranger. 5 M. & S. 38. And the rent must be in arrear at the time of the removal. 1 Saund. 284, a. 3 Esp. 15. 2 Saund. 2 n. b; *sed vid.* 4 Camp. 136.—CHITTY.

(42) If the lord come to distrain cattle which he sees within his fee, and the tenant, or any person, to prevent the lord from distraining, drive the cattle out of the lord's fee into some other place, yet he may pursue and take the cattle. Co. Litt. 161, a. But this rule does not hold to distresses damage-feasant, which must be made on the land. Id.—CHITTY.

(43) It may be as well here to observe that if a landlord come into a house and seize upon some goods as a distress, in the name of all the goods of the house, that will be a good seizure of all. 6 Mod. 215. 9 Vin. Abr. 127. But a fresh distress may be made on the same goods which have been replevied, for subsequent arrears of rent. 1 Taunt. 218. So, if the cattle distrained die in the pound, the loss will fall on the party distrained on, and not upon the distrainor. Burr. 1738. 1 Salk. 248. 11 East, 54.—CHITTY.

(44) Where the distress is excessive, an action on the case is the proper remedy. Jamison *v.* Reefsneider, 97 Pa. 141 (1881).

A pound (*parcus*, which signifies any enclosure) is either pound-*overt*, that is, open overhead; or pound-*covert*, that is, close. By the statute 1 & 2 P. and M. c. 12, no distress of cattle can be driven out of the hundred where it is taken, *unless to a pound-overt within the same shire, and   [*13 within three miles of the place where it was taken.(45)   This is for the benefit of the tenants, that they may know where to find and replevy the distress.   And by statute 11 Geo. II. c. 19, which was made for the benefit of landlords, any person distraining for rent may turn any part of the premises upon which a distress is taken into a pound, *pro hac vice*,(46) for securing of such distress. If a live distress of animals be impounded in a *common* pound-overt, the owner must take notice of it at his peril; but if in any *special* pound-overt, so constituted for this particular purpose, the distrainor must give notice to the owner: and in both these cases the owner, and not the distrainor, is bound to provide the beasts with food and necessaries.   But if they are put in a pound-covert, in a stable, or the like, the landlord or distrainor must feed and sustain them.(*m*)(47)   A distress of household goods, or other dead chattels, which are liable to be stolen or damaged by weather, ought to be impounded in a pound-covert; else the distrainor must answer for the consequences.

When impounded, the goods were formerly, as was before observed, only in the nature of a pledge or security to compel the performance of satisfaction, and upon this account it hath been held(*n*) that the distrainor is not at liberty to work or use a distrained beast.   And thus the law still continues with regard to beasts taken damage-feasant, and distresses for suit or services; which must remain impounded till the owner makes satisfaction, or contests the right of distraining by replevying the chattels.   To *replevy* (*replegiare*, that is, to take back the pledge) is when a person distrained upon applies to the sheriff or his officers, and has the distress returned into his own possession, upon giving good security to try the right of taking it in a suit of law, and, if that be determined against him, to return the cattle or goods once more into the hands of the distrainor.   This is called a replevin, of which more will be said hereafter.   At present I shall only observe that, as a distress is at common *law only in nature of a security for   [*14 the rent or damages done, a replevin answers the same end to the distrainor as the distress itself, since the party replevying gives security to return the distress if the right be determined against him.(48)

This kind of distress, though it puts the owner to inconvenience, and is therefore a punishment to *him*, yet if he continues obstinate and will make no satisfaction or payment, it is no remedy at all to the distrainor.   But for a debt due to the crown, unless paid within forty days, the distress was always salable at common law.(*o*)   And for an amercement imposed at a court-leet, the lord may also sell the distress:(*p*) partly because, being the king's court of record, its process partakes of the royal prerogative;(*q*) but

(*m*) Co. Litt. 47.
(*n*) Cro. Jac. 148.
(*o*) Bro. Abr. tit. *distress*, 71.

(*p*) 8 Rep. 41.
(*q*) Bro. ibid. 12 Mod. 330.

---

(45) 1 Woodfall's L. & T. 473.
(46) [For this occasion.]
(47) The distrainor cannot tie up cattle impounded; and if he tie a beast and it is strangled, he will be liable in damages. 1 Salk. 248. If the distress be lost by act of God, as by death, the distrainor may distrain again. 11 East, 51. Burr. 1738.—CHITTY. Field *v.* Coleman, 5 Cush. 267, 268 (1850). One entitled to the possession of property which was taken from him unlawfully may retake it wherever he may find it. Bowler *v.* Eldridge, 18 Conn. 1, 18 (1846).
(48) Owen *v.* Boyle, 22 Me. 45, 68 (1844).

principally because it is in the nature of an execution to levy a legal debt. And so, in the several statute-distresses before mentioned, which are also in the nature of executions, the power of sale is likewise usually given, to effectuate and complete the remedy. And in like manner, by several acts of parliament,(r) in all cases of distress for rent, if the tenant or owner do not, within five days after the distress is taken,(49) and notice of the cause thereof given him, replevy the same with sufficient security, the distrainor, with the sheriff or constable, shall cause the same to be appraised by two sworn appraisers, and sell the same towards satisfaction of the rent and charges; rendering the overplus, if any, to the owner himself. And by this means a full and entire satisfaction may now be had for rent in arrere by the mere act of the party himself, viz., by distress, the remedy given at common law; and sale consequent thereon, which is added by act of parliament.(50)

Before I quit this article, I must observe, that the many particulars which attend the taking of a distress used formerly to make it a hazardous *15] kind of proceeding: for if any *one irregularity was committed it vitiated the whole and made the distrainors trespassers *ab initio.*(s) But now, by the statute 11 Geo. II. c. 19, it is provided, that for any unlawful act done the whole shall not be unlawful, or the parties trespassers *ab initio:* but that the party grieved shall only have an action for the real damage sustained, and not even that if tender of amends is made before any action is brought.(51)

VI. The seizing of heriots, when due on the death of a tenant, is also another species of self-remedy, not much unlike that of taking cattle or goods in distress. As for that division of heriots which is called heriot-service, and is only a species of rent, the lord may distrain for this as well as seize: but for heriot-custom (which Sir Edward Coke says(t) lies only in *prender,*(52) and not in *render*) the lord may seize the identical thing itself, but cannot distrain any other chattel for it.(u) The like speedy and effectual remedy of

(r) 2 W. and M. c. 5. 8 Anne, c. 14. 4 Geo. II. c. 28. 11 Geo. II. c. 19.
(s) 1 Ventr. 37.
(t) Cop. § 25.
(u) Cro. Eliz. 590. Cro. Car. 260.

---

(49) 4 B. & A. 208; *sed vid.* 1 H. Bla. 15. The five days are reckoned inclusive of the day of sale; as if the goods are distrained on the first, they must not be sold before the sixth. 1 H. Bla. 13. An action lies on the equity of this act for selling within the five days. Semb. id. If the distrainor continue in possession more than a reasonable time beyond the five days, an action of case or trespass lies on the equity of the statute. 11 East, 395. Stra. 717. 4 B. & A. 208. 1 B. & C. 145. Though the act authorizes a sale after the five days, it does not take away the right to replevy after the five days in case the distress is not sold; but it would be otherwise after a sale. 5 Taunt. 451. 1 Marsh. 135. By the consent of the tenant, the landlord may continue in possession longer than the five days without incurring any liability; and his so continuing in possession will not of itself create any presumption of collusion between him and the tenant to defeat an execution. 7 Price, 690.—CHITTY. The landlord is obliged to ascertain the amount of damage done, within a reasonable time before impounding or selling the chattels, otherwise he is a trespasser *ab initio* [From the beginning]. Sackrider *v.* McDonald, 10 Johnson (N. Y.) 523 (1813).

(50) The common law character of distress as a process of seizure and detainer has by statute in Georgia become a process of seizure and sale, and such a remedy, although not founded upon a judgment, is in the nature of an execution which a tax collector has power to issue in case of arrears for taxes. In such a case the land of the defaulter is not liable to be seized and sold for taxes until his goods and chattels are first exhausted. Gladney *et al. v.* Deavers, 11 Georgia 79 (1852).

(51) A collector of duties who makes a distress to obtain the amount due upon a carriage, and sells it without having given the notice of sale required by law, is a trespasser *ab initio* [From the beginning], and the sale is illegal.

(52) [In taking.] But where money payment is due in lieu of heriots and reliefs by custom, there must be a custom of distress which must be alleged positively in the bill. Mayor of Basingstoke *v.* Lord Bolton, Dreweys Rep. 270, 291 (1852).

seizing is given with regard to many things that are said to lie in franchise; as waifs, wrecks, estrays, deodands, and the like; all which the person entitled thereto may seize without the formal process of a suit or action. Not that they are debarred of this remedy by action; but have also the other and more speedy one, for the better asserting their property; the thing to be claimed being frequently of such a nature as might be out of the reach of the law before any action could be brought.

These are the several species of remedies which may be had by the *mere act* of the *party injured*. I shall next briefly mention such as arise from the *joint act of all the parties* together. And these are only two, *accord* and *arbitration*.

I. Accord is a satisfaction agreed upon between the party injuring and the party injured; which, when performed, is a bar of all actions upon this account. As if a man contract *to build a house or deliver a [*16 horse, and fail in it; this is an injury for which the sufferer may have his remedy by action; but if the party injured accepts a sum of money or other thing as a satisfaction, this is a redress of that injury, and entirely takes away the action.(*w*)(53) By several late statutes, (particularly 11

(*w*) 9 Rep. 79.

---

(53) See Com. Dig. Accord, Bac. Abr. Accord. Owens *v.* White, 3 Tex. 161, 166 (1848). The mere consent of the parties to accept in satisfaction without actually receiving it is not a bar. Accord to be a bar must be received and accepted in satisfaction of the thing demanded. Sieber *v.* Amunson, 78 Wisc. 679, 683 (1891). Mitchell *v.* Porter, 3 Md. (Bl'd) 490, 498 (1834). Campbell *v.* Hard, 8 N. Y. 235, 238 (1893). It should be certain, complete, and executed; the terms and conditions must have been strictly performed. Ætna Insurance Co. *v.* Stevens, 48 Ill. 30, 33 (1868). Woodford *v.* Marshall, 72 Wis. 129, 133 (1888). And where accord and satisfaction is made and executed by one of several joint defendants for a tort or other injury, the plaintiff's right of action is extinguished as to all of the co-defendants. Ballard and others *v.* Noaks, 2 Pike (Arkansas) 45 (1839). 9 Rep. 79, b. Likewise accord and satisfaction to one of several co-plaintiffs will act as a bar as to the others. 13 Edw. IV. 6. 5 Co. 117, b. The satisfaction must be a reasonable one. Generally speaking, the mere acceptance of a less sum is not in law a satisfaction of a greater sum, (5 East, 230;) and this though an additional security be given. 1 Stra. 426. An agreement between a debtor and creditor that part of a larger sum due should be paid by the debtor, and accepted by the creditor as a satisfaction for the whole, might, under special circumstances, operate as a discharge of the whole; but then the legal effect of such an agreement might be considered to be the same as if the whole debt had been paid, and part had been returned as a gift to the party paying. Per Holroyd, J., 2 B. & C. 481. A debtor's assignment of all his effects to a trustee, to raise a fund for the payment of a composition to his creditors, is a sufficient satisfaction, (2 T. R. 24;) so if a third person guarantees the payment of the less sum. 11 East, 390. So if a creditor, by his undertaking to accept a composition, induce the debtor to part with his property to his creditors, or induce other creditors to discharge the debtor, to enter into a composition-deed, or deliver up securities to him, such creditor would be bound by such undertaking. 2 Stark. Rep. 407. 2 M. & S. 120. 1 Esp. 236. And where several creditors, with the knowledge of each other, agree on the faith of each others' undertaking to give time to, or accept a composition from, a debtor, the agreement will be binding on every creditor who is party to it. 3 Camp. 175. 2 M. & S. 122. 16 Ves. 374; and see further, as to composition with creditors, 3 Chitty's Com. L. 687 to 698. It should be here also observed that when a bond or other security under seal has been given and accepted in satisfaction of a simple contract-debt, the latter is merged in such higher security, and no action can be supported for the non-performance of the simple contract, (Cro. Car. 415. Bac. Abr. Debt, G.,) unless indeed such new security be void; but the mere taking of an instrument of a higher order as a *collateral* or *additional* security does not preclude the debtor from suing on the original contract, and this though judgment be obtained on such security. 2 Leon. 110. 6 T. R. 176, 177. Payment and acceptance of a part of a debt before the day it falls due, or at a place where the whole debt was not payable, in satisfaction of the whole, is a good satisfaction, (Co. Litt. 212, b.;) and so if the debtor give a chose in possession for a chose in action, (2 T. R. 24,) as the gift of a horse, or other property in specie. Co. Litt. 212, b. The mere fulfilment of an act which a party

Geo. II. c. 19, in case of irregularity in the method of distraining, and 24 Geo. II. c. 24, in case of mistakes committed by justices of the peace,) even *tender* of sufficient amends to the party injured, is a bar of all actions, whether he thinks proper to accept such amends or no.(54)

II. Arbitration is where the parties injuring and injured submit all matters in dispute, concerning any personal chattels or personal wrong, to the judgment of two or more *arbitrators*, who are to decide the controversy; and if they do not agree, it is usual to add, that another person be called in as *umpire*, (*imperator* or *impar*,)(x) to whose sole judgment it is then referred: or frequently there is only one arbitrator originally appointed. This decision, in any of these cases, is called an *award*.(55) And thereby the question is as fully determined, and the right transferred or settled, as it could have been by the agreement of the parties or the judgment of a court of justice.(y) But the right of real property cannot thus pass by a mere award:(z) which subtilty in point of form (for it is now reduced to nothing else) had its rise from feodal principles; for if this had been permitted the land might have been aliened collusively without the consent of the superior.(56) Yet doubtless an arbitrator may now award a conveyance or a release of land; and it will be a breach of the arbitration-bond to refuse compliance. For though originally the submission to arbitration used to be by word, or by deed, yet, both of these being revocable in their nature, it is now become the practice to enter into mutual bonds with condition to stand to the award or arbitration

---

(x) Whart. *Angl. Saer.* i. 772. Nicols. Scot. Hist. Libr. ch. 1, *prope finem.*

(y) Brownl. 55. 1 Freem. 410.

(z) 1 Roll. Abr. 242. 1 Lord Raym. 115.

---

is bound in law to do is no satisfaction. Per Grose, J., 5 East, 302. A release of an equity of redemption is no satisfaction. 2 Wils. 86. Conferring a benefit to a third person at the debtor's request is sufficient. See Skin. Rep. 391.

The satisfaction should proceed from the party who wishes to avail himself of it; for when it proceeds entirely from a stranger it will be a nullity. See 5 East, 294. 1 Smith, 515. Cro. Eliz. 541.—CHITTY.

Concerning the acceptance of a less sum in satisfaction of a greater, see Foersch *v.* Blackwell, 14 N. Y. (Barb.) 607, 609 (1853) and Pepper & Watson *v.* Aiken, 2 Bush. (Ky.) 251 (1867). Fowler, ex'r *v.* Smith, 153 Pa. 639 (1893).

(54) By several statutes, (particularly 11 Geo. II. c. 19, in case of irregularity in the method of distraining, and 11 & 12 Vict. c. 44, in case of mistakes committed by justices of the peace,) a *tender* of amends to the party injured is a bar to the action, if the party thinks proper to accept such tender. If the party injured does not accept the amends tendered, and the jury, on the trial of the action, think the sum offered sufficient, their verdict must be for the defendant. By the Common Law Procedure Act, 1852, s. 70, the defendant in all actions (except actions for assault and battery, false imprisonment, libel, slander, malicious arrest or prosecution, criminal conversation, or debauchery of the plaintiff's daughter or servant) may pay into court a sum of money by way of compensation or amends. And, by statute 6 & 7 Vict. c. 96, s. 2, in action for a libel contained in any newspaper or periodical publication, the defendant may plead that it was inserted without malice or gross negligence, and that an apology had been offered to be published. The defendant may with the plea pay money into court as amends By s. 4, the offer of apology is admissible in evidence in mitigation of damages.—STEWART. Lowrie *v.* Verner, 3 Watts, 117.

(55) Binn's Justice (Brightly, 10 ed.) 68.

(56) An award of arbitrators, although it can not *proprio vigore* [Of its own force] transfer title to land, yet it may decide in whom the title is vested, and it will conclude the party against whom it is made and those claiming under him from setting up a claim against such a title again. Shelton *v.* Alcox *et al.*, 11 Connecticut, 239, 243–44 (1836). 3 East, 15. But an award declaring the right of real property was held to be void in Drane *v.* Hodges, 1 Harris & McHenry (Md.) 262 (1768).

An award will not be good as a statutory award unless the arbitrator have complied with all the provisions of the statute. Owens *v.* Withee, 3 Texas, 161. But an arbitration and award at common law is still good notwithstanding the statute. Collins *v.* Karatopsky, 36 Arkansas, 317, 327 (1880).

of the arbitrators *or umpire therein named.(a)(57)   And experience [*17 having shown the great use of these peaceable and domestic tribunals, especially in settling matters of account, and other mercantile transactions, which are difficult and almost impossible to be adjusted on a trial at law, the legislature has now established the use of them as well in controversies where causes are depending as in those where no action is brought: enacting, by statute 9 & 10 W. III. c. 15, that all merchants and others who desire to end any controversy, suit, or quarrel, (for which there is no other remedy but by personal action or suit in equity,) may agree that their submission of the

(a) Append. No. III. § 6.

---

(57) If the parties intend to refer all disputes, the terms of the reference should be, "of all matters in difference between the parties." When the reference is only intended to be of the matter in a particular cause, it should be, "of all matters in difference in the cause." 3 T. R. 628. A time should in all cases be mentioned within which the award is to be made; but, if no time be mentioned, the award should be made in a reasonable time. 2 Keb. 10, 20. 3 M. & S. 145. It is usual to vest in the arbitrators a power of enlarging the time for making their award; but it should be stipulated that this enlargement be made a rule of court. It is best to provide that the arbitration is not to be defeated by the death of either party. 7 Taunt. 571. 2 B. & A. 394. 3 D. & R. 184, 608. In some cases the court will amend an order of reference. 5 Moore, 167.

A court of chancery will not decree a specific performance, (19 Ves. 431. 6 Ves. 815,) and no action lies for not appointing an arbitrator, (2 B. & P. 13;) but if a party has agreed not to revoke, or has covenanted to perform an award, and the award be made, he will be liable to an action for a breach of the agreement or covenant if he revoke or refuse to perform the award, (see 5 B. & A. 507. 1 D. & R. 106. 2 Chit. R. 316. 5 East, 266; and see 4 B. & C. 103;) and an attachment for a contempt of court sometimes lies, where the submission is a rule of court. Crompt. Prac. 262. 1 Stra. 593. 7 East, 607.

With respect to the *revocation* of the arbitrator's authority, it is a rule of law that every species of authority, being a delegated power, although by express words made irrevocable, is nevertheless in general revocable. See 8 Co. 82. A submission to arbitration may be revoked by the act of God, by operation of law, or by the act of the parties.

The *death* of either or any of the parties before the award is delivered in general vacates the submission, unless it contain a stipulation to the contrary, (see 1 Marsh. 366. 7 Taunt. 571. 1 Moore, 287, S. C. 2 B. & A. 394;) but where all matters in difference in a cause are referred by order of nisi prius to arbitration, the death of one of the parties at any time before award made is a revocation of the arbitrator's authority and the court will set aside an award made after his death; or, in other words, it should seem, if the cause of action is referred, the death abates the action, but not so if other matters besides the cause of action are referred. 3 D. & R. 608. 2 B. & A. 394.

If a feme-sole submit to arbitration, and marry before the award is delivered, such *marriage* is in effect a revocation, without notice to the arbitrators, (2 Keb. 865. Jones, 388. Roll. Abr. 331;) but the husband and wife may be sued on their bond for such revoking. 5 East, 266.

Bankruptcy of one of the parties is no revocation. 2 Chit. Rep. 43. 4 B. & A. 250.

The *death of the arbitrators*, or one of them, will defeat the reference, unless there be a clause in the submission to the contrary, (see 4 Moore, 3;) so if the arbitrators do not make the award within the limited time, or they disagree, or refuse to act or intermeddle any further. 1 Roll. Abr. 261. 2 Saund. 129. Tidd, 8 ed. 877.

The parties themselves, as we have just seen, may revoke the arbitrators' authority before the award is made: the revocation must follow the nature of the submission: if the latter be by parol, so may the revocation. 2 Keb. 64. If the submission be by deed, so must the revocation. 8 Co. 72; and see T. Jones, 134. Notice of the revocation by the act of the parties must be given to the arbitrators in order to render it effectual. Roll. Abr. 331.   Vin. Abr. Authority, 13; and see 5 B. & A. 507.

The law relating to the proceedings during the conduct of the arbitration, and the duties of arbitrators and umpires, will be found in 3 Chit. Com. Law, 650 to 656, and Caldw. on Arb. 42, 45, etc. As to the power, etc. of awarding costs, see Tidd, 8 ed. 883 to 887. As to when a court of equity will compel an arbitrator to proceed, see 1 Swanst. 40. As to the general requisites of an award and how it will be construed, see 3 Chit. Com. Law, 656 to 660. Tidd, 8 ed. 882. For the remedy to compel the performance of an award, see Tidd, Prac. 8 ed. 887 to 894. 3 Chit. Com. Law, 600 to 665; and for the relief against an improper award, see 3 Chit. Com. Law, 665 to 668. Tidd, Prac. 8 ed. 894 to 898.

suit to arbitration or umpirage shall be made a rule of any of the king's courts of record, and may insert such agreement in their submission or promise, or condition of the arbitration-bond: which agreement being proved upon oath by one of the witnesses thereto, the court shall make a rule that such submission and award shall be conclusive: and, after such rule made, the parties disobeying the award shall be liable to be punished as for a contempt of the court; unless such award shall be set aside for corruption or other misbehavior in the arbitrators or umpire, proved on oath to the court within one term after the award is made. (58) And, in consequence of this statute, it is now become a considerable part of the business of the superior courts to set aside such awards when partially or illegally made; or to enforce their execution, when legal, by the same process of contempt as is awarded for disobedience to those rules and orders which are issued by the courts themselves. (59)

CHAPTER II.

OF REDRESS BY THE MERE OPERATION OF LAW.

THE remedies for private wrongs which are effected by the mere operation of the law will fall within a very narrow compass; there being only two instances of this sort that at present occur to my recollection: the one that of *retainer*, where a creditor is made executor or administrator to his debtor; the other in the case of what the law calls a *remitter*.

I. If a person indebted to another makes his creditor or debtee his executor, or if such a creditor obtains letters of administration to his debtor; in these cases the law gives him a remedy for his debt by allowing him to *retain* so much as will pay himself, before any other creditors whose debts are of equal degree. (a)(1) This is a remedy by the mere act of law, and

---

(a) 1 Roll. Abr. 922. Plowd. 513. See book ii. page 511.

---

(58) Corruption or misbehavior of the arbitrators must be clearly proved. Wikoff *et al.* *v.* Coxe *et al.*, 1 Yeates (Pa.) 353 (1891). But if the award is palpably against law and the arbitrators intended to conform to what equity and good conscience required of the parties the award should be confirmed, it being immaterial whether the conclusion of the arbitrators conformed to law or not. Byrd *v.* Odem, 9 Alabama, 751 (1846). Sumner *v.* Lyman, 1 Conn. (Kirby) 241, 245 (1787).

(59) There have been two important recent statutes passed in England upon the subject of arbitration. The one in 1854 has been largely followed and also much modified by the last, passed in 1889, August 26, and known as the "Arbitration Act, 1889." (52 & 53 Vict. c. 49). This last act provides for two methods of arbitration, called respectively, "References by Consent out of Court," and "References under Order of Court." It is provided under the first method that the submission shall be irrevocable, unless otherwise intended, and shall have the effect of an order of court; that in certain specified cases the court may appoint an arbitrator, or umpire, or third arbitrator; that in certain other cases a party may supply a vacancy, subject, however, to have his appointee set aside by the court; that witnesses may be summoned by subpœna *ad testificandum* [To testify], or *duces te eum* [Bring with you], and may be punished for perjury. Further provision is made for setting aside the award for misconduct of arbitrators.

Under the second method the proceedings authorized differ little from those of references to an officer of the court to hear and determine. The court may refer any question arising in any cause (other than criminal) "to any official or special referee." The "questions" specially mentioned those requiring "prolonged examination of documents" and "matters of account." See Chitty's English Statutes, 1894, vol. 1, tit. arbitration.

(1) Toller, 4 ed. 295, 298. So if a creditor be made a co-executor. 1 B. & P. 630. The same law as to an administrator (8 T. R. 407) or heir. 2 Vern. 62. So if a debtor be

grounded upon this reason: that the executor cannot, without an apparent absurdity, commence a suit against himself, as a representative of the deceased, to recover that which is due to him in his own private capacity: but, having the whole personal estate in his hands, so much as is sufficient to answer his own demand is, by operation of law, applied to that particular purpose.(2) Else, by being made executor *he would be [*19 put in a worse condition than all the rest of the world besides. For though a ratable payment of all the debts of the deceased, in equal degree, is clearly the most equitable method, yet, as every scheme for a proportionable distribution of the assets among all the creditors hath been hitherto found to be impracticable, and productive of more mischiefs than it would remedy, so that the creditor who first commences his suit is entitled to a preference in payment; it follows that, as the executor can commence no suit, he must be paid the last of any, and of course must lose his debt, in case the estate of his testator should prove insolvent, unless he be allowed to retain it.(3) The doctrine of *retainer* is therefore the necessary consequence of that other doctrine of the law, the priority of such creditor who first commences his action. But the executor shall not retain his own debt, in prejudice to those of a higher degree; for the law only puts him in the same situation as if he had sued himself as executor and recovered his debt; which he never could be supposed to have done while debts of a higher nature subsisted. Neither shall one executor be allowed to retain his own debt in prejudice to that of his co-executor in equal degree; but both shall be discharged in proportion.(b) Nor shall an executor of his own wrong be in any case permitted to retain. (c)

II. Remitter is where he who hath the true property or *jus proprietatis* in lands, but is out of possession thereof, and hath no right to enter without recovering possession in an action, hath afterwards the freehold cast upon him by some subsequent, and of course defective, title; in this case he is remitted, or sent back by operation of law, to his ancient and more certain title.(d)(4) The right of entry, which he hath gained by a bad title, shall be

---

(b) Vin. Abr. tit. *executors*, D. 2.
(c) 5 Rep. 36.

(d) Litt. § 659.

---

made executor of creditor, it is a release at law. *Ante*, 2 book, 512. Plowd. 184. Salk. 299.—CHITTY.

A somewhat recent statute in England has abolished the distinction as to priority of payment between specialty and simple contract debts of deceased persons. 32 & 33 Vict. c. 46. Aug. 2, 1869—"Hinde Palmer's Act." Hence the limitation of the right of retainer mentioned in the text would no longer apply. It has been decided that the right is not otherwise affected by the act. Crowder *v.* Stewart, L. R. 16 ch. D. 368.

(2) The common law doctrine of retainer is recognized and upheld in all its vigor by the Supreme Court of U. S. (Page *v.* Patton, 5 Pet. 304) and by some of the states. Others have abolished it by statute. The law, where still in force, presumes that the executor or administrator retained the amount of his debt out of the decedent's estate, although he may prove the contrary and in that case recover. Smith *v.* Watkins, 8 Humphreys (Tenn.) 331, 340 (1847). But the mere fact of a creditor's being executor or administrator does not absolutely extinguish the debt. Hall *v.* Pratt, 5 Hammond (Ohio, 1831) 72. Draughon *v.* French's adm'r, 4 Porter (Ala.) 352, 364 (1837). In New York, no part of the property of the deceased can be retained by an executor or administrator, in satisfaction of his own debt or claim, until it shall have been proved to, and allowed by, the surrogate; and such debt or claim is not entitled to any preference over others of the same class. 2 Barb. Rights of Pers. and Prop. 784.

(3) It is recognized generally throughout the state of Florida that the doctrine of retainer does not apply to insolvent estates. Our insolvent laws require a distribution *pro rata* [Ratably] of an insolvent estate among all the creditors, and in such case the right of retainer does not exist. Sealey *v.* Thomas *et al.*, 6 Florida 25, 29 (1855).

(4) 1 Shep. Touch. Preston, 156. 2 Barb. Rights of Pers. and Prop. 786.

ipso facto annexed to his own inherent good one: and his defeasible estate shall be utterly defeated and annulled, by the instantaneous act of law, without his participation or consent.(*e*) As if A. disseizes B., that

*20]   *is, turns him out of possession, and dies, leaving a son C.; hereby the estate descends to C. the son of A., and B. is barred from entering thereon till he proves his right in an action; now, if afterwards C., the heir of the disseizor, makes a lease for life to D., with remainder to B. the disseizee for life, and D. dies; hereby the remainder accrues to B., the disseizee: who, thus gaining a new freehold by virtue of the remainder, which is a bad title, is by act of law *remitted*, or in of his former and surer estate.(*f*) For he hath hereby gained a new right of possession, to which the law immediately annexes his ancient right of property.

If the subsequent estate, or right of possession, be gained by a man's own act or consent, as by immediate purchase being of full age, he shall not be remitted. For the taking such subsequent estate was his own folly, and shall be looked upon as a waiver of his prior right.(*g*) Therefore it is to be observed, that to every remitter there are regularly these incidents: an ancient right, and a new defeasible estate of freehold, uniting in one and the same person; which defeasible estate must be *cast upon* the tenant, not gained by his own act or folly.(5) The reason given by Littleton,(*h*) why this remedy, which operates silently, and by the mere act of law, was allowed, is somewhat similar to that given in the preceding article; because otherwise he who hath right would be deprived of all remedy. For, as he himself is the person in possession of the freehold, there is no other person against whom he can bring an action, to establish his prior right. And for this cause the law doth adjudge him in by remitter; that is, in such plight as if he had lawfully recovered the same land by suit. For, as lord Bacon observes,(*i*) the benignity of the law is such, as when, to preserve the principles and grounds of law, it depriveth a man of his remedy without his own fault, it will rather put him in a better degree and condition than in a worse.

Nam quod remedio destituitur, ipsa re valet, si culpa absit.(6) But

*21]   there shall be no *remitter to a right for which the party has no remedy by action:(*k*) as if the issue in tail be barred by the fine or warranty of his ancestors,(7) and the freehold is afterwards cast upon him, he shall not be remitted to his estate-tail:(*l*) for the operation of the remitter is exactly the same, after the union of the two rights, as that of a real action would have been before it. As therefore the issue in tail could not by any action have recovered his ancient estate, he shall not recover it by remitter.

And thus much for these extrajudicial remedies, as well for real as personal injuries, which are furnished or permitted by the law, where the parties are so peculiarly circumstanced as not to make it eligible, or in some cases even possible, to apply for redress in the usual and ordinary methods to the courts of public justice.

(*e*) Co. Litt. 358. Cro. Jac. 489.
(*f*) Finch, L. 194. Litt. § 683.
(*g*) Co. Litt. 348, 350.
(*h*) § 661.

(*i*) Elem. c. 9.
(*k*) Co. Litt. 340.
(*l*) Moor. 115. 1 Ann. 186.

---

(5) 1 Lomax's Dig. 557. 2 Greenleaf's Cruise on Real Property, 133.

(6) [For that which is without remedy is by that very circumstance strengthened if it be free from fault.]

(7) The issue is no longer liable to be barred by these means. Stat. 3 & 4 W. IV. c. 74.—STEWART.

Where the statute of limitation bars the right there is no remitter. See Daniel *v.* Woodroffu, 10 M. & W. 608 (1842).

CHAPTER III.

OF COURTS IN GENERAL.

THE next, and principal, object of our inquiries is the redress of injuries by *suit in courts:* wherein the act of the parties and the act of law co-operate; the act of the parties being necessary to set the law in motion, and the process of the law being in general the only instrument by which the parties are enabled to procure a certain and adequate redress.

And here it will not be improper to observe, that although, in the several cases of redress by the act of the parties mentioned in a former chapter,(*a*) the law allows an extrajudicial remedy, yet that does not exclude the ordinary course of justice: but it is only an additional weapon put into the hands of certain persons in particular instances, where natural equity or the peculiar circumstances of their situation required a more expeditious remedy than the formal process of any court of judicature can furnish. Therefore, though I may defend myself, or relations, from external violence, I yet am afterwards entitled to an action of assault and battery: though I may retake my goods if I have a fair and peaceable opportunity, this power of recaption does not debar me from my action of trover or detinue: I may either enter on the lands on which I have a right of entry, or may demand possession by a real action: I may either abate a nuisance by my own authority, or call upon the law to do it for me: I may distrain for rent, or have an action of debt, at my own *option: if I do not dis-   [*23 train my neighbor's cattle *damage-feasant*, I may compel him by action of trespass to make me a fair satisfaction: if a heriot, or a deodand, be withheld from me by fraud or force, I may recover it though I never seized it. And with regard to accords and arbitrations, these, in their nature being merely an agreement or compromise, most indisputably suppose a previous right of obtaining redress some other way; which is given up by such agreement. But as to remedies by the mere operation of law, those are indeed given, because no remedy *can* be ministered by suit or action, without running into the palpable absurdity of a man's bringing an action against himself; the two cases wherein they happen being such wherein the only possible legal remedy would be directed against the very person himself who seeks relief.

In all other cases it is a general and indisputable rule, that where there is a legal right there is also a legal remedy, by suit or action at law, whenever that right is invaded.(1) And in treating of these remedies by suit in courts, I shall pursue the following method: *first*, I shall consider the nature and

(*a*) Ch. 1.

---

(1) Craigie *v.* Hepburn & Alves, 15 Sc. Fac. Decis. 481 (folio) (1809). Arrington *v.* Liscom *et al.*, 34 Hale (California) 365–384 (1868). Hubgh *v.* N. O. & C. R. R. Co., 6 Louisiana Annual Rep. 495–511 (1851). Ins. Co. *v.* Perrue, 3 N. J. 402, 408 (1852). Where a general assembly is the exclusive tribunal which has cognizance of the election of a governor only in a manner and time appointed by the constitution and the assembly refuses to act, the courts have jurisdiction. To claim that they have not would be to afford an instance where a flagrant wrong was without a remedy. State *ex rel.* Morris *v.* Bulkeley, 61 Connecticut, 287, 373 (1892). The legal obligation of a contract is the legal remedy for enforcing it. The constitutional provision, which prohibits a state from passing laws impairing the obligations of contracts, is defined to mean any law which weakens the obligations of a contract previously made or renders it less operative. Tapsley *v.* Brashears and Bar. etc., 4 Littell's Annual Rep. (Ky.) 50, 59 (1824). Emerick *v.* Harris, 1 Binney (Pa.) 416–420 (1808).

several species of courts of justice; and, *secondly*, I shall point out in which of these courts, and in what manner, the proper remedy may be had for any private injury; or, in other words, what injuries are cognizable, and how redressed, in each respective species of courts.

First, then, of courts of justice. And herein we will consider, *first*, their nature and incidents in general; and then, the several species of them, erected and acknowledged by the laws of England.

A court is defined to be a place wherein justice is judicially administered. (*b*)

(2) And, as by our excellent constitution the sole executive power of the laws is vested in the person of the king, it will follow that all courts of jus-
*24] tice which are *the medium by which he administers the laws, are derived from the power of the crown. (*c*)(3) For, whether created by act of parliament, or letters-patent, or subsisting by prescription, (the only methods by which any court of judicature(*d*) can exist,) the king's consent in the two former is expressly, and in the latter impliedly, given. In all these courts the king is supposed in contemplation of law to be always present; but, as that is in fact impossible, he is there represented by his judges, whose power is only an emanation of the royal prerogative.

For the more speedy, universal, and impartial administration of justice between subject and subject, the law hath appointed a prodigious variety of courts, some with a more limited, others with a more extensive, jurisdiction; some constituted to inquire only, others to hear and determine; some to determine in the first instance, others upon appeal and by way of review. All these in their turns will be taken notice of in their respective places: and I shall therefore here only mention one distinction, that runs throughout them all; viz., that some of them are courts *of record*, others *not of record*. A court of record is that where the acts and judicial proceedings are enrolled in parchment for a perpetual memorial and testimony:(4) which rolls are called the records of the court, and are of such high and supereminent authority that their truth is not to be called in question. For it is a settled rule and maxim that nothing shall be averred against a record, nor shall any plea, or even proof, be admitted to the contrary.(*e*)(5) And if the existence of a record be denied, it

(b) Co. Litt. 58.
(c) See book i. ch. 27.

(d) Co. Litt. 260.
(e) Ibid.

---

(2) Von Schmidt *v.* Widber, 99 Cal. 511, 512 (1893). The People *v.* Wilson, 15 Ill. 388, 391 (1854). This definition obviously wants fulness; it is limited to the *place* of a court in its expression. In addition to the place there must be the presence of the officers constituting the court, the judge or judges certainly and probably the clerk authorized to record the action of the court; time must be regarded, too, for the officers of the court must be present at the place and at the time appointed by law in order to constitute a court. McClerkin *v.* State, 20 Fla. 879, 885 (1885); and see Levey *et al. v.* Bigelow, 6 Ind. 677, 682 (1893).

(3) McClerkin *v.* State, 20 Florida, 879. Union Colony *et al. v.* Elliott, 5 Colorado, 371. Shoultz *v.* McPheeters, 79 Indiana, 373, 375 (1881). Jarvis *v.* Sewall, 40 Barbours (N. Y.) 449.

(4) If we stick to the letter of the law, few, if any, of our courts are according to the definition "courts of record," as their proceedings are not enrolled on parchment. Bailey's Onus Probandi, 163.

(5) Lacaze *et al. v.* State, 1 Addison (Pa.) 59. Schouler's Personal Property, vol. 1 (2 ed.) 420. Wait's Actions and Defences, vol. 1, p. 430. To constitute a court of record it is not sufficient that the court have a clerk and seal. It must be one the proceedings of which are enrolled for a perpetual memorial and testimony. The minutes of the court do not become part of the record until they are enrolled. Hutkoff *v.* Demorest, 103 N. Y. 377, 386 (1886). Adams *v.* Betz, 1 Watts (Pa.) 425, 427 (1834). Hall *v.* Hudson, 20 Alabama (Shepherd) 286 (1852). Dudley *v.* Butler, 10 New Hampshire, 281, 289, (1839). Bank *v.* Chipley and others, 1 Ga. Decisions, 50 (1842). Edwards *v.* Moody, 60 Me. (Virgin) 255.

shall be tried by nothing but itself;(6) that is, upon bare inspection whether there be any such record or no; else there would be no end of disputes.(7) But, if there appear any mistake of the clerk in making up such record, the court will direct him to amend it. All courts of record are the king's courts, in right of his crown and royal dignity,(*f*) and therefore no other court hath authority to fine or imprison; so that the very erection
*of a new jurisdiction with the power of fine or imprisonment makes   [*25
it instantly a court of record.(*g*)(8) A court not of record is the court of a private man; whom the law will not entrust with any discretionary power over the fortune or liberty of his fellow subjects. Such are the courts-baron incident to every manor, and other inferior jurisdictions: where the proceedings are not enrolled or recorded; but as well their existence as the truth of the matters therein contained shall, if disputed, be tried and determined by a jury. These courts can hold no plea of matters cognizable by the common law, unless under the value of 40*s*., nor of any forcible injury whatsoever, not having any process to arrest the person of the defendant.(*h*)(9)

In every court there must be at least three constituent parts, the *actor*, *reus*, and *judex:* the *actor*, or plaintiff, who complains of an injury done; the *reus*, or defendant, who is called upon to make satisfaction for it; and the *judex*, or judicial power, which is to examine the truth of the fact, to determine the law arising upon that fact, and, if any injury appears to have been done, to ascertain, and by its officer to apply, the remedy.(10) It is also

(*f*) Finch, L. 231.
(*g*) Salk. 200. 12 Mod. 388.

(*h*) 2 Inst. 311.

---

(6) This rule is subject to some exceptions; for in the case of a judgment signed on a warrant of attorney given upon an unlawful consideration or obtained by fraud, upon an affidavit thereof, the court will afford relief upon a summary application. Doug. 196. Cowp. 727. 1 Hen. Bla. 75. And equity will relieve against a judgment obtained by fraud or collusion. 1 Anst. 8. 3 Ves. & B. 42. And third persons who have been defrauded by a collusive judgment may show such fraud, so as to prevent themselves from being prejudiced by it. 2 Marsh. 392. 7 Taunt. 97. 13 Eliz. c. 5.—CHITTY. If a question arises as to the existence of the record, it may be proved by its production or by a sworn or office copy. Bellas *v.* McCarty, 10 Watts (Pa.) 25 (1841). Thompson *v.* Lyle, 3 Watts and Sergeants (Pa.) 166, 169 (1842). Bradley *v.* Vail, 48 Connecticut, 375, 381 (1880). Hahn *v.* Kelly, 34 California (Hale) 391, 422, 424 (1868).

(7) Wheaton *v.* Fellows, 23 Wend. (N. Y.) 375, 377 (1840). If there have been any mistake in making up a record, the court upon application will direct an amendment, and it can be altered or controlled in no other way. Claggett *v.* Simms, 21 N. H. 22, 33 (1855).

(8) Lacaze *v.* State, 1 Addison (Pa.) 59. State *v.* Connor, 5 Blackf. (Ind.) 325, 326 (1840). But every court of record has not necessarily a power to fine and imprison. 1 Sid. 145. There are several of the king's courts not of record, as the court of equity in chancery, the admiralty courts, etc. 4 Inst. 84. 37 H. 6, 14, b. Yelv. 227. Com. Dig. tit. Chancery, C. 2.—CHITTY. Crim *v.* Kessing, 89 Cal. (Pomeroy) 479, 484 (1891). Schouler's Pers. Prop. vol. 1, p. 357 (1884). Van Daren *v.* Horton, 1 Dutchers (N. J.) 205, 207 (1855). Withers *v.* The State, 36 Ala. 252, 263 (1860). Crockett *v.* Routon, 1 Dudley (Ga.) 254, 255 (1833). Delovis *v.* Boits, 7 Fed. Cases, 418, 438 (1815). Bow. Eng. Const. (2 ed.) 236.

(9) A judicial act is one performed by the court, touching the rights of parties or property brought before it by voluntary appearance, or by prior action of ministerial officers. Acts done out of court, in bringing the parties into court are, as a general proposition, ministerial acts; those done by the court in session in adjudicating between the parties or upon the right of one in court *ex parte* [On his behalf] are judicial acts. Flournoy *v.* The City of Jeffersonville, 17 Indiana, 186 (1861). Where a judge is illegally elected or appointed, his acts while performing the judicial functions are valid and binding upon the public. State *v.* Gleason, 12 Florida, 191 (1867).

(10) Fong Yue Ting *v.* U. S., 149 U. S. 698–729 (1892). Union Colony *v.* Elliott, 5 Colo. 371, 381 (1880). Regina *v.* Bunting, 7 Ontario, 118, 125 (1884). An attorney at

usual in the superior courts to have attorneys, and advocates or counsel, as assistants.(11)

An attorney at law answers to the *procurator*, or proctor, of the civilians and canonists.(i)(12) And he is one who is put in the place, stead, or *turn* of another, to manage his matters of law.(13) Formerly every suitor was obliged to appear in person, to prosecute or defend his suit, (according to the old Gothic constitution,)(k) unless by special license under the king's letters-patent.(l) This is still the law in criminal cases.(14) And an idiot cannot to this day appear by attorney, but in person;(m) for he hath not dis-
*26 cretion to enable him to appoint *a proper substitute: and upon his being brought before the court in so defenceless a condition, the judges are bound to take care of his interests, and they shall admit the best plea in his behalf that any one present can suggest.(n) But, as in the Roman law, "*cum olim in usu fuisset, alterius nomine agi non posse, sed, quia hoc non minimam incommoditatem habebat, cæperunt homines per procuratores litigare,*"(o)(15) so with us, upon the same principle of convenience, it is now permitted in general, by divers ancient statutes, whereof the first is statute Westm. 3, c. 10, that attorneys may be made to prosecute or defend any action in the absence of the parties to the suit. These attorneys are now formed into a regular corps; they are admitted to the execution of their office by the superior courts of Westminster hall, and are in all points officers of the respective courts of which they are admitted; and, as they have many privileges on account of their attendance there, so they are peculiarly subject to the censure and animadversion of the judges.(16) No man can practice

---

(i) Pope Boniface VIII. in 6 *Decretal. l.* 3, *t.* 16, § 3, speaks of "*procuratoribus, qui in aliquibus partibus attornati nuncupantur.*" ["Proctors who are in some places called attorneys."]
(k) Stiernhook *de jure Goth. l.* 1, c. 6.

(l) F. N. B. 25.
(m) F. N. B. 27.
(n) Bro. Abr. tit. *Idiot,* 1.
(o) Inst. 4, tit. 10.

---

law is not one of such officers as are contemplated by the act of November 16, 1863, and therefore he need not comply with the provisions of the act concerning the taking of the oath prescribed there.

(11) Bow. Eng. Const. (2 ed.) 236.

(12) Blackstone uses procurator and proctor as synonymous. There appear, however, to have been two kinds, covered by this wide expression—the *progmatici* and the *procuratores*. The *progmatici* are described as persons who assisted the advocates when they were pleading and instructed them in points of law. The *procuratores* seem to have resembled attorneys amongst us. 2 Beven on Negligence (2 ed.) 1414.

(13) Binn's Justice (Brightley) (10 ed.) 69, 213. Allen *v.* Rand, 5 Conn. 322, 325 (1824). An attorney is a public officer. *Ex parte* Falkner, 1 W. Va. (Hog.) 269, 297 (1866). *In re* Ole Mosness, 39 Wis. 509, 510 (1876). Leigh's Case, 1 Mumford (Va.) 468, 479 (1810).

(14) This is not universally so; for in prosecutions and informations for misdemeanors, especially in the court of King's Bench, a defendant may, and usually does, appear and plead by his attorney or clerk in court. 1 Chitty's Crim. Law. But an attorney has no right to be present during the investigation of a charge of felony before a magistrate against his client. 3 B. & A. 432; and see 1 B. & C. 37.—CHITTY. But the contrary is now the law in such cases in both England and the United States.

(15) ["Although formerly it had been the custom for no one to act in the name of another; yet as this was attended with great inconvenience, men began to carry on law suits by proctors."]

(16) The relation of attorney, or solicitor and client is governed in great degree by the same rules which are applicable to other cases of agency. The client is the principal and the attorney is the agent, clothed with an apparent general authority in the management of the cause. The attorney's duty is to follow his client's instructions; to observe every limitation placed upon his general authority; and to act with perfect good faith, and with a single view to his client's interests, and with the usual skill of members of his profession. If he violates his duty, he is liable to an action by his client although he acted within the scope of his apparent authority. Such is the oath and such the doctrine prescribed to lawyers in the days of Justinian Cod. Lib. 3, tit. 1, 1. 14, § 1. How well worthy is the doctrine for the consideration of Christian lawyers in our day. Story on

as an attorney in any of those courts, but such as is admitted and sworn an attorney of that particular court: an attorney of the court of king's bench cannot practice in the court of common pleas; nor *vice versa*. To practice in the court of chancery it is also necessary to be admitted a solicitor therein: and by the statute 22 Geo. II., c. 40, no person shall act as an attorney at the court of quarter-sessions but such as has been regularly admitted in some superior court of record. So early as the statute 4 Henry IV. c. 18, it was enacted, that attorneys should be examined by the judges, and none admitted but such as were virtuous, learned, and sworn to do their duty. And many subsequent statutes(*p*) have laid them under further regulations.(17)

Of advocates, or (as we generally call them) counsel, there are two species or degrees; barristers, and sergeants. The former are admitted after a considerable period of study, or at least standing, in the inns of court;(*q*) and are in our old books *styled apprentices, *apprenticii ad legem,*(18)　[*27 being looked upon as merely learners, and not qualified to execute the full office of an advocate till they were sixteen years standing, at which time, according to Fortesque,(*r*) they might be called to the state and degree of sergeants, or *servientes ad legem.*(19) How ancient and honorable this state and degree is, with the form, splendor, and profits attending it, hath been so fully displayed by many learned writers,(*s*) that it need not be here enlarged on. I shall only observe, that sergeants at law are bound by a solemn oath(*t*) to do their duty to their clients: and that by custom(*u*) the judges of the courts of Westminster are always admitted into this venerable order before they are advanced to the bench; the original of which was probably to qualify the *puisnè* barons of the exchequer to become justices of assize, according to the exigence of the statute of 14 Edw. III. c. 16.(20) From both these degrees some are usually selected to be his majesty's counsel learned in the law; the two principal of whom are called his attorney and solicitor-general. The first king's counsel under the degree of sergeant was Sir Francis Bacon, who was made so *honoris causa,*(21) without either patent

---

(*p*) 3 Jac. I. c. 7.　12 Geo. I. c. 29.　2 Geo. II. c. 23. 22 Geo. II. c. 46.　23 Geo. II. c. 26.
(*q*) See book i. introd. § 1.
(*r*) *De LL.* c. 50.
(*s*) Fortesc. ibid.　10 Rep. pref. Dugd. *Orig. Jurid.* To which may be added a tract by the late sergeant

Wynne, printed in 1765, entitled "Observations touching the Antiquity and Dignity of the Degree of Sergeant-at-Law."
(*t*) 2 Inst. 214.
(*u*) Fortesc. c. 50.

Agency (9 ed.) 24-25. In nearly all the states of the union attorneys and counsellors are regulated by statutes which require in general an examination for admission, a good moral character and a solemn oath to uphold the constitutions and faithfully to perform their professional duties. State *v.* Garesche, 36 Missouri, 256 (1866). The courts exercise jurisdiction over attorneys wherever their employment is of a professional capacity or arises from their professional character. Hughes *v.* Meyer, 3 T. R. 275. *In re* Aitkin, 4 B. & A. 47. Luxmoore *v.* Lethbridge, 5 B. & A. 898. An attorney is liable to an action for damages wherever his client is injured by his negligence or deficiency. 4 Bur. 2061. 4 B. & A. 202. 2 Wils. 325. 1 Bing. 347.

(17) In the early stages of the law attorneys were appointed orally in court; later they were appointed by warrant out of court, which warrant was required to be filed. But these rules have become to a great extent relaxed, until, at the present day, we find it well settled that although an attorney cannot admit service of process without authority, yet his authority will be presumed. But where one is represented by an unauthorized attorney he may find relief either by motion or bill in equity. Harshey *v.* Blackmarr, 20 Iowa (Withrow) 161, 171 (1866). An attorney's purchase from his client of the subject-matter of the litigation cannot be enforced. Wood *v.* Downes, 18 Vesey Jr. 119 (1811). West *v.* Raymond, 21 Ind. 305 (1863).

(18) [Apprentices to the law.]
(19) [Sergeants at law.]
(20) [The statute 9 & 10 Vict. c. 54 extended the privileges of sergeant in the court of Common Pleas to all barristers.
(21) [As a mark of honor.]

or fee;(w) so that the first of the modern order (who are now the sworn servants of the crown, with a standing salary) seems to have been Sir Francis North, afterwards lord-keeper of the great seal to king Charles II.(x) These king's counsel answer, in some measure, to the advocates of the revenue, *advocati fisci*, among the Romans. For they must not be employed in any cause against the crown without special license;(22) in which restriction they agree with the advocates of the fisc:(y) but in the imperial law the prohibition was carried still further, and perhaps was more for the dignity of the sovereign: for, excepting some peculiar causes, the fiscal advocates *28] were not permitted to be at all concerned *in private suits between subject and subject.(z) A custom has of late years prevailed of granting letters-patent of precedence to such barrister as the crown thinks proper to honor with that mark of distinction: whereby they are entitled to such rank and pre-audience(a) as are assigned in their respective patents; sometimes next after the king's attorney-general, but usually next after his majesty's counsel then being. These (as well as the queen's attorney and solicitor-general)(b) rank promiscuously with the king's counsel, and together with them sit within the bar of the respective courts; but receive no salaries, and are not sworn, and therefore are at liberty to be retained in causes against the crown. And all other sergeants and barristers indiscriminately (except in the court of common pleas, where only sergeants are admitted)(23) may take upon them the protection and defence of any suitors, whether plaintiff or defendant; who are therefore called their *clients*, like the dependants upon the ancient Roman orators. Those indeed practiced *gratis*, for honor merely, or at most for the sake of gaining influence: and so likewise it is established with us,(c) that a counsel can maintain no action for his fees; which are given, not as *locatio vel conductio*, but as *quiddam honorarium;*(24) not as a salary or hire, but as a mere gratuity, which a counsellor cannot demand without doing wrong to his reputation:(d)(25) as is also laid

(w) See his letters, 256.
(x) See his life by Roger North, 37.
(y) Cod. 2, 9, 1.
(z) Ibid. 2, 7, 13.
(a) Pre-audience in the courts is reckoned of so much consequence that it may not be amiss to subjoin a short table of the precedence which usually obtains among the practicers.
1. The king's premier sergeant, (so constituted by special patent).
2. The king's ancient sergeant, or the eldest among the king's sergeants.
3. The king's advocate-general.
4. The king's attorney-general. }
5. The king's solicitor-general. } (26)

6. The king's sergeants.
7. The king's counsel, with the queen's attorney and solicitor.
8. Sergeants at law.
9. The recorder of London.
10. Advocates of the civil law.
11. Barristers.
In the courts of exchequer, two of the most experienced barristers, called the *post*-man and the *tub*-man, (from the places in which they sit,) have also a precedence in motions.
(b) Seld. tit. *Hon.* 1, 6, 7.
(c) Davis, pref. 22. 1 Ch. Rep. 38.
(d) Davis, 23.

(22) Hence none of the king's counsel can publicly plead in court for a prisoner, or a defendant in a criminal prosecution, without a license,—which is never refused, but an expense of about nine pounds must be incurred in obtaining it.—CHITTY.

(23) That is, in bank; for at trials at nisi prius in Common Pleas a barrister who is not a sergeant may even lead a cause.—CHITTY.

(24) Story on Agency (9 ed.) 42.

(25) Upon the same principle a physician cannot maintain an action for his fees. 4 Term Rep. 317. It has also been held that no action lies to recover back a fee given to a barrister to argue a cause which he did not attend. Peake's R. 122. Formerly it was considered that if a counsel disclosed his client's case or neglected to attend to it, he was liable to be sued. See Vin. Abr. Actions of Assumpsit, P. But in more modern times it has been considered that no such action is sustainable. Peake's R. 96.
On the other hand, sergeants and barristers are entitled to certain privileges. Each is an esquire; and his eldest son is qualified to kill game. 1 T. R. 44. They are entitled when sued separately to have the venue laid in any action against them in Middlesex, (1 Stra. 610,) and are privileged from arrest and from being taken in execution whilst they are on their proper circuit and when they are attending the sittings at Nisi Prius. 1 Hen. Bla. 636.—CHITTY. See Bow. Eng. Const. (2 ed.) 239.

(26) By the king's mandate, 14th Dec. 1811, the king's attorney and solicitor-general are now to have a place and audience before the king's premier sergeant.—CHITTY.

down with regard to advocates in the civil law, (e) whose *honorarium* was directed by a decree of the senate not to exceed in any case ten thousand sesterces,*or about 8o*l.* of English money. (f)(27) And, in order   [*29 to encourage due freedom of speech in the lawful defence of their clients, and at the same time to give a check to the unseemly licentiousness of prostitute and illiberal men, (a few of whom may sometimes insinuate themselves even into the most honorable professions,) it hath been holden that a counsel is not answerable for any matter by him spoken relative to the cause in hand and suggested in his client's instructions, although it should reflect upon the reputation of another, and even prove absolutely groundless; but if he mentions an untruth of his own invention, or even upon instructions, if it be impertinent to the cause in hand, he is then liable to an action from the party injured. (g)(28) And counsel guilty of deceit or collusion are punishable by the statute Westm. 1, 3 Edw. I. c. 28, with imprisonment for a year and a day, and perpetual silence in the courts; a punishment still sometimes inflicted for gross misdemeanors in practice. (h)

CHAPTER IV.

OF THE PUBLIC COURTS OF COMMON LAW AND EQUITY.

WE are next to consider the several species and distinctions of courts of justice which are acknowledged and used in this kingdom.   And these are,

(e) *Ff.* 11, 6, 1.
(f) Tac. *Ann. l.* 11.

(g) Cro. Jac. 90.
(h) Sir T. Raym. 376.

(27) The circumstances which led to this decree, as recorded by Tacitus, deserve to be mentioned. Samius, a Roman knight of distinction, having given Suilius a fee of three thousand guineas to undertake his defence, and finding that he was betrayed by his advocate, *ferro in domo ejus incubuit* [He went home and fell upon his sword]. In consequence of this, the senate insisted upon enforcing the Cincian law, *quâ cavetur antiquitûs, nequis ob causam orandam pecuniam donumve accipiat* [By which it was anciently provided that no one should receive money or presents for pleading a cause].
   Tacitus then recites the arguments of those who spoke against the payment of fees and of those who supported the practice, and concludes with telling us that Claudius Cæsar, thinking that there was more reason, though less liberality, in the arguments of the latter, *capiendis pecuniis posuit modum, usque ad dena sestertia, quem egressi repetundarum tenerentur* [He fixed the amount of the sum to be received at ten thousand sesterces, to exceed which was considered as bribery]. 1 Ann. lib. 11, c. 5.
   But, besides the acceptance of such immense fees, the perfidy of advocates had become a common traffic; for Tacitus introduces the subject by observing, *nec quidquam publicæ mercis tam venale fuit quam advocatorum perfidia* [Nor was there any public traffic so venal as the perfidy of advocates]. To the honor of our courts, the corruption of judges and the treachery of counsel are crimes unheard of in this country. *Quid enim est jus civile? Quod neque inflecti gratiâ, neque perfringi potentiâ, neque adulterari pecuniâ possit* [For what is the civil law? That which can neither be biased by favor, violated by power, nor corrupted by money]. Cic. pro. Cæcina.—CHRISTIAN. See 2 Comyn on Contracts, 378. Adams *v.* Stevens and Cagger, 26 N. Y. (Wend.) 451, 453 (1841). It is now generally conceded throughout the United States that an attorney has a right of action for a reasonable compensation for services rendered. Stevens *v.* Adams, 23 Wendell, 57 S. C. 26. Ibid. 451. Newman *v.* Washington, Martin & Yerger, 79. Stevens *v.* Monges, 1 Harrington, 127. Bayard *v.* McLane, 3 Harrington, 217 (1844). Duncan *v.* Beishaupt, 1 McCord, 149. Downing *v.* Major, 2 Dana, 228. Christy *v.* Douglas, Wright's Ch. Rep. 485. Webb *v.* Hepp, 14 Missouri, 354. Vilas *v.* Downer, 12 Vermont, 419. Lecat *v.* Saller, 3 Porter, 115. Gray *v.* Brackenridge, 2 Penna. Rep. 181. Foster *v.* Jack, 4 Watts, 33. Wait's Actions and Defences, vol. 1, p. 450 (1877). But in N. J. counsel fees cannot be recovered *eo nomini* [Under that name], but by contract only. Seeley *et al. v.* Crane, 3 Green (N. J.) 35, 36 (1835).
   (28) See 1 B. & A. 232. 1 Saund. Rep. 130. When a client is present when his counsel speaks slanderous words and does not disavow them, the client is responsible for any

either such as are of public and general jurisdiction throughout the whole realm, or such as are only of a private and special jurisdiction in some particular parts of it. Of the former there are four sorts: the universally established courts of common law and equity; the ecclesiastical courts; the courts military; and courts maritime.(1) And, first, of such public courts as are courts of common law and equity.

The policy of our ancient constitution, as regulated and established by the great Alfred, was to bring justice home to every man's door, by constituting as many courts of judicature as there are manors and townships in the kingdom, wherein injuries were redressed in an easy and expeditious manner by the suffrage of neighbors and friends. These little courts, however, communicated with others of a larger jurisdiction, and those with others of a still greater power; ascending gradually from the lowest to the supreme courts, which were respectively constituted to correct the errors of the inferior ones, and to determine such causes as by reason of their weight and difficulty *31]   demanded a more solemn discussion. *The course of justice flowing in large streams from the king, as the fountain, to his superior courts of record; and being then subdivided into smaller channels, till the whole and every part of the kingdom were plentifully watered and refreshed. An institution that seems highly agreeable to the dictates of natural reason, as well as of more enlightened policy; being equally similar to that which prevailed in Mexico and Peru before they were discovered by the Spaniards, and to that which was established in the Jewish republic by Moses. In Mexico each town and province had its proper judges, who heard and decided causes, except when the point in litigation was too intricate for their determination; and then it was remitted to the supreme court of the empire, established in the capital, and consisting of *twelve* judges.(a) Peru, according to Garcilasso de Vega, (an historian descended from the ancient Incas of that country,) was divided into small districts containing *ten* families each, all registered and under one magistrate, who had authority to decide little differences and punish petty crimes. Five of these composed a higher class, of *fifty* families; and two of these last composed another, called a *hundred*. Ten hundreds constituted the largest division, consisting of a *thousand* families; and each division had its separate judge or magistrate, with a proper degree of subordination.(b) In like manner, we read of Moses, that, finding the sole administration of justice too heavy for him, he "chose able men out of all Israel, such as feared God, men of truth, hating covetousness: and made them heads over the people, rulers of thousands, rulers of hundreds, rulers of fifties, and rulers of tens; and they judged the people at all seasons: the hard causes they brought unto Moses; but every small matter they judged themselves."(c) These inferior courts, at least the name and form of them, still continue in our legal constitution; but as the superior courts of record have in practice obtained a concurrent original jurisdiction with these; and as there is, besides, a power of removing plaints or actions thither from all the inferior jurisdictions; upon these accounts (amongst others) it has *32]   happened that *these petty tribunals have fallen into decay, and almost into oblivion; whether for the better or the worse, may be matter of some speculation, when we consider on the one hand the increase of expense

(a) Mod. Un. Hist. xxxviii. 469.   (c) Exod. xviii.
(b) Ibid. xxxix. 14.

injury suffered, whether or not he authorized the use of such words. Stackpole *v.* Hennen, vol. 4 (part of 6 & 7, 8, n. s.). C. Rep. La. 27, 31 (1828). See also Ring *v.* Wheeler, 7 Cow. (N. Y.) 725. Jennings *v.* Paine, 4 Wisc. 358. McMillan *v.* Birch, 1 Binn. 178.

(1) Lacaze *v.* State, 1 Add. (Pa.) 59, 81 (1800).

and delay, and on the other the more able and impartial decision, that follow from this change of jurisdiction.

The order I shall observe in discoursing on these several courts, constituted for the redress of *civil* injuries, (for with those of a jurisdiction merely *criminal* I shall not at present concern myself,) will be by beginning with the lowest, and those whose jurisdiction, though public and generally dispersed throughout the kingdom, is yet (with regard to each particular court) confined to very narrow limits; and so ascending gradually to those of the most extensive and transcendent power.

I. The lowest, and at the same time the most expeditious, court of justice known to the law of England, is the court of *piepoudre curia, pedis pulverizati;* so called from the dusty feet of the suitors; or, according to Sir Edward Coke,(*d*) because justice is there done as speedily as dust can fall from the foot; upon the same principle that justice among the Jews was administered in the gate of the city,(*e*) that the proceedings might be the more speedy as well as public. But the etymology given us by a learned modern writer(*f*) is much more ingenious and satisfactory; it being derived, according to him, from *pied puldreaux*, (a pedler, in old French,) and therefore signifying the court of such petty chapmen as resort to fairs or markets. It is a court of record, incident to every fair and market, of which the steward of him who owns or has the toll of the market is the judge; and its jurisdiction extends to administer justice for all commercial injuries done in that very fair or market, and not in any preceding one. So that the injury must be done, complained of, heard, and determined within the compass of one and the same day, unless the fair continues longer. The court hath cognizance of *all matters of contract that can possibly arise within the   [*33 precinct of that fair or market; and the plaintiff must make oath that the cause of action arose there.(*g*) From this court a writ of error lies, in the nature of an appeal, to the courts at Westminster;(*h*) which are now also bound by the statute 19 Geo. III. c. 70 to issue writs of execution, in aid of its process after judgment, where the person or effects of the defendant are not within the limits of this inferior jurisdiction; which may possibly occasion the revival of the practice and proceedings in these courts, which are now in a manner forgotten.(2) The reason of their original institution seems to have been to do justice expeditiously among the variety of persons that resort from distant places to a fair or market; since it is probable that no other inferior court might be able to serve its process, or execute its judgments, on both, or perhaps either, of the parties; and therefore, unless this court had been erected, the complainant must necessarily have resorted, even in the first instance, to some superior judicature.

II. The *court-baron* is a court incident to every manor in the kingdom, to be holden by the steward within the said manor. This court-baron is of two natures:(*i*) the one is a customary court, of which we formerly spoke,(*k*) appertaining entirely to the copyholders, in which their estates are transferred by surrender and admittance, and other matters transacted relative to their tenures only. The other, of which we now speak, is a court of common law, and it is the court of the barons, by which name the freeholders were sometimes anciently called:(3) for that it is held before the freeholders who

---

(*d*) 4 Inst. 272.
(*e*) Ruth iv.
(*f*) Barrington's Observat. on the stat. 337.
(*g*) Stat. 17 Edw. IV. c. 2.

(*h*) Cro. Eliz. 773.
(*i*) Co. Lit. 58.
(*k*) Book ii. ch. 4, 6, and 22.

---

(2) Bow. Eng. Const. (2 ed.) 241.

(3) All the freeholders of the king were called barons; but the editor is not aware that it appears from any authority that this word was ever applied to those who held freeholds of a subject. See an account of the ancient barons, *ante*, 1 book, 399, n. 5.—CHRISTIAN.

owe suit and service to the manor, the steward being rather the registrar than the judge. These courts, though in their nature distinct, are frequently confounded together. The court we are now considering, viz., the free-holders' court, was composed of the lord's tenants, who were the *pares*(4) of each other, and were bound by their feodal tenure to assist their lord in the dispensation of domestic justice. This was formerly held every three weeks; and its most important business is to determine, by writ of right, all controversies relating to the right of lands within the manor.(5) It may

*34]   also hold plea of any personal actions of debt, trespass on the case, or the like, where the debt or damages do not *amount to forty shillings;(*l*) which is the same sum, or three marks, that bounded the jurisdiction of the ancient Gothic courts in their lowest instance, or *fierding-courts,* so called because four were instituted within every superior district or hundred.(*m*) But the proceedings on a writ of right may be removed into the county-court by a precept from the sheriff called a *tolt,*(*n*) "*quia tollit atque eximit causam e curia baronum.*"(*o*)(6) And the proceedings in all other actions may be removed into the superior courts by the king's writs of *pone,*(*p*) or *accedas ad curiam,*(7) according to the nature of the suit.(*q*) After judgment given, a writ also of *false judgment*(*r*) lies to the courts at Westminster to rehear and review the cause, and not a writ of *error;* for this is not a court of record: and therefore, in some of these writs of removal, the first direction given is to cause the plaint to be recorded, *recordari facias loquelam.*(8)

III. A hundred-court is only a larger court-baron, being held for all the inhabitants of a particular hundred instead of a manor. The free suitors are here also the judges, and the steward the registrar, as in the case of a court-baron. It is likewise no court of record; resembling the former in all points, except that in point of territory it is of greater jurisdiction.(*s*) This is said by Sir Edward Coke to have been derived out of the county-court for the ease of the people, that they might have justice done to them at their own doors, without any charge or loss of time;(*t*) but its institution was probably coeval with that of hundreds themselves, which were formerly observed(*u*) to have been introduced, though not invented, by Alfred, being derived from the polity of the ancient Germans. The *centeni,* we may re-

*35]   member, were the principal inhabitants of a district composed of different villages, originally in number a *hundred,* but afterwards only *called by that name;(*v*) and who probably gave the same denomination to the district out of which they were chosen. Cæsar speaks positively of the judicial power exercised in *their* hundred-courts and courts-baron. "*Principes regionum atque pagorum*" (which we may fairly construe, the lords of hundreds and manors) "*inter suos jus dicunt, controversiasque minuunt.*"(*w*)(9)

(*l*) Finch, 248.
(*m*) Stiernhook *de jure Goth. l.* 1, c. 2.
(*n*) F. N. B. 3, 4. See Append. No. I. § 2.
(*o*) 3 Rep. pref.
(*p*) See Append. No. I. § 3.
(*q*) F. N. B. 4, 70. Finch, L. 444, 445.
(*r*) F. N. B. 18.
(*s*) Finch, L. 243. 4 Inst. 267.
(*t*) 2 Inst. 71.

(*u*) Book i. p. 116.
(*v*) *Centeni ex singulis pagis sunt, idque ipsum inter suos vocantur, et, quod primo numeris fuit, jam nomen et honor est.* [Each village is divided into hundreds, and are so called by their inhabitants; and that which first was a mere number has now become both a name and an honor.] Tac. *de Mor. Germ.* c. 6.
(*w*) *De Bell. Gall. l.* 6, c. 22.

(4) [Peers or equals.]
(5) The writ of right having been abolished, (3 & 4 W. IV. c. 27, s. 36,) this branch of its jurisdiction no longer exists.—KERR.
(6) ["Because it tolls, *i. e.* takes away and removes the cause from the court barons."]
(7) [You may come to the court.]
(8) [That you cause the plaint to be recorded.] See Bow. Eng. Const. (2 ed.) 241.
(9) ["Declare the law among their dependents and abate controversies."]

And Tacitus, who had examined their constitution still more attentively, informs us not only of the authority of the lords, but that of the *centeni*, the hundredors, or jury; who were taken out of the common freeholders, and had themselves a share in the determination. "*Eliguntur in conciliis et principes, qui jura per pagos vicosque reddunt: centeni singulis, ex plebe comites, consilium simul et auctoritas, absunt.*"(*x*)(10) This hundred court was denominated *hæreda* in the Gothic constitution.(*y*) But this court, as causes are equally liable to removal from hence, as from the common court-baron, and by the same writs, and may also be reviewed by writ of false judgment, is therefore fallen into equal disuse with regard to the trial of actions.(11)

IV. The county-court(12) is a court incident to the jurisdiction of the sheriff. It is not a court of record, but may hold pleas of debt or damages under the value of forty shillings.(*z*)(13) Over some of which causes these inferior courts have, by the express words of the statute of Gloucester,(*a*) a jurisdiction totally exclusive of the king's superior courts. For in order to be entitled to sue an action of trespass for goods before the king's justiciars, the plaintiff is directed to make affidavit that the cause of action does really and *bonâ fide* amount to 40*s.*; which affidavit is now unaccountably disused,(*b*) except in the court of exchequer.(14) The statute also 43 Eliz. c. 6, which gives the judges in many personal actions, where the jury assess less damages than 40*s.*, a power to certify the same and *abridge the   [*36 plaintiff of his full costs, was also meant to prevent vexation by litigious plaintiffs; who for purposes of mere oppression might be inclinable to institute suits in the superior courts for injuries of a trifling value. The county-court may also hold plea of many real actions, and of all personal actions to any amount, by virtue of a special writ called a *justicies;* which is a writ empowering the sheriff for the sake of despatch to do the same justice

---

(*x*) *De Morib. Germ.* c. 13.
(*y*) Stiernhook, *l.* 1, c. 2.
(*z*) 4 Inst. 266.

(*a*) 6 Edw. I. c. 8.
(*b*) 2 Inst. 391. 3 T. R. 363. Bac. Abr. Court of King's Bench, A. 2.

---

(10) ["The lords are also chosen in their councils who administer justice through the towns and districts. The jury for each hundred are chosen by the people, and have both council and authority."]

(11) The courts-baron and hundred-courts have long been entirely obsolete as courts of civil jurisdiction; and the statute 9 & 10 Vict. c. 95 has accordingly empowered the lords of any hundred, or of any honor, manor, or liberty having any court in right thereof in which debts or demands may be recovered, to surrender the right of holding such courts to the crown, after which surrender the right of holding such courts is to cease and determine.—KERR.

(12) 6 T. R. 175. 8 T. R. 235. 1 Bos. & P. 75. 1 B. & A. 223. Com. Dig. County C. 8. See also Com. Dig. County Courts, 3. Bac. Abr. Court, County Court. Vin. Abr. Court, County, 7, vol. 5. 4 Inst. 266. Cole *v.* Driskell, 1 Blackfords (Indiana) 16 (1818).

(13) A county court may hold pleas in many real actions and in all personal actions to any amount. Shaw *v.* Dutcher, 19 Wend. (N. Y.) 216 (1838).

(14) Where the debt is shown to be less than 40*s.* a superior court will not proceed in the action unless it is shown that the defendant is a non-resident of the county. 3 Burr. 1592. 4 T. R. 495. 5 id. 64. Tid. Pract. 8. 2 Bla. Rep. 754. 6 T. R. 175. 8 T. R. 235. 1 B. & P. 75. 1 Dowl. & R. 359.

The statute 9 & 10 Vict. c. 95, created a new county court, which is a court of record, and which had jurisdiction over debt and damage not exceeding 20*l.* They had jurisdiction over such cases as would arise under partnership accounts, legacies, and cases between landlord and tenant where the rent did not exceed 50*l.* They have no jurisdiction over actions for seduction, breach of promise to marry, libel and slander, malicious prosecution, or criminal conversation.

The judges decided both law and fact unless one of the parties demanded a jury, to which he was entitled if the amount involved exceeded 5*l.*

in his county-court, as might otherwise be had at Westminster.(*c*)(15) The freeholders of the county are the real judges in this court, and the sheriff is the ministerial officer. The great conflux of freeholders which are supposed always to attend at the county court (which Spelman calls *forum plebeiæ justiciæ et theatrum comitivæ potestatis*)(*d*)(16) is the reason why all acts of parliament at the end of every session were wont to be there published by the sheriff ; why all outlawries of absconding offenders are there proclaimed; and why all popular elections which the freeholders are to make, as formerly of sheriffs and conservators of the peace, and still of coroners, verderors, and knights of the shire, must ever be made *in pleno comitatu*, or in full county-court. By the statute 2 Edw. VI. c. 25, no county-court shall be adjourned longer than for one month, consisting of twenty-eight days. And this was also the ancient usage, as appears from the laws of king Edward the elder;(*e*) "*præpositus* (that is, the sheriff) *ad quartam circiter septimanam frequentem populi concionem celebrato: cuique jus dicito; litesque singulas dirimito.*"(17) In those times the county-court was a court of great dignity and splendor, the bishop and the earldorman, (or earl,) with the principal men of the shire, sitting therein to administer justice both in lay and ecclesiastical causes.(*f*) But its dignity was much impaired when the bishop was prohibited and the earl neglected to attend it.   And, in modern times, as proceedings are

*37]   removable from hence into the king's superior courts, by writ of *pone* or *recordari*,(*g*)(18) in the same manner as from *hundred-courts and courts-baron; and as the same writ of false judgment may be had, in nature of a writ of error; this has occasioned the same disuse of bringing actions therein.

These are the several species of common-law courts, which, though dispersed universally throughout the realm, are nevertheless of a partial jurisdiction, and confined to particular districts, yet communicating with, and, as it were, members of, the superior courts of a more extended and general nature; which are calculated for the administration of redress, not in any one lordship, hundred, or county only, but throughout the whole kingdom at large. Of which sort is,

V. The court of *common pleas*, or, as it is frequently termed in law, the court of *common bench*.

By the ancient Saxon constitution, there was only one superior court of justice in the kingdom; and that court had cognizance both of civil and spiritual causes: viz., the *wittena-gemote*, or general council, which assembled annually or oftener, wherever the king kept his Christmas, Easter, or Whitsuntide, as well to do private justice as to consult upon public business. At the conquest the ecclesiastical jurisdiction was diverted into another channel; and the Conqueror, fearing danger from these annual parliaments, contrived also to separate their ministerial power, as judges, from their deliberative, as counsellors to the crown. He therefore established a constant court in his own hall, thence called by Bracton,(*h*) and other ancient authors, *aula regia*, or *aula regis*.(19) This court was composed of the king's great

---

(*c*) Finch, 318. F. N. B. 152.
(*d*) *Gloss. v. comitatus.*
(*e*) C. 11.

(*f*) *LL. Eadgari*, c. 5.
(*g*) F. N. B. 70. Finch. 445.
(*h*) *L*. 3, *tr*. 1, c. 7.

---

(15) Shaw *v.* Dutcher, 19 Wend. (N. Y.) 216, 219 (1838).
(16) [The court of justice for the common people and the theatre of the power of the county.]
(17) ["Let the sheriff hold a full assembly of the people about once a month; declare the law to every one; and severally determine suits."]
(18) Bow. Eng. Const. (2 ed.) 243.
(19) [The King's Bench.]

officers of state resident in his palace, and usually attendant on his person; such as the lord high constable and lord mareschal, who chiefly presided in matters of honor and of arms; determining according to the law military and the law of nations. Besides these, there were the lord high steward, and lord great chamberlain; the steward of the household; the lord chancellor, whose peculiar *business it was to keep the king's seal, and ex-   [*38 amine all such writs, grants, and letters as were to pass under that authority; and the lord high treasurer, who was the principal adviser in all matters relating to the revenue.   These high officers were assisted by certain persons learned in the laws, who were called the king's justiciars or justices, and by the greater barons of parliament, all of whom had a seat in the *aula regia*, and formed a kind of court of appeal, or rather of advice, in matters of great moment and difficulty. All these in their several departments transacted all secular business both criminal and civil, and likewise the matters of the revenue: and over all presided one special magistrate, called the chief justiciar, or *capitalis justiciarius totius Angliæ;*(20) who was also the principal minister of state, the second man in the kingdom, and by virtue of his office guardian of the realm in the king's absence. And this officer it was who principally determined all the vast variety of causes that arose in this extensive jurisdiction, and from the plenitude of his power grew at length both obnoxious to the people, and dangerous to the government which employed him.(*i*)(21)

This great universal court being bound to follow the king's household in all his progress and expeditions, the trial of common causes therein was found very burdensome to the subject. Wherefore king John, who dreaded also the power of the justiciar, very readily consented to that article which now forms the eleventh chapter of *magna carta*, and enacts, "that *communia placita non sequantur curiam regis, sed teneantur in aliquo loco cerio.*"(22) This certain place was established in Westminster hall, the place where the *aula regis* originally sat, when the king resided in that city; and there it hath ever since continued. And the court being thus rendered fixed and stationary, the judges became so too, and a chief with other justices of the common pleas was thereupon appointed; with jurisdiction to hear and determine all pleas of land, and injuries merely civil, between subject and subject. Which critical establishment of this principal court of *common law,   [*39 at that particular juncture and that particular place, gave rise to the inns of court in its neighborhood; and, thereby collecting together the whole body of the common lawyers, enabled the law itself to withstand the attacks of the canonists and civilians, who labored to extirpate and destroy it.(*j*) This precedent was soon after copied by king Philip the Fair in France, who about the year 1302 fixed the parliament at Paris to abide constantly in that metropolis; which before used to follow the person of the king wherever he went, and in which he himself used frequently to decide the causes that were there depending; but all were then referred to the sole cognizance of the parliament and its learned judges.(*k*) And thus also in 1495 the emperor Maximilian I. fixed the imperial chamber (which before always travelled with the court and household) to be constantly held at Worms, from whence it was afterwards translated to Spires.(*l*)

(*i*) Spelm. Gloss. 331, 332, 333. Gilb. Hist. C. P. introd. 17.
(*j*) See book i. introd. § 1.

(*k*) Mod. Un. Hist. xxiii. 396.
(*l*) Ibid. xxix. 46.

---

(20) [Chief justiciary of all England.]
(21) Bow. Eng. Const. (2 ed.) 242, 243. [*Aula regia*—The King's Bench.]
(22) ["Let not the common pleas follow the king's court, but be held in some fixed place."]

The *aula regia* being thus stripped of so considerable a branch of its jurisdiction, and the power of the chief justiciar being also considerably curbed by many articles in the great charter, the authority of both began to decline apace under the long and troublesome reign of king Henry III. And, in further pursuance of this example, the other several officers of the chief justiciar were, under Edward the First, (who new-modelled the whole frame of our judicial polity,) subdivided and broken into distinct courts of judicature. A court of chivalry was erected, over which the constable and mareschal presided; as did the steward of the household over another, constituted to regulate the king's domestic servants. The high steward, with the barons of parliament, formed an august tribunal for the trial of delinquent peers; and the barons reserved to themselves in parliament the right of reviewing the sentences of other courts in the last resort. The distribution of common justice between man and man was thrown into so provident an order,

*40]   that the great judicial officers were *made to form a check upon each other: the court of chancery issuing all original writs under the great seal to the other courts; the common pleas being allowed to determine all causes between private subjects; the exchequer managing the king's revenue; and the court of king's bench retaining all the jurisdiction which was not cantoned out to other courts, and particularly the superintendence of all the rest by way of appeal; and the sole cognizance of pleas of the crown or criminal causes. For pleas or suits are regularly divided into two sorts: *pleas of the crown*, which comprehend all crimes and misdemeanors, wherein the king (on behalf of the public) is the plaintiff; and *common pleas*, which include all civil actions depending between subject and subject.(23) The former of these were the proper object of the jurisdiction of the court of king's bench; the latter of the court of common pleas, which is a court of record, and is styled by Sir Edward Coke (*m*) the lock and key of the common law; for herein only can real actions, that is, actions which concern the right of freehold or the realty, be originally brought: and all other, or personal, pleas between man and man, are likewise here determined; though in most of *them* the king's bench has also a concurrent authority.(24)

The judges of this court are at present(*n*) four in number, one chief and three *puisne* justices, created by the king's letters-patent, who sit every day in the four terms to hear and determine all matters of law arising in civil causes, whether real or personal, or mixed and compounded of both. These it takes cognizance of, as well originally as upon removal from the inferior courts before mentioned. But a writ of error, in the nature of an appeal, lies from this court into the court of king's bench.(25)

*41]   *VI. The court of king's bench (so called because the king used

(m) 4 Inst. 99.
(n) King James I. during the greater part of his reign appointed five judges in the courts of King's Bench and Common Pleas, for the benefit of a casting voice in case of a difference in opinion, and that the circuits might at all times be fully supplied with judges of the superior courts. And in subsequent reigns, upon the permanent indisposition of a judge, a fifth hath been sometimes appointed. Sir T. Raym. 475.

(23) Territory *v.* Flowers, 2 Mon. 531, 536 (1877).
(24) The court of King's Bench has not jurisdiction over mere real actions, yet it may try an action of ejectment, nor has the court of Common Pleas jurisdiction over felony and treason. Hawk, b. 2, ch. 1, 34. Bac. Abr. Courts, A. The courts of the United States and of the several states of the union, like the courts of King's Bench and Common Pleas, have concurrent jurisdiction over many subjects. Territory *v.* Flowers, 2 Mon. 531, 536 (1877).
(25) The court now consists of five judges, one chief and four *puisne* justices. Until the statute 11 Geo. IV. and 1 W. IV. c. 70, an appeal lay from the judgment of this court to the court of King's Bench; but now the appeal for error in law is to the justices of the court of Queen's Bench and barons of the exchequer, in the exchequer-chamber, from whose judgment an appeal lies only to the house of lords.—STEWART.

formerly to sit there in person,(*o*) the style of the court still being *coram ipso rege*)(26) is the supreme court of common law in the kingdom; consisting of a chief justice and three *puisne*(27) justices, who are by their office the sovereign conservators of the peace and supreme coroners of the land. Yet, though the king himself used to sit in this court, and still is supposed so to do, he did not, neither by law is he empowered (*p*) to, determine any cause or motion, but by the mouth of his judges, to whom he hath committed his whole judicial authority.(*q*)(28)

This court, which (as we have said) is the remnant of the *aula regia*, is not, nor can be, from the very nature and constitution of it, fixed to any certain place, but may follow the king's person wherever he goes: for which reason all process issuing out of this court in the king's name is returnable *"ubicunque fuerimus in Anglia."*(29) It hath indeed, for some centuries past, usually sat at Westminster, being an ancient palace of the crown; but might remove with the king to York or Exeter, if he thought proper to command it. And we find that, after Edward I. had conquered Scotland, it actually sat at Roxburgh.(*r*) And this movable quality, as well as its dignity and power, are fully expressed by Bracton when he says that the justices of this court are *"capitales, generales, perpetui, et majores; a latere regis residentes, qui omnium aliorum corrigere tenentur injurias et errores."*(*s*)(30) And it is moreover especially provided in the *articuli super cartas,*(*t*) that the king's chancellor, and the justices of his bench, shall follow him, so that he may have at all times near unto him some that be learned in the laws.

*The jurisdiction of this court is very high and transcendent. It   [*42 keeps all inferior jurisdictions within the bounds of their authority, and may either remove their proceedings to be determined here, or prohibit their progress below. It superintends all civil corporations in the kingdom.

(*o*) 4 Inst. 73.
(*p*) See book 1. ch. 7. The king used to decide causes in person in the *aula regia*. *" In curia domini regis ipse in propria persona jura decernit "* [The king in person judges in his own court]. *Dial. de Scacch. l.* 1, § 4. After its dissolution king Edward I. frequently sat in the court of King's Bench, (see the records cited in 2 Burr. 851;) and in later times

James I. is said to have sat there in person, but was informed by his judges that he could not deliver an opinion.
(*q*) 4 Inst. 71.
(*r*) M. 20. 21 Edw. I. Hale, Hist. C. L. 200.
(*s*) L. 3, c. 10.
(*t*) 28 Edw. I. c. 5. [Articles on the charters.]

---

(26) [Before the king himself.] This court is called the Queen's Bench in the reign of a queen; and during the protectorate of Cromwell it was styled the upper bench.— CHRISTIAN.

(27) [Younger.] [*Aula regia*—The king's hall of justice.]

(28) Lord Mansfield, in 2 Burr. 851, does not mean to say, nor do the records there cited warrant the conclusion, that Edward I. actually sat in the King's Bench. Dr. Henry, in his very accurate History of Great Britain, informs us that he has found no instance of any of our kings sitting in the court of justice before Edward IV. "And Edward IV.," he says, "in the second year of his reign, sat three days together during Michaelmas Term in the court of King's Bench; but it is not said that he interfered in the business of the court; and, as he was then a very young man, it is probable that it was his intention to learn in what manner justice was administered, rather than to act the part of a judge." 5 vol. 282, 4to edit. Lord Coke says that the words in *magna carta*, (c. 29,) *nec super eum ibimus nec super eum mittemus nisi*, etc., signify that we shall not sit in judgment ourselves, nor send our commissioners or judges to try him. 2 Inst. 46. But that this is an erroneous construction of these words appears from a charter granted by king John in the sixteenth year of his reign, which is thus expressed:—*Nec super eos per vim vel per arma ibimus nisi per arma ibimus nisi per legem regni nostri vel per judicium parium suorum.* [Nor will we proceed against them by force or arms unless warranted by the law of our kingdom or the judgment of their peers.] See Introd. to Bl. Mag. Ch. p. 13. Statutes and charters in *pari materia* [Of the same subject-matter] must be construed by a reference to each other; and in the more ancient charter the meaning is clear that the king will not proceed with violence against his subjects unless justified by the law of his kingdom or by a judgment of their peers.—CHRISTIAN.

(29) [" In whatever part of England we shall be."]

(30) ["Chief, general, perpetual and elder; accompanying the king who are appointed to redress the injuries and correct the errors of all others."]

It commands magistrates and others to do what their duty requires, in every case where there is no other specific remedy.(31) It protects the liberty of the subject, by speedy and summary interposition. It takes cognizance both of criminal and civil causes: the former in what is called the crown side, or crown office; the latter in the plea side of the court. The jurisdiction of the crown side is not our present business to consider: that will be more properly discussed in the ensuing book. But on the plea side, or civil branch, it hath an original jurisdiction and cognizance of all actions of trespass or other injury alleged to be committed *vi et armis*(32); of actions for forgery of deeds; maintenance, conspiracy, deceit, and actions on the case which allege any falsity or fraud; all of which savor of a criminal nature, although the action is brought for a civil remedy; and make the defendant liable in strictness to pay a fine to the king, as well as damages to the injured party.(*u*) The same doctrine is also now extended to all actions on the case whatsoever: (*w*) but no action of debt or detinue, or other mere civil action, can by the *common law* be prosecuted by any subject in this court by *original* writ out of chancery;(*x*)(33) though an action of debt given by *statute* may be brought in the king's bench as well as in the common pleas.(*y*) And yet this court might always have held plea of any civil action, (other than actions real,) provided the defendant was an officer of the court; or in the custody of the marshal, or prison-keeper, of this court, for a breach of the peace or any other offence.(*z*) And, in process of time, it began by a fiction to hold plea of all personal actions whatsoever, and has continued to do so for ages:(*a*) it being surmised that the defendant is arrested for

*43]   *a supposed trespass, which he never has in reality committed; and, being thus in the custody of the marshal of the court, the plaintiff is at liberty to proceed against him for any other personal injury: which surmise, of being in the marshal's custody, the defendant is not at liberty to dispute.(*b*) And these fictions of law, though at first they may startle the student, he will find upon further consideration to be highly beneficial and useful; especially as this maxim is ever invariably observed, that no fiction shall extend to work an injury; its proper operation being to prevent a mischief, or remedy an inconvenience, that might result from the general rule of law.(*c*) So true it is, that *in fictione juris semper subsistit æquitas.*(*d*)(34) In the present case, it gives the suitor his choice of more than one tribunal before which he may institute his action; and prevents the circuity and delay of justice, by allowing that suit to be originally, and in the first instance,

(*u*) Finch, L. 198. 2 Inst. 23. *Dyversite de courtes c. bank le roy.*
(*w*) F. N. B. 86, 92. 1 Lilly, Pract. Reg. 503.
(*x*) 4 Inst. 76. Trye's Jus Filizar. 101.
(*y*) Carth. 234.
(*z*) 4 Inst. 71.
(*a*) Ibid. 71.
(*b*) Thus too in the civil law; *contra fictionem non admittitur probatio: quid enim efficeret probatio veritatis, ubi fictio adversus veritatem fingit. Nam fictio nihil aliud est, quam legis adversus veritatem in re possibili ex justa causa dispositio. Gothofred. in Ff. l. 22, t. 3.* [Proof is not admitted to contradict a fiction, for what would the proof of truth avail where fiction counterfeits truth? For fiction is simply a supposition by the law for a just cause of something possible which is contrary to the truth.]
(*c*) 3 Rep. 30. 2 Roll. Rep. 502.
(*d*) 11 Rep. 51. Co. Litt. 150.

(31) The writ of mandamus is confined only to the King's Bench as it has general supervision over all inferior courts and is co-extensive with judicial sovereignty. The same theory exist in all our state governments where the common law is adopted, and the power of issuing the writ is generally confided to the highest court of original jurisdiction. Swift *v.* Richardson, 7 Huston (Del.) 338, 356 (1886). *Ex parte* Henderson, 6 Florida, 279, 292 (1855). Chumasero *v.* Potts, 2 Blake (Montana) 242, 269 (1875). Thomas *v.* Mead *et al.*, 36 Whittelsey (Missouri) 232, 247 (1866). Cox *et al. v.* Brendlove *et al.*, 2 Yerger (Tenn.) 499, 506 (1831).
(32) [With force and arms.] Berry *v.* Hamill, 12 S. & R. 213 (1824).
(33) This is not the present practice. R. T. Hardw. 317. Tidd's Prac. 8 ed. 97.— CHITTY.
(34) [A fiction of law is always founded in equity.] Hibbard *v.* Smith, 67 Cal. 547, 561 (1885).

commenced in this court, which, after a determination in another, might ultimately be brought before it on a writ of error.(35)

For this court is likewise a court of appeal, into which may be removed by writ of error all determinations of the court of common pleas, and of all inferior courts of record in England; and to which a writ of error lies also from the court of king's bench in Ireland.(36) Yet even this so high and honorable court is not the *dernier resort*(37) of the subject; for, if he be not satisfied with any determination here, he may remove it by writ of error into the house of lords, or the court of exchequer chamber, as the case may happen, according to the nature of the suit and the manner in which it has been prosecuted.(38)

VII. The court of exchequer is inferior in rank not only to the court of king's bench, but to the common pleas also: but I have chosen to consider it in this order on account of its double capacity as a court of law and a court of equity *also. It is a very ancient court of record, set up [*44 by William the Conqueror,(e) as a part of the *aula regia*,(f) though regulated and reduced to its present order by king Edward I.,(g) and intended principally to order the revenues of the crown, and to recover the king's debts and duties.(h) It is called the exchequer, *scaccharium* from the checked cloth, resembling a chess-board, which covers the table there, and on which, when certain of the king's accounts are made up, the sums are marked and scored with counters. It consists of two divisions: the receipt of the exchequer, which manages the royal revenue, and with which these commentaries have no concern; and the court or judicial part of it, which is again subdivided into a court of equity and a court of common law.(39)

The court of equity is held in the exchequer chamber before the lord treasurer, the chancellor of the exchequer, the chief baron, and three *puisne* ones. These Mr. Selden conjectures(i) to have been anciently made out of such as were barons of the kingdom, or parliamentary barons; and thence to to have derived their name; which conjecture receives great strength from Bracton's explanation of *magna carta*, c. 14, which directs that the earls and barons be amerced by their peers; that is, says he, by the barons of the exchequer.(k) The primary and original business of this court is to call

(e) Lamb. *Archeion.* 24.
(f) Madox Hist. Exch. 109.
(g) Spelm. *Guil. I. in cod. leg. vet. apud* Wilkins.

(h) 4 Inst. 103-116.
(i) Tit. Hon. 2, 5, 16.
(k) L. 3, tr. 2, c. 1, § 8.

---

(35) But, as there is no reason for doing that indirectly which may be done directly, it was considered expedient to abolish this among other legal fictions, (2 W. IV. c. 39,) and the mode of commencing an action has for some time been and is now, uniform in all the superior courts.—STEWART.

(36) Upon *certiorari* under section 47, of the 2d Rev. Statutes, p. 49, providing that "Whenever any authority shall be exercised by any of the officers pursuant to any provision of this title, the proceedings may be removed into the Supreme Court by certiorari and there examined and corrected." The authority and duty of such court is to review and correct all errors in matters of law committed in the exercise of this extraordinary jurisdiction and not simply to review the record or the proceedings in the nature thereof, brought to it upon such writ. Morewood *v.* Hollister, 2 N. Y. App. (Seld.) 309, 312 (1852). A *certiorari* lies upon all final adjudications of an inferior court or officer invested by the legislature with power to decide on the property or rights of citizens and which court or officer acts in a summary way or in a new course different from the common law. Stone *et al. v.* The Mayor etc. of N. Y., 25 Wend. 157, 167 (1840).

(37) [The last resort.]

(38) Daniel *v.* Warren Co., 1 Bibb. (Ky.) 496, 498 (1840). The appeal from the King's or Queen's Bench is now in all cases to the justices of the Common Pleas and barons of the exchequer, in the exchequer-chamber, from whose judgment an appeal lies to the house of lords.—STEWART. [*Aula regia*—King's Bench.]

(39) This court has exclusive jurisdiction in fiscal matters, although it is of inferior rank to the court of Common Pleas and the King's Bench. 1 Austr. 205. Hardr. 176. Parker, 143. 1 Price, 206. 8 Price, 584. Manning's Exchequer Prac. 161, 164, n.

the king's debtors to account, by bill filed by the attorney-general; and to recover any lands, tenements, or hereditaments, any goods, chattels, or other profits or benefits, belonging to the crown. So that by their original constitution the jurisdiction of the court of common pleas, king's bench, and exchequer was entirely separate and distinct: the common pleas being intended to decide all controversies between subject and subject; the king's bench to correct all crimes and misdemeanors that amount to a breach of the peace, the king being then plaintiff, as such offences are in open derogation of the *jura regalia*(40) of his crown; and the exchequer to adjust *and recover his revenue, wherein the king also is plaintiff, as the withholding and non-payment thereof is an injury to his *jura fiscalia.* (41) But, as by a fiction almost all sorts of civil actions are now allowed to be brought in the king's bench, in like manner by another fiction all kinds of personal suits may be prosecuted in the court of exchequer. For as all the officers and ministers of this court have, like those of other superior courts, the privilege of suing and being sued only in their own court; so also the king's debtors and farmers, and all accomptants of the exchequer, are privileged to sue and implead all manner of persons in the same court of equity that they themselves are called into. They have likewise privilege to sue and implead one another, or any stranger, in the same kind of common-law actions (where the personalty only is concerned) as are prosecuted in the court of common pleas.

*45]

This gives original to the common-law part of their jurisdiction, which was established merely for the benefit of the king's accomptants, and is exercised by the barons only of the exchequer, and not the treasurer or chancellor. The writ upon which all proceedings here are grounded is called a *quo minus:* in which the plaintiff suggests that he is the king's farmer or debtor, and that the defendant hath done him the injury or damage complained of; *quo minus sufficiens existit,*(42) by which he is less able to pay the king his debt or rent. And these suits are expressly directed, by what is called the statute of Rutland,(*l*) to be confined to such matters only as specially concern the king or his ministers of the exchequer. And by the *articuli super cartas,*(*m*)(43) it is enacted, that no common pleas be thenceforth holden in the exchequer contrary to the form of the great charter. But now, by the suggestion of privilege, any person may be admitted to sue in the exchequer as well as the king's accomptant. The surmise, of being debtor to the king, is therefore become matter of form and mere words of course, and the court is open to all the nation equally.(44) The same holds with regard to the equity side of the court: for there any *46] person may file *a bill against another upon a bare suggestion that he is the king's accomptant; but whether he is so, or not, is never controverted. In this court on the equity side, the clergy have long used to exhibit their bills for the non-payment of tithes; in which case the surmise of being the king's debtor is no fiction, they being bound to pay him their first-fruits and annual tenths. But the chancery has of late years obtained a large share in this business.(45)

(*l*) 10 Edw. I. c. 11.   (*m*) 28 Edw. I. c. 4.

(40) [Regal rights.]
(41) [Fiscal rights.]
(42) [Whereby he is less able.]
(43) [Articles upon the charters.]
(44) This fiction has been for some time abolished. 2 W. IV. c. 39.—STEWART.
(45) This jurisdiction was transferred to the High Court of Chancery by st. 5 Vict. c. 5.
1 Quincy (Mass.) 470 (1761).

An appeal from the equity side of this court lies immediately to the house of peers; but from the common-law side, in pursuance of the statute 31 Edw. III. c. 12, a writ of error must first be brought into the court of exchequer chamber. And from the determination there had, there lies, in the *dernier resort*, a writ of error to the house of lords.(46)

VIII. The high court of chancery is the only remaining, and in matters of civil property by much the most important of any, of the king's superior and original courts of justice. It has its name of chancery, *cancellaria*, from the judge who presides here, the lord chancellor, or *cancellarius;* who, Sir Edward Coke tells us, is so termed *a cancellando*, from cancelling the king's letters patent when granted contrary to law, which is the highest point of his jurisdiction.(*n*)(47) But the office and name of chancellor (however derived) was certainly known to the courts of the Roman emperors: where it originally seems to have signified a chief scribe or secretary, who was afterwards invested with several judicial powers, and a general superintendency over the rest of the officers of the prince. From the Roman empire it passed to the Roman church, ever emulous of imperial state; and hence every bishop has to this day his chancellor, the principal judge of his consistory. And when the modern kingdoms of Europe were established upon the ruins of the empire, almost every state preserved its chancellor, with different jurisdictions and dignities, according to their different constitutions. But in all of them he seems to have had the supervision of all charters, letters, and such other public instruments of the crown as were authenticated in the most solemn manner; and therefore *when seals came in use, he   [*47 had always the custody of the king's great seal. So that the office of chancellor, or lord keeper,(48) (whose authority by statute 5 Eliz. c. 18, is declared to be exactly the same,) is with us at this day created by the mere delivery of the king's great seal into his custody:(*o*) whereby he becomes,

(*n*) 4 Inst. 88.   (*o*) Lamb. *Archeion.* 65.

(46) [Last resort.] By the 31 Edward III. c. 12, this court of appeal is to consist of the chancellor and treasurer, and such justices and sage persons as they shall think fit. It is altered by 31 Eliz. c. 1, 16 Car. II. c. 2, 20 Car. II. c. 4, from which it appears that the court may consist of both the chief justices, or one of them, or of the chancellor, provided the chancellor is present when the judgment is given. See the proceedings in the case of Johnstone *v.* Sutton in this court. 1 T. R. 493.—CHITTY.

But by statute 5 Vict. c. 5 its jurisdiction as a court of equity was transferred to the court of chancery; and it is now only a court of law and revenue, with five judges,—a chief and four puisnè barons,—like the courts of Queen's Bench and Common Pleas. From the judgment of this court an appeal lies to the justices of the Queen's Bench and Common Pleas, sitting as the court of exchequer chamber; and from that court an appeal lies to the house of lords.—KERR. See Bow. Eng. Const. (2 ed.) 248.

(47) According to the opinion of several learned authors, (as Mr. Cambden, in his Britannia, and Dr. Cowell, in his Interpreter, have observed,) the chancery had its name originally from certain bars laid one over another crosswise, like a lattice, wherewith it was environed to keep off the press of the people, and not to hinder the view of those officers who sat therein,—such gates or crossbars being by the Latins called *cancelli. Vid.* Dugd. 32. Cambden, Cowell, Cassiod. ep. 6, lib. 11. Pet. Pythæus, lib. 2, advers. c. 12. 1 Harr. Ch. 1. Dr. Johnson seems also inclined to this definition; and it indeed appears the most reasonable, for we have also the word "chancel," which signifies that part of the church formerly *barred* off from the body of it.—CHITTY.

(48) King Henry V. had two great seals, one of gold, which he delivered to the bishop of Durham and made him lord chancellor, another of silver, which he delivered to the bishop of London to keep; and historians often confound chancellors and keepers, (1 Harr. Ch. 68, note. 4 Inst. 88;) but at this day, there being but one great seal, there cannot be both a chancellor and a lord keeper of the great seal at one time, because both are but one office, as is declared by the stat. 5 Eliz. 4 Inst. 88, and the taking away the seal determines the office. 1 Sid. 338. It seems that it is not inconsistent for the lord chancellor also to hold the office of chief justice of the King's Bench. Lord Hardwicke held both offices from 20th February till 7th June. 1 Sid. 338. Com. Dig. tit. Chancery, (B. 1).—CHITTY. Chancellor's case, 1 Bland. (Md. Ch.) 596, 623 (1855).

without writ or patent, an officer of the greatest weight and power of any now subsisting in the kingdom, and superior in point of precedency to every temporal lord.(p) He is privy counsellor by his office,(q) and, according to lord chancellor Ellesmere,(r) prolocutor of the house of lords by prescription. To him belongs the appointment of all justices of the peace throughout the kingdom. Being formerly usually an ecclesiastic, (for none else were then capable of an office so conversant in writings,) and presiding over the royal chapel,(s) he became keeper of the king's conscience; visitor in right of the king, of all hospitals and colleges of the king's foundation; and patron of all the king's livings under the value of twenty marks(t) *per annum* in the king's books.(49) He is the general guardian of all infants,

(p) Stat. 31 Hen. VIII. c. 10.
(q) Selden, Office of Lord Chanc. § 3.
(r) Of the office of lord chancellor, edit. 1651.

(s) Madox, Hist. of Exch. 42.
(t) 38 Edw. III. 3 F. N. B. 35, though Hobart (214) extends this value to twenty *pounds*.

(49) With regard to the chancellor's patronage there seems to be some inaccuracy in the learned judge's text and references. I humbly conceive that a truer statement is this,—viz., that it appears from the rolls of parliament in the time of Edward III. that it had been the usage before that time for the chancellors to give all the king's livings taxed (by the subsidy assessments) at twenty marks or under, to the clerks, who were then actually *cleri* or clergymen, who had long labored in the court of chancery; but that the bishop of Lincoln, when he was chancellor, had given such livings to his own and other clerks, contrary to the pleasure of the king and the ancient usage; and therefore it is recommended to the king by the council to command the chancellor to give such livings only to the clerks of chancery, the exchequer, and the other two benches or courts of Westminster hall. 4 Edw. III. n. 51. But since the new valuation of benefices, or the king's books, in the time of Henry the Eighth, and the clerks ceased to be in orders, the chancellor has had the absolute disposal of all the king's livings, even where the presentation devolves to the crown by lapse, of the value of twenty pounds a year or under in the king's books. It does not appear how this enlarged patronage has been obtained by the chancellor: but it is probably by a private grant of the crown, from a consideration that the twenty marks in the time of Edward III. were equivalent to twenty pounds in the time of Henry VIII. Gibs. 764. 1 Burn, Ec. Law, 129.

Concerning chancellor's salary, see Chancellor case, 1 Bland. (Md.) 596, 623 (1835). So far this was the note in my first edition; but a reverend gentleman has been so obliging as to suggest to me that, having once had occasion to examine the subject, he was inclined to think that the chancellor's patronage was confined to benefices under 20*l.* a year, and that livings exactly of that value belonged to the king, to be presented to by himself or his minister. Having, in consequence, looked more attentively into the subject, I am still of opinion that the authorities support what is advanced in the preceding part of the note. It cannot be doubted that since the new *valor beneficiorum* [The value of benefices], *pounds* were intended to be substituted for *marks*, and this is expressly stated by bishop Gibson, p. 764. In the 4 Edw. III., cited above, the chancellor's patronage is stated to be of all livings of 20 marks and under, *del tax de vint marces et dedeyns* [Of the rate of twenty marks and under]. In the 1 Hen. VI. note 25, Rolls of Parliament, there is a record appointing the duke of Bedford protector, and the duke of Gloucestor protector in his absence; and amongst other privileges it grants the protector, for the time-being, the patronage of all the livings belonging to the crown, *ultra taxam viginti marcarum usque ad taxam triginta marcarum inclusivè* [Beyond the rate of twenty marks to the rate of thirty marks inclusive]; and reserves the rest of the royal patronage to the king, except the benefices belonging to the chancellor, *virtute officii sui* [By virtue of his office]. The word *inclusivè* can only apply to the words *usque ad triginta* [To thirty]; it cannot be reconciled with *ultra*, which was intended to leave the chancellor 20 or under. This is also clearly expressed in the Registrum Brevium 307, where there is an ancient writ called *de primo beneficio ecclesiastico habendo. Volumus quod idem A. ad primum beneficium ecclesiasticum (taxationem viginti marcarum excedens) vacaturum, quod ad præsentionem nostram pertinuerit,* etc. [Of possessing the first ecclesiastical. We will that the same A. be presented to the first vacant ecclesiastical benefice (exceeding the rate of twenty marks) which shall be in our presentation.]

In the year-book, 38 Edw. III. 3, it is laid down as law that the king shall present to *toutz esglises que passent l'extent de 20 marcs* [All churches which exceed the amount of twenty marks]; and in the next line it is said that the chancellor shall present to all not taxed at 20 marks, and having understood that the living in question was taxed at 40s. he had presented to it, but as, in fact, it was taxed at 40*l.*, the king claimed it. The words in French state the general law; the rest only apply to the particular case. Yet Watson is so careless as to state the chancellor's patronage to be under 20 marks and

idiots, and lunatics; and has the general superintendence of all charitable uses in the kingdom.(50) And all this over and above the vast and extensive jurisdiction which he exercises in his *judicial* capacity in the court of chancery; wherein, as in the exchequer, there are two distinct tribunals: the one ordinary, being a court of common law; the other extraordinary, being a court of equity.

The ordinary legal court is much more ancient than the court of equity. Its jurisdiction is to hold plea upon a *scire facias* to repeal and cancel the king's letters-patent, when made against law or upon untrue suggestions; and to hold plea of petitions, *monstrans de droit*,(51) traverses of offices, and the like; when the king hath been advised to do any act, or is put in possession of any lands or goods, in prejudice of a subject's right.(*u*)(52). On proof of which, as the king can never *be supposed intentionally to　　[*48 do any wrong, the law questions not but he will immediately redress the injury, and refers that conscientious task to the chancellor, the keeper of his conscience. It also appertains to this court to hold plea of all personal actions, where any officer or minister of the court is a party.(*v*) It might likewise hold plea (by *scire facias*) of partitions of land in coparcenery,(*w*) and of dower,(*x*) where any ward of the crown was concerned in interest, so long as the military tenures subsisted: as it now may also do of the tithes of forest land, where granted by the king, and claimed by a stranger against the grantee of the crown;(*y*) and of executions on statutes, or recognizances in nature thereof, by the statute 23 Henry VIII. c. 6.(*z*) But if any cause comes to issue in this court, that is, if any fact be disputed between the parties, the chancellor cannot try it, having no power to summon a jury;

(*u*) 4 Rep. 54.
(*v*) 4 Inst. 80.
(*w*) Co. Litt. 171. F. N. B. 62.

(*x*) Bro. Abr. tit. *Dower*, 66. Moor. 565.
(*y*) Bro. Abr. tit. *Dismes*, 10.
(*z*) 2 Roll. Abr. 469.

---

under 20*l.*, and refers to this authority, ch. 9. But it is correctly cited by Comyns to support the position that the chancellor has the patronage of 20 marks or 20*l.* Dig. tit. Esgl. H. 5. In Fitz. N. B. 35 it is stated to be *under* 20 marks, without taking any notice of 20 exactly. And in a case of Hob. 214 the word is *under*. In that case the chancellor had presented to a living lapsed to the crown above 20*l.* a year, and it was held that the king could have no remedy, because the presentation had passed the great seal, and therefore apparently made by the king himself; but if the presentation had stated that the benefice was under the value of 20*l.*, then it would have been void, because the chancellor must have been deceived. In this case there was no occasion to state the instance of a living of the exact value of 20*l.* This was a benefice which had devolved to the crown by lapse; but no objection is made on that ground, and there seems to be no reason for any distinction, whether the benefice devolves to the king by lapse or by promotion of the incumbent, or it is part of his original patronage. I have stated the authorities which expressly give the chancellor the patronage of the value of 20 marks, or now 20*l.*, and I have referred to those which state it to be *under;* and, I cannot but observe, so far they are all consistent, as I find no authority in opposition to those above, declaring that livings of the value of 20*l.* belong to the king and not to the chancellor.

The gentleman who wished me to examine the authorities upon this subject was so obliging as to inform me that the crown has the patronage of five livings of the exact value of 20*l.* in the king's books, but that several others of that value occasionally devolve to the crown by lapse and promotion; that he has examined the church-book in the secretary of state's office, and that he finds within the last century many instances of presentations to those livings by the crown; but he admits in some modern instances where the right to the presentation has been claimed both by the chancellor and the minister, that the latter has yielded to the former. From the whole, one is led to conclude that these presentations made by the crown were owing either to the inattention or the accommodation of the chancellor.—CHRISTIAN.

(50) But such is not the case in the United States. Robertson *v.* Bullions, 9 Barb. (N. Y.) 64, 91 (1850).

(51) [A manifestation or plea of right.]

(52) The jurisdiction of chancery according to equity and good conscience, extends to all cases cognizable in equity and the party objecting to its exercise must show that some other court of equity has cognizance of the case. Magill *v.* Brown, 1 Brightly (Pa.) 397.

but must deliver the record *propria manu*(53) into the court of king's bench, where it shall be tried by the country, and judgment shall be there given thereon.(a)(54) And when judgment is given in chancery upon demurrer or the like, a writ of error in nature of an appeal lies out of this ordinary court into the court of king's bench:(b) though so little is usually done on the common-law side of the court, that I have met with no traces of any writ of error(c) being actually brought, since the fourteenth year of queen Elizabeth, A. D. 1572.(55)

In this ordinary or legal court is also kept the *officina justitiæ*:(56) out of which all original writs that pass under the great seal, all commissions of charitable uses, sewers, bankruptcy, idiotcy, lunacy, and the like, do issue; and for which it is always open to the subject, who may there at any time demand and have, *ex debito justitiæ*,(57) any writ that his occasions *49] *may call for. These writs (relating to the business of the subject) and the returns to them were, according to the simplicity of ancient times, originally kept in a hamper, *in hanaperio;* and the others (relating to such matters wherein the crown is immediately or mediately concerned) were preserved in a little sack or bag, in *parva baga:* and thence hath arisen the distinction of the *hanaper* office and *petty bag* office, which both belong to the common-law court in chancery.

But the extraordinary court, or court of equity, is now become the court of the greatest judicial consequence. This distinction between law and equity, as administered in different courts, is not at present known, nor seems to have ever been known, in any other country at any time:(d) and yet the difference of one from the other, when administered by the same tribunal, was perfectly familiar to the Romans;(e) the *jus prætorium*, or discretion of the prætor, being distinct from the *leges*, or standing laws,(f)

(a) Cro. Jac. 12. Latch. 112.
(b) Year-book, 18 Edw. III. 25. 17 Ass. 24. 29 Ass. 47. Dyer, 315. 1 Roll. Rep. 287. 4 Inst. 80.
(c) The opinion of lord-keeper North, in 1682, (1 Vern. 131. 1 Eq. Ca. Abr. 129.) that no such writ of error lay, and that an injunction might be issued against it, seems not to have been well considered.
(d) The *Council of Conscience*, instituted by John III. king of Portugal, to review the sentence of all inferior courts and moderate them by equity, (Mod. Un. Hist. xxii. 237,) seems rather to have been a court of appeal.
(e) Thus too the parliament of Paris, the court of session in Scotland, and every other jurisdiction in Europe of which we have any tolerable account, found all their decisions as well upon principles of equity as those of positive law. Lord Kaimes's Histor. Law Tracts, i. 325, 330: Princ. of Equity, 44.
(f) Thus Cicero: "*jam illis promissis, non esse standum, quis non videt, quæ coactus quis metu et deceptus dolo promiserit? quæ quidem plerumque jure prætorio liberantur, nonnulla legibus.*" Offic. l. 1. [To whom is it not evident that promises made through fear or fraud are of no validity? some of which are dissolved at the discretion of the judge, and some by the laws.]

(53) [With his own hand.]
(54) But on the equity side of the court questions of fact may be decided without an issue; but this jurisdiction ought to be exercised very tenderly and sparingly. 9 Vesey, 168. On the trial of an issue directed out of chancery, if either party be desirous of having a special jury, it is said to be proper to move the court of chancery for that purpose. See Prec. Ch. 264. 2 P. Wms. 68. 4 M. & S. 195, 196.—CHITTY.

It is important to confine this observation (which is not always done) to the common-law side of the court of chancery. Sitting as a judge at common law and trying causes according to the rules of the common law, the lord chancellor cannot decide by himself a disputed fact, and has no power of issuing process to the sheriff or other officer for summoning a jury. But on the equity side of the court, where the jurisdiction of the lord chancellor is placed entirely on other grounds than those of the common law, he is equally competent to decide on disputed facts as on disputed law; and it is matter of discretion only when he either orders or permits the parties to submit the trial of such fact to the cognizance of a jury. For the manner in which this is done, see *post*, 452. According to the later precedents, when a record comes into the King's Bench from chancery, the chancellor does not deliver it *propria manu* [With his own hands], but sends it by the clerk of the petty bag. 1 Eq. Ca. Abr. 128.—COLERIDGE. Cunningham *v.* Browning, 1 Bland (Md. Ch.) 299, 304 (1835).

And now, by 12 & 13 Vict. c. 109, any issue, either of fact or law, must be sent to one of the three superior courts of law, there to be determined according to the ordinary course of proceeding in those courts.—STEWART.

(55) Bow. Eng. Const. (2 ed.) 250.
(56) [The magazine of justice.]
(57) [As due to justice.]

but the power of both centred in one and the same magistrate, who was equally intrusted to pronounce the rule of law, and to apply it to particular cases by the principles of equity. With us, too, the *aula regia*(58), which was the supreme court of judicature, undoubtedly administered equal justice according to the rules of both or either, as the case might chance to require: and, when that was broken to pieces, the idea of a court of equity, as distinguished from a court of law, did not subsist in the original plan of partition. For though equity is mentioned by Bracton(*g*) as a thing contrasted to strict law, yet neither in that writer, nor in Glanvil or Fleta, nor yet in Britton, (composed under the auspices and in the name of Edward I., and *treating particularly of courts and their several jurisdictions,) is   [*50 there a syllable to be found relating to the equitable jurisdiction of the court of chancery. It seems therefore probable, that when the courts of law, proceeding merely upon the ground of the king's original writs, and confining themselves strictly to that bottom, gave a harsh or imperfect judgment, the application for redress used to be to the king in person assisted by his privy-council, (from whence also arose the jurisdiction of the court of requests,(*h*) which was virtually abolished by the statute 16 Car I. c. 10;) and they were wont to refer the matter either to the chancellor and a select committee, or by degrees to the chancellor only, who mitigated the severity or supplied the defects of the judgments pronounced in the courts of law, upon weighing the circumstances of the case. This was the custom not only among our Saxon ancestors, before the institution of the *aula regia*,(*i*) but also after its dissolution, in the reign of king Edward I.;(*k*) and perhaps, during its continuance, in that of Henry II.(*l*)

In these early times the chief judicial employment of the chancellor must have been in devising new writs, directed to the courts of common law, to give remedy in cases where none was before administered.(59) And to quicken the diligence of the clerks in the chancery, who were too much attached to ancient precedents, it is provided by statute Westm. 2, 13 Edw. I. c. 24, that " whensoever from thenceforth in one case a writ shall be found in the chancery, and in a like case falling under the same right and requiring like remedy *no precedent of a writ can be produced, the   [*51 clerks in chancery shall agree in forming a new one; and, if they cannot agree, it shall be adjourned to the next parliament, where a writ shall be framed by consent of the learned in the law,(*m*) lest it happen for the future that the court of our lord the king be deficient in doing justice to the suitors.'' And this accounts for the very great variety of writs of trespass on the case to be met with in the register; whereby the suitor had ready relief, according to the exigency of his business, and adapted to the specialty, reason, and equity of his very case.(*n*) Which provision (with a little accuracy in the clerks of the chancery, and a little liberality in the

---

(*g*) L. 2, c. 7, fol. 23.
(*h*) The matters cognizable in this court, immediately before its dissolution, were " almost all suits that, by color of equity, or supplication made to the prince, might be brought before him; but originally and properly all poor men's suits, which were made to his majesty by supplication, and upon which they were entitled to have right, without payment of any money for the same." Smith's Commonwealth, b. 3, c. 7.
(*i*) *Nemo ad regem appellet pro aliqua lite, nisi jus domi consequi non possit. Si jus nimis severum sit, alleviatio deinde quæratur apud regem* [No one may appeal to the king in any suit, unless he cannot obtain justice at home. If the decision be too severe,

then a mitigation of it may be prayed from the king]. *LL. Edg.* c. 2.
(*k*) Lambard. *Archeion.* 59.
(*l*) Joannes Sarisburiensis, (who died A. D. 1182, 26 Hen. II.,) speaking of the chancellor's office in the verses prefixed to his *polycraticon*, has these lines:—
    Hic est, qui leges regni cancellat iniquas
    Et mandata pii principis æqua facit.
[It is he who cancels the unequitable laws of the kingdom, and executes the just mandates of a righteous prince.]
(*m*) A great variety of new precedents of writs, in cases before unprovided for, are given by this very statute of Westm. 2.
(*n*) Lamb. *Archeion.* 61.

---

(58) [King's Bench.]
(59) Cobbey on Replevin, p. 319, § 607 (1890).

judges, by extending rather than narrowing the remedial effects of the writ) might have effectually answered all the purposes of a court of equity;(o) except that of obtaining a discovery by the oath of the defendant.

But when, about the end of the reign of king Edward III., uses of land were introduced (p) and, though totally discountenanced by the courts of common law, were considered as fiduciary deposits and binding in conscience by the clergy, the separate jurisdiction of the chancery as a court of equity began to be established;(q) and John Waltham, who was bishop of Salisbury and chancellor to king Richard II., by a strained interpretation of the above-mentioned statute of Westm. 2, devised the writ of *subpœna*, returnable in the court of chancery only, to make the feoffee to uses accountable to his *cestuy que use*(60): which process was afterwards extended to other matters wholly determinable at the common law, upon false and fictitious suggestions; for which therefore the chancellor himself is, by statute 17 Ric.

*52]   II. c. 6, directed to give damages to the party unjustly aggrieved. But as the *clergy, so early as the reign of king Stephen, had attempted to turn their ecclesiastical courts into courts of equity, by entertaining suits *pro læsione fidei*,(61) as a spiritual offence against conscience, in case of non-payment of debts or any breach of civil contracts;(r) till checked by the constitutions of Clarendon,(s) which declared that "*placita de debitis quæ fide interposita debentur, vel absque interpositione fidei, sint in justitia regis*:"(62) therefore probably the ecclesiastical chancellors, who then held the seal, were remiss in abridging their own new-acquired jurisdiction; especially as the spiritual courts continued(t) to grasp at the same authority as before in suits *pro læsione fidei* so late as the fifteenth century,(u) till finally prohibited by the unanimous concurrence of all the judges. However, it appears from the parliament rolls,(w) that in the reigns of Henry IV. and V. the commons were repeatedly urgent to have the writ of *subpœna* entirely suppressed, as being a novelty devised by the subtlety of chancellor Waltham against the form of the common law; whereby no plea could be determined unless by examination on oath of the parties, according to the form of the law civil, and the law of holy church, in subversion of the common law. But though Henry IV., being then hardly warm in his throne, gave a palliating answer to their petitions, and actually passed the statute 4 Hen. IV. c. 23, whereby judgments at law are declared irrevocable unless by attaint or writ of error, yet his son put a negative at once upon their whole application: and in Edward IV.'s time the process by bill and *subpœna*, was become the daily practice of the court.(x)

*53]   *But this did not extend very far: for in the ancient treatise entitled *diversité des courtes*,(y) supposed to be written very early in the

---

(o) This was the opinion of Fairfax, a very learned judge in the time of Edward the Fourth. "*Le subpœna* (says he) *ne serroit ore cy souventment use come il est ore, si nous attendames tiels actions sur les cases, et mainteinames le jurisdiction de ceo court, et d'outer courts.*" Year-book, 21 Edw. IV. 23. [" The subpœna would not be so often used here as it is if we were to pay attention to actions on the case, and maintain the jurisdiction of this or other courts.]
(p) See book ii. ch. 20.
(q) Spelm. Gloss. 106.   1 Lev. 242
(r) Lord Lyttelt. Hen. II. b. iii. p. 361, note.
(s) 10 Hen. II. c. 15.   Speed. 458.
(t) In 4 Hen. III., suits in court Christian *pro læsione fidei* upon temporal contracts were adjudged to be contrary to law. Fitz. Abr. tit. *Prohibition*, 15. But in the statute or writ of *circumspecte agatis* [That you act cautiously], supposed by some to

have issued 13 Edw. I., but more probably (3 Pryn. Rec. 336) 9 Edw. II., suits *pro læsione fidei* were allowed to the ecclesiastical courts; according to some ancient copies, (Berthelet *stat. antiq.* Lond. 1531, 9d, b. 3 Pryn. Rec. 386,) and the common English translation of that statute; though in Lyndewode's copy (*Prov. l. 2, t. 2,*) and in the Cotton MS. (*Chaud. D. 2*) that clause is omitted.
(u) Year-book, 2 Hen. IV. 10.   11 Hen. IV. 88. 38 Hen. VI. 29.   20 Edw. IV. 10.
(w) *Rot. Parl.* 1 Hen. IV. N° 78 and 110.   3 Hen. V. N° 16, cited in Prynne's Abr. of Cotton's Records, 410, 422, 424, 548.   4 Inst. 83.   1 Roll. Abr. 370, 371, 372.
(x) *Rot. Parl.* 11 Edw. IV. N° 33, (not 11 Edw. III,) as cited 1 Roll. Abr. 370, etc.
(y) Tit. *Chancery*, fol. 296.   Rastell's edit. A. D. 1534. [Diversity of the courts.]

---

(60) [Beneficiary's use]
(61) [For a breach of faith.]
(62) ["Let those pleas of debts which are due with or without the interposition of a trust, be in the king's jurisdiction."]

sixteenth century, we have a catalogue of the matters of conscience then cognizable by *subpœna* in chancery, which fall within a very narrow compass. No regular judicial system at that time prevailed in the court; but the suitor, when he thought himself aggrieved, found a desultory and uncertain remedy, according to the private opinion of the chancellor, who was generally an ecclesiastic, or sometimes (though rarely) a statesman: no lawyer having sat in the court of chancery from the times of the chief justices Thorp and Knyvet, successively chancellors to king Edward III. in 1372 and 1373,(*z*) to the promotion of Sir Thomas More by king Henry VIII. in 1530. After which the great seal was indiscriminately committed to the custody of lawyers, or courtiers,(*a*) or churchmen,(*b*) according as the convenience of the times and the disposition of the prince required, till sergeant Puckering was made lord keeper in 1592; from which time to the present the court of chancery has always been filled by a lawyer, excepting the interval from 1621 to 1625, when the seal was intrusted to Dr. Williams, then dean of Westminster, but afterwards bishop of Lincoln, who had been chaplain to lord Ellesmere when chancellor.(*c*)(63)

In the time of lord Ellesmere (A. D. 1616) arose that notable dispute between the courts of law and equity, set on foot by Sir Edward Coke, then chief justice of the court of king's bench; whether a court of equity could give relief after or against a judgment at the common law? This contest was so warmly carried on, that indictments were preferred against the suitors, solicitors, the counsel, and even a master in chancery, for having incurred a *præmunire*(64) by questioning in a court of equity a judgment in the court of king's bench obtained by gross fraud and imposition.(*d*) This matter, being brought before the king, was by him referred *to his learned [*54 counsel for their advice and opinion; who reported so strongly in favor of the courts of equity,(*e*) that his majesty gave judgment in their behalf; but, not contented with the irrefragable reasons and precedents produced by his counsel, (for the chief justice was clearly in the wrong,) he chose rather to decide the question by referring it to the plenitude of his royal prerogative.(*f*) Sir Edward Coke submitted to the decision,(*g*) and thereby made atonement for his error: but this struggle, together with the business of *commendams*, (in which he acted a very noble part,)(*h*) and his controlling the commissioners of sewers,(*i*) were the open and avowed causes,(*k*) first of his suspension, and soon after of his removal, from his office.

Lord Bacon, who succeeded lord Ellesmere, reduced the practice of the court into a more regular system; but did not sit long enough to effect any considerable revolution in the science itself: and few of his decrees which have reached us are of any great consequence to posterity. His successors,

(*z*) Spelm. Gloss. 111. Dugd. *Chron. Ser.* 50.
(*a*) Wriothesly, St. John, and Hatton.
(*b*) Goodrick, Gardiner, and Heath.
(*c*) Biog. Brit. 4278.
(*d*) Bacon's Works, iv. 611, 612, 682.
(*e*) Whitelocke of Parl. ii. 390. 1 Chanc. Rep. Append. 11.
(*f*) "For that it appertaineth to our princely office only to judge over all judges, and to discern and determine such differences as at any time may and shall arise between our several courts touching their jurisdiction, and the same to settle and determine as we in our princely wisdom shall find to stand most with our honor," etc. 1 Chanc. Rep. Append. 26.
(*g*) See the entry in the council-book, 26 July, 1616. Biog. Brit. 1390.
(*h*) In a cause of the bishop of Winchester, touching a *commendam* [A recommendation to elect a

bishop], king James, conceiving that the matter affected his prerogative, sent letters to the judges not to proceed in it till himself had been first consulted. The twelve judges joined in a memorial to his majesty, declaring that their compliance would be contrary to their oaths and the law; but, upon being brought before the king and council, they all retracted and promised obedience in every such case for the future, except Sir Edward Coke, who said "that, when the case happened, he would do his duty." Biog. Brit. 1388.
(*i*) See that article in ch. 6.
(*k*) See lord Ellesmere's speech to Sir Henry Montague, the new chief justice, 15 Nov. 1616, Moor's Reports, 828. Though Sir Edward might probably have retained his seat, if, during his suspension, he would have complimented lord Villiers (the new favorite) with the disposal of the most lucrative office in his court. Biog. Brit. 1391.

(63) Winder *v.* Diffendefer, 2 Bland (Md.) 188 (1840).
(64) A writ so called by which certain offenders are put out of the protection of the law.

in the reign of Charles I., did little to improve upon his plan; and even after the restoration the seal was committed to the earl of Clarendon, who had withdrawn from practice, as a lawyer, near twenty years; and afterwards to the earl of Shaftesbury, who (though a lawyer by education) had never *55] practiced at all. Sir Heneage Finch, who succeeded in 1673, *and became afterwards earl of Nottingham, was a person of the greatest abilities and most uncorrupted integrity; a thorough master and zealous defender of the laws and constitution of his country; and endued with a pervading genius that enabled him to discover and to pursue the true spirit of justice, notwithstanding the embarrassments raised by the narrow and technical notions which then prevailed in the courts of law, and the imperfect ideas of redress which had possessed the courts of equity. The reason and necessities of mankind, arising from the great change in property by the extension of trade and the abolition of military tenures, co-operated in establishing his plan, and enabled him, in the course of nine years, to build a system of jurisprudence and jurisdiction upon wide and rational foundations; which have also been extended and improved by many great men who have since presided in chancery. And from that time to this, the power and business of the court have increased to an amazing degree.(65)

---

(65) Besides the chancellor, the *master of the rolls* has jurisdiction of judging causes on the extraordinary side of the court of chancery. Cardinal Wolsey was, it is said, the first who introduced this power, though then much objected to; yet now it seems he is authorized by special commission under the great seal. Wyatt, Prac. Reg. 278. Com. Dig. Chancery, B. 4. The time and place of his sitting are usually at six o'clock in the evening at his own court in the rolls yard. All decrees made by him must be signed by the lord chancellor before they are enrolled. 3 Geo. II. c. 30, s. 1. By statute 23 Geo. II. c. 25, s. 6, a yearly sum of 1200*l.* was granted to him; and by the late act 6 Geo. IV. c. 84 his salary is raised to 7000*l.* He holds his office by patent for life, and takes the oath prescribed by 18 Edw. III. in open court. Wyatt, Prac. Reg. 277. He takes precedence next after the chancellor, before all other of the judges.

Owing to the great increase of business, and which is still increasing, it was provided, by the 53 Geo. III. c. 24, that his majesty might appoint an additional judge-assistant, called the *vice-chancellor*, to assist the chancellor, who must be a barrister of fifteen years' standing, to hold his office during good behavior, subject to removal upon the address of both houses. By sect. 2, he shall hear such cases as the chancellor shall direct. His decrees shall be subject to reversal by the chancellor, and must be signed by the latter before they are enrolled. By sect. 3, he cannot alter or vary a decree of chancellor or master of rolls. Sect. 4 directs in what court he shall sit; and he is to rank next after the master of rolls. Sect. 5 appoints his officers. Sect. 6, how he is to be removed. Sect. 7, oath of office. Sect. 8, his salary, (5000*l.*, increased by 6 Geo. IV. c. 84 to 6000*l.*) Sect. 12, that he and his officers shall receive no fees for business done. Query, Whether the vice-chancellor has power to hear, by consent, a motion to discharge or alter an order made by the lord chancellor? See 1 J. & W. 429. If he is authorized to discharge it, he is not to alter it. Id. ib. When sitting *for* the lord chancellor, he has no jurisdiction to alter or discharge orders made by the chancellor. Id. 431.

Besides the master of the rolls, (the chief,) there are eleven other *masters in chancery.* Com. Dig. Chancery, B. 5. All answers and affidavits are sworn before one of them and signed; all matters of account, exceptions to answers, etc., irregularities, contempts, and such like, are referred to them. 13 Car. II. st. 6. 12 Geo. I. c. 32. 5 Geo. III. c. 28. 32 Geo. III. c. 42. 9 Geo. III. c. 19. 46 Geo. III. c. 128. Besides these, there are *masters extraordinary*, appointed in the country to take affidavits, etc. Next in precedence are the *six clerks*, each of whom has ten sworn clerks under him. The six clerks are principally concerned in matters in equity, and it is their business to transact and file all proceedings by bill and answer, and also to issue certain patents which pass the great seal, as pardons of men for chance medley, patents for ambassadors, sheriff's patents, and some others. All these matters are transacted by their under-clerks. 1 Harr. Ch. P. 75. Though formerly otherwise, clients are now at liberty to choose their own clerks. Ord. Ch. 107. They claim, besides fees of six clerks' offices, others as comptrollers of the hanaper, and for enrolling warrants, for patents, grants, and other matters passing under the great seal and returned into hanaper office. Six clerks and three clerks of petty bag are by letters-patent (16 Eliz.) incorporated and styled clerks of the enrolment of the high court of chancery, and have two deputies. See 14 & 15 Hen. VIII. c. 8.

From this court of equity in chancery, as from the other superior courts, an appeal lies to the house of peers. But there are these differences between appeals from a court of equity, and writs of error from a court of law: 1. That the former may be brought upon any interlocutory matter; the latter upon nothing but only a definitive judgment. 2. That on writs of error the house of lords pronounces the judgment; on appeals it gives direction to the court below to rectify its own decree.(66)

IX. The next court that I shall mention is one that hath no original jurisdiction, but is only a court of appeal, to correct the errors of other jurisdictions. This is the court of exchequer; which was first erected by statute 31

The office of *registrar* of this court is of great importance. Com. Dig. Chancery, B. 6. The registrar has four deputies, two of whom always sit in court and take notes of orders and decrees, etc.; and before the same are entered he signs them. 45 Geo. III. c. 75. Besides these, there are the master of the subpoena office, registrar of affidavits, examiners, ushers, accountant-general, (12 Geo. I. c. 32. 12 Geo. II. c. 24. 9 Geo. III. c. 19. 32 Geo. III. c. 42. 46 Geo. III. c. 129. 54 Geo. III. c. 14,) cursitors, clerks of the petty-bag office, sergeant-at-arms, warden of the fleet, clerk of the chapel of the rolls, etc. —CHITTY.

The master of the rolls has long administered justice according to the rules of equity, in a separate court. He is appointed by letters-patent, and was formerly the chief merely of the masters in chancery, who carried out the decrees and performed the ministerial functions of the courts of equity. A recent statute (15 & 16 Vict. c. 80) has provided, however, for the gradual abolition of the masters in chancery and the transference of their functions, under an amended procedure, to the judges and their chief clerks. The jurisdiction of the master of the rolls is regulated by the statute 3 Geo. II. c. 30, by which all decrees and orders made by him, except in matters of bankruptcy and lunacy, which, when this statute was passed, were appropriated exclusively to the lord chancellor, are to be valid, subject, however, to their being discharged or altered on appeal to the lord chancellor. His jurisdiction is extended by the 3 & 4 W. IV. c. 94; and an appeal now lies from his judgment, to the lord chancellor, or to the court of appeal in chancery. The master of rolls is, by 1 & 2 Vict. c. 94, the custodier of the public records.

In 1813, an additional judge in chancery, or vice-chancellor, was created, with power to hear and determine all matters depending in the court of chancery, according to the direction of the lord chancellor. This additional assistance was soon found insufficient to keep under the business which flowed into this court; and in 1832 it was relieved from the jurisdiction in bankruptcy, which it had previously exercised, and which was then transferred to the courts of bankruptcy, an appeal, however, being still open to one of the vice-chancellors appointed to sit in bankruptcy. But this appeal must now be made to the court of appeal in chancery. It was still, however, generally admitted that the court of chancery was inadequate to relieve the crowd of suitors who awaited its judgments, and an increase of judges was loudly called for. Accordingly, when the equity jurisdiction of the court of exchequer was transferred to the court of chancery in 1841, two additional vice-chancellors were appointed, (5 Vict. c. 5;) and a third vice-chancellor's court has since been created. 14 & 15 Vict. c. 4. 15 & 16 Vict. c. 80. These judges are to hear and determine all matters depending in the court of chancery,—either as a court of law or equity,—or which have been or shall be submitted to the jurisdiction of the said court or of the lord chancellor by the special authority of any act of parliament.

There is an appeal from the judgment of any of the vice-chancellors, either to the lord chancellor or to the court of appeal in chancery.

The court of appeal in chancery was created by the stat. 14 & 15 Vict. c. 83. It consists of two lords-justices, appointed by letters-patent, with whom the lord chancellor sometimes sits to form a full court, but who, with or without the lord chancellor, exercise all the jurisdiction in equity possessed by him, without prejudice to his sitting alone and exercising such jurisdiction alone as formerly. This court may consist of the lord chancellor and the two lords-justices, or of the chancellor and one of such judges, or of the two lords-justices sitting together. The appeal in bankruptcy, formerly to one of the vice-chancellors, is now to the two lords-justices, who, together and exclusive of the lord chancellor, constitute the court of appeal in bankruptcy, whose judgment in such cases is final. An appeal from any judgment or order of the master of the rolls or any of the vice-chancellors lies to this court or to the lord chancellor.

From these courts of equity in chancery, as from the other superior courts, an appeal lies to the house of peers.—STEWART.

(66) Clason v. Shotwell, 12 Johnson (N. Y.) 30, 49 (1814). See further Jurisdiction of Chancery, McCarthy v. Orphan Asylum Society, 9 Cowen (N. Y.) 437.

Edw. III. c. 12 to determine causes by writs of error from the common-law side of the court of exchequer. And to that end it consists of the lord chancellor and lord treasurer, taking unto them the justices of the king's bench and common pleas. In imitation of which, a second court of exchequer chamber was erected by statute 27 Eliz. c. 8, consisting of the justices of the common pleas, and the barons of the exchequer, before
*56]　whom writs of error may be brought to reverse judgments *in certain suits(*l*) originally begun in the court of king's bench.(67) Into the court also of exchequer chamber (which then consists of all the judges of the three superior courts, and now and then the lord chancellor also) are sometimes adjourned from the other courts such causes as the judges upon argument find to be of great weight and difficulty, before any judgment is given upon them in the court below.(*m*)

From all the branches of this court of exchequer chamber a writ of error lies to

X. The house of peers, which is the supreme court of judicature in the kingdom, having at present no original jurisdiction over causes, but only upon appeals and writs of error, to rectify any injustice or mistake of the law committed by the courts below. To this authority this august tribunal succeeded of course upon the dissolution of the *aula regia*. For, as the barons of parliament were constituent members of that court; and the rest of its jurisdiction was dealt out to other tribunals, over which the great officers who accompanied those barons were respectively delegated to preside; it followed, that the right of receiving appeals, and superintending all other jurisdictions, still remained in the residue of that noble assembly, from which every other great court was derived. They are therefore in all causes the last resort, from whose judgment no further appeal is permitted; but every subordinate tribunal must conform to their determinations; the law reposing an entire confidence in the honor and conscience of the noble persons who compose this important assembly, that (if possible) they will make themselves masters of those questions which they undertake to decide, and in all dubious cases refer themselves to the opinions of the judges who are summoned by writ to advise them, since upon their decision all property must finally depend.(68)

(*l*) See ch. xxv. p. 411.　　　　　　　　　　　(*m*) 4 Inst. 119. 2 Bulst. 146.

---

(67) By the stat. 11 Geo. IV. and 1 W. IV. c. 70, these courts have been abolished, and the court of exchequer chamber, as it now exists, constituted in their place. Error brought upon (that is to say, an appeal presented against) any judgment given by the courts of Queen's Bench, Common Pleas, or Exchequer is to be heard and determined only by the judges—or judges and barons, as the case may be—of the other two courts in the exchequer chamber, from the judgment of which court no error lies except to the house of lords.—STEWART. [*Aula regia*—The king's hall of justice.]

(68) It is to be observed that it is not now the practice of the whole body of the house of peers to attend to its judicial business. This is usually transacted entirely by the lord chancellor, or other peers who have filled judicial stations. Deputy speakers of the legal profession not members of the body have been appointed at various times to preside in the absence of the lord chancellor. The attendance of three other lay peers during these sessions of the house is a matter of form settled by rotation; but the lay peers, although thus present, properly abstain from voting on judicial matters,—the arguments on which it would be unreasonable to suppose that they can perfectly understand, and to which they have not always entirely attended. The propriety of their so abstaining has been recently recognized in a case of great importance.—O'Connell *v.* The Queen, 11 C. & F. 421. The appellate jurisdiction of the house of lords must, however, be admitted to be in an unsettled and unsatisfactory state. 1 Stewart's Blackst. 9.

"There can be no doubt," says Mr. Lewis, "that, both recently and of old, well-founded complaints have been heard of defects in the constitution of the upper house as the final court of appeal and error. The paucity of its legal members, the absence of any constitutional obligation upon their legal members (excepting the chancellor) to

Hitherto may also be referred the tribunal established by statute 14 Edw. III. c. 5, consisting (though now out of use) of one prelate, two earls, and two barons, who are to be chosen at every new parliament, to hear complaints of grievances and delays of justice in the king's courts, and (with the advice of the chancellor, treasurer, and justices of both benches) to give directions for remedying these *inconveniences in the courts below.   [*57 This committee seems to have been established lest there should be a defect of justice for want of a supreme court of appeal during any long intermission or recess of parliament; for the statute further directs, that if the difficulty be so great that it may not well be determined without assent of parliament, it shall be brought by the said prelate, earls and barons, unto the *next* parliament, who shall finally determine the same.

XI. Before I conclude this chapter, I must also mention an eleventh species of courts of general jurisdiction and use, which are derived out of, and act as collateral auxiliaries to, the foregoing. I mean the courts of assize and *nisi prius.*

These are composed of two or more commissioners, who are twice in every year sent by the king's special commission all round the kingdom, (except London and Middlesex, where courts of *nisi prius* are holden in and after every term, before the chief or other judge of the several superior courts;(69)

---

attend the transaction of the judicial business, the irregularity of attendance which the engrossing avocations of those who hold judicial office elsewhere renders in their case unavoidable, the advanced years to which most have in general attained who by success in forensic life reach the peerage,—these various circumstances have led to a want of confidence in the constitution of this high court, and a feeling of uncertainty in its administration of justice, which has occasionally been justified by the spectacle of one peer sitting in error from the judgment of a court composed of a plurality of judges; or, again, the decision of judges specially versed and accomplished, it may be, in the branch of jurisprudence involved, reviewed by a peer or peers having no such experience and endowed with no such special knowledge; or, again, two peers only attending and differing,—the one agreeing in and the other dissenting from the decision under review and thus in effect nullifying the suitor's right to a decision by leaving the case precisely where it was; or, lastly, (and which is perhaps more to be regretted than all,) a single legal peer sitting alone in one character to adjudicate upon a complaint against the decision already pronounced by him in another.'' Papers of Juridical Society, vol. 1. p. 142. With the view of strengthening the judicial staff in the house of peers, baron Parke was recently made a peer for life only, with the title of lord Wensleydale, the object being that hereafter eminent lawyers may be introduced into the highest court without involving any *permanent* addition to the hereditary peerage or to the aristocratic section of the legislature, and without entailing the burden of a hereditary title when there may not be adequate means of supporting it. Great dissatisfaction having been expressed at this movement, as tending to subject the house of peers to the influence and power of the crown and to injuriously affect the balance of the constitution, a patent has been since issued to lord Wensleydale in the usual form.

In New York and New Jersey, and some other states, the plan of investing the Senate or the more permanent branch of the legislature with the functions of a high court of errors and appeals has been fairly tried, and, after an experience of many years in the two states named, has been abandoned. To subject the decisions of lawyers to be reversed in the highest courts by the votes of laymen was found to be productive of confusion and uncertainty, and consequent insecurity to titles and property,—than which a greater evil cannot afflict any community.—SHARSWOOD. See Republic v. Smith, 1 Dallam (Tex.) 407 (1841). Gibson and Moore v. Rogers, 2 Pike (Ark.) 335 (1839). For the present English law on this subject see note 75, p. 1071, *infra.*

(69) The courts of *Nisi Prius* [Unless before] in London and Middlesex are called *sittings.* Those for Middlesex were established by the legislature in the reign of queen Elizabeth. In ancient times all issues in action brought in that county were tried at Westminster in the terms, at the bar of the court in which the action was instituted; but when the business of the courts increased these trials were found so great an inconvenience that it was enacted, by the 18 Eliz. c. 12, that the chief-justice of the King's Bench should be empowered to try within the term, or within four days after the end of the term, all the issues joined in the court of chancery and King's Bench; and that the chief-justice of the Common Pleas and the chief-baron should try in like manner the issues

and except the four northern countries, where the assizes are holden only once a year,) to try by a jury of the respective counties the truth of such matters of fact as are then under dispute in the courts of Westminster hall. These judges of assize came into use in the room of the ancient justices in eyre, *justiciarii in itinere*, who were regularly established, if not first appointed, by the parliament of Northampton, A.D. 1176, 22 Hen. II.,(*n*) with a delegated power from the king's great court, or *aula regia*, being looked upon as members thereof; and they afterwards made their circuit round the kingdom once in seven years for the purpose of trying causes.(*o*) They were afterwards directed, by *magna carta*, c. 12, to be sent into every county once a year to take (or receive the verdict of the jurors or recognitors in certain actions, then called) recognitions or assizes; the most difficult of which they are directed to adjourn into the court of common pleas to be there determined. The itinerant justices were sometimes mere justices *58] of assize, or of dower, or of gaol-delivery, and the like; and *they had sometimes a more general commission to determine all manner of causes, being constituted *justiciarii ad omnia placita:*(*p*)(70) but the present justices of assize and *nisi prius* are more immediately derived from the statute Westm. 2, 13 Edw. I. c. 30, which directs them to be assigned out of the king's sworn justices, associating to themselves one or two discreet knights of each county. By statute 27 Edw. I. c. 4, (explained by 12 Edw. II. c. 3,) assizes and inquests were allowed to be taken before any one justice of the court in which the plea was brought, associating to him one knight or other approved man of the county. And lastly, by statute 14 Edw. III. c. 16, inquests of *nisi prius* may be taken before any justice of either bench, (though the plea be not depending in his own court,) or before the chief baron of the exchequer, if he be a man of the law; or otherwise before the justices of assize, so that one of such justices be a judge of the king's bench or common pleas, or the king's sergeant sworn.(71) They usually make their circuits in the respective vacations after Hilary and Trinity terms; assizes being allowed to be taken in the holy time of lent by consent of the bishops at the king's request, as expressed in statute Westm. 1, 3 Edw. I. c. 51. And it was also usual, during the times of popery, for the prelates to grant annual licenses to the justices of assize to administer oaths in holy times; for, oaths being of a sacred nature, the logic of those deluded ages concluded that they must be of ecclesiastical cognizance.(*q*) The prudent jealousy of our ancestors ordained(*r*) that no man of law should be judge of assize in his own county, wherein he was born or doth

(n) Seld. *Jan. l.* 2, § 5. Spelm. *Cod.* 309.
(o) Co. Litt. 293.—Anno 1261, *justiciarii itinerantes venerunt apud Wigorniam in octavis S. Johannes Baptistæ:—et totus comitatus eos admittere recusavit, quod septem anni nondum erant elapsi, postquam justiciarii ibidem ultimosederunt.* [The judges in Eyre came to Worcester on the octave of *Saint John the Baptist;* and the whole county refused to admit them, because seven years had not elapsed since the judges had

sat in the same place.] *Annal. Eccl. Wigorn. in Whart. Angl. Sacr.* i. 495.
(p) Bract. *l.* 3, *tr.* 1, c. 11.
(q) Instances hereof may be met with in the appendix to Spelman's original of the terms, and in Mr. Parker's Antiquities, 209.
(r) Stat. 4 Edw. III. c. 2. 8 Ric. II. c. 2. 33 Hen. VIII. c. 24.

joined in their respective courts. In the absence of any one of the chiefs, the same authority was given to two of the judges or barons of his court. The statute 12 Geo. I. c 31 extended the time to eight days after term, and empowered one judge or baron to sit in the absence of the chief. The 24 Geo. II. c. 18 has extended the time after term still further to fourteen days.—CHRISTIAN.

And the time was afterwards, and still continues, unlimited during the vacation next after the term, by the 1 Geo. IV. c. 55. Before the passing of the 1 Geo. IV. c. 21, the nisi prius sittings in Middlesex were confined to Westminster hall; but by that act they may be held at any other fit place within the city of Westminster.—CHITTY.

(70) [Justices of all pleas.]

(71) And now, by 1 Geo. IV. c. 55, s. 5, any judge or baron may, on his circuit, amend a record and make any order in any cause, although it was not in a suit depending in his own court.—CHITTY.

inhabit;(72) and a similar prohibition is found in the civil law,(s) which has carried this principle so far that it is equivalent to the crime of sacrilege for a man to be governor of the province in which he was born or has any civil connection.(t)

The judges upon their circuits now sit by virtue of five several authorities. 1. The commission of the *peace*. 2. A commission of *oyer* and *terminer*. 3. A commission of general *gaol-delivery*. The consideration of all which belongs properly *to the subsequent book of these commentaries. But   [*59 the fourth commission is, 4. A commission of *assize*, directed to the justices and sergeants therein named, to take (together with their associates) assizes in the several counties,—that is, to take the verdict of a peculiar species of jury, called an assize, and summoned for the trial of *landed* disputes, of which hereafter. The other authority is, 5. That of *nisi prius*,(73) which is a consequence of the commission of *assize*,(u) being annexed to the office of those justices by the statute of Westm. 2, 13 Edw. I. c. 30, and it empowers them to try all questions of fact issuing out of the courts of Westminster that are then ripe for trial by jury.(74) These, by the course of the courts,(w) are usually appointed to be tried at Westminster in some Eastern or Michaelmas Term, by a jury returned from the county wherein the cause of action arises; but with this proviso, *nisi prius, unless before* the day prefixed the judges of assize come into the county in question. This they are sure to do in the vacations preceding each Easter and Michaelmas Term, which saves much expense and trouble. These commissions are constantly accompanied by writs of *association*, in pursuance of the statutes of Edward I. and II. before mentioned; whereby certain persons (usually the clerk of assize and his subordinate officers) are directed to associate themselves with the justices and sergeants, and they are required to admit the said persons into their society, in order to take the assizes, etc., that a sufficient supply of commissioners may never be wanting. But, to prevent the delay of justice by the absence of any of them, there is also issued of course a writ of *si non omnes*, directing that if all cannot be present, any two of them (a justice or a sergeant being one) may proceed to execute the commission.

These are the several courts of common law and equity which are of public and general jurisdiction throughout the kingdom.(75) And, upon the whole,

(s) *Ff.* 1,3 .2 2,
(t) C. 9, 29, 4.

(u) Salk. 454.
(w) See ch. xxii. p. 353.

---

(72) The statute 12 Geo. II. c. 27 withdrew this restriction from the commissioners of oyer and terminer, and 49 Geo. III. c. 91 withdrew it as to commissioners of assize and nisi prius.

(73) [Unless before.]

(74) An important act, the 3 Geo. IV. c. 10, was lately passed to remedy the defect of the commission not being opened on the day appointed; by which it is enacted that the commission may be opened on the succeeding day to the one appointed; and if such succeeding day be a Sunday, or any other day of public rest, then on the next following day, provided the opening the commission on the appointed day was prevented by the pressure of business elsewhere, or by some unforeseen cause or accident.—CHITTY.

(75) "The Supreme Court of Judicature Act of 1873 & 1875," has effected a complete reorganization of the English courts. The act declares that the high court of chancery, the court of queen's bench, of common pleas at Westminster, of exchequer, of admiralty, of probate, and of divorce and matrimonial causes shall be consolidated together, and shall constitute one supreme court of judicature.

This supreme court is then divided into two permanent divisions: "Her Majesty's High Court of Justice," and "Her Majesty's Court of Appeal." For convenience and for business of a special character, the former is subdivided into three parts: 1. Chancery; 2. Queen's bench (embracing the common pleas and exchequer); 3. Probate, divorce, and admiralty.

The court of appeal, while not subdivided, usually sits in two divisions of three judges each.

we cannot but admire the wise economy and admirable provision of our ancestors in settling the distribution of justice in a method so well calculated for cheapness, expedition, and ease. By the constitution which they established, all trivial debts and injuries of small consequence were to be *60] recovered or redressed in every *man's own county, hundred, or perhaps parish. Pleas of freehold, and more important disputes of property, were adjourned to the king's court of common pleas, which was fixed in one place for the benefit of the whole kingdom. Crimes and misdemeanors were to be examined in a court by themselves, and matters of the revenue in another distinct jurisdiction. Now indeed, for the ease of the subject and greater despatch of causes, methods have been found to open all the three superior courts for the redress of private wrongs; which have remedied many inconveniences, and yet preserved the forms and boundaries handed down to us from high antiquity. If facts are disputed, they are sent down to be tried in the country by the neighbors; but the law arising upon those facts is determined by the judges above: and, if they are mistaken in point of law, there remain in both cases two successive courts of appeal to rectify such their mistakes. If the rigor of general rules does in any case bear hard upon individuals, courts of equity are open to supply the defects, but not sap the fundamentals, of the law. Lastly, there presides over all

---

As to jurisdiction, that of the high court of justice corresponds in its several divisions to the jurisdiction anciently possessed by each. The judges in any division may sit in any other; and any relief which might be given by any of the courts constituting the several divisions may now be given by any other division or by any judge of any division. Where rules of equity, common law, or admiralty conflict, the act states which rule shall prevail, and, in cases not otherwise provided for, enacts that when law and equity conflict, equity shall prevail.

The high court of justice exercises chiefly original jurisdiction; the court of appeal only appellate. The house of lords is retained as the highest court of appeals.

As to the number of judges in each division: the chancery consists of the lord chancellor, *president*, and five *justices;* the queen's bench division, of the lord chief-justice and fourteen justices; the probate, divorce, and admiralty, of two judges, the president and another. Chitty's Eng. Statutes, vol. 7, *Judicature.*

In the United States there are two systems of courts, separate and distinct, growing out of the peculiar nature of our form of government. "America is a commonwealth of commonwealths, a republic of republics, a state which, while one is nevertheless composed of other states," each covering a legislative domain, sovereign and independent, limited in its powers only by the broader powers of the federal government.

1. State courts. Between the courts of the several states there is a striking family resemblance. Each has its highest court of last resort, and its system of inferior courts of various grades and names, with powers and jurisdictions definitely marked out.

2. The federal courts are provided for by the constitution of the United States and statutes passed by congress from time to time under authority originally conferred by the constitution "to establish inferior courts."

The highest federal court is the supreme court, composed at the present time of nine judges—one chief justice and eight associate justices—sitting at the national capital, holding one term a year. The justices are appointed by the president, for life, subject to removal for misbehavior only.

The jurisdiction of this court, as of all federal courts, is accurately defined by the constitution and statutes. In brief, it extends to questions arising under the constitution, laws, and treaties of the United States; to questions affecting ambassadors, other public ministers, and consuls; to cases of admiralty and maritime jurisdiction; to cases in which the United States is a party; to controversies between states, between citizens of different states, and between states or citizens thereof and foreign states, citizens, or subjects. In cases affecting ambassadors, and where a state is a party, the jurisdiction of this court is original; in other cases, appellate. It is in some matters exclusive of, in others concurrent with, the jurisdiction of the state courts.

The constitution provides that the judicial power of the federal government shall extend to all cases at law or in equity arising under the constitution. As a consequence, law and equity have never been merged as in England and in many of the states, but if an equitable remedy is sought, it must be under equity practice, which is based upon that of the English high court of chancery.

one great court of appeal, which is the last resort in matters of both law and equity, and which will therefore take care to preserve a uniformity and *equilibrium* among all the inferior jurisdictions: a court composed of prelates selected for their piety, and of nobles advanced to that honor for their personal merit, or deriving both honor and merit from an illustrious train of ancestors; who are formed by their education, interested by their property, and bound upon their conscience and honor, to be skilled in the laws of their country. This is a faithful sketch of the English juridical constitution, as designed by the masterly hand of our forefathers, of which the great original lines are still strong and visible; and if any of its minuter strokes are by the length of time at all obscured or decayed, they may still be with ease restored to their pristine vigor; and that not so much by fanciful alterations and wild experiments (so frequent in this fertile age) as by closely adhering to the wisdom of the ancient plan, concerted by Alfred and perfected by Edward I., and by attending to the spirit, without neglecting the forms, of their excellent and venerable institutions.

CHAPTER V.

OF COURTS ECCLESIASTICAL, MILITARY, AND MARITIME.

BESIDES the several courts which were treated of in the preceding chapter, and in which all injuries are redressed that fall under the cognizance of the common law of England, or that spirit of equity which ought to be its constant attendant, there still remain some other courts of a jurisdiction equally

---

The inferior federal courts are the following:

1. The district courts. The territory of the United States is divided in judicial districts, usually co-extensive with the several states, but some of the larger states having two or three districts. At the present time (1897) there are in all about seventy, each having a district court presided over by one judge, who is appointed by the president, and must live in his district. The jurisdiction of the district courts embraces admiralty and maritime causes; penalties under the United States laws; the postal service; actions against national banks; crimes, less than capital, against United States laws, and many others. Appeals formerly went to the circuit court or to the supreme court; but now go to the recently established circuit court of appeals or to the supreme court.

2. The circuit courts. The territory covered by the 69 districts is also covered by nine circuits, each having its court. Each circuit consists of several states. Each of the nine justices of the supreme court is allotted to one of the circuits, and a special circuit judge is appointed on each circuit, and recently (1891) it was found advisable to appoint a second judge in each circuit.

Circuit courts are held by the justice of the supreme court assigned to the circuit, or by a circuit judge, assisted, in some cases, by a district judge. The jurisdiction of these courts was, before 1891, both appellate and original. But the act creating the circuit court of appeals took from them all appellate jurisdiction, and vested it in the latter.

3. The circuit courts of appeal. It was found advisable in 1891 (act of Mar. 3) to create a court of appeals, standing between the circuit and district courts and the supreme court, and to send to it much of the work formerly done by the latter.

There is a circuit court of appeals created for each of the nine circuits. It consists of three judges, of whom two shall constitute a quorum. The chief justice and associate justices of the supreme court assigned to each circuit, and the circuit judges in each circuit, and the several district judges within each circuit, are competent to sit as judges in the circuit court of appeals. But no judge may sit in a cause originally tried before him.

The act of 1891 provides for a division of the appellate jurisdiction between this court and the supreme court. It may be stated generally that to the latter are sent cases involving the jurisdiction of the former; prize causes; capital convictions; constitutional questions, either federal or state, and appeals from state courts. All other cases go to the circuit court of appeals. The judgment of this court is final, with the exception that it may, at any time, "certify to the supreme court any questions or propositions of law concerning which it desires the instruction of that court for its proper decision." There-

public and general, which take cognizance of other species of injuries of an ecclesiastical, military, and maritime nature; and therefore are properly distinguished by the title of ecclesiastical courts, courts military, and maritime.

I. Before I descend to consider particular ecclesiastical courts, I must first of all in general premise that in the time of our Saxon ancestors there was no sort of distinction between the lay and the ecclesiastical jurisdiction: the county-court was as much a spiritual as a temporal tribunal: the rights of the church were ascertained and asserted at the same time, and by the same judges, as the rights of the laity.(1) For this purpose the bishop of the diocese, and the alderman, or in his absence the sheriff of the county, used to sit together in the county-court, and had there the cognizance of all causes, as well ecclesiastical as civil: a superior deference being paid to the bishop's opinion in spiritual matters, and to that of the lay judges in temporal.(a)

This union of power was very advantageous to them both; the pres-
*62] ence of the *bishop added weight and reverence to the sheriff's proceedings; and the authority of the sheriff was equally useful to the bishop, by enforcing obedience to his decrees in such refractory offenders as would otherwise have despised the thunder of mere ecclesiastical censures.

But so moderate and rational a plan was wholly inconsistent with those views of ambition that were then forming by the court of Rome. It soon became an established maxim in the papal system of policy, that all ecclesiastical persons and all ecclesiastical causes should be solely and entirely subject to ecclesiastical jurisdiction only; which jurisdiction was supposed to be lodged in the first place and immediately in the pope, by divine indefeasible right and investiture from Christ himself, and derived from the pope to all inferior tribunals. Hence the canon law lays it down as a rule, that "sacerdotes a regibus honorandi sunt, non judicandi,"(b)(2) and places an emphatic reliance on a fabulous tale which it tells of the emperor Constantine, that when some petitions were brought to him, imploring the aid of his authority against certain of his bishops accused of oppression and injustice, he caused (says the holy canon) the petitions to be burnt in their presence, dismissing them with this valediction, "ite et inter vos causas vestras discutite, quia dignum non est ut nos judicemus Deos."(c)(3)

It was not, however, till after the Norman conquest that this doctrine was received in England; when William I. (whose title was warmly espoused by the monasteries, which he liberally endowed, and by the foreign clergy, whom he brought over in shoals from France and Italy and planted in the best preferments of the English church) was at length prevailed upon to establish this fatal encroachment, and separate the ecclesiastical court from the civil: whether actuated by principles of bigotry, or by those of a more

refined policy, in order to discountenance the laws of king Edward,
*63] abounding with the spirit of Saxon liberty, is not altogether *certain.

(a) Celeberrimo huic conventui episcopus et aldermannus inter sunto; quorum alter jura divina, alter humana populum edoceto. [Let the bishop and alderman be present at this illustrious assembly; of whom let the one instruct the people in divine, the other in human laws.] Ll. Eadgar. c. 5.
(b) Decret. part. 2, caus. 11, qu. 1, c. 41.
(c) Ibid.

upon the supreme court may send down binding legal instructions, or may have the whole record sent up to it for final determination as upon an original appeal.

The only other federal courts are a court of claims, five judges; a court of private land claims, five judges; a court of appeals of the District of Columbia, three judges; and a supreme court of the District of Columbia, six judges.

(1) 3 Moore's Priv. Cro. Cases, 177, 192 (1838). The ecclesiastical as separate from the civil courts is foreign to our institutions, and has no place in our jurisprudence. Here all wrongs are redressed, and all remedies furnished in the civil tribunals. Short v. Stotts, 58 Ind. 29, 36 (1877).

(2) ["The priests are to be honored, not judged, by kings."]

(3) ["Go and discuss your causes among yourselves, for it is not meet that we should judge the gods."]

But the latter, if not the cause, was undoubtedly the consequence, of this separation; for the Saxon laws were soon overborne by the Norman judiciaries, when the county-court fell into disregard by the bishop's withdrawing his presence, in obedience to the charter of the Conqueror;(*d*) which prohibited any spiritual cause from being tried in the secular courts, and commanded the suitors to appear before the bishop only, whose decisions were directed to conform to the canon law.(*e*)

King Henry the First, at his accession, among other restorations of the laws of king Edward the Confessor, revived this of the union of the civil and ecclesiastical courts.(*f*) Which was, according to Sir Edward Coke,(*g*) after the great heat of the conquest was past, only a restitution of the ancient law of England. This, however, was ill relished by the popish clergy, who, under the guidance of that arrogant prelate, archbishop Anselm, very early disapproved of a measure that put them on a level with the profane laity, and subjected spiritual men and causes to the inspection of the secular magistrates: and therefore in their synod at Westminster, 3 Hen. I., they ordained that no bishop should attend the discussion of temporal causes;(*h*) which soon dissolved this newly-effected union. And when, upon the death of king Henry the First, *the usurper Stephen was brought in   [*64 and supported by the clergy, we find one article of the oath which they imposed upon him was, that ecclesiastical persons and ecclesiastical causes should be subject only to the bishop's jurisdiction.(*i*) And as it was about that time that the contest and emulation began between the laws of England and those of Rome,(*k*) the temporal courts adhering to the former, and the spiritual adopting the latter as their rule of proceeding, this widened the breach between them, and made a coalition afterwards impracticable; which probably would else have been effected at the general reformation of the church.

In briefly recounting the various species of ecclesiastical courts, or, as they are often styled, courts christian, (*curiæ christianitatis*,) I shall begin with the lowest, and so ascend gradually to the supreme court of appeal.(*l*)

1. The *archdeacon's* court is the most inferior court in the whole ecclesiastical polity. It is held in the archdeacon's absence before a judge appointed by himself, and called his official; and its jurisdiction is sometimes in concurrence with, sometimes in exclusion of, the bishop's court of the diocese. From hence, however, by statute 24 Hen. VIII. c. 12, an appeal lies to that of the bishop.

2. The *consistory* court of every diocesan bishop is held in their several cathedrals, for the trial of all ecclesiastical causes arising within their respec-

(*d*) Hale, Hist. C. L. 102. Selden, in *Eadm.* p. 6, *l.* 24. 4 Inst. 259. Wilk. *LL. Angl. Sax.* 292.

(*e*) *Nullus episcopus vel archidiaconus de legibus episcopalibus amplius in hundret placita teneant, nec causam, quæ ad regimen animarum pertinet ad judicium secularium hominum adducant: sed quicunque secundum episcopales leges, de quacunque causa vel culpa interpellatus fuerit, ad locum, quem ad hoc episcopus elegerit et nominaverit, veniat; ibique de causa sua respondeat; et non secundum hundred, sed secundum canones et episcopales leges, rectum Deo et episcopo suo faciat.* [No bishop or archdeacon shall longer hold pleas in the hundred court that are to be decided by episcopal laws, nor bring any cause which relates to spiritual matters (the government of souls) for the judgment of secular persons; but whoever shall be sued according to the episcopal laws, for any cause or offence, shall come to the place chosen and appointed by the bishop for that purpose, and there make his own defence; to the end that right may be done to God and his bishops, according to the canon and episcopal laws, and not those of the hundred.]

(*f*) *Volo et præcipio, ut omnes de comitatu eant ad comitatus et hundreda, sicut fecerint tempore regis Edwardi. Cart. Hen. I. in Spelm. Cod. vet. legum,* 305.

[I will and command that all persons belonging to the county, attend the county and hundred courts as they did in the time of King Edward.] And what is here obscurely hinted at is fully explained by his code of laws extant in the red book of the exchequer, though in general but of doubtful authority. *Cap.* 8. *Generalia comitatuum placita certis locis et vicibus teneantur. Intersint autem episcopi. comites, etc.; et agantur primo debita veræ christianitatis jura, secunda regis placita, postremo causæ singulorum dignis satisfactionibus expleantur.* [Let the general pleas of the counties be held in certain places and districts; and the bishops and courts, etc., be present: and first let all affairs concerning religion be transacted; next the pleas of the crown, and lastly let the causes of individuals be heard and justly determined.]

(*g*) 2 Inst. 70.

(*h*) *Ne episcopi secularium placitorum officium suscipiant.* [Let no bishop take charge of secular pleas.] Spelm. *Cod.* 301.

(*i*) Spelm. *Cod.* 301.

(*k*) See book i. introd. § 1.

(*l*) For further particulars, see Burn's Ecclesiastical Law, Wood's Institute of the Common Law, and Oughton's *Ordo Judiciorum.*

tive dioceses. The bishop's chancellor, or his commissary, is the judge; and from his sentence an appeal lies, by virtue of the same statute, to the archbishop of each province respectively.

3. The court of *arches* is a court of appeal belonging to the arch-
*65] bishop of Canterbury; whereof the judge is called *the *dean of the arches*, because he anciently held his court in the church of Saint Mary *le bow*, (*sancta Maria de arcubus*,) though all the principal spiritual courts are now holden at doctors' commons. His proper jurisdiction is only over the thirteen peculiar parishes belonging to the archbishop in London; but the office of dean of the arches having been for a long time united with that of the archbishop's principal official, he now, in right of the last-mentioned office, (as doth also the official principal of the archbishop of York,) receives and determines appeals from the sentences of all inferior ecclesiastical courts within the province. And from him an appeal lies to the king in chancery, (that is, to a court of delegates appointed under the king's great seal,) by statute 25 Hen. VIII. c. 19, as supreme head of the English church, in the place of the bishop of Rome, who formerly exercised this jurisdiction; which circumstance alone will furnish the reason why the popish clergy were so anxious to separate the spiritual court from the temporal.

4. The court of *peculiars* is a branch of and annexed to the court of arches. It has a jurisdiction over all those parishes dispersed through the province of Canterbury in the midst of other dioceses, which are exempt from the ordinary's jurisdiction and subject to the metropolitan only. All ecclesiastical causes arising within these peculiar or exempt jurisdictions are, originally, cognizable by this court; from which an appeal lay formerly to the pope, but now, by the statute 25 Hen. VIII. c. 19, to the king in chancery.

5. The *prerogative* court is established for the trial of all testamentary causes where the deceased hath left *bona notabilia*(4) within two different dioceses. In which case the probate of wills belongs, as we have formerly seen, (*m*) to the archbishop of the province, by way of special prerogative. And all causes relating to the wills, administrations, or legacies of such
persons are, originally, cognizable herein, before a judge appointed
*66] by the archbishop, called the judge *of the prerogative court: from whom an appeal lies, by statute 25 Hen. VIII. c. 19, to the king in chancery, instead of the pope, as formerly.

I pass by such ecclesiastical courts as have only what is called a *voluntary*, and not a *contentious*, jurisdiction; which are merely concerned in doing or selling what no one opposes, and which keep an open office for that purpose, (as granting dispensations, licenses, faculties, and other remnants of the papal extortions,) but do not concern themselves with administering redress to any injury: and shall proceed to

6. The great court of appeal in all ecclesiastical causes, viz., the court of *delegates, judices delegati,*(5) appointed by the king's commission under his great seal, and issuing out of chancery, to represent his royal person, and hear all appeals to him made by virtue of the before-mentioned statute of Henry VIII. This commission is frequently filled with lords, spiritual and temporal, and always with judges of the courts at Westminster, and doctors of the civil law. Appeals to Rome were always looked upon by the English

(*m*) Book ii. ch. 32.

(4) [Goods of notable value, *i. e.* goods of a person to the value of one hundred shillings, lying in another house than that in which he died, and hereby rendered cognizable by probate before the archbishop of the province, unless by special custom it be otherwise.] See Bowyer's Com. Const. Law of Eng. 267.
(5) [Delegated judges.] See Bowyer's Com. Const. Law of Eng. p. 281.

nation, even in the times of popery, with an evil eye, as being contrary to the liberty of the subject, the honor of the crown, and the independence o. the whole realm; and were first introduced in very turbulent times in the sixteenth year of king Stephen, (A. D. 1151,) at the same period (Sir Henry Spelman observes) that the civil and canon laws were first imported into England.(*n*)   But, in a few years after, to obviate this growing practice, the constitutions made at Clarendon, 11 Hen. II., on account of the disturbances raised by archbishop Becket and other zealots of the holy see, expressly declare,(*o*) that appeals in causes ecclesiastical ought to lie, from the archdeacon to the diocesan; from the diocesan to the archbishop of the province; and from the archbishop to the king; and are not to proceed any further without special license from the crown.   But the unhappy advantage that was given, in the reigns of king John and his son Henry the Third, to the encroaching *power of the pope, who was ever vigilant to   [*67 improve all opportunities of extending his jurisdiction hither, at length riveted the custom of appealing to Rome in causes ecclesiastical so strongly, that it never could be thoroughly broken off till the grand rupture happened in the reign of Henry the Eighth; when all the jurisdiction usurped by the pope in matters ecclesiastical was restored to the crown, to which it originally belonged: so that the statute 25 Hen. VIII. was but declaratory of the ancient law of the realm.(*p*)   But in case the king himself be party in any of these suits, the appeal does not then lie to him in chancery, which would be absurd; but, by the statute 24 Hen. VIII. c. 12, to all the bishops of the realm, assembled in the upper house of convocation.(6)

7. A commission of *review* is a commission sometimes granted, in extraordinary cases, to revise the sentence of the court of delegates, when it is apprehended they have been led into a material error.   This commission the king may grant, although the statutes 24 & 25 Hen. VIII. before cited, declare the sentence of the delegates definitive: because the pope, as supreme head by the canon law, used to grant such commission of review; and such authority as the pope heretofore exerted is now annexed to the crown (*q*) by statutes 26 Hen. VIII. c. 1, and 1 Eliz. c. 1.   But it is not matter of right, which the subject may demand *ex debito justitiæ*,(7) but merely a matter of favor, and which therefore is often denied.

These are now the principal courts of ecclesiastical jurisdiction: none of which are allowed to be courts of record; no more than was another much more formidable jurisdiction, but now deservedly annihilated, viz., the court of the king's *high commission* in causes ecclesiastical. This court was erected and united to the legal power(*r*) by virtue of the statute 1 Eliz. c. 1, instead

(*n*) *Cod. vet. leg.* 315.
(*o*) Ch. 8.
(*p*) 4 Inst. 341.

(*q*) Ibid.
(*r*) 4 Inst. 324.

---

(6) No such assembly can exist as all the bishops of the realm in any house of convocation.   But the statute says that the appeal shall be to the bishops, abbots, and priors of the upper house of the convocation of the province in which the cause of the *suit* *arises.*   Therefore, in the province of York, the appeal lies now to the archbishop and his three bishops; in the province of Canterbury, to the rest of the bench of bishops. See 1 Book, 280, n. 36.   When the delegates are equally divided in opinion, so that no judgment can be pronounced, a commission of adjuncts may issue.   See an instance referred to in 4 Burr. 2254.   A commission of review was applied for in the court of chancery in Michaelmas Term, 1798, when the chancellor, upon hearing the arguments of civilians and barristers respecting the judgment of the delegates, determined to recommend to the king to grant a commission of review.   See 4 Ves. Jr. 186.—CHRISTIAN.   The statutes 2 & 3 W. IV. c. 92 and 3 & 4 W. IV. c. 41 have transferred the jurisdiction of the court of delegates to the judicial committee of the privy council.   This is a court of record having power to award costs, and have them taxed, to punish contempts and enforce its decrees.   Three members are necessary to hear all appeals.   6 & 7 Vict. c. 38.
(7) [By or on account of a debt due to justice.]

of a larger jurisdiction which had before been exercised under the
*68]   pope's authority.   It was intended *to vindicate the dignity and peace
of the church, by reforming, ordering, and correcting the ecclesiastical
state and persons, and all manner of errors, heresies, schisms, abuses,
offences, contempts, and enormities.   Under the shelter of which very general words, means were found, in that and the two succeeding reigns, to vest
in the high commissioners extraordinary and almost despotic powers of fining
and imprisoning; which they exerted much beyond the degree of the offence
itself, and frequently over offences by no means of spiritual cognizance.   For
these reasons this court was justly abolished by statute 16 Car. I. c. 11.   And
the weak and illegal attempt that was made to revive it, during the reign of
king James the Second, served only to hasten that infatuated prince's ruin.

II. Next, as to the courts military.   The only court of this kind known to,
and established by, the permanent laws of the land, is the court of *chivalry*,(8)
formerly held before the lord high constable and earl marshal of England
jointly, but since the attainder of Stafford, duke of Buckingham, under
Henry VIII., and the consequent extinguishment of the office of lord high
constable, it hath usually, with respect to civil matters, been held before the
earl marshal only.(s)   This court, by statute 13 Ric. II. c. 2, hath cognizance of contracts and other matters touching deeds of arms and war, as well
out of the realm as within it.   And from its sentences an appeal lies immediately to the king in person.(t)   This court was in great reputation in the
times of pure chivalry, and afterwards during our connections with the continent, by the territories which our princes held in France: but is now grown
almost entirely out of use, on account of the feebleness of its jurisdiction,
and want of power to enforce its judgments, as it can neither fine nor
imprison, not being a court of record. (u).

III. The maritime courts, or such as have power and jurisdiction to
*69]   determine all maritime injuries, arising upon the *seas, or in parts
out of the reach of the common law, are only the court of admiralty
and its courts of appeal.(9)   The court of admiralty is held before the lord
high admiral of England, or his deputy, who is called the judge of the court.
According to Sir Henry Spelman,(w) and Lambard,(x) it was first of all
erected by king Edward the Third.   Its proceedings are according to the
method of the civil law, like those of the ecclesiastical courts; upon which
account it is usually held at the same place with the superior ecclesiastical
courts, at doctors' commons in London.   It is no court of record, any more
than the spiritual courts.   From the sentences of the admiralty judge an
appeal always lay, in ordinary course, to the king in chancery, as may be
collected from statute 25 Hen. VIII. c. 19 which directs the appeal from the
archbishop's courts to be determined by persons named in the king's commission, "like as in case of appeal from the admiral court."   But this is also

(s) 1 Lev. 230. Show. Parl. Cas. 60.
(t) 4 Inst. 125.
(u) 7 Mod. 127.

(w) Gloss. 13.
(x) *Archeion.* 41.

(8) The practice of the court of admiralty has been improved and its jurisdiction
extended by statute 3 & 4 Vict. c. 65.—STEWART.   It is supposed that courts martial
were intended originally to be a partial substitute for the courts of *chivalry*.   Their consti-
tutionality as established in this country is not open to question.   *Ex parte* Reed, 100
U. S. 13, 21 (1879).

(9) The statute 3 & 4 Vict. extended the jurisdiction of the court of admiralty, and
improved its practice.   The regulations of the United States navy for the administration
of law and justice, established by the secretary of the navy, with the approval of the president, has the force of law.   *Ex parte* Read, 10 U. S. 13.   See Lacaze *v.* The State, 1
Add. (Pa.) 59, 81 (1800).   Bains *v.* The James & Catherine, 2 Fed. Rep. 413 (1832).   N. J.
S. Nav. Co. *v.* The Bank, 6 How. (U. S) 344.   Bailey's Onus Probandi, 590 (1886).
Bowyer's Com. Const. Law of Eng. p. 283.

expressly declared by statute 8 Eliz. c. 5, which enacts, that upon appeal made to the chancery, the sentence definitive of the delegates appointed by commission shall be final.

Appeals from the vice-admiralty courts in America, and our other plantations and settlements, may be brought before the courts of admiralty in England, as being a branch of the admiral's jurisdiction, though they may also be brought before the king in council. But in case of prize vessels, taken in time of war, in any part of the world, and condemned in any courts of admiralty or vice-admiralty as lawful prize, the appeal lies to certain commissioners of appeals consisting chiefly of the privy council, and not to judges delegates. And this by virtue of divers treaties with foreign nations; by which particular courts are established in all the maritime countries of Europe for the decision of this question, whether lawful prize or not;(10) for, this being a question between subjects of different states, it belongs entirely to the law of nations, and not to the municipal laws of either country, to determine it. The original court, to which this question is *permitted in England, is the court of admiralty;(11) and the court [*70 of appeal is in effect the king's privy council, the members of which are, in consequence of treaties, commissioned under the great seal for this purpose. In 1748, for the more speedy determination of appeals, the judges of the courts of Westminster hall, though not privy counsellors, were added to the commission then in being. But doubts being conceived concerning the validity of that commission on account of such addition, the same was confirmed by statute 22 Geo. II. c. 3, with a proviso that no sentence given under it should be valid unless a majority of the commissioners present were actually privy counsellors. But this did not, I apprehend, extend to any future commissions: and such an addition became indeed totally unnecessary in the course of the war which commenced in 1756; since during the whole of that war, the commission of appeals was regularly attended and all its decisions conducted by a judge whose masterly acquaintance with the law of nations was known and revered by every state in Europe.(y)(12)

CHAPTER VI.

OF COURTS OF A SPECIAL JURISDICTION.

In the two preceding chapters we have considered the several courts whose jurisdiction is public and general, and which are so contrived that some or

(y) See the sentiments of the president Montesquieu and M. Vattel (a subject of the king of Prussia) on the answer transmitted by the English court to his Prussian majesty's *Exposition des Motifs*, etc. A. D. 1753. Montesquieu's Letters, 5 Mar. 1753. Vattel's *droit de gens l.* 2, c. 7, § 81.

---

(10) Bowyer's Const. Law of Eng. 282. All appeals from a court of admiralty of the queen's dominions abroad must be made to the queen in council. 3 & 4 W. IV. c. 41. It is usually necessary that ships taken as prize should be condemned in a court of admiralty. 19 Geo. III. c. 67. 1 Wils. 229. 4 Rob. 55.

(11) The question of prize is tried in the prize court and although the judges of the admiralty preside at the prize court they should be distinguished. The prize court is authorized to consider all captures, seizures, prize, and reprisal, and to determine according to the law of nations and the course of the admiralty. Talbot qui tam etc. v. Commanders etc. of Three Brigs, 1 Dallas (Pa.) 103. Doug. 594 and 614. The district courts of the United States have cognizance over all cases of admiralty and maritime jurisdiction occurring within a marine league of its shores. Appeal is taken from these courts to the circuit courts and thence to the U. S. Supreme Court. See Constitution of U. S., act of Congress, September 24, 1789, s. 9; also Story's Laws of U. S.

(12) Lord Mansfield is here alluded to. The answer to the *Exposition des Motifs*, etc. is signed by Sir G. Lee, judge of the prerogative court, Dr. Paul, advocate-general, Sir

other of them may administer redress to every possible injury that can arise in the kingdom at large. There yet remain certain others, whose jurisdiction is private and special, confined to particular spots, or instituted only to redress particular injuries. These are,

I. The forest courts, instituted for the government of the king's forests in different parts of the kingdom, and for the punishment of all injuries done to the king's deer or *venison*, to the *vert* or greensward, and to the *covert* in which such deer are lodged. These are the courts of *attachments*, of *regard*, of *sweinmote*, and of *justice-seat*. 1. The court of *attachments, wood-motes*, or forty-days court is to be held before the verderors of the forest once in every forty days;(a) and is instituted to inquire into all offenders against vert and venison;(b) who may be attached by their bodies, if taken with the mainor, (or *mainoeuvre, a manu*,) that is, in the very act of killing venison, or stealing wood, or preparing so to do, or by fresh and immediate pursuit after the act is done;(c) else they must be attached by their goods. And in this forty-days court the foresters or keepers are to bring their attachments, or presentments *de viridi et venatione;*(1) and the verderors are to receive the same, and to enroll them, and to certify them under their seals to the court of justice-seat or sweinmote:(d) for this court can only inquire of, but not convict, offenders. 2. The court of *regard*, or survey of dogs, is to be holden every third year for the lawing or expedition of mastiffs, which is

*72] done by cutting off the claws and ball (or *pelote) of the forefect, to prevent them from running after deer.(e) No other dogs but mastiffs are to be thus lawed or expeditated, for none others were permitted to be kept within the precincts of the forest; it being supposed that the keeping of these, and these only, was necessary for the defence of a man's house.(f) 3. The court of *sweinmote* is to be holden before the verderors, as judges, by the steward of the sweinmote, thrice in every year,(g) the sweins or freeholders within the forest composing the jury. The principal jurisdiction of this court is, first, to inquire into the oppressions and grievances committed by the officers of the forest; "*de super-oneratione forestariorum, et aliorum ministrorum forestæ; et de eorum oppressionibus populo regis illatis;*"(2) and, secondly, to receive and try presentments certified from the court of attachment against offences in vert and venison.(h) And this court may not only inquire, but convict also, which conviction shall be certified to the court of justice-seat under the seals of the jury; for this court cannot proceed to judgment.(i) But the principal court is, 4, The court of *justice-seat*, which is held before the chief justice in eyre, or chief itinerant judge, *capitalis justiciarius in itinere*, or his deputy; to hear and determine all trespasses within the forest, and all claims of franchises, liberties, and privileges, and all pleas and causes whatsoever therein arising.(k) It may also proceed to try presentments in the inferior courts of the forests, and to give judgment upon conviction of the sweinmote. And the chief justice may therefore, after presentment made, or indictment found, but not before,(l) issue his warrant to the officers of the forest to apprehend the offenders. It may be held every

---

(a) *Cart. de forest.* 9 Hen. III. c. 8.
(b) 1 Inst. 289.
(c) Carth. 79.
(d) *Cart. de forest.* c. 16.
(e) Ibid.
(f) 4 Inst. 308.

(g) *Cart. de forest.* c. 8.
(h) Stat. 34 Edw. I. c. 1.
(i) 4 Inst. 289.
(k) 4 Inst. 291.
(l) Stat. 1 Edw. III. c. 8. 7 Ric. II. c. 4.

D. Ryder, attorney, and Sir W. Murray, solicitor-general; but lord Mansfield frequently declared to his friends that it was entirely his own composition. Holliday's Life of Lord M. p. 424. Montesquieu calls it *une réponse sans replique* [An answer without a reply]. —COLERIDGE.

(1) [Of vert and venison.]

(2) ["Concerning the imposition of the foresters, and other officers of the forest; and their oppression on the king's people."]

third year; and forty days' notice ought to be given of its sitting. This court may fine and imprison for offences within the forest,(*m*) it being a court of record: and therefore a writ of error lies from hence to the court of *king's bench, to rectify and redress any mal-administrations of jus-   [*73 tice;(*n*) or the chief justice in eyre may adjourn any matter of law into the court of king's bench.(*o*)   These justices in eyre were instituted by king Henry II., A. D. 1184,(*p*)(3) and their courts were formerly very regularly held: but the last court of justice-seat of any note was that holden in the reign of Charles I., before the earl of Holland; the rigorous proceedings at which are reported by Sir William Jones.   After the restoration another was held, *pro forma* only, before the earl of Oxford;(*q*) but since the era of the revolution in 1688, the forest laws have fallen into total disuse, to the great advantage of the subject.(4)

II. A second species of restricted courts is that of commissioners of *sewers*. This is a temporary tribunal, erected by virtue of a commission under the great seal; which formerly used to be granted *pro re nata*(5) at the pleasure of the crown,(*r*) but now at the discretion and nomination of the lord chancellor, lord treasurer, and chief justices, pursuant to the statute 23 Hen. VIII. c. 5.   Their jurisdiction is to overlook the repairs of sea-banks and sea-walls, and the cleansing of rivers, public streams, ditches, and other conduits whereby any waters are carried off: and is confined to such county, or particular district, as the commission shall expressly name.   The commissioners are a court of record, and may fine and imprison for contempt;(*s*) and in the execution of their duty may proceed by jury, or upon their own view, and may take order for the removal of any annoyances, or the safeguard and conservation of the sewers within their commission, either according to the laws and customs of Romney marsh,(*t*) or otherwise at their own discretion. They may also assess such rates, or scots, upon the owners of lands within their district as they shall judge necessary; and, if any person refuses to pay them, the commissioners may levy the same by distress of his goods and chattels; or they may, by statute 23 Hen. VIII. c. 5, sell his freehold lands (and, by the 7 Anne, c. 10, his copyhold also) in order to pay such *scots or assessments.   But their conduct is under the control of the   [*74 court of king's bench, which will prevent or punish any illegal or tyrannical proceedings.(*u*)   And yet, in the reign of king James I., (8 Nov. 1616,) the privy counsel took upon them to order that no action or complaint should be prosecuted against the commissioners unless before that board; and committed several to prison, who had brought such actions at common law, till they should release the same: and one of the reasons for discharging Sir Edward Coke from his office of lord chief justice was for countenancing

(*m*) 4 Inst. 313.
(*n*) Ibid. 297.
(*o*) Ibid. 295.
(*p*) Hoveden.
(*q*) North's Life of Lord Guildford, 45.
(*r*) F. N. B. 118.
(*s*) Sid. 145.
(*t*) Romney marsh, in the county of Kent, a tract

containing 24,000 acres, is governed by certain ancient and equitable laws of sewers, composed by Henry de Bathe, a venerable judge in the reign of king Henry the Third, from which laws all commissioners of sewers in England may receive light and direction. 4 Inst. 276.
(*u*) Cro. Jac. 336.

(3) By the 57 Geo. III. c. 61, the offices of these justices are abolished on the termination of their then existing interests, and the salaries of the abolished offices are to make part of the consolidated fund.—CHITTY.

(4) [As a matter of form.]   All the forests which were made after the conquest, except New Forest in Hampshire, created by William the Conqueror, were disafforested by the *charta de foresta* [The charters of the forest]. The forest of Hampshire Court was established by the authority of parliament in the reign of Hen. VIII.   The number of forests in England is sixty-nine. 4 Inst. 319. Charles I. enforced the odious forest laws, as a source of revenue independent of the parliament.—CHRISTIAN. See Bowyer's Com. Const. Law of Eng. 285.

(5) [According to circumstances—for the occasion.]

those legal proceedings.(*v*) The pretence for which arbitrary measures was no other than the tyrant's plea(*w*) of the *necessity* of unlimited powers in works of evident utility to the public, "the supreme reason above all reasons, which is the salvation of the king's lands and people." But now it is clearly held, that this (as well as all other inferior jurisdictions) is subject to the discretionary coercion of his majesty's court of king's bench.(*x*)(6)

III. The court of *policies of insurance*, when subsisting, is erected in pursuance of the statute 43 Eliz. c. 12, which recites the immemorial usage of policies of assurance, "by means whereof it cometh to pass, upon the loss or perishing of any ship, there followeth not the undoing of any man, but the loss lighteth rather easily upon many than heavy upon few, and rather upon them that adventure not than upon those that do adventure: whereby all merchants, especially those of the younger sort, are allured to venture more willingly and more freely: and that heretofore such assurers had used to stand so justly and precisely upon their credits as few or no controversies had arisen thereupon; and if any had grown, the same had from time to time been ended and ordered by certain grave and discreet merchants appointed by the lord mayor of the city of London; as men by reason of their experience fittest to understand and speedily decide those causes:" but that of late years divers persons had withdrawn themselves from that course of arbitration, and had driven the assured to bring separate actions at law against each assurer: *75] it therefore enables the *lord chancellor yearly to grant a standing commission to the judge of the admiralty, the recorder of London, two doctors of the civil law, two common lawyers, and eight merchants; any three of which, one being a civilian or a barrister, are thereby and by the statute 13 & 14 Car. II. c. 23, empowered to determine in a summary way all causes concerning policies of assurance in London, with an appeal (by way of bill) to the court of chancery. But the jurisdiction being somewhat defective, as extending only to London, and to no other assurances but those on merchandise,(*y*) and to suits brought by the assured only, and not by the insurers,(*z*) no such commission has of late years issued: but insurance causes are now usually determined by the verdict of a jury of merchants, and the opinion of the judges in case of any legal doubts; whereby the decision is more speedy, satisfactory, and final: though it is to be wished that some of the parliamentary powers invested in these commissions, especially for the examination of witnesses, either beyond the seas or speedily going out of the kingdom,(*a*) could at present be adopted by the courts of Westminster hall, without requiring the consent of parties.(7)

IV. The court of the *marshalsea*, and the *palace-court* at Westminster, though two distinct courts, are frequently confounded together. The former was originally holden before the steward and marshal of the king's house, and was instituted to administer justice between the king's domestic servants, that they might not be drawn into other courts and thereby the king lose their service.(*b*) It was formerly held in, though not a part of, the *aula regis*,(*c*) and, when that was subdivided, remained a distinct jurisdiction: holding plea of all trespasses committed within the verge of the court, where only one of the parties is in the king's domestic service, (in which case the inquest shall be taken by a jury of the country,) and of all debts, contracts, and covenants where both of the contracting parties belong to the royal

(*v*) Moor. 825, 826. See page 55.
(*w*) Milt. Paradise Lost, iv. 393.
(*x*) 1 Ventr. 66. Salk. 146.
(*y*) Styl. 166.

(*z*) 1 Show. 396.
(*a*) Stat. 13 & 14 Car. II. c. 22, §§ 3, 4.
(*b*) 1 Bulstr. 211.
(*c*) Flet. *l.* 2, c. 2. [The king's hall of justice.]

(6) For the present powers and duties of these commissioners, see statutes 3 & 4 Wm. IV. c. 22 (1833) and 4 & 5 Vict. c. 45 (1841).
(7) These courts now possess the former power.

household; and then the inquest shall be composed of men of the house*hold only.(*d*)　By the statute of 13 Ric. II. st. 1, c. 3, (in　[*76 affirmance of the common law,)(*e*) the verge of the court in this respect extends for twelve miles round the king's place of residence.(*f*)　And, as this tribunal was never subject to the jurisdiction of the chief justiciary, no writ of error lay from it (though a court of record) to the king's bench, but only to parliament,(*g*) till the statutes of 5 Edw. III. c. 2, and 10 Edw. III. st. 2, c. 3, which allowed such writ of error before the king in his palace. But this court being ambulatory, and obliged to follow the king in all his progresses, so that by the removal of the household actions were frequently discontinued,(*h*) and doubts having arisen as to the extent of its jurisdiction(*i*) king Charles I., in the sixth year of his reign, by his letters-patent erected a new court of record, called the *curia palatii*, or *palace-court*, to be held before the steward of the household and knight-marshal, and the steward of the court, or his deputy, with jurisdiction to hold plea of all manner of personal actions whatsoever which shall arise between any parties within twelve miles of his majesty's palace at Whitehall.(*k*)　The court is now held once a week, together with the ancient court of marshalsea, in the borough of Southwark: and a writ of error lies from thence to the court of king's bench.　But if the cause is of any considerable consequence, it is usually removed on its first commencement, together with the custody of the defendant, either into the king's bench or common pleas, by a writ of *habeas corpus cum causa*:(8) and the inferior business of the court hath of late years been much reduced by the new courts of conscience erected in the environs of London; in consideration of which, the four counsel belonging to these courts had salaries granted them for their lives by the statute 23 Geo. II. c. 27.(9)

V. *A fifth species of private courts of a limited, though extensive,　[*77 jurisdiction, are those of the principality of Wales, which, upon its thorough reduction, and the settling of its polity in the reign of Henry the Eighth,(*l*) were erected all over the country; principally by the statute 34 & 35 Hen. VIII. c. 26, though much had been done before, and the way prepared, by the statute of Wales, 12 Edw. I., and other statutes.　By the statute of Henry the Eighth before mentioned, court-barons, hundred, and county courts are there established, as in England.　A session is also to be held twice in every year in each county, by judges(*m*) appointed by the king, to be called the great sessions of the several counties in Wales: in which all pleas of real and personal actions shall be held, with the same form of process, and in as ample a manner, as in the court of common pleas at Westminster:(*n*) and writs of error shall lie from judgments therein (it being a court of record) to the court of king's bench at Westminster.　But the ordinary original writs of process of the king's courts at Westminster do not run into the principality of Wales:(*o*) though process of execution

---

(*d*) *Artic. sup. cart.* 28 Edw. I. c. 3. Stat. 5 Edw. III. c. 2. 10 Edw. III. st. 2, c. 2.
(*e*) 2 Inst. 548.
(*f*) By the ancient Saxon constitution, the *pax regia*, or privilege of the king's palace, extended from his palace-gate to the distance of three miles, three furlongs, three acres, nine feet, nine palms, and nine barley-corns, as appears from a fragment of the *Textus Roffensis* cited in Dr. Hickes's *Dissertat. Epistol.* 114.

(*g*) 1 Bulstr. 211.　10 Rep. 79.
(*h*) F. N. B. 241.　2 Inst. 548.
(*i*) 1 Bulstr. 208.
(*k*) 1 Sid. 180.　Salk. 439.
(*l*) See book i. introd. § 4.
(*m*) Stat. 18 Eliz. c. 8.
(*n*) See, for further regulations of the practice of these courts, stat. 5 Eliz. c. 25.　8 Eliz. c. 20.　8 Geo. I. c. 25, § 6.　6 Geo. II. c. 14.　13 Geo. III. c. 51.
(*o*) 2 Roll. Rep. 141.

---

(8) [That you have the body with the cause of detention.]
(9) The business of the court was much reduced,—first, by the erection of courts of conscience in the environs of London, and next by the establishment of the county courts; and the court itself was finally abolished by statute 12 & 13 Vict. c. 101.—KERR. Browne's View of the Civil Law, 76, 83.

does;(*p*) as do also prerogative writs, as writs of *certiorari*, *quo minus*, *mandamus*, and the like.(*q*) And even in causes between subject and subject, to prevent injustice through family factions or prejudices, it is held lawful (in causes of freehold at least, and it is usual in all others) to bring an action in the English courts, and try the same in the next English county adjoining to that part of Wales where the cause arises,(*r*) and where the venue is laid. But, on the other hand, to prevent trifling and frivolous suits, it is enacted, by statute 13 Geo. III. c. 51, that in *personal* actions, *tried* in any English county where the cause of action arose, and the defendant resides in Wales, if the plaintiff shall not recover a verdict for ten pounds, he shall be nonsuited and pay the defendant's costs, unless it be certified by the judge that the freehold or title came principally in question, or that the cause was proper *to be tried, in such English county. And if any *78] *transitory* action, the cause whereof arose and the defendant is resident in Wales, shall be *brought* in any English county, and the plaintiff shall not recover a verdict for ten pounds, the plaintiff shall be nonsuited, and shall pay the defendant's costs, deducting thereout the sum recovered by the verdict.(10)

VI. The court of the duchy chamber of Lancaster is another special jurisdiction, held before the chancellor of the duchy or his deputy, concerning all matter of equity relating to lands holden of the king in right of the duchy of Lancaster:(*s*) which is a thing very distinct from the county palatine, (which hath also its separate chancery, for sealing of writs, and the like,(*t*) and comprises much territory which lies at a vast distance from it; as particularly a very large district surrounded by the city of Westminster. The proceedings in this court are the same as on the equity side in the courts of exchequer and chancery;(*u*) so that it seems not to be a court of record; and indeed it has been holden that those courts have a concurrent jurisdiction with the duchy court, and may take cognizance of the same causes.(*v*)

VII. Another species of private courts, which are of a limited local jurisdiction, and have at the same time an exclusive cognizance of pleas, in matters of both law and civil equity,(*w*) are those which appertain to the counties palatine of Chester, Lancaster, and Durham, and the royal franchise of Ely.(*x*)(11) In all these, as in the principality of Wales, the king's ordinary writs, issuing under the great seal out of chancery, do not run; that

---

(*p*) 2 Bulstr. 15. 26 Saund. 193. Raym. 206.
(*q*) Cro. Jac. 484.
(*r*) Vaugh. 413. Hardr. 66.
(*s*) Hob. 77. 2 Lev. 24.
(*t*) 1 Ventr. 257.

(*u*) 4 Inst. 206.
(*v*) 1 Ch. Rep. 55. Toth. 145. Hardr. 171.
(*w*) 4 Inst. 213. 218. Finch, R. 452.
(*x*) See book i. introd. § 4.

---

(10) But these distinctions are now entirely abolished; for, by stat. 11 Geo. IV. and 1 W. IV. c. 70, s. 14, it is enacted that from the 12th of October, 1830, all power and jurisdiction of the judges and courts of great sessions, both at law and in equity, shall cease, and that all suits in equity then depending should be transferred into the court of exchequer; and, by s. 13, it is enacted that the king's writ shall be directed and obeyed, and the jurisdiction of the courts of common law and the judges thereof shall extend and be exercised in like manner as the jurisdiction of such courts is now exercised in and over the counties of England. The administration of justice in Wales is thus and by subsequent statutes (5 Vict. s. 2, c. 33, 8. Vict. c. 11) rendered uniform in every respect with that of England.—STEWART.

See construction of this act, Tidd, 8 ed. index, tit. Wales. If goods be delivered in London to be carried into Wales, the debt, though under 10*l.*, may be sued for in London. 2 Starkie, 33.—CHITTY.

(11) The two former of which are now united to the crown, (6 W. IV. c. 19,) while that of Chester has been, by stat. 11 Geo. IV. and 7 W. IV. c. 70, abolished, and that of Ely, by stat. 6 & 7 W. IV. c. 87, and 7 W. IV. and 1 Vict. c. 53, also extinguished.—STEWART. See Bowyer's Coms. on the Const. Law of Eng. 287–289.

is, they are of no force. For as originally all *jura regalia*(12) were granted to the lords of these counties palatine, they had of course the sole administration of justice by their own judges, appointed by themselves and not by the crown. It would therefore be incongruous for the king to send his writ to direct the judge of another's court in what manner to administer justice between the suitors. But when the privilege of these counties palatine and franchises were abridged by statute 27 Hen. VIII. c. 24, it was *also enacted that all writs and process should be made in the king's 　[*79 name, but should be *tested* or witnessed in the name of the owner of the franchise. Wherefore all writs whereon actions are founded and which have current authority here must be under the seal of the respective franchises; the two former of which are now united to the crown, and the two latter under the government of their several bishops. And the judges of assize who sit therein sit by virtue of a special commission from the owners of the several franchises, and under the seal thereof, and not by the usual commission under the great seal of England. Hither also may be referred the courts of the *cinque ports*, or five most important havens, as they formerly were esteemed, in the kingdom, viz., Dover, Sandwich, Romney, Hastings, and Hythe, to which Winchelsea and Rye have been since added, which have also similar franchises in many respects(*y*) with the counties palatine, and particularly an exclusive jurisdiction, (before the mayor and jurats of the ports,) in which exclusive jurisdiction the king's ordinary writ does not run. A writ of error lies from the mayor and jurats of each port to the lord warden of the *cinque ports* in his court of *Shepway*, and from the court of *Shepway* to the king's bench.(*z*) So likewise a writ of error lies from all the other jurisdictions to the same supreme court of judicature,(*a*) as an ensign of superiority reserved to the crown at the original creation of the franchises. And all prerogative writs (as those of *habeas corpus*, prohibition, *certiorari*, and *mandamus*) may issue for the same reason to all these exempt jurisdictions;(*b*) because the privilege, that the king's writ runs not, must be intended between party and party, for there can be no such privilege against the king.(*c*)

VIII. The stannary courts in Devonshire and Cornwall, for the administration of justice among the tinners therein, are also courts of record, but of the same private and exclusive nature. They are held before the lord warden and his substitutes, in virtue of a privilege granted to the workers in the *tin-mines there to sue and be sued only in their own 　[*80 courts, that they may not be drawn from their business, which is highly profitable to the public, by attending their law-suits in other courts.(*d*) The privileges of the tinners are confirmed by a charter, 33 Edw. I., and fully expounded by a private statute,(*e*) 50 Edw. III., which has since been explained by a public act, 16 Car. I. c. 15. What relates to our present purpose is only this,—that all tinners and laborers in and about the stannaries shall, during the time of their working therein *bona fide*, be privileged from suits of other courts, and be only impleaded in the stannary court in all matters, excepting pleas of land, life, and member. No writ of error lies from hence to any court in Westminster hall, as was agreed by all the judges(*f*) in 4 Jac. I. But an appeal lies from the steward of the court to the under-warden; and from him to the lord-warden; and thence to the privy council of the prince of Wales, as duke of Cornwall,(*g*) when he hath had

(*y*) 1 Sid. 106.
(*z*) Jenk. 71. *Dyversyte des courtes*, tit. *bank le roy.* 1 Sid. 356.
(*a*) Bro. Abr. tit. *error*, 74, 101. Davis, 62. 4 Inst. 38, 214, 218.
(*b*) 1 Sid. 92.

(*c*) Cro. Jac. 543.
(*d*) 4 Inst. 232.
(*e*) See this at length in 4 Inst. 232.
(*f*) 4 Inst. 231.
(*g*) Ibid. 230.

(12) [Royal rights.]

livery or investiture of the same.(*h*)   And from thence the appeal lies to the king himself in the last resort.(*i*)

IX. The several courts within the city of London,(*j*) and other cities, boroughs, and corporations throughout the kingdom, held by prescription, charter, or act of parliament, are also of the same private and limited species. It would exceed the design and compass of our present inquiries, if I were to enter into a particular detail of these, and to examine the nature and extent of their several jurisdictions. It may, in general, be sufficient to say that they arose originally from the favor of the crown to those particular districts wherein we find them erected, upon the same principle that hundred-courts, and the like, were established for the convenience of the inhabi-

*81]   tants, that they may prosecute their suits and *receive justice at home: that, for the most part, the courts at Westminster hall have a concurrent jurisdiction with these, or else a superintendency over them,(*k*) and are bound by the statute 19 Geo. III. c. 70 to give assistance to such of them as are courts of record, by issuing writs of execution, where the person or effects of the defendant are not within the inferior jurisdiction: and that the proceedings in these special courts ought to be according to the course of the common law, unless otherwise ordered by parliament; for though the king may erect new courts, yet he cannot alter the established course of law.

But there is one species of courts, constituted by act of parliament, in the city of London, and other trading and populous districts, which in their proceedings so vary from the course of common law that they may deserve a more particular consideration. I mean the courts of requests, or courts of conscience, for the recovery of small debts.(13) The first of these was established in London, so early as the reign of Henry the Eighth, by an act of their common council; which, however, was certainly insufficient for that purpose and illegal, till confirmed by statute 3 Jac. I. c. 15, which has since been explained and amended by statute 14 Geo. II. c. 10.(14) The constitution is this: two aldermen, and four commoners, sit twice a week to hear all causes of debt not exceeding the value of forty shillings; which they examine in a summary way, by the oath of the parties or other witnesses, and make such order therein as is consonant to equity and good conscience. The time and expense of obtaining this summary redress are very inconsiderable, which make it a great benefit to trade; and thereupon divers trading towns and other districts have obtained acts of parliament, for establishing in them courts of conscience upon nearly the same plan as that in the city of London.(15)

*82]   *The anxious desire that has been shown to obtain these several acts, proves clearly that the nation in general is truly sensible of the

---

(*h*) 3 Bulstr. 183.
(*i*) Doddridge, Hist. of Cornw. 94.
(*j*) The chief of those in London are the *sheriffs' courts*, holden before their steward or judge, from which a writ of error lies to the *court of hustings*, before the mayor, recorder, and sheriffs, and from

thence to justices appointed by the king's commission, who used to sit in the church of St. Martin le Grand, (F. N. B. 32:) and from the judgment of those justices a writ of error lies immediately to the house of lords.
(*k*) Salk. 144, 263.

---

(13) See Tidd's Prac. (8 ed.) 889 to 896. The justice courts throughout the several states correspond, to a great extent, to courts of conscience. Johnson *v.* Nelms, 21 Georgia (Martin) 192.

(14) The act is still further extended by the 39 and 40 Geo. III. c. 104. Tidd's Prac. (8 ed.) 988—CHITTY.

(15) By the 25 Geo. III. c. 45 and 26 Geo. III. c. 38, no debtor or defendant, in any court for the recovery of small debts, where the debt does not exceed 20*s.*, shall be committed to prison for more than twenty days, and if the debt does not exceed 40*s.*, for more than forty days, unless it be proved to the satisfaction of the court that he has money or goods which he fraudulently conceals; and in the first case the imprisonment may be extended to thirty days, and in the latter to sixty. See Bowyer's Coms. on Const. Law of Eng. 292.

great inconvenience arising from the disuse of the ancient county and hundred courts; wherein causes of this small value were always formerly decided, with very little trouble and expense to the parties. But it is to be feared, that the general remedy which of late hath been principally applied to this inconvenience (the erecting these new jurisdictions) may itself be attended in time with very ill consequences: as the method of proceeding therein is entirely in derogation of the common law; as their large discretionary powers create a petty tyranny in a set of standing commissioners; and as the disuse of the trial by jury may tend to estrange the minds of the people from that valuable prerogative of Englishmen, which has already been more than sufficiently excluded in many instances. How much rather is it to be wished, that the proceedings in the county and hundred courts could again be revived, without burdening the freeholders with too frequent and tedious attendances; and *at the same time removing the delays that have insensibly 　[*83 crept into their proceedings, and the power that either party have of transferring at pleasure their suits to the courts at Westminster! And we may with satisfaction observe, that this experiment has been actually tried, and has succeeded, in the populous county of Middlesex; which might serve as an example for others. For by statute 23 Geo. II. c. 33, it is enacted, 1. That a special county-court should be held, at least once a month, in every hundred of the county of Middlesex, by the county-clerk. 2. That twelve freeholders of that hundred, qualified to serve on juries, and struck by the sheriff, shall be summoned to appear at such court by rotation; so as none shall be summoned oftener than once a year. 3. That in all causes not exceeding the value of forty shillings, the county-clerk and twelve suitors shall proceed in a summary way, examining the parties and witnesses on oath, without the formal process anciently used; and shall make such order therein as they shall judge agreeable to conscience. 4. That no plaints shall be removed out of this court by any process whatsoever; but the determination herein shall be final. 5. That if any action be brought in any of the superior courts against a person resident in Middlesex, for a debt or contract, upon the trial whereof the jury shall find less than 40s. damages, the plaintiff shall recover no costs, but shall pay the defendant double costs; unless upon some special circumstances, to be certified by the judge who tried it. 6. Lastly, a table of very moderate fees is prescribed and set down in the act; which are not to be exceeded upon any account whatsoever. This is a plan entirely agreeable to the constitution and genius of the nation; calculated to prevent a multitude of vexatious actions in the superior courts, and at the same time to give honest creditors an opportunity of recovering small sums; which now they are frequently deterred from by the expense of a suit at law; a plan which, one would think, wants only to be generally known, in order to its universal reception.

X. There is yet another species of private courts, which I must not pass over in silence: *viz.*, the chancellor's courts in the two universities of England.(16)　Which two learned bodies enjoy the sole jurisdiction,

---

(16) As the object of the privilege is that students and others connected with the universities should not be distracted from the studies and duties to be there performed, the party proceeded against must in general be a resident member of the university, and that fact must be expressly sworn, or be collected from the affidavit. The privilege of Cambridge differs from that of Oxford: in the former it only extends to causes of action accruing in the town and its suburbs; but in Oxford it extends to all personal causes arising anywhere. R. T. Hardw. 241. 2 Wils. 406. Bac. Abr. Universities. The claim of conusance must be made in due form and in due time. 2 Wils. 406. Claim of conusance of an action of trespass, brought in King's Bench against a resident member of the university of *Cambridge*, for a cause of action verified by affidavit not to have arisen within the town and suburbs of Cambridge, was allowed upon the claim of the vice-chancellor on

*84] in exclusion of the king's *courts, over all civil actions and suits whatsoever, when a scholar or privileged person is one of the parties; excepting in such cases where the right of freehold is concerned. And these by the university charter they are at liberty to try and determine, either according to the common law of the land, or according to their own local customs, at their discretion; which has generally led them to carry on their process in a course much conformed to the civil law, for reasons sufficiently explained in a former book.(*l*)

These privileges were granted, that the students might not be distracted from their studies by legal process from distant courts, and other forensic avocations. And privileges of this kind are of very high antiquity, being generally enjoyed by all foreign universities as well as our own, in consequence (I apprehend) of a constitution of the emperor Frederick, A.D. 1158.(*m*) But as to England in particular, the oldest charter that I have seen, containing this grant to the university of Oxford, was 28 Hen. III. A.D. 1244. And the same privileges were confirmed and enlarged by almost every succeeding prince, down to Henry the Eighth; in the fourteenth year of whose reign the largest and most extensive charter of all was granted. One similar to which was afterwards granted to Cambridge in the third year of queen Elizabeth. But yet, notwithstanding these charters, the privileges granted therein, of proceeding in a course different from the law of the land, were of so high a nature that they were held to be invalid; for though the king might erect new courts, yet he could not alter the course of law by his letters-patent. Therefore in the reign of queen Elizabeth an act of parliament was obtained,(*n*) confirming all the charters of the two universities, and those of 14 Hen. VIII. and 3 Eliz. by name. Which *blessed act*, as Sir Edward Coke entitles it,(*o*) established this high privilege without any doubt or opposition:(*p*) or, as Sir Matthew Hale(*q*) very fully expressed the
*85] sense *of the common law and the operation of the act of parliament, "although king Henry the Eighth, 14 *A. R. sui*, granted to the university a liberal charter, to proceed according to the use of the university; *viz.*, by a course much conformed to the civil law, yet that charter had not been sufficient to have warranted such proceedings without the help of an act of parliament. And therefore in 13 Eliz. an act passed, whereby that charter was in effect enacted; and it is thereby that at this day they have a kind of civil-law procedure, even in matters that are of themselves of common-law cognizance, where either of the parties is privileged."

This privilege, so far as it relates to civil causes, is exercised at Oxford in the chancellor's court; the judge of which is the vice-chancellor, his deputy or assessor. From his sentence an appeal lies to delegates appointed by the congregation; from thence to other delegates of the house of convocation; and if they all three concur in the same sentence it is final at least by the

<hr>

(*l*) Book I. introd. § 1.
(*m*) Cod. 4, *tit.* 13.
(*n*) 13 Eliz. c. 29.
(*o*) 4 Inst. 227.

(*p*) Jenk. Cent. 2, pl. 88; Cent. 3, pl. 88. Hardr. 504. Godbolt. 201.
(*q*) Hist. C. L. 33.

<hr>

behalf of the chancellor, masters, and scholars of the university, entered on the roll in due form, setting out their jurisdictions under charters confirmed by statute, and averring that the cause of action arose within such jurisdiction. 12 East, 12. And claim of consance by the university of *Oxford* was allowed in an action of trespass in King's Bench against a proctor, a pro-proctor, and the marshal of the university, though the affidavit of the latter, describing him as of a parish in the suburbs of Oxford, only verified that he then was, and had been for the last fourteen years, a common servant of the university, called marshal of the university, and that he was sued for an act done by him in the discharge of his duty, and in obedience to the orders of the other two defendants, without stating that he resided within the university, or was matriculated. 15 East, 634.—CHITTY.

See Bowyer's Coms. Const. Law of Eng. 292.

statutes of the university, (r) according to the rule of the civil law. (s)   But, if there be any discordance or variation in any of the three sentences, an appeal lies in the last resort to judges delegates appointed by the crown under the great seal in chancery.

I have now gone through the several species of private, or special, courts, of the greatest note in the kingdom, instituted for the local redress of private wrongs; and must, in the close of all, make one general observation from Sir Edward Coke: (t) that these particular jurisdictions, derogating from the general jurisdiction of the courts of common law, are ever strictly restrained, and cannot be extended further than the express letter of their privileges will most explicitly warrant.

CHAPTER VII.

OF THE COGNIZANCE OF PRIVATE WRONGS.

*WE now proceed to the cognizance of private wrongs; that is, to   [*86 consider in which of the vast variety of courts, mentioned in the three preceding chapters, every possible injury that can be offered to a man's person or property is certain of meeting with redress.

The authority of the several courts of private and special jurisdiction, or of what wrongs such courts have cognizance, was necessarily remarked as those respective tribunals were enumerated, and therefore need not be here again repeated; which will confine our present inquiry to the cognizance of civil injuries in the several courts of public and general jurisdiction.   And the order in which I shall pursue this injury will be by showing: 1. What actions may be brought, or what injuries remedied, in the ecclesiastical courts. 2. What in the military. 3. What in the maritime. And 4. What in the courts of common law.

And, with regard to the three first of these particulars, I must beg leave not so much to consider what hath at any time been *claimed* or pretended to belong to their jurisdiction, by the officers and judges of those respective courts; but what the common law *allows* and permits to be so.   For these eccentrical tribunals, (which are principally guided by the rules of the imperial and canon laws,) as they subsist and are *admitted in Eng-   [*87 land, not by any right of their own, (a) but upon bare sufferance and toleration from the municipal laws, must have recourse to the laws of that country wherein they are thus adopted, to be informed how far their juris-diction extends, or what causes are permitted, and what forbidden, to be discussed or drawn in question before them.   It matters not therefore what the pandects of Justinian, or the decretals of Gregory, have ordained.   They are here of no more intrinsic authority than the laws of Solon and Lycurgus: curious perhaps for their antiquity, respectable for their equity, and fre-quently of admirable use in illustrating a point of history.   Nor is it at all material in what light other nations may consider this matter of jurisdiction. Every nation must and will abide by its own municipal laws; which various accidents conspire to render different in almost every country in Europe. We permit some kinds of suits to be of ecclesiastical cognizance, which other nations have referred entirely to the temporal courts; as concerning wills and successions to intestates' chattels; and perhaps we may in our turn prohibit

(r) Tit. 21, § 19.   (t) 2 Inst. 548.
(s) Cod. 7, 70, 1.   (a) See book i. introd. § 1.

them from interfering in some controversies, which on the continent may be looked upon as merely spiritual. In short, the common law of England is the one uniform rule to determine the jurisdiction of our courts: and, if any tribunals whatsoever attempt to exceed the limits so prescribed them, the king's courts of common law may and do prohibit them; and in some cases punish their judges.(*b*)

Having premised this general caution, I proceed now to consider,

I. The wrongs or injuries cognizable by the ecclesiastical courts. I mean such as are offered to private persons or individuals; which are cognizable by the ecclesiastical court, not for reformation of the offender himself or party *injuring*, (*pro salute animæ*,(1) as is the case with immoralities in general, when unconnected with private injuries,) but for the sake of the party *injured*, to make him a satisfaction and redress for *the damage which he has sustained. And these I shall reduce under three general heads; of causes *pecuniary*, causes *matrimonial*, and causes *testamentary*.

*88]

1. Pecuniary causes, cognizable in the ecclesiastical courts, are such as arise either from the withholding ecclesiastical dues, or the doing or neglecting some act relating to the church, whereby some damage accrues to the plaintiff; towards obtaining a satisfaction for which he is permitted to institute a suit in the spiritual court.

The principal of these is the subtraction or withholding of *tithes* from the parson or vicar, whether the former be a clergyman or a lay appropriator.(*c*) But herein a distinction must be taken: for the ecclesiastical courts have no jurisdiction to try the *right* of tithes unless between spiritual persons;(*d*) but, in ordinary cases between spiritual men and lay men, are only to compel the payment of them, when the right is not disputed.(*e*) By the statute, or rather writ,(*f*) of *circumspecte agatis*,(*g*)(2) it is declared that the court Christian shall not be prohibited from holding plea, "*si rector petat versus parochianos oblationes et decimas debitas et consuetas:*"(3) so that if any dispute arises whether such tithes be *due* and *accustomed*, this cannot be determined in the ecclesiastical court, but before the king's court of the common

<hr/>

(*b*) Hal. Hist. C. L. c. 2.
(*c*) Stat. 32 Hen. VIII. c. 7.
(*d*) 2 Roll. Abr. 309, 310. Bro. Abr. c. *Jurisdiction*, 85.

(*e*) 2 Inst. 364, 489, 490.
(*f*) See Barrington, 123. 3 Pryn. Rec. 336.
(*g*) 13 Edw. I. st. 4, or rather 9 Edw. II.

<hr/>

(1) [For the safety of the soul.] See, in general, Bac. Abr. tit. Courts Ecclesiastical, D. and tit. Slander; Com. Dig. Prohibition; where see G. when the ecclesiastical court has jurisdiction and when not. The ecclesiastical court has no jurisdiction over trusts; and therefore, where a party sued as a trustee was arrested on a writ *de contumace capiendo*, [For taking the contumacious,] the court of King's Bench discharged him out of custody. 1 B. & C. 655.

Suits for *defamation may be added* to the three heads above considered. As to these in general, see Burn, Eccl. L. Defamation. Com. Dig. Prohibition, G. 14. Bac. Abr. Slander, T. U. Stark on slander, 32, 464. Words imputing an offence merely *spiritual* are not in themselves actionable at law, unless followed by special damage, and the party slandered can only institute a suit in the spiritual court; and though the law discourages suits of this kind, yet redress for the insult and injury is not denied. 2 Phil. Ec. Cases, 106. *Words* which impute an offence merely cognizable in a spiritual court may be punished in that court, as calling a person heretic, adulterer, fornicator, whore, etc.; but if the words are coupled with others for which an action at law would lie, as calling a woman a whore and a thief, the ecclesiastical court has no jurisdiction, and a prohibition lies. 2 Roll. Abr. 297. 1 Sid. 404. 3 Mod. 74. 1 Hagg. Rep. 463, in notes. So a suit cannot be instituted in the spiritual court for a written libel, because any slander of a person reduced into writing, and which can be the subject of any proceeding, is actionable or indictable. Comb. 71. Bac. Abr. Courts Ecclesiastical, D. The power of the ecclesiastical court is confined to the infliction of penance *pro salute animæ* [For the safety of the soul] and awarding costs, and does not extend to the awarding damages to the injured party. 4 Co. 20. 2 Inst. 492.—CHITTY. See Bowyer's Coms. Const. Law of Eng., 274.

(2) [That you proceed carefully.]

(3) ["If the rector sue his parishioners for oblations and tithes due and accustomed."]

law; as such question affects the temporal inheritance, and the determination must bind the real property. But where the *right* does not come into question, but only the *fact* whether or no the tithes allowed to be due are really subtracted or withdrawn, this is a transient personal injury, for which the remedy may properly be had in the spiritual court; viz., the recovery of the tithes, or their equivalent. By statute 2 & 3 Edw. IV. c. 13, it is enacted, that if any person shall carry off his predial tithes (viz., of corn, hay, or the like) before the tenth part *is duly set forth, or agreement is [*89 made with the proprietor, or shall willingly withdraw his tithes of the same, or shall stop or hinder the proprietor of the tithes, or his deputy, from viewing or carrying them away; such offender shall pay *double* the value of the tithes, with costs to be recovered before the ecclesiastical judge, according to the king's ecclesiastical laws. By a former clause of the same statute, the *treble* value of the tithes, so subtracted or withheld, may be sued for in the temporal courts, which is equivalent to the *double* value to be sued for in the ecclesiastical. For one may sue for and recover in the ecclesiastical courts the tithes themselves, or a recompense for them, by the ancient law; to which the suit for the *double* value is superadded by the statute. But as no suit lay in the temporal courts for the subtraction of tithes themselves, therefore the statute gave a *treble* forfeiture, if sued for there; in order to make the course of justice uniform, by giving the same reparation in one court as in the other.(*h*)(4) However, it now seldom happens that tithes are sued for at all in the spiritual court; for if the defendant pleads any custom, *modus*, composition, or other matter whereby the right of tithing is called in question, this takes it out of the jurisdiction of the ecclesiastical judges: for the law will not suffer the existence of such a right to be decided by the sentence of any single, much less an ecclesiastical, judge; without the verdict of a jury. But a more summary method than either of recovering small tithes under the value of 40s. is given by statute 7 & 8 W. III. c. 6, by complaint to two justices of the peace; and, by another statute of the same year, c. 34, the same remedy is extended to all tithes withheld by Quakers under the value of ten pounds.(5)

Another pecuniary injury, cognizable in the spiritual courts, is the *non-payment* of other ecclesiastical *dues* to the clergy; as pensions, mortuaries, compositions, offerings, and whatsoever falls under the denomination of surplice-fees, for marriages or other ministerial offices of the church: all which injuries are redressed by a decree for their actual *payment. [*90 Besides which, all offerings, oblations, and obventions not exceeding the value of 40s. may be recovered in a summary way before two justices of

(*h*) 2 Inst. 250,

(4) This statute enacts that every person shall justly divide, set out, yield, and pay all manner of predial tithes in such manner as they have been of right yielded and paid within forty years, or of right or custom ought to have been paid, before the making of that act, under the forfeiture of treble value of the tithes so carried away; and in an action upon this statute, in which the declaration stated that the tithes were within forty years before the statute yielded and payable, and yielded and paid, it was held that evidence that the land had been, as far as any witness knew, in pasture, and that it was never known to pay in predial tithe, was not sufficient to defeat the action. The same action might also be supported to recover tithes of lands enclosed out of wastes, which never paid tithes before. Mitchell *v.* Walker, 5 T. R. 260.—CHRISTIAN. See Bowyer's Com. Const. Law of Eng., 274.

(5) The 53 Geo. III. c. 127 extends the jurisdiction of the two justices to tithes, oblations, and compositions, of the value of 10l; and in respect of tithes and church-rates, due from Quakers, to 50l., see statute and proceedings, Burn, J., Tithes. The 54 Geo. III. c. 68 extends the same provisions to Ireland.—CHITTY.

It is hardly necessary to observe that the commutation of tithes, under the provisions of the statute 6 & 7 W. IV. c. 71 and numerous subsequent statutes, will eventually put an end to all suits for the subtraction of tithes.—STEWART.

the peace.(*i*) But care must be taken that these are real and not imaginary dues: for, if they be contrary to the common law, a prohibition will issue out of the temporal courts to stop all suits concerning them. As where a fee was demanded by the minister of the parish for the baptism of a child, which was administered in another place;(*j*) this, however authorized by the canon, is contrary to common right: for of common right, no fee is due to the minister even for performing such branches of his duty, and it can only be supported by a special custom;(*k*) but no custom can support the demand of a fee without performing them at all.

For *fees* also, settled and acknowledged to be due to the officers of the ecclesiastical courts, a suit will lie therein: but not if the *right* of the fees is at all disputable; for then it must be decided by the common law.(*l*) It is also said, that if a curate be licensed, and his salary appointed by the bishop, and he be not paid, the curate has a remedy in the ecclesiastical court;(*m*) but, if he be not licensed, or hath no such salary appointed, or hath made a special agreement with the rector, he must sue for a satisfaction at common law;(*n*) either by proving such special agreement, or else by leaving it to a jury to give damages upon a *quantum meruit*, that is, in consideration of what he reasonably deserved in proportion to the service performed.

Under this head of pecuniary injuries may also be reduced the several matters of spoliation, dilapidations, and neglect of repairing the church and things thereunto belonging; for which a satisfaction may be sued for in the ecclesiastical court.

Spoliation is an injury done by one clerk or incumbent to another *91] in taking the fruits of his benefice without any *right thereunto, but under a pretended title. It is remedied by a decree to account for the profits so taken. This injury, when the *jus patronatus* or right of advowson does not come in debate, is cognizable in the spiritual court: as if a patron first presents A. to a benefice, who is instituted and inducted thereto; and then, upon pretence of a vacancy, *the same* patron presents B. to the same living, and he also obtains institution and induction. Now, if the fact of the vacancy be disputed, then, that clerk who is kept out of the profits of the living, whichever it be, may sue the other in the spiritual court for spoliation, or taking the profits of his benefice. And it shall there be tried, whether the living were or were not vacant: upon which the validity of the second clerk's pretensions must depend.(*o*) But if the right of patronage comes at all into dispute, as if one patron presented A., and another patron presented B., there the ecclesiastical court hath no cognizance, provided the tithes sued for amount to a fourth part of the value of the living, but may be prohibited at the instance of the patron by the king's writ of *indicavit*.(*p*)(6) So also if a clerk, without any color of title, ejects another from his parsonage, this injury must be redressed in the temporal courts: for it depends upon no question determinable by the spiritual law, (as plurality of benefices or no plurality, vacancy or no vacancy,) but is merely a civil injury.

For *dilapidations*, which are a kind of ecclesiastical waste, either voluntary, by pulling down; or permissive, by suffering the chancel, parsonage-house, and other buildings thereunto belonging, to decay; an action also lies, either in the spiritual court by the canon law, or in the courts of common law,(*q*) and it may be brought by the successor against the predecessor, if living, or,

(*i*) Stat. 7 & 8 W. III. c. 6.
(*j*) Salk. 332.
(*k*) Ibid. 334. Lord Raym. 450, 1558. Fitz. 55.
(*l*) 1 Ventr. 165.
(*m*) 1 Burn, Eccl. Law, 438.

(*n*) 1 Freem. 70.
(*o*) F. N. B. 36.
(*p*) *Circumspecte agatis;* 13 Edw. I. st. 4, *Artic. cleri.* 9 Edw. II. c. 2. F. N. B. 45.
(*q*) Cart. 224. 3 Lev. 268.

(6) [He showed.]

if dead, then against his executors.   It is also said to be good cause of deprivation, if the bishop, parson, vicar, or other ecclesiastical person, dilapidates
the buildings, or cuts down timber growing on the patrimony of
*the church, unless for necessary repairs:(r)(7) and that a writ of pro-   [*92
hibition will also lie against him in the courts of common law.(s)(8)
By statute 13 Eliz. c. 10, if any spiritual person makes over or alienates his
goods with intent to defeat his successors of their remedy for dilapidations,
the successor shall have such remedy against the alienee, in the ecclesiastical
court, as if he were the executor of his predecessor.   And by statute 14
Eliz. c. 11, all money recovered for dilapidations shall within two years be
employed upon the buildings in respect whereof it was recovered, on penalty
of forfeiting double the value to the crown.

As to the neglect of reparations of the church, churchyard, and the like,
the spiritual court has undoubted cognizance thereof;(t) and a suit may be
brought therein for non-payment of a rate made by the church-wardens for
that purpose.   And these are the principal pecuniary injuries, which are
cognizable, or for which suits may be instituted, in ecclesiastical courts.

2. Matrimonial causes, or injuries respecting the rights of marriage, are
another, and a much more undisturbed, branch of the ecclesiastical jurisdiction.(9)   Though if we consider marriages in the light of mere civil contracts, they do not seem to be properly of spiritual cognizance.(u)   But the
Romanists having very early converted this contract into a holy sacramental
ordinance, the church of course took it under her protection, upon the
division of the two jurisdictions.   And in the hands of such able politicians,
it soon became an engine of great importance to the papal scheme of a universal monarchy over Christendom.   The numberless canonical impediments
that were invented, and occasionally dispensed with, by the holy see, not only
enriched the coffers of the church, but gave it a vast ascendant over princes
of all denominations; whose marriages were sanctified or reprobated, their
issue legitimated or bastardized, and the succession to their thrones
established or rendered precarious, according *to the humor or inter-   [*93
est of the reigning pontiff: besides a thousand nice and difficult
scruples, with which the clergy of those ages puzzled the understandings,
and loaded the consciences of the inferior orders of the laity; and which
could only be unravelled and removed by these their spiritual guides.   Yet,
abstracted from this universal influence, which affords so good a reason for
their conduct, one might otherwise be led to wonder that the same authority,
which enjoined the strictest celibacy to the priesthood, should think them
the proper judges in causes between man and wife.   These causes indeed,
partly from the nature of the injuries complained of, and partly from the
clerical method of treating them,(v) soon became too gross for the modesty

(r) 1 Roll. Rep. 86.   11 Rep. 98.   Godb. 259.
(s) 3 Bulstr. 138.   1 Roll. Rep. 335.
(t) *Circumspecte agatis.*   [That you proceed carefully.]   5 Rep. 66.

(u) Warb. Alliance, 173.
(v) Some of the impurest books that are extant in
any language are those written by the popish clergy
on the subjects of matrimony and divorce.

(7) See Radcliffe v. D'Oyley, 2 T. R. 630 (1788) for the common law remedy of action
on the case.

(8) A summary remedy before two justices of the peace may now be had.   Rex v. The
Church Wardens of Milnrow.   5 M. & S. 248 (1816).

(9) There is no uniformity in the American States as to the courts that shall take cognizance of applications for divorce; but this may be said in general, that divorce is sometimes a proceeding in the common law courts, sometimes in equity courts, and may
sometimes be had in the courts exercising probate powers.   The question of divorce
jurisdiction, when not determined by the State constitution, seems to have been always
regarded as one addressed to legislative discretion.   Whitmore v. Hardin, 3 Utah, 121,
128 (1881).   See Bowyer's Coms. Const. Law of Eng. 275.   Bright's Husb. and Wife, 361,

of a lay tribunal. And causes matrimonial are now so peculiarly ecclesiastical that the temporal courts will never interfere in controversies of this kind, unless in some particular cases. As if the spiritual court do proceed to call a marriage in question after the death of either of the parties; this the courts of common law will prohibit, because it tends to bastardize and disinherit the issue; who cannot so well defend the marriage, as the parties themselves, when both of them living, might have done.(w)

Of matrimonial causes, one of the first and principal is, 1. *Causa jactitationis matrimonii;* when one of the parties boasts(10) or gives out that he or she is married to the other, whereby a common reputation of their matrimony may ensue. On this ground the party injured may libel the other in the spiritual court; and, unless the defendant undertakes and makes out a proof of the actual marriage, he or she is enjoined perpetual silence upon that head; which is the only remedy the ecclesiastical courts can give for this injury. 2. Another species of matrimonial causes was, when a party contracted to another brought a suit in the ecclesiastical court to compel a celebration of the marriage in pursuance of such contract; but this branch of causes is now cut off entirely by the act for preventing clandestine
*94] marriages, 26 Geo. II. *c. 33, which enacts, that for the future no suit shall be had in any ecclesiastical court, to compel a celebration of marriage *in facie ecclesiæ*(11) for or because of any *contract* of matrimony whatsoever. 3. The suit for *restitution of conjugal rights* is also another species of matrimonial causes: which is brought whenever either the husband or wife is guilty of the injury of subtraction, or lives separate from the other without any sufficient reason; in which case the ecclesiastical jurisdiction will compel them to come together again, if either party be weak enough to desire it, contrary to the inclination of the other. 4. *Divorces* also, of which, and their several distinctions, we treated at large in a former book, (x) are causes thoroughly matrimonial, and cognizable by the ecclesiastical judge. If it becomes improper, through some supervenient cause arising *ex post facto,*(12) that the parties should live together any longer; as through intolerable cruelty,(13) adultery, a perpetual disease, and the like; this unfitness or inability for the marriage state may be looked upon as an injury to the suffering party; and for this the ecclesiastical law administers the remedy of separation, or a divorce *a mensa et thoro.*(14) But if the case existed previous to the marriage, and was such a one as rendered the marriage unlawful *ab initio,*(15) as consanguinity, corporal imbecility, or the like; in this case

(w) Inst. 614.   (x) Book i. ch. 15.

---

(10) The boasting must be malicious as well as false. Lord Hawke having permitted the party to assume the character of lady Hawke, in his presence, and having introduced and acknowledged her as such, the court dismissed the suit. Lord Hawke *v.* Corri, 2 Dr. Hagg. 220. See McKee *v.* Ingalls, 4 Scam. (Ill.) 30.
(11) [In the face of the church.]
(12) [After the fact.]
(13) A husband or a wife may sustain a suit for divorce on account of cruelty, even in a single instance, when dangerous to life, limb, or health—and threats of such danger are sufficient. But irritability, coldness, insult, or even desertion, is not alone sufficient ground for divorce. Evans *v.* Evans, 1 Hagg. Rep. 36, 364, 409, 458. 2 id. 154, 158. 2 Phil. Ec. c. 132. See Bowyer's Coms. Const. Law of Eng. 277. It has been determined by the court of delegates that the public infamy of the husband, arising from a judicial conviction of an attempt to commit an unnatural crime, is a sufficient cause for the ecclesiastical courts to decree a separation *a mensa et thoro* [From bed and board]. Feb. 1794.—CHRISTIAN. In this country the action for divorce on the ground of desertion is a substitute for the English proceeding for the restitution of conjugal rights. Fritz *v.* Fritz, 138 Ill. 436, 442 (1891). Segelbaum *v.* Segelbaum, 39 Minn. 258, 259 (1888).
(14) [From bed and board.]
(15) [From the beginning.] Lea *v.* Lea, 104 N. C. 603, 606 (1889).

the law looks upon the marriage to have been always null and void, being contracted *in fraudem legis*,(16) and decrees not only a separation from bed and board, but *a vinculo matrimonii*(17) itself. 5. The last species of matrimonial causes is a consequence drawn from one of the species of divorce, that *a mensa et thoro;*(18) which is the suit for *alimony,*(19) a term which signifies maintenance: which suit the wife, in case of separation, may have against her husband, if he neglects or refuses to make her an allowance suitable to their station in life. This is an injury to the wife, and the court Christian will redress it by assigning her a competent maintenance, and compelling the husband by ecclesiastical censures to pay it. But no alimony will be assigned in case of a divorce for adultery on her part; for as that amounts to a forfeiture of her *dower after his death, it is also a   [*95 sufficient reason why she should not be partaker of his estate when living.

3. Testamentary causes are the only remaining species belonging to the ecclesiastical jurisdiction;(20) which, as they are certainly of a mere temporal

---

(16) [Unlawfully.]

(17) [From the bonds of matrimony.]

(18) [From bed and board.]

(19) Alimony is a vested right, arising out of the marriage contract, and exists although the parties live separate, if there be no criminality on the part of the wife. Garland *v.* Garland, 50 Miss. 694, 710. A court of chancery will grant alimony when the misconduct of the husband renders it unsafe for the wife to live with him; or he turns her out of his home; but she has no claim to specific property. Almond *v.* Almond, 4 Rand. (Va.) 662.

(20) Com. Dig. Prohibition, G. 16. Although the ecclesiastical courts have by length of time acquired the orignal jurisdiction *in rebus testamentariis*, [In testamentary causes,] courts of equity have nevertheless obtained a concurrent jurisdiction with them in determinations upon personal bequests, as relief in those cases is generally dependent upon a discovery and an account of assets. And an executor being considered a trustee for the several legatees named in the testament, the execution of trusts is never refused by courts of equity. 1 P. Wms. 544, 575. These courts, indeed, in some other instances which frequently occur upon the present subject, exercise a jurisdiction in exclusion of the ecclesiastical, inasmuch as the relief given by the former is more efficient than that administered by the latter. One of these cases happens when a *husband* endeavors to obtain payment of his wife's legacy: equity will oblige him to make a proper settlement upon her, before a decree will be made for payment of the money to him; but this the ecclesiastical court cannot do: therefore, if the baron libel in that court for his wife's legacy, the court of chancery will grant an injunction to stay proceedings in it, he not having made any settlement or provision for her. 1 Dick. Rep. 373. Also 1 Atk. 491, 516. 2 Atk. 420. Prec. Cha. 548, S. P. Another of those instances occurs when legacies are given to *infants;* for equity will protect their interests, and give proper directions for securing and improving the fund for their benefit, which could not be effected in the ecclesiastical court. 1 Vern. 26. It has been already observed that the probate of wills belongs exclusively to the ecclesiastical court, except in the instance above adduced; whence it follows that, if a probate has been granted of a will obtained by fraud, the ecclesiastical court alone can revoke it, (2 Vern. 8. 1 P. Wms. 388;) and a person cannot be convicted of forging a will of a deceased person of personal property until the probate thereof has been sealed by the ecclesiastical court. 3 T. R. 127.

Although a court of equity cannot set aside a will of personal estate the probate of which has been obtained from the spiritual court, yet the court will interfere when a probate has been granted by the fraud of the person obtaining it, and either convert the wrong-doer into a *trustee*, in respect of such probate, or oblige him to consent to a repeal or revocation of it in the court from which it was granted. 1 Ves. 119, 284, 287. A court of equity will also interfere and prevent a person from taking an undue advantage by contesting the validity of a probate, when such person *has acted under it* and *admitted facts* material to its validity. 1 Atk. 628.

The jurisdiction of the ecclesiastical courts is confined to testaments merely, or, in other words, to dispositions of personalty: if, therefore, real estate be the subject of a devise to be sold for payment of debts or portions, these courts cannot hold plea in relation to such bequests, but the proper forum is a court of equity. Dyer, 151, b. Palm. 120, S. P. But the ecclesiastical courts' jurisdiction may extend to affect interests arising out of real property, when those interests are less than freehold, as in devises of terms for years, or of rents payable out of them; for such dispositions relate to *chattels real* only. 2 Keb. 8. Cro. J. 279. Buls. 153. If a legatee alter the nature of his demand,

nature, (*y*) may seem at first view a little oddly ranked among matters of a spiritual cognizance. And indeed (as was in some degree observed in a former book,)(*z*) they were originally cognizable in the king's courts of common law, viz., the county-courts;(*a*) and afterwards transferred to the jurisdiction of the church, by the favor of the crown, as a natural consequence of granting to the bishops the administration of intestates' effects.

This spiritual jurisdiction of testamentary causes is a peculiar constitution of this island; for in almost all other (even in popish) countries all matters testamentary are under the jurisdiction of the civil magistrate. And that this privilege is enjoyed by the clergy in England, not as a matter of ecclesiastical right, but by the special favor and indulgence of the municipal law, and as it should seem by some public act of the great council, is freely acknowledged by Lindewode, the ablest canonist of the fifteenth century. Testamentary causes, he observes, belong to the ecclesiastical courts "*de consuetudine Angliæ, et super consensu regio et suorum procerum in talibus ab antiquo concesso.*"(*b*)(21) The same was, about a century before, very openly professed in a canon of archbishop Stratford, viz., that the administration of intestates' goods was "*ab olim*"(22) granted to the ordinary, "*consensu regio et magnatum regni Angliæ.*"(*c*)(23) The constitutions of cardinal Othobon also testify that this provision "*olim a prælatis cum approbatione regis et baronum dicitur emanasse.*"(*d*)(24) And archbishop Parker,(*e*) in queen Elizabeth's time, affirms in express words, that originally in matters testamentary "*non ullam habebant episcopi auctoritatem, prætere a quam a rege acceptam referebant. Jus testamenti probandi non*

(*y*) Warburt. Alliance, 173.
(*z*) Book ii. ch. 32.
(*a*) Hickes's *Dissert Epistolar.* p. 8, 58.
(*b*) *Provincial, l.* 3, *t.* 13, *fol.* 176.

(*c*) Ibid. *l.* 3, *t.* 38, *fol.* 203.
(*d*) *Cap.* 28.
(*e*) See 9 Rep. 38.

---

and change it into a debt or duty, as by accepting a bond from the executor for payment of the legacy, it seems that the effect of the transaction will be either to deprive the ecclesiastical court of its jurisdiction, or to give an option to the person entitled, to sue in that or in a temporal court, at his discretion. 2 Roll. R. 160. Yelv. 39. 8 Mod. 327.

Cases have occurred in which *courts of common law* have assumed jurisdiction of testamentary matters, and permitted actions to be instituted for the recovery of legacies, upon proof of an express *assumpsit* or undertaking by the executor to pay them. Sid. 45. 11 Mod. 91. Ventr. 120. 2 Lev. 3. Cowp. 284. But it seems to be the opinion of modern judges that this jurisdiction extends to cases of *specific* legacies only; for when the executor assents to those bequests, the legal interests vest in the legatees, which enable them to enforce their rights at law. 3 East. R. 120. It seems to be the better opinion that when the legacy is not specific, but merely a gift out of the *general* assets, and particularly when a *married woman* is the legatee, a court of common law will not entertain jurisdiction to compel payment of such a legacy, upon the ground that a court of common law is, from its rules, incompetent that complete justice to the parties which courts of equity have the power, and are in the constant habit, of doing. 5 Term Rep. K. B. 690. 7 T. R. 667. 2 P. Wms. 641. Peake's C. N. P. 73. There is one case in the books where the declaration states that, in consideration of a forbearance by the plaintiff to sue, the executor promised to pay the legacy, and the court held that the action might be be maintained; but the circumstance of that action being brought on a promise, in consideration of forbearance, shows that it was understood that the bare possession of assets was not alone sufficient. 5 T. R. 693. 2 Lev. 3. But it has been suggested that it should seem that upon an express promise and admission of assets an executor may be sued. 2 Saund. by Patteson, 137, note a.—CHITTY.

(21) ["By the custom of England, and the consent of the king and his nobles anciently granted in such cases."]

(22) ["Formerly."]

(23) ["By command of the king and the peers of the kingdom of England."]

(24) ["It is said to have emanated formerly from the prelates with the approbation of the king and barons."]

*habebant: administrationis potestatem cuique delegare non poter-   [*96
ant.''(25)

At what period of time the ecclesiastical jurisdiction of testaments and
intestacies began in England, is not ascertained by any ancient writer: and
Lindewode(*f*) very fairly confesses, "*cujus regis temporibus hoc ordinatum
sit, non reperio.*''(26)   We find it indeed frequently asserted in our common-
law books, that it is but of *late years* that the church hath had the probate
of wills.(*g*)   But this must be understood to mean that it hath not *always*
had this prerogative: for certainly it is of very high antiquity.   Lindewode,
we have seen, declares that it was "*ab antiquo;*''(27) Stratford, in the reign
of king Edward III., mentions it as "*ab olim ordinatum;*''(28) and cardinal
Othobon, in the 52 Hen. III., speaks of it as an ancient tradition.   Bracton
holds it for clear law, in the same reign of Henry III., that matters testamentary belonged to the spiritual court.(*h*)   And, yet earlier, the disposition of
intestates' goods "*per visum ecclesiæ*''(29) was one of the articles confirmed
to the prelates by king John's *magna carta.*(*i*)   Matthew Paris also informs
us that king Richard I. ordained in Normandy "*quod distributio rerum quæ
in testamento relinquuntur auctoritate ecclesiæ fiet.*''(30)   And even this
ordinance of king Richard was only an introduction of the same law into his
ducal dominions, which before prevailed in this kingdom; for in the reign of
his father Henry II. Glanvil is express, that "*si quis aliquid dixerit contra
testamentum, placitum illud in curia christianitatis audiri debet et termi-
nari.*''(*j*)(31)   And the Scots book, called *regiam majestatem*, agrees
verbatim with Glanvil in this point.(*k*)

It appears that the foreign clergy were pretty early ambitious of
this branch of power; but their attempts to assume *it on the continent   [*97
were effectually curbed by the edict of the emperor Justin,(*l*) which
restrained the insinuation or probate of testaments (as formerly) to the office
of the *magister census:*(32) for which the emperor subjoins this reason:
"*absurdum et enim clericis est, immo etiam opprobriosum, si peritos se velint
ostendere disceptationum esse forensium.*''(33)   But afterwards by the canon
law(*m*) it was allowed that the bishop might compel by ecclesiastical censures
the performance of a bequest to *pious uses.*   And therefore, as that was
considered as a cause *quæ secundum canones et episcopales legis ad regimen
animarum pertinuit;*(34) it fell within the jurisdiction of the spiritual courts
by the express words of the charter of king William I., which separated those
courts from the temporal.   And afterwards, when king Henry I. by his
coronation-charter directed that the goods of an intestate should be divided

---

(*f*) Fol. 263.
(*g*) Fitz. Abr. tit. *testament*, pl. 4.   2 Roll. Abr. 217.
9 Rep. 37.   Vaugh. 207.
(*h*) L. 5, *de exceptionibus*, c. 10.
(*i*) Cap. 27, edit. *Oxon.*

(*j*) L. 7, c. 8.
(*k*) L. 2, c. 38.
(*l*) Cod. 1, 3, 41.
(*m*) Decretal. 3, 26, 17.   Gilb. Rep. 204, 205.

---

(25) ["The bishops had no other authority than what they received from the king. They
had not the right of proving wills; neither could they grant the power of administration."]

(26) ["I do not find in what king's reign this was ordained."]

(27) [" Anciently."]

(28) [" Ordained formerly."]

(29) [" Under the direction of the church."]

(30) ["That a distribution of the things which are left by will, be made by the authority
of the church."]

(31) ["If anything be averred against a will, that plea should be heard and determined
in the spiritual court."]

(32) [An officer for taking the value of estates.]

(33) ["For it is absurd, nay more, it is disgraceful for clergymen to wish to display their
skill in forensic disputes."]

(34) [Which according to the canon and episcopal laws, appertain to the cure of souls.]

for the good of his soul,(n) this made all intestacies immediately spiritual causes, as much as a legacy to pious uses had been before. This therefore, we may probably conjecture, was the era referred to by Stratford and Othobon when the king, by the advice of the prelates and with the consent of his barons, invested the church with this privilege. And accordingly in king Stephen's charter it is provided that the goods of an intestate ecclesiastic shall be distributed *pro salute animæ ejus, ecclesiæ consilio;*(o)(35) which latter words are equivalent to *per visum ecclesiæ* in the great charter of king John before mentioned. And the Danes and Swedes (who received the rudiments of Christianity and ecclesiastical discipline from England about the beginning of the twelfth century) have thence also adopted the spiritual cognizance of intestacies, testaments, and legacies.(p)

This jurisdiction, we have seen, is principally exercised with us in *98] the consistory courts of every diocesan *bishop, and in the prerogative court of the metropolitan, originally; and in the arches court and court of delegates by way of appeal. It is devisable into three branches; the probate of wills, the granting of administrations, and the suing for legacies. The two former of which, when no opposition is made, are granted merely *ex officio et debito justitiæ,*(36) and are then the object of what is called the *voluntary*, and not the *contentious*, jurisdiction. But when a *caveat* is entered against proving the will or granting administration, and a suit thereupon follows to determine either the validity of the testament, or who hath a right to administer; this claim and obstruction by the adverse party are an injury to the party entitled, and as such are remedied by the sentence of the spiritual court, either by establishing the will or granting the administration. Subtraction, the withholding or detaining of legacies, is also still more apparently injurious, by depriving the legatees of that right with which the laws of the land and the will of the deceased have invested them: and therefore, as a consequential part of testamentary jurisdiction, the spiritual court administers redress herein, by compelling the executor to pay them. But in this last case the courts of equity exercise a concurrent jurisdiction with the ecclesiastical courts, as incident to some other species of relief prayed by the complainant; as to compel the executor to account for the testator's effects, or assent to the legacy, or the like. For, as it is beneath the dignity of the king's courts to be merely ancillary to other inferior jurisdictions, the cause, when once brought there, receives there also its full determination.(37)

(n) *Si quis baronum seu hominum meorum,—pecuniam suam non dederit vel dare disposuerit, uxor sua, seu liberi, aut parentes et legitimi homines ejus, eam pro anima ejus dividant, sicut eis melius visum fuerit Text. Regibus. c. 34. p. 51.* [If any one of my barons or vassals shall not have disposed of his wealth, or directed the disposal of it, let his wife, children, or parents and proper persons divide it, for the good of his soul, as shall seem best to them.]

(o) Lord Lyttlet. Hen. II. vol. i. 539. Hearne *ad Gul. Neubr.* 711.

(p) Stiernhook, *de jure Sueon. l.* 2, c. 3.

(35) [For the good of his soul, by the advice and direction of the church.] [*Per visum ecclesiæ*—Under the inspection of the church.]

(36) [Officially and as in justice due.]

(37) See Randall *v.* Hodges, 3 Bland (Md.) 477, 484 (1832.) No action at law can be maintained against an executor for a legacy where there is no further proof of his assent to the legacy than what the law can infer from an acknowledgment by him of assets sufficient to pay it. Convenience is much in favor of this rule, because, if the person who was *legally* entitled could recover at *law*, he would do so *absolutely* and for his own use; and though the legacy might have been intended for the benefit of another, a court of law would have no means of compelling the legatee so to apply it, as in the case of a legacy to the wife, which would become the husband's absolutely; and the court of law could not oblige him, as a court of equity now will, to make provision for his wife out of it. Decks *v.* Strutt, 5 T. R. 690. But where the executor admits assets and expressly promises to pay in the case of a pecuniary legacy, or where the legacy being specific he assents to it, such promise and assent vests the property in the legatee, and he may maintain an action against the executor. Atkins *v.* Hill, Cowp. 284. Lord Say and Sele *v.* Guy, 3 E. R. 120.

It is omitted to be observed in the text that causes of defamation are within the jurisdiction of the ecclesiastical court. Suits of this kind are entertained for the use of words

These are the principal injuries for which the party grieved either must, or may, seek his remedy in the spiritual courts. But before I entirely dismiss this head, it may not be improper to add a short word concerning the *method of proceeding* in these tribunals, with regard to the redress of injuries.

It must (in the first place) be acknowledged, to the honor of the spiritual courts, that though they continue to this *day to decide many   [*99 questions which are properly of temporal cognizance, yet justice is in general so ably and impartially administered in those tribunals (especially of the superior kind) and the boundaries of this power are now so well known and established, that no material inconvenience at present arises from this jurisdiction still continuing in the ancient channel. And, should an alteration be attempted, great confusion would probably arise, in overturning long-established forms, and new-modeling a course of proceedings that has now prevailed for seven centuries.

The establishment of the civil-law process in all the ecclesiastical courts was indeed a masterpiece of papal discernment, as it made a coalition impracticable between them and the national tribunals, without manifest inconvenience and hazard. And this consideration had undoubtedly its weight in causing this measure to be adopted, though many other causes concurred. The time when the pandects of Justinian were discovered afresh, and rescued from the dust of antiquity, the eagerness with which they were studied by the popish ecclesiastics, and the consequent dissensions between the clergy and the laity of England, have formerly(*q*) been spoken to at large. I shall only now remark upon those collections, that their being written in the Latin tongue, and referring so much to the will of the prince and his delegated officers of justice, sufficiently recommended them to the court of Rome, exclusive of their intrinsic merit. To keep the laity in the darkest ignorance, and to monopolize the little science, which then existed, entirely among the monkish clergy, were deep-rooted principles of papal policy. And, as the bishops of Rome affected in all points to mimic the imperial grandeur, as the spiritual prerogatives were moulded on the pattern of the temporal, so the canon-law process was formed on the model of the civil law: the prelates embracing with the utmost ardor a method of judicial proceedings which was carried on in a language unknown to the bulk of the people, which banished the intervention of a jury, (that bulwark of *Gothic   [*100 liberty,) which placed an arbitrary power of decision in the breast of a single man.

The proceedings in the ecclesiastical courts are therefore regulated according to the practice of the civil and canon laws; or rather according to a mixture of both, corrected and new-modeled by their own particular usages, and the interposition of the courts of common law. For, if the proceedings in the spiritual court be ever so regularly consonant to the rules of the Roman law, yet if they be manifestly repugnant to the fundamental maxims of the municipal laws, to which upon principles of sound policy the ecclesiastical process ought in every state to conform,(*r*) (as if they require two witnesses to prove a fact, where one will suffice at common law;) in such cases a prohibition will be awarded against them.(*s*) But, under these restrictions, their ordinary course of proceeding is: first, by *citation*, to call the party injuring before them. Then, by *libel, libellus,* a little book, or by articles drawn out in a formal *allegation*, to set forth the complainant's ground of complaint. To

(*q*) Book i. introd. § 1.
(*r*) Warb. Alliance, 179.

(*s*) 2 Roll. Abr. 300, 302.

---

which, not importing or producing any temporal danger or loss, are not actionable in the courts of common law; and the use of them is punished by penance with or without costs, at the discretion of the court.—COLERIDGE.

this succeeds the *defendant's answer* upon oath, when, if he denies or extenuates the charge, they proceed to *proofs* by witnesses examined, and their depositions taken down in writing, by an officer of the court. If the defendant has any circumstances to offer in his defence, he must also propound them in what is called his *defensive allegation*, to which he is entitled in his turn to the *plaintiff's answer* upon oath, and may from thence proceed to *proofs* as well as his antagonist. The canonical doctrine of *purgation*, whereby the parties were obliged to answer upon oath to any matter, however criminal, that might be objected against them, (though long ago overruled in the court of chancery, the genius of the English law having broken through the bondage imposed on it by its clerical chancellors, and asserted the doctrines of judicial as well as civil liberty,) continued to the middle of the last century to be upheld by the spiritual courts; when the legislature was obliged to interpose, to teach them a lesson of similar moderation. By the
*101]   *statute of 13 Car. II. c. 12, it is enacted that it shall not be lawful for
any bishop or ecclesiastical judge to tender or administer, to any person whatsoever, the oath usually called the oath *ex officio*, [officially,] or any other oath whereby he may be compelled to confess, accuse, or purge himself of any criminal matter or thing, whereby he may be liable to any censure or punishment. When all the pleadings and proofs are concluded, they are referred to the consideration, not of a jury, but of a single judge; who *takes information* by hearing advocates on both sides, and thereupon forms his *interlocutory decree* or *definitive sentence* at his own discretion: from which there generally lies an *appeal*, in the several stages mentioned in a former chapter;(*t*) though if the same be not appealed from in fifteen days, it is final by the statute 25 Hen. VIII. c. 19.

But the point in which these jurisdictions are the most defective, is that of enforcing their sentences when pronounced; for which they have no other process but that of *excommunication;* which is described(*u*) to be twofold; the less, and the greater, excommunication. The less is an ecclesiastical censure, excluding the party from the participation of the sacraments; the greater proceeds further, and excludes him not only from these, but also from the company of all Christians. But, if the judge of any spiritual court excommunicates a man for a cause of which he hath not the legal cognizance, the party may have an action against him at common law, and he is also liable to be indicted at the suit of the king. (*w*)(38)

Heavy as the penalty of excommunication is, considered in a serious light, there are, notwithstanding, many obstinate or profligate men, who would despise the *brutum fulmen*(39) of mere ecclesiastical censures, especially

(*t*) Ch. 5.
(*u*) Co. Lit. 133.   (*w*) 2 Inst. 623.

---

(38) The recent act, 53 Geo. III. c. 127, prohibits excommunication and the writ *de excommunicato capiendo* [Writ for retaking an excommunicated person who had recovered his liberty without giving security to the church] as a mode of enforcing performance or obedience to ecclesiastical orders and decrees; and, instead of the sentence of excommunication in those cases, the court is to pronounce the defendant contumacious, and the ecclesiastical judge is to send his *significavit* in the prescribed form to the chancery, from which a *writ de contumace capiendo* [Writ for the arrest of certain vicious persons] is to issue in the prescribed form, and which is to have the same force as the ancient writ. There is a similar act as to Ireland, 54 Geo. III. c. 68. In other cases not of disobedience to the orders and decrees of the court, there may be excommunication, and a writ *de excommunicato capiendo*, as heretofore. In the proceedings under this statute, it must clearly appear that the ecclesiastical court had jurisdiction, and that the form of proceedings has been duly observed. 5 Bar. & Ald. 791. 3 Dowl. & R. 570, *ante*, 87, note 1.—
CHITTY. See Wait's Act. & Def. vol. 2, p. 265. Metcalf on Cont. p. 108 (Heard's ed.).
(39) [Empty sound.]

when pronounced by a petty surrogate in the country, for railing or con-
tumelious words, for non-payment of fees, or costs, or for other trivial
causes. The common law therefore compassionately steps in to *the   [*102
aid of the ecclesiastical jurisdiction, and kindly lends a supporting
hand to an otherwise tottering authority. Imitating herein the policy of our
British ancestors, among whom, according to Cæsar,(x) whoever were inter-
dicted by the Druids from their sacrifices, "*in numero impiorum ac scelerato-
rum habentur: ab iis omnes decedunt, aditum eorum sermonemque difugiunt,
ne quid ex contagione incommodi accipiant: neque iis petentibus jus redditur,
neque honos ullus communicatur.*"(40) And so with us by the common law an
excommunicated person is disabled to do any act that is required to be done
by one that is *probus et legalis homo.*(41) He cannot serve upon juries, cannot be a witness in any court, and, which is the worst of all, cannot bring an
action, either real or personal, to recover lands or money due to him.(y)(42)
Nor is this the whole: for if, within forty days after the sentence has been
published in the church, the offender does not submit and abide by the sentence of the spiritual court, the bishop may certify such contempt to the king
in chancery. Upon which there issues out a writ to the sheriff of the county,
called, from the bishop's certificates, a *significavit;* or, from its effects, a writ
de excommunicato capiendo(43) and the sheriff shall thereupon take the
offender, and imprison him in the county gaol, till he is reconciled to the
church, and such reconciliation certified by the bishop; under which another
writ, *de excommunicato deliberando*(44) issues out of chancery to deliver and
release him.(z) This process seems founded on the charter of separation (so
often referred to) of William the Conqueror. "*Si aliquis per superbiam
elatus ad justitiam episcopalem venire noluerit, vocetur semel, secundo, et tertio:
quod si nec ad emendationem venerit, excommuniceter; et, si opus fuerit, ad hoc
vindicandum fortitudo et justitia regis sive vicecomitis adhibeatur.*(45) And
in case of subtraction of tithes, a more summary and expeditious assistance
is given by the statutes of 27 Hen. VIII. c. 20, and 32 Hen. VIII. c. 7, which
enact, that upon complaint of any contempt or misbehavior of the ecclesiastical judge by the defendant in any suit for tithes, any privy counsellor, or any* two justices of the peace (or, in case of disobedience   [*103
to a definitive sentence, any two justices of the peace,) may commit
the party to prison without bail or mainprize, till he enters into a recognizance with sufficient sureties to give due obedience to the process and sentence
of the court. These timely aids, which the common and statute laws have
lent to the ecclesiastical jurisdiction, may serve to refute that groundless
notion which some are too apt to entertain, that the courts at Westminster
hall are at open variance with those at doctors' commons. It is true that
they are sometimes obliged to use a parental authority, in correcting the excesses of these inferior courts, and keeping them within their legal bounds;
but, on the other hand, they afford them a parental assistance in repressing

(x) *De bello Gall. l.* 6.   (z) F. N. B. 62.
(y) Litt. § 201.

---

(40) ["Are reckoned among the impious and wicked; all shun them, fly their approach,
and avoid all communication with them, lest they should receive some hurt from the
contagion, neither are they allowed to seek justice or preferment."]
(41) [A true and lawful man.]
(42) See Robertson *v.* Bullious, 9 Barb. (N. Y.) 64, 105 (1850).
(43) [For taking the excommunicated.]
(44) [For liberating the excommunicated.]
(45) ["If any one puffed up with pride come not to the episcopal court, let him be
summoned three times, and if he fail then to attend its correction, let him be excommunicated; and if necessary let the power and justice of the king, or sheriff, be exerted
to punish his contempt."]

the insolence of contumacious delinquents, and rescuing their jurisdiction from that contempt which for want of sufficient compulsive powers would otherwise be sure to attend it.(46)

II. I am next to consider the injuries cognizable in the *court military*, or court of *chivalry*. The jurisdiction of which is declared by statute 13 Ric. II. c. 2 to be this: "that it hath cognizance of contracts touching deeds of arms or of war, out of the realm, and also of things which touch war within the realm, which cannot be determined or discussed by the common law; together with other usages and customs to the same matters appertaining." So that wherever the common law can give redress, this court hath no jurisdiction: which has thrown it entirely out of use as to the matter of contracts, all such being usually cognizable in the courts of Westminster hall, if not directly, at least by fiction of law: as if a contract be made at Gibraltar, the plaintiff may suppose it made at Northampton; for the locality, or place of making it, is of no consequence with regard to the validity of the contract.

The words "other usages and customs" support the claim of this court, 1. To give relief to such of the nobility and gentry as think themselves aggrieved in matters of honor; and 2. To keep up the distinction of *104] degrees and *quality. Whence it follows, that the civil jurisdiction of this court of chivalry is principally in two points; the redressing injuries of honor, and correcting encroachments in matters of coat-armor, precedency, and other distinctions of families.

As a court of honor, it is to give satisfaction to all such as are aggrieved in that point; a point of a nature so nice and delicate, that its wrongs and injuries escape the notice of the common law, and yet are fit to be redressed somewhere.(47) Such, for instance, as calling a man a coward, or giving him the lie; for which, as they are productive of no immediate damage to his person or property, no action will lie in the courts of Westminster; and yet they are such injuries as will prompt every man of spirit to demand some honorable amends, which by the ancient law of the land was appointed to be given in the court of chivalry.(a) But modern resolutions have determined, that how much soever such a jurisdiction may be expedient, yet no action for words will at present lie therein.(b) And it hath always been most clearly holden,(c) that as this court cannot meddle with anything determinable by the common law, it therefore can give no pecuniary satisfaction or damages, inasmuch as the quantity and determination thereof is ever of common-law cognizance. And therefore this court of chivalry can at most only order reparation in point of honor; as, to compel the defendant *mendacium sibi ipsi imponere*, or to take the lie that he has given upon himself, or to make such other submission as the laws of honor may require.(d) Neither can this court, as to the point of reparation in honor, hold plea of any such word or thing wherein the party is relievable by the courts of common law. As if a man gives another a blow, or calls him thief or murderer; for in both these

---

(a) Year-book, 37 Hen. VI. 21. Selden of Duels, c. 10. Hal. Hist. C. L. 37.
(b) Salk. 533. 7 Mod. 125. 2 Hawk. P. C. 11.
(c) Hal. Hist. C. L. 37.
(d) 1 Roll. Abr. 128.

---

(46) In the ecclesiastical courts the maxim is that *nullum tempus occurrit ecclesiæ* [No time runs against the church], or that there is no limitation to a prosecution for a spiritual offence; and it was thought a great grievance that the peace of families might be disturbed by a prosecution for a crime of incontinence committed many years before. It was therefore enacted by the 27 Geo. III. c. 44 that no prosecution should be commenced in the spiritual courts for defamation after six months, or for fornication or incontinence, or for striking or brawling in a church or churchyard, after eight months; and that in no case parties who had intermarried should be prosecuted for their previous fornication.—CHRISTIAN.

(47) 1 Bishop's New Crim. Law, § 10.

cases the common law has pointed out his proper remedy by action.

*As to the other point of its civil jurisdiction, the redressing of   [*105 encroachments and usurpations in matters of heraldry and coat-armor; it is the business of this court, according to Sir Matthew Hale, to adjust the right of armorial ensigns, bearings, crests, supporters, pennons, etc.; and also rights of place or precedence, where the king's patent or act of parliament (which cannot be overruled by this court) have not already determined it.

The proceedings in this court are by petition, in a summary way; and the trial not by a jury of twelve men, but by witnesses, or by combat.(*e*)   But as it cannot imprison, not being a court of record, and as by the resolutions of the superior courts it is now confined to so narrow and restrained a jurisdiction, it has fallen into contempt and disuse.   The marshaling of coat-armor, which was formerly the pride and study of all the best families in the kingdom, is now greatly disregarded; and has fallen into the hands of certain officers and attendants upon this court, called heralds, who consider it only as a matter of lucre, and not of justice: whereby such falsity and confusion have crept into their records, (which ought to be the standing evidence of families, descents, and coat-armor,) that, though formerly some credit has been paid to their testimony, now even their common seal will not be received as evidence in any court of justice in the kingdom.(*f*)   But their original visitation books, compiled when progresses were solemnly and regularly made into every part of the kingdom, to inquire into the state of families, and to register such marriages and descents as were verified to them upon oath, are allowed to be good evidence of pedigrees.(*g*)   And it is much to be wished, that this practice of visitation at certain periods were revived; for the failure of inquisitions *post mortem*,(48) by the abolition of military tenures, combined with the negligence of the heralds in omitting their usual progresses, has rendered the proof of a modern descent, *for the recovery   [*106 of an estate or succession to a title of honor, more difficult than that of an ancient.   This will be indeed remedied for the future, with respect to claims of peerage, by a late standing order(*h*) of the house of lords; directing the heralds to take exact accounts, and preserve regular entries, of all peers and peeresses of England, and their respective descendants; and that an exact pedigree of each peer and his family shall, on the day of his first admission, be delivered to the house by garter the principal king-at-arms. But the general inconvenience, affecting more private successions, still continues without a remedy.

III. Injuries cognizable by the courts maritime, or admiralty courts, are the next object of our inquiries.   These courts have jurisdiction and power to try and determine all maritime causes; or such injuries which, though they are in their nature of common-law cognizance, yet being committed on the high seas, out of the reach of our ordinary courts of justice, are therefore to be remedied in a peculiar court of their own.   All admiralty causes must be therefore causes arising wholly upon the sea, and not within the precincts of any county.(*i*)(49)   For the statute 13 Ric. II. c. 5 directs that the admiral

(*e*) Co. Litt. 261.
(*f*) 2 Roll. Abr. 686. 2 Jon. 224.
(*g*) Comb. 63.

(*h*) 11 May, 1767.
(*i*) Co. Litt. 260. Hob. 79.

---

(48) [After death.]
(49) See much learning respecting the jurisdiction of the court of admiralty in the case of Le Caux *v.* Eden, Doug. 572.—CHRISTIAN.   See also for a learned and exhaustive discourse on the same subject, the opinion of Story, J., in De Lorie *v.* Boit *et al.*, 7 Fed. Cas. 418 (case 3776), in which he held that the district courts of the United States have jurisdiction over all maritime contracts wherever executed and over all torts and injuries committed on the high seas, and in ports and harbors within the ebb and flow of the tide.

and his deputy shall not meddle with anything, but only things done upon the sea; and the statute 15 Ric. II. c. 3 declares that the court of the admiral hath no manner of cognizance of any contract, or of any other thing, done within the body of any county either by land or water; nor of any wreck of the sea: for that must be cast on land before it becomes a wreck.(j)(50) But it is otherwise of things *flotsam, jetsam,* and *ligan;* for over them the admiral hath jurisdiction, as they are in and upon the sea.(k) If part of any contract, or other cause of action, doth arise upon the sea, and part upon the land, the common law excludes the admiralty court from its jurisdiction; for, part belonging properly to one cognizance and part to another, the

*107] common or general law takes place of the particular.(l) *Therefore, though pure maritime acquisitions, which are earned and become due on the high seas, as seamen's wages, are one proper object of the admiralty jurisdiction, even though the contract for them be made upon land;(m) yet, in general, if there be a contract made in England and to be executed upon the seas, as a charter-party or covenant that a ship shall sail to Jamaica, or shall be in such a latitude by such a day; or a contract made upon the sea to be performed in England, as a bond made on shipboard to pay money in London, or the like; these kinds of mixed contracts belong not to the admiralty jurisdiction, but to the courts of common law.(n) And indeed it hath been further holden, that the admiralty court cannot hold plea of any contract under seal.(o)(51)

(j) See book i. ch. 8.
(k) 5 Rep. 106.
(l) Co. Litt. 261.

(m) 1 Ventr. 146.
(n) Hob. 12. Hal. Hist. C. L. 35.
(o) Hob. 212.

In Chamberlain v. Chandler, 5 Fed. Cas. 413 (case 2575) (1823), it was held by the same judge that admiralty has jurisdiction of personal torts committed by the master of a ship, on the high seas, on a passenger, and that it was immaterial whether the tort was a direct or consequential wrong, whether an assault or a denial of necessaries. See contra as to the jurisdiction of admiralty of torts committed *infra corpus committatus* [Within the body of the county,] the dissenting opinion of Woodbury, J., in Waring v. Clarke, 5 How. U. S. 441, 467 (1847). For further discussion, see Ramsay v. Alegre, 12 Wheaton, 638. Bains v. Schooner James and Catherine, Baldwin, 544. Waring v. Clarke, 5 Howard, 441. New Jersey Steam Navigation Co. v. Merchant's Bank, 6 Howard, 344. Cutler v. Rae, 7 Howard, 729. United States v. The New Bedford Bridge, 1 Woodb. & Minot. Boylan *et al.* v. Steamboat Victory, 4 Missouri (Wittelsey) 245. Talbot v. Owners of Three Brigs, 1 Dallas (Pa.) 95. Connelly v. The Steamboat Bee, 40 Mo. 263-4 (1867). Martin v. Commonwealth *et al.*, 1 Mass. 347. Angell on Carriers, § 610, n. (1877).

(50) Brantley's Pers. Prop. § 138, p. 219

(51) The case referred to in the text is that of Palmer v. Pope, Hobart's Rep. p. 79 and p. 212; but it does not seem to warrant the position. The libel in the admiralty court there stated an agreement, made *super altum mare* [Upon the high seas], that Pope should carry certain sugars, and that the agreement was after put in writing, in the port of Gado, on the coast of Barbary; a breach was then assigned. The court resolved "that a prohibition lay, because the original contract, though it were made at sea, yet was changed when it was put in writing and sealed, *which, being at land*, changed the jurisdiction; but if it had been a writing only without seal, a mere remembrance of the agreement, it had made no change." But this is to be understood that the sealed contract destroyed the original parol contract, which a mere writing would not have done; and as that new contract was made *on land*, though out of the king's dominions, still it was not within the admiralty jurisdiction. It cannot, therefore, be inferred from this case that the admiralty court cannot hold plea of *any* contract under seal. The same point, however, is undoubtedly laid down in Opy v. Addison and others, 12 Mod. 38. S. C. Salk. 31. Day v. Searle, 2 Strange, 968, (which, however, was decided only on the authority of the preceding case,) and Howe v. Nappier, 4 Burr, 1950. Perhaps, however, upon an examination of the authorities, it would appear that there is nothing to warrant the position that the admiralty court has not jurisdiction where the specialty contract is made *on the sea*, and to be performed on the sea, or where it relates to a subject-matter over which the court has jurisdiction. The 4 Inst. p. 135, which has been cited to support this, does not go so far; and the case of Menetone v. Gibbons, 3 T. R. 267, virtually overruled the cases on which lord Mansfield relied in Howe v. Nappier, because there it was determined

And also, as the courts of common law have obtained a concurrent jurisdiction with the court of chivalry with regard to foreign contracts, by supposing them made in England; so it is no uncommon thing for a plaintiff to feign that a contract, really made at sea, was made at the royal exchange, or other inland place, in order to draw the cognizance of the suit from the courts of admiralty to those of Westminster hall.(*p*) This the civilians exclaim against loudly, as inequitable and absurd; and Sir Thomas Ridley(*q*) hath very gravely proved it to be impossible for the ship in which such cause of

(*p*) 4 Inst. 134.　　　　　　　　　　(*q*) View of the Civil Law, b. iii. p. 1, § 8.

that the admiralty court *had* jurisdiction respecting an hypothecation *bond*, though executed on land and under seal, *because* it had jurisdiction over the subject-matter of the hypothecation of ships, and it was expressly negatived that the circumstance of the instrument being under seal could deprive them of their jurisdiction. Now, the cases alluded to were suits for mariners' wages, and it was admitted that the admiralty had jurisdiction over the subject-matter; but it was said that the special agreement and the seal took it away.

It will be observed that the reasoning in this note on the case of Palmer *v.* Pope proceeds further than the text, and assumes that in the case of contracts it is not necessary to bring the matter within the precincts of a county in order to oust the admiralty of jurisdiction. In that case it is expressly laid down that the jurisdiction is limited to the *seas* only, that the libel must allege the matter to have arisen *super altum mare* [Upon the high seas], and that if it arise upon any continent, port, or haven, in the world, of the king's dominions, the statutes take away the jurisdiction. This must be qualified, it is conceived, by the principle laid down in Menetone *v.* Gibbons. See H. C. L. c. 2.—COLERIDGE.

And now, by stat. 3 & 4 Vict. c. 65, s. 6, the court may in certain cases adjudicate on claims for services and repairs, although not on the high seas: and by 9 & 10 Vict. c. 99 its jurisdiction in matters of wreck and salvage is regulated.—STEWART.

All civil injuries cognizable in the court of admiralty in England are in like manner cognizable in the district courts of the United States, which are courts of admiralty *quoad hoc* [As to this]. Captures within the waters of the United States or within a marine league of the coasts, by whomsoever made, are likewise cognizable therein,—saving to suitors, in all cases, the right of a common-law remedy where the common law is competent to give it. Act Sept. 24, 1789, 1 Story's Laws, 56. Act of June 5, 1794, 1 Story's Laws, 353. Seamen's wages are there also recoverable; and a summary method of compelling payment, by application to the district judge, or, in case of his residence being more than three miles from the place, or of his absence, to any judge or justice of the peace, is given by the act for the government of seamen in the merchants' service; saving to them the right of maintaining an action at common law. Act of July 20, 1790, 1 Story's Laws, 105.

It was at first questioned whether the district courts had jurisdiction under the act of Congress as prize courts, in virtue of the clause vesting in them all civil causes of admiralty jurisdiction. The Supreme Court of the United States settled this question by deciding that the district courts of the United States possessed all the powers of courts of admiralty, whether considered as instance or as prize courts. Glass *v.* The Sloop Betsy, 3 Dallas, 6.

In regard to the powers of the district courts as instance courts, it seems to be settled that the federal courts, as courts of admiralty, can only exercise such criminal jurisdiction as is expressly conferred upon them by acts of Congress. United States *v.* Hudson & Goodwin, 7 Cranch, 32. United States *v.* Coolidge, 1 Wheaton, 415. The Judiciary Act of 1789 provides that the trial of all issues in fact in the district courts, in all causes except civil causes of admiralty and maritime jurisdiction, shall be by jury.

In regard to the extent of the powers of the district courts in civil causes of admiralty jurisdiction, it was held, in De Lovio *v.* Boit and others, 2 Gallison, 398, that the admiralty has jurisdiction over all maritime contracts, wheresoever the same may be made or executed, and whatever may be the form of the stipulations; that it has also jurisdiction over all torts and injuries committed upon the high seas and in ports or harbors within the ebb and flow of the tide; and that the like causes are within the jurisdiction of the district courts of the United States, by virtue of the delegation of authority in all civil causes of admiralty and maritime jurisdiction. The doctrines of this case have been denied, and the question has been much discussed in subsequent cases. Ramsay *v.* Allegre, 12 Wheat. 638. Bains *v.* The Schooner James and Catherine, Baldwin, 544. Waring *v.* Clarke, 5 Howard, 441. New Jersey Steam. Nav. Co. *v.* Merchants' Bank, 6 ibid. 344. Cutler *v.* Rae, 7 ibid. 729. United States *v.* The New Bedford Bridge, 1 Wood and Minot, 401.—SHARSWOOD.

action arises to be really at the royal exchange in Cornhill. But our lawyers justify this fiction, by alleging (as before) that the locality of such contracts is not at all essential to the merits of them; and that learned civilian himself seems to have forgotten how much such fictions are adopted and encouraged in the Roman law: that a son killed in battle is supposed to live forever for the benefit of his parents;(r) and that, by the fiction of *postliminium* and the *lex Cornelia*,(52) captives, when freed from bondage, were held to have never been prisoners,(s) and such as died in captivity were supposed to have died in their own country.(t)

*108]   *Where the admiral's court hath no original jurisdiction of the cause, though there should arise in it a question that is proper for the cognizance of the court, yet that doth not alter nor take away the exclusive jurisdiction of the common law.(u) And so, *vice versa*, if it hath jurisdiction of the original, it hath also jurisdiction of all consequential questions, though properly determinable at common law.(v) Wherefore, among other reasons, a suit for beaconage of a beacon standing on a rock in the sea may be brought in the court of admiralty, the admiral having an original jurisdiction over beacons.(w) In case of prizes also in time of war, between our own nation and another, or between two other nations, which are taken at sea, and brought into our ports, the courts of admiralty have an undisturbed and exclusive jurisdiction to determine the same according to the law of nations.(x)(53)

(r) Iust. 1, tit. 25.
(s) *Ff.* 49, 15, 12, § 6.
(t) *Ff.* 49, 15, 18.
(u) Comb. 462.

(v) 13 Rep. 53.   2 Lev. 25.   Hardr. 183
(w) 1 Sid. 158.
(x) 2 Show. 232.   Comb. 474.

(52) [A reprisal and the Cornelian law.]

(53) The author takes no notice of what is very material,—that there are in fact two courts, the admiralty court, or more properly the instance court, of which he has hitherto been speaking, and which the statutes of Richard were made to restrain, but which has no jurisdiction in matters of prize, and the prize court. Both courts have, indeed, the same judge; but in the former he sits by virtue of a commission under the great seal, which enumerates the objects of his jurisdiction but specifies nothing relative to prize; while in the latter he sits by virtue of a commission which issues in every war, under the great seal, to the lord high admiral, requiring the court of admiralty and the lieutenant and judge of the same court "to proceed upon all and all manner of captures, seizures, prizes, and reprisals of all ships and goods that are or shall be taken, and to hear and determine according to the course of the admiralty and the law of nations;" and upon this a warrant issues to the judge. The manners of proceeding and the systems of litigation and jurisprudence are different in the two courts. The jurisdiction of this last court is exclusive; for it has been determined solemnly, that though for taking a ship on the high seas an action will lie at common law, yet when it is taken *as prize*, though wrongfully taken and there were no color for the taking, no action can be maintained. Nor is the jurisdiction confined to captures *at sea*. Captures in port or on land, where the surrender has been to a naval force or a mixed force of the army and navy, are equally and exclusively triable by the prize court. The reasonableness and convenience of these determinations are beautifully enforced, in the judgments of Mr. J. Buller in Le Caux *v.* Eden, and of lord Mansfield in Lindo *v.* Rodney and another, Douglas's Rep. 594, 620. Though the prize court proceeds under a commission issuing at the commencement of each war, its jurisdiction is not peremptorily terminated by the peace, but all questions of prize between the two nations will still be tried by this court. Thus, where a vessel, having been captured by an American privateer in time of war, was recaptured after the period prescribed for the cessation of hostilities by the treaty of peace, and the American commander claimed the vessel to be restored to him by suit in the prize court, the jurisdiction of the court was affirmed and a prohibition refused. *Ex parte* Lynch, 1 Maddock's R. 15. The Harmony, S. C. 2 Dodson's R. 78.—COLERIDGE.

The court of admiralty has now, by stat. 3 & 4 Vict. c. 65, an express jurisdiction to try questions of booty at war; and by 13 & 14 Vict. cc. 26, 27, jurisdiction in questions relating to the attack and capture of pirates is vested in the admiralty court here and in all vice-admiralty courts abroad. Offences committed within the jurisdiction of the admiralty courts may now be tried in the ordinary criminal courts. 7 & 8 Vict. c. 2. 12 & 13 Vict. c. 96.—STEWART.

The proceedings of the courts of admiralty bear much resemblance to those of the civil law, but are not entirely founded thereon; and they likewise adopt and make use of other laws, as occasion requires; such as the Rhodian laws and the laws of Oleron.(*y*) For the law of England, as has frequently been observed, doth not acknowledge or pay any deference to the civil law, considered as such; but merely permits its use in such cases where it judged its determinations equitable, and therefore blends it, in the present instance, with other marine laws: the whole being corrected, altered, and amended by acts of parliament and common usage; so that out of this composition a body of jurisprudence is extracted, which owes its authority only to its reception here by consent of the crown and people. The first process in these courts is frequently by arrest of the defendant's person;(*z*) and they also take recognizances or stipulations of certain fidejussors in the nature of bail,(*a*) and in case of default may *imprison both them and their   [*109 principal.(*b*) They may also fine and imprison for a contempt in the face of the court.(*c*) And all this is supported by immemorial usage, grounded on the necessity of supporting a jurisdiction so extensive;(*d*) though opposite to the usual doctrines of the common law: these being no courts of record, because in general their process is much conformed to that of the civil law.(*e*)

IV. I am next to consider such injuries as are cognizable by the courts of the common law. And herein I shall for the present only remark, that all possible injuries whatsoever that did not fall within the exclusive cognizance of either the ecclesiastical, military, or maritime tribunals, are, for that very reason, within the cognizance of the common-law courts of justice.(54) For it is a settled and invariable principle in the laws of England, that every right when withheld must have a remedy, and every injury its proper redress. The definition and explication of these numerous injuries, and their respective legal remedies, will employ our attention for many subsequent chapters. But before we conclude the present, I shall just mention two species of injuries, which will properly fall now within our immediate consideration: and which are, either when justice is delayed by an inferior court which has proper cognizance of the cause; or, when such inferior court takes upon itself to examine a cause and decide the merits without a legal authority.

1. The first of these injuries, refusal or neglect of justice, is remedied either by writ of *procedendo*, or of *mandamus*. A writ of *procedendo ad judicium*(55) issues out of the court of chancery, where judges of any sub-

(*y*) Hale, Hist. C. L. 36. Co. Litt. 11.
(*z*) Clerke *prax. cur. adm.* § 13.
(*a*) Ibid. § 11. 1 Roll. Abr. 531. Raym. 78. Lord Raym. 1286.
(*b*) 1 Roll. Abr. 531. Godb. 193, 260.
(*c*) 1 Ventr. 1.
(*d*) 1 Keb. 552.
(*e*) Bro. Abr. tit. *Error*, 177.

The text is incorrect in stating that in prizes "between two other nations which are taken at sea and brought into our ports" the courts of admiralty have jurisdiction to determine the same according to the law of nations. The condemnation of property thus taken in war must be pronounced by a prize court of the government of the captor, sitting either in the country of the captor or of his ally. The prize court of an ally cannot condemn. Prize or no prize is a question belonging exclusively to the courts of the country of the captor. The reason of this rule is said to be that the sovereign of the captors has a right to inspect their behavior, for he is answerable to other states for the acts of the captor. The prize court of the captor may sit in the territory of the ally; but it is not lawful for such a court to act in a neutral territory. Neutral ports are not intended to be auxiliary to the operations of the powers at war; and the law of nations has clearly ordained that a prize court of a belligerent captor cannot exercise jurisdiction in a neutral country. This prohibition rests not merely on the unfitness and danger of making neutral ports the theatre of hostile proceedings, but it stands on the ground of the usage of nations. 1 Kent's Com. 103.—SHARSWOOD.

(54) State *ex rel.* Morris v. Buckley, 61 Conn. 287, 374 (1892).

(55) [In proceeding to judgment.] The supreme court of the United States has power to issue writs of *mandamus* in cases warranted by the principles and usages of law, to any

ordinate court do delay the parties; for that they will not give judgment
either on the one side or the other, when they ought so to do. In this case a
writ of *procedendo* shall be awarded, commanding them in the king's name
to proceed to judgment; but without specifying any particular judg-
*110]   ment, for that (if erroneous) may *be set aside in the course of appeal,
or by writ of error or false judgment: and upon further neglect or
refusal, the judges of the inferior court may be punished for their contempt
by writ of attachment returnable in the king's bench of common pleas.(*f*)

A writ of *mandamus*(56) is, in general, a command issuing in the king's
name from the court of king's bench, and directed to any person, corporation,
or inferior court of judicature within the king's dominions, requiring them
to do some *particular* thing therein specified, which appertains to their office
and duty, and which the court of king's bench has previously determined, or
at least supposes, to be consonant to right and justice. It is a high prerogative writ, of a most extensively remedial nature; and may be issued in
some cases where the injured party has also another more tedious method of
redress, as in the case of admission or restitution of an office; but it issues in
all cases where the party hath a right to have any thing done, and hath no
other specific means of compelling its performance. A *mandamus* therefore
lies to compel the admission or restoration of the party applying to any office
or franchise of a public nature, whether spiritual or temporal; to academical
degrees; to the use of a meeting-house, etc.:(57) it lies for the production,

(*f*) F. N. B. 153, 154, 240.

courts appointed or persons holding office under the authority of the United States. Act
of Cong. Sep. 24, 1789. 1 Story's Laws, 59.—SHARSWOOD. 2 Barb. Rights of Pers. and
Prop. 895. Bowyer's Const. Law Eng. 246.

Bliss on Code Pl. § 443. Where there is an adequate remedy at law, a *mandamus*
does not lie. Rex *v.* Severn & W. R. R. Co., 2 B. & A. 646. *Ex parte* Trapnall, 1
Eng. (Ark.) 2 (1845). Trustees *v.* State, 11 Tanner (Ind.) 205 (1858). Lother *v.*
Davis, 33 W. Va. 132 (1889). Taylor *v.* Governor, 1 Pike (Ark.) 21 (1837). State
ex rel. Railroad Co., 59 Ala. 321 (1877). State *v.* Layton, 4 Dutch. (N. J.) 244
(1859). People *v.* Martin, 62 Barb. (N. Y.) 570 (1872). Nor will it lie where the right
is a private one. Rex *v.* Bank of Eng., 2 B. & A. 620. Rex *v.* London Ins. Co.,
5 B. & A. 599. Hamilton *v.* State, 3 Ind. 452 (1852). Richards *v.* Swift, 7 Houston
(Del.) 137. Mandamus does not lie to determine the ultimate right to an office. Warner
v Meyer, 3 Wils. (Ore.) 218 (1869). But where a party has a *prima facie* right to an
office, it may be enforced by *mandamus*. State *ex rel. v.* Oates, 86 Wis. 634 (1893).
Dow *v.* Judges, 3 H. & M. (Va.) 23 (1808). Harwood *v.* Marshall, 9 Maryland (83).
State *v.* City, 1 Dutch. (N. J.) 536 (1856). Bradley *v.* McCrabb, 1 Dall. (Tex.) 504 (1843).
See also Swift *v.* Richardson, 7 Hous. (Del.) 338 (1886). Strong's Case, 1 Kirby (Conn.)
349 (1787). Mattox *v.* Neal, 45 Ark. 121 (1885). Parker *v.* Smith, 1 Gill. (Ill.) 411
(1844). People *ex rel. v.* Kilduff, 15 Ill. 492 (1854). It would not lie to compel a board
of county canvassers who had declared the result of an election and dissolved, to reor-
ganize for the purpose of correcting an error in the count. People *v.* Supervisors, 12
Barb. (N. Y.) 217 (1851). State *v.* Bruce *et al.*, 3 Bev. (S. C.) 264 (1812). An issue of
fact in a mandate must be tried by jury if either party demands it. The State *ex rel.*
McCalla *v.* The Brunsw. Turnp. Co., 97 Ind. 416 (1884). Yates *v.* People, 6 Johnson
(N. Y.) 337-463. See Woodstock *v.* Gallup, 28 Vt. (2 Williams) 587 (1856), where the
proper office of, and proceeding upon writs of *certiorari* and mandamus in the nature of
a *procedendo* are considered.

(56) [We command.]

(57) It lies to compel an inferior court to restore an attorney. People *v.* Turner, 9
Wils. (Cal.) 143 (1850); to compel judges to hold court, and officers of a county to keep
their offices at the county seat. Calaveras Co. *v.* Brockway, 30 Cal. 325 (1866): to correct
the actions of inferior courts, or judicial officers, or of a corporation, but the writ cannot
be used for the review or correction of judicial errors. Smythe *v.* Titcomb, 31 Me. 272
(1850). Nor to control judicial discretion, except where discretion has been abused.
Virginia *v.* Reeves, 100 U. S. 329 (1879). State *v.* City, 41 La. An. Rep. 156 (1889).
Mattox *v.* Graham, 2 Met. (Ky.) 56 (1859). State *ex rel. v.* Rois, 18 Mo. 23 (1893). *Ex
parte* Bradley, 7 Wall. (U. S.) 364 (1868). Goheen *v.* Myers, 18 Monroe (Ky.) 423
(1857). Daniel *v.* Warren Co. Court, 1 Bibb. (Ky.) 496, 499 (1809). Church *v.* Trustees,

inspection, or delivery of public books and papers; for the surrender of the *regalia* of a corporation; to oblige bodies corporate to affix their common seal; to compel the holding of a court; and for an infinite number of other purposes, which it is impossible to recite minutely. But at present we are more particular to remark, that it issues to the judges of any inferior court, commanding them to do justice according to the powers of their office, whenever the same is delayed. For it is the peculiar business of the court of king's bench to superintend all inferior tribunals, and therein to enforce the due exercise of those judicial or ministerial powers with which the crown or legislature have invested them: and this, not only by restraining their excesses, but also by quickening *their negligence, and   [*111 obviating their denial of justice. A *mandamus* may therefore be had to the courts of the city of London, to enter up judgment;(*g*) to the spiritual courts to grant an administration, to swear a church-warden, and the like. This writ is grounded on a suggestion, by the oath of the party injured, of his own right, and the denial of justice below: whereupon, in order more fully to satisfy the court that there is a probable ground for such interposition, a rule is made, (except in some general cases where the probable ground is manifest,) directing the party complained of to show cause why a writ of *mandamus* should not issue: and, if he shows no sufficient cause, the writ itself is issued, at first in the alternative, either to do thus, or signify some reason to the contrary; to which a return, or answer, must be made at a certain day. And, if the inferior judge, or other person to whom the writ is directed, returns or signifies an insufficient reason, then there issues in the second place a *peremptory mandamus*, to do the thing absolutely; to which no other return will be admitted, but a certificate of perfect obedience and due execution of the writ. If the inferior judge or other person makes no return, or fails in his respect and obedience, he is punishable for his contempt by attachment. But if he, at the first, returns a sufficient cause, although it should be false in fact, the court of king's bench will not try the truth of the fact upon affidavits; but will for the present believe him, and proceed no further on the *mandamus*. But then the party injured may have an action against him for his false return, and (if found to be false by the jury) shall recover damages equivalent to the injury sustained; together with a *peremptory mandamus* to the defendant to do his duty.(58) Thus much for the injury of neglect or refusal of justice.

2. The other injury, which is that of encroachment of jurisdiction, or calling one *coram non judice*,(59) to answer in a court that has no legal cogni-

(*g*) Raym. 214.

6 Hamm. (Ohio) 446 (1834). Richards *v.* Wheeler, 2 Ailsens (Ver.) 369 (1827). Cartelyon *v.* Ten Eyck, 2 Zab. (N. J.) 45 (1849). Kimbal *v.* Lampey, 19 N. H. 215, 221 (1848). Atty.-Gen. *v.* Blossoms, 1 Wis. 317, 319 (1853). Wilson *v.* Supervisors, 12 Johns. (N. Y.) 415 (1815). Treat *v.* Middleton, 8 Conn. 243, 246 (1830). People *ex rel.* Faite *v.* Ferris, 16 Hun. (N. Y.) 219, 225 (1878). Lawson's Rights, Rem. and Prac. vol. 7, p. 6330. In this country it is a constitutional writ and may issue from the supreme or circuit court. Webb & Estil *v.* Hauger, 1 Ark. 121, 123 (1838).

(58) However, by stat. 1 W. IV. c. 21, s. 3, the prosecutor may now in all cases of *mandamus* (as he could by stat. 9 Anne, c. 20, in certain special cases) plead to or traverse the matters in any return, and proceed and obtain damages as in an action for a false return, without the necessity of bringing such action as heretofore; and, by s. 6, the costs on all applications for *mandamus* are to be in the discretion of the court. And now, by stat. 6 & 7 Vict. c. 67, on such return being made, the person prosecuting the writ may object to the validity of such return by way of demurrer, and thereupon the writ and return and the demurrer shall be entered upon record, and proceedings shall be taken as upon a demurrer to pleadings: and, by s. 2, upon judgment being given thereon, error may be brought for reversing the same in like manner as in ordinary civil actions. —STEWART.

(59) [Before a judge unauthorized to take cognizance of the affair.]

zance of the cause, is also a grievance for which the common law has provided a remedy by the writ of *prohibition.*

[*112   *A prohibition is a writ issuing properly only out of the court of king's bench, being the king's prerogative writ; but, for the furtherance of justice, it may now also be had in some cases out of the court of chancery, (h) common pleas, (i) or exchequer; (k) directed to the judge and parties of a suit in any inferior court, commanding them to cease from the prosecution thereof, upon a suggestion that either the cause originally, or some collateral matter arising therein, does not belong to that jurisdiction, but to the cognizance of some other court. This writ may issue either to inferior courts of common law; as, to the courts of the counties palatine or principality of Wales, if they hold plea of land or other matters not lying within their respective franchises; (l) to the county-courts or courts-baron, where they attempt to hold plea of any matter of the value of forty shillings: (m) or it may be directed to the courts Christian, the university courts, the court of chivalry, or the court of admiralty, where they concern themselves with any matter not within their jurisdiction; as if the first should attempt to try the validity of a custom pleaded, or the latter a contract made or to be executed within this kingdom. Or if, in handling of matters clearly within their cognizance, they transgress the bounds prescribed to them by the laws of England; as where they require two witnesses to prove the payment of a legacy, a release of tithes, (n) or the like; in such cases also a prohibition will be awarded. For, as the fact of signing a release, or of actual payment, is not properly a spiritual question, but only allowed to be decided in those courts because incident or accessory to some original question clearly within their jurisdiction; it ought therefore, where the two laws differ, to be decided not according to the spiritual, but the temporal, law; else the same question might be determined different ways, according to the court in which the suit is depending: an impropriety

*113]   which no wise government can or ought to endure, *and which is therefore a ground of prohibition. And if either the judge or the party shall proceed after such prohibition, an attachment may be had against them, to punish them for the contempt, at the discretion of the court that awarded it; (o) and an action will lie against them, to repair the party injured in damages. (60)

(h) 1 P. Wms. 476.
(i) Hob. 15.
(k) Palmer, 523.
(l) Lord Raym. 1408.

(m) Finch, L. 451.
(n) Cro. Eliz. 666. Hob. 188.
(o) F. N. B. 40.

---

(60) Yates *v.* People, 6 Johns. (N. Y) 437, 463 (1810). Brown *v.* Rowe, 10 Tex. 184 (1853). State *v.* Benton, 12 Mont. 66 (1892). State *ex rel. v.* Gary, 33 Wis. 93 (1873). Smith *v.* Whitney, 116 U. S. 167 (1886). *Ex parte* Row, 1 Charl. (Ga.) 41 (1805). Board of Com. *v.* Spitler, 13 Ind. 240 (1859). *Ex parte* Smith, 23 Ala. 94 (1853). Clayton *v.* Heidelberg, 9 S. & M. (Miss.) 623 (1848). State *v.* McDuffie, 52 Ala. 6 (1875). Thomas *v.* Mead, 36 Mo. 232 (1866). Howe Ins. Co. *v.* Flint, 13 Minn. 244, 246 (1868). People *v.* Supervisors, 1 Hill (N. Y.) 195 (1841). It would not lie as to commissioners of highways. *Ex parte* Withers, 3 Brevard (S. C.) 83 (1812). Nor the mayor of a city. Burch *v.* Hardwick, 23 Gratt. (Va.) 51 (1873). See also C. R. R. Co. *v.* County, 127 Mass. 50 (1879). A preliminary order to show cause why the writ should not issue, should be issued before the writ itself. Mayor *v.* James, 12 Gratt. (Va.) 17 (1855). A judge of a circuit court has no authority to issue the writ during vacation. Raye *v.* Defoe, 45 Ala. 15 (1871). In Tennessee, the Supreme Court has no power to issue a writ of prohibition to restrain an inferior court from usurping jurisdiction. Memphis *v.* Halsey, 12 Heiskell (Tenn.) 210 (1873). The writ may be issued against referees. State *ex rel. v.* Stackhouse, 14 S. C. 417 (1880). As to power of a court to issue a prohibition to a court-martial, see Smith *v.* Whitney, 116 U. S. 167 (1886), and Washburn *v.* Phillips, 43 Mass. 299 (1841). Sere *v.* Armitage, 1 Cond. Rep. Sup. Ct. La. 750. Bowyer's Const. Law Eng. 280. 2 Barb. Rights of Pers. & Prop. 903. Congress has empowered the Supreme Court of the U. S. to issue writs of prohibition to the district courts " when proceeding as

So long as the idea continued among the clergy, that the ecclesiastical state was wholly independent of the civil, great struggles were constantly maintained between the temporal courts and the spiritual, concerning the writ of prohibition and the proper object of it; even from the time of the constitutions of Clarendon, made in opposition to the claims of archbishop Becket in 10 Hen. II., to the exhibition of certain articles of complaint to the king by archbishop Bancroft in 3 Jac. I., on behalf of the ecclesiastical courts: from which, and from the answers to them signed by all the judges of Westminster hall,(*p*) much may be collected concerning the reasons of granting and methods of proceeding upon prohibitions. A short summary of the latter is as follows: The party aggrieved in the court below applies to the superior court, setting forth in a suggestion upon record the nature and cause of his complaint, in being drawn *ad aliud examen*,(61) by a jurisdiction or manner of process disallowed by the laws of the kingdom; upon which, if the matter alleged appears to the court to be sufficient, the writ of prohibition immediately issues; commanding the judge not to hold, and the party not to prosecute, the plea. But sometimes the point may be too nice and doubtful to be decided upon merely a motion; and then, for the more solemn determination of the question, the party applying for the prohibition is directed by the court to *declare* a prohibition; that is, to prosecute an action, by filing a declaration, against the other, upon a supposition or fiction (which is not traversable)(*q*) that he has proceeded in the suit below, notwithstanding the writ of prohibition. And if, upon demurrer and argument, the court shall finally be of opinion that the matter suggested is a good and sufficient ground of *prohibition in point of law, then   [*114 judgment with nominal damages shall be given for the party complaining, and the defendant, and also the inferior court, shall be prohibited from proceeding any further. On the other hand, if the superior court shall think it no competent ground for restraining the inferior jurisdiction, then judgment shall be given against him who applied for the prohibition in the court above, and a writ of *consultation* shall be awarded; so called, because, upon deliberation and consultation had, the judges find the prohibition to be ill founded, and therefore by this writ they return the cause to its original jurisdiction, to be there determined, in the inferior court. And, even in ordinary cases, the writ of prohibition is not absolutely final and conclusive. For though the ground be a proper one in point of *law*, for granting the prohibition, yet if the *fact* that gave rise to it be afterwards falsified, the cause shall be remanded to the prior jurisdiction. If, for instance, a custom be pleaded in the spiritual court; a prohibition ought to go, because that court has no authority to try it: but, if the fact of such a custom be brought to a competent trial, and be there found false, a writ of consultation will be granted. For this purpose the party prohibited may appear to the prohibition, and take a declaration, (which must always pursue the suggestion,) and so plead to issue upon it; denying the contempt, and traversing the custom upon which the prohibition was grounded; and if that issue be found for the defendant, he shall then have a writ of *consultation*. The writ of *consultation* may also be, and is frequently, granted by the court without any action brought; when, after a prohibition issued, upon more mature consideration the court are of opinion that the matter suggested is not a good and sufficient ground to stop the proceedings below. Thus careful has the law

(*p*) 2 Inst. 601–618.   (*q*) Barn. Not. 4to, 148.

---

courts of admiralty and maritime jurisdiction." Conkl. Treatise (5 ed.) 56. *Ex parte* Easton, 95 U. S. 68 (1871).

(61) [To another examination or trial.]

been, in compelling the inferior courts to do ample and speedy justice; in preventing them from transgressing their due bounds; and in allowing them the undisturbed cognizance of such causes as by right, founded on the usage of the kingdom or act of parliament, do properly belong to their jurisdiction.(62)

CHAPTER VIII.

OF WRONGS, AND THEIR REMEDIES, RESPECTING THE RIGHTS OF PERSONS.

*115]   *THE former chapters of this part of our commentaries having been employed in describing the several methods of redressing private wrongs, either by the mere act of the parties, or the mere operation of law; and in treating of the nature and several species of courts; together with the cognizance of wrongs or injuries by private or special tribunals, and the public ecclesiastical, military, and maritime jurisdictions of this kingdom; I come now to consider at large, and in a more particular manner, the respective remedies, in the public and general courts of common law, for injuries or private wrongs of any denomination whatsoever, not exclusively appropriated to any of the former tribunals. And herein I shall, first, define the several injuries cognizable by the courts of common law, with the respective remedies applicable to each particular injury; and shall, secondly, describe the method of pursuing and obtaining these remedies in the several courts.

First, then, as to the several injuries cognizable by the courts of common law, with the respective remedies applicable to each particular injury. And, in treating of these, I shall at present confine myself to such wrongs as may be committed in the mutual intercourse between subject and subject; which the king, as the fountain of justice, is officially bound to redress in *116] the ordinary forms of law: reserving such *injuries or encroachments as may occur between the crown and the subject, to be distinctly considered hereafter, as the remedy in such cases is generally of a peculiar and eccentrical nature.

Now, since all wrongs may be considered as merely a privation of right, the plain natural remedy for every species of wrong is the being put in possession of that right whereof the party injured is deprived. This may either be effected by a specific delivery or restoration of the subject-matter in dispute to the legal owner; as when lands or personal chattels are unjustly withheld or invaded; or, where that is not a possible, or at least not an adequate, remedy, by making the sufferer a pecuniary satisfaction in damages; as in case of assault, breach of contract, etc.: to which damages the party injured has acquired an incomplete or inchoate right the instant he receives the injury,(a) though such right be not fully ascertained till they are assessed by the intervention of the law. The instruments whereby this remedy is

(a) See book ii. ch. 29.

---

(62) Since the statute of 1 Wm. IV. (1831) ch. 21, sec. 1, the old practice has become obsolete in England, and the practice in the United States has conformed to the later English. The initial step in modern proceedings is an order to the defendant to show cause why the writ should not be granted. State *ex rel.* Macklin *v.* Rombauer, 104 Mo. 619, 629 (1891). The Supreme Court of the United States has power to issue writs of prohibition to the federal district court, when proceeding as courts of admiralty and maritime jurisdiction. Act of Cong. Sep. 24, 1789. 1 Story's Laws, 59.—SHARSWOOD.

obtained (which are sometimes considered in the light of the remedy itself)
are a diversity of suits and actions, which are defined by the Mirror(*b*) to be
"the lawful demand of one's right;"(1) or, as Bracton and Fleta express it,
in the words of Justinian,(*c*) *jus prosequendi in judicio quod alicui debetur.*(2)

The Romans introduced, pretty early, set forms for actions and suits in
their law, after the example of the Greeks; and made it a rule, that each
injury should be redressed by its proper remedy only. "*Actiones,*" say the
pandects, "*compositæ sunt, quibus inter se homines disceptarent: quas actiones,
ne populus prout vellet institueret, certas solennesque esse voluerunt.*"(*d*)(3)
The forms of these actions were originally preserved in the books of the
pontifical college, as choice and inestimable secrets; till one Cneius Flavius,
the secretary of Appius Claudius, stole a copy and published them
to the people.(*c*)   The *concealment was ridiculous; but the estab-   [*117
lishment of some standard was undoubtedly necessary, to fix the true
state of a question of right; lest in a long and arbitrary process it might be
shifted continually, and be at length no longer discernible.   Or, as Cicero
expresses it,(*f*) "*sunt jura, sunt formulæ, de omnibus rebus constitutæ, ne
quis aut in genere injuriæ, aut in ratione actionis, errare posit. Expressæ
enim sunt ex uniuscujusque damno, dolore, incommodo, calamitate, injuria,
publicæ a prætore formulæ, ad quas privata lis accomodatur.*"(4)   And in the
the same manner our Bracton, speaking of the original writs upon which all
our actions are founded, declares them to be fixed and immutable, unless by
authority of parliament.(*g*)   And all the modern legislators of Europe have
found it expedient, from the same reasons, to fall into the same or a similar
method.   With us in England the several suits, or remedial instruments of
justice, are from the subject of them distinguished into three kinds: actions
personal, real, and *mixed.*

Personal actions are such whereby a man claims a debt, or personal duty,
or damages in lieu thereof; and, likewise, whereby a man claims a satisfaction
in damages for some injury done to his person or property.(5)   The former
are said to be founded on contracts, the latter upon *torts* or wrongs; and they
are the same which the civil law calls "*actiones in personam, quæ adversus
eum intenduntur, qui ex contractu vel delicto obligatus est aliquid dare vel con-
cedere.*"(*h*)(6)   Of the former nature are all actions upon debt or promises;

(*b*) C. 2, § 1.
(*c*) Inst. 4, 6, pr.
(*d*) Ff. 1, 2, 2, § 6.
(*e*) Cic. pro Muræna, § 11, de orat. l. c. 41.
(*f*) Pro. Qu. Roscio. § 8.
(*g*) Sunt quædam brevia formata super certis casibus
de cursu, et de communi consilio totius regni approbata

*et concessa, quæ quidem nullatenus mutari poterint
absque contensu et voluntate eorum.* [There are some
writs formed on certain cases, granted and approved
by the common council of the kingdom, which can
in no wise be changed without its will and consent.]
L. 5, de exceptionibus, c. 17, § 2.
(*h*) Inst. 4, 6, 15.

---

(1) Harlin's heirs *v.* Eastland, 1 Harding (Ky.) 310 (1808). Sanford *v.* Sanford, 28
Conn. 6 (1859). McBride's Appeal, 72 Penn. 480 (1873).   Lightfoot *v.* Grove, 5 Heiskell
(Tenn.) 473 (1871).   Badger *v.* Gilmore, 37 N. H. (Fogg) 457 (1859).   *Ex parte* Davis,
41 Maine, 56 (1856).   People *v.* Clarke, 10 Barb. (N. Y.) 120 (1850).   Wait's Actions and
Defences, vol. 2, ch. 34, sec. 2.   Co. Litt. 285.   Miller *v.* Wiley *et al.* 16 Upp. Can. C. P.
529, 531 (1866).

(2) [The right of prosecuting to judgment for what is due to any one.]

(3) ["Forms of actions were settled by which men might argue their differences, which
forms were established and made certain that the people might not on their own motion
institute their own modes of proceeding."]

(4) ["There are rights, there are forms appointed for all things, lest anyone should mistake either the kind of injury or the mode of redress.   For public forms are composed by
the prætor from every kind of loss, trouble, inconvenience, calamity, and injury, for the
accommodation of private suits."]

(5) Marlatt *v.* Perrine, 17 N. J. Eq. 49-50 (1863).   Magill *v.* Parsons, 4 Conn. 317-322
(1822).

(6) ["Personal actions which are commenced against him who by contract, or through
the commission of some offence, is bound to give or surrender something."] The Law of
Torts, Hilliard (3 ed.) vol. 1, p. 1.

of the latter, all actions for trespasses, nuisances, assaults, defamatory words, and the like.(7)

Real actions, (or, as they are called in the Mirror,(*i*) *feodal* actions,) which concern real property only, are such whereby the plaintiff, here called the demandant, claims title to have any lands or tenements, rents, com-

*118]   mons, or other *hereditaments, in fee-simple, fee-tail, or for term of life.(8) By these actions formerly all disputes concerning real estates were decided; but they are now pretty generally laid aside in practice, upon account of the great nicety required in their management, and the inconvenient length of their process: a much more expeditious method of trying titles being since introduced, by other actions personal and mixed.(9)

Mixed actions are suits partaking of the nature of the other two, wherein some real property is demanded, and also personal damages for a wrong sustained.(10) As for instance an action of waste: which is brought by him who hath the inheritance in remainder or reversion, against the tenant for life who hath committed waste therein, to recover not only the land wasted, which would make it merely a *real* action; but also treble damages, in pursuance of the statute of Gloucester,(*k*) which is a *personal* recompense; and so both, being joined together, denominate it a *mixed* action.(11)

Under these three heads may every species of remedy by suit or action in the courts of common law be comprised. But in order effectually to apply the remedy it is first necessary to ascertain the complaint. I proceed, therefore, now to enumerate the several kinds, and to inquire into the respective nature, of all private wrongs, or civil injuries, which may be offered to the rights of either a man's person or his property; recounting at the same time the respective remedies which are furnished by the law for every infraction of right. But I must first beg leave to premise that all civil injuries are of two kinds, the one *without force* or violence, as slander or breach of contract; the other coupled *with force* and violence, as batteries or false imprisonment.(*l*)(12) Which latter species savor something of the criminal kind, being always attended with some violation of the peace; for which

*119]   in strictness of law a fine ought to be paid to the king, as *well as a private satisfaction to the party injured.(*m*) And this distinction of private wrongs, into injuries *with* and *without* force, we shall find to run through all the variety of which we are now to treat. In considering of which, I shall follow the same method that was pursued with regard to the distribution of rights: for, as these are nothing else but an infringement or breach of those rights which we have before laid down and explained, it will follow that this negative system, of *wrongs*, must correspond and tally with

---

(*i*) C. 2. 3 6.
(*k*) 6 Edw. I. c. 5.

(*l*) Finch. L. 184.
(*m*) Finch. L. 198. Jenk. Cent. 185.

---

(7) Williams on Pers. Prop. 64 (1872).

(8) Sedgwick and Wait on Title to Land (2 ed.) 34.

(9) Blakeley *v.* Tyler, 55 Conn. 397 (1887). Hill *et ux.* Davis, 4 Mass. 139 (1808). Hitchcock *v.* Munger, 15 N. H. 97 (1844).

(10) Browne on Actions of Law, 317.

(11) 2 Barb. Rights of Pers. and Prop. 788. Lippincott *v.* Fuller, 57 Me. 406 (1869). Real actions, with the exception of three,—dower, right of dower, and *quare impedit*,— [Wherefore or why did he hinder or disturb—the name of a writ which lies for many purposes] were entirely abolished by stat. 3 & 4 W. IV. c. 27, s. 36. All mixed actions, with one exception,—the action of ejectment,—were abolished by the same statute. The action of ejectment thus preserved has now, by the Common-Law Procedure Act 1852, been also swept away, and a new procedure or action of ejectment substituted in its place.— STEWART.

(12) Webb's Pollock on Torts, enl. Am. ed. 5 (1894).

the former positive system, of *rights*. As therefore we divide(*n*) all rights into those of *persons* and those of *things*, so we must make the same general distribution of injuries into such as affect the *rights of persons*, and such as affect the *rights of property*.

The rights of *persons*, we may remember, were distributed into *absolute* and *relative*: *absolute*, which were such as appertained and belong to private men, considered merely as individuals, or single persons; and *relative*, which were incident to them as members of society and connected to each other by various ties and relations. And the absolute rights of each individual were defined to be the right of personal security, the right of personal liberty, and the right of private property, so that the wrongs or injuries affecting them must consequently be of a corresponding nature.

I. As to injuries which affect the *personal security* of individuals, they are either injuries against their lives, their limbs, their bodies, their health, or their reputations.

1. With regard to the first subdivision, or injuries affecting the life of man, they do not fall under our present contemplation; being one of the most atrocious species of crimes, the subject of the next book of our commentaries.(13)

(n) See book i. ch. 1.

---

(13) For injury to life, in general, cannot be the subject of a civil action, the civil remedy being merged in the offence to the public. Therefore an action will not lie for battery of wife or servant, whereby death ensued. Styles, 347. 1 Lev. 247. Yelv. 89, 90. 1 Lord, 339. The remedy is by indictment for murder, or, formerly, by appeal, which the wife might have for killing her husband, provided she married not again before or pending her appeal; or the *heir male* for the death of his ancestor, and which differed principally from an indictment in respect of its not being in the power of the king to pardon the offender without the appellor's consent. See *post*, 4 book 312, 6. 5 Burr. 2643. But appeals of murder, treason, felony, and other offences were abolished by 59 Geo. III. c. 46, s. 1. In general, all felonies suspend the civil remedies, (Styles, 346, 347;) and before conviction of the offender there is no remedy against him at law or in equity, (id. ibid. 17 Ves. 331;) but after conviction and punishment on an indictment of the party for stealing, the party robbed may support trespass or trover against the offender. Styles, 347. Latch. 144. Sir Wm. Jones, 147. 1 Lev. 247. Bro. Abr. tit. Trespass. And after an acquittal of the defendant upon an indictment for a felonious assault upon a party by stabbing him, the latter may maintain trespass to recover damages for the civil injury, if it be not shown that he colluded in procuring such acquittal. 12 East, 409. In some cases, by express enactment, the civil remedy is not affected by the criminality of the offender. Thus it is provided by 52 Geo. III. c. 63, s. 5, that where bankers, etc. have been guilty of embezzlement, they may be prosecuted, but the civil remedy shall not be affected. The 21 Hen. VIII. c. 11 directs that goods stolen shall be restored to the owner upon certain conditions,—namely, that he shall give or produce evidence against the felons, and that the felon be prosecuted to conviction thereon. Upon performance of these, the right of the owner, which was before suspended, becomes perfect and absolute; but he cannot recover the value from a person who purchased them in market overt and sold them again before the conviction of the felon, notwithstanding the owner gave such person notice of the robbery while they were in his possession; but he must proceed against the original felon, or against the person who has the chattel in his possession at the time of the conviction. 2 T. R. 750. And the above act does not extend to goods obtained by false pretences. 5 T. R. 175. See, further, 1 Chitty's Crim. L. 5.—CHITTY.

By the common law, the wife or husband, parent or child, of the party killed, cannot recover any pecuniary compensation for the injury sustained by the death of the relative, (Baker *v.* Bolton, 1 Camp. 493;) and this was the law till the stat. 9 & 10 Vict. c. 93 enacted that whenever the death of a person shall be caused by such wrongful act, neglect, or default as would, if death had not ensued, have entitled the party injured to maintain an action for damages, the person who would have been liable to such action may be sued by the executor or administrator for the benefit of the wife, husband, parent, or child of the person deceased. The jury, in any such action, may give damages proportionable to the injury resulting from the death, to be divided among the parties for whose benefit the action is brought, in shares as the jury shall direct. Blake *v.* Midland Railway Company, 21 L. J. R. 233, Q. B. S. C. 18 Ad. & El. 93.—STEWART.

The doctrine that the civil remedy cannot be pursued until the criminal has been found guilty, is not generally applicable in the United States.

*120]   *2, 3. The two next species of injuries, affecting the limbs or
          bodies of individuals, I shall consider in one and the same view.
And these may be committed, 1. By *threats* and menaces of bodily hurt,
through fear of which a man's business is interrupted. A menace alone,
without a consequent inconvenience, makes not the injury: but, to complete
the wrong, there must be both of them together.(*o*)(14) The remedy for
this is in pecuniary damages, to be recovered by action of *trespass vi et
armis;*(*p*)(15) this being an inchoate, though not an absolute, violence.(16)
2. By *assault;* which is an attempt or offer to beat another, without touching
him; as if one lifts up his cane, or his fist, in a threatening manner at
another; or strikes at him but misses him; this is an assault, *insultus*, which
Finch(*q*) describes to be "an unlawful setting upon one's person." This also
is an inchoate violence, amounting considerably higher than bare threats;
and therefore, though no actual suffering is proved, yet the party injured
may have redress by action of *trespass vi et armis;* wherein he shall recover
damages as a compensation for the injury.(17) 3. By *battery;* which is the
unlawful beating of another. The least touching of another's person wilfully,
or in anger, is a battery; for the law cannot draw the line between different
degrees of violence, and therefore totally prohibits the first and lowest stage

(*o*) Finch, L. 202.   (*q*) Finch, L. 202.
(*p*) Regist. 104. 27 Ass. 11. 7 Edw. IV. 21.

---

(14) Browne on Actions at Law, 395, 396.
(15) [Trespass with force and arms.]
(16) If the menace be not actionable alone, but only in conjunction with the injurious
consequence, it seems contrary to principle that the remedy should be by trespass *vi et
armis*, and not by trespass on the case. On examination, none of the authorities cited
for the position satisfactorily bear it out; and, in the same book of Edw. IV. 21, one of
the same judges (Choke) says, *Si home fait a moy manace en ma person come d'empris-
oner ou de maimer, jeo avera action sur mon case.*—COLERIDGE. [If a man makes a threat
against me, as to imprison or to maim me, I will have (a right) of action on the case.]
(17) See, in general, Com. Dig. Battery, C. Bac. Abr. Assault and Battery, A. An
assault is an attempt or offer, accompanied by a degree of violence, to commit some
bodily harm, by any means calculated to produce the end if carried into execution.
Leveling a gun at another within a distance from which, supposing it to have been
loaded, the contents might wound, is an assault. Bac. Abr. Assault, A. Abusive words
alone cannot constitute an assault, and indeed may sometimes so explain the aggressor's
intent as to prevent an act *prima facie* an assault from amounting to such an injury; as
where a man, during assize-time, in a threatening posture, half drew his sword from its
scabbard, and said, "If it were not that it is assize-time, I would run you through the
body," this was held to be no assault, the words explaining that the party did not mean
any immediate injury. 1 Mod. 3. 3 Bul. N. P. 15. Vin. Abr. Trespass, A. 2. The
intention as well as *the act* constitute an assault. 1 Mod. 3, case 13. Assault for money
won at play is particularly punishable by 9 Anne, c. 14. 4 East, 174.—CHITTY.
An assault may consist in shaking the fist at a person, or presenting a gun or other
weapon within such distance as that a hurt might be inflicted, or by drawing and brand-
ishing a sword; provided the act is done with intent to do some corporal injury. United
States *v.* Myers, 1 Cranch (C. C.) 310. Murray *v.* Boyne, 42 Mo. 472. State *v.* Hampton,
63 N. C. 13. To constitute an assault with a gun or a pistol, it is not necessary that it
should be loaded if the plaintiff was ignorant on the point. Commonwealth *v.* White,
110 Mass. 407-18. Crow *v.* State, 41 Tex. 468. To strike with a stick the horse which
another is driving is an assault. De Marentille *v.* Oliver, 1 Pennington (N. J.) 380 (1806).
Mere threats, alone, do not constitute an assault and words accompanying a threatening gesture may deprive the gesture of the character of an assault, as where the defendant
raised his whip and shook it at the plaintiff within striking distance of him and made
use of the words: "Were you not an old man I would knock you down." The drawing
a pistol, without presenting or cocking it, does not amount to an assault. Waits Actions
and Defences, 332-4. And where the defendant presented a gun, within shooting distance
of, and against the prosecutor who was then armed with a knife, and was about to attack
the defendant, there being no attempt to use the gun, or intention of using it unless first
assailed with the knife, it was held that the defendant was not guilty of an assault. Governor to use *v.* Powall, 9 Ala. 83 (1846).

of it; every man's person being sacred, and no other having a right to meddle with it in any the slightest manner.(18)   And therefore upon a similar principle the Cornelian law *de injuriis*(19) prohibited *pulsation* as well as *verberation;* distinguishing verberation, which was accompanied with pain, from pulsation, which was attended with none.(*r*)   But battery is, in some cases, justifiable or lawful; as where one who hath authority, a parent, or master, gives moderate correction to his child, his scholar, or his apprentice.   So also on the principle of self-defence: for if one strikes me first, or even only assaults me, I may strike in my own defence; and, if sued for it, may plead *son assault demesne*, or that it was the plaintiff's *own original   [*121 assault that occasioned it.(20)   So likewise in defence of my goods or possession, if a man endeavors to deprive me of them I may justify laying hands upon him to prevent him; and in case he persists with violence, I may proceed to beat him away.(*s*)(21)   Thus too in the exercise of an office, as that of church-warden or beadle, a man may lay hands upon another to turn him out of church, and prevent his disturbing the congregation.(*t*)   And, if sued for this or the like battery, he may set forth the whole case, and plead that he laid hands upon him gently, *molliter manus imposuit*,(22) for this purpose.   On account of these causes of justification, battery is defined to be the *unlawful* beating of another;(23) for which the remedy is, as for assault, by action of *trespass vi et armis*:(24) wherein the jury will give adequate damages.   4. By *wounding;* which consists in giving another some dangerous hurt, and is only an aggravated species of battery.   5. By *mayhem;* which is an injury still more atrocious, and consists in violently depriving another of the use of a member proper for his defence in fight.   This is a battery attended with this aggravating circumstance, that thereby the party injured is forever disabled from making so good a defence against future external injuries, as he otherwise might have done.(25)   Among these

(*r*) Ff. 47, 10, 5.   (*t*) 1 Sid. 301.
(*s*) 1 Finch, L. 203.

---

(18) Com. Dig. Battery, A. Bac. Abr. Assault and Battery. B. A battery is any unlawful touching the person of another by the aggressor himself, or any other substance put in motion by him. 1 Saund. 29, b., n. 1. Id. 13 and 14, n. 3. Taking a hat off the head of another is no battery. 1 Saund. 14. It must be either *wilfully* commited, or proceed from want of due care, (Stra. 596. Hob. 134. Plowd. 19,) otherwise it is *damnum absque injuriâ*, [Loss without injury,] and the party aggrieved is without remedy, (3 Wils. 303. Bac. Abr. Assault and Battery, B.;) but the absence of intention to commit the injury constitutes no excuse where there has been a want of due care. Stra. 596. Hob. 134. Plowd. 19. But if a person unintentionally push against a person in the street, or if without any default in the rider a horse runs away and goes against another, no action lies. 4 Mod. 405. Every battery includes an assault, (Co. Litt. 253;) and the plaintiff may recover for the assault only, though he declares for an assault and battery. 4 Mod. 405.—CHITTY. See also, 1 Russell on Crimes, chap. 10. Waits Actions & Defences, chap. 13. Assault and battery may be committed by striking one's cane while in his hand; striking the skirt of his coat while on his person; spitting upon a person; striking a horse which a man is riding, whereby the man is thrown. And it is a battery for an officer to handcuff a prisoner previous to his conviction, when there is no attempt to escape nor any reasonable ground to fear a rescue. Wait's Actions & Defences, 335-6. Webb's Pollock on Torts, enl. Am. ed., 249 (1894). Johnson *v.* State, 17 Tex. 515-517 (1856).
(19) [Of injuries.]
(20) Wait's Actions & Defences, vol. 1, 337 (1877). Browne on Actions at Law, 398.
(21) Hilliard's Law of Torts (3 ed.) vol. 1, 184. Care must be taken not to exceed the bounds of mere defence, prevention, or recovery; for beyond that there is no justification. Baldwin *v.* Hayden *et al.*, 6 Conn. 453, 457 (1827). Com. *v.* Donahue, 148 Mass. 529 (1889).
(22) Binn's Justice (10 ed.) p. 78 (1895).
(23) If there is any doubt whether or not the battery was justifiable the defendant is entitled to acquittal. Com. *v.* McKee, 67 Mass. 61, 63 (1854).
(24) [Trespass with force and arms.]
(25) As to whether breaking the skull is *mayhem*, see the statutes and authori-

defensive members are reckoned not only arms and legs, but a finger, an eye, and a foretooth,(*u*) and also some others.(*v*) But the loss of one of the jaw-teeth, the ear, or the nose, is no mayhem at common law, as they can be of no use in fighting. The same remedial action of *trespass vi et armis* lies also to recover damages for this injury, an injury which (when wilful) no motive can justify but necessary self-preservation.(26) If the ear be cut off, treble damages are given by statute 37 Hen. VIII. c. 6, though this is not mayhem at common law.(27) And here I must observe that for these four last injuries, assault, battery, wounding, and mayhem, an indictment may be brought as well as an action, and frequently both are accordingly prosecuted, the one at the suit of the crown for the crime against the public, the *other at the suit of the party injured, to make him a reparation in damages.(28)

*122]

(*u*) Finch. L. 204.   (*v*) 1 Hawk. P. C. 111.

---

ties defining the crime of mayhem, collated and discussed in Foster *v.* The People, 50 N. Y. Ct. App. (Sickels) 598 (1873).

(26) This is expressed with great correctness and caution: it is not intended to convey the notion that no mayhem can be justified under the plea of *son assault demesne* [His own assault], except where that assault threatened the life of the party, but that no mayhem can be justified except under such circumstances, if it was wilful and deliberate. In the case of Cockroft *v.* Smith, stated in 1 Lord Raym. 177, and reported in Salkeld, 642, and 11 Mod. 43, the plaintiff had either tilted up the form on which the defendant was sitting, or run his finger towards his eye, and the defendant immediately bit off his finger: *son assault demesne* was held to be a good plea; and lord Holt there laid down the principle thus:—"If A. strike B. and B. strike again, and they close immediately, and in the scuffle B. mayhems A., that is *son assault;* but if, upon a little blow given by A. to B., B. gives him a blow that mayhems him, that is not *son assault demesne.*" To this Powell, J., agreed. It seems that the party must always intend to act in self-defence, which intention is to be collected from the circumstances, in the blow which he gives to the plaintiff.—COLERIDGE.

Son assault demesne [His own assault] is a good defence to an indictment for mayhem; but the defence can only be sustained by proof that the resistance was in proportion to the injury offered. Hayden *v.* The State, 4 Blackford, 546.

Any thing attached to the person partakes of its inviolability. A blow on the skirt of one's coat, when upon his person, is an assault and battery. So of striking one's cane while in his hand. Respublica *v.* Longchamps, 1 Dall. 114. State *v.* Davis, 1 Hill, 46. So to strike the horse which a person is riding or driving is an assault. De Marentille *v.* Oliver, 1 Pennington, 380. No words of provocation will justify an assault, although they may constitute a ground for the reduction of damages. Cushman *v.* Ryan, 1 Story, 91.—SHARSWOOD.

One remarkable property is peculiar to the action for a mayhem,—viz., that the court in which the action is brought have a discretionary power to increase the damages, if they think the jury at the trial have not been sufficiently liberal to the plaintiff; but this must be done *super visum vulneris* [On view of the wound], and upon proof that it is the same wound concerning which evidence was given to the jury. 1 Wils. 5. Barnes, 106, 153. 3 Salkeld, 115. 1 Ld. Raym. 176, 339.—CHRISTIAN. 1 Wharton's Crim. Law, § 581 (1885). [*Vi et armis*—with force and arms.]

(27) And the prosecutor cannot be forced to make an election to proceed in one way only. State *v.* Frost, 1 S. Car. Law (Brevard) 300–1 (1804). But if the battery be justifiable, the defendant can neither be punished criminally nor held responsible for damages in a civil action. N. O. & N. E. Railroad Co. *v.* Jopes, 142 U. S. Rep. 18–24 (1891). In a civil action for assault and battery, *son assault demesne* [His own assault] must be specially pleaded. Norris *v.* Casel, 9 Indiana, 143 (1883). Meyers *v.* Moore, 3 Indiana App. Ct. Rep. 226 (1891).

(28) The party injured may proceed by indictment and by action at the same time, and the court will not compel him to stay proceedings in either. 1 Bos. & P. 191. But in general the adoption of both proceedings is considered vexatious, and will induce the jury to give smaller damages in the action. The legislature has discouraged actions for trifling injuries of this nature, by enacting that in all actions of trespass for assault and battery, in case the jury should find a verdict for damages under forty shillings, the plaintiff shall have no more costs than damages, unless the judge at the trial shall certify that an assault and battery was sufficiently proved. See constructions on the statute, Tidd's Prac. (8 ed.) 998.—CHITTY.

4. Injuries affecting a man's *health* are where, by any unwholesome practices of another, a man sustains any apparent damage in his vigor or constitution.　As by selling him bad provisions or wine;(*w*) by the exercise of a noisome trade, which infects the air in his neighborhood;(*x*) or by the neglect or unskilful management of his physician, surgeon, or apothecary.　For it hath been solemnly resolved,(*y*) that *mala praxis*(29) is a great misdemeanor and offence at common law, whether it be for curiosity and experiment, or by neglect; because it breaks the trust which the party had placed in his physician, and tends to the patient's destruction.(30)　Thus, also, in

---

(*w*) 1 Roll. Abr. 90　　　　　　　　　　(*y*) Lord Raym. 214.
(*x*) 9 Rep. 82.　Hutt. 135.

The injuries affecting the person above mentioned are all in their nature direct.　There are others which do not come within any of the above definitions, and which may in contradistinction be termed *consequential*, as resulting occasionally, although not necessarily, from wrongful acts or neglects.

The personal injuries which may be considered *consequential* only are such generally as arise from the neglect or default of others in the performance of the duties they have undertaken to discharge.　Thus, if a passenger is injured by the want of care of the driver of a coach, or a person sustains an injury owing to the negligence of a carman, (Lynch *v.* Hurdin, 2 B. 29,) the owner of the coach in the first case, the carman's master in the second, will be liable in an action for damages; for it was the duty of the owner and master in each case to employ careful servants.　If, on the other hand, the driver or the carman did the injury *wilfully*, even if in the master's service, he, and not the owner or master, will be liable.　Gordon *v.* Rolt, 4 Exc. 365.　Consequential injuries may also be sustained from a bull, ram, monkey, or other animal being left at large or not properly taken care of, (Jackson *v.* Smithson, 15 M. & W. 563.　May *v.* Burdett, 9 Q. B. 101,) and the owner will in such case be liable to the party injured.　The owner must, however, be shown to have been aware of the mischievous propensities of the animal before he can be made liable, (Hudson *v.* Roberts, 6 Exc. 497;) and if the party injured have imprudently exposed himself, he cannot maintain an action.　Cattlin *v.* Hills, 8 C. B. 115.—KERR.

(29) [Bad practice.]

(30) The law implies a contract on the part of a medical man, as well as those of other professions, to discharge their duty in a skilful and attentive manner; and the law will grant redress to the party injured by their *neglect* or ignorance, by an action on the case, as for a tortious misconduct.　1 Saund. 312, n. 2.　1 Ld. Raym. 213, 214.　Reg. Brevium, 205, 206.　2 Wils. 359.　8 East, 348.　And in that case the surgeon could not recover any fees.　Peake, C. N. P. 59.　See 2 New Rep. 136.　But in the case of a physician whose profession is honorary, he is not liable to an action, (Peake, C. N. P. 96, 123.　4 T. R. 317,) though he may be punished by the college of physicians.　Com. Dig. tit. Physician.　Vin. Abr. tit. Physician.　According to Hawkins, P. C., if any person, not duly authorized to practice, undertake to cure, and should kill his patient, he is guilty of felony, though clergyable.　And such person so employed cannot recover in an action for the medicines supplied.　See 55 Geo. III. c. 194.　However, if the party employ a person as surgeon, knowing him not to be one, he has no civil remedy.　1 Hen. B. 161.　Bac. Abr. Action on the Case, F.　2 Wils. 359.　Reg. Brev. 105.　8 East, 348.

Though the law does not in general imply a warranty as to the goodness and quality of any personal chattel, it is otherwise with regard to food and liquors, in which, especially in the case of a publican, the law implies a warranty.　1 Roll. Abr. 90, pl. 1, 2.　2 East, 314.

With regard to private nuisances, it is particularly observable that the law regards the health of the individual, though it will not afford a remedy for malicious and ill-natured acts tending to destroy the beauty of situation, such as stopping a prospect, etc.　9 Co. 58, b.　In complaining of a nuisance in stopping ancient lights, etc., the consequent injury must be stated to have been the deprivation of light and air, which are considered as conducive to health.　Peake, 91.　Com. Dig. tit. Action on the Case for a Nuisance.　As to ancient lights in general, see *ante.*

Public Nuisance.　With respect to the injuries to health, as a consequence of a public nuisance, it seems that if the injury be attributable to the inhabitants of a county, no action is sustainable.　2 T. R. 667.　9 Co. 112, b., 117, a.　But if the special injury be occasioned by an individual, an action lies.　Bac. Abr. Action on the Case.　1 Salk. 15, 16.—CHITTY.

A physician, however, ignorant of medical science, who prescribes with the honest intention of curing, is not guilty of murder or manslaughter, if, through the physician's ignorance of the qualities of the medicine prescribed, or of the nature of the disease, the

the civil law,(z) neglect or want of skill in physicians or surgeons, "*culpæ adnumerantur, veluti si medicus curationem dereliquerit, male quempian secuerit, aut perperam ei medicamentum dederit.*"(31) These are wrongs or injuries unaccompanied by force, for which there is a remedy in damages by a special action of *trespass upon the case.*(32) This action of *trespass*, or transgression, *on the case*, is a universal remedy, given for all personal wrongs and injuries without force; so called because the plaintiff's whole case or cause of complaint is set forth at length in the original writ.(a)(33) For though in general there are methods prescribed, and forms of actions previously settled, for redressing those wrongs, which most usually occur, and in which the very act itself is immediately prejudicial or injurious to the plaintiff's person or property, battery, non-payment of debts,
*123] detaining one's goods, or the like; yet where *any special consequential damage arises, which could not be foreseen and provided for in the ordinary course of justice, the party injured is allowed, both by common law and the statute of Westm. 2, c. 24, to bring a special action on his own case, by a writ formed according to the peculiar circumstances of his own particular grievance.(b) For wherever the common law gives a right or prohibits an injury, it also gives a remedy by action;(c)(34) and, therefore, wherever a new injury is done, a new method of remedy must be pursued.(d)(35) And it is a settled distinction,(e) that where an act is done which is in itself an *immediate* injury to another's person or property, there the remedy is usually by an action of trespass *vi et armis;*(36) but where there is no act done, but only a culpable omission, or where the act is not immediately injurious, but only by *consequence* and collaterally; there no action of trespass *vi et armis* will lie, but an action on the special case, for the damages consequent on such omission or act.(37)

(z) Inst. 4, 3, 6, 7.
(a) For example: "*Rex vicecomiti salutem, Si A. fecerit te securum de clamore suo prosequendo, tunc pone per vadium et salvos plegios B. quod sit coram justitiariis nostris apud Westmonasterium in octabis sancti Michaelis, ostensurus quare cum idem B. ad dextrum oculum ipsius A. casualiter læsum bene et competenter curandum insum A. assumpsisset, idem B. curam suam circa oculum prædictum tam negligenter et improvide apposuit, quod idem A. defectu ipsius B. visum oculi prædicti totaliter amisit, ad damnum ipsius A. viginti librarum, ut dicit. Et habeas ibi nomina plegiorum et hoc breve. Teste meipso apud Westmonasterium,*" etc. ["The king to the sheriff sends greeting. If A. give you security that he will prosecute his claim, then*

put B., by gage and safe pledges, to appear before our justices at Westminster on the octave of St. Michael, to show cause why, when the said B. had at S. undertaken, for a certain sum of money paid beforehand, well and completely to cure the right eye of the said A., accidentally hurt, the said B. attended to the said eye so negligently and carelessly, that the said A. by the default of the said B., totally lost the sight of the said eye, to the damage of the said A. (as he says) of twenty pounds. And have you there the names of the pledges and this writ. Witness myself at Westminster," etc.] *Registr. Brev.* 105.
(b) See page 52.
(c) 1 Salk. 20. 6 Mod. 54.
(d) Cro. Jac. 478.
(e) 11 Mod. 130. Lord Raym. 1402. Stra. 635.

patient die in consequence of the treatment. But if the physician has such knowledge of the nature of the medicine that it may be presumed that he acted from an obstinate, wilful rashness, and not an intention to cure, he is guilty of manslaughter, although he had no intention to injure the patient. Rice *v.* State, 8 Missouri (Bay, 1844). And a physician is liable to a civil action if he be guilty of negligence, or want of skill, but he is not responsible for a mistake of judgment. Graham *v.* Gautier, 21 Texas, 111 (1858). Long *v.* Morrison, 14 Indiana (Tanner) 596 (1860).
(31) ["They are reckoned faults, as if a medical man neglect his patient, perform an amputation unskilfully, or administer medicine unadvisedly."]
(32) Webb's Pollock on Torts, enl. Am. ed. 14 (1894). Newton *v.* N. Y. & N. Eng. R. R. Co., 56 Conn. 21, 24 (1888).
(33) Landlord and Tenant in Pennsylvania, Jackson and Gross, 192 (1884).
(34) Hendricks *v.* Cook, 4 Ga. 241, 261 (1848). Adams *v.* Paige, 7 Pick. (Mass.) 542, 550 (1829). Garing *v.* Fraser, 76 Me. 37. 41 (1855).
(35) Wootten *v.* Gwinn, 56 Miss. 422, 438 (1879). Long *v.* Long, 1 Watts (Pa.) 265, 267 (1834).
(36) [With force and arms.]
(37) See the author's celebrated judgment in the case of Scott *v.* Shepherd, 2 Bl. Rep. 892, the principle of which has been since repeatedly recognized. No distinction arises from the lawfulness or unlawfulness of the act. If one turning round suddenly were to

5. Lastly; injuries affecting a man's *reputation* or good name are, first, by malicious, scandalous, and slanderous *words*, tending to his damage and derogation.(38)   As if a man maliciously and falsely utter any slander or false tale of another; which may either endanger him in law, by impeaching him of some heinous crime, as to say that a man hath poisoned another, or is perjured;(*f*) or which may exclude him from society, as to charge him with having an infectious disease, or which may impair or hurt his trade or livelihood, as to call a tradesman a bankrupt, a physician a quack, or a lawyer a knave.(*g*)   Words spoken in derogation of a peer, a judge, or other great officer of the realm, which are called *scandalum magnatum*,(39) are held to be still more heinous:(*h*) and though they be such as would not be actionable in the case of a common person, yet when spoken in disgrace of such high and respectable characters, they amount to an atrocious injury: *which is redressed by an action on the case founded on many ancient   [*124 statutes,(*i*) as well on behalf of the crown, to inflict the punishment of imprisonment on the slanderer, as on behalf of the party, to recover damages for the injury sustained.(40)   Words also tending to scandalize a magistrate, or person in a public trust, are reputed more highly injurious than when spoken of a private man.(*k*)(41)   It is said, that formerly no actions were brought for words, unless the slander was such as (if true) would endanger the life of the object of it.(*l*)   But, too great encouragement being given by this lenity to false and malicious slanderers, it is now held that for scandalous words of the several species before mentioned, (that may endanger a man by subjecting him to the penalties of the law, may exclude him from society, may impair his trade, or may affect a peer of the realm, a magistrate, or one in public trust,) an action on the case may be had, without proving any particular damage to have happened, but merely upon the probability that it might happen.   But with regard to words that do not

---

(*f*) Finch, L. 185.
(*g*) Finch, L., 186.
(*h*) 1 Ventr. 60.
(*i*) Westm. 1. 3 Edw. I. c. 34. 2 Ric. II. c. 5. 12

Ric. II. c. 11.
(*k*) Lord Raym. 1369.
(*l*) 2 Ventr. 28.

---

knock another down, whom he did not see, without intending it, no doubt, said Mr. J. Lawrence, the action must be trespass *vi et armis*. Neither will it vary the case that besides the immediate injury there is an ulterior consequential injury; for it is the former on which the action is supported: the latter is merely in aggravation of the damages. Leame *v.* Bray, 3 East's Rep. 593.—COLERIDGE. 1 Waterman on Trespass, 31 (1875). Leighton *v.* Sargent, 27 N. H. 460, 469 (1853). Long *v.* Morrison, 14 Ind. 596, 600 (1860). Graham *v.* Gautier, 21 Tex. 111, 117 (1858).

(38) Terwilliger *v.* Wands, 17 N. Y. Ct. App. 54, 59 (1858).

(39) [Scandal against the peerage.] Stout *v.* Keyes, 2 Mich. Doug. 184, 187 (1846). Marshall ads. White, 1 S. Car. (Harper) 122, 124 (1824).

(40) This action or public prosecution (for it partakes of both) for *scandalum magnatum* is totally different from the action of slander in the case of common persons. The *scandalum magnatum* is reduced to no rule or certain definition, but it may be whatever the courts in their discretion shall judge to be derogatory to the high character of the person of whom it was spoken: as it was held to be *scandalum magnatum* to say of a peer, "he was no more to be valued than a dog;" which words would have been perfectly harmless if uttered of any inferor person. Bull. N. P. 4. This action is now seldom resorted to. By the two first statutes upon which it is founded, (3 Edw. I. c. 34 and 2 Ric. II. st. 2, c. 5,) the defendant may be imprisoned till he produces the first author of the scandal. Hence probably is the origin of the vulgar notion that a person who has propagated slander may be compelled to give up his author.—CHITTY. See also Sharff *v.* Comm., 2 Binney (Pa.) 514, 519 (1810). Bowyer's Comm. on Const. of Eng. 467.

(41) Many words which are not slanderous when applied to private persons, become so, when applied to them in their official character; but then the words must impute a defect of understanding, ability, or integrity, to make them actionable. Buller's *Nisi Prius*, 4-5 (1806). 1 Salk. 695. McCuen *v.* Ludlum, 2 Harrison (N. J.) 12-19 (1839). Gove *v.* Blethen, 21 Minn. 80-81 (1874), and authorities there cited.

thus apparently, and upon the face of them, import such defamation as will of course be injurious, it is necessary that the plaintiff should aver some particular damage to have happened; which is called laying his action with a *per quod*.(42) As if I say that such a clergyman is a bastard, he cannot for this bring any action against me, unless he can show some special loss by it; in which case he may bring his action against me for saying he was a bastard, *per quod* he lost the presentation to such a living. (*m*) In like manner, to *slander another man's title,* by spreading such injurious reports as, if true, would deprive him of his estate, (as to call the issue in tail, or one who hath land by descent, a bastard,) is actionable, provided any special damage accrues to the proprietor thereby; as if he loses an opportunity of selling the land.(*n*) But mere scurrility, or opprobrious words, which neither in themselves import, nor are in fact attended with, any injurious effects will not

support an action. So scandals, which concern matters merely
*125] spiritual, as to call a *man heretic or adulterer, are cognizable only in the ecclesiastical court;(*o*) unless any temporal damage ensues, which may be a foundation for a *per quod.* Words of heat and passion, as to call a man a rogue and rascal, if productive of no ill consequence, and not of any of the dangerous species before mentioned, are not actionable; (43) neither are words spoken in a friendly manner, as by way of advice, admonition, or concern, without any tincture or circumstance of ill will: for, in both these cases, they are not *maliciously* spoken, which is part of the definition of slander.(*p*) Neither (as was formerly hinted)(*q*) are any reflecting words made use of in legal proceedings, and pertinent to the cause in hand, a sufficient cause of action for slander.(*r*)(44) Also, if the defendant be able to justify, and prove the words to be true, no action will lie,(*s*)(45) even though special damage hath ensued: for then it is no slander or false tale. As if I can prove the tradesman a bankrupt, the physician a quack, the lawyer a knave, and the divine a heretic, this will destroy their respective actions; for though there may be damage sufficient accruing from it, yet, if the fact be true, it is *damnum absque injuria;*(46) and where there is no injury the law gives no remedy. And this is agreeable to the reasoning of the civil law:(*t*)(47) "*eum qui nocentem infamat, non est æquum et bonum ob eam rem condemnari; delicta enim nocentium nota esse oportet et expedit.*"(48)

(*m*) 4 Rep. 17. 1 Lev. 248.
(*n*) Cro. Jac. 213. Cro. Eliz. 197.
(*o*) Noye 64. 1 Freem. 277.
(*p*) Finch, L. 186. 1 Lev. 82. Cro. Jac. 91.

(*q*) Page 29.
(*r*) Dyer, 285. Cro. Jac. 90.
(*s*) 4 Rep. 13.
(*t*) *ff.* 47, 10, 18.

(42) [Whereby.] Terwilliger *v.* Wands, 17 N. Y. Ct. App. 54-60 (1858).
(43) McKee *v.* Ingalls, 4 Scammon (Ill.) 30-31 (1842).
(44) And now, by stat. 6 & 7 Vict. c. 96, (amended by stat. 8 & 9 Vict. c. 75,) in any action for defamation, the offer of an apology is admissible in evidence in mitigation of damages, and in an action against a newspaper for libel the defendant may plead that it was inserted without malice.—STEWART.
   It seems that in this country evidence of this nature has been deemed by the courts admissible in mitigation of damages without waiting for the interference of the legislature. See the language of the court in Larned *v.* Buffinton, 3 Mass. 546, as qualified in Alderman *v.* French, 1 Pick. 19. See, also, what was said by Chief-Justice Savage in Mapes *v.* Weeks, 4 Wendell, 663, and the intimation of Nelson, C. J., in Hotchkiss *v.* Oliphant, 2 Hill, 515, that a withdrawal or recantation of the charges by way of atonement would be admissible in evidence in mitigation of damages. See, also, Starkie on Slander, vol. 2, p. 99, n. a. and n. 1, American edition of 1843.—WENDELL.
   (45) Shull *v.* Raymond, 23 Minn. 66-68 (1876). Commons *v.* Walters, 1 Porter (Ala.).
   (46) [Damage without injury.]
   (47) Castle *v.* Houston, 19 Kan. 417-424 (1877); 323-327 (1835).
   (48) ["It is not just and right that he who exposes the faults of a guilty person should be condemned on that account; for it is proper and expedient that the offences of the guilty should be known."]

A second way of affecting a man's reputation is by printed or written libels, pictures, signs, and the like; which set him in an odious or ridiculous(*u*) light, and thereby diminish his reputation.(49) With regard to libels in general, there are, as in many other cases, two remedies: one by indictment, and the other by action. The former for the *public* offence; for every libel has a tendency to the breach of the peace, by provoking the person libelled to break it: which offence is the same (in point of law) whether *the matter contained be true or false; and therefore the defendant,   [*126 on an indictment for publishing a libel, is not allowed to allege the truth of it by way of justification.(*w*)(50) But in the remedy by action on the case, which is to repair the *party* in damages for the injury done him, the defendant may, as for words *spoken*, justify the truth of the facts, and show that the plaintiff has received no injury at all.(*x*)(51) What was said with regard to words spoken will also hold in every particular with regard to libels by writing or printing, and the civil actions consequent thereupon; but as to signs or pictures, it seems necessary always to show, by proper *innuendoes* and averments of the defendant's meaning, the import and application of the scandal, and that some special damage has followed; otherwise it cannot appear that such libel by picture was understood to be levelled at the plaintiff, or that it was attended with any actionable consequences.(52)

A third way of destroying or injuring a man's reputation is by preferring malicious indictments or prosecutions against him;(53) which, under the

(*u*) 2 Show. 314. 11 Mod. 99.   (*x*) Hob. 53. 11 Mod. 99.
(*w*) 5 Rep. 125.

---

(49) Cooper *v.* Greeley, 1 Denio (N. Y.) 347–359 (1845).

(50) But now, by stat. 6 & 7 Vict. c. 96, s. 6, on the trial of any indictment or information for a libel, the defendant having pleaded such plea as therein mentioned, the truth of the matter charged may be inquired into, but shall not amount to a defence unless it was for the public benefit that the matter charged should be published. To entitle the defendant to give evidence of the truth of the matters charged as a defence to such indictment or information, it is necessary for the defendant, in pleading to the indictment or information, to allege the truth of the said matters, and also that it was for the public benefit that the matters charged should be published,—to which plea the prosecutor may reply generally; and if after such plea the defendant is convicted, the court may, in pronouncing sentence, consider whether the guilt of the defendant is aggravated or mitigated by the plea.—STEWART.

In an action of slander, the defendant was not allowed to give in evidence, in mitigation of damages, facts and circumstances which induced him to believe that the charges which he made were true, when such facts and circumstances tended to prove the charges or formed a link in the chain of evidence to establish a justification, though the defendant expressly disavowed a justification and fully admitted the falsity of the charges. Purple *v.* Horton, 13 Wend. 9. Petrie *v.* Rose, 5 Watts & Serg. 364. Regnier *v.* Cabot, 2 Gilman, 34. Watson *v.* Moore, 2 Cushing, 133. It has been since held, however, that the defendant may prove, in mitigation of damages, circumstances which induced him erroneously to make the charge complained of, and thereby rebut the presumption of malice, provided the evidence do not necessarily imply the truth of the charge or tend to prove it true. Minesinger *v.* Kerr, 9 Barr. 312.—SHARSWOOD.

(51) Bailey's Onus Probandi, 186 (1886). Castle *v.* Houston, 19 Webb (Kansas) 417 (1877).

(52) The printer or publisher, as well as the writer, is liable in an action for damages. It is no defence that the printer did not know, or had no personal malice against, the party libelled, nor that he did not know of the publication, nor that the libel was accompanied with the name of the author. Rundle *v.* Meyer, 3 Yeates, 518. Dexter *v.* Spear, 4 Mason, 115. Andre *v.* Wells, 7 Johns. 260. Dole *v.* Lyon, 10 Johns. 447. The publication in a newspaper of rumors is not justified by the fact that such rumors existed; but such fact is admissible in mitigation of damages. Skinner *v.* Powers, 1 Wend. 451.—SHARSWOOD.

In the United States, if the truth be published with good motives and ends that are justifiable, it is a good defence in a criminal prosecution.

(53) An action for malicious prosecution will not be sustained unless it be shown, first: that the action was instituted without suitable cause; second, that the motive which prompted its institution was malicious; and third, that the defendant was acquitted of

mask of justice and public spirit, are sometimes made the engines of private spite and enmity. For this, however, the law has given a very adequate remedy in damages,(54) either by an action of *conspiracy*,(*y*) which cannot be brought but against two at the least;(55) or, which is the more usual way, by a special action on the case for a false and malicious prosecution.(*z*)(56) In order to carry on the former, (which gives a recompense for the danger to which the party has been exposed,) it is necessary that the plaintiff should obtain a copy of the record of his indictment and acquittal;(57) but, in prosecutions for felony, it is usual to deny a copy of the indictment, where there is any the least probable cause to found such prosecution upon.(*a*)(58) For it would be a very great discouragement to the public justice of the kingdom, if prosecutors, who had a tolerable ground of suspicion, were liable to be sued at law whenever their indictments

*127]   miscarried. *But an action on the case for a malicious prosecution may be founded upon an indictment whereon no acquittal can be had; as if it be rejected by the grand jury, or be *coram non judice*,(59) or be insufficiently drawn. For it is not the danger of the plaintiff, but the scandal, vexation, and expense, upon which this action is founded.(*b*)(60) However, any probable cause for preferring it is sufficient to justify the defendant.

II. We are next to consider the violation of the right of personal liberty. This is effected by the injury of false imprisonment,(61) for which the law has not only decreed a punishment, as a heinous public crime, but has also given a private reparation to the party; as well by removing the actual confinement for the present, as, after it is over, by subjecting the wrong-doer to

---

(*y*) Finch. L. 305.
(*z*) F. N. B. 116.

(*a*) Carth. 421. Lord. Raym. 253.
(*b*) 10 Mod. 219, 220. Stra. 691.

---

the offence charged against him. Bacon *v.* Prone, 4 Cuth. 217 (1849). Malice may be inferred sometimes from want of suitable cause, where there is nothing to rebut the inference; but such inference is only one of fact, and not of law. Sietz *v.* Langfett, 63 Pa. 234 (1869).

(54) Bailey's Onus Probandi, 186 (1886). Shore *v.* Smith, 15 Ohio (Critch.) 173 (1864).

(55) Dicey on Parties to Actions. Truman's Notes, 54 (1876).

(56) Whipple *v.* Fuller, 11 Conn. 581-585 (1836). Bailey's Onus Probandi, 184 (1886). Gugy *v.* McGuire, 13 Lower Can. 33, 56 (1863).

(57) Dunlap *v.* Gliddon *et al.*, 31 Me. 435-438 (1850).

(58) Gray *v.* Pentland, 2 Sergt. & Rawle (Pa.) 23-34 (1815).   1 Waterman's Crim. Prac. 745.

(59) [Before a judge who has not jurisdiction of the affair.]

(60) A corporation having no personal character, cannot recover in a suit for malicious prosecution without proving some special damage to its property. Supreme Lodge Amer. Protect. League *v.* Univerzagt *et al.*, 76 Md. 104 (1892). And where the subject-matter of an offence charged on the accused is wholly beyond the jurisdiction of the committing magistrate, only an action for false imprisonment, and not an action for malicious prosecution, will lie. Castro *v.* De Uriarte, 12 Fed. Rep. 250 (1882).

(61) But the merely giving charge of a person to a peace-officer, not followed by any actual apprehension of the person, does not amount to an imprisonment, though the party to avoid it attend at a police-office, (1 Esp. Rep. 431. 2 New Rep. 211;) and in Gardner *v.* Wedd and others, Easter Term, 1825, on a motion for a new trial, the court of Common Pleas held that the lifting up a person in his chair and carrying him out of the room in which he was sitting with others, and excluding him from the room, was not a false imprisonment so as to entitle the plaintiff to a verdict on a count for false imprisonment. The circumstance of an imprisonment being committed under a mistake constitutes no excuse. 3 Wils. 309. And it has been decided that if A. tell an officer who has a warrant against B. that his (A.'s) name is B., and thereupon the officer arrests A., it is false imprisonment, (Moore, 457. Hardr. 323; but see 3 Camp. 108;) and this doctrine was overruled in a late case on the western circuit, on the principle *volenti non fit injuriam* [An injury cannot be done to a willing person], and that such a fraud upon legal proceedings cannot give a right of action.—CHITTY.

a civil action, on account of the damage sustained by the loss of time and liberty.

To constitute the injury of false imprisonment there are two points requisite: 1. The detention of the person; and, 2. The unlawfulness of such detention. Every confinement of the person is an imprisonment, whether it be in a common prison, or in a private house, or in the stocks, or even by forcibly detaining one in the public streets.(c) (62)   Unlawful, or false, imprisonment consists in such confinement or detention without sufficient authority: which authority may arise either from some process from the courts of justice, or from some warrant from a legal officer having power to commit, under his hand and seal, and expressing the cause of such commitment;(d) or from some other special cause warranted, for the necessity of the thing, either by common law, or act of parliament;(63) such as the arresting of a felon by a private person without warrant, the impressing of mariners for the public service, or the apprehending of wagoners for misbehavior in the public highways.(e) False imprisonment also may arise by executing a lawful warrant or process at an *unlawful time, as on a Sunday;(f) for the   [*128 statute hath declared that such service or process shall be void.(64)
This is the injury.   Let us next see the remedy: which is of two sorts; the one *removing* the injury, the other *making satisfaction* for it.

The means of *removing* the actual injury of false imprisonment are fourfold.   1. By writ of *mainprize*.   2. By writ *de odio et atia*.(65)   3. By writ *de homine replegiando*.(66)   4. By writ of *habeas corpus*.

1. The writ of *mainprize, manucaptio*, is a writ directed to the sheriff, (either generally, when any man is imprisoned for a bailable offence and bail has been refused; or specially, when the offence or cause of commitment is not properly bailable below,) commanding him to take sureties for the prisoner's appearance, usually called *mainpernors*, and to set him at large.(g) Mainpernors differ from bail, in that a man's bail may imprison or surrender him up before the stipulated day of appearance; mainpernors can do neither, but are barely sureties for his appearance at the day: bail are only sureties that the party be answerable for the special matter for which they stipulate; mainpernors are bound to produce him to answer all charges whatsoever.(h)

2. The writ *de odio et atia* was anciently used to be directed to the sheriff, commanding him to inquire whether a prisoner charged with murder was

---

(c) 2 Inst. 589.
(d) Ibid. 46.
(e) Stat. Geo. III. c. 78.
(f) Stat. Car. II. c. 7.   Salk. 78.   5 Mod. 95.

(g) F. N. B. 250.   1 Hal. P. C. 141.   Coke on Bail and Mainp. ch. 10.
(h) Coke on Bail and Mainp. ch. 3.   4 Inst. 197.

---

(62) False imprisonment is a wrongful interference with the personal liberty of the individual. The wrong may be committed by words alone, or by acts alone, or by both, and by merely operating on the will of the individual, or by personal violence, or by both, it is not necessary that the wrongful act be committed with malice, or ill will, or with the slightest wrongful intention; nor is it necessary that the act be under the color of any legal or judical proceedings. All that is necessary is, that the individual be restrained of his liberty without any legal cause, and by words or acts which he fears to disregard. Webb's Pollock on Torts, 259 (1894). It is the fact of compulsory submission which brings a person into imprisonment. Lawson's Rights, Remedies and Practice, vol. 3, § 1064 (1890). State v. Lemsford, 81 N. C. 528. Johnson v. Tomkins, 1 Baldwin, 571. Pike v. Hanson, 9 N. H. 49.

(63) 1 Russell on Crimes, 1024 (1877).

(64) But the statute has excepted cases of treason, felony, and breach of the peace, in which the execution of a lawful warrant or process is allowed upon a Sunday.—CHITTY.

(65) [Of hatred and ill will.]   Of the two first-mentioned writs nothing is now known in practice, their use and application being entirely superseded by summary resort to magistrates, or, upon their refusal, to a judge of the court, as the case may require.—CHITTY.

(66) [Of replevying a man.]

committed upon just cause of suspicion, or merely *propter odium et atiam,* for hatred and ill will; and if upon the inquisition due cause of suspicion did not appear, then there issued another writ for the sheriff to admit him to bail. This writ, according to Bracton,(*i*) ought not to be denied to any man, it being expressly ordered to be made out *gratis,* without any denial, by

magna carta, c. 26, and statute Westm. 2, 13 Edw. I. c. 29. But *129]   the statute *of Gloucester, 6 Edw. I. c. 9, restrained it in the case of killing by misadventure or self-defence, and the statute 28 Edw. III. c. 9 abolished it in all cases whatsoever: but as the statute 42 Edw. III. c. 1 repealed all statutes then in being, contrary to the great charter, Sir Edward Coke is of opinion(*k*) that the writ *de odio et atia* was thereby revived.

3. The writ *de homine replegiando*(*l*)(67) lies to replevy a man out of prison, or out of the custody of any private person, (in the same manner that chattels taken in distress may be replevied, of which in the next chapter,) upon giving security to the sheriff that the man shall be forthcoming to answer any charge against him. And if the person be conveyed out of the sheriff's jurisdiction, the sheriff may return that he is eloigned, *elongatis;* upon which a process issues (called a *capias in withernam*)(68) to imprison the defendant himself, without bail or main-prize,(*m*) till he produces the party. But this writ is guarded with so many exceptions,(*n*) that it is not an effectual remedy in numerous instances, especially where the crown is concerned. The incapacity therefore of these three remedies to give complete relief in every case hath almost entirely antiquated them, and hath caused a general recourse to be had, in behalf of persons aggrieved by illegal imprisonment, to

4. The writ of *habeas corpus,* the most celebrated writ in the English law. Of this there are various kinds made use of by the courts at Westminster, for removing prisoners from one court into another for the more easy administration of justice. Such is the *habeas corpus ad respondendum,*(69) when a man hath a cause of action against one who is confined by the process of some inferior court; in order to remove the prisoner, and charge him with

this new action in the court above.(*o*) Such is that *ad satisfacien-* *130]   dum,*(70) when a prisoner hath *had judgment against him in an action, and the plaintiff is desirous to bring him up to some superior court to charge him with process of execution.(*p*) Such also are those *ad prosquendum, testificandum, deliberandum,* etc;(71) which issue when it is necessary to remove a prisoner, in order to prosecute or bear testimony in any court, or to be tried in the proper jurisdiction wherein the fact was committed.(72) Such is, lastly, the common writ *ad faciendum et recipien-*

(*i*) *L.* 3, *tr.* 2, c. 8.
(*k*) 2 Inst. 43, 55, 315. [Of hatred and malice.]
(*l*) F. N. B. 66.
(*m*) Raym. 474.
(*n*) *Nisi captus est per speciale præceptum nostrum, vel capitalis justiciarii nostri, vel pro morte hominis, vel pro foresta nostra, vel pro aliquo alio retto, quare secundum consuetudinem Angliæ non sit replegiabilis.* [Un-

less he be taken by our special command, or by that of our chief justice, for the death of a man, for a breach of the forest laws, or any other offence for which, according to the custom of England, he may not be repleviable.] *Registr.* 77.

(*o*) 2 Mod. 198.
(*p*) 2 Lilly Prac. Reg. 4.

---

(67) [Of replevying a man.]
(68) [That you take in withernam.]
(69) [That you have the body to answer.]
(70) [To satisfy.]
(71) [To prosecute, testify, deliberate, etc.]
(72) By 44 Geo. III. c. 102, any of the judges of England or Ireland may award a writ of *habeas corpus ad testificandum* [That you have the body to testify] to bring a prisoner detained in any gaol to be examined as a witness in any court of record or sitting at nisi prius.—CHITTY.

dum,(73) which issues out of any of the courts of Westminster hall, when a person is sued in some inferior jurisdiction, and is desirous to remove the action into the superior court; commanding the inferior judges to produce the body of the defendant, together with the day and cause of his caption and detainer, (whence the writ is frequently denominated an *habeas corpus cum causa,*)(74) to *do and receive* whatsoever the king's court shall consider in that behalf.   This is a writ grantable of common right, without any motion in court,(*q*) and it instantly supersedes all proceedings in the court below.   But in order to prevent the surreptitious discharge of prisoners, it is ordered by statute 1 & 2 P. and M. c. 13 that no *habeas corpus* shall issue to remove any prisoner out of any gaol, unless signed by some judge of the court out of which it is awarded.   And to avoid vexatious delays by removal of frivolous causes, it is enacted by statute 21 Jac. I. c. 23 that, where the judge of an inferior court of record is a barrister of three years' standing, no cause shall be removed from thence by *habeas corpus* or other writ, after issue or demurrer deliberately joined; that no cause, if once remanded to the inferior court by writ of *procedendo* or otherwise, shall ever afterwards be again removed; and that no cause shall be removed at all, if the debt or damages laid in the declaration do not amount to the sum of five pounds.   But an *expedient*(*r*) having been found out to elude the latter branch of the statute, by procuring a nominal plaintiff to bring another action for five pounds or upwards, (and then, by the course of the court, the *habeas corpus* removed both actions together,) it is therefore enacted by statute 12 Geo. I. c. 29, that the inferior *court may proceed in   [*131 such actions as are under the value of five pounds, notwithstanding other actions may be brought against the same defendant to a greater amount. And by statute 19 Geo. III. c. 70, no cause under the value of ten pounds(75) shall be removed by *habeas corpus*: or otherwise, into any superior court, unless the defendant so removing the same shall give special bail for payment of the debt and costs.

But the great and efficacious writ, in all manner of illegal confinement, is that of *habeas corpus ad subjiciendum;* directed to the person detaining another, and commanding him to produce the body of the prisoner, with the day and cause of his caption and detention, *ad faciendum, subjiciendum, et recipiendum,* to do, submit to, and receive whatsoever the judge or court awarding such writ shall consider in that behalf.(*s*)(76)   This is a high prerogative writ, and therefore by the common law issuing out of the court of king's bench not only in term-time, but also during the vacation,(*t*) by a *fiat* from the chief justice or any other of the judges, and running into all parts of the king's dominions;(77) for the king is at all times entitled to have an

---

(*q*) 2 Mod. 306.
(*r*) Bohun. *Instit. Legal.* 85, edit. 1708.
(*s*) St. Trials, viii. 142.
(*t*) The *pluries habeas corpus* directed to Berwick in 43 Eliz. (cited 4 Burr. 856) was *teste'd die Jovis prox' post quinden' Sancti Martini.* [The Thursday

next after the quindena (November 25) of St. Martin.]   It appears, by referring to the dominical letter of that year, that this *quindena* (Nov. 25) happened that year on a Saturday.   The Thursday after was therefore the 30th of November,—two days after the expiration of the term.

---

(73) [To do and receive.]

(74) [That you have the body with the cause of detention.]

(75) By statute 57 Geo. III. c. 124, extended to 15*l.*, and by statute 7 & 8 Geo. IV. c. 71, § 6, extended to 20*l.*—CHITTY.

(76) Both federal and state constitutions in the United States declare that "the privilege of the writ of *habeas corpus* shall not be suspended, unless, when in case of rebellion or invasion, the public safety may require its suspension."   2 Barb. on Pers. Prop. 894. 1 Archibald Crim. Pr. and Pl. 200.   2 Barb. Cr. Law (3 ed.) 574.   State *v.* Ward, 3 Halstead (N. J.) 120-122 (1825).   Yeates *v.* The People, 6 Johns. (N. Y.) 337-454 (1810).   *Ex parte* Holman, 28 Iowa, 88-128 (1869).   State *v.* Cheeseman, 2 Southard (N. J.) 445-447 (1819).

(77) State *v.* Glenn, 54 Md. 572-598 (1880).   People *v.* Bradley, 60 Ill. 390-398 (1871). State *v.* Hill, 10 Minn. 63-66 (1865).

account why the liberty of any of his subjects is restrained, (u) wherever that restraint may be inflicted. If it issues in vacation, it is usually returnable before the judge himself who awarded it, and he proceeds by himself thereon;(v) unless the term shall intervene, and then it may be returned in court.(w) Indeed, if the party were privileged in the courts of common pleas and exchequer, as being (or supposed to be) an officer or suitor of the court, an *habeas corpus ad subjiciendum*(78) might also by common law have been awarded from thence;(x) and, if the cause of imprisonment were palpably illegal, they might have discharged him:(y) but, if he were committed for any criminal matter, they could only have remanded him, or taken bail for his appearance in the court of king's bench,(z) which *132]   *occasioned the common pleas for some time to discountenance such applications. But since the mention of the king's bench and common pleas, as co-ordinate in this jurisdiction, by statute 16 Car. I. c. 10, it hath been holden, that every subject of the kingdom is equally entitled to the benefit of the common-law writ, in either of those courts, at his option.(a) It hath also been said, and by very respectable authorities,(b) that the like *habeas corpus* may issue out of the court of chancery in vacation; but upon the famous application to lord Nottingham by Jenks, notwithstanding the most diligent searches, no precedent could be found where the chancellor had issued such a writ in vacation;(c) and therefore his lordship refused it.(79)

(u) Cro. Jac. 543.
(v) 4 Burr. 856.
(w) Ibid. 460, 542, 606.
(x) 2 Inst. 55, 4 Inst. 290. 2 Hal. P. C. 141. 2 Ventr. 21.

(y) Vaugh. 155.
(z) Carter, 221. 2 Jon. 13.
(a) 2 Mod. 198. Wood's Case, C. B. Hill. 11 Geo. III.
(b) 4 Inst. 182. 2 Hal. P. C. 147.
(c) Lord Nott. MSS. Rep. July, 1676.

(78) [That you have the body to answer.]
(79) It was determined, after a very elaborate investigation of all the authorities by lord Eldon in Crowley's case, that the lord chancellor can issue the writ of habeas corpus at common law in vacation, overruling the decision in Jenks's case. See 2 Swanst. I.
By two modern statutes, the 43 Geo. III. c. 140 and 44 Geo. III. c. 102, the habeas corpus *ad testificandum* [To testify] has been rendered more efficient. By the first, a judge may award the writ for the purpose of bringing any prisoner from any gaol in England or Ireland as a witness, before any court-martial, commissioners of bankrupt or for auditing public accounts, or other commissioners, under any commission or warrant from his majesty: (the statute has the same application to the habeas corpus *ad deliberandum*) [A writ to remove a prisoner from one county to another]. By the other statute, a similar power is given for bringing up any prisoner as a witness before any of the courts, or any justice of oyer and terminer, or gaol-delivery, or sitting at nisi prius, in England or Ireland.
The benefit of the writ of habeas corpus, which was limited by the former acts to cases of commitment or detainer for criminal, or supposed criminal, matter, has been still further extended by the 59 Geo. III. c. 100, which enacts that any one of the judges may issue a writ of habeas corpus in vacation, returnable immediately, before himself or any other judge of the same court, in cases other than for criminal matter or for debt; and the non-observance of such writ is to be deemed a contempt of court. But if the writ be awarded so late in the vacation that the return cannot be conveniently made before term, then it is to be made returnable in court at a day certain. And if the writ be awarded late in term, it may be made returnable in vacation in like manner. The act applies to Ireland as well as England, and the writ may run into counties palatine, cinque ports, and privileged places, etc., Berwick-upon-Tweed, and the isles of Guernsey, Jersey, or Man.
The writ of habeas corpus is the privilege of the British subject only, and therefore cannot be obtained by an alien enemy or a prisoner of war. See the case of the three Spanish sailors, 2 Blk. 1324. 2 Burr. 765. The relief in such cases is by application to the secretary at war. On a commitment by either house of parliament for contempt or breach of privilege, the courts at Westminster cannot discharge on a habeas corpus, although, on the return of the writ, such commitment should appear illegal; for they have no power to control the privileges of parliament. 2 Hawk. c. 15, s. 73. 8 T. R. 314.
The writ of habeas corpus, whether at common law or under 31 Car. II. c. 2, does not issue, as a matter of course, upon application in the first instance, but must be grounded

In the king's bench and common pleas it is necessary to apply for it by motion to the court,(*d*) as in the case of all other prerogative writs,

(*d*) 2 Mod. 306. 1 Lev. 1.

on an affidavit, upon which the court are to exercise their discretion whether the writ shall issue or not. 3 B. & A. 420. 2 Chitty R. 207. A habeas corpus *cum causa* [With the cause (why he is arrested)] does not lie to remove proceedings from an inferior jurisdiction into the court of King's Bench, unless it appears that the defendant is actually or virtually in the custody of the court below. 1 B. & C. 513. 2 Dowl. & R. 722. The court of King's Bench will grant a habeas corpus to the warden of the Fleet, to take a prisoner confined there for debt before a magistrate, to be examined from day to day respecting a charge of felony or misdemeanor. 5 B. & A. 730. The court of exchequer will not grant a habeas corpus to enable the defendant in an information, who is confined in a county gaol for a libel under the sentence of another court, to attend at Westminster to conduct his defence in person: the application should be made to the court by whom the defendant was sentenced. 9 Price, 147. Nor will the court of King's Bench grant a writ of habeas corpus to bring up a defendant under sentence of imprisonment for a misdemeanor, to enable him to show cause in person against a rule for a criminal information. 3 B. & A. 679, n. Where there are articles of separation between the husband and wife, if the husband afterwards confine her, she may have a habeas corpus and be set at liberty. 13 East, 173, n. A habeas corpus will be granted in the first instance, to bring up an infant who had absconded from his father and was detained by a third person without his consent. 4 Moore, 366. The court will not grant a habeas corpus to bring up the body of a feme-covert on an affidavit that she is desirous of disposing of her separate property, and that her husband will not admit the necessary parties, and that she is confined by illness and not likely to live long; nor will they, under such circumstances, grant a rule to show cause why the necessary parties should not be admitted to see her; for if there be no restraint of personal liberty, the matter is only cognizable in a court of equity. 1 Chitty R. 654. Where application had been made for the discharge of an impressed seaman, before the two years of his protection by the stat. 13 Geo. II. c. 17 were expired, which was then ineffectual, because the facts were not verified with sufficient certainty, yet, the doubt being removed by another affidavit, the court granted a writ of habeas corpus for the purpose of liberating him, though the two years were expired. 8 East, 27. The court on affidavit, suggesting probable cause to believe that a helpless and ignorant female foreigner was exhibited for money without her consent, granted a rule on her keepers to show cause why a writ of habeas corpus should not issue to bring her before the court, and directed an examination before the coroner and attorney of the court, in the presence of the parties applying and applied against. *Ex parte* Hottentot Venus, 13 East, 195. The writ will be granted to a military officer under arrest for charges of misconduct, if he be not brought to trial pursuant to the articles of war, as soon as a court-martial can be conveniently assembled, unless the delay is satisfactorily explained. 2 M. & S. 428. The court will grant a habeas corpus to bring up the body of a bastard child within the age of nurture, for the purpose of restoring it to its mother, from whom it had been taken, first by fraud, and then by force, without prejudice to the question of guardianship, which belongs to the lord chancellor. 7 East, 579. Where a prisoner is brought up under a habeas corpus issued at common law, he may controvert the truth of the return by virtue of the 56 Geo. III. c. 100, s. 4. 4 B. & C. 136. Prisoner committed for manslaughter, upon the return of the habeas corpus, was allowed to give bail in the country, by reason of his poverty, which rendered him unable to appear with bail in court. 6 M. & S. 108. 1 B. & A. 209. 2 Chit. Rep. 110.

With respect to the *Return*. A return in the following words, "I had not, at the time of receiving this writ, nor have I since, had the body of A. B. *detained* in my custody, so that I *could not* have her, etc." was holden bad, and an attachment was granted against the party who made it. 5 T. R. 89. It seems sufficient to set forth that the defendant is in custody under the sentence of a court of competent jurisdiction to inquire of the offence and pass such sentence, without setting forth the particular circumstances necessary to warrant such a sentence. 1 East, 306. 5 Dowl. 199, 200. The court will not extend matter dehors the return, in support of the sentence or proceeding against the defendant, (2 M. & S. 226,) nor go into the merits, but decide upon the return of a regular conviction *prima facie*. 7 East, 376. Where a defendant was committed by an ecclesiastical judge of appeal for contumacy in not paying costs, and the significavit only described the suit to be "a certain cause of appeal and complaint of nullity," without showing that the defendant was committed for a cause within the jurisdiction of the spiritual judge, it was held that the defendant was entitled to be discharged on habeas corpus. 5 B. & A. 791. 1 Dowl. & Ry. 460.—CHITTY. See Territory *v.* Ashenfether, 4 N. Mex. 85, 91, 93 (1885). Bethuram *v.* Black, 11 Ky. 628, 632 (1874). Bowyer's Com. on Cons. Eng. p. 426.

(*certiorari*, prohibition, *mandamus*, etc.,) which do not issue as of mere course, without showing some probable cause why the extraordinary power of the crown is called in to the party's assistance. For, as was argued by lord chief justice Vaughan,(*e*) "it is granted on motion, because it cannot be had of course, and there is therefore no *necessity* to grant it; for the court ought to be satisfied that the party hath a probable cause to be delivered." And this seems the more reasonable because (when once granted) the person to whom it is directed can return no satisfactory excuse for not bringing up the body of the prisoner.(*f*) So that if it issued of mere course, without showing to the court or judge some reasonable ground for awarding it, a traitor or felon under sentence of death, a soldier or mariner in the king's service, a wife, a child, a relation, or a domestic confined for insanity or other prudential reasons, might obtain a temporary *enlargement
*133] by suing out a *habeas corpus*, though sure to be remanded as soon as brought up to the court. And therefore Sir Edward Coke, when chief justice, did not scruple in 13 Jac. I. to deny a *habeas corpus* to one confined by the court of admiralty for piracy; there appearing, upon his own showing, sufficient grounds to confine him.(*g*) On the other hand, if a probable ground be shown that the party is imprisoned without just cause,(*h*) and therefore hath a right to be delivered, the writ of *habeas corpus* is then a writ of right, which "may not be denied, but ought to be granted to every man that is committed or detained in prison, or otherwise restrained, though it be by the command of the king, the privy council, or any other."(*i*)

In a former part of these commentaries,(*k*) we expatiated at large on the personal liberty of the subject. This was shown to be a natural inherent right, which could not be surrendered or forfeited unless by the commission of some great and atrocious crime, and which ought not to be abridged in any case without the special permission of law. A doctrine coeval with the first rudiments of the English constitution, and handed down to us from our Saxon ancestors, notwithstanding all their struggles with the Danes and the violence of the Norman conquest; asserted afterwards and confirmed by the Conqueror himself and his descendants; and though sometimes a little impaired by the ferocity of the times, and the occasional despotism of jealous or usurping princes, yet established on the firmest basis by the provisions of *magna carta*, and a long succession of statutes enacted under Edward III. To assert an absolute exemption from imprisonment in all cases is inconsistent with every idea of law and political society; and in the end would destroy all civil liberty by rendering its protection impossible: but the glory of the Eng-
*134] lish law consists in clearly defining the times, the causes, and the extent, when, wherefore, and to what degree, the *imprisonment of the subject may be lawful. This it is which induces the absolute necessity of expressing upon every commitment the reason for which it is made: that the court upon a *habeas corpus* may examine into its validity, and, according to the circumstances of the case, may discharge, admit to bail, or remand the prisoner.(80)

(*e*) Bushel's case, 2 Jon. 13.
(*f*) Cro. Jac. 543.
(*g*) 3 Bulstr. 27. See also 2 Roll. Rep. 138.

(*h*) 2 Inst. 615.
(*i*) Com. Jour. 1 Apr. 1628.
(*k*) Book i. ch. 1.

---

(80) It has been decided by the Supreme Court of the United States that that tribunal has authority to issue a habeas corpus where a person is imprisoned under the warrant or order of any other court. It is in the nature of a writ of error to examine the legality of the commitment. As it is the exercise of the appellate power of the court to award the writ, it is within its jurisdiction to do so. It is revising the effect of the process of the inferior court under which the prisoner is detained, and is not the exercise of original jurisdiction. But the Supreme Court has no appellate jurisdiction in criminal

And yet, early in the reign of Charles I., the court of king's bench, relying on some arbitrary precedents, (and those perhaps misunderstood,) determined(*l*) that they could not upon a *habeas corpus* either bail or deliver a prisoner, though committed without any cause assigned, in case he was committed by the special command of the king, or by the lords of the privy council. This drew on a parliamentary inquiry, and produced the *petition of right*, 3 Car. I. which recites this illegal judgment, and enacts that no freeman hereafter shall be so imprisoned or detained. But when, in the following year, Mr. Selden and others were committed by the lords of the council, in pursuance of his majesty's special command, under a general charge of "notable contempts and stirring up sedition against the king and government," the judges delayed for two terms (including also the long vacation) to deliver an opinion how far such a charge was bailable. And when at length they agreed that it was, they, however, annexed a condition of finding sureties for the good behavior, which still protracted their imprisonment, the chief justice, Sir Nicholas Hyde, at the same time declaring (*m*) that "if they were again remanded for that cause perhaps the court would not afterwards grant a *habeas corpus*, being already made acquainted with the cause of the imprisonment." But this was heard with indignation and astonishment by every lawyer present: according to Mr. Selden's own(*n*) account of the matter, whose *resentment was not cooled at the dis-　[*135 tance of four-and-twenty years.

These pitiful evasions gave rise to the statute 16 Car. I. c. 10, § 8, whereby it is enacted that if any person be committed by the king himself in person, or by his privy council, or by any of the members thereof, he shall have granted unto him, without any delay upon any pretence whatsoever, a writ of *habeas corpus*, upon demand or motion made to the court of king's bench *or common pleas;* who shall thereupon, within three court-days after the return is made, examine and determine the legality of such commitment, and do what to justice shall appertain, in delivering, bailing, or remanding such prisoner. Yet still, in the case of Jenks, before alluded to,(*o*) who in 1676 was committed by the king in council for a turbulent speech at Guildhall,(*p*) new shifts and devices were made use of to prevent his enlargement by law, the chief justice (as well as the chancellor) declining to award a writ of *habeas corpus ad subjiciendum* in vacation, though at last

(*l*) State Tr. vii. 136.
(*m*) Ibid. 240.
(*n*) "*Etiam judicum tunc primarius, nisi illud faceremus, rescripti illius forensis, qui libertatis personalis omnimodæ vindex legitimus est fere solus, usum omnimodum palam pronuntiavit (sui semper similis) nobis perpetuo in posterum denegandum. Quod, ut odiosissimum juris prodigium, scientioribus hic universis censitum.*" [Then also the chief justice, (always the same,) openly declared that unless we could do it

(find sureties for good behavior) the use of this forensic rescript, which is almost the only lawful protection of every kind of personal liberty, would forever after be denied us, which was considered by all the lawyers present as a most odious and monstrous declaration."] *Vindic Mar. claus edit.* A. D. 1653.
(*o*) Page 132.
(*p*) State Tr. vii. 471.

---

cases confided to it by the laws of the United States, and hence will not grant a habeas corpus where a party has been committed for a contempt adjudged by a court of competent jurisdiction, nor inquire into the sufficiency of the cause of commitment. *Ex parte* Kearney, 7 Wheat. 38. *Ex parte* Tobias Watkins, 3 Peters, 193. S. C. 7 Peters, 568. But neither the Supreme Court, nor any other court of the United States, nor judge thereof, can issue a *habeas corpus* to bring up a prisoner who is in custody under a sentence or execution of a state court for any other purpose than to be used as a witness. *Ex parte* Dorr, 3 Howard, 103. The court on a *habeas corpus* cannot look behind the sentence where the court had jurisdiction. Johnson v. The United States, 3 McLean, 89.—SHARSWOOD. See also Beckwith v. Bean, 98 U. S. 266, 296 (1878). *Ex parte* Yerger, 8 Wallace, 85 (1868). State v. Ward, 3 N. J. (Hal.) 120-121 (1825). *Ex parte* Davis, 7 Fed. Cases, 45. 2 B. & A. 420. 20 Chitty, R. 207. See also *ex parte* Holman, 28 Iowa, 88 (1869), where the right of a state court to issue a writ of *habeas corpus* in behalf of a prisoner held in custody under the order of a federal court is discussed.

he thought proper to award the usual writs *ad deliberandum*,(81) etc., whereby the prisoner was discharged at the Old Bailey. Other abuses had also crept into daily practice which had in some measure defeated the benefit of this great constitutional remedy. The party imprisoning was at liberty to delay his obedience to the first writ, and might wait till a second and a third, called an *alias* and a *pluries*, were issued, before he produced the party, and many other vexatious shifts were practiced to detain state-prisoners in custody. But whoever will attentively consider the English history may observe that the flagrant abuse of any power by the crown or its ministers has always been productive of a struggle, which either discovers the exercise of that power to be contrary to law, or (if legal) restrains it for the future. This was the case in the present instance. The oppression of an obscure individual gave birth to the famous *habeas corpus* act, 31

*136]   Car. II. c. 2, which is frequently *considered as another *magna carta*(*q*) of the kingdom; and by consequence and analogy has also in subsequent times reduced the general method of proceedings on these writs (though not within the reach of that statute, but issuing merely at the common law) to the true standard of law and liberty.(82)

The statute itself enacts, 1. That on complaint and request in writing by or on behalf of any person committed and charged with any *crime*, (unless committed for treason or felony expressed in the warrant; or as accessory, or on suspicion of being accessory, before the fact, to any petit-treason or felony; or upon suspicion of such petit-treason or felony, plainly expressed in the warrant; or unless he is convicted or charged in execution by legal process,) the lord chancellor or any of the twelve judges, in vacation, upon viewing a copy of the warrant, or affidavit that a copy is denied, shall (unless the party has neglected for two terms to apply to any court for his enlargement) award a *habeas corpus* for such prisoner, returnable immediately before himself or any other of the judges; and upon the return made shall discharge the party, if bailable, upon giving security to appear and answer to the accusation in the proper court of judicature. 2. That such writs shall be endorsed as granted in pursuance of this act, and signed by the person awarding them. 3. That the writ shall be returned and the prisoner brought up within a limited time, according to the distance, not exceeding in any case twenty days. 4. That officers and keepers neglecting to make due returns, or not delivering to the prisoner or his agent within six hours after demand a copy of the warrant of commitment, or shifting the custody of a prisoner from one to another without sufficient reason or authority, (specified in the act,) shall for the first offence forfeit 100*l.*, and for the second offence 200*l.*, to the party grieved, and be disabled to hold his office. 5. That no person once delivered by *habeas corpus* shall be recommitted for the same offence, on penalty of 500*l.* 6. That every person committed for treason or felony shall, if he requires it the first week of the next

(*q*) See book i. ch. 1.

(81) *Vide supra*, p. 131.
(82) People *ex rel.* Tweed *v.* Liscomb, 60 N. Y. (Sickles) 559, 566 (1875). It was brought to America by the colonists, and claimed as among the immemorial rights descended to them from their ancestors. On the adoption of the constitution the writ was embodied in that instrument in these words, "The privilege of the writ of *habeas corpus* shall not be suspended, unless when in cases of rebellion or invasion the public safety may require it." Const. U. S. Art. 1, § ix. *Ex parte* Yerger, 8 Wall. 85, 95 (1868). The president has no power to suspend the privilege of the writ without an act of Congress to authorize it. Binns's Justice (Brightly) 10 ed. p. 22 (1895). See also State *v.* Fenderson, 28 La. 82, 83 (1876).

term, or the first day of the next session of *oyer and terminer*, be   [*137
indicted in that term or session, or else admitted to bail: unless the
king's witnesses cannot be produced at that time: and if acquitted, or if not
indicted and tried in the second term or session, he shall be discharged from
his imprisonment for such imputed offence: but that no person, after the
assizes shall be open for the county in which he is detained, shall be removed
by *habeas corpus*, till after the assizes are ended, but shall be left to the
justice of the judges of assize.   7. That any such prisoner may move for
and obtain his *habeas corpus* as well out of the chancery or exchequer as out
of the king's bench or common pleas; and the lord chancellor or judges
denying the same, on sight of the warrant or oath that the same is refused,
forfeit severally to the party grieved the sum of 500*l*.   8. That this writ of
habeas corpus shall run into the counties palatine, cinque ports, and other
privileged places, and the islands of Jersey and Guernsey.   9. That no inhabitant of England (except persons contracting, or convicts praying, to be
transported, or having committed some capital offence in the place to which
they are sent) shall be sent prisoner to Scotland, Ireland, Jersey, Guernsey, or
any places beyond the seas, within or without the king's dominions, on pain
that the party committing, his advisers, aiders, and assistants, shall forfeit to
the party aggrieved a sum not less than 500*l*., to be recovered with treble
costs; shall be disabled to bear any office of trust or profit; shall incur the
penalties of *præmunire;* and shall be incapable of the king's pardon.

This is the substance of that great and important statute: which extends
(we may observe) only to the case of commitments for such criminal charge,
as can produce no inconvenience to public justice by a temporary enlargement
of the prisoner: all other cases of unjust imprisonment being left to the
habeas corpus at common law.   But even upon writs at the common law it is
now expected by the court, agreeable to ancient precedents(*r*) and the spirit
of the act of parliament, that the writ should be immediately obeyed,
without waiting for any *alias* or *pluries;* otherwise an attachment   [*138
will issue.   By which admirable regulations, judicial as well as parliamentary, the remedy is now complete for *removing* the injury of unjust
and illegal confinement.   A remedy the more necessary, because the oppression does not always arise from the ill-nature, but sometimes from the mere
inattention, of government.   For it frequently happens in foreign countries
(and has happened in England during temporary suspensions(*s*) of the
statute) that persons apprehended upon suspicion have suffered a long
imprisonment, merely because they were forgotten.(83)

(*r*) 4 Burr. 856.   (*s*) See book i. page 136.

---

(83) Besides the efficacy of the writ of *habeas corpus* in liberating the subject from
illegal confinement in a public prison, it also extends its influence to remove every unjust restraint of personal freedom in private life, though imposed by a husband or a
father; but when women and infants are brought before the court by a *habeas corpus*,
the court will only set them free from an unmerited or unreasonable confinement, and
will not determine the validity of a marriage, or the right to the guardianship, but will
leave them at liberty to choose where they will go; and if there be any reason to apprehend that they will be seized in returning from the court, they will be sent home under
the protection of an officer.   But if a child is too young to have any discretion of its
own, then the court will deliver it into the custody of its parent or the person who appears to be its legal guardian.   See 3 Burr. 1434, where all the prior cases are considered
by lord Mansfield.   In a late case (Moore and Fitzgibbon) the court refused to permit
an inquiry whether a child born during wedlock was the offspring of the former or the
latter, but on a writ of *habeas corpus* directed that the child, an infant under three years
of age, should be restored to the former, who was the husband of the child's mother M.
T. 1825, K. B.

The *satisfactory* remedy for this injury of false imprisonment, is by an action of trespass *vi et armis*, usually called an action of false imprisonment; which is generally, and almost unavoidably, accompanied with a charge of assault and battery also; and therein the party shall recover damages for the injury he has received; and also the defendant is, as for all other injuries committed with force, or *vi et armis*, liable to pay a fine to the king for the violation of the public peace.(84)

III. With regard to the third absolute right of individuals, or that of private property, though the enjoyment of it, when acquired, is strictly a personal right; yet as its nature and original, and the means of its acquisition or loss, fell more directly under our second general division, of the *rights of things;* and as, of course, the wrongs that affect these rights must be referred to the corresponding division in the present book of our commentaries; I conceive it will be more commodious and easy to consider together, rather than in a separate view, the injuries that may be offered to the *enjoyment*, as well as to the *rights* of property. And therefore I shall here conclude the head of injuries affecting the *absolute* rights of individuals.

We are next to contemplate those which affect their *relative* rights; or such as are incident to persons considered as members of society, and connected to each other by various *ties and relations; and, in particular, such injuries as may be done to persons under the four following relations: husband and wife, parent and child, guardian and ward, master and servant.

*139]

I. Injuries that may be offered to a person, considered as a *husband*, are principally three: *abduction*, or taking away a man's wife; *adultery*, or criminal conversation with her; and *beating* or otherwise abusing her. 1. As to the first sort, *abduction*, or taking her away, this may either be by fraud and persuasion, or open violence: though the law in both cases supposes force and constraint, the wife having no power to consent; and therefore gives a remedy by writ of *ravishment*, or action of *trespass vi et armis, de uxore rapta et abducta.*(t)(85) This action lay at the common law; and thereby the husband shall recover, not the possession(u) of his wife, but damages for taking her away: and by statute Westm. 1, 3 Edw. I. c. 13, the offender shall also be imprisoned two years, and be fined at the pleasure of the king. Both the king and the husband may therefore have this action;(w) and the husband is also entitled to recover damages in an action on the case against such as persuade and entice the wife to live separate from him without a suf-

---

(t) F. N. B. 89.   (w) Ibid.
(u) 2 Inst. 434.

If an equivocal return is made to a *habeas corpus*, the court will immediately grant an attachment. 5 T. R. 89.—CHRISTIAN. See Yates v. The People, 6 Johns (N. Y.) 337, 480 (1810).

In the United States the writ of *habeas corpus* generally issues from the supreme court, and frequently from some of the inferior courts and their justices and judges of the state, where the protection of the personal liberty of a person within its jurisdiction requires it. But the authority to issue this writ is not confined to these jurisdictions alone. Where a person is in custody under or by order of the authority of the United States, or is committed for trial before one of its courts, or is in custody for adherence to one of its laws, or for obedience to a mandate or decree of a court thereof, or for the breach of one of its customs or treaties, or for some act or omission depending for its validity upon the law of nations, the supreme, a circuit or district court, as the case may be, within the jurisdiction of one or another of them, has power to issue a writ of *habeas corpus* for the protection of the liberty of the person in custody.

(84) [With force and arms.] Since the Common-Law Procedure Act, 1852, this fine to the king (for which formerly judgment was awarded by the court as a matter of form) no longer appears in the judgment.—STEWART.

(85) [For the ravishment and abduction of his wife.]

ficient cause.(*x*) The old law was so strict in this point, that if one's wife missed her way upon the road, it was not lawful for another man to take her into his house, unless she was benighted and in danger of being lost or drowned;(*y*) but a stranger might carry her behind him on horseback to market to a justice of the peace for a warrant against her husband, or to the spiritual court to sue for a divorce.(*z*)(86). 2. *Adultery*, or criminal conversation with a man's wife, though it is, as a public crime, left by our laws to the coercion of the spiritual courts; yet, considered as a civil injury, (and surely there can be no greater,) the law gives a satisfaction to the husband for it by action of trespass *vi et armis* against the adulterer, wherein the damages recovered are usually *very large and exemplary.(87)　　[*140 But these are properly increased and diminished by circumstances;(*a*) as the rank and fortune of the plaintiff and defendant;(88) the relation or connection between them; the seduction or otherwise of the wife, founded on her previous behavior and character; and the husband's obligation, by settlement or otherwise, to provide for those children, which he cannot but suspect to be spurious. In this case, and upon indictments for polygamy, a marriage *in fact* must be proved; though generally, in other cases, reputation and cohabitation are sufficient evidence of marriage.(*b*) The third injury is that of *beating* a man's wife, or otherwise ill using her; for which, if it be a common assault, battery, or imprisonment, the law gives the usual remedy to recover damages, by action of trespass *vi et armis*, which must be brought in the names of the husband and wife *jointly;*(89) but if the beating or other mal-treatment be very enormous, so that thereby the husband is deprived for any time of the company and assistance of his wife, the law then gives him a *separate* remedy by an action of trespass, in nature of an action upon the case, for this ill usage, *per quod consortium amisit;*(90) in which he shall recover a satisfaction in damages.(*c*)

II. Injuries that may be offered to a person considered in the relation of a *parent*(91) were likewise of two kinds: 1. *Abduction*, or taking his children

---

(*x*) Law of *Nisi Prius*, 74.
(*y*) Bro. Abr. tit. *Trespass*, 213.
(*z*) Bro. Abr. 207, 440.

(*a*) Law of *Nisi Prius*, 26.
(*b*) Burr. 2057.
(*c*) Cro. Jac. 501, 538.

---

(86) 2 Waterman on Crim. Proc. 148.

(87) [With force and arms.] Bedan *v.* Turney, 99 Cal. 649–653 (1893). Jacobson *v.* Siddel, 12 Ore. 280, 285 (1885). Webb's Pollock on Torts, enl. Am. ed. 276 (1894). Bishop on Stat. Crimes, ¿ 614 (1883). The early theory of the common law, though contrary to the ecclesiastical law, was that to constitute adultery, the carnal intercourse must be such as might produce a spurious issue in a family, (Buller's N. P. 26,) consequently the intercourse of a married man with a maid, was not adultery in the man. The authorities in the various states of the Union are conflicting on the question. See State *v.* Searle, 56 Vt. 516 (1884). State *v.* Lash. 1 Harrison, N. J. 380 (1838). Hood *v.* State, 56 Ind. 263–273 (1877). Actions for criminal conversation were abolished in England on the establishment of the Divorce Court in 1857, 20, 21 Vict. c. 85, ¿¿ 33, 59, but damages can be claimed on the same principles in proceedings for a dissolution of marriage, or judicial separation. Webb's Pollock on Torts, enl. Am. ed. p. 274 (1894).

(88) "This dictum has been echoed from Butler to Blackstone, from Blackstone to Espinasse, and from Espinasse to Swift, and it is worthy of remark that these learned compilers do not quote a single authority in support of this doctrine. It may, therefore, be doubted, even in England, and *a fortiori* in this country, where it is considered a self-evident truth that all men are created free and equal." Per Peters, J., in Norton *v.* Warner, 9 Conn. 172–174 (1832). Evidence of defendant's wealth is inadmissible. Peters *v.* Lake, 66 Ill. 206 (1872).

(89) Barb. Parties to Actions, 288. Broom's Parties to Actions, 236.

(90) [By which means he lost his wife.] See Drew *v.* Rue, 93 Pa. 234 (1880). Webb's Pollock on Torts, enl. Am. ed. p. 273 (1894). Barb. Parties to Actions, 283 (2 ed.). Broom's Parties to Actions, 231.

(91) See in general, Bac. Abr. Master & Servant, O. Selw. N. P. Master & Servant. It

away; and, 2. *Marrying* his son and heir without the father's consent, whereby during the continuance of the military tenures he lost the value of his marriage. But this last injury is now ceased, together with the right upon which it is grounded; for, the father being no longer entitled to the value of the marriage, the marrying his heir does him no sort of injury for which a civil action will lie. As to the other, of abduction, or taking away the children from the father, that is also a matter of doubt whether it be a civil injury or no; for, before the abolition of the tenure in chivalry, it was equally

*141]   a doubt whether an action would lie for taking and carrying away *any other child besides the heir; some holding that it would not, upon the supposition that the only ground or cause of action was losing the value of the heir's marriage; and others holding that an action would lie for taking away *any* of the children, for that the parent hath an interest in them

---

has been disputed, but the better opinion is, that the father has an interest in his legitimate child, sufficient to enable him to support an action in that character, for taking the child away, he being entitled to the custody of it. Cro. Eliz. 770. 23 Vin. 451. 2 P. Wms. 116. 3 Co. 38. 5 East, 221. No modern instance, however, of such action can be adduced; and it is now usual for the father to bring his action for any injury done to his child, as for debauching her, or beating him or her, in the character of master, *per quod servitium amisit*, [By which he was deprived of service,] in which case some evidence must be adduced of service. 5 T. R. 360. 361.

In an action for debauching plaintiff's daughter, as his servant, it is necessary to prove her residence with him; and some acts of service, though the most trifling, are sufficient. See 2 T. R. 167. 2 N. R. 476. 6 East, 387. It is unnecessary to prove any contract of service. Peake's R. 253. But if the seduction take place while she is residing elsewhere, and she in consequence return to her father, he cannot maintain the action, (5 East, 45,) unless she be absent with his consent, and with the intention of returning, although she be of age, (ib. 47, n.;) or if the defendant engaged her as his servant, and induced her to live in his house as such, with intent to seduce her. 2 Starkie Rep. 493. If she live in another family, the person with whom she resides may maintain the action, (11 East, 24. 5 East, 45. 2 T. R. 4;) and the jury are not limited in their verdict to the mere loss of service. 11 East, 24. The daughter is a competent witness, (2 Stra. 1064,) and, though not essential, the omission to call her would be open to observation. Holt's Rep. 451. Expenses actually incurred should be proved, and a physician's fee, unless actually paid, cannot be recovered. 1 Starkie R. 287. The state and situation of the family at the time should be proved in aggravation of damages, (3 Esp. R. 119;) and, if so, that the defendant professed to visit the family and was received as the suitor of the daughter. 5 Price, 641. It has been said that evidence to prove that defendant prevailed by a promise of marriage is inadmissible. 3 Camp. 519. Peake L. E. 355. See 5 Price, 641. And no evidence of the daughter's general character for chastity is admissible, unless it is impugned. 1 Camp. 460. 3 Camp. 519. The defendant may, in mitigation of damages, adduce any evidence of the improper, negligent, and imprudent conduct of the plaintiff himself; as where he knew that defendant was a married man, and allowed his visits in the probability of a divorce, lord Kenyon held the action could not be maintained. Peake R. 240. And evidence may be given, on an inquisition of damages in an action for seduction, that the defendant visited at the plaintiff's house for the purpose of paying his addresses to the daughter, with an intention of marriage. 5 Price, 641.— CHITTY.

Gray *v.* Corland, 51 Sickels (N. Y.) 424 (1873). Hudkins *v.* Huskins, 22 W. Va. 645 (1843). Parker *v.* Meak, 3 Sneed (Tenn.) 30 (1855). Ream *v.* Rank, 3 S. & R. (Pa.) 215 (1817). Moran *v.* Dawes, 4 Cowen (N. Y.) 412 (1825). Sergeant *v.* ——, 5 Cowen (N. Y.) 106 (1825). Where a step-daughter leaves the house of her step-father, and is seduced while in the service of a third person, the step-father cannot maintain an action for the seduction, although before the birth of the child she returns to his house, engages in his service, and is there nursed during her confinement. Bartley *v.* Richtmeyer, 4 Comstock (N. Y.) 38 (1850). There is discrepancy between the English and American authorities as to whether it needs to be shown that the person seduced was in the actual employ of the father; the English authorities point to the affirmative, while some respectable American authorities point the other way. The true rule seems to be that if the daughter be a minor, and the plaintiff has a right to *command* her services *at any time*, as if she be in the temporary employment of another, with the parent's assent, the action lies. Bailey's Onus Probandi, 208–9.

all, to provide for their education.(*d*)(92)   If, therefore, before the abolition of these tenures, it was an injury to the father to take away the rest of his children, as well as his heir, (as I am inclined to think it was,) it still remains an injury, and is remediable by writ of *ravishment* or action of *trespass vi et armis, de filio, vel filia, rapto vel abducto;*(*e*)(93) in the same manner as the husband may have it on account of the abduction of his wife.

III.   Of a similar nature to the last is the relation of *guardian* and *ward;* and the like actions *mutatis mutandis,*(94) as are given to fathers, the guardian also has for recovery of damages, when his ward is stolen or ravished away from him.(*f*)(95) And though guardianship in chivalry is now totally abolished, which was the only beneficial kind of guardianship to the guardian, yet the guardian in socage was always(*g*) and is still entitled to an action of *ravishment,* if his ward or pupil be taken from him; but then he must account to his pupil for the damages which he so recovers.(*h*)(96)   And, as a guardian in socage was also entitled at common law to a writ of *right of ward, de custodia terræ et hæredis,*(97) in order to recover the possession and custody of the infant,(*i*) so I apprehend that he is still entitled to sue out this antiquated right.   But a more speedy and summary method of redressing all complaints relative to wards and guardians hath of late obtained by an application to the court of chancery; which is the supreme guardian, and has the superintendent jurisdiction, of all the infants in the kingdom.(98)   And it is expressly provided by statute 12 Car. II. c. 24 that testamentary guardians may maintain an action of ravishment or trespass, for recovery of *any of their wards, and also for damages to be applied to the use   [*142 and benefit of the infants.(*k*)

IV.   To the relation between *master* and *servant,* and the rights accruing therefrom, there are two species of injuries incident.   The one is, retaining a man's hired servant before his time is expired; the other is, beating or confining him in such a manner that he is not able to perform his work.(99)   As to the first, the retaining another person's servant during the time he has agreed to serve his present master; this, as it is an ungentlemanlike, so it is also an illegal, act.(100)   For every master has by his contract purchased for a valuable consideration the service of his domestics for a limited time: the inveigling or hiring his servant, which induces a breach of this contract, is therefore an injury to the master; and for that injury the law has given him a remedy by a special action on the case; and he may also have an action against the servant for the non-performance of his agreement.(*l*)(101)   But, if the new master was not apprised of the former contract, no action lies against *him,*(*m*) unless he refuses to restore the servant, upon demand.(102)

(*d*) Cro. Eliz. 770.
(*e*) F. N. B. 90.
(*f*) F. N. B. 139.
(*g*) Ibid.
(*h*) Hale on F. N. B. 139.

(*i*) F. N. B. 139.
(*k*) 2 P. Wms. 108.
(*l*) F. N. B. 167.
(*m*) Ibid. Winch. 51.

(92) The law seems to be now settled that the father cannot recover damages for the abduction of his children; the uniform language in the cases being, that he can only sustain an action on the case where there has been actually or constructively a loss of service.   Magee *v.* Holland, 3 Dutch. (N. J.) 86 (1858).
(93) [For the ravishment, or the abduction of the son or daughter.]
(94) [Changing with changing circumstances.]
(95) Broom's Parties to Actions, p. 227.
(96) Barber's Parties to Actions (2 ed.) 263.
(97) [For the custody of the land and heir]
(98) Linton *v.* Walker, 8 Fla. 144, 153 (1858).
(99) Woodward *v.* Washburn, 3 Denio (N. Y.) 369, 372 (1846).
(100) Haight *v.* Badgeley, 15 Barb. (N. Y.) 499, 503 (1853).
(101) Broom's Parties to Actions, 226, 227. Barb. Parties to Actions, 294.
(102) Ferguson *v.* Tucker, 2 H. & G. (Md.) 182, 190 (1828). Bailey's Onus Probandi, 208.

The other point of injury is that of beating, confining, or disabling a man's servant, which depends upon the same principle as the last; viz., the property which the master has by his contract acquired in the labor of the servant. In this case, besides the remedy of an action of battery or imprisonment, which the servant himself as an individual may have against the aggressor, the master also, as a recompense for *his* immediate loss, may maintain an action of trespass *vi et armis;* in which he must allege and prove the special damage he has sustained by the beating of his servant, *per quod servitium amisit;*(*n*)(103) and then the jury will make him a proportionable pecuniary satisfaction.(104) A similar practice to which we find also to have obtained among the Athenians; where masters were entitled to an action against such as beat or ill treated their servants.(*o*)(105)

(*n*) 9 Rep. 113. 10 Rep. 330.   (*o*) Pott. Antiq. b. i. c. 26.

(103) [With force and arms.] [By which means he lost his service.]
(104) Even in case of debauching, beating, or injuring a child, the father cannot sue without alleging and proving that he sustained some loss of service, or at least that he was obliged to incur expense in endeavoring to cure his child. 5 East, 45. 6 East, 391. 11 East, 23. Sir T. Raym. 259. And if it appear in evidence that the child was of such tender years as to be incapable of affording any assistance, then he cannot sustain any action. The rules and principles in support of this doctrine were elucidated in the case of Hall *v.* Hollander, decided 14th November, 1825, M. T., and in which the plaintiff declared in trespass for driving a chaise on the highway against plaintiff's son and servant, by means whereof he was thrown down and his skull fractured.
The lord chief-justice was of opinion that the action could not be maintained in this form, inasmuch as the declaration was founded upon the loss of the services of a child who, from his tender years, (being only two years of age,) was incapable of performing any acts of service, and therefore directed a nonsuit; which was confirmed by the court. —CHITTY. Magre *v.* Holland, 3 Dutch. (N. J., 1858). Ames *v.* Railway Co., 117 Mass. 541, 544 (1875).
(105) It appears to be a remarkable omission in the law of England, which with such scrupulous solicitude guards the rights of individuals and secures the morals and good order of the community, that it should have afforded so little protection to female chastity. It is true that it has defended it by the punishment of death, from force and violence, but has left it exposed to perhaps greater danger from the artifices and solicitations of seduction. In no case whatever, unless she has had a promise of marriage, can a woman herself obtain any reparation for the injury she has sustained from the seducer of her virtue. And even where her weakness and credulity have been imposed upon by the most solemn promises of marriage, unless they have been overheard or made in writing, she cannot recover any compensation, being incapable of giving evidence in her own cause. Nor can a parent maintain any action in the temporal courts against the person who has done this wrong to his family, and to his honor and happiness, but by stating and proving that from the consequences of the seduction his daughter is less able to assist him as a servant, or that the seducer, in the pursuit of his daughter, was a trespasser upon his premises. Hence no action can be maintained for the seduction of a daughter, which is not attended with a loss of service or an injury to property. Therefore, in that action for seduction which is in most general use, viz., a *per quod servitium amisit,* [By which he was deprived of service,] the father must prove that his daughter, when seduced, actually assisted in some degree, however inconsiderable, in the housewifery of his family; and that she has been rendered less serviceable to him by her pregnancy; or the action would probably be sustained upon the evidence of a consumption, or any other disorder, contracted by the daughter, in consequence of her seduction, or of her shame and sorrow for the violation of her honor. It is immaterial what is the age of the daughter; but it is necessary that at the time of the seduction she should be living in, or be considered part of, her father's family. 4 Burr. 1878. 3 Wils. 18. It should seem that this action may be brought by a grandfather, brother, uncle, aunt, or any relation under the protection of whom, *in loco parentis* [In place of the parent], a woman resides, especially if the case be such that she can bring no action herself; but the courts would not permit a person to be punished twice by exemplary damages for the same injury. 2 T. R. 4.
Another action for seduction is a common action for trespass, which may be brought when the seducer has illegally entered the father's house; in which action the debauching his daughter may be stated and proved as an aggravation of the trespass. 2 T. R.

*We may observe that in these relative injuries, notice is only   [*143
taken of the wrong done to the superior of the parties related, by the
breach and dissolution of either the relation itself, or at least the advantages
accruing therefrom; while the loss of the inferior by such injuries is totally
unregarded.(106)   One reason for which may be this: that the inferior hath
no kind of property in the company, care, or assistance of the superior, as
the superior is held to have in those of the inferior; and therefore the inferior
can suffer no loss or injury.(107)   The wife cannot recover damages for beating her husband, for she hath no separate interest in any thing during her
coverture.   The child hath no property in his father or guardian, as they
have in him, for the sake of giving him education and nurture.   Yet the wife
or the child, if the husband or parent be slain, have a peculiar species of
criminal prosecution allowed them, in the nature of a civil satisfaction; which
is called an *appeal*,(108) and which will be considered in the next book.
And so the servant, whose master is disabled, does not thereby lose his maintenance or wages.(109)   He had no property in his master; and if he receives
his part of the stipulated contract, he suffers no injury, and is therefore
entitled to no action, for any battery or imprisonment which such master may
happen to endure.''(110)

CHAPTER IX.

OF INJURIES TO PERSONAL PROPERTY.

*IN the preceding chapter we considered the wrongs or injuries   [*144
that affected the rights of persons, either considered as individuals,
or as related to each other; and are at present to enter upon the discussion

---

166.   Or where the seducer carries off the daughter from the father's house, an action
might be brought for enticing away his servant,—though I have never known an instance
of an action of this nature.

In the two last-mentioned actions the seduction may be proved, though it may not
have been followed by the consequences of pregnancy.

These are the only actions which have been extended by the modern ingenuity of the
courts to enable an unhappy parent to recover a recompense, under certain circumstances,
for the injury he has sustained by the seduction of his daughter.—CHRISTIAN.

(106) Barb. Parties to Actions, 263 (2 ed.).   The tendency and aim of the legislation
and judicial decisions in the states of this union, has been toward the abrogation of the
common law unity of husband and wife, and in many of the states it is held that a
married woman may maintain an action for the alienation of the affections of her husband.   Of course the enforcement of this right is still limited to cases where, by statute,
she has been enabled to sue alone, as from the very nature of such cases it is seldom, if
ever, practicable that the husband should join her in the action.   See Postlewaite v. Postlewaite, 1 Ind. App. 473 (1891).   Simmons v. Simmons, 21 Abb. (N. C.) 469.   Jaynes v.
Jaynes, 39 Hun. (N. Y.) 40.   Fort v. Cord, 58 Conn. 1.   Bassett v. Bassett, 20 Ill. App.
543.   Sever v. Adams. (N. H.) 19 Atl. Rep. 776.   Westlake v. Westlake, 34 Ohio, 621.
Mehrhoff v. Mehrhoff, 26 Fed. Rep. 13.   See *contra*.   Duffies v. Duffies, 31 Cent. L. J.
29, and cases there cited.

(107) Adams v. Main, 3 Ind. App. 232, 236 (1891).
(108) Now abolished by stat. 59 Geo. III. c. 46.—CHITTY.
(109) See Browne on Actions of Law, p. 173.
(110) The wife or the child, if the husband or parent were slain, had, indeed, until
lately, a peculiar species of criminal prosecution allowed them, in the nature of a civil
satisfaction, which was called an *appeal*.   See Public Wrongs, vol. 4, c. 27.   Ashford v.
Thornton, 1 B. & A. 405.

This is now abolished, (59 Geo. III. c. 46;) but they can recover damages for the
injury sustained by the death of the husband or parent, under the 9 & 10 Vict. c. 93.—
STEWART.   Broom's Parties to Actions, p. 229.

of such injuries as affect the rights of property, together with the remedies which the law has given to repair or redress them.

And here again we must follow our former division (*a*) of property into personal and real: *personal*, which consists in goods, money, and all other movable chattels, and things thereunto incident; a property which may attend a man's person wherever he goes, and from thence receives its denomination: and *real* property, which consists of such things as are permanent, fixed, and immovable: as lands, tenements, and hereditaments of all kinds, which are not annexed to the person, nor can be moved from the place in which they subsist.

*145]   *First, then, we are to consider the injuries that may be offered to the rights of *personal* property; and, of these, first the rights of personal property in *possession*, and then those that are in *action* only.(*b*)

I. The rights of personal property in *possession* are liable to two species of injuries: the amotion or deprivation of that possession; and the abuse or damage of the chattels while the possession continues in the legal owner. The former, or deprivation of possession, is also divisible into two branches; the unjust and unlawful *taking* them away; and the unjust *detaining* them, though the original taking might be lawful.

1. And first of an unlawful *taking*. The right of property in all external things being solely acquired by occupancy, as has been formerly stated, and preserved and transferred by grants, deeds, and wills, which are a continuation of that occupancy; it follows, as a necessary consequence, that when I have once gained a rightful possession of any goods or chattels, either by a just occupancy or by a legal transfer, whoever either by fraud or force dispossesses me of them, is guilty of a transgression against the law of society, which is a kind of secondary law of nature. For there must be an end of all social commerce between man and man, unless private possessions be secured from unjust invasions: and, if an acquisition of goods by either force or fraud were allowed to be a sufficient title, all property would soon be confined to the most strong, or the most cunning; and the weak and simple-minded part of mankind (which is by far the most numerous division) could never be secure of their possessions.

The wrongful taking of goods being thus most clearly an injury, the next consideration is, what remedy the law of England has given for it. And *146]   this is, in the first place, the restitution of the goods themselves so wrongfully taken, with *damages for the loss sustained by such unjust invasion; which is effected by action of *replevin;* an institution which the Mirror(*c*) ascribes to Glanvil, chief justice to king Henry the Second. This obtains only in one instance of an unlawful taking, that of a wrongful distress:(1) and this and the action of *detinue* (of which I shall

(*a*) See book ii. ch. 2.
(*b*) Book ii. ch. 25.

(*c*) C. 2, § 6.

---

(1) See Leake's Dig. Laws Prop. 9. In Virginia the writ was abolished by statute of Oct., 1823, in all cases except in distress for rent. Vaiden *v.* Bell, 3 Rand. 448, 451 (1826). While the general rule in the United States accords with the law established in England, that replevin, though not confined to cases of distress for rent, only lies where there has been an unlawful taking. Pangburn *v.* Patridge, 7 Johns. 140. Byrd *v.* O'Hanlin, 1 Rep. Con. Ct. 401. Daggett *v.* Robbins, 2 Blackf. 415. Wright *v.* Armstrong, Brun. 130. Rector *v.* Chevelier, 1 Missouri, 345. Yet in some of the states it is allowed, and used as a remedy wherever one man claims goods in the possession of another, and seeks to recover them specifically. Weaver *v.* Lawrence, 1 Dall. 156. Cullum *v.* Bevans, 6 Har. & J. 460.

It is either in the *detinet* or *detinuit* [He detains or has detained]. Where the sheriff delivers the goods to the plaintiff the declaration is in the *detinuit*, and the

presently say more) are almost the only actions in which the actual specific possession of the identical personal chattel is restored to the proper owner.(2) For things personal are looked upon by the law as of a nature so transitory and perishable, that it is for the most part impossible either to ascertain their identity, or to restore them in the same condition as when they came to the hands of the wrongful possessor. And, since it is a maxim that "*lex neminem cogit ad vana seu impossibilia,*"(3) it therefore contents itself in general with restoring, not the thing itself, but a pecuniary equivalent, to the party injured; by giving him a satisfaction in damages. But in the case of a *distress*, the goods are from the first taking in the custody of the law, and not merely in that of the distrainor; and therefore they may not only be identified, but also restored to their first possessor, without any material change in their condition. And, being thus in the custody of the law, the taking them back by force is looked upon as an atrocious injury, and denominated a *rescous*, for which the distrainor has a remedy in damages, either by writ of *rescous*,(d) in case they were going to the pound, or by writ *de parco fracto*, or *pound-breach*,(e) in case they were actually impounded. He may also at his option bring an action on the case for this injury; and shall therein, if the distress were taken for rent, recover treble damages.(f) The term *rescous* is likewise applied to the forcible delivery of a defendant, when arrested, from the officer who is carrying him to prison.(4) In which circumstances the plaintiff has a similar remedy by action on the case, or of *rescous*:(g)(5) or, if the sheriff makes a return of such **rescous*   [*147 to the court out of which the process issued, the rescuer will be punished by attachment.(h)

An action of replevin, the regular way of contesting the validity of the transaction, is founded, I said, upon a distress taken wrongfully and without sufficient cause; being a re-delivery of the pledge,(i) or thing taken in distress, to the owner, upon his giving security to try the right of the distress,

(d) F. N. B. 101.
(e) Ibid. 100.
(f) Stat. 2 W. and M. Sess. 1, c. 5.

(g) 6 Mod. 211.
(h) Cro. Jac. 419. Salk. 586.
(i) See page 13.

plaintiff recovers only damages for the detention. In such case, if the defendant recover, there is a general verdict for the defendant and damages for the detention, on which there is a judgment *pro retorno habendo* [To have the return] and for the damages. Easton *v.* Worthington, 5 Serg. & R. 130. Where the goods are not delivered to the plaintiff, but are allowed to remain in the defendant's possession upon his claim of property and giving a bond for their forthcoming, or where the goods have been eloigned, the declaration is in the *detinet*. The plaintiff recovers the value of the goods in damages; or, if the defendant recovers, it is by a general verdict in his favor. Bower *v.* Tallman, 5 Watts & Serg. 556.—SHARSWOOD.

See also Cummings *v.* Vorce, 3 Hill (N. Y.) 282 (1842). Coursey *v.* Wright, 1 H. & McH. (Md.) 394 (1771). Hall *v.* Tuttle, 2 Wend. 475 (1829). Mansfield's Case, 1 Mollay's Rep. 278 (1828). Harwood *v.* Smethurst, 5 Dutch. (N. J.) 195 (1861). Demand is not necessary before bringing suit. Sharon *v.* Nunan, 63 Cal. 234 (1883). In the code states the old action of replevin is abolished, and the provisional remedy, claim and delivery, is in use. But the name is still in use even in these states. Cobbey on Rep. § 19, p. 13. Williams on Pers. Prop. p. 2, note 1 (4 ed.). Chambers *v.* Hunt, 3 Harrison (N. J.) 339. 357 (1841).

(2) The writ will not lie for the recovery of an undivided interest or share. Low *v.* Martin, 18 Ill. 286, 288 (1857). It will lie for a title deed. Wilson *v.* Rybolt, 17 Ind. 391 (1861). An article of personal ornament cannot be taken on a writ of replevin from the person of the defendant, without his consent, even if worn by him for the sole purpose of keeping it beyond the reach of legal process. Maxham *v.* Day, 16 Gray (Mass.) 213 (1871).

(3) ["The law compels no one to do anything which is useless or impossible."]

(4) See Adams *v.* Woods, 51 Mich. 411, 413 (1854).

(5) The latter action now is seldom brought.

and to restore it if the right be adjudged against him:(*j*) after which the distrainor may keep it till tender made of sufficient amends; but must then re-deliver it to the owner.(*k*) And formerly, when the party distrained upon intended to dispute the right of the distress, he had no other process by the old common law than by a writ of replevin, *replegiari facias;*(*l*)(6) which issued out of chancery, commanding the sheriff to deliver the distress to the owner, and afterwards to do justice in respect of the matter in dispute in his own county-court. But this being a tedious method of proceeding, the beasts or other goods were long detained from the owner, to his great loss and damage.(*m*) For which reason the statute of Marlbridge(*n*) directs that (without suing a writ out of the chancery) the sheriff immediately upon plaint to him made shall proceed to replevy the goods.(7) And, for the greater ease of the parties, it is further provided, by statute 1 P. & M. c. 12, that the sheriff shall make at least four deputies in each county, for the sole purpose of making replevins. Upon application therefore, either to the sheriff or one of his said deputies, security is to be given, in pursuance of the statute of Westm. 2, 13 Edw. I. c. 2: 1. That the party replevying will pursue his action against the distrainor, for which purpose he puts in *plegios de prosequendo,* or pledges to prosecute; and, 2. That if the right be deter-
*148]   mined against him he will return the distress again; for which pur-pose he is also bound to find *plegios de retorno *habendo.*(8) Besides these pledges, the sufficiency of which is discretionary and at the peril of the sheriff, the statute 11 Geo. II. c. 19 requires that the officer granting a replevin on a distress for rent shall take a bond with two sureties in a sum of double the value of the goods distrained, conditioned to prose-cute the suit with effect and without delay, and for the return of the goods; which bond shall be assigned to the avowant or person making cognizance, on request made to the officer; and if forfeited may be sued in the name of the assignee.(9) And certainly, as the end of all distresses is only to compel

---

(*j*) Co. Litt. 145.   (*m*) 2 Inst. 139.
(*k*) 8 Rep. 147.   (*n*) 52 Hen. III. c. 21.
(*l*) F. N. B. 68.

---

(6) [That you cause to be replevied.] See Brown's Actions of Law, p. 449.
(7) Bardwell *v.* Stubbert, 17 Neb. 485, 487 (1885). Coursey *v.* Wright, 1 H. & McH. (Md.) 394, 397 (1771).
(8) [Pledges to have the return.]
(9) But for the greater ease of the parties it is now provided, by stat. 19 & 20 Vict. c. 108, §§ 63-66, that the registrar of the county court of the district in which the distress is taken shall grant replevins. Upon application therefore to the registrar, security is to be given by the replevisor for such an amount as the registrar shall deem sufficient to cover the rent or damage, in respect of which the distress was made and the costs of the action which is to follow, that he will pursue his action against the distrainor either in one of the superior courts of law or in the county court.
If the replevisor elects to sue in a superior court, the bond must be conditioned,—1, that the party replevying shall commence an action of replevin within one week, and prosecute the same with effect and without delay; 2, that, unless judgment be obtained by default, he shall prove *either* that he had good ground for believing, that the *title* to some corporeal or incorporeal hereditament, or to some toll-market, fair, or franchise, was in question, *or* that the rent or damage in respect of which the distress was made exceeded twenty pounds; and, 3, that he shall make a return of the goods, if a return thereof shall be adjudged.
If the replevisor elects to sue in the county court, the bond shall be conditioned,—1, to commence the action within one month and to prosecute the same without delay; and, 2, to make a return of the goods, if a return be ordered.—KERR.
The property turned over to the plaintiff on his bond is generally regarded to be still in the custody of the law. The statutes of the different states are not uniform, but in most of them the property is not subject to sale, and the Supreme Court of the United States held that it is as free from process as if it had been in the hands of an officer, but

the party distrained upon to satisfy the debt or duty owing from him, this end is as well answered by such sufficient sureties as by retaining the very distress, which might frequently occasion great inconvenience to the owner; and that the law never wantonly inflicts.   The sheriff on receiving such security is immediately, by his officers, to cause the chattels taken in distress to be restored into the possession of the party distrained upon; unless the distrainor claims a property in the goods so taken.   For if by this method of distress the distrainor happens to come again into possession of his own property in goods which before he had lost, the law allows him to keep them, without any reference to the manner by which he thus has gained possession, being a kind of personal *remitter*.(o)   If therefore the distrainor claims any such property, the party replevying must sue out a writ *de proprietate probanda*,(10) in which the sheriff is to try, by an inquest, in whom the property previous to the distress subsisted.(p)   And if it be found to be in the distrainor, the sheriff can proceed no further, but must return the claim of property to the court of king's bench or common pleas, to be there further prosecuted, if thought advisable, and there finally determined.(q)

But if no claim of property be put in, or if (upon trial) the sheriff's inquest determines it against the distrainor; then the sheriff is to replevy the goods (making use of even force, *if the distrainor makes resist-   [*149 ance)(r) in case the goods be found within his county.   But if the distress be carried out of the county, or concealed, then the sheriff may return that the goods, or beasts, are *eloigned, elongata*, carried to a distance, to places to him unknown; and thereupon the party replevying shall have a writ of *capias in withernam, in vetito* (or more properly *repetito*) *namio;* a term which signifies a second or reciprocal distress,(s) in lieu of the first which was eloigned.   It is therefore a command to the sheriff to take other goods of the distrainor in lieu of the distress formerly taken, and eloigned, or withheld from the owner.(t)   So that here is now distress against distress: one being taken to answer the other by way of reprisal,(u) and as a punishment for the illegal behavior of the original distrainor.   For which reason goods taken in *withernam* cannot be replevied till the original distress is forthcoming.(v)(11)

But in common cases the goods are delivered back to the party replevying, who is then bound to bring his action of replevin, which may be prosecuted in the county-court, be the distress of what value it may.(w)   But either party may remove it to the superior courts of king's bench or common pleas, by writ of *recordari* or *pone;*(x) the plaintiff at pleasure, the defendant upon reasonable cause;(y) and also, if in the course of proceeding any right of

(o) See page 19.
(p) Finch. L. 316.
(q) Co. Lit. 145.   Finch, L. 450.
(r) 2 Inst. 193.
(s) Smith's Commonw. b. iii. c. 10.   2 Inst. 141. Hickes's *Thesaur.* 164.
(t) F. N. B. 69, 73.
(u) In the old northern languages the word *withernam* is used as equivalent to *reprisals.* Stiernhook, *de jure Sueon. l.* 1, c. 10.
(v) Raym. 475.   The substance of this rule composed the terms of that famous question with which

Sir Thomas More (when a student on his travels) is said to have puzzled a pragmatical professor in the University of Bruges, in Flanders, who gave a universal challenge to dispute with any person in any science; *in omni scibili, et de qualibet ente.*   Upon which Mr. More sent him this question—"*utrum averia caruca, capta in vetito namio, sint irreplegibilia,*" whether beasts of the plough, taken in *withernam,* are incapable of being replevied.   Hoddesd. c. 5.
(w) 2 Inst. 139.
(x) Ibid. 23.
(y) F. N. B. 69, 70.

---

where a defendant in an attachment suit is allowed to replevy, it was held that the other creditors may attach the same property.   Cobbey on Replevin, 373.

(10) [For proving the ownership.]   See Maxham *v.* Day, 16 Gray (Mass.) 213, 215 (1860).   Binn's Justice, p. 80 (10 ed.).   See Brown on Actions of Law, 449-451.

(11) Browne on Actions at Law, 456.   The use of the capias in withernam is not inconsistent with our laws, and it is necessary to give full effect to an action of replevin.   In this country this writ follows the return of elongata [the goods eloigned] of the original writ.   Bennett *v.* Berry, 8 Blackford's (Indiana) 2 (1846).   In New York this writ has been abolished by statute.

freehold comes in question, the sheriff can proceed no further,(z) so that it
is usual to carry it up in the first instance to the courts of West-
*150]   minster hall.(12) *Upon this action brought, and declaration de-
livered, the distrainor, who is now the defendant, makes *avowry;*
that is, he *avows* taking the distress in his own right, or the right of his
wife;(a)(13) and sets forth the reason of it, as for rent-arrere, damage done,
or other cause: or else, if he justifies in another's right as his baliff or servant,
he is said to make *cognizance;* that is, he *acknowledges* the taking, but insists
that such taking was legal, as he acted by the command of one who had a
right to distrain; and on the truth and legal merits of this avowry or cognizance the cause is determined.   If it be determined for the plaintiff; viz., that
the distress was wrongfully taken; he has already got his goods back into his
own possession, and shall keep them, and moreover recover damages.(b)
But if the defendant prevails, by the default or nonsuit of the plaintiff, then
he shall have a writ *de retorno habendo,* whereby the goods or chattels (which
were distrained and then replevied) are returned again into his custody,
to be sold, or otherwise disposed of, as if no replevin hath been made.   And
at the common law, the plaintiff might have brought another replevin, and
so *in infinitum,* to the intolerable vexation of the defendant.   Wherefore
the statute of Westm. 2, c. 2 restrains the plaintiff, when nonsuited, from
suing out any fresh replevin; but allows him a *judicial* writ issuing out of the
original record, and called a writ of *second deliverance,* in order to have the
same distress again delivered to him, on giving the like security as before.
And, if the plaintiff be a second time nonsuit, or if the defendant has judgment upon verdict or demurrer in the first replevin, he shall have a writ of
return irreplevisable; after which no writ of second deliverance shall be
allowed.(c)   But in case of a distress for rent-arrere, the writ of second
deliverance is, in effect,(d) taken away by statute 17 Car. II. c. 7, which
directs that if the plaintiff be nonsuit before issue joined, then upon suggestion
made on the record in nature of an avowry or cognizance; or if judgment be
given against him on demurrer, then, without any such suggestion,
*151]   the defendant may have *a writ to inquire into the value of the dis-
tress by a jury, and shall recover the amount of it in damages, if less
than the arrear of rent; or, if more, then so much as shall be equal to such
arrear, with costs; or, if the nonsuit be after issue joined, or if a verdict be
against the plaintiff, then the jury impanelled to try the cause shall assess
such arrears for the defendant: and if (in any of these cases) the distress be
insufficient to answer the arrears distrained for, the defendant may take a
further distress or distresses.(e)   But otherwise, if pending a replevin for a
former distress, a man distrains again for the same rent or service, then the

(z) Finch, L. 317.
(a) 2 Saund. 195.
(b) F. N. B. 69.

(c) 2 Inst. 340.
(d) 1 Ventr. 64.
(e) Stat. 17 Car. II. c. 7.

(12) Now, however, by stat. 9 & 10 Vict. c. 95, s. 119, all actions of replevin in cases
of distress for rent in arrear or damage-feasant shall be brought without writ in the New
County Court and (s. 120) in the court holden for the district wherein the distress was
taken.   But (s. 121) in case either party declare to the court that the title to any hereditament or to any toll-market, fair, or franchise is in question, or that the rent or damage in
respect of which the distress was taken exceeds 20l., and becomes bound with two sureties
to prosecute the suit without delay and to prove that such title was in dispute, or that
there was ground for believing the rent or damage to exceed 20l., - then the action may
be removed before any court competent to try the same, which is done not by *recordari,*
but by writ of *certiorari,* the new county courts being courts of record, which the schire-
motes were not.— STEWART. See Browne on Actions of Law, 451-453.
(13) Newell Univ. Mill Co. *v.* Muxlon, 115 N. Y. 170, 174 (1889). Kilburn *v.* Lowe, 44
Hun. (N. Y.) 237, 240 (1885).

party is not driven to his action of replevin, but shall have a writ of *recaption*,(*f*) and recover damages for the defendant the re-distrainor's contempt of the process of the law.

In like manner, other remedies for other unlawful takings of a man's goods consist only in recovering a satisfaction in damages. And if a man takes the goods of another out of his actual or virtual possession, without having a lawful title so to do, it is an injury, which though it doth not amount to felony unless it be done *animo furandi*,(14) is nevertheless a transgression for which an action of *trespass vi et armis*(15) will lie; wherein the plaintiff shall not recover the thing itself, but only damages for the loss of it. Or, if committed without force, the party may, at his choice, have another remedy in damages by action of *trover* and *conversion*, of which I shall presently say more.

2. Deprivation of possession may also be an unjust *detainer* of another's goods, though the original *taking* was lawful.(16)(17) As if I distrain another's cattle damage-feasant, and before they are impounded he tenders me sufficient amends; now, though the original taking was lawful, my subsequent detainment of them after tender of amends is wrongful, and he shall have an action of *replevin* against me to recover them:(*g*) in which he shall recover damages only for the *detention* and not *for the *caption*, because   [*152 the original taking was lawful. Or, if I lend a man a horse, and he afterwards refuses to restore it, this injury consists in the detaining and not in the original taking, and the regular method for me to recover possession is by action of *detinue*.(*h*) In this action of *detinue* it is necessary to ascertain the thing detained, in such manner as that it may be specifically known and recovered. Therefore it cannot be brought for money, corn, or the like, for that cannot be known from other money or corn, unless it be in a bag or a sack, for then it may be distinguishably marked.(18) In order therefore to ground an action of detinue, which is only for the *detaining*, these points are necessary:(*i*) 1. That the defendant came lawfully into possession of the goods as either by delivery to him, or finding them; 2. That the plaintiff have a property; 3. That the goods themselves be of some value; and 4. That they be ascertained in point of identity. Upon this the jury, if they find for the plaintiff, assess the respective values of the several parcels detained, and also damages for the detention. And the judgment is conditional;(19) that the plaintiff recover the said goods, or (if they cannot be

(*f*) F. N. B. 71.
(*g*) F. N. B. 69. 3 Red. 147.

(*h*) F. N. B. 138.
(*i*) Co. Litt. 286.

(14) [With the design of stealing them,] Browne on Actions of Law, 453.
(15) [Trespass with force and arms.]
(16) Detinue will lie in all cases where the plaintiff prefers the recovery of the specific article, rather than damages for its conversion. Peirce v. Hill, 9 Porter (Ala.) 151 (1840). Wright v. Ross, 2 Greene (Iowa) 266 (1849). Charles v. Elliott, 4 D. & B. (N. C.) 468 (1839). Collier v. Bickley, 33 Ohio 523 (1878). If the taking has not been wrongful, demand for their return must be made before suit. Adams v. Woods, 5 Mich. 413 (1854). Caldwell v. West, 1 Zab. (N. J.) 411 (1848). Chambers v. Hunt, 3 Harr. (N. J.) 411 (1848).
(17) When the goods are taken by force the plaintiff may waive his right to proceed for the violence and recover the value in trover or *assumpsit*. Cummings v. Vorce, 3 Hill (N. Y.) 282, 286 (1842). And as a general principle the owner of a chattel may take it from any person whose possession is unlawful—unless it is in the custody of the law—or has been taken from him by replevin. Badger v. Phinney, 15 Tyng (Mass.) 359, 362 (1819). Baker v. Fales, 16 Tyng (Mass.) 146, 152 (1819). See further, Osgood v. Green, 30 N. H. 210, 215. Danby v. Edwards, 1 Pike (Ark.) 444 (1839). Wildey v. Doe, 26 Miss. 35, 40 (1853). Angell on Limitations, p. 326 (6 ed.). Com. Dig. Detinue. 1 Chitty on Pl., 4 ed., 110 to 114. Cobbey on Replevin, pp. 10, 12.
(18) Beven on Negligence, p. 919 (2 ed.). Skidmore v. Taylor, 29 Cal. 619 (1866). Sharon v. Nunan, 63 Cal. 235 (1883).
(19) See Charles v. Elliott, 4 D. & B. (N. C.) 469 (1839). McCormick v. Stevenson, 13 Neb. 70, 73 (1882). Slade v. Washburn, 2 Ired. (N. C.) 415 (1842).

had) their respective values, and also the damages for detaining them.(*j*) But there is one disadvantage which attends this action, viz., that the defendant is herein permitted to wage his law, that is, to exculpate himself by oath,(*k*) and thereby defeat the plaintiff of his remedy: which privilege is grounded on the confidence originally reposed in the bailee by the bailor, in the borrower by the lender, and the like; from whence arose a strong presumptive evidence that in the plaintiff's own opinion the defendant was worthy of credit. But, for this reason, the action itself is of late much disused, and has given place to the action of trover.(20)

This action of *trover* and *conversion* was in its original an action of trespass upon the case, for the recovery of damages against such person as had *found* another's goods and refused to deliver them on demand, but *converted* *153] them to his own *use; from which finding and converting it is called an action of *trover* and *conversion*. The freedom of this action from wager of law,(21) and the less degree of certainty requisite in describing the goods,(*l*) gave it so considerable an advantage over the action of *detinue*, that by a fiction of law actions of *trover* were at length permitted to be brought against any man who had in his possession by any means whatsoever the personal goods of another, and sold them or used them without the consent of the owner, or refused to deliver them when demanded. The injury lies in the conversion; for any man may take the goods of another into possession, if he finds them; but no finder is allowed to acquire a property therein, unless the owner be forever unknown:(*m*) and therefore he must not convert them to his own use, which the law presumes him to do if he refuses them to the owner: for which reason such refusal also is, *prima facie*, sufficient evidence of a conversion.(*n*)(22) The fact of the finding or *trover* is therefore now totally immaterial; for the plaintiff needs only to suggest (as words of form) that he lost such goods, and that the defendant found them; and if he proves that the goods are *his* property and that the defendant had them in his possession, it is sufficient. But a conversion must be fully proved; and then in this action the plaintiff shall recover damages, equal to the value of the thing converted, but not the thing itself; which nothing will recover but an action of *detinue* or *replevin*.

(*j*) Co. Entr. 170. Cro. Jac. 681.
(*k*) Co. Litt. 295.
(*l*) Salk. 654.

(*m*) See book i. ch. 8; book ii. ch. 1 and 26.
(*n*) 10 Rep. 56.

(20) Formerly the defendant in an action of detinue always had it in his power to retain the chattels upon payment of the value as assessed by the jury. The remedy at law was in this respect incomplete, and it became usual to apply to the court of chancery, which from a very early period interfered to compel the return of the chattels themselves. This jurisdiction seems originally to have been confined in its exercise to cases where the chattels were of peculiar value to the owner, as, for instance, heirlooms, jewelry, articles of curiosity or antiquity, family pictures, etc. But latterly it has been decided that the right to be protected in the use or beneficial enjoyment of property in *specie* is not confined to articles possessing any peculiar or intrinsic value. The damages recovered in an action, although equal to the intrinsic value of the article detained, may be infinitely less than that at which it is estimated by the owner, so that damages may not be any thing like adequate compensation to him for the loss. And accordingly the courts of common law have now (by a peculiar process of execution) the same powers as the court of chancery to compel the return of the chattel itself. Com. Law Proc. Act, 1854, s. 79. *Regulæ Generales*, Michaelmas Vacation, 1854.—KERR.

This action can be maintained only when the plaintiff has been in possession of the goods, or has such a property in them as draws to it the right of possession. Williams on Pers. Prop. p. 24 (4 ed.). Webb's Pollock on Torts, enlg'd Am. ed. p. 426. A levy upon property under a void writ of attachment, is such a tortious taking as will support trover. Jones *v.* Buzzard. 2 Pike (Ark.) 415, 445 (1839.)

(21) Wager of law was abolished by stat. 3 & 4 W. IV. c. 42, § 13.—STEWART.
(22) See Angell on Lim. p. 323 (6 ed.).

As to the damage that may be offered to things personal while in the possession of the owner, as hunting a man's deer, shooting his dogs, poisoning his cattle, or in any wise taking from the value of any of his chattels or making them in a worse condition than before, these are injuries too obvious to need explication. I have only therefore to mention the remedies given by the law to redress them, which are in two shapes; by action of *trespass vi et armis*,(23) where the act is in itself *immediately* *injurious [*154 to another's property, and therefore necessarily accompanied with some degree of force; and by special action *on the case*, where the act is in itself indifferent, and the injury only *consequential*, and therefore arising without any breach of the peace. In both of which suits the plaintiff shall recover damages, in proportion to the injury which he proves that his property has sustained. And it is not material whether the damage be done by the defendant himself, or his servants by his direction; for the action will lie against the master as well as the servant.(o) And, if a man keeps a dog or other brute animal, used to do mischief, as by worrying sheep, or the like, the owner must answer for the consequences, if he knows of such evil habit.(p)(24)

II. Hitherto of injuries affecting the right of things personal in *possession*. We are next to consider those which regard things in *action* only: or such rights as are founded on, and arise from, *contracts;* the nature and several divisions of which were explained in the preceding volume.(q) The violation, or non-performance, of these contracts might be extended into as great a variety of wrongs, as the rights which we then considered: but I shall now consider them in a more comprehensive view, by here making only a twofold division of contracts; viz., contracts *express*, and contracts *implied;* and pointing out the injuries that arise from the violation of each, with their respective remedies.

Express contracts include three distinct species; debts, covenants, and promises.

1. The legal acceptation of *debt* is, a sum of money due by certain and express agreement: as, by a bond for a determinate sum; a bill or note; a special bargain; or a rent reserved on a lease; where the quantity is fixed and specific, and does not depend upon any subsequent valuation to settle it.(25)

(o) Noy's Max. c. 44.
(p) Cro. Car. 254, 487.

(q) See book ii. ch. 30.

---

(23) [Trespass by force and arms.]

(24) As to what is evidence of knowledge see 4 Camp. 198. 2 Stra. 1264. 2 Esp. 482. But the owner is not answerable for the first mischief done by a dog, a bull, or other tame animal. Bull. N. P. 77. 12 Mod. 333. Ld. Raym. 608. Yet if he should carry his dog into a field where he himself is a trespasser, and the dog should kill sheep, this, though the first offence, might be stated and proved as an aggravation of the trespass. Burr. 2092. 2 Lev. 172. But where a fierce and vicious dog is kept chained for the defence of the premises, and any one incautiously, or not knowing of it, should go so near as to be injured by it, no action can be maintained by the person injured, though he was seeking the owner, with whom he had business. Bates v. Crosbie, M. T. 1798, in the King's Bench. If a man sets traps in his own grounds, but baited with such strong-scented articles as allure the neighboring dogs from the premises of the owners or from the highways, the owner of a dog injured may maintain an action upon the case. 9 East, 227; but see Ilot v. Wilkes, 3 Bar. & Ald. 304.—CHITTY. And see Hewes v. McNamara, 106 Mass. 281 (1874). Durden v. Barnett, 7 Ala. 169 (1844), and Keitlinger v. Egan, 65 Ill. 235 (1872).

(25) The word debt has a broader meaning than is here given. Properly it is used to denote all that is due a man, under any form of obligation or promise,—whether it be a lien upon an estate; or secured by pledge, pawn, or mortgage, or without security. Schouler's Pers. Prop. vol. 1, § 59, p. 64. § 354, p. 417. Debt will lie on a decree of a court of a sister state, if it be for a gross sum, and no acts are to be performed by the

*155]   The non-payment of these is an injury, for which the proper remedy *is by action of *debt*,(r) to compel the performance of the contract and recover the specific sum due.(s)   This is the shortest and surest remedy; particularly where the debt arises upon a specialty, that is, upon a deed or instrument under seal.   So also, if I verbally agree to pay a man a certain price for a certain parcel of goods, and fail in the performance, an action of debt lies against me; for this is also a *determinate* contract: but if I agree for no settled price I am not liable to an action of debt, but a special action on the case, according to the nature of my contract. And indeed actions of debt are now seldom brought but upon special contracts under seal; wherein the sum due is clearly and precisely expressed: for, in case of such an action upon a simple contract, the plaintiff labors under two difficulties.   First, the defendant has here the same advantage as in action of *detinue*, that of waging his law, or purging himself of the debt by oath, if he thinks proper.(t)   Secondly in an action of debt the plaintiff must prove the whole debt he claims, or recover nothing at all.   For the debt is one single cause of action, fixed and determined; and which therefore, if the proof varies from the claim, cannot be looked upon as the same contract whereof the performance is sued for.   If therefore I bring an action of debt for 30l., I am not at liberty to prove a debt of 20l. and recover a verdict thereon:(u) any more than if I bring an action of *detinue* for a horse I can thereby recover an ox.   For I fail in the proof of that contract, which my action or complaint has alleged to be specific, express, and determinate.(26)   But in an action on the case, on what is called an *indebitatus assumpsit*,(27) which is not brought to compel a specific performance of the contract, but to recover damages for its non-performance, the implied *assumpsit*, and consequently the damages for the breach of it, are in their nature indeterminate; and will therefore adapt and proportion themselves to the truth of the case which shall be proved, without being confined *156] to the precise demand stated in the declaration.   *For if *any* debt be proved, however less than the sum demanded, the law will raise a promise *pro tanto*,(28) and the damages will of course be proportioned to the actual debt.   So that I may declare that the defendant, *being indebted to*

(r) F. N. B. 119.
(s) See Appendix, No. III. § 1.
(t) 4 Rep. 94.

(u) Bro. *Ley gager*, 93. Dyer, 219. 2 Roll. Abr. 706. 1 Show. 215.

plaintiff—if payment is to be made to several persons, the action may be joint. Post v. Neafil, 3 Caines (N. Y.) 22 (1805). The omission to pay a liquidated sum causes it to become fixed and determinate. Barrett v. Twombly, 23 Me. 329 (1843). Liability is not always a debt, but it is a duty which the law will compel to be performed. Choate v. Quinchett, 12 Heiskell (Tenn.) 427 (1873). State v. Becht, 23 Minn. 1 (1876). Immature liabilities of a stockholder of a corporation are debts. Leggett v. Bank, 10 Sm. Ap. (N. Y.) 283 (1862), and if the liability be for unliquidated damages it relates to the time of its origin and not to the time of its liquidation. Carver v. Braintree Mfg. Co., 5 Fed. Cases, 235 (1843). See also Hall v. Hall, 3 Call (Va.) 421 (1803). Schouler's Pers. Prop. vol. 1, p. 319. Dunlop v. Silver, 1 Cranch. (U. S.) 27 (1801). Respub. v. Lecaze, 1 Yeates (Pa.) 55 (1791). Thompson's Heirs v. Thompson's Devisees, 16 Yerg. (Tenn.) 97, 102 (1826). Spellman v. Parkersburg, 35 W. Va. 614 (1891). Gardner v. Clark, 1 Murphy (N. C.) 283, 286 (1809). In Missouri it has been decided that a bank, incorporated under the law of that state, might consider each bank bill a separate and distinct demand. Boatman's Saving Ins. v. Bank of the State, 33 Mo. 497, 518 (1863).

(26) This is no longer the case; for it is now completely settled that the plaintiff in an action of debt may prove and recover less than the sum demanded in the writ. See Bla. R. 1221. 1 Hen. Bla. 249. 11 East. 62. - ARCHBOLD.

The judgment being final in the first instance (suing a writ of injury and wager of law having become almost obsolete) renders debt on simple contract, as well as specialty, a favorite form of action, and it is of daily occurrence.—CHITTY.

(27) [Being indebted, he undertook.]

(28) [For so much.] See Lewis v. Long, 3 Munf. (Va.) 136, 157 (1816).

me in 30*l.*, *undertook* or promised to pay it, but failed; and lay my damages arising from such failure at what sum I please: and the jury will, according to the nature of my proof, allow me either the whole in damages, or any inferior sum. And, even in actions of *debt*, where the contract is proved or admitted, if the defendant can show that he has discharged any part of it, the plaintiff shall recover the residue. (*v*)

The form of the writ of *debt* is sometimes in the *debet* and *detinet*, and sometimes in the *detinet* only: that is, the writ states, either that the defendant *owes* and unjustly *detains* the debt or thing in question, or only that he unjustly *detains* it. It is brought in the *debet* as well as *detinet*, when sued by one of the original contracting parties who personally gave the credit, against the other who personally incurred the debt, or against his heirs, if they are bound to the payment; as by the obligee against the obligor, the landlord against the tenant, etc. But, if it be brought by or against an executor for a debt due to or from the testator, this, not being his own debt, shall be sued for in the *detinet* only. (*w*) So also if the action be for goods, or corn, or a horse, the writ shall be in the *detinet* only; for nothing but a sum of money, for which I (or my ancestors in my name) have personally contracted, is properly considered as my *debt*. And indeed a writ of *debt* in the *detinet* only for goods and chattels, is neither more nor less than a mere writ of *detinue;* and is followed by the very same judgment. (*x*)

2. A covenant also, contained in a deed, to do a direct act or to omit one, is another species of express contract, the violation or breach of which is a civil injury. As if a man covenants to be at York by such a day, or not to exercise a trade in a particular place, and is not at York at the time appointed, or *carries on his trade in the place forbidden, these are [*157 direct breaches of his covenant; and may be perhaps greatly to the disadvantage and loss of the covenantee. (29) The remedy for this is by a writ of *covenant:* (*y*) which directs the sheriff to command the defendant generally to keep his covenant with the plaintiff, (without specifying the nature of the covenant,) or show good cause to the contrary: and if he continues refractory, or the covenant is already so broken that it cannot now be specifically performed, then the subsequent proceedings set forth with precision the covenant, the breach, and the loss which has happened thereby; whereupon the jury will give damages in proportion to the injury sustained

---

(*v*) 1 Roll. Rep. 257. Salk. 664.
(*w*) F. N. B. 119.

(*x*) Rast. Entr. 174.
(*y*) F. N. B. 145.

---

(29) Pollard *v.* Shaffer, 1 Dall. (Pa.) 232 (1787). By an express covenant a man is bound to perform what he covenants at all events. Thus, where in a lease there is an express unqualified covenant on the part of the tenant to pay rent, he is obliged to pay it during the term, although the house be burned down and he do not enjoy the use of it. Shudbrick *v.* Salmond, 3 Burr. 1637. Belfour *v.* Weston, 1 T. R. 310. This is certainly a great hardship to lessees where they are not by the provisions of their lease obliged to rebuild; and in such cases we accordingly find that recourse has been had to a court of equity to obtain an injunction against the lessor proceeding at law for the recovery of the rent,—which has generally been granted, on condition of the lessee's surrendering the lease. Cambden *v.* Morton, in Canc. E. 4 Geo. III. MS. Selw. N. P. 472. Brown *v.* Quilter, Ambl. 619.

The covenantor is also answerable for even the act of God, as damage by lightning, etc., if he have not excepted it in his covenant. Brecknock and Abergavenny Canal Navigation *v.* Pritchard, 6 T. R. 750.

It may not be unnecessary to point out a distinction between covenants in general and those secured by a penalty or forfeiture. In the latter case the obligee has his election either to bring an action of debt for the penalty, or to proceed upon the covenant and recover in damages more or less than the penalty *toties quoties*, [As often as;] but he cannot have recourse to both. Lowe *v.* Peers, 4 Burr. 2228. See, further, on covenants, in Harg. & Butler's Notes on Co. Litt.—ARCHBOLD.

by the plaintiff, and occasioned by such breach of the defendant's contract.(30)

There is one species of covenant of a different nature from the rest; and that is a covenant *real*,(31) to convey or dispose of lands, which seems to be partly of a personal and partly of a real nature.(*z*) For this the remedy is by a special writ of covenant, for a specific performance of the contract concerning certain lands particularly described in the writ. It therefore directs the sheriff to command the defendant, here called the deforciant, to keep the covenant made between the plaintiff and him concerning the identical lands in question: and upon this process it is that fines of land are usually levied at common law,(*a*) the plaintiff, or person to whom the fine is levied, bringing a writ of covenant, in which he suggests some agreement to have been made between him and the deforciant, touching those particular lands, for the completion of which he brings this action. And, for the end of this supposed difference, the fine or *finalis concordia*(32) is made, whereby the deforciant (now called the cognizor) acknowledges the tenements to be the right of the plaintiff, now called the cognizee. And moreover, as leases for years were formerly considered only as contracts(*b*) or covenants for the enjoyment of the rents and profits, and not as the conveyance of any real interest in the land, *the ancient remedy for the lessee, if ejected, was by a writ of covenant against the lessor to recover the term (if in being) and damages, in case the ouster was committed by the lessor himself: or if the term was expired, or the ouster was committed by a stranger claiming by an elder title, then to recover damages only.(*c*)

*158]

No person could at common law take advantage of any covenant or condition, except such as were parties or privies thereto; and, of course, no grantee or assignee of any reversion or rent. To remedy which, and more effectually to secure to the king's grantees the spoils of the monasteries then newly dissolved, the statute 32 Hen. VIII. c. 34 gives the assignee of a reversion (after notice of such assignment)(*d*) the same remedies against the particular tenant, by entry or action, for waste or other forfeitures, non-payment of rent, and non-performance of conditions, covenants, and agreements, as the assignor himself might have had; and makes him equally liable, on the other hand, for acts agreed to be performed by the assignor, except in the case of warranty.

3. A promise is in the nature of a verbal covenant, and wants nothing but the solemnity of writing and sealing to make it absolutely the same. If therefore it be to do any explicit act, it is an express contract, as much as any covenant; and the breach of it is an equal injury.(33) The remedy indeed is not exactly the same: since, instead of an action of covenant, there only lies an action upon the case for what is called the *assumpsit* or undertaking of the defendant; the failure of performing which is the wrong or injury done to the plaintiff, the damages whereof a jury are to estimate and settle. As if a builder promises, undertakes, or assumes to Caius that he will build and cover his house within a time limited, and fails to do it; Caius

(*z*) Hob. on F. N. B. 146.
(*a*) See book ii. ch. 21.
(*b*) See book ii. ch. 9.

(*c*) Bro. Abr. tit. *covenant*, 33.   F. N. B. 476.
(*d*) Co. Litt. 215.   Moor. 876.   Cro. Jac. 145.

(30) Stout *v*. Jackson, 2 Rand. (Va.) 132, 161 (1823).

(31) The stat. 3 & 4 W. IV. c. 27, § 36, abolished the writ of covenant real, together with nearly all other real actions. See Hare on Cont. p. 92.

(32) [Final agreement.]

(33) If one voluntarily and without consideration becomes the agent of another, and does not perform the act agreed upon, he will not be liable to his principal; but if he performs part of the agreement, and neglects to complete it, then he will be liable for misfeasance. Story on Agency, 589 (9 ed.).

has an action on the case against the builder, for this breach of his express promise, undertaking, or *assumpsit;* and shall recover a pecuniary satisfaction for the injury sustained by such delay.(34)   So also in the case before mentioned, of *a debt by simple contract, if the debtor prom-   [*159 ises to pay it and does not, this breach of promise entitles the creditor to his action on the case, instead of being driven to an action of debt.(*e*) Thus, likewise, a promissory note, or note of hand not under seal, to pay money at a day certain, is an express *assumpsit;* and the payee at common law, or by custom and act of parliament the endorsee,(*f*) may recover the value of the note in damages, if it remains unpaid.   Some agreements indeed, though never so expressly made, are deemed of so important a nature that they ought not to rest in verbal promise only, which cannot be proved but by the memory (which sometimes will induce the perjury) of witnesses.   To prevent which, the statute of frauds and perjuries, 29 Car. II. c. 3, enacts, that in the five following cases no verbal promise shall be sufficient to ground an action upon, but at the least some note or *memorandum* of it shall be made in writing, and signed by the party to be charged therewith: 1. Where an executor or administrator promises to answer damages out of his own estate. 2. Where a man undertakes to answer for the debt, default, or miscarriage of another.   3. Where any agreement is made upon consideration of marriage.   4. Where any contract or sale is made of lands, tenements, or hereditaments, or any interest therein.   5. And lastly, where there is any agreement that is not to be performed within a year from the making thereof. In all these cases a mere verbal *assumpsit* is void.(35)

(*e*) 4 Rep. 99.   (*f*) See book ii. ch. 30.

---

(34) It is worthy of remark that the learned commentator has not either named, described, or even alluded to the consideration requisite to support an assumpsit; and, what is more remarkable, the example put by him in the text in order to illustrate the nature of the action is, in the terms in which it is there stated, a case of *nudum pactum* [Barren contract].   (See 1 Roll. Abr. 9, 1, 41. Doct. & Stud. ii. ch. 24, and 5 T. R. 143 that the action will not lie for a mere non-feasance unless the promise is founded on a consideration.)   This remark ought not—neither was it intended—to derogate from the merit of a justly-celebrated writer, who for comprehensive design, luminous arrangement, and elegance of diction is unrivalled.   Selw. N. P. 45.—CHITTY.

(35) These provisions in the statute have produced many decisions, both in the courts of law and equity.   See 3 Chitty's Com. L. *per tot.*   It is now settled that if two persons go to a shop, and one order goods, and the other say, "If he does not pay, I will," or, "I will see you paid," he is not bound unless his engagement is reduced into writing.   In all such cases the question is who is the buyer, or to whom the credit is given, and who is the surety; and that question, from all the circumstances, must be ascertained by the jury; for if the person for whose use the goods are furnished be liable at all, any promise by a third person to discharge the debt must be in writing, otherwise it is void.   2 T. R. 80.   1 H. Bl. Rep. 120.   1 Bos. & Pul. 158.   Mutual promises to marry need not be in writing: the statute relates only to agreements made in consideration of the marriage. A lease not exceeding three years from the making thereof, and in which the rent reserved amounts to two-thirds of the improved value, is good without writing; but all other parol leases or agreements for any interest in lands have the effect of estates at will only.   Bull. N. P. 279.   All declarations of trusts, except such as result by implication of law, must be made in writing.   29 Car. II. c. 3, ss. 7, 8.   If a promise depends upon a contingency which may or may not fall within a year, it is not within the statute, as a promise to pay a sum of money upon a death or marriage, or upon the return of a ship, or to leave a legacy by will, is good by parol; for such a promise may by possibility be performed within the year.   3 Burr. 1278.   1 Salk. 280.   3 Salk. 9, etc.   Partial performance within the year, where the original understanding is that the whole is to extend to a longer period, does not take the case out of the statute.   11 East, 142.   But even a written undertaking to pay the debt of another is void, unless a good consideration appears in the writing; and the consideration, if any, cannot be proved by parol evidence.   5 East, 10. If a growing crop is purchased without writing, the agreement, before part execution, may be put an end to by parol notice.   6 East, 602.   But a court of equity will decree a specific performance of a verbal contract when it is confessed by a defendant in his answer, or when there has been a part performance of it, as by payment of part of the

From these *express* contracts the transition is easy to those that are only *implied* by law; which are such as reason and justice dictate, and which therefore the law presumes that every man has contracted to perform, and upon this presumption makes him answerable to such persons as suffer by his non-performance. (36)

Of this nature are, first, such as are necessarily implied by the fundamental constitution of government, to which every man is a contracting party.

*160]   And thus it is that every person *is bound and hath virtually agreed to pay such particular sums of money as are charged on him by the sentence, or assessed by the interpretation, of the law. For it is a part of the original contract, entered into by all mankind who partake the benefits of society, to submit in all points to the municipal constitutions and local ordinances of that state of which each individual is a member. Whatever therefore the laws order any one to pay, that becomes instantly a debt, which he hath beforehand contracted to discharge. (37) And this implied agreement it is that gives the plaintiff a right to institute a second action, founded merely on the general contract, in order to recover such damages, or sum of money, as are assessed by the jury and adjudged by the court to be due from the defendant to the plaintiff in any former action. So that if he hath once obtained a judgment against another for a certain sum, and neglects to take out execution thereupon, he may afterwards bring an action of debt upon this judgment, (g) and shall not be put upon the proof of the original cause of action; but upon showing the judgment once obtained still in full force and yet unsatisfied, the law immediately implies, that by the original contract of society the defendant hath contracted a debt, and is bound to pay it. (38)

(g) Roll. Abr. 600, 601.

---

consideration-money, or by entering and expending money upon the estate; for such acts preclude the party from denying the existence of the contract, and prove that there can be no fraud or perjury in obtaining the execution of it. 3 Ves. Jr. 39, 378, 712. But lord Eldon seems to think that a specific performance cannot be decreed if the defendant in his answer admits a parol agreement, and at the same time insists upon the benefit of the statute. 6 Ves Jr. 37. If one party only signs an agreement, he is bound by it; and if an agreement is by parol, but it is agreed it shall be reduced into writing, and this is prevented by the fraud of one of the parties, performance of it will be decreed. 2 Bro. 564, 565, 566. See 3 Woodd. Lect. lvii. and Fonblanque Tr. of Eq. b. i. c. 3, ss. 8, 9, where this subject is fully and learnedly discussed.—CHITTY.

(36) Brackett v. Norton, 4 Day (Conn.) 517, 524 (1823).

(37) Bowen v. Hoxie, 137 Mass. 527, 531 (1884). Dryden v. Kellogg, 2 Berry (Mo.) 87, 94 (1876). King v. Nottingham O. W. Works, 6 A. & E. 363 (1839). We do not subscribe to this doctrine. It was a convenient fiction in the beginning, and can never arise to the dignity of reality. The authorities are overwhelmingly in favor of the conclusion, that taxes are not debts in the sense that they are liabilities arising out of contracts express or implied, and in the true sense are not debts at all, but are the enforced proportional contribution of each citizen and his estate, levied by authority of the state, for all public needs; that they owe their existence to the action of the legislative power, and do not depend for their validity and enforcement upon the individual assent of the taxpayer, but operate *in invitum* [Unwillingly]. Per Leonard, J., in Nevada v. Y. J. S. M. Co., citing Cooley on Tax. 13. Bliss on Code Pleading. 128. Johnson v. Howard, 41 Vermont, 125. 26 id. 486. City of Augusta v. North, 57 Me. 394. Green v. Gruber, 26 La. An. 697. Loan Ass'n v. Topeka, 20 Wall. 664. Peirce v. City of Boston, 3 Met. 420, and other authorities. See also U. S. v. Mundel, 6 Call. (Va.) 1795. City v. R. R. Co., 39 Iowa, 56 (1874). Town of Decorah v. Dunston, 34 Iowa, 360 (1872). Denison v. Williams, 4 Conn. 402 (1822). State v. Delain, 8 Wis. 259 (1891). Boswell v. Robinson, 4 Vroom (N. J.) 273. Joseph v. Bank, 46 Ind. 59. Brunswick v. Windsor, 3 Hal. (N. J.) 64 (1824). Chitty on Cont. c. 3, § 1, p. 57 (12 ed.).

(38) Action may be maintained upon a judgment, although it is in full force and effect, and the time within which an execution might issue has not expired. Hummer v. Lamphear, 32 Kan. 441 (1884). Linton v. Hurley, 114 Mass. 76. But the institution of such an action, as it is incompatible with, and cannot be prosecuted at the same time, and

This method seems to have been invented when *real* actions were more in use than at present, and damages were permitted to be recovered thereon; in order to have the benefit of a writ of *capias* to take the defendant's body in execution for those damages, which process was allowable in an action of debt, (in consequence of the statute 25 Edw. III. c. 17,) but not in an action real. Wherefore, since the disuse of those real actions, actions of debt upon judgment in personal suits have been pretty much discountenanced by the courts, as being generally vexatious and oppressive, by harassing the defendant with the costs of two actions instead of one.

On the same principle it is (of an implied original contract to submit to the rules of the community whereof we are members) *that a [*161 forfeiture imposed by the by-laws and private ordinances of a corporation upon any that belong to the body, or an amercement set in a court-leet or court-baron upon any of the suitors to the court, (for otherwise it will not be binding,)(*h*) immediately creates a debt in the eye of the law; and such forfeiture or amercement, if unpaid, works an injury to the party or parties entitled to receive it: for which the remedy is by action of debt.(*i*)

The same reason may with equal justice be applied to all penal statutes, that is, such acts of parliament whereby a forfeiture is inflicted for transgressing the provisions therein enacted. The party offending is here bound by the fundamental contract of society to obey the directions of the legislature, and pay the forfeiture incurred to such persons as the law requires.(39) The usual application of this forfeiture is either to the party aggrieved, or else to any of the king's subjects in general. Of the former sort is the forfeiture inflicted by the statute of Winchester(*k*) (explained and enforced by several subsequent statutes)(*l*) upon the hundred wherein a man is robbed, which is meant to oblige the hundredors to make hue and cry after the felon; for if they take him they stand excused. But otherwise the party robbed is entitled to prosecute them by a special action on the case, for damages equivalent to his loss. And of the same nature is the action given by statute 9 Geo. I. c. 22, commonly called the black act, against the inhabitants of any hundred, in order to make satisfaction in damages to all persons who have suffered by the offences enumerated and made felony by that act. But more usually these forfeitures created by statute are given at large to any common informer;(40) or, in other words, to any such person or persons as will sue for the same: and hence such actions are called *popular* actions, because they are given to the people in general.(*m*) Sometimes one part is given to the

(*h*) Law of Nisi Prius, 155.
(*i*) 5 Rep. 61. Hob. 279.
(*k*) 13 Edw. I. c. 1.

(*l*) 27 Eliz. c. 13. 29 Car. II. c. 7. 8 Geo. II. c. 16. 22 Geo. II. c. 24.
(*m*) See book ii. ch. 29.

---

together with an execution upon the judgment, amounts to a waiver of the lien arising from the right to issue execution; or an admission that no such lien then exists. Coombs *v.* Jordan, 3 Bland's Ch. (Md.) 284, 327 (1831). Carver *v.* Braintree M. Co., 5 Fed. Cases, 235, 240 (1894). See further on this subject, Denison *v.* Williams, 4 Conn. 402 (1822). Lightfoot's Adm'r *v.* Polgrann's Adm'r, 13 S. & R. (Pa.) 400. McKim *v.* Odom, 12 Fairf. (Me.) 94 (1835). Lockwood *v.* Barefield, 7 Ga. 393 (1847). The effect of the evidence is not qualified by the fact that the court rendering the judgment is not a court of record. Hence transcript of judgment, in the court of justice of the peace, is in the nature of a specialty, and entitled to the same credit in a sister state as within the state in which the judgment was rendered. Stockwell *v.* Coleman, 10 Critchf. (Ohio) 33, 37 (1859).

(39) Payne *v.* The People, 6 Johns. (N. Y.) 101, 103 (1810). Robertson *v.* Kettrell, 64 N. H. 430 (1887). W. U. T. Co. *v.* Bright, 90 Va. 778, 780 (1894). An insolvent debtor's right of action for recovery of a penalty for usury, passes by assignment of his estate, and his assignee may maintain a bill in equity to recover it. Gray *v.* Bennettt, 3 Metc. (Mass.) 522, 526 (1842).

(40) In the popular action for penalty given by the statute, the one bringing suit first attaches a right in himself which no other common informer, by subsequent suit, can divest. Dozier *v.* Williams *et al.*, 47 Mississippi 605 (1873).

king, to the poor, or to some public use, and the other part to the
*162]   *informer or prosecutor: and then the suit is called a *qui tam* action,
because it is brought by a person "*qui tam pro domino rege, etc., quam
pro se ipso in hac parte sequitur.*"(41)   If the king therefore himself commences this suit, he shall have the whole forfeiture.(n)   But if any one hath
begun a *qui tam*, or *popular* action, no other person can pursue it: and the
verdict passed upon the defendant in the first suit is a bar to all others, and
conclusive even to the king himself.   This has frequently occasioned offenders
to procure their own friends to begin a suit, in order to forestall and prevent
other actions: which practice is in some measure prevented by a statute made
in the reign of a very sharp-sighted prince in penal laws, 4 Hen. VII. c. 20,
which enacts that no recovery, otherwise than by verdict, obtained by collusion in an action popular, shall be a bar to any other action prosecuted *bona
fide*.   A provision that seems borrowed from the rule of the Roman law, that
if a person was acquitted of any accusation merely by the prevarication of the
accuser, a new prosecution might be commenced against him.(o)

A second class of implied contracts are such as do not arise from the
express determination of any court, or the positive direction of any statute;
but from natural reason, and the just construction of law.   Which class
extends to all presumptive undertakings or *assumpsits;* which though never
perhaps actually made, yet constantly arise from the general implication and
intendment of the courts of judicature, that every man hath engaged to perform what his duty or justice requires.   Thus,(42)

1. If I employ a person to transact any business for me, or perform any
work, the law implies that I undertook or assumed to pay him so much as
his labor deserved.   And if I neglect to make him amends, he has a remedy
for this injury by bringing his action on the case upon this implied *assumpsit;*
wherein he is at liberty to suggest that I promised to pay him as
*163]   *much as he reasonably deserved, and then to aver that his trouble
was really worth such a particular sum, which the defendant has
omitted to pay. But this valuation of his trouble is submitted to the determination of a jury; who will assess such a sum in damages as they think he
really merited.   This is called an *assumpsit* on a *quantum meruit*.(43)

2. There is also an implied *assumpsit* on a *quantum valebat*,(44) which is
very similar to the former, being only where one takes up goods or wares of a
tradesman, without expressly agreeing for the price.   There the law concludes, that both parties did intentionally agree that the real value of the
goods should be paid; and an action on the case may be brought accordingly,
if the vendee refuses to pay that value.

3. A third species of implied *assumpsits* is when one has had and received
money belonging to another, without any valuable consideration given on
the receiver's part; for the law construes this to be money had and received
for the use of the owner only; and implies that the person so receiving promised, and undertook, to account for it to the true proprietor.   And, if he
unjustly detains it, an action on the case lies against him for the breach of
such implied promise and undertaking; and he will be made to repay the

---

(n) 2 Hawk. P. C. 268.   (o) Ff. 47, 15, 3.

(41) ["Who prosecutes this suit as well for the king, etc., as for himself."] See The State
v. Williams, 7 Rob. (La.) 252, 311 (1844).
(42) Hart v. Smith, 1 Conn. 127, 131 (Kirby 1786).   Crane v. Bandoine, 65 Barb. (N.
Y.) 260 (1873).   If one intended to perform services for another free of charge a recovery
cannot be had.   Rea v. Flathers, 31 Stiles (Iowa) 545 (1871).
(43) [As much as he deserved.] Binn's Justice, p. 79 (10 ed).
(44) [As much as it was worth.] Wharton's Law of Contracts, p. 80, § 708.   Smith v.
Griffith, 3 Hill (N. Y.) 333 (1842).

owner in damages, equivalent to what he has detained in violation of such his promise.   This is a very extensive and beneficial remedy, applicable to almost every case where the defendant has received money which *ex æquo et bono*(45) he ought to refund.   It lies for money paid by mistake, or on a consideration which happens to fail, or through imposition, extortion, or oppression, or where any undue advantage is taken of the plaintiff's situation.(*p*)

4. Where a person has laid out and expended his own money for the use of another, at his request, the law implies a promise of repayment, and an action will lie on this *assumpsit.*(*q*)(46)

5. *Likewise, fifthly, upon a stated account between two merchants,   [*164 or other persons, the law implies that he, against whom the balance appears, has engaged to pay it to the other; though there be not any actual promise.   And from this implication it is frequent for actions on the case to be brought, declaring that the plaintiff and defendant had settled their accounts together, *insimul computassent,* (which gives name to this species of *assumpsit,*) and that the defendant engaged to pay the plaintiff the balance, but has since neglected to do it.   But if no account has been made up, then the legal remedy is by bringing a writ of *account de computo;*(*r*) commanding the defendant to render a just account to the plaintiff, or show the court good cause to the contrary.   In this action, if the plaintiff succeeds, there are two judgments: the first is, that the defendant do account (*quod computet*) before auditors appointed by the court; and, when such account is finished, then the second judgment is, that he do pay the plaintiff so much as he is found in arrear.   This action, by the old common law,(*s*) lay only against the parties themselves, and not their executors; because matters of account rested solely on their own knowledge.   But this defect, after many fruitless attempts in parliament, was at last remedied by statute 4 Anne, c. 16, which gives an action of account against the executors and administrators.(47) But, however, it is found by experience, that the most ready and effectual way to settle these matters of account is by bill in a court of equity, where a discovery may be had on the defendant's oath, without relying merely on the evidence which the plaintiff may be able to produce.   Wherefore actions of account, to compel a man to bring in and settle his accounts, are now very seldom used; though, when an account is once stated, nothing is more common than an action upon the implied *assumpsit* to pay the balance.(48)

(*p*) 4 Burr. 1012.
(*q*) Carth. 446. 2 Keb. 99.

(*r*) F. N. B. 116.
(*s*) Co. Litt. 90.

(45) [By equity and right.]
(46) If a surety in a bond pays the debt of the principal, he may recover it back from the principal in an action of *assumpsit* for so much money paid and advanced to his use. Yet in ancient times this action could not be maintained; and it is said that the first case of the kind in which the plaintiff succeeded was tried before the late Mr. J. Gould, at Dorchester.   But this is perfectly consistent with the equitable principles of an *assumpsit.* 2 T. R. 105.—CHITTY.   Webb's Pollock on Torts, p. 659. 2 Comyn on Contracts, 3. Ritchie *v.* Smith, 1 Kirby (Conn.) 127 (1786). Freer *v.* Denton, 61 Sickels (N. Y.) 492 (1875).   Shaw *v.* Gardner, 3 Stiles (Iowa) 111 (1870).   Ward & May *v.* Bull & Shine, 1 Fla. 278 (Branch, 1847). Shaw *v.* Gardner, 30 Iowa 111, 113 (1870).   Cobb *v.* Dows, 341 Seld. (N. Y.) 335, 341 (1852). Ritchie *v.* Summers, 3 Yeates (Pa.) 531, 539 (1803).

(47) By statute 3 & 4 Wm. IV. c. 42, executors or administrators may sue for injuries to real estate of their decedent, and be sued for injuries to property, both real and personal, by their testator.   In case of action for injury to the decedent's real estate, it must be instituted within a year of the death of the owner, and in the other case within six calendar months.

(48) State *v.* Bookover, 22 W. Va. 214 (1883).   Tiller *v.* Cook, 77 Va. 477 (1883). Wait's Actions & Def., vol. 1, p. 174. 2 Com. on Const. 205. Action of account by

*165]   6. *The last class of contracts, implied by reason and construction
of law, arises upon this supposition, that every one who undertakes
any office, employment, trust, or duty, contracts with those who employ or
intrust him, to perform it with integrity, diligence, and skill. And, if by
his want of either of those qualities any injury accrues to individuals, they
have therefore their remedy in damages by a special action on the case. A
few instances will fully illustrate this matter. If an officer of the public is
guilty of neglect of duty, or a palpable breach of it, of non-feasance or of
mis-feasance; as, if the sheriff does not execute a writ sent to him, or if he
wilfully makes a false return thereof; in both these cases the party aggrieved
shall have an action *on the case* for damages to be assessed by a jury.(*t*)(49)
If a sheriff or gaoler suffers a prisoner, who is taken upon mesne process,
(that is, during the pendency of a suit,) to escape, he is liable to an action
on the case.(*u*) But if, after judgment, a gaoler or a sheriff permits a debtor
to escape, who is charged in execution for a certain sum, the debt immediately becomes his own, and he is compellable by action of *debt*, being for a
sum liquidated and ascertained, to satisfy the creditor his whole demand;
which doctrine is grounded(*w*) on the equity of the statute of Westm. 2, 13
Edw. I. c. 11, and 1 Ric. II. c. 12. An advocate or attorney that betray the
cause of their client, or, being retained, neglect to appear at the trial, by
which the cause miscarries, are liable to an action on the case for a reparation to
their injured client.(*x*)(50)   There is also in law always an implied contract

---

(*t*) Moor. 431. 11 Rep. 99.   (*w*) Bro. Abr. tit. *Parliament*, 19. 2 Inst. 382.
(*u*) Cro. Eliz. 625. Comb. 69.   (*x*) Finch, L. 183.

statute, as in New York and Virginia, would lie against a joint tenant or tenant in common of real estate for receiving more than his share. At common law it would not lie
against a joint tenant unless he received all the profits for the common benefit of both,
and not for his own use merely; nor could it be brought by or against an executor or
administrator. Wait's Actions & Def., vol. 1, p. 173. It now seems to be entirely settled
that it is not essential that there should be mutual or counter accounts between the parties to support an action for an account stated. A bill of items rendered, or even a single
item presented to a party and acknowledged to be correct, will constitute such an account.
Weigell *v.* Hartman, 51 N. J. 446, 451 (1889).

(49) An action of *assumpsit*, as implied by law, is never the proper remedy against a
public officer for neglect or misbehavior in his office. Bailey *v.* Butterfield, 14 Shep.
(Me.) 112, 115 (1836).

In an action against a jailor for the escape of a debtor, the jury may give what damages
they deem just. If the debtor be insolvent the jury might award a shilling. But if he
was solvent and likely to pay, the measure of damages would be the amount of the debt.
Deliesseline *v.* King & Jones, 1 Har. (S. C.) 357 (1824). The action against a recorder of
mortgages for furnishing a false certificate arises *ex contractu* [From or by contract]. Brown
v. Penn, 1 McG. (La.) 265, 269 (1881). See also Fogarty *v.* Furday, 10 Cal. 239 (1858).

(50) The authority cited for this position falls short of maintaining it to its full extent.
Finch merely lays down the law in the case of an attorney for the tenant in a real action
making default; and F. N. B. 96, which is *his* authority, goes no further. As the advocate can maintain no action for his fees, (see *ante*, p. 28,) there would be some hardship
in exposing him to an action for what his client might consider want of proper zeal,
industry, or knowledge in the conduct of his cause. In two cases (Fell *v.* Brown and
Turner *v.* Phillips, Peake's N. P. C. 131, 166) lord Kenyon, at Nisi Prius, held such
actions not to be maintainable. —COLERIDGE.

In the United States there is no distinction between attorneys and advocates. The
same persons fulfil the duties of both. Hence no difference is made between their right
to recover compensation for services in the one capacity or the other. The attorney is
liable for want of ordinary care and skill. When he disobeys the lawful instructions of
his client, and a loss ensues, for that loss he is responsible. But a client has no right to
control his attorney in the due and orderly conduct of a suit; and it is his duty to do
what the court would order to be done, though his client instruct him otherwise. Gilbert *v.* Williams, 8 Mass. 57. Holmes *v.* Peck, 1 Rhode Island, 245. Cox *v.* Sullivan, 7
Georgia, 144. Cox *v.* Livingston, 2 W. & S. 103. Wilcox *v.* Plummer, 4 Peters, 172.
Anon., 1 Wendell, 108.—SHARSWOOD. Baugh *v.* McDaniel & Strong, 42 Ga. 641, 655
(1871). South. Exp. Co. *v.* Shea, 38 Ga. 519, 527 (1868). The liability of a bailee
depends upon his wilful or careless participation in the loss or injury of the chattels.
Bailey's Onus Probandi, p. 93.

with a common inn-keeper to secure his guest's goods in his inn; with a
common carrier, or bargemaster, to be answerable for the goods he carries;
(51) with a common farrier, that he shoes a horse well, without laming him;
with a common tailor, or other workman, that he performs his business in a
workmanlike manner; in which, if they fail, an action on the case
lies to recover damages for *such breach of their general undertak-   [*166
ing.(y)(52)   But if I employ a person to transact any of these concerns, whose common profession and business it is not, the law implies no
such *general* undertaking; but, in order to charge him with damages, a
special agreement is required.   Also, if an inn-keeper, or other victualler,
hangs out a sign and opens his house for travelers, it is an implied engagement to entertain all persons who travel that way; and upon this universal
assumpsit an action on the case will lie against him for damages if he, without good reason, refuses to admit a traveler.(z)   If any one cheats me with
false cards or dice, or by false weights and measures, or by selling me one
commodity for another, an action on the case also lies against him for damages, upon the contract which the law always implies, that every transaction
is fair and honest.(a)

In contracts, likewise, for sales, it is constantly understood that the seller
undertakes that the commodity he sells is his own;(53) and if it proves

(y) 11 Rep. 54.   1 Saund. 324.   (a) 10 Rep. 56.
(z) 1 Ventr. 333.

(51) See Story on Cont. p. 47 (5 ed.).   Verplanck's Doct. Cont. 205.   As to the liabilities of innkeepers, see Bailey's Onus Prob. p. 306.   Lawson's Crim. Def. vol. 4, p. 846.
Brightley's Binns' Justice, p. 550 (5 ed.).   Comyn on Cont. p. 6.   State *v.* Moore, 12 N.
H. (McF.) 45 (1845).
(52) Comyn on Contracts, p. 263.   Emmerson *v.* Brigham, 10 Rand. (Mass.) 196, 201
(1813).   Searl *v.* Prentice, 8 East, 449 (Wharton, 1785).   Hare on Contracts, p. 155
(1887).   Edwards on Bailments, pp. 323, 339, 426, 444 (3 ed. 1893).   Copeland *v.* Draper,
157 Mass. 558, 560 (1892).   Purviance *v.* Angus, 1 Dall. (Pa.) 193, 197 (1786).   In an
action brought to recover damages for a deceit practiced, the burden is on the plaintiff
to prove: 1. That the defendant by words or acts represented a certain condition or
status with reference to the subject matter, or some contract or transaction to exist,
which, 2. is material, and known by the defendant to be false; 3. of which falsity the
plaintiff being ignorant, believed to be true. 4. That it was made with intent to deceive,
or that it should be acted on, and, 5. being acted on plaintiff was damaged—6. proxi-
mately by the deception.   Bailey's Onus Probandi, p. 77 (1886).   Parsons on Contracts,
v. 1, *p. 573 (8 ed. 1893).   Ricks *v.* Dillahunty, 8 Porter (Ala.) 134, 137 (1838).   As to
innkeepers' implied contracts, see Bonner *v.* Welborn, 7 Ga. 296, 333 (1849).   The acceptance of every office is upon an implied contract that the acceptor will perform its duties
with integrity, diligence and skill, and it is further a familiar principle that offices like
franchises may be forfeited by mis-user and non-user.   The State *v.* Allen, 21 Ind. 516,
522 (1863).
(53) As to warranties in general, see Bac. Abr. Actions on the Case, E.   A warranty on
the sale of a personal chattel, as to the right thereto, is generally implied, (*ante*, 2 book,
451.   3 id. 166.   3 T. R. 57.   Peake C. N. P. 94.   Cro. Jac. 474.   1 Roll. Abr. 90.   1
Salk. 210.   Doug. 18;) but not as to the right of real property, (Doug. 654.   2 B. & P. 13.
3 B. & P. 166.) if a regular conveyance has been executed.   6 T. R. 606.   Nor is a warranty of soundness, goodness, or value of a horse, or other personalty, implied, (3 Camp.
351.   2 East, 314, 448.   *Ante*, 2 book, 451; and see further, 2 Roll. Rep. 5.   F. N. B. 94,
acc. Wooddes. 415.   3 Id. 199, *cont.*;) and if a ship be sold with all faults, the vendor
will not be liable to an action in respect to latent defects which he knows of, unless he
used some artifice to conceal them from the purchaser.   3 Camp. 154, 506.   But if it is
the usage of the trade to specify defects, (as in case of sales of drugs if they are sea-dam-
aged,) and none are specified, an implied warranty arises, (4 Taunt. 847;) and warranty
may be implied from the production of a sample, in a parol sale by sample, (4 Camp. 22,
144, 169.   4 B. & A. 387.   3 Stark. 32; and see notes;) and if the bulk of the goods do
not correspond with the sample, it would be a breach of the warranty.   If the contract
describe the goods as of a particular denomination, there is an implied warranty that
they shall be of a merchantable quality of the denomination mentioned in the contract.
4 Camp. 144.   3 Chit. Com. Law, 303.   1 Stark. 504.   4 Taunt. 853.   5 B. & A. 240.   In

otherwise, an action on the case lies against him, to exact damages for this deceit. In contracts for provisions, it is always implied that they are wholesome; and if they be not, the same remedy may be had.(54)   Also if he, that selleth any thing, doth upon the sale warrant it to be good, the law annexes a tacit contract to his warranty, that if it be not so, he shall make compensation to the buyer; else it is an injury to good faith, for which an action on the case will lie to recover damages.(*b*)   The warranty must be *upon the sale;* for if it be made *after,* and not *at,* the time of the sale, it is a void warranty:(*c*) for it is then made without any consideration; neither does the buyer then take the goods upon the credit of the vendor.(55)   Also, the warranty can only reach to things in being at the time of the warranty made, and not to things *in futuro;* as, that a horse *is* sound at the buying of him, not that he *will be* sound two years hence.(56)   But if the vendor **165]   knew the goods **to be unsound, and hath used any art to disguise them,(*d*) or if they are in any shape different from what he represents them to be to the buyer, this artifice shall be equivalent to an express

(*b*) F. N. B. 94.
(*c*) Finch, L. 189.

(*d*) 2 Roll. Rep. 5.

all contracts for the sale of provisions there is an implied contract that they shall be wholesome.   1 Stark. 384.   2 Camp. 391.   3 Camp. 286.   An implied warranty arises in the sale of goods where no opportunity of an inspection is given, (4 Camp. 144, 169.   6 Taunt. 108;) and if goods are ordered to be manufactured, a stipulation that they shall be proper is implied, (4 Camp. 144.   6 Taunt. 108,) especially if for a foreign market.   4 Camp. 169.   5 Taunt. 108.   As to what is an express warranty, see 3 Chit. Com. Law, 305. Where a horse has been warranted sound, any infirmity rendering it unfit for immediate use is an unsoundness.   1 Stark. 127.   The question of unsoundness is for the opinion of a jury.   7 Taunt. 153.   It is not necessary for the purchaser to return the horse, unless it be expressly stipulated that he should do so.   2 Hen. Bla. 573.   2 T. R. 745.   If not so stipulated, an action for the *breach of warranty* may be supported without returning the horse, or even giving notice of the unsoundness, and although the purchaser have re-sold the horse.   1 Hen. Bla. 17.   1 T. R. 136.   2 T. R. 745.   But unless the horse be returned as soon as the defect is discovered, or if the horse has been long worked, the purchaser cannot recover back the purchase-money on the count for money had and received, (1 T. R. 136.   5 East, 449.   1 East, 274.   2 Camp. 410.   1 New Rep. 260;) and in all cases the vendee should object within a reasonable time, (1 J. B. Moore, 166;) and in these cases, or when the purchaser has doctored the horse, he has no defence to an action by the vendor for the price, but must proceed in a cross-action on the warranty, (1 T. R. 136.   5 East, 449.   7 id. 274.   2 Camp. 410.   1 N. R. 260.   3 Esp. Rep. 82.   4 Esp. Rep. 95;) and in these cases, if the vendee has accepted a bill or given any other security, it should seem that the breach of warranty is no defence to an action thereon, but he must proceed by cross-action.   2 Taunt. 2.   1 Stark. 51.   3 Camp. 38.   S. C., 14 East, 486.   3 Stark. 175.   But it would be otherwise if the vendee entirely repudiated the contract, (2 Taunt. 2,) as if he in the first instance, on discovery of the breach of warranty, returned or tendered back the horse.   2 Taunt. 2; and see 14 East, 484.   3 Camp. 38.   Peake's C. N. P. 38.   For what damage defendant is liable in this action, see 2 J. B. Moore, 106.—CHITTY.

(54) The responsibility of a victualler, vintner, brewer, butcher, or cook for selling unwholesome food does not arise from contract, or implied warranty, but is a responsibility imposed by statute, that they shall make good any *damage caused* by the sale of unwholesome food.   Benjamin on Sales, pp. 769, 770, § 671 (4 Am. ed.).   Cord's Mar. Wom. vol. 2, § 1041, p. 280 (2 ed.).   Schouler's Pers. Prop. vol. 2, p. 344 (2 ed.).   Smith's Merc. Law, p. 531 and note.   Story on Sales, p. 457.   Moses *v.* Mead, 1 Den. (N. Y.) 378, 387 (1845).

(55) This must be understood to mean statements made after the bargain which seek the protection of the original consideration; for any warranty made after the original sale, is valid, like any substituted agreement of parties.   Cougar *v.* Chamberlain, 14 Wis. 258 (1861).

(56) There seems to be no good reason for holding that a warranty can have no prospective operation, Lord Mansfield has said "there is no doubt, but you may warrant a future event."   And it has been expressly held that the vendor's warranty, reaching the quality of the subject-matter sold, is as good as a warranty of present quality.   Schouler's Pers. Prop. vol. 2. § 333, p. 326.   Biddle's Warranties, p. 63.   Smith's Merc. Law, 636 (3 ed.).   As to implied warranty of title, see Biddle's Warranties, p. 227.

warranty, and the vendor is answerable for their goodness.(57)   A general warranty will not extend to guard against defects that are plainly and obviously the object of one's senses, as if a horse be warranted perfect, and wants either a tail or an ear, unless the buyer in this case be blind.(58)   But if cloth is warranted to be of such a length, when it is not, there an action on the case lies for damages; for that cannot be discerned by sight, but only by a collateral proof, the measuring it.(e)   Also, if a horse is warranted sound, and he wants the sight of an eye, though this seems to be the object of one's senses, yet, as the discernment of such defects is frequently matter of skill, it hath been held that an action on the case lieth to recover damages for this imposition.(f)(59)

Besides the special action on the case, there is also a peculiar remedy, entitled an action of *deceit;*(g) to give damages in some particular cases of fraud; and principally where one man does any thing in the name of another, by which he is deceived or injured;(h) as if one brings an action in another's name, and then suffers a nonsuit, whereby the plaintiff becomes liable to costs; or where one obtains or suffers a fraudulent recovery of lands, tenements, or chattels, to the prejudice of him that hath right.   As when, by collusion, the attorney of the tenant makes default in a real action, or where the sheriff returns that the tenant was summoned when he was not so, and in either case he loses the land, the writ of *deceit* lies against the demandant, and also the attorney or the sheriff and his officers; to annul the former proceedings, and recover back the land.(i)   It also lies in the cases of warranty before mentioned, and other personal injuries committed contrary to good faith and honesty.(k)(60)   But an action *on the case*, for damages, in nature of a writ of *deceit*, is more usually brought upon these occasions.(l)

And indeed it is the only(m) **remedy for a lord of a manor, in or   [**166 out of ancient demesne, to reverse a fine or recovery had in the king's courts of lands lying within his jurisdiction; which would otherwise be thereby turned into frank-fee.   And this may be brought by the lord against the parties and *cestuy que use* (61) of such fine or recovery; and thereby

(e) Finch, L. 189.
(f) Salk. 611.
(g) F. N. B. 95.
(h) Law of Nisi Prius, 30.
(i) Booth, Real Actions, 251.   Rast. Entr. 221, 222.

See page 405.
(k) F. N. B. 98.
(l) Booth, 253.   Co. Entr. 8.
(m) 3 Lev. 419.

(57) Where the sale is by an executor or administrator a warranty is not implied unless there is evidence of fraud.   Rick's Adm'r v. Dellahantey, 8 Porter (Ala.) 134 (1838). A mere expression of opinion will not render the seller liable unless it was made with a knowledge of its falsity.   Id.   When the goods are in view of the purchaser, a warranty will not be implied, where none is expressed, except in case of provisions.   Van Bracklein v. Fonda, 12 Johns. (N. Y.) 468 (1815).   Getty v. Rountree, 2 Punney (Wis.) 379 (1850).   Connersville v. Wadleigh, 7 Blackf. (Ind.) 102.   Copeland v. Draper, 157 Mass. 558 (1892).   Hoe v. Sanburn, 21 Smith (N. Y.) 552 (1860).   Schouler's Pers. Prop. Story on Sales, c. 12, § 374, p. 324.   Crowder v. Langdon, 3 Ired. (N. C.) 476, 485 (1845). Pres. etc. of Connellsville v. Wadleigh, 7 Blackf. (Ind.) 104 (1843).   If an action be brought for breach of warranty of soundness, proof of the warranty is indispensable, and it is immaterial whether the defendant knew of the unsoundness or not.   But if brought for fraud by representations which the defendant knew were false, such knowledge is an essential ingredient and must be proved.   Bartholomew v. Bushnell, 20 Day (Conn.) 271, 280 (1850).   Where there is no express warranty, nor fraud, an action will not lie because the goods are not fit for every purpose for which they may be used.   Wright v. Hart, 18 Wend. (N. Y.) 449 (1837).

(58) It has been held that this rule may apply as well to the title, as to the quality. The vendee knowing the title to be bad, takes it at his risk.   Sibley v. Beard, 5 Kell. & Cobb. (Ga.) 550, 554 (1849).   Otherwise want of title in the vendor would be a good defence to an action for the purchase money.   Sweetman v. Prince, 62 Barb. (N. Y.) 256 (1862).   Ritchie v. Summers, 3 Yeates (Pa.) 531.

(59) See Comyn on Cont. 274.   Long on Sales, 203 (Rand's ed.).

(60) The writ of *deceit* was abolished by statute 3 & 4 Will. IV. c. 27.—KERR.

(61) [Beneficiary.]

he shall obtain judgment not only for damages, (which are usually remitted,) but also to recover his court, and jurisdiction over the lands, and to annul the former proceedings. (*n*)

Thus much for the non-performance of contracts, express or implied; which includes every possible injury to what is by far the most considerable species of personal property, viz., that which consists in action merely, and not in possession. Which finishes our inquiries into such wrongs as may be offered to *personal* property, with their several remedies by suit or action.

CHAPTER X.

OF INJURIES TO REAL PROPERTY; AND FIRST OF DISPOSSESSION, OR OUSTER OF THE FREEHOLD.

*167]   *I COME now to consider such *injuries* as affect that species of property which the laws of England have denominated *real;* as being of a more substantial and permanent nature than those transitory rights of which personal chattels are the object. (1)

(*n*) Rast. Entr. 100, b.   3 Lev. 415.   Lutw. 711, 749.

---

(1) "The different degrees of title which a person dispossessing another of his lands acquires in them in the eye of the law, (independently of any anterior right,) according to the length of time and other circumstances which intervene from the time such dispossession is made, form different degrees of presumption in favor of the title of the dispossessor; and in proportion as that presumption increases, his title is strengthened. The modes by which the possession may be recovered vary; and more, or rather different, proof is required from the person dispossessed to establish his title to recover. Thus, if A. is disseised by B., while the possession continues in B. it is a *mere naked possession,* unsupported by any right, and A. may restore his own possession, and put a total end to the possession of B., by an *entry* on the lands, without any previous action. But if B. dies, the possession descends on the heir by act of law. In this case the heir comes to the land by lawful title, and acquires in the eye of the law an apparent *right of possession,* which is so far good against the person disseised that he has lost his right to recover the possession by entry, and can only recover it by *an action at law.* The actions used in these cases are called *possessory actions,* and the original writs by which the proceedings upon them are instituted are called writs of entry. But if A. permits the possession to be withheld from him beyond a certain period of time without claiming it, or suffers judgment in a possessory action to be given against him, by default or upon the merits,—in all these cases B.'s title, in the eye of the law, is strengthened, and A. can no longer recover by a possessory action, and his only remedy then is by an action on the right. These last actions are called *droiturel actions,* in contradistinction to *possessory actions.* They are the ultimate resort of the person disseised, so that if he fails to bring his writ of right within the time limited for the bringing of such writ, he is remediless, and the title of the dispossessor is complete. The original writs by which droiturel actions are instituted are called writs of right. The dilatoriness and niceties in these processes introduced the writ of assize. The invention of this proceeding is attributed to Glanville, chief justice to Henry II. See Mr. Reeve's History of the English Law, part 1, ch. 3. It was found so convenient a remedy that persons, to avail themselves of it, frequently supposed or admitted themselves to be disseised by acts which did not, in strictness, amount to a disseisin. This disseisin, being such only by the will of the party, is called a *disseisin by election,* in opposition to an *actual disseisin:* it is only a disseisin as between the disseisor and disseisee, the disseisee still continuing the freeholder as to all persons but the disseisor. The old books, particularly the reports of assize, when they mention disseisins, generally relate to those cases where the owner admits himself disseised. See 1 Burr. 111; and see Bract. 1. b. 4, cap. 3. As the processes upon writs of entry were superseded by the assize, so the assize and all other real actions have been since superseded by the modern process of ejectment. This was introduced as a mode of trying titles to lands in the reign of Henry VII. From the ease and expedition with which the proceedings in it are conducted, it is now become the general remedy in these cases. Booth, who wrote about the end of the last century, mentions real actions as *then* worn

Real injuries, then, or injuries affecting real rights, are principally six:—1. Ouster; 2. Trespass; 3. Nuisance; 4. Waste; 5. Subtraction; 6. Disturbance.

Ouster, or dispossession, is a wrong or injury that carries with it the amotion of possession; for thereby the wrong-doer gets into the actual occupation of the land or hereditament, and obliges him that hath a right, to seek his legal remedy in order to gain possession and damages for the injury sustained.(2)　And such ouster, or dispossession, may either be of the *freehold*, or of *chattels real*. Ouster of the *freehold* is effected by one of the following methods:—1. Abatement; 2. Intrusion; 3. Disseisin; 4. Discontinuance; 5. Deforcement. All of which, in their order, and afterwards their respective remedies, will be considered in the present chapter.

I. And first, an *abatement* is where a person dies seised of an inheritance and before the heir or devisee enters, a stranger *who [*168 has no right makes entry and gets possession of the freehold.(3)

This entry of him is called an abatement, and he himself is denominated an abator.(a) It is to be observed that this expression of *abating*, which is derived from the French, and signifies to quash, beat down, or destroy, is used by our law in three senses. The first, which seems to be the primitive sense, is that of abating or beating down a nuisance, of which we spoke in the beginning of this book;(b) and in a like sense it is used in statute Westm. 1, 3 Edw. I. c. 17, where mention is made of abating a castle or fortress; in which case it clearly signifies to pull it down and .level it with the ground. The second signification of abatement is that of abating a writ or action, of which we shall say more hereafter; here it is taken figuratively, and signifies the overthrow or defeating of such writ by some fatal exception to it. The last species of abatement is that we have now before us; which is also a figurative expression, to denote that the rightful possession or freehold of the heir or devisee is overthrown by the rude intervention of a stranger.

This abatement of a freehold is somewhat similar to an immediate occupancy in a state of nature, which is effected by taking possession of the land the same instant that the prior occupant by his death relinquishes it. But this, however agreeable to natural justice, considering man merely as an individual, is diametrically opposite to the law of society, and particularly the law of England; which, for the preservation of public peace, hath prohibited as far as possible all acquisitions by mere occupancy, and hath directed that lands on the death of the present possessor should immediately vest either in some person expressly named and appointed by the deceased as his devisee,

---

(a) Finch, L. 195.　　　　　　　　(b) Page 5.

---

out of use. It is rather singular that this should be the fact, as many cases must frequently have occurred in which a writ of ejectment was not a sufficient remedy. Within these few years past, some attempts have been made to revive real actions; and the most remarkable of these are the case of Tissen *v.* Clarke, reported in 3 Wils. 419, 541, and that of Carlos & Shuttleworth *v.* Lord Dormer. The writ of summons in this last case is dated the 1st day of December, 1775. The summons to the four knights to proceed to the election of the grand assize is dated the 22d day of May, 1780. To this summons the sheriff made his return; and there the matter rested. The last instance in which a real action was used is the case of Sidney *v.* Perry. All these were actions on the right. The part of Sir William Blackstone's Commentary which treats upon real actions is not the least valuable part of that most excellent work." See Co. Litt. 239, a., note 1. In M. T. 1825, a writ of right stood for trial in the court of Common Pleas; but, the four knights summoned for the purpose not appearing, the case was adjourned to the next term.—CHITTY.

(2) See Emerson *v.* Goodwin, 9 Day (Conn.) 421, 429 (1833). Brown *v.* Burdick, 25 Ohio, 260 (1874). Angell on Limitations, p. 395 (6 ed.).

(3) Brown's Law of Lim. 448. Graham *v.* Luddington, 19 Hun. (N. Y.) 246, 251 (1879). Bright's Husb. & Wife, 324.

or, on default of such appointment, in such of his next relations as the law hath selected and pointed out as his natural representative or heir. Every entry, therefore, of a mere stranger by way of intervention between the ancestor and heir or person next entitled, which keeps the heir or devisee out of possession, is one of the highest injuries to the right of real property.(4)

*169]   *2. The second species of injury by ouster, or amotion of possession from the freehold, is by *intrusion;*(5) which is the entry of a stranger, after a particular estate of freehold is determined, before him in remainder or reversion. And it happens where a tenant for term of life dieth seised of certain lands and tenements, and a stranger entereth thereon, after such death of the tenant, and before any entry of him in remainder or reversion.(c) This entry and interposition of the stranger differ from an abatement in this; that an abatement is always to the prejudice of the heir or immediate devisee; an intrusion is always to the prejudice of him in remainder or reversion. For example; if A. dies seised of lands in fee-simple, and before the entry of B. his heir, C. enters thereon, this is an abatement; but if A. be tenant for life, with remainder to B. in fee-simple, and after the death of A., C. enters, this is an intrusion. Also if A. be tenant for life on lease from B., or his ancestors, or be tenant by the curtesy, or in dower, the reversion being vested in B. and after the death of A., C. enters and keeps B. out of possession, this is likewise an intrusion. So that an intrusion is always immediately consequent upon the determination of a particular estate; an abatement is always consequent upon the descent or devise of an estate in fee-simple. And in either case the injury is equally great to him whose possession is defeated by this unlawful occupancy.(6)

3. The third species of injury by ouster, or privation of the freehold, is by *disseisin*. Disseisin is a wrongful putting out of him that is seised of the freehold.(d)(7) The two former species of injury were by a wrongful entry where the possession was vacant; but this is an attack upon him who is in actual possession, and turning him out of it. Those were an ouster from a freehold in law; this is an ouster from a freehold in deed. Disseisin *170] may be effected either in corporeal inheritances, *or incorporeal.

Disseisin of things corporeal, as of houses, lands, etc., must be by entry and actual dispossession of the freehold;(e)(8) as if a man enters either by force or fraud into the house of another, and turns, or at least keeps, him or his servants out of possession. Disseisin of incorporeal hereditaments cannot be an actual dispossession: for the subject itself is neither capable of actual bodily possession, or dispossession; but it depends on their respective natures, and various kinds; being in general nothing more than a disturbance of the owner in the means of coming at or enjoying them.(9) With regard to freehold rent in particular, our ancient law-books(f) mentioned five methods of

(c) Co. Litt. 277. F. N. B. 203, 204.
(d) Co. Litt. 277.

(e) Ibid. 181.
(f) 1 Finch, L. 165, 166. Litt. § 237, etc.

(4) A disseisor has the right of possession against all men except the owner, and may recover against a subsequent intruder without having actual adverse possession for twenty years. Hoey v. Furman, 1 Barr. (Pa.) 295 (1845). See Angell on Limitations, 380.

(5) Where the intrusion is made upon the land of an infant, it would be considered in equity a trust for the benefit of the infant; but a tenant of the intruder, without knowledge of the infant's title, would not be considered a trustee. Baylan *et al.* v. Deinzer *et al.*, 45 New Jersey, 485 (1889).

(6) People v. Conklin, 2 Hill (N. Y.) 67 (1841).

(7) Weston v. Reading, 5 Day (Conn.) 255, 257 (1824). Unger v. Mooney, 63 Cal. 586, 590 (1883). Rockwell v. Bradley, 2 Conn. 11 (Day, 1816). Dyett v. Pendleton, 8 Cowan (N. Y.) 743 (1826).

(8) Mitchell v. Warner, 5 Day (Conn.) 497, 526 (1825). Newell on Ejectment, p. 414.

(9) Sedgwick on Title to Land, § 146, p. 83 (2 ed.).

working a disseisin thereof: 1. By *enclosure;* where the tenant so encloseth the house or land, that the lord cannot come to distrain thereon, or demand it: 2. By *forestaller*, or lying in wait, when the tenant besetteth the way with force and arms, or by menaces of bodily hurt affrights the lessor from coming: 3. By *rescous;* that is, either by violently retaking a distress taken, or by preventing the lord with force and arms from taking any at all: 4. By *replevin;* when the tenant replevies the distress at such time when his rent is really due: 5. By *denial;* which is when the rent being lawfully demanded is not paid.(10) All or any of these circumstances amount to a disseisin of rent; that is, they wrongfully put the owner out of the only possession, of which the subject-matter is capable, namely, the receipt of it. But all these disseisins, of hereditaments, incorporeal, are only so at the election and choice of the party injured; if, for the sake of more easily trying the right, he is pleased to suppose himself disseised. (*g*) Otherwise, as there can be no actual dispossession, he cannot be compulsively disseised of any incorporeal hereditament.

And so, too, even in corporeal hereditaments, a man may frequently suppose himself to be disseised, when he is not so in fact, for the sake of entitling himself to the more easy and commodious remedy of an assize of *novel disseisin,* (which will be explained in the sequel of this chapter,) instead of being *driven to the more tedious process of a writ of entry.(*h*)   [*171 The true injury of compulsive disseisin seems to be that of dispossessing the tenant, and substituting oneself to be the tenant of the lord in his stead; in order to which in the times of pure feodal tenure the consent or connivance of the lord, who upon every descent or alienation personally gave, and who therefore alone could change, the seisin or investiture, seems to have been considered as necessary. But when in process of time the feodal form of alienations wore off, and the lord was no longer the instrument of giving actual seisin, it is probable that the lord's acceptance of rent or service, from him who had dispossessed another, might constitute a complete disseisin. Afterwards, no regard was had to the lord's concurrence, but the dispossessor himself was considered as the sole disseisor: and this wrong was then allowed to be remedied by entry only, without any form of law, as against the disseisor himself; but required a legal process against his heir or alienee. And when the remedy by assize was introduced under Henry II. to redress such disseisins as had been committed within a few years next preceding, the facility of that remedy induced others, who were wrongfully kept out of the freehold, to feign or allow themselves to be disseised, merely for the sake of the remedy.

These three species of injury, *abatement, intrusion,* and *disseisin,* are such wherein the entry of the tenant *ab initio,* as well as the continuance of his possession afterwards, is unlawful. But the two remaining species are where the entry of the tenant was at first lawful, but the wrong consists in the detaining of possession afterwards.

4. Such is, fourthly, the injury of *discontinuance;*(11) which happens when he who hath an estate-tail maketh a larger estate of the land than by law he

---

(*g*) Litt. §§ 588, 589.   (*h*) Hengh. parv. c. 7. 4 Burr. 110.

---

(10) If the tenant deny the holding; refuses to pay the rent; forbids distress, and provides the means of resisting it; no regular demand at the time specified in the lease is necessary. Farley *v.* Craig, 6 Hals. (N. J.) 262 (1830). See also Rockwell *v.* Bradley, 2 Conn. 1 (1816). [*Ab initio*—From the beginning].

(11) See, in general, Adams on Ejectment, 35 to 41. Com. Dig. Discontinuance. Bac. Abr. Discontinuance. Vin. Abr. Discontinuance. Cru. Dig. Index, Discontinuance.

is entitled to do:(i) in which case the estate is good, so far as his power extends who made it, but no further. As if tenant in tail makes a feoff-

*172] ment in fee-simple, or for the life of the feoffee, or in tail; all *which
are beyond his power to make, for that by the common law extends
no further than to make a lease for his own life; in such case the entry of the
feoffee is lawful during the life of the feoffor; but if he retains the possession
after the death of the feoffor, it is an injury, which is termed a discontinuance:
the ancient legal estate, which ought to have survived to the heir in tail,
being gone, or at least suspended, and for a while discontinued. (12) For, in
this case, on the death of the alienors, neither the heir in tail, nor they in
remainder or reversion expectant on the determination of the estate-tail, can
enter on and possess the lands so alienated. Also, by the common law, the
alienation of a husband who was seised in the right of his wife, worked a
discontinuance of the wife's estate, till the statute 32 Hen. VIII. c. 28 provided, that no act by the husband alone shall work a discontinuance of, or
prejudice, the inheritance or freehold of the wife; but that, after his death,
she or her heirs may enter on the lands in question. Formerly, also, if an
alienation was made by a sole corporation, as a bishop or dean, without consent of the chapter, this was a discontinuance.(j) But this is now quite
antiquated by the disabling statutes of 1 Eliz. c. 19 and 13 Eliz. c. 10, which

(i) Finch, L. 190.   (j) F. N. B. 194.

Co. Litt. 325. 2 Saund. Index, tit. Discontinuance. The term "discontinuance" is used
to distinguish those cases where the party whose freehold is ousted can restore it by
action only from those in which he may restore it by entry. Now, things which lie in
grant cannot either be devested or restored by entry. The owner therefore of any thing
which lies in grant has in no stage, and under no circumstances, any other remedy but
by action. The books often mention both disseisins and discontinuances of incorporeal
hereditaments; but these disseisins and discontinuances are only at the election of the
party, for the purpose of availing himself of the remedy by action. Co. Litt. 330, b., n.
But a disseisin or discontinuance of corporeal hereditaments necessarily operates as a
disseisin or discontinuance of all the incorporeal rights or incidents which the disseisee
or discontinuee has himself in, upon, or out of the land affected by the disseisin or discontinuance. Ib. 332, a., n. 1. Conveyances by feoffment and livery, or by fine or
recovery by tenant in tail in possession, work a discontinuance; but if by covenants to
stand seised to uses, under the statute, lease and release, bargain and sale, they do not,
(Co. Litt. 330, a., n. 1,) unless accompanied with a fine, as one and the same assurance
in the two latter instances, (10 Co. 95;) but if the fine be a *distinct* assurance it is otherwise. 2 Burr. 704. See *ante*, 2 book, 301. See, further, Adams on Ejectment, 35, etc.
2 Saund. Index, Discontinuance. See 2 D. & R. 373. 1 B. & C. 238.—CHITTY.

The alienation by a husband who was seised in right of his wife worked a discontinuance of the wife's estate, until the stat. 32 Hen. VIII. c. 28, which provided that no act
of the husband alone should have that effect. Wildey *v.* Doe, 26 Miss. 35 (1853). See
also Sheppard's Touchstone (Preston) p. 33.

(12) Bacon (New Abr. tit. Discontinuance) defines it to be "such an alienation of the
possession whereby he who has a right to the inheritance cannot enter, but is driven to his
action." The question whether any particular act has this effect depends not so much
on the quantity of estate which the wrong-doer has, as upon the mode of conveyance by
which he has done it. For example, by the old law the disseisor, who has but a naked
possession, might, by feoffment and livery of seisin to a third person, discontinue the
lawful estate of the disseisee,—that is, take from him his right to revest it by mere entry;
on the other hand, the tenant in tail, who has all but the fee-simple, may by lease and
release profess to convey the inheritance in fee to one and his heirs, and yet discontinue
no estate, the form of the instrument operating to pass only whatever he lawfully can
grant.

In order to effect a *general* discontinuance, the alienation must be made with livery of
seisin, or what is equivalent to it,—though the estates of particular persons may be discontinued by other modes, in order to avoid circuity, as lease and release by tenant in tail
with *warranty* will displace the estate of the issue on whom the warranty descends. See
ante, vol. ii. p. 301. Litt. s. 592. Co. Litt. 325, a., n. 278, etc.—COLERIDGE.

declare all such alienations absolutely void *ab initio*, and therefore at present no discontinuance can be thereby occasioned.(13)

5. The fifth and last species of injuries by ouster or privation of the freehold, where the entry of the present tenant or possessor was originally lawful, but his detainer is now become unlawful, is that by *deforcement*.(14) This, in its most extensive sense, is *nomen generalissimum;*(15) a much larger and more comprehensive expression than any of the former: it then signifying the holding of any lands or tenements to which another person hath a right.(*k*) So that this includes as well an abatement, an intrusion, a disseisin, or a discontinuance, as any other species of wrong whatsoever, whereby he that hath right to the freehold is kept out of possession. But, as contradistinguished from the former, it is only such a detainer of the *freehold from him that hath the right of property, but never   [*173 had any possession under that right, as falls within none of the injuries which we have before explained. As in case where a lord has a seignory, and lands escheat to him *propter defectum sanguinis,*(16) but the seisin of the lands is withheld from him; here the injury is not *abatement*, for the right vests not in the lord as heir or devisee; nor is it *intrusion*, for it vests not in him who hath the remainder or reversion; nor is it *disseisin*, for the lord was never seised; nor does it at all bear the nature of any species of *discontinuance;* but, being neither of these four, it is therefore a *deforcement.*(*l*) If a man marries a woman, and during the coverture is seised of lands, and alienes, and dies; is disseised, and dies; or dies in possession; and the alienee, disseisor, or heir enters on the tenements and doth not assign the widow her dower; this is also a deforcement to the widow, by withholding lands to which she hath a right.(*m*)(17) In like manner, if a man lease lands to another for term of years, or for the life of a third person, and the term expires by surrender, efflux of time, or death of the *cestuy que vie;*(18) and the lessee or any stranger, who was at the expiration of the term in possession, holds over, and refuses to deliver the possession to him in remainder or reversion, this is likewise a deforcement.(*n*)(19) Deforcements may also arise upon the breach of a condition in law: as if a woman gives lands to a man by deed, to the intent that he marry her, and he will not when thereunto required, but continues to hold the lands: this is such a fraud on the man's part, that the law will not allow it to devest the woman's right of possession; though, his entry being lawful, it does devest the actual possession, and thereby becomes a deforcement.(*o*)(20) Deforcements may

(*k*) Co. Litt. 277.
(*l*) F. N. B. 143.
(*m*) F. N. B. 8, 147.

(*n*) Finch, L. 263.   F. N. B. 201, 205, 206, 207. See book ii. ch. 9, p. 151.
(*o*) F. N. B. 205.

(13) [From the beginning.] But now, by stat. 3 & 4 W. IV. c. 27, s. 39, no discontinuance shall defeat any right of entry or action for the recovery of land; and, by stat. 8 & 9 Vict. c. 106, s. 4, a feoffment made after October 1, 1845, shall not have a tortious operation, so as to create an estate *by wrong;* and therefore a *discontinuance* would seem now to be impossible.—STEWART.

(14) City of Pella *v.* Schotte, 24 Stiles (Iowa) 283 (1868). Lessee of Ruggie *v.* Ellis, 1 Bay (S. C.) 110 (1790). Gresham *v.* Webb, 29 Ga. 320 (1859). Hoye *v.* Swan's Lessee, 5 Mill. (Md.) 237.

(15) [A most general name.]

(16) [Through failure of issue.]

(17) Hopper *v.* Hopper, 1 Zab. 543 (1848).

(18) [The person for whose life property is held in trust.]

(19) Thus where land conveyed for a specific purpose, is used for a different one. Clark *v.* Holton, 57 Ind. 564 (1877). Or it is conditioned for the payment of an annuity, which is not paid. Chalker *v.* Chalker, 1 Conn. 79 (1814). Hamilton *v.* Elliott, 5 S. & R. (Pa.) 375 (1819). Sheppard's Touchstone, p. 135 (Preston).

(20) On the other hand, if a man should, after much solicitation and hesitancy, convey land without adequate pecuniary consideration, to a woman who had promised to marry him, and had thereby gained great influence over him; her refusal to marry him would

also be grounded on the disability of the party deforced: as if an infant do make an alienation of his lands, and the alienee enters and keeps possession: now, as the alienation is voidable, this possession as against the infant (or, in case of his decease, as against his heir) is after avoidance wrongful, *174] and therefore a deforcement.(_p_) The same happens *when one of non-sane memory alienes his lands or tenements, and the alienee enters and holds possession; this may also be a deforcement.(_q_) Another species of deforcement is, where two persons have the same title to land, and one of them enters and keeps possession against the other: as where the ancestor dies seised of an estate in fee-simple, which descends to two sisters as coparceners, and one of them enters before the other, and will not suffer her sister to enter and enjoy her moiety; this is also a deforcement.(_r_) Deforcement may also be grounded on the non-performance of a covenant real: as if a man, seised of lands, covenants to convey them to another, and neglects or refuses so to do, but continues possession against him; this possession, being wrongful, is a deforcement:(_s_) whence, in levying a fine of lands, the person against whom the fictitious action is brought upon a supposed breach of covenant is called the _deforciant_.(21) And, lastly, by way of analogy, keeping a man by any means out of a freehold office is construed to be a deforcement; though, being an incorporeal hereditament, the deforciant has no corporeal possession. So that whatever injury (withholding the possession of a freehold) is not included under one of the four former heads, is comprised under this of deforcement.

The several species and degrees of injury by _ouster_ being thus ascertained and defined, the next consideration is the remedy; which is, universally, the _restitution_ or _delivery of possession_ to the right owner; and in some cases, _damages_ also for the unjust amotion. The methods, whereby these remedies, or either of them, may be obtained, are various.

1. The first is that extrajudicial and summary one, which we slightly touched in the first chapter of the present book,(_t_) of _entry_ by the legal owner, when another person, who hath no right, hath previously taken possession of lands or tenements. In this case the party entitled may make a formal, but peaceable, entry thereon, declaring that thereby he takes possession; which notorious act of ownership is equivalent to a feodal *175] investiture by the lord;(_u_)(22) or he may enter on any *part of it in the same county, declaring it to be in the name of the whole;(_v_) but if it lies in different counties he must make different entries; for the notoriety of such entry or claim to the _pares_ or freeholders of Westmoreland

(_p_) Finch, L. 264. F. N. B. 192.
(_q_) Finch. ibid. F. N. B. 202.
(_r_) Finch, L. 293, 294. F. N. B. 197.
(_s_) F. N. B. 146.

(_t_) See page 5.
(_u_) See book ii. ch. 14, p 209.
(_v_) Litt. § 417.

afford him ground for rescinding the conveyance. Rockafellow _v._ Newcomet, 57 Ill. 186. Bigelow on Frauds, vol. 1, p. 271, § 12 (1877).

(21) Sheppard's Touchstone, p. 3 (Preston).

(22) Barb. Rights of Pers. & Prop. 778. Byrne _v._ Lowry, 19 Ga. (Cobb) 27, 30 (1855). Jackson _v._ Stanbury, 9 Wend. (N. Y.) 202 (1832). It was the abuse of this summary power to right one's self by entry which gave rise to the numerous English statutes against forcible entry and detainer and from which our American statutes are in general derived; out of which our modern law-makers have endeavored to legislate a remedy more suitable than the action of ejectment. Newell on Ejectmt. p. 853, c. 26, § 1 (1892). Under our system of jurisprudence, a demand of possession is equivalent to an entry on the premises. Clark _v._ Holton, 57 Ind. 564, 567 (1877). In Georgia a conveyance of land by one against whom the land conveyed, is held adversely, under claim of title is void. Gresham _v._ Webb, 29 Ga. 320, 327 (1859). Every forcible entry is forbidden, but a forcible detainer after a peaceable entry is not forbidden unless the detainer be unlawful. Hoffman _v._ Harrington, 22 Mich. 52, 56 (1870).

is not any notoriety to the *pares* or freeholders of Sussex. Also if there be *two* disseisors, the party disseised must make his entry on *both;* or if *one* disseisor has conveyed the lands with livery to *two* distinct feoffees, entry must be made on *both:*(*w*)(23) for as their seisin is distinct, so also must be the act which devests that seisin. If the claimant be deterred from entering by menaces or bodily fear, he may make *claim* as near to the estate as he can, with the like forms and solemnities; which claim is in force for only a year and a day.(*x*) And this claim, if it be repeated once in the space of every year and a day, (which is called *continual claim,*) has the same effect with, and in all respects amounts to, a legal entry.(*y*)(24) Such an entry gives a man seisin,(*z*) or puts into immediate possession him that hath right of entry on the estate, and thereby makes him complete owner, and capable of conveying it from himself by either descent or purchase.(25)

This remedy by entry takes place in three only of the five species of ouster, viz., abatement, intrusion, and disseisin;(*a*) for as in these the original entry of the wrong-doer was unlawful, they may therefore be remedied by the mere entry of him who hath right. But, upon a discontinuance or deforcement, the owner of the estate cannot enter, but is driven to his action;(26) for herein, the original entry being lawful, and thereby an apparent right of possession being gained, the law will not suffer that right to be overthrown by the mere act or entry of the claimant. Yet a man may enter(*b*) on his tenant by sufferance: for such tenant hath no freehold, but only a bare possession; which may be defeated, like a tenancy at will, by the mere entry of the owner. But if the owner thinks it more expedient to suppose or admit(*c*) such tenant to have *gained a tortious freehold, he is [*176 remediable by writ of entry, *ad terminum qui præteriit.*(27)

On the other hand, in case of abatement, intrusion, or disseisin, where entries are generally lawful, this right of entry may be *tolled,* that is, taken away by descent.(28) Descents which take away entries(*d*) are when any

(*w*) Co. Litt. 252.	(*a*) Ibid. 237, 238.
(*x*) Litt. § 422.	(*b*) See book ii. page 150.
(*y*) Litt. §§ 419, 423.	(*c*) Co. Litt. 57.
(*z*) Co. Litt. 15.	(*d*) Litt. § 385-413.

(23) Barb. Rights of Pers. & Prop. 778.

(24) Chalker *v.* Chalker, 1 Day (Conn.) 79, 85 (1814). Martinsdale's Lessee *v.* Troop, 3 H. & McH. (Md.) 244, 249 (1793).

(25) But now, by statute 3 & 4 W. IV. c. 27, s. 10, no person shall be deemed to have been in possession of any land within the meaning of that act, merely by reason of having made an entry thereon; and, by s. 11, no continual or other claim upon or near any land shall preserve any right of making an entry. The distinction between the law as laid down by Blackstone and the present law as to an entry is, that by the former a bare entry on land was attended with a certain effect in keeping a right alive, whereas by the latter it has no effect whatever unless there be a change of possession. When this takes place, the remedy by entry is still in operation; when not, an entry is of no avail, and this remedy no longer exists.—STEWART. See also French *v.* Gray, 2 Day (Conn.) 92, 112 (1816). Lawrence *v.* Hunter, 9 Watts (Pa.) 64, 84 (1841). Newton *v.* Harland, 1 Scott's New Rep. (Eng.) 474, 494 (1840).

(26) Lessee of Rugge, 1 Bay (S. C.) 107, 111 (1790). Richardson *v.* Anthony, 12 Weston (Ver.) 273, 283 (1841). Williams *v.* Snidon, 4 Leigh (Va.) 14, 19 (1852).

(27) [For the term which has passed.]

(28) See the doctrine as to *descents cast* clearly explained in Adams on Ejectment, 41 to 45; and see H. Chitty on Descents, 25, 43, 56. Taylor *v.* Horde, 1 Burr. 60. 12 East, 141. Watkins on Descents. Com. Dig. Descents. Bac. Abr. Descents. It is scarcely possible to suggest a case in which the doctrine of descent cast can be now so applied as to prevent a claimant from maintaining ejectment. Adams, 41, note e. We have before seen that where the entry of the party or his ancestor was originally lawful, and the continuance in possession only unlawful, the entry is not tolled. See Dowl. & R. 41. "If a disseisor make a lease for term of his own life, and dieth, this descent shall not take away the entry of the disseisee; for though the fee and franktenement descend to the heir of the disseisor, yet the disseisor died not seised of the fee and franktenement;

one, seised by any means whatsoever of the inheritance of a corporeal here-ditament, dies;(29) whereby the same descends to his heir:(30) in this case, however feeble the right of the ancestor might be, the entry of any other person who claims title to the freehold is taken away, and he cannot recover possession against the heir by this summary method, but is driven to his action to gain a legal seisin of the estate.(31) And this, first, because the heir comes to the estate by act of law, and not by his own act; the law there-fore protects his title, and will not suffer his possession to be devested till the claimant hath proved a better right.(32) Secondly, because the heir may not suddenly know the true state of his title; and therefore the law, which is ever indulgent to heirs, takes away the entry of such claimant as neglected to enter on the ancestor, who was well able to defend his title; and leaves the claimant only the remedy of an action against the heir.(e) Thirdly, this was admirably adapted to the military spirit of the feodal tenures, and tended to make the feudatory bold in war, since his children could not by any mere entry of another be dispossessed of the lands whereof he died seised. And, lastly, it is agreeable to the dictates of reason and the general principles of law.(33)

For, in every complete title(f) to lands, there are two things necessary: the possession or seisin, and the right of property therein;(g) or, as it is expressed in Fleta, *juris et seisinæ conjunctio*.(h)(34) Now, if the possession be severed from the property, if A. has the *jus proprietatis*,(35) and B. by some unlawful means has gained possession of the lands, this is an *injury to A., for which the law gives a remedy by putting *him in possession, but does it by different means according to the circum-stances of the case. Thus, as B., who was himself the wrong-doer, and hath obtained the possession by either fraud or force, hath only a *bare* or *naked possession*, without any shadow of right, A., therefore, who hath both the *right* of property and the *right* of possession, may put an end to his title at once by the summary method of *entry*. But if B. the wrong-doer dies seised of the lands, then B.'s heir advances one step further towards a good title; he hath not only a *bare* possession, but also an apparent *jus possessionis*, or *right* of possession. For the law presumes that the possession which is

*177]

(e) Co. Litt. 237.
(f) See book ii. ch. 13.

(g) Mirror, c. 2, § 27.
(h) L. 3, c. 15, § 5.

and Littleton saith, unless he hath the fee and franktenement at the time of his decease, such descent shall not take away the entry." Co. Litt. 239, b., c. It was laid down in Carter v. Tash, by Holt, C. J., that if a feme-covert be disseisee, and after her husband dies she takes a second husband, and then the descent happens, this descent shall take away the entry of the feme, for she might have entered before the second marriage and prevented the descent. 1 Salk, 241. See also 4 T. R. 300.—CHITTY.

(29) He must die seised of the *freehold;* for if disseisor make a lease for *life* of the premises, retaining a reversion, and die, this descent does not take away the entry of the disseisee; because the disseisor died not possessed of the *freehold*, but merely of the re-version. Co. Litt. 239, b.—ARCHBOLD.

(30) This descent must be *immediate;* for if any other estate intervene between the death of the disseisor and the descent to the heir, it will not be a descent capable of toll-ing entry. Thus, if a woman be seised of an estate upon which another has a right of entry, and she marry, have issue, and die, her husband remaining tenant by the curtesy, —if upon the husband's death the issue enter, this descent does not toll entry, because it is not *immediate* from the mother, the estate by the curtesy intervening. See Litt. s. 394.—ARCHBOLD.

(31) Willard on Real Pr. & Conv. p, 358 (2 ed.).
(32) Jackson v. Bodle, 20 Johns. (N. Y.) 181 (1822).
(33) Doe *ex dem. v.* McLoskey, 1 Judges (Ala.) 708 (1840). Brown v. Potter, 17 Wen-dell, 164 (1837).
(34) [The joinder of right and possession.]
(35) [Right of property.]

transmitted from the ancestor to the heir is a rightful possession until the contrary be shown; and therefore the mere entry of A. is not allowed to evict the heir of B.; but A. is driven to his action at law to remove the possession of the heir, though his entry alone would have dispossessed the ancestor.(36)

So that, in general, it appears that no man can recover possession by mere entry on lands which another hath by descent.(37) Yet this rule hath some exceptions(i) wherein those reasons cease upon which the general doctrine is grounded; especially if the claimant were under any legal disabilities during the life of the ancestor, either of infancy, coverture, imprisonment, insanity, or being out of the realm: in all which cases there is no neglect or *laches* in the claimant, and therefore no descent shall bar or take away his entry.(k) And this title of taking away entries by descent is still further narrowed by the statute 32 Hen. VIII. c. 33, which enacts that, if any person disseises or turns another out of possession, no descent to the heir of the disseisor shall take away the entry of him that has a right to the land, unless the disseisor had peaceable possession five years next after the disseisin. But the statute extendeth not to any feoffee or donee of the disseisor, mediate or immediate;(l) because such a one by the genuine feodal constitutions always came into the tenure solemnly *and with the lord's con-　[*178 currence, by actual delivery of seisin, that is, open and public investiture. On the other hand, it is enacted by the statute of limitations, 21 Jac. I. c. 16, that no entry shall be made by any man upon lands, unless within twenty years after his right shall accrue.(38) And by statute 4 & 5 Anne, c. 16, no entry shall be of force to satisfy the said statute of limitations, or to avoid a fine levied of lands, unless an action be thereupon commenced within one year after, and prosecuted with effect.(39)

(i) See the particular cases mentioned by Littleton, b. iii. ch. 6, the principles of which are well explained in Gilbert's Law of Tenures.

(k) Co. Litt. 246.
(l) Ibid. 256.

---

(36) See Brown's Law of Lim. p. 69. But this distinction is now entirely abolished, having been found to lead to many useless subtleties in practice, it being enacted, by stat. 3 & 4 W. IV. c. 27, s. 39, that no descent which may happen to be made after the 31st of December, 1833, shall toll or defeat any right of entry for the recovery of land.—STEWART.

(37) This doctrine needs to be qualified a little. If a person be found in possession of land claiming it as his own in fee, it is *prima facie* evidence of his ownership and seisin of the inheritance. It is not, however, the possession, but the possession accompanied with the claim of the fee, that gives this effect by construction of law, to the acts of the party. Possession *per se* [By itself] evidences no more than the mere fact of present occupation by right; for the law will not presume a wrong: and that possession is just as consistent with a present interest under a lease for years, or for life, as in fee. From the very nature of the case, therefore, it must depend upon the collateral circumstances what is the quality and extent of interest claimed by the party; and to that extent, and that only, will the presumption of law go in his favor. Tyler on Ejectments, p. 71 (1871). Doe *ex dem.* Duval's Heirs *v.* McLoskey, 1 Judges (Ala.) 708, 738 (1840). City of Peda *v.* Schotte. 24 Iowa, 283, 296, 297 (1868).

(38) But by the second section, the same exceptions as are enumerated above, of infancy, coverture, imprisonment, insanity, and absence beyond seas, are made, in which case the party entitled may enter within ten years after the disability ceases, notwithstanding the twenty years should have elapsed after his title first accrued; and to *his heir* the statute gives ten years after the death of such party dying under the disability. It gives the heir ten years and no more, whatever disability he may labor under during all that time. 6 East, 85. And in 4 T. R. 300, it was agreed by the court that in every statute of limitations, if a disability be once removed, the time must continue to run notwithstanding any subsequent disability, either voluntary or involuntary. And in 5 B. & A., Abbott, C. J., said, the several statutes of limitation, being all in *pari materia* [Upon the same subject], ought to receive a uniform construction notwithstanding any slight variations of phrase, the object and intention being the same.—CHITTY. Johnson *v.* Howard, 1 Md. 281, 295, H. & McH. (1768).

(39) However, by stat. 3 & 4 W. IV. c. 27, one period of limitation is established for all

Upon an ouster by the discontinuance of tenant in tail, we have said that no remedy by mere entry is allowed; but that, when tenant in tail alienes the lands entailed, this takes away the entry of the issue in tail, and drives him to his action at law to recover the possession.(m)   For, as in the former cases, the law will not suppose, without proof, that the ancestor of him in possession acquired the estate by wrong, and therefore, after five years' peaceable possession, and a descent cast, will not suffer the possession of the heir to be disturbed by mere entry without action; so here the law will not suppose the discontinuor to have aliened the estate without power so to do, and therefore leaves the heir in tail to his action at law, and permits not his entry to be lawful.   Besides, the alienee, who came into possession by a lawful conveyance, which was at least good for the life of the alienor, hath not only a *bare* possession, but also an *apparent right* of possession; which is not allowed to be devested by the mere entry of the claimant, but continues in force till a better right be shown, and recognized by a legal determination.   And something also perhaps, in framing this rule of law, may be allowed to the inclination of the courts of justice, to go as far as they could in making estates-tail alienable, by declaring such alienations to be voidable only, and not absolutely void.

In case of deforcement also, where the deforciant had originally a lawful possession of the land, but now detains it wrongfully, he still continues to have the presumptive *prima *facie* evidence of right; that
*179] is, possession lawfully gained.   Which possession shall not be overturned by the mere entry of another; but only by the demandant's showing a better right in a course of law.

This remedy by entry must be pursued, according to statute 5 Ric. II. st. 1, c. 8, in a peaceable and easy manner; and not with force or strong hand. For, if one turns or keeps another out of possession forcibly, this is an injury of both a civil and a criminal nature.(40)   The civil is remedied by immediate restitution, which puts the ancient possessor *in statu quo:*(41) the criminal injury, or public wrong, by breach of the king's peace, is punished by fine to the king.   For by the statute 8 Hen. VI. c. 9, upon complaint made to any justice of the peace, of a forcible entry, with strong hand, on lands or tenements; or a forcible detainer after a peaceable entry; he shall try the truth of the complaint by jury, and, upon force found, shall restore the possession to the party so put out:(42) and in such case, or if any alienation be made to defraud the possessor of his right, (which is likewise declared to be absolutely void,) the offender shall forfeit, for the force found, treble damages to the party grieved, and make fine and ransom to the king.   But this does

(m) Co. Litt. 325.

---

lands and rents; and it is enacted by s. 2, that after the 31st of December, 1883, no person shall make an entry or bring an action to recover any land but within twenty years next after the time at which the right to make such entry or bring such action shall have first accrued to some person through whom he claims, or, if such right shall not have accrued to any person through whom he claims, then within twenty years next after the time at which the right to make such entry or bring such action shall have first accrued to the person making or bringing the same.—STEWART.

(40) Norvell *v.* Gray's Lessee, 1 Swanst. (Tenn.) 97.   Jackson *v.* Elsworth, 20 Johns. (N. Y.) 180 (1822).   Newton *v.* Harland, 1 Man. & Ch. (Eng.) 644 (1848).   French *v.* Gray, 2 Conn. 92 (1816).   Binn's Justice, p. 252 (10 ed.).   Lyon's Heirs *v.* Mottuse, 19 Ala. 185.   Exr's of Adam *v.* Robeson, Murphy (N. C.) 393 (1810).   State *v.* Morgan, 59 N. H. 323 (1879).

(41) [In the original state.]

(42) The question of title could not be considered in such an action of trespass, and judgment was no bar to any subsequent action.   Myers *v.* Koenig, 5 Neb. 419, 422 (1877).

not extend to such as endeavor to keep possession *manu forti*,(43) after three years' peaceable enjoyment of either themselves, their ancestors, or those under whom they claim; by a subsequent clause of the same statute, enforced by statute 31 Eliz. c. 11.(44)

II. Thus far of remedies, when tenant or occupier of the land hath gained only a *mere* possession, and no apparent shadow of right. Next follow another class, which are in use where the title of the tenant or occupier is advanced one step nearer to perfection; so that he hath in him not only a bare possession, which may be destroyed by a bare entry, but also an *apparent right of possession*, which cannot be removed but by orderly course of law; in the process of which it must be shown, that though he hath at present possession, and therefore hath *the presumptive right, yet   [*180 there is a right of possession, superior to his, residing in him who brings the action.

These remedies are either by a *writ of entry*, or an *assize;* which are actions merely *possessory;* serving only to regain that possession, whereof the demandant (that is, he who sues for the land) or his ancestors have been unjustly deprived by the tenant or possessor of the freehold, or those under whom he claims.   They decide nothing with respect to the *right of property;* only restoring the demandant to that state or situation, in which he was (or by law ought to have been) before the dispossession committed.   But this without any prejudice to the right of ownership; for, if the dispossessor has any legal claim, he may afterwards exert it, notwithstanding a recovery against him in these possessory actions.   Only the law will not suffer him to be his own judge, and either take or maintain possession of the lands, until he hath recovered them by legal means:(*n*) rather presuming the right to have accompanied the ancient seisin, than to reside in one who had no such evidence in his favor.

1. The first of these possessory remedies is by *writ of entry;*(45) which is that which disproves the title of the tenant or possessor, by showing the

(*n*) Mir. c. 4, § 24.

---

(43) [With a strong hand.]

(44) It was doubted whether, under the statutes mentioned in the text, any but a freeholder could have restitution; and therefore the 21 Jac. I. c. 25 applied the power conferred by them to the restitution of possession of which tenants for terms of years, tenants by copy of court-roll, guardian by knight-service, and tenants by elegit, statute-merchant, or statute-staple, had been forcibly deprived.   The justices of the peace are bound to grant a writ of restitution; but when the indictment is found at the assizes the judge may exercise his discretion.   The Queen *v.* Harland, 8 Add. & Ell. 326.   2 Moo. & Rob. 141.   In an indictment made under the statutes, the prosecutor's interest in the premises must be stated, (Rex *v.* Wilson, 8 T. R. 360, 362;) whence it seems to follow that where a tenant, wrongfully holding over after the expiration of his term, is forcibly dispossessed by the landlord, the case is not within them: otherwise the justices would be compellable to award restitution to the tenant, although his previous possession would not have supported an action of trespass *quare clausum fregit* [Wherefore he broke the close] against the landlord.   Turner *v.* Meymott, 1 Bing. 158; Taunton *v.* Costar, 7 T. R. 431.   Perhaps, however, the landlord may be indicted for a forcible entry at common law.   It is laid down, indeed, by Hawkins that no indictment for a forcible entry lay at common law where the party had lawful right of entry.   But in the King *v.* Bathurst, Sayer's Rep. 225, a forcible entry into a dwelling-house was held indictable at common law; and the correctness of what Hawkins said may be doubted.   See per lord Kenyon, Rex *v.* Wilson, *supra*, 364.   The landlord is undoubtedly liable to an action for a trespass to the person of the tenant, or to an indictment, if the entry be attended with circumstances that of themselves amount to a breach of the peace.   Rex *v.* Storr, 3 Burr. 1678. Rex *v.* Bake, id., 1731.   Newton *v.* Harland, 1 M. & G. 644.—COUCH.

(45) In Massachusetts and in Maine the demandant in a writ of entry must declare on his own seisin within twenty years, then past without specifying any particular day and must allege disseisin by the tenant, but need not aver the taking of the profits.   The demandant is not required to prove an actual entry under his title; but, if he is entitled to such an estate as he claims in the premises, whether as heir, or devisee, purchaser, or

unlawful means by which he entered or continues possession.(o)   The writ is directed to the sheriff, requiring him to "command the tenant of the land that he render (in Latin, *præcipe quod reddat*) to the demandant the land in question, which he claims to be his right and inheritance; and into which, as he saith, the said tenant had not entry but by (or after) a disseisin, intrusion, or the like, made to the said demandant, within the time limited by law for such actions; or that upon refusal he do appear in court on such a day, to show wherefore he hath not done it."(p)   This is the original process, the *præcipe* upon which all the rest of the suit is grounded: wherein it

*181]   appears, that the tenant is required, either to deliver *seisin of the lands, or to show cause why he will not.   This cause may be either a denial of the fact of having entered by or under such means as are suggested, or a justification of his entry by reason of title in himself or in those under whom he makes claim: whereupon the possession of the land is awarded to him who produces the clearest right to possess it.

In our ancient books we find frequent mention of the *degrees* within which writs of entry are brought.   If they be brought against the party himself that did the wrong, then they only charge the tenant himself with the injury: "*non habuit ingressum nisi per intrusionem quam ipse fecit.*" (46) But if the intruder, disseisor, or the like has made any alienation of the land to a third person, or it has descended to his heir, that circumstance must be alleged in the writ, for the action must always be brought against the tenant of the land; and the defect of his possessory title, whether arising from his own wrong or that of those under whom he claims, must be set forth.   One such alienation or descent makes the first(q) degree, which is called the *per*, because then the form of a writ of entry is this; that the tenant had not entry but by the original wrong-doer, who alienated the land, or from whom it descended to him: "*non habuit ingressum nisi per Gulielmum, qui se in illud intrusit, et illud tenenti dimisit.*" (r)(47) A second alienation or descent makes another degree, called the *per* and *cui;* because the form of a writ of entry, in that case, is, that the tenant had not entry but *by* or *under* a prior alienee, *to* whom the intruder demised it; "*non habuit ingressum nisi* per *Ricardum*, cui *Gulielmus illud dimisit, qui se in illud intrusit.*"(s)(48) These degrees thus state the original wrong, and the title of the tenant who claims under such wrong.   If more than two degrees (that is, two alienations or descents) were past, there lay no writ of entry at the com-

*182]   mon law.   For as it was provided, for the *quietness of men's inheritances, that no one, even though he had the true right of possession, should enter upon him who had the apparent right by descent or otherwise, but he was driven to his *writ of entry* to gain possession; so, after

---

(o) Finch, L. 261.
(p) See book ii. Append. No. V. § 1.
(q) Finch. L. 262. Booth indeed (of Real Actions, 172) makes the first degree to consist in the original

wrong done, the second in the *per*, and the third in the *per* and *cui*. But the difference is immaterial.
(r) Booth, 181.
(s) Finch, L. 263. F. N. B. 203, 204.

---

otherwise, and also that he has a right of entry therein, it shall be sufficient proof of his seisin. Angell on Limitations, p. 368.

(46) ["He had no entry but by the intrusion, which he himself made."] Jackson v. Slausbury, 9 Wend. (N. Y.) 203 (1832). It is now well settled that when a contract of tenancy is consummated the tenant has exclusive right of possession and for any injury to the possession during the tenancy, lies in the tenant and not the landlord. Yet the landlord still has a right of action for any injury done to his reversionary interest. Walden v. Conn, 84 Kentucky, 312 (1886). Angell on Lim. p. 367 (6 ed.)

(47) ["He had no entry but through William, who intruded himself on it, and demised it to his tenant."]

(48) ["He had no entry but through Richard, to whom William, who had intruded on the lands, demised it."]

more than two descents or two conveyances were passed, the demandant, even though he had the right both of possession and property, was not allowed this *possessory* action; but was driven to his *writ of right*, a long and final remedy, to punish his neglect in not sooner putting in his claim, while the degree subsisted, and for the ending of suits and quieting of all controversies. (*t*) But by the statute of Marlberge, 52 Hen. III. c. 30, it was provided, that when the number of alienations or descents exceeded the usual degrees, a new writ should be allowed without any mention of degrees at all.   And accordingly a new writ has been framed, called a writ of entry in the *post*, which only alleges the injury of the wrong-doer, without deducing all the intermediate title from him to the tenant: stating it in this manner; that the tenant had not entry unless *after*, or subsequent to, the ouster or injury done by the original dispossessor; "*non habuit ingressum nisi* post *intrusionem quam Gulielmus in illud fecit;*"(49) and rightly concluding, that if the original title was wrongful, all claims derived from thence must participate of the same wrong.   Upon the latter of these writs it is (the writ of entry *sur disseisin* in the *post*) that the form of our common recoveries of landed estates(*u*) is usually grounded; which, we may remember, were observed in the preceding volume(*v*) to be fictitious actions brought against the tenant of the freehold, (usually called the tenant to the *præcipe*, or writ of entry;) in which by collusion the demandant recovers the land.

This remedial instrument, or writ of entry, is applicable to all the cases of ouster before mentioned, except that of discontinuance by tenant in tail, and some peculiar species of deforcements.   Such is that of deforcement of dower, by not assigning *any* dower to the widow within the time limited by *law; for which she has her remedy by writ of *dower*,   [*183 *unde nihil habet.*(*w*)(50)   But if she be deforced of part only of her dower, she cannot then say that *nihil habet;*(51) and therefore she may have recourse to another action, by writ of *right of dower;* which is a more general remedy, extending either to part or the whole; and is (with regard to her claim) of the same nature as the grand writ of right, whereof we shall presently speak, is with regard to claims in fee simple.(*x*)   On the other hand, if the heir (being within age) or his guardian assign her more than she ought to have, they may be remedied by a writ of *admeasurement of dower.*(*y*)   But in general the writ of entry is the universal remedy to recover possession, when wrongfully withheld from the owner.   It were therefore endless to recount all the several divisions of writs of entry, which the different circumstances of the respective demandants may require, and which are furnished by the laws of England:(*z*) being plainly and clearly

(*t*) 2 Inst. 153.
(*u*) See book ii. Append. No. V.
(*v*) Book ii. ch. 21.
(*w*) F. N. B. 147.
(*x*) Ibid. 16.
(*y*) F. N. B. 148.   Finch, L. 314.   Stat. Westm. 2, 13 Edw. I. c. 7.
(*z*) See Bracton, *l.* 4. *tr.* 7, c. 6, §4.   Britton, c. 114, fol. 264.   The most usual were,—1. The writs of entry *sur disseisin* [On disseisin] and of *intrusion*, (F. N. B. 191, 203,) which are brought to remedy either of those species of ouster. 2. The writs of *dum fuit*

infra ætatem [While he was under age] and *dum fuit non compos mentis*, [While he was of unsound mind,] (ibid. 192, 202,) which lie for a person of full age, or one who hath recovered his understanding, after having (when under age or insane) aliened his lands, or for the heirs of such alienor. 3. The writs of *cui in vita* [Whom in his life time] and *cui ante divortium*, [Whom before divorce,] (ibid. 193, 204,) for a woman, when a widow or divorced, whose husband during the coverture (*cui in vita sua, vel cui ante divortium, ipsa contradicere non potuit*) [Whom in his lifetime, or whom before divorce she could not con-

(49) ["He had no entry except after the intrusion William made therein."]

(50) [Whereby she has nothing.]   Dower is not within the statute of limitations of Henry or of James.   In New Hampshire, Georgia, North Carolina and Tennessee it is also considered as not within the statute and in Maryland it has been held that the statute was not a bar.   Dower may be recovered by a bill in equity as well as an action at law, and in many states the courts of probate are empowered to appoint commissioners to set off the dower.   Angell on Limitations, p. 369.

(51) 1 Lomax Dig. 98.

chalked out in that most ancient and highly venerable collection of legal forms, the *registrum omnium brevium*, or register of such writs as are

*184]   suable out of the king's court, upon which Fitzherbert's *natura brevium*(52) is a comment; and in which every man who *is injured will be sure to find a method of relief, exactly adapted to his own case, described in the compass of a few lines, and yet without the omission of any material circumstance.   So that the wise and equitable provision of the statute Westm. 2, 13 Edw. I. c. 24, for framing new writs when wanted, is almost rendered useless by the very great perfection of the ancient forms. And indeed I know not whether it is a greater credit to our laws, to have such a provision contained in them, or not to have occasion, or at least very rarely, to use it.(53)

In the times of our Saxon ancestors the right of possession seems only to have been recoverable by writ of entry,(a) which was then usually brought in the county-court.   And it is to be observed that the proceedings in these actions were not then so tedious when the courts were held and process issued from and was returnable therein at the end of every three weeks, as they became after the conquest, when all causes were drawn into the king's courts, and process issued only from term to term; which was found exceedingly dilatory, being at least four times as slow as the other.   And hence a new remedy was invented in many cases, to do justice to the people and to determine the possession in the proper counties, and yet by the king's judges.   This was the remedy by *assize*, which is called, by statute Westm. 2, 13 Edw. I. c. 24, *festinum remedium*,(54) in comparison with that by a writ of entry; it not admitting of many dilatory pleas and proceedings to which other real actions are subject.(b)(55)

2. The writ of *assize* is said to have been invented by Glanvil, chief justice to Henry the Second;(c) and if so, it seems to owe its introduction to the parliament held at Northampton in the twenty-second year of that prince's

*185]   reign; when justices in eyre were appointed to go round the kingdom in order to take these assizes: and the assizes themselves *(particularly those of *mort d'ancestor* and *novel disseisin*) were clearly pointed out and described.(d)   As a writ of entry is a real action which *disproves* the title of the tenant by showing the unlawful commencement of his possession, so an assize is a real action which *proves* the title of the demandant merely

---

tradict] hath aliened her estate. 4. The writ *ad communem legem*, [At common law] (ibid. 207,) for the reversioner, after the alienation and death of the particular tenant for life. 5. The writs *in causa proviso* [In the case provided] and *in consimili casu*, [In the like case,] (ibid. 205, 206), which lay not *ad communem legem* [At common law,] but are given, by stat. Gloc. 6 Edw. I. c. 7, and Westm. 2, 13 Edw. I. c. 21, for the reversioner after the alienation, but during the life, of the tenant in dower or other tenant for life. 6. The writ *ad terminum qui præter iit*, [For an expired term,] (ibid. 201,) for the reversioner, when the possession is withheld by the lessee or a stranger after the determination of a lease for years.   7. The writ *causa matrimonii prælocuti*, [In consideration of marriage before agreed upon,] (ibid. 205,) for a woman who giveth land to a man in fee or for life, to the intent that he may marry her, and he doth not.   And the like in case of other deforcements.

(a) Gilb. Ten. 42.
(b) Booth, 202.

(c) Mirror, c. 2, § 25.
(d) § 9. *Si dominus feodi negat hæredibus defuncti saisi non ejusdem feodi, justiciarii domini regis faciant inde fieri, recognitionem per xii. legales homines, qualem saisinam defunctus inde habuit, die qua fuit vivus et mortuus; et, sicut recognitum fuerit, ita hæredibus ejus restituant.* § 10. *Justiciarii domini regis faciant fieri recognitionem de dissaisinis factis super assisam, a tempore quo dominis rex venit in Angliam proxime post pacem factam inter ipsum et regem filium suum.* [If the lord of the fee refuse to the heirs of the deceased seisin of the same fee, the king's justices may cause an inquiry to be made by twelve lawful men, of what seisin the deceased had on the day of his death, and according to the result of such inquiry it shall be restored to his heirs. S. 10. The king's justices shall cause an inquiry to be made of the disseisins made upon assize, from the time at which the king came into England, next after the peace made between him and his son.] Spelm. *Cod.* 350.

---

(52) [Natural writs.]
(53) Sedgwick on Title to Land, p. 7 (2 ed.).
(54) [The speedy remedy.]
(55) The remedy by writ of entry was abolished by 3 & 4 W. IV. c. 27, s. 36.—
STEWART.

by showing his or his ancestor's possession:(e) and these two remedies are in all other respects so totally alike that a judgment or recovery in one is a bar against the other; so that when a man's possession is once established by either of these possessory actions it can never be disturbed by the same antagonist in any other of them. The word *assize* is derived by Sir Edward Coke (f) from the Latin *assideo*, to sit together; and it signifies, originally, the jury who try the cause and sit together for that purpose. By a figure it is now made to signify the court or jurisdiction which summons this jury together by a commission of assize, or *ad assisas capiendas;* and hence the judicial assemblies held by the king's commission in every county, as well to take these writs of assize, as to try causes at *nisi prius*, are termed in common speech the *assizes*. By another somewhat similar figure the name of assize is also applied to this action, for recovering possession of lands; for the reason, saith Littleton,(g) why such writs at the beginning were called assize, was, for that in these writs the sheriff is ordered to summon a jury or assize; which is not expressed in any other original writ.(h)

This remedy, by writ of assize, is only applicable to two species of injury by ouster, viz., *abatement*, and a recent or *novel disseisin*. If the abatement happened upon the death of the demandant's father or mother, brother or sister, uncle or aunt, nephew or niece, the remedy is by an assize of *mort d'ancestor*, or death of one's ancestor. This *writ directs the [*186 sheriff to summon a jury or assize, who shall view the land in question, and recognize whether such ancestor was seised thereof on the day of his death, and whether the demandant be the next heir:(i) soon after which the judges come down by the king's commission to take the recognition of assize: when, if these points are found in the affirmative, the law immediately transfers the possession from the tenant to the demandant. If the abatement happened on the death of one's grandfather or grandmother, then an assize of *mort d'ancestor* no longer lies, but a writ of *ayle* or *de avo:*(56) if on the death of the great-grandfather or great-grandmother, then a writ of *besayle* or *de proavo:*(57) but if it mounts one degree higher, to the *tresayle*, or grandfather's grandfather, or if the abatement happened upon the death of any collateral relation other than those before mentioned, the writ is called a writ of *cosinage* or *de consanguineo.*(k) And the same points shall be inquired of in all these actions *ancestrel* as in an assize of *mort d'ancestor;* they being of the very same nature:(l) though they differ in this point of form, that these *ancestrel* writs (like all other writs of *præcipe*) expressly assert a title in the demandant, (viz., the seisin of the ancestor at his death, and his own right of inheritance,) the assize asserts nothing directly, but only prays an inquiry whether these points be so.(m) There is also another ancestrel writ, denominated a *nuper obiit*,(58) to establish an equal division of the land in question, where, on the death of an ancestor who has several heirs, one enters and holds the others out of possession.(n) But a man is not allowed to have any of these actions ancestrel for an abatement consequent on the death of any collateral relation beyond the fourth degree;(o) though in the lineal ascent he may proceed *ad infinitum.*(p)(59) For there must be some boundary, or else the privilege would be universal; which is

(e) Finch, L. 284.
(f) 1 Inst. 153.
(g) 2 234.
(h) Co. Litt. 159.
(i) F. N. B. 195. Finch, L. 290.
(k) Finch, L. 266, 267.

(l) Stat. Westm. 2, 13 Edw. I. c. 20.
(m) 2 Inst. 399.
(n) F. N. B. 197. Finch, L. 298.
(o) Hale on F. N. B. 221.
(p) Fitz. Abr. tit. *cosinage*, 15.

(56) [From the grandfather.]
(57) [From the great-grandfather.]
(58) [He lately died.]
(59) [Indefinitely.]

absurd: and therefore the law pays no regard to the possession of a collateral ancestor who was no nearer than the fifth degree. (60)

*187]   *It was always held to be a law (q) that where lands were devisable in a man's last will by the custom of the place, there an assize of *mort d'ancestor* did not lie. For where lands were so devisable, the right of possession could never be determined by a process which inquired only of these two points, the seisin of the ancestor and the heirship of the demandant. And hence it may be reasonable to conclude, that when the statute of wills, 32 Hen. VIII. c. 1, made all socage-lands devisable, an assize of *mort d'ancestor* no longer could be brought of lands held in socage; (r) and that now, since the statute 12 Car. II. c. 24, (which converts all tenures, a few only excepted, into free and common socage,) no assize of *mort d'ancestor* can be brought of any lands in the kingdom, but that, in case of abatements, recourse must be properly had to the writs of entry. (61)

An assize of *novel* (or recent) *disseisin* is an action of the same nature with the assize of *mort d'ancestor*, (62) before mentioned, in that herein the demandant's possession must be shown. But it differs considerably in other points; particularly in that it recites a complaint by the demandant of the disseisin committed, in terms of direct averment; whereupon the sheriff is commanded to reseize the land and all the chattels thereon, and keep the same in his custody till the arrival of the justices of assize, (which in fact hath been usually omitted;) (s) and in the meantime to summon a jury to view the premises, and make recognition of the assize before the justices. (t) At which time the tenant may plead either the general issues *nul tort, nul disseisin*, (63) or any special plea. And if, upon the general issue, the recognitors find an actual seisin in the demandant, and his subsequent disseisin by the present tenant, he shall have judgment to recover his seisin, and damages for the injury sustained: being the only case in which damages were recoverable in any possessory actions at the common law; (u) the tenant being in
*188]   all other cases allowed to retain the intermediate profits of the *land, to enable him to perform the feudal service. But costs and damages were annexed to many other possessory actions by the statutes of Marlberge, 52 Hen. III. c. 16, and Glocester, 6 Edw. I. c. 1. And to prevent frequent and vexatious disseisins, it is enacted by the statute of Merton, 20 Hen. III. c. 3, that if a person disseised recover seisin of the land again by assize of *novel disseisin*, and be again disseised of the same tenements by the same disseisor, he shall have a writ of *re-disseisin;* and if he recover therein, the re-disseisor shall be imprisoned; and by the statute of Marlberge, 52 Hen. III. c. 8, shall also pay a fine to the king: to which the statute Westm. 2, 13 Edw. I. c. 26 hath superadded double damages to the party aggrieved. In like manner, by the same statute of Merton, when any lands or tenements are recovered by assize of *mort d'ancestor*, or other injury, or any judgment

---

(q) Bracton, l. 4, *de assis. mortis antecessoris*, c. 13, § 3. F. N. B. 196.
(r) See 1 Leon. 267.

(s) Booth, 211. Bract. 4, 1, 19, § 7.
(t) F. N. B. 177.
(u) Bract. 187. Stat. Marlbr. c. 16.

---

(60) The revised statutes of New York provide that no person shall be precluded from an inheritance by reason of the alienation of any ancestor of such a person. McCarthy *v.* Marsh, 1 Selden (N. Y.) 263 (1851). (And so in other states.)

(61) In Launder *v.* Brooks and others, Cro. Car. 562, the court of King's Bench "resolved that an assize of *mort d'ancestor* lies of lands devisable; but if the defendant plead that the land is by custom devisable, *and was devised to him*, it is a good bar to the action." This seems more sensible than to deny generally a form of action to the heir because in a particular case there may be a good bar to his right.—COLERIDGE. See Angell on Limitations, p. 367 (6 ed.)

(62) [Death of an ancestor.]

(63) [No wrong, no disseisin.]

of the court, if the party be afterwards disseised by the same person against whom judgment was obtained, he shall have a writ of *post-disseisin* against him; which subjects the post-disseisor to the same penalties as a re-disseisor. The reason of all which, as given by Sir Edward Coke,(*w*) is because such proceeding is a contempt of the king's courts, and in despite of the law; or, as Bracton more fully expresses it,(*x*) " *talis qui ita convictus fuerit, dupliciter delinquit contra regem: quia facit disseisinam et roberiam contra pacem suam; et etiam ausu temerario irrita facit ea, quæ in curia domini regis rite acta sunt: et propter duplex delictum merito sustinere debet pœnam duplicatam.*"(64)

In all these possessory actions there is a time of limitation settled, beyond which no man shall avail himself of the possession of himself or his ancestors, or take advantage of the wrongful possession of his adversary.(65) For, if he be negligent for a long and unreasonable time, the law refuses afterwards to lend him any assistance, to recover the possession merely; both to punish his neglect, (*nam leges vigilantibus, non dormientibus, subvenient,*)(66) and also because it is presumed that the supposed wrong-doer has in such a length of time procured a legal title, otherwise *he would [*189 sooner have been sued. This time of limitation by the statute of Merton, 20 Hen. III. c. 8, and Westm. 1, 3 Edw. I. c. 39, was successively dated from particular eras, viz., from the return of king John from Ireland, and from the coronation, etc., of king Henry the Third. But this date of limitation continued so long unaltered that it became indeed no limitation at all; it being above three hundred years from Henry the Third's coronation to the year 1540, when the present statute of limitations(*y*) was made. This, instead of limiting actions from the date of a particular event, as before, which in process of years grew absurd, took another and more direct course, which might endure forever: by limiting a certain period, as fifty years for lands, and the like period(*z*) for customary and prescriptive rents, suits, and services, (for there is no time of limitation upon rents created by deed, or reserved on a particular estate,)(*a*) and enacting that no person should bring any possessory action, to recover possession thereof merely upon the seisin, or dispossession of his ancestors, beyond such certain period. But this does not extend to services which by common possibility may not happen to become due more than once in the lord's or tenant's life; as fealty, and the like.(*b*) And all writs, grounded upon the possession of the demandant himself, are directed to be sued out within thirty years after the disseisin complained of; for if it be an older date, it can with no propriety be called a fresh, recent, or *novel disseisin;* which name Sir Edward Coke informs us was originally given to this proceeding, because the disseisin must have been since the last *eyre* or circuit of the justices, which happened once in seven years, otherwise the action was gone.(*c*) And we may observe,(*d*) that the

---

(*w*) 2 Inst. 83, 84.
(*x*) L. 4, c. 49.
(*y*) 32 Hen. VIII. c. 2.
(*z*) So Berthelet's original edition of the statute, A. D. 1540, and Cay's, Pickering's, and Ruffhead's editions, examined with the record. Rastell's and other intermediate editions, which Sir Edward Coke

(2 Inst. 95) and other subsequent writers have followed, make it only *forty* years for rents, etc.
(*a*) 8 Rep. 65.
(*b*) Co. Litt. 115.
(*c*) 1 Inst. 153. Booth, 210.
(*d*) See page 184.

---

(64) ["He who is so convicted offends doubly against the king; first, because he makes a disseisin and robbery against his peace; and secondly, by a rash undertaking sets at defiance the just decisions of the king's court: and for this double offence he deserves a double punishment."] Costs are now regulated in the federal courts of the United States by act of congress, and are recoverable by the prevailing party. Goodyear *v.* Sawyer, 17 Federal Reporter, 2 (1883).

(65) The landlord may, after a recovery in ejectment, bring an action for rents and profits recovered by the disseisor. Nelson *v.* Allen and Harris, 1 Yerger (Tenn.) 360 (1830).

(66) [For the laws aid the vigilant, not the slothful.]

limitation, prescribed by Henry the Second at the first institution of the assize of *novel disseisin*, was from his own return into England, after the peace made between him and the young king his son; which was but the year before.(67)

*190]   *What has been here observed may throw some light on the doctrine of *remitter*, which we spoke of in the second chapter of this book; and which we may remember was where one who hath right to lands, but is out of possession, hath afterwards the freehold cast upon him by some subsequent defective title, and enters by virtue of that title. In this case the law remits him to his ancient and more certain right, and by an equitable fiction supposes him to have gained possession in consequence and by virtue thereof: and this, because he cannot possibly obtain judgment at law to be restored to his prior right, since he is himself the tenant of the land, and therefore hath nobody against whom to bring his action. This determination of the law might seem superfluous to a hasty observer; who perhaps would imagine, that since the tenant hath now both the right and also the possession, it little signifies by what means such possession shall be said to be gained. But the wisdom of our ancient law determined nothing in vain. As the tenant's possession was gained by a defective title, it was liable to be overturned by showing that defect in a writ of entry; and then he must have been driven to his writ of right, to recover his just inheritance: which would have been doubly hard, because during the time he was himself tenant he could not establish his prior title by any possessory actions. The law therefore remits him to his prior title, or puts him in the same condition as if he had recovered the land by writ of entry. Without the remitter, he would have had *jus, et seisinam*(68) separate; a good right, but a bad possession: now, by the remitter, he hath the most perfect of all titles, *juris et seisinæ conjunctionem.*(69)

III. By these several possessory remedies the right of possession may be restored to him that is unjustly deprived thereof. But the right of *possession* (though it carries with it a strong presumption) is not always conclusive evidence of the right of *property*, which may still subsist in another *191]   man. For, as *one man may have the *possession*, and another the *right of possession*, which is recovered by these possessory actions; so one man may have the *right of possession*, and so not be liable to eviction by any possessory action, and another may have the *right of property*, which cannot be otherwise asserted than by the great and final remedy of a writ of right, or such correspondent writs as are in the nature of a writ of right.

---

(67) But all these distinctions are now chiefly of interest as matters of antiquity; for all writs of assize are abolished. 3 & 4 W. IV. c. 27, s. 36.—STEWART.

Adverse possession to be effective must be continuous; one cannot vacate the land, and after a lapse of time return and claim the benefit of the statute; yet where one builds part of a house and departs, but returns in a short time and finishes the house, the statute begins to run from the time in which he first took possession. Byrne *v*. Lowry, 19 Cobb (Ga.) 27 (1855). But where one holds possession for a time insufficient to give title, and another succeeds him in possession, the imperfect possession of the former cannot be united to the possession of the latter, and make the possession continuous and exclusive against the owner. Hoye *v*. Swan's lessee, 5 Maryland (Miller's) 237 (1853). In order to avoid the statute of limitations, the owner must make actual and peaceful re-entry *animo clamando* [With intention of claiming]. He must declare his intention of re-entering for the purpose of claiming his land. Johnson *v*. Howard, 1 Harris and McHenry's (Md.) 281 (1763). Norvell *v*. Gray's lessee, 1 Swan. (Tenn.) 96 (1851). Angell on Limitations, 356, 374. Cunningham *v*. Frandtzen, 2 Texas, 34 (1861). Jacob *v*. Rice, 33 Illinois, 369 (1864). Pinckney *et al. v*. Burrage *et al.*, 2 Vroom (N. J.) 21 (1864). Greenleaf's Cruise on Real Prop. vol. 2, p. 238 (1856). 2 Barb. Rights of Pers. & Prop. p. 786.

(68) [A right and seisin.]
(69) [The conjunction of right and seisin.]

This happens principally in four cases: 1. Upon discontinuance by the alienation of tenant in tail: whereby he who had the right of possession hath transferred it to the alienee; and therefore his issue, or those in remainder or reversion, shall not be allowed to recover by virtue of that possession, which the tenant hath so voluntarily transferred. 2, 3. In case of judgment given against either party, whether by his own default, or upon trial of the merits, in any possessory action: for such judgment, if obtained by him who hath not the true ownership, is held to be a species of deforcement; which, however, binds the right of possession, and suffers it not to be ever again disputed, unless the right of property be also proved. 4. In case the demandant, who claims the right, is barred from these possessory actions by length of time and the statute of limitations before mentioned: for an undisturbed possession for fifty years ought not to be devested by any thing but a very clear proof of the absolute right of property. In these four cases the law applies the remedial instruments of either the writ of right itself, or such other writs as are said to be of the same nature.

1. And first, upon an alienation by tenant in tail, whereby the estate-tail is *discontinued*, and the remainder or reversion is by failure of the particular estate displaced, and turned into a mere right, the remedy is by action of *formedon*, (*secundum formam doni*,)(70) which is in nature of a writ of right,(*e*) and is the highest action that tenant in tail can have.(*f*) For he cannot have an absolute writ of right, which is confined only to such as claim in fee-simple: and for that reason this writ of *formedon* was granted him by the statute *de donis* or *Westm. 2, 13 Edw. I. c. 1, which is   [*192 therefore emphatically called *his* writ of right.(*g*) This writ is distinguished into three species: a *formedon* in the *descender*, in the *remainder*, and in the *reverter*. A writ of *formedon* in the *descender* lieth, where a gift in tail is made, and the tenant in tail alienes the lands entailed, or is disseised of them, and dies; in this case the heir in tail shall have this writ of *formedon* in the *descender*, to recover these lands so given in tail against him who is then the actual tenant of the freehold.(*h*) In which action the demandant is bound to state the manner and form of the gift in tail, and to prove himself heir *secundum forman doni*. A *formedon* in the *remainder* lieth, where a man giveth lands to another for life or in tail, with remainder to a third person in tail or in fee, and he who hath the particular estate dieth without issue inheritable, and a stranger intrudes upon him in remainder and keeps him out of possession.(*i*) In this case the remainder-man shall have his writ of *formedon* in the *remainder*, wherein the whole form of the gift is stated, and the happening of the event upon which the remainder depended. This writ is not given in express words by the statute *de donis;* but is founded upon the equity of the statute, and upon this maxim in law, that if any one hath a right to the land, he ought also to have an action to recover it. A *formedon* in the *reverter* lieth, where there is a gift in tail, and afterwards by the death of the donee or his heirs without issue of his body the reversion falls in upon the donor, his heirs, or assigns: in such case the reversioner shall have his writ to recover the lands, wherein he shall suggest the gift, his own title to the reversion minutely derived from the donor, and the failure of issue upon which his reversion takes place.(*k*) This lay at common law,

---

(*e*) Finch. L. 267.
(*f*) Co. Litt. 316.
(*g*) F. N. B. 255.

(*h*) F. N. B. 211, 212.
(*i*) Ibid. 217.
(*k*) Ibid. 219. 8 Rep. 88.

---

(70) ["According to the form of the gift."] See Martindale's Lessee *v.* Troop, 3 H. & McH. (Md.) 244, 305 (1793). Lyon's Heirs *v.* Motuse, 19 Ala. 463 (1851). Lecate *v.* Ins. Co., 16 Ala. 463 (1849). Angell's Limitations, 358. [*De donis*—Of gifts.]

before the statute *de donis*, if the donee aliened before he had performed the condition of the gift, by having issue, and afterwards died without any.(*l*)

The time of limitation in a *formedon*, by statute 21 Jac. I. c. 16, *193] is twenty years;(71) within *which space of time after his title accrues, the demandant must bring his action, or else he is forever barred.(72)

2. In the second case; if the owners of a particular estate, as for life, in dower, by the curtesy, or in fee-tail, are barred of the right of possession by a recovery had against them, through their default or non-appearance in a possessory action, they were absolutely without any remedy at the common law: as a writ of right does not lie for any but such as claim to be tenants of the fee-simple. Therefore the statute Westm. 2, 13 Edw. I. c. 4 gives a new writ for such persons, after their lands have been so recovered against them by default, called a *quod ei deforceat;*(73) which, though not strictly a writ of right, so far partakes of the nature of one, as that it will restore the right to him who has been thus unwarily deforced by his own default.(*m*) But in case the recovery were not had by his own default, but upon defence in the inferior possessory action, this still remains final with regard to these particular estates, as at the common law: and hence it is, that a common recovery (on writ of entry in the *post*) had, not by default of the tenant himself, but (after his defence made and voucher of a third person to warranty) by default of such vouchee, is now the usual bar to cut off an estate-tail.(*n*)

3, 4. Thirdly, in case the right of possession be barred by a recovery upon the merits in a possessory action, or lastly by the statute of limitations, a claimant in fee simple may have a *mere writ of right;* which is in its nature the highest writ in the law,(*o*) and lieth only of an estate in fee-simple, and not for him who hath a less estate.(74) This writ lies *concurrently* with all other real actions, in which an estate of fee-simple may be recovered: and it also lies *after* them, being as it were an appeal to the mere right, when judgment hath been had as to the possession in an inferior possessory *194] *action.(*p*) But though a writ of right may be brought, where the demandant is entitled to the possession, yet it rarely is advisable to be brought in such cases, as a more expeditious and easy remedy is had, without meddling with the property, by proving the demandant's own, or his ancestor's, possession, and their illegal ouster, in one of the possessory

(*l*) Finch, L. 268.
(*m*) F. N. B. 155.
(*n*) See book ii. ch. 21.

(*o*) F. N. B. 1.
(*p*) Ibid. 1, 5.

---

(71) The twenty years within which a *formedon* in the *descender* ought to be commenced under the 21 Jac. I. c. 16, begin to run when the title descends to the first heir in tail, unless he lie under a disability; and the heirs of such person who suffers the twenty years to elapse without commencing the formedon are utterly excluded, and the right of entry is forever lost. 3 Brod. & Bing. 217. 6 East, 83; and see note 38, *ante*, 1169.—CHITTY.

(72) It might seem, and has been contended, that a fresh title accrues to the issue in tail of a person who has been barred by the lapse of time, and therefore that such issue would have another twenty years in which to bring his *formedon*. But if this construction prevailed at all, it is obvious that it would equally prevail through any number of descents, and would virtually repeal the statute in the most pernicious manner. In the case of Tolson *v.* Kaye, 3 Brod. & Bing. 217, the court of Common Pleas, therefore, determined that the *first* descent of the title, within twenty years after which the statute requires the *formedon* to be sued out, is the descent upon that claimant who, being free from any disability, suffers twenty years to elapse without asserting his right; and, consequently, that the bar which operates upon him equally concludes all claiming as his heirs.—COLERIDGE.

(73) [That he deforced him.]

(74) Henry *v.* Thorpe, 14 Ala. 103, 109 (1848). Angell on Limitations, p. 357 (1876).

actions. But in case the right of possession be lost by length of time, or by judgment against the true owner in one of these inferior suits, there is no other choice: this is then the only remedy that can be had; and it is of so forcible a nature, that it overcomes all obstacles, and clears all objections that may have arisen to cloud and obscure the title. And, after issue once joined in a writ of right, the judgment is absolutely final; so that a recovery had in this action may be pleaded in bar of any other claim or demand. (*q*)

The pure, proper, or mere writ of right lies only, we have said, to recover lands in fee-simple, unjustly withheld from the true proprietor.(75) But there are also some other writs which are said to be *in the nature of* a writ of right, because their process and proceedings do mostly (though not entirely) agree with the writ of right: but in some of them the fee-simple is not demanded; and in others not land, but some incorporeal hereditament. Some of these have been already mentioned, as the writ of *right of dower*, *of formedon*, etc., and the others will hereafter be taken notice of under their proper divisions. Nor is the mere writ of right alone, or always, applicable to every case of a claim of lands in fee-simple: for if the lord's tenant in fee-simple dies without heir, whereby an escheat accrues, the lord shall have a writ of *escheat*,(*r*) which is in the nature of a writ of right.(*s*) And if one of two of more coparceners deforces the other, by usurping the sole possession, the party aggrieved shall have a writ of right, *de rationabili parte*,(*t*)(76) which may be grounded on the *seisin of the ancestor   [*195 at any time during his life; whereas in a *nuper obiit* (which is a possessory remedy)(*u*) he must be seised at the time of his death. But, waiving these and other minute distinctions, let us now return to the general writ of right.

This writ ought to be first brought in the court-baron (*w*) of the lord, of whom the lands are holden; and then it is open or *patent:* but if he holds no court, or hath waived his right, *remisit curiam suam*, it may be brought in the king's courts by writ of *præcipe* originally;(*x*) and then it is a writ of right *close;* (*y*) being directed to the sheriff and not the lord.(*z*) Also, when one of the king's immediate tenants *in capite* is deforced, his writ of right is called a writ of *præcipe in capite*,(77) (the improper use of which, as well as of the former *præcipe quia dominus remisit curiam*,(78) so as to oust the lord of his jurisdiction, is restrained by *magna carta*,)(*a*) and, being directed to the sheriff and originally returnable in the king's courts, is also a writ of right *close*.(*b*) There is likewise a little writ of *right close*, *secundum consuetudinem manerii*,(79) which lies for the king's tenants in ancient demesne,(*c*) and others of a similar nature,(*d*) to try the right of their lands and tenements in the court of the lord exclusively.(*e*) But the writ of *right patent* itself may also at any time be removed into the county-court, by writ of *tolt*,(*f*) and from thence into the king's courts by writ of

(*q*) F. N. B. 6. Co. Litt. 158.
(*r*) F. N. B. 143.
(*s*) Booth. 135.
(*t*) F. N. B. 9.
(*u*) See page 186.
(*w*) Append. No. I. § 1.
(*x*) F. N. B. 2. Finch, L. 313.
(*y*) Booth, 91.
(*z*) Append. No. I. § 4.

(*a*) C. 24.
(*b*) F. N. B. 5.
(*c*) See book ii. ch. 6.
(*d*) Kitchen, tit. *Copyhold*.
(*e*) Bracton, *l.* 1, c. 11, *l.* 4, *tr.* 1, c. 9, and *tr.* 3, c. 13, § 9. Old Tenur. t. *tenir en socage*. Old N. B. t. *garde*, and t. *briefe de recto claus*. F. N. B. 11.
(*f*) Append. No. I. § 2.

(75) Speed *v.* Buford, 3 Bibb. (Ky.) 57 (1813). Henry *v.* Thorpe, 14 Alabama, 103 (1848).
(76) [For the reasonable part.]
(77) [Command for the tenant in capite.]
(78) [Because the lord has waived his court.]
(79) [According to the custom of the manor.]

pone(*g*) or *recordari facias*,(80) at the suggestion of either party that there is a delay or defect of justice.(*h*)

In the progress of this action,(*i*) the demandant must allege some seisin of the lands and tenements in himself,(81) or else in some person
*196]   under whom he claims, and then derive the right *from the person so seised to himself; to which the tenant may answer by denying the demandant's right, and averring that he has more right to hold the lands than the demandant has to demand them: and this right of the tenant being shown, it then puts the demandant upon the proof of his title: in which, if he fails, or if the tenant hath shown a better, the demandant and his heirs are personally barred of their claim; but if he can make it appear that his right is superior to the tenant's, he shall recover the land against the tenant and his heirs forever. But even this writ of right, however superior to any other, cannot be sued out at any distance of time. For by the ancient law no seisin could be alleged by the demandant, but from the time of Henry the First;(*k*) by the statute of Merton, 20 Hen. III. c. 8, from the time of Henry the Second; by the statute of Westm. 1, 3 Edward I. c. 39, from the time of Richard the First; and now, by statute 32 Henry VIII. c. 2, seisin in a writ of right shall be within sixty years. So that the possession of lands in fee-simple uninterruptedly, for threescore years, is at present a sufficient title against all the world; and cannot be impeached by any dormant claim whatsoever.(82)

I have now gone through the several species of injury by ouster and dispossession of the freehold, with the remedies applicable to each. In consid-

---

(*g*) Ibid. § 3.
(*h*) F. N. B. 3, 4.

(*i*) Append. No. I. § 5.
(*k*) Glanv. *l*. 2, c. 3. Co. Litt. 114.

---

(80) [That you cause to be recorded.]
(81) A writ of right cannot be maintained without showing *an actual seisin by taking the esplees*, either in the demandant himself or the ancestor from whom he claims. 1 H. B. 1. And the demandant must allege in his count that his ancestor was seised *of right*, as well as that he was seised in his demesne as of fee. 2 B. & P. 570. 5 East, 272. And if the count state that the lands descended to four women, as nieces and co-heirs of J. S., it must also show how they were nieces. 3 B. & P. 453. 1 N. R. 66. Proof of possession of land and pernancy of the rents is *prima facie* evidence of a seisin in fee of the pernor. But proof of forty years' subsequent possession by a daughter, while a son and heir lived near and knew the fact, is much stronger evidence that the first possessor had only a particular estate. 5 Taunt. 326. 1 Marsh. 68. The court requires a strict observance of the prescribed forms in this proceeding, and will not assist the demandant who applies to rectify omissions or irregularities. 2 N. R. 429. 1 Marsh, 602. 1 Taunt. 415. 1 Bing. 208. The court will not permit the mise joined in a writ of right to be tried by a jury instead of the grand assize, though both parties desire it. 1 B. & P. 192. As to summoning and swearing the four knights, see 3 Moore, 249. 1 Taunt. & Brod. 17. They may be summoned from the grand jury when present at the assizes. Ib. As to the tender of the demymark, and what the demandant must prove previous to the tenant being put upon proof of his title, see Holt C. N. P. 657; and see the precedents in pleading. 3 Chitty on Pl. 4 ed. 1355 to 1390.—CHITTY. See also Liter *v.* Green, 2 Wheaton (N. S.) 305 (1817).
(82) This is far from being universally true; for an uninterrupted possession for sixty years will not create a title where the claimant or demandant had no right to enter within that time; as where an estate in tail, for life, or for years continues above sixty years, still the reversioner may enter and recover the estate; the possession must be adverse, and lord Coke says, "It has been resolved that although a man has been out of possession of land for sixty years, yet if his entry is not tolled he may enter and bring any action of his own possession; and if his entry be congeable, and he enter, he may have an action of his own possession." 4 Co. 11, b.—CHRISTIAN. See Willard on Real Est. & Conv. 527 (2 ed.). Williams on Real Prop. 196, 450, 451 (6 ed.) Brown's Limitations, 736. Angell on Limitations, 374 (6 ed.). Eakin *v.* Ramb, 12 S. & R. (Pa.) 330, 366 (1825). Jacobs *v.* Rice, 33 Ill. 369, 371 (1864). Pinckney & Bruen *v.* Burrage & Stephens, 2 Vroom (N. J.) 21, 24 (1864). Cunningham *v.* Fraudtzen, 26 B. & J. (Tex.) 34, 42 (1867). Moore *v.* The State, 14 Vroom (N. J.) 203, 206 (1881).

ering which I have been unavoidably led to touch upon such obsolete and abstruse learning, as it lies intermixed with, and alone can explain the reason of, those parts of the law which are now more generally in use. For, without contemplating the whole fabric together, it is impossible to form any clear idea of the meaning and connection of those disjointed parts which still form a considerable branch of the modern law; such as the doctrine of entries and remitter, the levying of fines, and the suffering of common recoveries. Neither indeed is any considerable part of that, which I have selected in this chapter from among the venerable monuments of our ancestors, so *absolutely antiquated as to be out of *force*, though the   [*197 whole is certainly out of *use:* there being but a very few instances for more than a century past of prosecuting any real action for land by writ of *entry, assize, formedon,* writ of right, or otherwise. The forms are indeed preserved in the practice of common recoveries; but they are forms and nothing else; for which the very clerks that pass them are seldom capable to assign the reason. But the title of lands is now usually tried in actions of *ejectment* or *trespass;* of which in the following chapters.(83)

CHAPTER XI.

OF DISPOSSESSION, OR OUSTER, OF CHATTELS REAL.

*Having in the preceding chapter considered with some attention   [*198 the several species of injury by dispossession or ouster of the *freehold*, together with the regular and well-connected scheme of remedies by actions real, which are given to the subject by the common law, either to recover the possession only, or else to recover at once the possession, and also to establish the right of property: the method which I there marked out leads me next to consider injuries by ouster of *chattels real;* that is, by amoving the possession of the tenant from an estate by statute-merchant, statute-staple, recognizance in the nature of it, or *elegit;*(1) or from an estate for years.

I. Ouster, or amotion of possession, from estates held by statute, recognizance, or *elegit*, is only liable to happen by a species of disseisin, or turning out of the legal proprietor, before his estate is determined by raising the sum for which it is given him in pledge. And for such ouster, though the estate be merely a chattel interest, the owner shall have the same remedy as for an injury to a freehold; viz., by assize of *novel disseisin.*(a)   But this depends upon the several statutes which *create these respective   [*199 interests,(b) and which expressly provide and allow this remedy in case of dispossession. Upon which account it is that Sir Edward Coke observes,(c) that these tenants are said to hold their estates *ut liberum tene-*

(a) F. N. B. 178.
(b) Stat. Westm. 2. 13 Edw. I. c. 18. Stat. *de mercatoribus,* [Of merchants,] 27 Edw. III. c. 9. Stat. 23
Hen. VII. c. 6, § 9.
(c) 1 Inst. 43.

---

(83) All the real actions which have been mentioned in this chapter, and all others whatsoever, with the exceptions of the writ of *right of dower*, the writ of *dower unde nihil habet* [From whence she derives no interest], and writ of *quare impedit* [Wherefore did he hinder], have been abolished; and the title to lands is now *always* tried, as it was *usually* in the time of Blackstone, by an action of *ejectment* or of *trespass.*—STEWART. In the United States all real and mixed actions are generally abolished except ejectment which is the common law remedy to try the title to lands.

(1) [He hath chosen.]

mentum,(2) until their debts are paid: because by the statutes they shall have an assize, as tenants of the freehold shall have; and in that respect they have the similitude of a freehold.(*d*)(3)

II. As for *ouster*, or amotion of possession, from an *estate for years;* this happens only by a like kind of disseisin, ejection, or turning out, of the tenant from the occupation of the land during the continuance of his term. (4) For this injury the law has provided him with two remedies, according to the circumstances and situation of the wrong-doer: the writ of *ejectione firmæ;*(5) which lies against any one, the lessor, reversioner, remainder-man, or any stranger, who is himself the wrong-doer and has committed the injury complained of; and the writ of *quare ejecit infra terminum*,(6) which lies not against the wrong-doer or ejector himself, but his feoffee or other person claiming under him. These are mixed actions, somewhat between real and personal: for therein are two things recovered, as well restitution of the term of years, as damages for the ouster or wrong.

1. A writ then of *ejectione firmæ*, or action of trespass in *ejectment*,(7) lieth where lands or tenements are let for a term of years; and afterwards the lessor, reversioner, remainder-man, or any stranger, doth eject or oust the lessee of his term.(*e*) In this case he shall have his writ of *ejection* to call the defendant to answer for entering on the lands so demised to the plaintiff for a term that is not yet expired, and ejecting him.(*f*)(8) And by this writ the plaintiff shall recover back his term, or the remainder of it, with damages.(9)

(*d*) See book ii. ch. 10.
(*e*) F. N. B. 220.

(*f*) See Appendix, No. II. § 1.

(2) [As a freehold.]

(3) The assize of novel disseisin, as we have seen in the notes to the last chapter, is now abolished. These tenants therefore have the same remedy for the ouster of their possession as the tenant of the freehold,—an ejectment.—STEWART.

(4) One objection in England to the action of ejectment was that it would not lie for rents, commons and incorporeal hereditaments; but in Pennsylvania the supreme court has held that ejectment may be maintained notwithstanding the grant under a lease may have been an incorporeal interest. Landl. and Ten. in Pa. (Jackson & Gross, 1884) p. 731-32. Angell on Limitations, p. 372 (6 ed. 1876).

(5) ["In trespass for a form;" trespass in ejectment.] Thorn *v.* Reed, 1 Pike (Ark.) 490 (1839).

(6) [Why he hath ejected within the term.] Sedgwick on Title to Lands (2 ed.) § 21, p. 12.

(7) See, in general, Adams on Ejectment. Tidd Prac. (8 ed.) 518, etc. Runington on Ejectment, by Ballatine. Com. Dig. Ejectment. 1 Chitty on Pl. (4 ed.) 172.

In general, ejectment will lie to recover possession of any thing whereon an entry can be made, and whereof the sheriff can deliver possession. But an ejectment cannot be maintained for a close, (11 Rep. 55. Godb. 53,) a manor, without describing the quantity of land therein, (Latch. 61. Lutw. Rep. 301. Hetl. 146,) a messuage *and tenement*, (1 East, 441. Stra. 834;) but after verdict (even pending a rule to arrest the judgment on this ground) the court will give leave to enter the verdict according to the judge's notes for the messuage only, (8 East, 357;) nor a messuage *or tenement*, (3 Wils. 23,) nor a messuage situate in the parishes of A. *and* B., *or one of them*, (7 Mod. 457,) nor for things that lie merely in grant, not capable of being delivered in execution, as an advowson, common in gross, (Cro. Jac. 146,) a piscary. Ib. Cro. Car. 492. 8 Mod. 277. 1 Brownl. 142. *Contra, per* Ashurst, J., 1 T. R. 361. And where the owner of the fee by indenture granted to A. free liberty to dig for tin, and all other metals, throughout certain lands thereby described, and the use of all water, water-courses, and to make adits, etc., reserving to himself liberty to drive any new adit and to carry any new water-course over the premises granted, habendum for twenty-one years, with right of re-entry for breach of covenants, this deed, it was held, did not amount to a lease, but contained a mere license to dig, etc., and the grantee could not maintain ejectment for mines lying within the limits of the set but not connected with the workings of the grantee. 2 B. & A. 724—CHITTY.

(8) Redfield *v.* U. and S. R. R. Co., 25 Barb. 57 (1857).

(9) Cook *v.* Thornton, 6 Va. 17 (1827) (Rand.). Beach *v.* Beach, 18 Vt. 298 (1846).

*Since the disuse of real actions, this mixed proceeding is become   [*200 the common method of trying the title to lands or tenements.(10)

It may not therefore be improper to delineate, with some degree of minuteness, its history, the manner of its process, and the principles whereon it is grounded.

We have before seen, (g) that the writ of covenant, for breach of the contract contained in the lease for years, was anciently the only specific remedy for recovering against the lessor a term from which he had ejected his lessee, together with damages for the ouster.(11)   But if the lessee was ejected by a stranger, claiming under a title superior(h) to that of the lessor, or by a grantee of the reversion, (who might at any time by a common recovery have destroyed the term,)(i) though the lessee might still maintain an action of covenant against the lessor for non-performance of his contract or lease, yet he could not by any means recover the term itself.   If the ouster was committed by a mere stranger, without any title to the land, the lessor might indeed by a real action recover possession of the freehold, but the lessee had no other remedy against the ejector but in damages, by a writ of *ejectione firmæ*, for the trespass committed in ejecting him from his farm.(k) But afterwards, when the courts of equity began to oblige the ejector to make a specific restitution of the land to the party immediately injured, the courts of law also adopted the same method of doing complete justice:(12) and, in the prosecution of a writ of ejectment, introduced a species of remedy not warranted by the original writ nor prayed by the declaration, (which are *calculated for damages merely, and are silent as to any   [*201 restitution,) viz., a judgment to recover the term, and a writ of possession thereupon.(l)   This method seems to have been settled as early as the reign of Edward IV.;(m) though it hath been said(n) to have first begun under Henry VII., because it probably was then first applied to its present principal use, that of trying the title to the land.

The better to apprehend the contrivance whereby this end is effected, we must recollect that the remedy by ejectment is in its original an action brought by one who hath a lease for years, to repair the injury done him by dispossession.(13)   In order therefore to convert it into a method of trying titles to the freehold, it is first necessary that the claimant do take possession of the lands, to empower him to constitute a lessee for years, that may be capable of receiving this injury of dispossession.   For it would be an offence,

---

(g) See page 157.
(h) F. N. B. 145.
(i) See book ii. ch. 9.
(k) P. 6, Ric. II. *Ejectione firmæ n'est que un action de trespass en son nature, et le plaintiff ne recovera son terme que est a venir, nient plus que en trespass home recovera damages pur tresspass nient fait, mes a feser; mes il convient a suer par action de covenant al comen law: a recoverer son terme: quod tota curia concessit. Et per Belknap, la comen ley est, lou home est ouste de son terme par estranger, il avera ejectione firmæ versus cesty queluy ouste: et sil soit ouste par son lessor, briefe de covenant; et si par lessee ou grantee de reversion, briefe de covenant versus son lessor, et countera especial count,* etc.   [A writ of *ejectione firmæ* is in its nature merely an action of trespass, and the plaintiff can only recover that part of the term which is unexpired, the same as in trespass, a man shall recover no damages for trespass not committed, but to be committed.   But to recover his terms he must sue by an action of covenant at common law; to which the whole court assented.   And per Belknap, where a man is ousted from his term by a stranger, the common law is that he shall have a writ of *ejectione firmæ* against him who ousted him; and if he be ousted by his lessor, a writ of covenant; and if by the lessee or grantee of the reversion, a writ of covenant against his lessor and he shall count a special count, etc.]   Fitz. Abr. tit. *eject. firm* 2.   See Bract. l. 4, tr. 1, c. 36.

(l) See Append. No. II. § 4, *prope fin.*
(m) 7 Edw. IV. 6.   *Per Fairfax si home port ejectione firmæ, le plaintiff recovera son terme qui est arere, si bien come in quare ejecit infra terminum; et, si nul soit arere, donques tout in damages.*   [If a plaintiff bring a writ of *ejectione firmæ* he shall recover the remainder of his term as well as in a *quare ejecit infra terminum*, and, if it be all run out, he shall recover the whole in damages.]   Bro. Abr. tit. *quare ejecit infra terminum*, 6.
(n) F. N. B. 220.

---

(10) Farley v. Craeg, 3 N. J. 201, Green (1836).
(11) Sedgwick and Wait on Trial of Title to Land (2 ed.) 9.   Leake's Dig. of Law, R. P. 45.
(12) Sedgwick and Wait on Trial of Title to Land (2 ed.) 13.
(13) Chalker v. Chalker, 1 Conn. 79, 92 (1814).   Brown on Actions of Law, 458.

called in our law *maintenance*, (of which in the next book,) to convey a title to another, when the grantor is not in possession of the land; and indeed it was doubted at first, whether this occasional possession, taken merely for the purpose of conveying the title, excused the lessor from the legal guilt of maintenance. (*o*)(14) When therefore a person, who hath right of entry into lands, determines to acquire that possession, which is wrongfully withheld by the present tenant, he makes (as by law he may) a formal entry on the premises; and being so in the possession of the soil, he there, upon the land, seals and delivers a lease for years to some third person or lessee; and, having thus given him entry, leaves him in possession of the premises. This lessee is to stay upon the land till the prior tenant, or he who had the previous possession, enters thereon afresh and ousts him; or till some other person (either by accident or by agreement beforehand) comes upon the land, and *202]* turns him *out or ejects him. For this injury the lessee is entitled to his action of ejectment against the tenant, or this *casual ejector*, whichever it was that ousted him, to recover back his term and damages. But where this action is brought against such a casual ejector as is before mentioned, and not against the very tenant in possession, the court will not suffer the tenant to lose his possession without any opportunity to defend it. Wherefore it is a standing rule, that no plaintiff shall proceed in ejectment to recover land against a casual ejector, without notice given to the tenant in possession, (if any there be,) and making him a defendant if he pleases.(15) And, in order to maintain the action, the plaintiff must, in case of any defence, make out four points before the court; viz., *title, lease, entry*, and *ouster*.(16) First, he must show a good *title* in his lessor, which brings the matter of right entirely before the court; then, that the lessor, being seised or possessed by virtue of such title, did make him the *lease* for the present term; thirdly, that he, the lessee or plaintiff, did *enter* or take possession in consequence of such lease; and then, lastly, that the defendant *ousted* or ejected him.(17) Whereupon he shall have judgment to recover his term and damages; and shall, in consequence, have a *writ of possession*, which the sheriff is to execute by delivering him the undisturbed and peaceable possession of his term.

This is the regular method of bringing an action of ejectment, in which the title of the lessor comes collaterally and incidentally before the court, in order to show the injury done to the lessee by this ouster. This method must be still continued in due form and strictness, save only as to the notice to the tenant, whenever the possession is vacant, or there is no actual occupant of the premises; and also in some other cases.(18) But, as much trouble and formality were found to attend the actual making of the *lease, entry*, and *ouster*, a new and more easy method of trying titles by writ of ejectment, where there is any actual tenant or occupier of the premises in

(*o*) 1 Ch. Rep. Append. 39.

(14) Browne of Actions of Law, 459.
(15) Sedgwick and Wait on Trial of Title to Land, 16.
(16) Evans *v.* Hinds, 2 Hill, 206 (S. C. 1834).
(17) He was also compelled to prove that the defendant was in actual possession at the time of the commencement of his suit. Redfield *v.* U. and S. R. R. Co. 25 Barber 57 (1857).
(18) When the remedy by ejectment is pursued in an inferior court, the fictions of the modern system are not applicable; for inferior courts have not the power of framing rules for confessing lease, entry, and ouster, nor the means, if such rules were entered into, of enforcing obedience to them. 1 Keb. 690, 795. Gilb. Eject. 38. Adams on Eject. 173. If the rule requiring service of notice upon the tenant in possession cannot be observed on account of his having quitted, and his place of residence is unknown, (2 Stra. 1064. 4 T. R. 464,) the claimant must resort to the ancient practice. (Ad. Eject. 181,) except in particular cases, provided for by the 4 Geo. II. c. 28, 11 Geo. II. c. 19, and 57 Geo. III. c. 52.—CHITTY.

dispute, was invented somewhat more than a century ago, by the lord chief justice Rolle, (*p*) who then sat in the court of *upper* bench; so called during the exile of king Charles the *Second.   This new method   [*203 entirely depends upon a string of legal fictions; no actual lease is made, no actual entry by the plaintiff, no actual ouster by the defendant; but all are merely ideal, for the sole purpose of trying the title.(19)   To this end, in the proceedings(*q*) a lease for a term of years is stated to have been made, by him who claims title, to the plaintiff who brings the action, as by John Rogers to Richard Smith, which plaintiff ought to be some real person, and not merely an ideal fictitious one who hath no existence, as is frequently though unwarrantably practiced;(*r*)(20) it is also stated that Smith the lessee entered; and that the defendant William Stiles, who is called the *casual ejector*, ousted him; for which ouster he brings this action.   As soon as this action is brought, and the complaint fully stated in the declaration,(*s*) Stiles, the casual ejector, or defendant, sends a written notice to the tenant in possession of the lands, as George Saunders, informing him of the action brought by Richard Smith, and transmitting him a copy of the declaration; withal assuring him that he, Stiles the defendant, has no title at all to the premises, and shall make no defence; and therefore advising the tenant to appear in court and defend his own title: otherwise he, the casual ejector, will suffer judgment to be had against him; and thereby the actual tenant Saunders will inevitably be turned out of possession.(*t*)(21)   On receipt of this friendly caution, if the tenant in possession does not within a limited time apply to the court to be admitted a defendant in the stead of Stiles, he is supposed to have no right at all; and, upon judgment being had against Stiles the casual ejector, Saunders the real tenant will be turned out of possession by the sheriff.

But, if the tenant in possession applies to be made a defendant, it is allowed him upon this condition; that he enter into a rule of court(*u*) to confess, at the trial of the cause, three of the four requisites for the maintenance of the plaintiff's action; viz., the *lease* of Rogers the lessor, the *entry* of Smith *the plaintiff, and his *ouster* by Saunders himself, now made   [*204 the defendant instead of Stiles: which requisites being wholly fictitious, should the defendant put the plaintiff to prove them, he must of course be non-suited for want of evidence; but by such stipulated confession of *lease*, *entry*, and *ouster*, the trial will now stand upon the merits of the *title* only.(22)

(*p*) Styl. Pract. Reg. 108, edit. 1657.
(*q*) See Append. No. II. §§ 1, 2.
(*r*) 6 Mod. 309.

(*s*) Append. No. II. § 2.
(*t*) Ibid.
(*u*) Ibid. § 3.

---

(19) An actual entry is necessary to avoid a fine levied with proclamations, according to the statute 4 Hen. VII. c. 24, (see book 2, p. 352;) and the demise laid in the ejectment must be subsequent to the entry; but that is the only case in which an actual entry is required, (2 Stra. 1086. Doug. 468.   1 T. R. 741.   4 Bro. P. C. 353.   3 Burr. 1895.   7 T. R. 433.   1 Prest. Conv. 207.   9 East, 17;) unless it is an ejectment brought to recover on a vacant possession, and not by a landlord upon a right of re-entry under the 4 Geo. II. c. 28; in which case the lessor or his attorney must actually seal a lease upon the premises to the plaintiff, who must be ejected by a real person.   See the mode of proceeding, 2 Crompt. Prac. 198.—CHRISTIAN.   The action of trespass in ejectment has qeen instituted for the sole purpose of trying the title to lands or tenements.   Doe *v.* G. R. R. & Bkg. Co., 1 Kelly 524, 533 (1846).

(20) The practice was reprobated, because it was considered that it provided no responsibility for costs in case the defendant succeeded.   But this objection is now obviated by its being always part of the consent rule that in such case the lessor of the plaintiff will pay the costs, and an attachment will lie against him for disobedience of this as of every other rule of court.   Adams on Eject. 235, 298.—CHITTY.

(21) Browne on Actions of Law, 460.   Sedgwick and Wait on Trial of Title to Land, 19.

(22) It has been determined that no ejectment can be maintained where the lessor of the plaintiff has not a legal right of entry; and the heir at law was barred from recover-

This done, the declaration is altered by inserting the name of George Saunders instead of William Stiles, and the cause goes down to trial under the name of Smith, (the plaintiff,) on the demise of Rogers, (the lessor,) against Saunders, the new defendant. And therein the lessor of the plaintiff is bound to make out a clear title; otherwise his fictitious lessee cannot obtain judgment to have possession of the land for the term supposed to be granted.(23) But, if the lessor makes out his title in a satisfactory manner, then judgment and a writ of possession shall go for Richard Smith the nominal plaintiff, who by this trial has proved the right of John Rogers, his supposed lessor. Yet, to prevent fraudulent recoveries of the possession, by collusion with the tenant of the land, all tenants are obliged by statute 11 Geo. II. c. 19, on pain of forfeiting three years' rent, to give notice to their landlords, when served with any declaration in ejectment; and any landlord may by leave of the court be made a co-defendant to the action, in case the tenant himself appears to it; or, if he makes default, though judgment must be then signed against the casual ejector, yet execution shall be stayed, in case the landlord applies to be made a defendant, and enters into the common rule;(24) a right which indeed the landlord had, long before the provision of this statute;(v) in like manner as (previous to the statute of Westm. 2, c. 3) if in a real action the tenant of the freehold made default, the remainder-man or reversioner had a right to come in and defend the possession; lest, if judgment were had against the tenant, the estate of those behind should be turned to a naked right.(w)(25) But, if the new defendants, whether landlord or tenant, or both, after entering into the common rule, fail to appear at the trial, and to confess lease, entry, and ouster, the plaintiff, Smith, must indeed be

(v) Styl. Pract. Reg. 108, 111, 265. 7 Mod. 70. Salk. 257. Burr. 1301.   (w) Bracton, l. 5, c. 10, § 14.

---

ing in ejectment, where there was an unsatisfied term raised for the purpose of securing an annuity, though the heir claimed the estate subject to that charge. But a satisfied term may be presumed to be surrendered. 2 T. R. 695. 1 T. R. 758. In Doe on the demise of Bowerman v. Sybourn, 7 T. R. 2, lord Kenyon declared that in all cases where trustees ought to convey to the beneficial owner he would leave it to the jury to presume, where such a presumption might reasonably be made, that they had conveyed accordingly, in order to prevent a just title from being defeated by a matter of form. But if such a presumption cannot be made, he who has only the equitable estate cannot recover in ejectment. Jones v. Jones, 7 T. R. 46. The doctrine respecting the presumption of a surrender of a term, though assigned to attend the inheritance, still prevails. 2 B. & A. 710, 782. 3 Bar. & Cres. 616; but see Mr. Sugden's able essay on the subject of presuming the surrender of a term. A person who claims under an *elegit* sued out against the landlord cannot recover in ejectment against the tenant whose lease was granted prior to the plaintiff's judgment. 8 T. R. 2.—CHRISTIAN.

(23) Before the following rules it was necessary for lessor of plaintiff to prove on the trial the defendant's possession of the premises in question, although the defendant had entered into the general consent rule, to confess lease, entry, and ouster. 7 T. R. 327. 1 B. & P. 573. But by rule in King's Bench, M. T. 1820, it was ordered that in every action of ejectment the defendant shall specify in the consent rule for what premises he intends to defend, and shall consent in such rule to confess upon the trial that the defendant (if he defends as tenant, or, in case he defends as landlord, that his tenant) was, at the time of the service of the declaration, in the possession of such premises; and that if upon the trial the defendant shall not confess such possession, as well as lease, entry, and ouster, whereby the plaintiff shall not be able further to prosecute his suit against the said defendant, then no costs shall be allowed for not further prosecuting the same, but the said defendant shall pay costs to the plaintiff, in that case to be taxed. In the following year the same rule was adopted by the court of Common Pleas. See 2 Brod. & Bing. 470.—CHITTY.

(24) *Ex parte* Black, 2 Bail. 9 (S. C. 1830). Township of Union v. Bayliss, 11 Vroom, 60, 61 (N. J. 1877).

(25) A devisee, although he has never been in possession, has been permitted to defend as a landlord under this statute. 11 Geo. II. c. 19. 4 T. R. 122.—CHITTY. Newell on Ejectment, 3–7 (1892).

there *non-suited, for want of proving those requisites; but judgment   [*205
will in the end be entered against the casual ejector Stiles; for the
condition on which Saunders, or his landlord, was admitted a defendant is
broken, and therefore the plaintiff is put again in the same situation as if he
never had appeared at all; the consequence of which (we have seen) would
have been, that judgment would have been entered for the plaintiff, and the
sheriff, by virtue of a writ for that purpose, would have turned out Saunders,
and delivered possession to Smith.   The same process therefore as would
have been had, provided no conditional rule had been ever made, must now
be pursued as soon as the condition is broken.(26)

The damages recovered in these actions, though formerly their only intent,
are now usually (since the title has been considered as the principal question)
very small and inadequate, amounting commonly to one shilling, or some
other trivial sum.   In order therefore to complete the remedy when the possession has been long detained from him that hath the right to it, an action
of trespass also lies, after a recovery in ejectment, to recover the mesne profits
which the tenant in possession has wrongfully received.(27)   Which action

---

(26) Where an ejectment is defended merely to continue the possession of the premises
and no defence is made at the trial, the practice is for the crier of the court, first, to call
the defendant to confess lease, entry, and ouster, and then the plaintiff, as in other cases
of nonsuits, to come forth, or he will lose his writ of nisi prius. Though in this case the
judgment is given against the casual ejector, yet the costs are taxed as in other cases,
and if the real defendant refuses to pay them the court will grant an attachment against
him. Salk. 259. In like manner, if there be a verdict for the defendant, or the nominal
plaintiff be non-suited without the default of the defendant, the defendant must tax his
costs and sue out a writ of execution against the nominal plaintiff; and if, upon serving
the lessor of the plaintiff with his writ and a copy of the rule to confess lease, entry, and
ouster, the lessor of the plaintiff does not pay the costs, the court will grant an attachment against him. 2 Cromp. Pract. 214. In ejectment the unsuccessful party may
re-try the same question as often as he pleases without the leave of the court; for by making a fresh demise to another nominal character, it becomes the action of a new plaintiff
upon another right, and the courts of law cannot any further prevent this repetition of
the action than by ordering the proceedings in one ejectment to be stayed till the costs
of a former ejectment, though brought in another court, be discharged. 2 Bla. Rep.
1158. Barnes, 133. But a court of equity, in some instances where there have been
several trials in ejectment for the same premises, though the title was entirely legal, has
granted a perpetual injunction. 1 P. Wms. 672.—CHRISTIAN.

New proceedings for the recovery of land have been created by the Common-Law
Procedure Act, 1852, and the former action of ejectment has given place altogether to
this new procedure.

The form of action which has been abolished was valuable in this respect,—that it
allowed no questions to be raised except that of title. If the person who brought the
action had a right to possession, he was entitled to recover, without regard to whether the
person in possession or who took defence to the action had ousted him or not. The new
action is also an action for recovery of the land, without regard to any other claim which
may exist between the parties.

An action of ejectment is now commenced by the issue of a writ directed to the persons
in possession by name, and to all persons entitled to defend the possession of the property claimed, which property must be described in the writ with reasonable certainty.

The writ must state the names of all the persons in whom the title is alleged to be; and
it commands the persons to whom it is directed to appear, within sixteen days after service
in the court from which it issued, to defend the possession of the property sued for, or
such part thereof as they may think fit. It must also contain a notice that in default of
appearance they may be turned out of possession.—STEWART.

It has not been deemed necessary to pursue the new procedure further than is contained
in the foregoing extract. The action has been divested of its cumbrous fictions, and all
the ends of real justice are attained by a simple and intelligible process. Many of the
United States had long preceded England in this valuable reform; but several still continue to employ the ancient form; and in the circuit courts of the United States, in
those states in which it was in use when those courts were established, it is still
employed.—SHARSWOOD.

(27) Beach v. Beach, 20 Vt. 83, 89 (1847). But with reference to mesne profits accrued
up to the day of the verdict, and in cases where the tenancy existed under lease or agree-

may be brought in the name of either the nominal plaintiff in the ejectment, or his lessor, against the tenant in possession, whether he be made party to the ejectment or suffers judgment to go by default.(x) In this case the judgment in ejectment is conclusive evidence against the defendant for all profits which have accrued since the date of the demise stated in the former declaration of the plaintiff; but if the plaintiff sues for any antecedent profits the defendant may make a new defence.(28)

(*x*) 4 Burr. 668.

ment, resort to this separate action is superseded by sect. 2 of stat. 1 Geo. IV. c. 87, which enacts, "Wherever thereafter it shall appear on the trial of any ejectment, at the suit of a landlord against a tenant, that such tenant or his attorney hath been served with due notice of trial, the plaintiff shall not be non-suited for default of the defendant's appearance, or of confession of lease, entry, and ouster; but the production of the consent rule and undertaking of the defendant shall in all such cases be sufficient evidence of lease, entry, and ouster; and the judge before whom such cause shall come on to be tried shall, whether the defendant shall appear upon such trial or not, permit the plaintiff on the trial, after proof of his right to recover possession of the whole or of any part of the premises mentioned in the declaration, to go into evidence of the mesne profits thereof which shall or might have accrued from the day of the expiration or determination of the tenant's interest in the same down to the time of the verdict given in the cause, or to some preceding day, to be specially mentioned therein; and the jury on the trial finding for the plaintiff shall in such case give their verdict upon the whole matter, both as to the recovery of the whole or any part of the premises, and also as to the amount of the damages to be paid for such mesne profits. The said act not to bar the landlord from bringing trespass for the mesne profits to accrue from the verdict or the day so specified therein down to the day of the delivery of possession of the premises recovered in the ejectment."—CHITTY.

The action to recover *mesne* profits is an action *quare clausum fregit* [Why did he break the close], and cannot be maintained without proof of the trespass. Thompson *v.* Bower, 60 Barb. 463, 478 (N. Y. 1871). City of Apalachicola *v.* Apalachicola Land Co., 9 Fla. 340, 349 (1861).

(28) Sumter *v.* Lehie, 1 Treadw. 102, 105 (S. C. 1812). The defendant may plead the statute of limitations, and by that means protect himself from the payment of all mesne profits except those which have accrued within the last six years. Bull. N. P. 88.

The common remedy by ejectment is generally treated as a mixed action, the party interested thereby recovering his *estate* and *damages* for the ouster; but as those damages are nominal, and the claimant must in order to recover the intermediate profits resort to an action of trespass, such action of ejectment is in substance merely for the recovery of the estate. But in one instance, in favor of landlords, a remedy by ejectment is given nearly resembling the ancient and mixed action; for it is enacted by 1 Geo. IV. c. 87, that upon refusal by a late tenant to deliver up possession upon the expiration of his tenancy by lease or *written* agreement, and after lawful demand in writing, the landlord, on bringing an ejectment, may address a notice at the foot of the declaration to the tenant, requiring him to appear in court on the first day of the next term, or if in Wales, or the counties palatine of Chester, Lancaster, or Durham, on the first day of the assizes, or appearance-day, there to be made defendant, and to find bail; or in case of his non-appearance, upon production of the lease, agreement, etc. and the proper affidavits by the landlord, etc., the court may grant a rule, calling on the tenant to show cause why he should not, upon being admitted defendant, besides entering into the common rule, undertake, in case a verdict should pass against him, to give the plaintiff a judgment, to be entered up against the real defendant of the term next preceding the trial, and also why he should not enter into a recognizance by himself and two sufficient sureties in a reasonable sum (to be named) conditioned to pay the costs and damages which shall be recovered by the plaintiff in the action. Upon the rule being made absolute, if the tenant do not conform, judgment to be for the plaintiff. The act further provides that, whether the defendant appear or not at the trial, the plaintiff may go into proof, and the jury give damages for mesne profits down to the verdict or a day specified therein. See 1 Dowl. & Ryl. 433. But when the required undertaking is given, it is provided that if it appear to the judge that the finding of the jury was contrary to the evidence, he may order a stay of execution till the fifth day of the next term; and he is bound to make this order if the defendant desire it, upon his undertaking to give security not to commit any kind of waste, or sell the crops, etc. And if the result of the trial under this act be against the landlord, the tenant shall have judgment with double costs.

"It sufficiently appears on the whole record in the ejectment, that the plaintiff was in possession, that the defendant ousted him on a certain day, and detained the possession

Such is the modern way of obliquely bringing in question the title to lands and tenements, in order to try it in this collateral manner; a method which is now universally adopted in almost every case. It is founded on the same principle as the ancient writs of assize, being calculated to try the mere *possessory* title to an estate; and hath succeeded to those real actions, *as being infinitely more convenient for attaining the end of justice; [*206 because, the form of the proceeding being entirely fictitious, it is wholly in the power of the court to direct the application of that fiction so as to prevent fraud and chicane, and eviscerate the very truth of the title. The writ of ejectment and its nominal parties (as was resolved by all the judges)(*y*) are "judicially to be considered as the fictitious form of an action really brought by the lessor of the plaintiff against the tenant in possession: invented, under the control and power of the court, for the advancement of justice in many respects; and to force the parties to go to trial on the merits, without being entangled in the nicety of pleadings on either side."(29)

(*y*) Mich. 32 Geo. II.   4 Burr. 668.

---

until the trial; so that the action is not for a single act of trespass; and, therefore, the jury may well give damages for the whole time the wrong continued." Boyd's Lessee *v.* Cowan, 4 Dall. 138, 139 (Pa. 1794).

The judgment "is conclusive as to *title*, for the *whole time laid in the demise.* But if the plaintiff would recover the profits *beyond the time of the demise,* the defendant may put him to prove his title, because the record only shows that he recovered the term mentioned in the declaration. Bailey *v.* Fairplay, 6 Binn. 450, 455 (Pa. 1814).

The statute 1 Geo. IV. c. 87 does not extend to the case of a lessee holding over after notice to quit, given by himself, where his tenancy has not expired by the efflux of time. 1 Dowl. & Ryl. 540. And where a tenant holds from year to year, without a lease or agreement *in writing*, it is not within the first section of the statute, (1 Geo. IV. c. 87). 5 B. & A. 770. But an agreement *in writing*, for apartments for *three months* certain comes within the meaning of the words of the act, where the party holds for any term, or number of years certain, or from year to year. 5 B. & A. 766. 1 Dowl. & Ryl. 433. A tenant being in possession, under an agreement that the landlord should grant a lease for eight years, and that the tenant should pay 40s. for every day he held over, continued to hold the whole time, though the lease was never granted; and, upon his holding over, notice to quit and demand of possession, with notice of ejectment, was regularly served. It was held that the tenant was not to be treated as a tenant from year to year, and that the demand of possession was sufficient notice within the statute, so as to entitle the plaintiff to the benefit of the undertaking and security required by that statute. 2 Dowl. & Ryl. 565.

The rule nisi, calling on a tenant to enter into a recognizance under this statute, need not specify all the particulars thereby required, as the court may mould the rule according to its requisites, upon showing cause. 5 B. & A. 766. 1 Dowl. & Ryl. 433. The time within which the undertaking and security required by the statute shall be given is to be fixed by the court at the time the rule is granted. 2 Dowl. & Ryl. 688. After a rule granted in a cause entitled Doe, etc. *v.* Roe, to which the tenant in possession appeared, judgment was entered up and execution taken out against the tenant by *name*, and it was held not to be irregular. 3 Dowl. & Ryl. 230.

The court, on making a rule absolute under this act (no cause being shown) for the tenant's undertaking to give the plaintiff judgment, to be entered up against the real defendant, and to enter into a recognizance in a *reasonable sum* conditioned to pay the costs and damages which should be recovered by the plaintiff in the action, ordered the tenant to appear in the next succeeding term, to find such bail as was specified in the former rule; and, on no cause being shown to that order, they directed the rule for entering up judgment for the plaintiff to be made absolute. The court can only give a reasonable sum for the costs of the action, and not for the mesne profits, the amount of which must be ascertained by the prothonotary. 6 Moore, 54. See further, as to the proceedings on this statute. Tidd (8 ed.) 541, etc.—CHITTY.

(29) Read *v.* Read, 5 Call 160, 183 (Va. 1804). Actions of ejectment, as has been observed, have succeeded to those real actions called possessory actions; but an inconvenience was found to result from them which did not follow from real actions, to which it has been found necessary to apply a remedy. Real actions could not be brought twice for the same thing; but a person might bring as many ejectments as he pleased,—which rendered the rights of parties subject to endless litigation. To remedy this, therefore, when two or more verdicts have been had upon the same title, and to the satisfaction of

But a writ of ejectment is not an adequate means to try the title of all estates; for on those things whereon an entry cannot in fact be made, no entry shall be supposed by any fiction of the parties. Therefore an ejectment will not lie of an advowson, a rent, a common, or other incorporeal hereditament:(z)(30) except for tithes in the hands of lay appropriators, by the express purview of statute 32 Hen. VIII. c. 7,(31) which doctrine hath since been extended, by analogy, to tithes in the hands of the clergy:(a)(32) nor will it lie in such cases where the entry of him that hath the right is taken away by descent, discontinuance, twenty years' dispossession, or otherwise.

This action of ejectment is, however, rendered a very easy and expeditious remedy to landlords whose tenants are in arrear, by statute 4 Geo. II. c. 28, which enacts that every landlord who hath by his lease a right of re-entry in case of non-payment of rent, when half a year's rent is due and no sufficient distress is to be had, may serve a declaration in ejectment on his tenant, or fix the same upon some notorious part of the premises, which shall be valid without any formal re-entry or previous demand of rent. And a recovery in such ejectments shall be final and conclusive, both in law and equity, unless the rent and all costs be paid or tendered within six calendar months afterwards.(33)

(z) Brownl. 129. Cro. Car. 492. Stra. 54.   (a) Cro. Car. 301. 2 Lord Raym. 789.

---

the court, the courts of equity will now grant a perpetual injunction to restrain the party from bringing any further ejectment. See Barefoot v. Fry, Bunb. 158, pl. 228. Selw. N. P. 780.—ARCHBOLD.

Under all the changes of practice and the purposes to which the action of ejectment is applied, it has been permitted to be brought only against some person in possession, exercising acts of ownership, and claiming title; and this possession must be exclusive of the public, to authorize the action to be brought against an individual as occupant. Redfield v. U. & S. R. R. Co., 25 Barb. 54, 58 (N. Y. 1851). As a general rule, any real property for the recovery of which an action of ejectment will lie, may be held adversely, and any interest in lands for which the action will not lie cannot. Newell on Ejectment, 722 (1892.)

(30) Witherow v. Kellar, 11 S. & R. 271, 274 (Pa. 1824). *Den ex dem* Farley v. Craig, 3 Green 191, 128 (N. J. 1836). Redfield v. U. & S. R. R. Co., 25 Barb. 54, 60 (N. Y. 1851). Taylor's Landlord and Tenant, 588 (7 ed. 1879).

(31) Rowan v. Kelsey, 18 Barb. 484, 488 (N. Y. 1854).

(32) Browne on Actions of Law, 462.

(33) Where there is a sufficient distress upon the premises, the landlord cannot maintain an ejectment upon his right of re-entry for non-payment of rent under this statute; nor can he maintain an action of ejectment for a forfeiture at common law unless he has demanded the rent on the last of the specified days for the payment thereof, just before sunset. As where the proviso in a lease is, "that, if the rent shall be behind and unpaid by the space of thirty or any other number of days after the days of payment, it shall be lawful for the lessor to re-enter," a demand must be made of the precise rent in arrear on the thirtieth or other last day, a convenient time just before and until sunset, upon the land, or at the dwelling-house, or the *most* notorious place. 1 Saund. 287, n. 16. 7 T. R. 117.

The 11 Geo. II. c. 19, s. 16 gives the landlord a summary remedy, by application to two justices of the peace, where a tenant at rack-rent, or at full three-fourths of the yearly value, being in arrear a year's rent, deserts the premises and leaves the same uncultivated or unoccupied and no sufficient distress thereon. In such case, after fourteen days' notice, the justices may put the landlord in possession; and the 57 Geo. III. c. 52 extends the regulation to such tenants as are half a year in arrear. As to the proceeding of the justices under these acts, and how far the record of such proceedings will be conclusive in their behalf, see 3 Bar. & Cres. 649.

Difficulties having frequently arisen, and considerable expenses having been incurred, by reason of the refusal of persons who had been permitted to occupy, or who had intruded themselves into, *parish* houses, to deliver up possession of such houses, by stat. 59 Geo. III. c. 12, s. 24, two justices are empowered in such cases to cause possession to be delivered to church-wardens and overseers. The mode of proceeding is prescribed by this statute. The visitors and feoffees of a free grammar-school who have dismissed the school-master for misconduct cannot maintain ejectment for the school-house till they

*2. The writ of *quare ejecit infra terminum* (34) lieth, by the ancient   [*207
law, where the wrong-doer or ejector is not himself in possession of
the lands, but another who claims under him.   As where a man leaseth
lands to another for years, and, after, the lessor or reversioner entereth and
maketh a feoffment in fee, or for life, of the same lands to a stranger: now
the lessee cannot bring a writ of *ejectione firmæ* or ejectment against the
feoffee; because he did not eject him, but the reversioner; neither can he
have any such action to recover his term against the reversioner who did
oust him, because he is not now in possession.   And upon that account this
writ was devised, upon the equity of the statute of Westm. 2, c. 24, as in a
case where no adequate remedy was already provided.(*b*)   And the action
is brought against the feoffee for deforcing, or keeping out, the original lessee
during the continuance of his term; and herein, as in the ejectment, the
plaintiff shall recover so much of the term as remains, and also shall have
actual damages for that portion of it whereof he has been unjustly deprived.
But since the introduction of fictitious ousters, whereby the title may be
tried against any tenant in possession, (by what means soever he acquired it,)
and the subsequent recovery of damages by action of trespass for mesne profits, this action is fallen into disuse.(35)

CHAPTER XII.

OF TRESPASS.

*IN the two preceding chapters we have considered such injuries to   [*208
real property as consisted in an ouster or amotion of the possession.
Those which remain to be discussed are such as may be offered to a man's
real property without any amotion from it.
The second species, therefore, of real injuries, or wrongs that affect a man's
lands, tenements, or hereditaments, is that of *trespass*.   Trespass, in its
largest and most extensive sense, signifies any transgression or offence against
the law of nature, of society, or of the country in which we live, whether it
relates to a man's person or his property.(1)   Therefore, beating another
is a trespass, for which (as we have formerly seen) an action of trespass *vi et
armis* in assault and battery will lie; taking or detaining a man's goods are
respectively trespasses, for which an action of trespass *vi et armis*, or on the
case in trover and conversion, is given by the law,(2) so also, non-performance
of promises or undertakings is a trespass, upon which an action of trespass
on the case in *assumpsit* is grounded: and, in general, any misfeasance or act
of one man whereby another is injuriously treated or damnified is a transgression or trespass in its largest sense: for which we have already seen(*a*)
that whenever the act itself is directly and immediately injurious to
the person or property of *another, and therefore necessarily accom-   [*209
panied with some force, an action of trespass *vi et armis*(3) will lie;

(*b*) F. N. B. 198.   (*a*) See page 123.

---

have determined the master's interests therein, upon summons in the ordinary manner,
when he might be heard to answer the charges forming the ground of dismissal.   1 Bing.
357, 8 T. R. 109.—CHITTY.
   (34) [Wherefore or why did he eject within the term.]
   (35) And has now been for some time abolished.   3 & 4 W. IV. c. 27, s. 36.—STEWART.
   (1) Grunson *v.* The State, 89 Ind. 533, 536 (1883).   Watson *v.* State of Mississippi, 36
Miss. 593, 611 (1859).   See 1 Waterman on Trespass, 33, 34 (1875).
   (2) Robinson *v.* Woodford, 37 W. Va. 379 (1893).
   (3) [By force and arms.]

but, if the injury is only consequential, a special action of trespass *on the case* may be brought.(4)

But, in the limited and confined sense in which we are at present to consider it, it signifies no more than an entry on another man's ground without a lawful authority, and doing some damage, however inconsiderable, to his real property.(5) For the right of *meum* and *tuum*,(6) or property in lands, being once established, it follows as a necessary consequence that this right must be exclusive; that is that the owner may retain to himself the sole use and occupation of his soil: every entry, therefore, thereon without the owner's leave, and especially if contrary to his express order, is a trespass or transgression.(7) The Roman laws seem to have made a direct prohibition

---

(4) See these distinctions fully considered, 1 Chitty on Pl. 115 to 122 and 149 to 172. The distinctions between actions of trespass *vi et armis* for an immediate injury, and actions of trespass upon the case for a consequential damage, are frequently very subtle. See the subject much considered in 2 Bl. Rep. 892. In a case where an action of trespass *vi et armis* was brought against the defendant for throwing a lighted squib in a public market, which fell upon a stall, the owner of which, to defend himself and his goods, took it up and threw it to another part of the market, where it struck the plaintiff and put out his eye, the question was much discussed whether the person injured ought to have brought an action of trespass *vi et armis*, or an action upon the case; and one of the four judges strenuously contended that it ought to have been an action upon the case. But I should conceive that the question was more properly this,—viz., whether an action of trespass *vi et armis* lay against the original or the intermediate thrower, or whether the act of the second thrower was involuntary, (which seems to have been the opinion of the jury,) or wilful and mischievous, and, if so, whether the first thrower alone ought not to have been answerable for the consequences. For if A. throws a stone at B., which, after it lies quietly at his foot, B. takes up and throws again at C., it is presumed that C. has his action against B. only; but if it is thrown at B., and B., by warding it off from himself, gives it a different direction, in consequence of which it strikes C., in that case it is wholly the act of A., and B. must be considered merely as an inanimate object, which may chance to divert its course. In the case of Leame *v.* Bray, 3 East, 598, it was decided that if one man drives a carriage, being on the wrong side of the road, against another carriage, though unintentionally, the action ought to be trespass *vi et armis* [With force and arms].—CHRISTIAN.

If the injurious act be the immediate result of the force originally applied by the defendant, and the plaintiff be injured thereby, it is the subject of an action of trespass *vi et armis*, by all the cases, both ancient and modern, and it is immaterial whether the injury be *wilful or not.* Newsom *v.* Anderson, 2 Ired. 42, 43 (N. C. 1841). The contrary doctrine was expressed by chief-justice Shaw, of Massachusetts, in Brown *v.* Kendall (6 Cushing, 292). He says, "It is frequently stated by judges that where one receives injury from the direct act of another, trespass will lie. . . . These *dicta* are no authority, we think, for holding that damage received by a direct act of force from another will be sufficient to maintain an action of trespass, whether the act was lawful or unlawful, and neither wilful, intentional, or careless. We think as the result of all the authorities, that the rule is that the plaintiff must come prepared with evidence to show that the intention was unlawful, or that the defendant was in fault, for if the injury was unavoidable and the conduct of the defendant was free from blame, he will not be held liable." This is quoted with approval in Loser *v.* Buchanan, 51 N. Y. (6 Sickels). "The selling by a sheriff, under execution, of more of the goods of a defendant, than are sufficient to satisfy the process, will render him liable (to the extent of the additional goods sold) to the action of trespass." Roberts *v.* Beeson, 4 Porter, 164, 168 (Ala. 1836). Berry *v.* Mo. Pac. Ry. Co., 124 Mo. 223, 292 (1894). "The intent of the wrong-doer is not material to the form of the action; neither is it generally important whether the original act was or was not legal." 2 Greenleaf on Evidence, § 224. Bristol Mfg. Co. *v.* Gridley, 28 Conn. 201, 214 (1859).

(5) Landlord and Tenant in Pennsylvania, Jackson & Gross, 651 (2 ed. 1884). Binns' Justice, 83 (10 ed. Brightly, 1895). As water is a distinct thing from land, no action of trespass is sustainable for poisoning the water on a person's land. Mitchell *v.* Warner, 5 Conn. 497, 519 (1825).

(6) [Mine and thine.]

(7) Worrall *v.* Rhoads, 2 Whart. 427, 430 (Pa. 1837). Every entry on land without the owner's leave, or the license or authority of law, is a trespass. Newkirk *v.* Sabler, 9 Barb. 652, 654 (N. Y. 1850). Where A.'s servant by his order took his property on B.'s land after A. had been forbidden crossing the same, and B. detained the property, A. had no right to enter to regain possession after having been forbidden to do so by B. Newkirk

necessary in order to constitute this injury: "*qui alienum fundum ingreditur, potest a domino, si is præviderit, prohiberi ne ingrediatur.*"(*b*)(8) But the law of England, justly considering that much inconvenience may happen to the owner before he has an opportunity to forbid the entry, has carried the point much further, and has treated every entry upon another's lands (unless by the owner's leave, or in some very particular cases) as an injury or wrong, for satisfaction of which an action of trespass will lie; but determines the *quantum* of that satisfaction, by considering how far the offence was wilful, or inadvertent, and by estimating the value of the actual damage sustained. (9)

Every unwarrantable entry on another's soil the law entitles a trespass *by breaking his close:* the words of the writ of trespass commanding the defendant to show cause *quare clausum querentis fregit.*(10) For every man's land is, in the eye of the law, enclosed and set apart from his neighbor's; and that either by a visible and material fence, as one field is divided from another by a hedge, or by an ideal, invisible boundary, *existing   [*210 only in the contemplation of law, as when one man's land adjoins to another's in the same field.(11) And every such entry or breach of a man's close carries necessarily along with it some damage or other; for, if no other special loss can be assigned, yet still the words of the writ itself specify one general damage, viz., the treading down and bruising his herbage.(*c*)(12)

One must have a property (either absolute or temporary) in the soil, and actual possession by entry, to be able to maintain an action of trespass;(13)

(*b*) Inst. 2, 1, 12.   (*c*) F. N. B. 87, 88.

---

v. Sabler, 9 Barb. 652, 654 (N. Y. 1850). This rule has many exceptions. "I may enter my neighbor's close to succor his beast whose life is in danger; to prevent his beasts from being stolen, or to prevent his grain from being consumed or spoiled by cattle; or to carry away my tree which has been blown down upon his land, or to pick up my apples which have fallen from my trees upon his land, or to take my personal property which another has wrongfully taken and placed there, or to escape from one who threatens my life." Loree *v.* Buchanan, 51 N. Y. (6 Sickels) 476, 484 (1873).

(8) ["He who enters on another's land may be resisted by the owner if he shall have previously forbidden it."]

(9) Trespass for breaking a close is sustainable without previous notice; but it is most prudent to serve a notice and proceed for a subsequent trespass, upon which the judge on the trial will usually certify that the trespass was wilful, which will entitle plaintiff to full costs, though the damages be under 40*s*. 8 & 9 W. III. c. 11, s. 4. 3 Wils. 325. 6 T. R. 11. 7 T. R. 449. 3 East, 405.—CHITTY.

(10) [Wherefore he broke his close.] It matters not that there was no actual force, for the law implies force, and damage likewise, in every unauthorized entry. Norvell *v.* Gray's Lessee, 1 Swan, 96, 103 (Tenn. 1851).

(11) The Law of Torts; Clerk and Lindsell, 267. The Law of Torts; Hilliard (3 ed.) vol. 1, p. 523. In Pennsylvania, unless there be a fence around a man's land, built in accordance with the law, it is no trespass for wandering animals to enter therein, because it is the fault of the occupier of the ground to not fence them out. Landlord and Tenant in Pennsylvania, Jackson & Gross, 656 (2 ed. 1884).

(12) Hurd *v.* R. & B. R. R. Co, 25 Vt. 116, 122 (1853). 2 Waterman on Trespass, 294 (1875). In an action of trespass for entering the grounds of another person and sporting over them, the jury may take into consideration, in determining their verdict, not only the actual damage sustained by the plaintiff, but circumstances of aggravation and insult on the part of the defendant. Merest *v.* Harvey, 1 Marsh, 139. 5 Taunt. 442.—CHITTY.

(13) By the term "property either absolute or temporary" the student might be led to suppose that this action is only maintainable by one who is lawful owner or lawfully in possession. But the action is founded on possession, not on title. In his original complaint, the plaintiff relies only on his possession, and discloses no title; nor will he be bound to prove any, unless the defendant destroys the presumption arising from his possession by showing a title *prima facie* good in himself. Even if it should appear clearly that the plaintiff's possession was wrongful, he will recover damages in case the defendant is also a wrong-doer and has no title to rely on. Graham *v.* Peat, 1 East, 244. Catteris *v.* Cowper, 4 Taunt. 547.—COLERIDGE.

Where no one is in possession,—the land being vacant and uncultivated,—the party

or, at least, it is requisite that the party have a lease and possession of the vesture and herbage of the land.(*d*)(14)   Thus, if a meadow be divided annually among the parishioners by lot, then, after each person's several portion is allotted, they may be respectively capable of maintaining an action for the breach of their several closes:(*e*) for they have an exclusive interest and freehold therein for the time.   But before entry and actual possession one cannot maintain an action of trespass, though he hath the freehold in law.(*f*)(15)   And therefore an heir before entry cannot have this action against an abator; though a disseisee might have it against the disseisor, for the injury done by the disseisin itself, at which time the plaintiff was seised of the land;(16) but he cannot have it for any act done after the disseisin until he hath gained possession by re-entry,(17) and then he may well main-

---

(*d*) Dyer, 285. 2 Roll. Abr. 549.   (*f*) 2 Roll. Abr. 553.
(*e*) Cro. Eliz. 421.

---

having the title or right of possession may maintain trespass.   Gillespie *v.* Dew, 1 Stew. 229.   Aiken *v.* Buck, 1 Wend. 466.   Goodrich *v.* Hathaway, 1 Verm. 485.   It is settled that the owner of wild and uncultivated land is to be deemed in possession so as to maintain trespass until an adverse possession is clearly made out.   Mather *v.* Trinity Church, 3 Serg. & Rawle, 513.   Cook *v.* Foster, 2 Gilman, 652.   Smith *v.* Yell, 3 English, 470.   "In a mere uncultivated country, in wild and impenetrable woods, in the sullen and solitary haunts of beasts of prey, what notoriety could an entry, a gathering of a twig or an acorn, convey to civilized man at the distance of hundreds of miles?   The reason of the rule could not apply to such a state of things; and *cessante ratione, cessat ipsa lex* [The reason ceasing that law is (then) superseded].   We are entirely satisfied that a conveyance of wild or vacant lands gives a constructive seisin thereof in deed to the grantee: it attaches to him all the legal remedies incident to the estate."   Story, J., in Green *v.* Liter *et al.* 8 Cranch, 249.—SHARSWOOD.

(14) As to the possession and title essential, see Chitty on Pl. 159–166.   An exclusive interest in the crop, without an interest in the soil, is sufficient to sustain an action of trespass, (3 Burr. 1826.   Bro. Abr. Tresp. 273.   Bull. N. P. 85;) but possession, actual or constructive, must be proved.   1 East, 244.   4 Taunt. 547.   6 East, 602.   Trespass will not lie for entering a pew or seat, because the plaintiff has not the *exclusive* possession, the possession of the church being in the parson.   1 T. R. 430.   If trees are excepted in the lease, the land whereon they grow is necessarily excepted also: consequently the landlord may maintain trespass *for breaking his close*, if the tenant cut down the trees. Selw. N. P. 1287.   Where two fields are separated by a hedge and ditch, the hedge *prima facie* belongs to the owner of the field in which the ditch is not.   If there is a ditch on each side, the ownership of the hedge must be proved by acts of ownership.   Ib. 1288. A person may cut his ditch to the edge of his own land; but if he goes beyond, he is a trespasser on his neighbor's land, though he may cut as wide as he pleases on his own land.   3 Taunt. 138.—CHITTY.

(15) Clark *v.* Smith, 25 Pa. 137, 139 (1855).   Browne on Actions of Law, 418.   It is the settled law of England that constructive possession, alone, will not support the action. In America, however, the authorities are at variance.   Bailey's Onus Probandi, 291 (1886). A mere legal or constructive possession will not maintain an action of trespass.   McClain *v.* Todd's Heirs, 5 J. J. Marsh. 335, 336 (Ky. 1831).   The general rule is, that to maintain trespass *quare clausum fregit* [Why he broke the close], there must have been an actual possession in the plaintiff when the trespass was committed or a constructive possession in respect of the right being actually vested in him, the ground of the action being the injury to the possession.   Perry *v.* Carr, 44 N. H. 118, 120 (1862).   This doctrine does not apply in all cases in this country, for as an actual entry into wild and uncultivated land would give no notoriety to the possession or the change of property, it is declared to be an impracticable and an utterly useless thing, and of course a plaintiff may maintain trespass in such cases without actual possession of the premises—without ever having made an entry upon the land.   For not to give him such a right would be to expose his possession to serious and destructive injury without any adequate remedy or redress. For if he is seised by a lawful estate of inheritance or in fee, the law presumes that he is rightfully in possession to the extent of his boundary, and his seisin is not confined to his mere occupancy, or actual cultivation; but if he enters without title, he is then confined by metes and bounds strictly to his actual possession.   Wilson *v.* Bushnell, 1 Ark. 465, 470, 471 (1839).   Followed in Smith *v.* Yell, 8 Eng. 470, 473 (Ark.) (1848).

(16) Storrs *v.* Feick, 24 W. Va. 606, 608 (1884).

(17) Jones *v.* Leeman, 69 Me. 489, 490 (1879).   Holmes *v.* Seely, 19 Wend. 507, 509 (N. Y. 1838).   The owner of land cannot be made answerable in damages for dispossessing a trespasser divested of all title.   Muldrow *v.* Jones, 1 Rice, 64, 71 (S. C. 1838).

tain it for the intermediate damage done; for after his re-entry the law, by a kind of *jus postliminii*,(18) supposes the freehold to have all along continued in him.(g)(19) Neither, by the common law, in case of an intrusion or deforcement, could the party kept out of possession sue the wrong-doer by a mode of redress which was calculated merely for injuries committed against the land while *in the possession* of the owner. But now, by the statute 6 Anne, c. 18, if a guardian or trustee for any infant, a husband seised *jure uxoris*,(20) or a person having any estate or interest determinable upon a life or lives, shall, after the *determination of their respective   *211] interests, hold over and continue in possession of the lands or tenements without the consent of the person entitled thereto, they are adjudged to be trespassers; and any reversioner or remainder-man expectant on any life-estate may once in every year, by motion to the court of chancery, procure the *cestuy que vie* to be produced by the tenant to the land, or may enter thereon in case of his refusal or wilful neglect. And by the statutes of 4 Geo. II. c. 28, and 11 Geo. II. c. 19, in case, after the determination of any term of life, lives, or years, any person shall wilfully hold over the same, the lessor or reversioner is entitled to recover by action of debt, either at the rate of double the annual value of the premises in case he himself hath demanded and given notice in writing to the tenant to deliver the possession; or else double the usual rent in case the notice of quitting proceeds from the tenant himself, having power to determine his lease, and afterwards neglects to carry that notice into due execution.(21)

A man is answerable for not only his own trespass, but that of his cattle also; for, if by his negligent keeping they stray upon the land of another, (and much more if he permits or drives them on,) and they there tread down his neighbor's herbage and spoil his corn or his trees, this is a trespass for which the owner must answer in damages,(22) and the law gives the party

(g) 11 Rep. 5.

---

(18) [Remitter.]

(19) Cunningham *v.* Browning, 1 Bland, 299, 325 (Md.). Dewey *v.* Osborn, 4 Cow. 329, 338 (N. Y. 1825). Nelson *v.* Allen & Harris, 1 Yerg. 360, 365 (Tenn. 1830). Schermerhorn *v.* Buell, 4 Denio, 422, 425 (N. Y. 1847). Smith *v.* Wunderlich, 70 Ill. 426, 436 (1873). Fulner *v.* Langford, 11 Mo. 288 (1883). 2 Waterman on Trespass, 373, n. (1875). After an ouster and re-entry, the owner of the land may lay his action with a *continuando* [Continuance of the trespass] and recover *mesne* profits, as well as damages for the ouster. Smith *v* Wunderlich, 70 Ill. 426, 434 (1873). It does not matter whether the re-entry was by recovery in ejectment, or without the aid of the law. Emrich *v.* Ireland, 55 Miss. 390, 401 (1877). Ex'rs of Stevens *v.* Hollister, 18 Vt. 294, 298 (1846). The authorities extend the rule to an owner who never had any possession till his entry or recovery. Leland *v.* Tansey, 6 Hill, 328, 331 (N. Y. 1864).

(20) [In right of his wife.] [*Cestuy que vie*—The beneficiary.]

(21) See 2 Book, p. 151. Upon these statutes it has been determined that it is not necessary that the notice from the tenant should be in writing; but notice from the landlord to the tenant must. Burr. 1603. Bla. Rep. 533. And the 4 Geo. II. extends to cases where the tenant holds over fraudulently and perversely only, not where he continues his possession under a *bona fide* claim of right. 5 Esp. 203. See also ib. 215. The action for double rent may be maintained after recovery in ejectment. 9 East, 310. —CHITTY.

(22) Dolph *v.* Ferris, 7 W. & S. 367, 369 (Pa. 1844). L. & I. R. R. Co. *v.* Shriner, 6 Ind. 141, 145 (1855). C., St. L. & P. R. R. Co. *v.* Nash, 1 Ind. App. Co. Rep. 298, 313 (1890). Bulpit *v.* Matthews, 145 Ill. 345, 349 (1893). Bishop on Non-Contract Law, § 1220 (1889). 1 Hilliard's Law of Torts, 565 (3 ed). Unless the entry is through defect of fences, which the owner of the land entered ought to repair. Van Lewen *v.* Lyke, 1 Comstock, 515, 517 (1848). At common law, the owner of cattle is required to take care of them. If they trespass on a neighbor's land, he is responsible, though there is no fence. Such, in the absence of a statute, is the rule of law in most of our states. But in a few of them it is not accepted, so that owners are not responsible for the trespasses of their cattle running at large. And, pretty generally with us, there are statutes requiring fences. Bishop on Non-Contract Law, § 801 (1889). In Vermont, notwithstanding the statutes in

injured a double remedy in this case, by permitting him to distrain the cattle thus *damage-feasant*, or doing damage, till the owner shall make him satisfaction, or else by leaving him to the common remedy *in foro contentioso*,(23) by action. And the action that lies in either of these cases of trespass committed upon another's land either by a man himself or his cattle is, the action of trespass *vi et armis*, whereby a man is called upon to answer *quare vi et armis clausum ipsius A., apud B., fregit, et blada ipsius A., ad valentiam centum solidorum, ibidem nuper crescentia cum quibusdam averiis depastus*

---

relation to fences, the common law rule prevails, requiring the owners of cattle to take care of them. Keenan *v.* Cavanaugh, 44 Vt. 268. The liability is the same in Indiana, in the absence of an order of the board of county commissioners. Mich. Southern R. R. Co. *v.* Fisher, 27 Ind. 96.

In Missouri and Mississippi, the common law liability does not prevail. Gorman *v.* Pacific R. R. Co., 26 Mo. 441. Vicksburg & Jackson R. R. Co. *v.* Patton, 31 Miss. 156. In Massachusetts, where the parties are not adjoining owners, the common law rule prevails that each is bound to keep his cattle upon his own lands at his peril. Where, therefore, the mule of A. escaped from his field through an insufficient fence, which B. was bound to repair, into B.'s field, from that into the field of C., and thence into the field of D., through D.'s insufficient fence, and injured D.'s mare so that she died, it was held that A. was liable to D. for the injury, although he did not know that the mule was vicious. Lyons *v.* Merrick, 105 Mass. 71. In Kansas, where both parties choose to do otherwise than maintain a partition fence under the statute, the common law governs, and each must take care of his cattle, or be liable for all injuries they may commit by roaming. Baker *v.* Robbins, 9 Kan. 303. Wells *v.* Beal, ib. 597. 2 Waterman on Trespass, 279, n. (1875). This common law rule has never been in force in California. Merritt *v.* Hill, 104 Cal. 184, 185 (1894). This rule does not apply to damage done by cattle straying from a highway on which they are being lawfully driven; in such case the owner is liable only on proof of negligence; and the law is the same for a town street as for a country road. Webb's Pollock on Torts, 612 (Am. ed. 1894). As to injuries committed by stock running at large, the liability of the owner will depend upon whether the local law requires them to be kept up, as in England and many of our states, wherever what is commonly known as the "stock law" prevails, the breach of the duty to keep them up gives a right of action if they stray and commit damage, and in such cases the burden does not extend beyond proof of the ownership and damage. Bailey's Onus Probandi, 12 (1886). In Michigan, the Act of March 17, 1847 provided that: "No person shall be entitled to recover any sum of money, in any action for damages done upon lands by any beast or beasts, unless in cases where, by the by-laws of the proper township, such beasts are prohibited from running at large, except in cases where such lands are enclosed by a fence of the same height and description, as is required by the provisions of sect. 1, chap. 18, of R. S. of 1846." This was enacted only in reference to exterior fences; and the exception in the act relates to beasts running at large, and to lands enclosed as distinguished from that unenclosed or wild lands, and not to adjoining enclosures. Accordingly, where one of two owners of adjoining lands put cattle upon his own land, from which they entered upon the land of the other (there being no partition fence), he was liable to an action therefor. Johnson *v.* Wing, 3 Mich. 163, 170 (1854). In Nebraska, under the herd law, chap. 2 and 3, Compiled Statutes, persons having the custody of cattle, though not the owners, are liable for trespasses and damage by such cattle upon cultivated lands. The common law of England is not applicable as to trespasses by cattle upon open, uncultivated lands. Laflin *v.* Svoboda, 37 Neb. 368, 371 (1893). The exceptions to the common law rule are: (1) Where cattle are being driven along a highway, the owner is not liable in trespass if they break into adjoining grounds or houses, provided the driver of such cattle was not negligent, because such use of a highway is lawful. But the public has no right to use a highway for the purpose of pasturing cattle. And if animals straying upon the highway get upon the adjacent land, the owner is liable for the trespass. (2) There is no common law obligation to maintain division or partition fences between the lands of contiguous proprietors; but in some states there are statutory provisions concerning them. And if a division fence, established by statute, prescription, or agreement, is out of repair through the plaintiff's neglect, then the defendant is not liable for the resulting trespass of his cattle. The owner of a dog is not liable for its mere trespasses, unless he accompanies it, or knows that it is in the habit of doing damage. In some states, the common law rule is not in force, and it is held that where it is customary for cattle to run at large on unenclosed lands, they are not trespassing in doing so, because there is an implied license from the land owners. The application of these rules will determine what constitutes a trespass by animals. Brantley on Personal Property, § 81 (1891).

(23) [In a court of litigation.] 1 Beven on Negligence (2 ed.) 632.

fuit, conculcavit, et consumpsit, etc.:(h)(24) for the law always couples the idea of force with that of intrusion upon the property of another. And herein, if any unwarrantable act of the *defendant or his beasts   [*212 in coming upon the land be proved, it is an act of trespass for which the plaintiff must recover some damages; such, however, as the jury shall think proper to assess.

In trespasses of a permanent nature, where the injury is continually renewed, (as by spoiling or consuming the herbage with the defendant's cattle,) the declaration may allege the injury to have been committed by *continuation* from one given day to another, (which is called laying the action with a *continuando,*)(25) and the plaintiff shall not be compelled to bring separate actions for every day's separate offence.(i)   But where the trespass is by one or several acts, each of which terminates in itself, and being once done cannot be done again, it cannot be laid with a *continuando;* yet if there be repeated acts of trespass committed, (as cutting down a certain number of trees,) they may be laid to be done, not continually, but at divers days and times within a given period.(k)(26)

In some cases trespass is justifiable, or, rather, entry on another's land or house shall not in those cases be accounted trespass; as if a man comes thither to demand or pay money there payable, or to execute in a legal manner the process of the law.(27) Also, a man may justify entering into an inn or public house without the leave of the owner first specially asked, because when a man professes the keeping such inn or public house he thereby gives a general license to any person to enter his doors.(28) So a landlord may justify entering to distrain for rent; a commoner, to attend his cattle commoning on another's land; and a reversioner, to see if any waste be committed on the estate; for the apparent necessity of the thing.(l)(29) Also, it hath been said that, by the common law and custom of England, the poor are allowed to enter and glean upon another's ground after the harvest without *being guilty of trespass:(m) which humane   [*213 provision seems borrowed from the Mosaical law.(n)(30)

In like manner the common law warrants the hunting of ravenous beasts of prey, as badgers and foxes, in another man's land, because the destroying

---

(h) Registr. 94.
(i) 2 Roll. Abr. 545. Lord Raym. 240.
(k) Salk. 638, 639. Lord Raym. 823. 7 Mod. 152.

(l) 8 Rep. 146.
(m) Gilb. Ev. 253. Trials *per pais,* ch. 15, p. 438.
(n) Levit. xix. 9, and xxiii. 22. Deut. xxiv. 19, etc.

(24) [Wherefore he broke the close of the said A., at B., by force and arms, razed, trampled on, and consumed the grass of the said A., lately growing thereon, with certain beasts, to the value of twenty shillings, etc.]

(25) [By continuation.]

(26) Bucker *v.* McNeely, 4 Blackf. 179, 180 (Ind. 1836). The latter mode prevails in modern practice, and the form of declaring with a *continuando* has grown obsolete. Under the statement that the defendant, on a day named, and on divers other days and times between that day and the commencement of the suit, trespassed, the plaintiff may prove any number of trespasses within those limits, though none are specified except those on the earliest day named. 1 Stark. R. 351.—CHITTY.

(27) Binns' Justice, 78 (10 ed. Brightly).

(28) Newkirk *v.* Sabler, 9 Barb. 654 (N. Y. 1850). Bigelow on Torts, 194, 195.

(29) Landlord and Tenant in Pennsylvania, (Jackson & Gross) 653 (2 ed. 1884).

(30) Two actions of trespass have been brought in the Common Pleas against gleaners, with an intent to try the general question,—viz., whether such a right existed. In the first, the defendant pleaded that he, being a poor, necessitous, and indigent person, entered the plaintiff's close to glean; in the second, the defendant's plea was as before, with the addition that he was an inhabitant legally settled within the parish. To the plea in each case there was a general demurrer. Mr. J. Gould delivered a learned judgment in favor of gleaning, but the other three judges were clearly of opinion that this claim had no foundation in law; that the only authority to support it was an extra-judicial dictum of lord Hale; that it was a practice incompatible with the exclusive enjoyment of property, and was productive of vagrancy and many mischievous consequences. 1 H. Bl. Rep. 51, 52, n. (a.)—CHITTY.

such creatures is said to be profitable to the public. (*o*)(31) But in cases where a man misdemeans himself or makes an ill use of the authority with which the law intrusts him, he shall be accounted a trespasser *ab initio:*(*p*)(32) as if one comes into a tavern and will not go out in a reasonable time, but tarries there all night contrary to the inclinations of the owner; this wrongful act shall affect and have relation back, even to his first entry, and make the whole a trespass.(*q*) But a bare non-feasance, as not paying for the wine he calls for, will not make him a trespasser; for this is only a breach of contract, for which the taverner shall have an action of debt or *assumpsit* against him.(*r*) So, if a landlord distrained for rent and wilfully killed the distress, this, by the common law, made him a trespasser *ab initio:*(*s*) and so, indeed, would any other irregularity have done, till the statute 11 Geo. II. c. 19, which enacts that no subsequent irregularity of the landlord shall make his first entry a trespass; but the party injured shall have a special action of trespass or on the case, for the real specific injury sustained, unless tender of amends hath been made. But still, if a reversioner, who enters on pretence of seeing waste, breaks the house, or stays there all night; or if the commoner who comes to tend his cattle cuts down a tree; in these and similar cases the law judges that he entered for this unlawful purpose, and therefore, as the act which demonstrates such his purpose is a trespass, he shall be esteemed a trespasser *ab initio.*(*t*) So also, in the case of hunting the fox or the badger, a man cannot justify breaking the soil

*214] and digging him out of his earth; for though *the law warrants the hunting of such noxious animals for the public good, yet it is held(*u*) that such things must be done in an ordinary and usual manner; therefore, as there is an ordinary course to kill them, viz., by hunting, the court held that the digging for them was unlawful.

A man may also justify in an action of trespass, on account of the freehold and right of entry being in himself; and this defence brings the title of the estate in question.(33) This is therefore one of the ways devised, since the disuse of real actions, to try the property of estates; though it is not so usual as that by ejectment, because that, being now a mixed action, not only gives damages for the ejection, but also possession of the land: whereas in trespass, which is merely a personal suit, the right can be only ascertained, but no possession delivered; nothing being recovered but damages for the wrong committed.

In order to prevent trifling and vexatious actions of trespass, as well as other personal actions, it is (*inter alia*) enacted by statutes 43 Eliz. c. 6,

(*o*) Cro. Jac. 321.
(*p*) Finch, L. 47. Cro. Jac. 148.
(*q*) 2 Roll. Abr. 561.
(*r*) 8 Rep. 147.

(*s*) Finch, L. 47.
(*t*) 8 Rep. 146.
(*u*) Cro. Jac. 321.

(31) It has been determined that it is lawful to follow a fox with horses and hounds over another's grounds, if no more damage be done than is necessary for the destruction of the animal by such a pursuit, (1 T. R. 338;) but, in the Earl of Essex *v.* Capel, Hertford Assizes, A. D. 1809, 2 Chitty Game L. 1381, a different doctrine was laid down by lord Ellenborough, who said, "These pleasures are to be taken only when there is the consent of those who are likely to be injured by them; but they must be necessarily subservient to the consent of others. There may be such a public nuisance by a noxious animal as may justify the running him to his earth; but then you cannot justify the digging for him afterwards: that has been ascertained and settled to be law: but even if an animal may be pursued with dogs, it does not follow that fifty or sixty people have therefore a right to follow the dogs and trespass on other people's lands." The jury, under his lordship's direction, found a verdict for the plaintiff And see 1 Stark. 351.—
CHITTY.

(32) [From the beginning.] [*Inter alia*—Among other things.]
(33) Ming *v.* Compton, Penn. *345, *346, *347 (N. J. 1808). Gambling *v.* Prince, 2 Nott & McC. 138, 139 (S. C. 1819).

and 22 & 23 Car. II. c. 9, § 136, that where the jury, who try an action of trespass, give less damages than forty shillings, the plaintiff shall be allowed no more costs than damages, unless the judge shall certify under his hand that the freehold or title of the land came chiefly in question.(34)   But this rule now admits of two exceptions more, which have been made by subsequent statutes.   One is by statute 8 & 9 W. III. c. 11, which enacts, that in all actions of trespass, wherein it shall appear that the trespass was wilful and malicious, and it be so certified by the judge, the plaintiff shall recover full costs.(35)   Every trespass is *wilful*, where the defendant has notice, and is especially forewarned not to come on the land; as every trespass is *malicious*, though the damage may not amount to forty shillings, where the intent of the defendant plainly appears to *be to harass   [*215 and distress the plaintiff.   The other exception is by statute 4 & 5 W. and M. c. 23, which gives full costs against any inferior tradesman, apprentice, or other dissolute person, who is convicted of a trespass in hawking, hunting, fishing, or fowling, upon another's land.   Upon this statute it has been adjudged, that if a person be an inferior tradesman, as a clothier for instance, it matters not what qualification he may have in point of estate; but, if he be guilty of such trespass, he shall be liable to pay full costs.(w)(36)

CHAPTER XIII.

OF NUISANCE.

*A THIRD species of real injuries to a man's lands and tenements,   [*216 is by *nuisance*. Nuisance, *nocumentum*, or annoyance, signifies any thing that worketh hurt, inconvenience, or damage.(1)   And nuisances are of two kinds: *public* or *common* nuisances, which affect the public, and are

(w) Lord Raym. 149.

(34) And if this appears upon the face of the pleadings, it is considered tantamount to the judge's certificate, and the plaintiff is entitled to his full costs. 2 Lev. 234. 1 East, 350. Selw. N. P. 1324. 6 T. R. 281. 7 T. R. 650. See, also, *post*, 401, n. 21.—ARCHBOLD.

But by stat. 3 & 4 Vict. c. 24, explained by stat. 4 & 5 Vict. c. 28, these statutes are repealed, and their provisions are consolidated and extended; it being enacted that if the plaintiff in any action of trespass, either to the person, or to real or personal property, or for libel, slander, or malicious prosecution, brought in any of her Majesty's courts at Westminster, shall recover less damages than 40s., he shall not be entitled to recover any costs whatever, whether it shall be given upon any issue tried or judgment passed by default, unless the judge or presiding officer shall certify on the back of the record (if the action be in trespass) that the action was really brought to try a right besides the mere right to recover damages for the trespass or grievance for which the action shall have been brought.—STEWART.

(35) It has been supposed that the judge must certify in open court after the trial, otherwise the certificate is void, (2 Wils. 21;) but the contrary has recently been decided. 2 B. & C. 580, 621.—CHITTY.

(36) But now, by the stat. 1 & 2 W. IV. c. 32, s. 1, this act is repealed; and, by s. 6, all certificated persons are allowed to sport, subject to the law of trespass.—STEWART.

(1) State *v*. Matthews, 2 Dev. & Bat. 424, 425 (1837). Burnham *v*. Hotchkiss, 14 Conn. 311, 317 (1841). Lancaster Turnpike Co. *v*. Rogers, 2 Pa. 114, 115 (1845). State *v*. Haines, 17 Me. 65, 74 (1849). Carhart *v*. Gas Co., 22 Barb. 297, 310 (N. Y. 1856). Burditt *v*. Swenson, 17 Tex. 489, 502 (1856). Harvey *v*. Dewoody, 18 Ark. 252, 258 (1856). Rogers *v*. Barker, 31 Barb. 447, 452 (N. Y. 1860). Norcross *v*. Thorns, 51 Me. 503, 504 (1863). Griffith *v*. McCullum, 46 Barb. 568 (N. Y. 1866). Landlord and Tenant in Pennsylvania (Jackson & Gross) 741 (2 ed. 1884). 2 Barbour's Rights of Pers. & Prop. 779. A nuisance, of the sort which is redressed at the suit of the party, is anything done on one's premises or elsewhere, or put into circulation, or omitted to be done contrary to

annoyance to *all* the king's subjects:(2)for which reason we must refer them to the class of public wrongs, or crimes and misdemeanors: and *private* nuisances, which are the objects of our present consideration, and may be defined, any thing done to the hurt or annoyance of the lands, tenements, or hereditaments of another.(*a*)(3) We will therefore, first, mark out the several kinds of nuisances, and then their respective remedies.

I. In discussing the several kinds of nuisances, we will consider, first, such nuisances as may affect a man's corporeal hereditaments, and then those that may damage such as are incorporeal.

1. First, as to *corporeal* inheritances. If a man builds a house so close to mine that his roof overhangs my roof and throws the water off his roof upon mine, this is a nuisance, for which an action will lie.(*b*) Likewise to erect a house or other building so near to mine that it obstructs my ancient *217]   *lights and windows, is a nuisance of a similar nature.(*c*) But in this latter case it is necessary that the windows be *ancient*, that is, have subsisted there a long time without interruption; otherwise there is no injury done.(4) For he hath as much right to build a new edifice upon his ground as I have upon mine; since every man may erect what he pleases upon the upright or perpendicular of his own soil, so as not to prejudice what has long been enjoyed by another; and it was my folly to build so near another's ground.(*d*)(5) Also if a person keeps his hogs, or other

(*a*) Finch, L. 188.
(*b*) F. N. B. 181.

(*c*) 9 Rep. 58.
(*d*) Cro. Eliz. 118. Salk 459.

a legal duty, wherefrom, through the separate action of nature or of the common course of events, an injury follows to, or directly menaces another; or, it is any indictable nuisance which has wrought special harm to the individual. Bishop on Non-Contract Law, § 411 (1889). In Indiana, the statutory definition of a nuisance is this: "Whatever is injurious to health, or indecent, or offensive to the senses, or an obstruction to the free use of property, so as essentially to interfere with the comfortable enjoyment of life or property, is a nuisance, and the subject of an action." O. & M. Ry. Co. *v.* Simon, 40 Ind. 278, 285 (1872). A common tippling house, in and about which idle and dissolute persons are encouraged to assemble, and are permitted to drink, swear, quarrel, and shout by night as well as by day, is a nuisance. State *v.* Bertheol, 6 Blackf. 474, 475 (Ind. 1843).

(2) Ferguson *v.* City of Selma, 43 Ala. 398, 400 (1869).

(3) Caldwell *v.* Knott, 10 Yerg. 211 (Tenn. 1836). Carhart *v.* Auburn Gas Light Co., 22 Barb. 297, 310 (N. Y. 1856). Burditt *v.* Swenson, 17 Tex. 489, 502 (1856). Harvey *v.* Dewoody, 18 Ark. 252, 258 (1856). Veazie *v.* Dwinel, 50 Me. 479, 482 (1862). State *v.* Close, 35 Iowa, 570, 572 (1872). Paddock *v.* Somes, 102 Mo. 226, 237 (1890). Archbold's Crim. Pr. and Pl. 1751. Webb's Pollock on Torts, 492 (Am. ed. 1894). Binns' Justice, 78 (10 ed. Brightly, 1895). By hurt or annoyance here is meant, not a physical injury necessarily, but an injury to the owner or possessor thereof, as respects his dealing with, possessing or enjoying them. Cooley on Torts, 670 (2 ed. 1888). If a railroad company occupies a street by its side tracks and cars and engines, without authority of law, it is a public nuisance. And if a property owner suffers special damage in which the public does not participate, it becomes, as to such property owner, a private nuisance. Kavanagh *v.* M. & G. R. R. Co., 78 Ga. 271, 273 (1886).

(4) Robeson and Maxwell *v.* Pittenger, 1 Green, 57, 63 (N. J. 1838).

(5) Where A. had enjoyed lights made in a building not erected at the extremity of his land, looking upon the premises of B., without interruption for at least thirty-eight years, and there was no evidence of the time when the lights were first put out, and C., the purchaser of B.'s premises, erected in their stead a building which obstructed A.'s lights: held that an action was maintainable for the obstruction, though there was no proof of knowledge in B. or his agents of the existence of the windows. Cross *v.* Lewis, 2 B. & C. 686. 4 D. & R. 234. S. C. Where the plaintiff is entitled to lights by means of blinds fronting a garden of the defendant's, which he takes away, and opens an uninterrupted view into the garden, the defendant cannot justify making an erection to prevent the plaintiff from so doing, if he thereby render the plaintiff's house more dark than before. Cotterell *v.* Griffiths, 4 Esp. 69. A parol license to put a sky-light over the defendant's area (which impeded the light and air from coming to the plaintiff's dwelling-house through a window) cannot be recalled at pleasure after it has been executed at the defendant's expense,—at least not without tendering the expenses he had been put

noisome animals, so near the house of another that the stench of them incommodes him and makes the air unwholesome,(6) this is an injurious nuisance, as it tends to deprive him of the use and benefit of his house.(*e*)(7) A like injury is, if one's neighbor sets up and exercises an offensive trade; as a tanner's, a tallow-chandler's, or the like; for though these are lawful and necessary trades, yet they should be exercised in remote places; for the rule is, "*sic utere tuo, ut alienum non lædas:*"(8) this therefore is an actionable nuisance.(*f*) So that the nuisances which affect a man's *dwelling* may be reduced to these three: 1. Overhanging it; which is also a species of trespass, for *cujus est solum, ejus est usque ad cælum:*(9) 2. Stopping ancient lights: and 3. Corrupting the air with noisome smells· for light and air are two indispensable requisites to every dwelling.(10) But depriving one of a

(*e*) 9 Rep. 58.   (*f*) Cro. Car. 510.

---

to; and therefore no action lies as for a private nuisance in stopping the light and air, etc. and communicating a stench from the defendant's premises to the plaintiff's house by means of such sky-light. Winter *v.* Brockwell, 8 East, 308. If an ancient window be raised and enlarged, the owner of the adjoining land cannot lawfully obstruct the passage of light and air to any part of the space occupied by the ancient window, although a greater portion of light and air be admitted through the unobstructed part of the enlarged window than was anciently enjoyed. Chandler *v.* Thompson, 3 Camp. 80. Le Blanc, J. To constitute an illegal obstruction, by building, of the plaintiff's ancient lights, it is not sufficient that the plaintiff has less light than he had before, but there must be such a privation of light as will render the occupation of his house uncomfortable, and prevent him, if in trade, from carrying on his business as beneficially as he had previously done. Back *v.* Stacy, 2 C. & P. 485. Best, L. C. J. C. P. The occupier of one of two houses built nearly at the same time and purchased of the same proprietor may maintain a special action on the case against the tenant of the other for obstructing his window-lights by adding to his own building, however short the previous period of enjoyment by the plaintiff. Compton *v.* Richards, 1 Price, 27. And where the owner of a house divided into two tenements demised one of them to the defendant: held that he was liable to an action on the case for obstructing windows existing in the house at the time of the demise, although of recent construction, and though there was no stipulation against the obstruction. Rivieri *v.* Bower, 1 R. & M. 24. Abbott, [Lord Tenterden,] L. C. J. If an ancient light has been completely shut up with bricks and mortar above twenty years, it loses its privilege. Lawrence *v.* Obee, 3 Camp. 514. Lord Ellenborough, L. C. J.—CHITTY.

(6) Lord Mansfield has said that "it is not necessary that the smell should be unwholesome: it is enough if it renders the enjoyment of life and property uncomfortable." 1 Burr. 337.

So also it will be a nuisance if life is made uncomfortable by the apprehension of danger: it has therefore been held to be a nuisance, a misdemeanor, to keep great quantities of gunpowder near dwelling-houses. 2 Stra. 1167.—CHRISTIAN.

(7) Bonner *v.* Welborn, 7 Ga. 296, 311 (1849).

(8) ["So use your property that you do not injure that of another."]

(9) [He who owns the soil has it even to the sky.]

(10) The buildings in which the particular trades are carried on, or the houses which may be kept in a disorderly manner, or used for unlawful purposes, are not *per se* [By themselves] nuisances; but it is the *abuse* of them only which constitutes the nuisance. Miller *v.* Burch, 32 Tex. 208, 210 (1869). The keeping or manufacturing of gunpowder or of fireworks does not necessarily constitute a nuisance *per se*. That depends upon the locality, the quantity, and the surrounding circumstances, and not entirely upon the degree of care used. Heeg *v.* Licht, 80 N. Y. (35 Sickels) 579, 581 (1880).

Where defendant employed a steam-engine in his business, as a printer, which produced a continual noise and vibration in the plaintiff's apartment, which adjoined the premises of the defendant, it was held that this was a nuisance. Duke of Northumberland *v.* Clowes, C. P. at Westminster, A. D. 1824.—CHITTY.

A carriage factory which, by its proximity to a dwelling, injures the same is a nuisance. Whitney *v.* Bartholomew, 21 Conn. 213, 219 (1851). The keeping and standing of jacks and stallions within the immediate view of a private dwelling is a nuisance. Hayden *v.* Tucker, 37 Mo. 214, 217 (1866). Farrell *v.* Cook, 16 Neb. 483, 485 (1884).

But the following note of a case describes an injury not exactly coming within either of the above three sections. A. has immemorially had for watering his lands a channel through his own field, in a porous field, through the banks of which channel, when filled, the water percolates and thence passes through the contiguous soil of B. below the sur-

mere matter of pleasure, as of a fine prospect by building a wall, or the like: this, as it abridges nothing really convenient or necessary, is no injury to the sufferer, and is therefore not an actionable nuisance.(g)(11)

As to nuisance to one's *lands:* if one erects a smelting-house for lead so near the land of another, that the vapor and smoke kill his corn and grass, and damage his cattle therein, this is held to be a nuisance.(h) And by consequence it follows, that if one does any other act, in itself lawful, which yet being done in that place necessarily tends to the damage of another's property, it is a nuisance: for it is incumbent on *him to find some *218] other place to do that act, where it will be less offensive.(12) So also if my neighbor ought to scour a ditch, and does not, whereby my land is overflowed, this is an actionable nuisance.(i)(13)

With regard to *other* corporeal hereditaments: it is a nuisance to stop or divert water that used to run to another's meadow, or mill;(k)(14) to corrupt or poison a water-course, by erecting a dye-house or a lime-pit for the use of trade, in the upper part of the stream;(l) or, in short, to do any act therein that in its consequences must necessarily tend to the prejudice of one's neighbor. So closely does the law of England enforce that excellent rule of gospel morality, of "doing to others as we would they should do unto ourselves."(15)

2. As to *incorporeal* hereditaments, the law carries itself with the same equity.(16) If I have a way, annexed to my estate, across another's land, and he obstructs me in the use of it, either by totally stopping it, or putting logs across it, or ploughing over it, it is a nuisance: for in the first case I cannot enjoy my right at all, and in the latter I cannot enjoy it so commodiously as I ought.(m) Also, if I am entitled to hold a fair or market, and another person sets up a fair or market so near mine that he does me a preju-

---

(g) 9 Rep. 58.
(h) 1 Roll. Abr. 89.
(i) Hale on F. N. B. 427.

(k) F. N. B. 184.
(l) 9 Rep. 59. 2 Roll. Abr. 141.
(m) F. N. B. 183. 2 Roll. Abr. 140.

---

face without producing visible injury. B. builds a new house in his land below the level of his soil, in the current of the percolating water. Held that A. cannot now justify filling his channel, if the percolating water thereby injures the house of B. Cowper *v.* Barber, 3 Taunt. 99. —CHITTY.

(11) Am. and Eng. Enc. of Law, Title—Nuisance.

(12) Binns' Justice, 749 (10 ed. Brightly, 1895).

(13) One man has no right to erect a mill-dam on his own land, so as to throw the water back and overflow the land of another, without his consent. Dorman *v.* Ames & George, 12 Minn. 451, 461 (1867).

(14) Haymes *v.* Gault, 1 McCord, 543, 544 (S. C. 1822). After twenty years' uninterrupted enjoyment of a spring of water, an absolute right to it is gained by the occupier of the close in which it issues above ground; and the owner of an adjoining close cannot lawfully cut a drain whereby the supply of water by the spring is diminished. Balston *v.* Bensted, 1 Camp. 463. Lord Ellenborough, L. C. J. And see Bealey *v.* Shaw, 6 East, 208. 2 Smith, 321, S. C.—CHITTY.

The owner of premises may lawfully erect a mill-dam across a stream not navigable. In such case the dam will not *per se* be a nuisance, and this is so with any lawful business or erection. But, whenever they are erected, managed or carried on in such places or in such manner as to become prejudicial to the health or comfort of others, they become nuisances. State *v.* Close, 35 Iowa, 570, 573, 574 (1872).

(15) Burditt *v.* Swenson, 17 Tex. 489, 502 (1856).

(16) Here we should mention a recent change in the law which limits actions and suits relating to incorporeal hereditaments. The prescriptive rights to profits and easements over the soil of another were rendered very difficult of proof, as by the ancient rule of the common law enjoyment of such rights was to be proved from time whereof the memory of man ran not to the contrary, or during legal memory. This rule was partly alleviated by the modern practice of the courts and the doctrine of *presumption*, by which proof of enjoyment as far as living witnesses could speak was held sufficient to raise a presumption of enjoyment from a remote era, and a grant would be presumed; but still frequent difficulties arose, to obviate which the statute 2 & 3 W. IV. c. 71 has

dice, it is a nuisance to the freehold which I have in my market or fair.(*n*)(17) But, in order to make this out to be a nuisance, it is necessary, 1. That my market or fair be the elder, otherwise the nuisance lies at my own door. 2. That the market be erected within the third part of twenty miles from mine. For Sir Matthew Hale(*o*) construes the *dieta*, or reasonable day's journey, mentioned by Bracton,(*p*) to be twenty miles; as indeed it is usually understood, not only in our own law,(*q*) but also in the civil,(*r*) from which we probably borrowed it. So that if the new market be not within seven miles of the old one, it is no *nuisance: for it is held reason-   [*219 able that every man should have a market within one-third of a day's journey from his own home; that, the day being divided into three parts, he may spend one part in going, another in returning, and the third in transacting his necessary business there. If such market or fair be on the same day with mine, it is *prima facie* a nuisance to mine, and there needs no proof of it, but the law will intend it to be so; but if it be on any other day, it *may* be a nuisance: though whether it *is* so or not, cannot be intended or presumed, but I must make proof of it to the jury. If a ferry is erected on a river, so near another ancient ferry as to draw away its custom, it is a nuisance to the owner of the old one. For where there is a ferry by prescription, the owner is bound to keep it always in repair and readiness, for the ease of all the king's subjects; otherwise he may be grievously amerced:(*s*) it would be therefore extremely hard if a new ferry were suffered to share his profits which does not also share his burden.(18) But where the reason ceases, the law also ceases with it: therefore it is no nuisance to erect a mill so near mine as to draw away the custom, unless the miller also intercepts the water. Neither is it a nuisance to set up any trade, or a school, in a neighborhood or rivalship with another: for by such emulation the public are like to be gainers; and, if the new mill or school occasion a damage to the old one, it is *damnum absque injuria.*(*t*)(19)

II. Let us next attend to the remedies which the law has given for this injury of nuisance.(20) And here I must premise that the law gives no *private* remedy for anything but a *private* wrong. Therefore no *action* lies

---

(*n*) F. N. B. 148. 2 Roll. Abr. 140.
(*o*) Hale on F. N. B. 184.
(*p*) L. 3, c. 16.
(*q*) 2 Inst. 567.

(*r*) Ff. 2, 11, 1.
(*s*) 2 Roll. Abr. 140.
(*t*) Hale on F. N. B. 184.

---

been passed, under which the periods at which claims may be made for incorporeal hereditaments are much limited.—STEWART.

(17) Shepard *v.* Milwaukee Gas Light Co., 15 Wis. 318, 330 (1862). Bowyer's Com. on Const. Law of Eng. 176. The law on the subject of markets stands practically unaltered in any feature of public utility. Att'y-Gen'l *v.* Detroit, 71 Mich. 92, 103 (1888). This classification seems rather to depend on accidents of procedure than on any substantial resemblance between interference with peculiar rights of this kind and such injuries to the enjoyment of common rights of property as we have been considering. Webb's Pollock on Torts, 512 (Am. ed. 1894).

(18) Charles River Bridge *v.* Warren Bridge, 11 Peters, 422, 621 (U. S. 1837). Smith *v.* Harkins, 3 Ired. Eq. 613, 619 (N. C. 1845). Norris *v.* Farmers' & Teamsters' Co., 6 Cal. 590, 594 (1856). R. & D. B. R. R. Co. *et al. v.* D. & R. Canal *et al.*, 3 C. E. Green(18 N. J. Eq.) 546, 570 (1867). The grantee of a ferry privilege is entitled to an injunction against one who, having no license, undertakes to operate another ferry in competition with that which is licensed. Tugwell & Madison *v.* Eagle Pass Ferry Co., 74 Tex. 480, 493 (1888).

(19) [Damage without injury. A loss which does not give rise to an action of damages against the person causing it.]
This shows that the only ground upon which the owner of an ancient ferry can claim protection is the obligation he is under to keep the ferry always in a fit state for the use of the public. Letton *v.* Goodden, L. R. 2. Eq. Cus. 123, 133 (Eng. 1866).

(20) The Maine statute (R. S. c. 17, ₴ 8) does not define a nuisance, but simply provides a remedy for *certain* injuries arising from a nuisance at common law. It does not deprive a party of his remedy for *other* injuries arising from the same source, but leaves the

for a public or common nuisance, but an *indictment* only,(21) because, the damage being common to all the king's subjects, no *one* can assign his particular proportion of it; or, if he could, it would be extremely hard if every subject in the kingdom were allowed to harass the offender with separate actions.   For this reason, no person, natural or corporate, can have an action for a public nuisance, or punish it; but only the king in his public

*220]   *capacity of supreme governor and *pater-familias* of the kingdom.(*u*)

Yet this rule admits of one exception, where a private person suffers some extraordinary damage, beyond the rest of the king's subjects, by a public nuisance, in which case he shall have a private satisfaction by action.(22)   As if, by means of a ditch dug across the public way, which is a common nuisance, a man or his horse suffer any injury by falling therein; there, for this particular damage, which is not common to others, the party shall have his action.(*w*)(23)   Also, if a man hath abated or removed a nuisance which offended him, (as we may remember it was stated in the first chapter of this book that the party injured hath a right to do,)(24) in this case he is entitled to no action.(*x*)   For he had choice of two remedies: either without suit, by abating it himself by his own mere act and authority, or by suit, in which he may both recover damages and remove it by the aid of the law; but, having made his election of one remedy, he is totally precluded from the other.(25)

(*u*) Vaugh. 341, 342.   (*x*) 9 Rep. 55.
(*w*) Co. Litt. 56.   5 Rep. 73.

common law doctrine of nuisance in full force and effect.   Norcross *v.* Thomas, 51 Me. 503, 505 (1863).

(21) Harvey *v.* Dewoody, 18 Ark. 252, 258 (1856). S. C. R. R. Co. *v.* Moore & Philpot, 28 Ga. 398, 418 (1859). Shed *v.* Hawthorne, 3 Neb. 179, 185 (1874). Centre & Treadwell *v.* Davis, 39 Ga. 210, 217 (1869).

(22) Pittsburg *v.* Scott, 1 Pa. 309, 319 (1845).   Cole *v.* Sprowl, 35 Me. 161, 169 (1852). Justices etc. *v.* G. & W. P. R. R. Co., 15 Ga. 39, 62 (1854). S. C. R. R. *v.* Moore & Philpot, 28 Ga. 398, 418 (1859). Shed *v.* Hawthorne, 3 Neb. 139 (1873). City of Roseburg *v.* Abraham, 8 Ore. 509, 511, 512 (1880). Fossian *v.* Landry, 123 Ind. 136, 140, 141 (1889). Dicey on Parties to Actions, 75 (1876). Lansing *v.* Smith, 4 Wend. (N. Y. 19). Abbot *v.* Mills, 3 Vt. 529. Hughes *v.* Heiser, 1 Binn. 463.

(23) But the particular damage in this case must be direct, and not consequential, as by being delayed in a journey of importance. Bull. N. P. 26. Carth. 194. And if the plaintiff has not acted with ordinary care and skill, with a view to protect himself from the mischief, he cannot recover. 11 East, 60. 2 Taunt. 414. It is upon the same principle that parties suffering special damage by a public nuisance are entitled, under 5 W. and M. c. 11, s. 3, to receive their expenses in prosecuting an indictment against the party guilty of the nuisance. See 16 East, 196. Willes, 71. Cro. Eliz. 664. If a party living in the neighborhood, and who has been in the habit of passing to and fro on a highway, is obliged by a nuisance thereto to take a more circuitous route in his transit to and from the nearest market-town to his house, it is a private injury, for which he may sue as well as indict. 3 M. & S. 472. So, being delayed four hours by an obstruction in a highway, and being thereby prevented from performing the same journey as many times in a day as if the obstruction had not existed, is a sufficient injury to entitle a party to sue for the obstruction. 2 Bingh. 283. So, if the nuisance prevent the plaintiff navigating his barges on a public navigable creek, and compel him to convey his goods out of the same over a great distance of land, it is actionable. 4 M. & S. 101. But the mere obstruction of the plaintiff in his business. (1 Esp. N. C. 148. 4 M. & S. 103,) or delaying him a little while in a journey, (Carth. 191,) is not such a damage as will entitle the party to his action: the damage ought to be direct, not consequential. Carth. 191.

There are also various other injuries which partake of both a criminal and civil nature, for which both an indictment as well as an action will lie,—as for a forcible entry, enticing away a servant, using false weights, disobeying an order of justices, extortion, or for a libel, etc.—CHITTY.

(24) Amoskeag Mfg. Co. *v.* Goodale, 46 N. H. 53, 56 (1865).

(25) Griffith *v.* McCullum, 46 Barb. 561, 568 (1866). If one abates a private nuisance, he cannot afterwards maintain an assize of nuisance; but he may maintain an action on the case to recover damages. Tate *v.* Parrish, 7 T. B. Mon. 325, 328 (Ky. 1828.) Gleason *v.* Gary, 4 Conn. 418, 421 (1822).

The remedies by suit are, 1. By action *on the case* for damages, in which the party injured shall only recover a satisfaction for the injury sustained, but cannot thereby remove the nuisance.(26) Indeed, every continuance of a nuisance is held to be a fresh one;(*y*) and therefore a fresh action will lie,(27) and very exemplary damages will probably be given, if, after one verdict against him, the defendant has the hardiness to continue it.(28) Yet the founders of the law of England did not rely upon probabilities merely, in order to give relief to the injured. They have therefore provided two other actions: the *assize of nuisance*, and the writ of *quod permittat prosternere;*(29) which not only give the plaintiff satisfaction for his injury past, but also strike at the root and remove the cause itself, the nuisance that occasioned the injury. These two actions, however, can only be brought by the tenant of the freehold; so that a lessee for years is confined to his action upon the case.(*z*)(30)

*2. An *assize of nuisance* is a writ, wherein it is stated that the   [*221
party injured complains of some particular fact done, *ad nocumentum
liberi tenementi sui,*(31) and therefore commanding the sheriff to summon an assize, that is, a jury, and view the premises, and have them at the next commission of assizes, that justice may be done therein:(*a*) and if the assize is found for the plaintiff, he shall have judgment of two things: 1. To have the nuisance abated; and, 2. To recover damages.(*b*) Formerly an assize of nuisance only lay against the very wrong-doer himself who levied or did the nuisance, and did not lie against any person to whom he had alienated the tenements whereon the nuisance was situated.(32) This was the imme-

---

(*y*) 2 Leon. pl. 129. Cro. Eliz. 402.   (*a*) F. N. B. 183.
(*z*) Finch, L. 289.   (*b*) 9 Rep. 55.

---

(26) Harvey *v.* Dewoody, 18 Ark. 252, 258 (1856). Courtwright *v.* B. R. & A. W. & M. Co., 30 Cal. 573, 576 (1866). Spurr *v.* Hall, 2 L. B. Div. 615, 623 (Eng. 1877). In New Jersey, the remedy for a nuisance is only by an action on the case. Perrine *v.* Bergen, 2 Green's Law Rep. 355, 357 (N. J. 1834).

(27) Duncan *v.* Markley, Harp. 276, 278 (S. C. 1824). Caldwell *v.* Knott, 10 Yerg. 209, 211 (Tenn. 1836). Vedder *v.* Vedder, 1 Denio, 257, 261 (N. Y. 1845). Brady *v.* Weeks, 3 Barb. 157, 160 (N. Y. 1848). Brown *v.* C. & S. R. R. Co., 2 Kern, 486, 492 (N. Y. 1855). Miles *v.* Wingate, 6 Ind. 458, 459 (1855). Conhocton Stone Co. *v.* B. N. Y. & E. R. R. Co., 52 Barb. 390, 392 (N. Y. 1868). Pettis *v.* Johnson, 56 Ind. 139, 149 (1877). Stein *v.* City of Lafayette, 6 Ind. App. Ct. 414, 419 (1892). Though the party complaining cannot, in an action on the case, recover upon the original cause of action, after the expiration of six years, he may for its continuance any time before the right of entry is barred, and recover not only nominal damages, but such actual damage as has accrued any time within six years. Angell on Limitations, 321, 322 (6 ed. (1876),

(28) Miller *v.* Trueheart, 4 Leigh. 569 577 (Va. 1833). Webb's Pollock on Torts, 518, 519 (Am. ed. 1894). An action for continuing a nuisance cannot be maintained against him who did not erect it, without a previous request made to him to remove or abate it. Pierson *v.* Glean, 2 Green, 36.
Parties who cause a nuisance by acts done on the land of a stranger are liable for its continuance; and it is no defence that they cannot lawfully enter to abate the nuisance without rendering themselves liable to an action by the owner of the land. Smith *v.* Elliott, 9 Barr. 345. One who demises premises for carrying on a business necessarily injurious to the adjacent proprietors is liable as the author of the nuisance. Fish *v.* Dodge, 4 Denio, 317.—SHARSWOOD.

(29) [That he permit to abate or put down.] This action is no longer in use. *Vid.* n. 74, c. x. *supra.* Miller *v.* Trueheart, 4 Leigh. 569, 577 (Va. 1833).

(30) Great F. Co. *v.* Worster, 15 N. H. 436 (1844).

(31) [To the damage of his freehold.]

(32) The writ of nuisance given by the act of West. 2, 13, ed. 1, c. 24, went also against the erector of the nuisance and his alienee jointly. Brady *v.* Weeks, 3 Barb. 157, 161 (N. Y. 1848). By an English statute and by the New York statute a writ of nuisance can be brought against the original wrong-doer and his immediate alienee, and no other person. (2 R. S. 427, § 1, code § 453). Conhocton Stone Co. *v.* B. N. Y. & E. R. R. Co. 52 Barb. 390, 394 (N. Y. 1868). In New York, an action for damages must be brought against the person erecting at the time he was owner, and if he has aliened, against him and the

diate reason for making that equitable provision in statute Westm. 2, 13 Edw. I. c. 24, for granting a similar writ *in casu consimili,*(33) where no former precedent was to be found. The statute enacts that "*de cetero non recedant querentes a curia domini regis, pro eo quod tenementum transfertur de uno in alium;*"(34) and then gives the form of a new writ in this case; which only differs from the old one in this, that where the assize is brought against the very person only who levied the nuisance, it is said "*quod A.* [the wrong-doer] *injuste levavit tale nocumentum;*"(35) but, where the lands are aliened to another person, the complaint is against both, "*quod A.* [the wrong-doer] *et B.* [the alienee] *levaverunt.*"(*c*)(36) For every continuation, as was before said, is a fresh nuisance, and therefore the complaint is as well grounded against the alienee who continues it as against the alienor who first levied it.

3. Before this statute, the party injured, upon any alienation of the land wherein the nuisance was set up, was driven to his *quod permittat prosternere,* which is in the nature of a writ of right, and therefore subject to greater delays.(*d*) This is a writ commanding the defendant to permit the plaintiff to abate, *quod permittat prosternere,* the nuisance complained of;

*222] *and, unless he so permits, to summon him to appear in court, and show cause why he will not.(*e*) And this writ lies as well *for* the alienee of the party first injured, as *against* the alienee of the party first injuring; as hath been determined by all the judges.(*f*) And the plaintiff shall have judgment herein to abate the nuisance, and to recover damages against the defendant.

Both these actions of *assize of nuisance,* and of *quod permittat prosternere,* are now out of use,(37) and have given way to the action on the case; in which, as was before observed, no judgment can be had to abate the nuisance, but only to recover damages. Yet, as therein it is not necessary that the freehold should be in the plaintiff and defendant respectively, as it must be in these real actions,(38) but it is maintainable by one that hath possession only, against another that hath like possession, the process is therefore easier,(39) and the effect will be much the same, unless a man has a very obstinate as well as an ill-natured neighbor; who had rather continue to pay damages than remove his nuisance. For in such a case recourse must at last be had to the old and sure remedies, which will effectually conquer the defendant's

(*c*) 9 Rep. 55.
(*d*) 2 Inst. 405.

(*e*) F. N. B. 124.
(*f*) 5 Rep. 100, 101.

person or persons to whom he has transferred the title. To *abate the nuisance* the action must be against the owner in fee. Ellsworth *v.* Putnam, 16 Barb. 565, 569 (N. Y. 1853).

(33) [In a similar case.]

(34) ["Moreover the complainants shall not be obliged to abandon their action because the tenement is transferred to another."]

(35) ["That A. unjustly levied such a nuisance."]

(36) ["That A. and B. levied."]

(37) These were obsolete in practice long before they were abolished. Webb's Pollock on Torts, 518 (Am. ed. 1894); and were finally abolished by the statute 3 & 4 Wm. IV. c. 27, § 36. Waggoner *v.* Jermaine, 3 Denio, 306, 311 (N. Y. 1846). The writ of nuisance is abolished in New York (Code, § 453), but § 454 of the Code enacts that "injuries heretofore remediable by writ of nuisance are subjects of action as other injuries, and in such action there may be judgment for damages, or for the removal of the nuisance, or both." Ellsworth *v.* Putnam, 16 Barb. 565, 568 (N. Y. 1852).

(38) Great Falls Co. *v.* Worster, 15 N. H. 412, 436 (1844). As real actions can only be brought by a tenant in fee, a disseised tenant for years cannot sustain one. Landlord and Tenant in Pennsylvania (Jackson & Gross) 733 (2 ed. 1884).

(39) Bonner *v.* Welborn, 7 Ga. 296, 317 (1849). It must not be inferred from this that the reversioner cannot maintain this action, for if the nuisance be calculated to affect his reversionary interest, he can maintain an action on the case for damages as well as the person in possession. See Beddingfield *v.* Onslow, 3 Lev. 209. Leader *v.* Moxon, 3 Wils. 461. 3 Black. 924, S. C.—ARCHBOLD.

perverseness, by sending the sheriff with his *posse comitatus*, or power of the county, to level it.

CHAPTER XIV.

OF WASTE.

*THE fourth species of injury, that may be offered to one's real   [*223
property is by *waste*, or destruction in lands and tenements.   What
shall be called waste was considered at large in a former book,(*a*) as it was
a means of forfeiture, and thereby of transferring the property of real estates.
I shall, therefore, here only beg leave to remind the student, that waste is a
spoil and destruction of the estate, either in houses, woods, or lands; by
demolishing not the temporary profits only, but the very substance of the
thing; thereby rendering it wild and desolate,(1) which the common law
expresses very significantly by the word *vastum;* and that this *vastum*, or
waste, is either voluntary, or permissive; the one by an actual and designed
demolition of the lands, woods, and houses; the other arising from mere
negligence, and want of sufficient care in reparations, fences, and the like.
So that my only business is at present to show to whom this waste is an
injury; and of course who is entitled to any, and *what* remedy by action.

I.   The persons who may be injured by waste are such as have some *interest*
in the estate wasted; for if a man be the absolute tenant in fee-simple, without any encumbrance or charge on the premises, he may commit
whatever waste his *own indiscretion may prompt him to, without   [*224
being impeachable, or accountable for it to any one.(2)   And, though
his heir is sure to be the sufferer, yet *nemo est hæres viventis;*(3) no man is
certain of succeeding him, as well on account of the uncertainty which shall
die first, as also because he has it in his power to constitute what heir he
pleases, according to the civil-law notion of an *hæres natus*(4) and an *hæres
factus;*(5) or, in the more accurate phraseology of our English law, he may
aliene or devise his estate to whomever he thinks proper, and by such alienation or devise may disinherit his heir at law.   Into whose hands soever,
therefore, the estate wasted comes, after a tenant in fee-simple, though the
waste is undoubtedly *damnum*, it is *damnum absque injuria.* (6)

One species of interest which is injured by waste is that of a person who
has a right of common in the place wasted; especially if it be common of
estovers, or a right of cutting and carrying away wood for house-bote, plough-
bote, etc.   Here, if the owner of the wood demolishes the whole wood, and
thereby destroys all possibility of taking estovers, this is an injury to the
commoner, amounting to no less than a disseisin of his common of estovers,

(*a*) See book ii, ch. 18.

---

(1) Waste may be committed by destruction of any part of a tenement.   Davenport *v.*
Magoon, 13 Ore. 3, 6 (1884); or by alteration thereof.   Bandlow *v.* Thieme, 53 Wis. 57
60 (1881).   The act or omission to constitute waste must be either an invasion of the lord's
property, or at least be some act or neglect which tends materially to deteriorate the tenement or to destroy the evidence of its identity . . . and that the action is founded
partly upon the common law and partly upon the statute, and does not depend for its
support on any covenants of the tenant.   Moore *v.* Townshend, 33 N. J. 302, 306 (1869).
(2) Williams on Real Property, 79 (6 ed.).   A tenant in fee-tail has the same uncontrolled
and unlimited power in committing waste as a tenant in fee-simple.—CHRISTIAN.
(3) [No one is heir to the living.]
(4) [Heir born, or natural heir.]
(5) [Heir made, or appointed.]
(6) [Damage without injury.]

if he chooses so to consider it; for which he has his remedy to recover possession and damages by assize, if entitled to a freehold in such common; but if he has only a chattel interest, then he can only recover damages by an action on the case for this waste and destruction of the woods out of which his estovers were to issue.(b)

But the most usual and important interest, that is hurt by this commission of waste, is that of him who hath the remainder or reversion of the *inheritance*, after a particular estate for life or years in being. Here, if the particular tenant, (be it the tenant in dower or by curtesy, who was answerable

*225] for waste at the common law,(c) or the lessee for life or years, *who was first made liable by the statutes of Marlberge(d) and of Glocester,)(e) if the particular tenant, I say, commits or suffers any waste, it is a manifest injury to him that has the inheritance, as it tends to mangle and dismember it of its most desirable incidents and ornaments, among which timber and houses may justly be reckoned the principal. To him therefore in remainder and reversion, to whom the *inheritance* appertains in expectancy,(f) the law hath given an adequate remedy. For he, who hath the remainder *for life* only, is not entitled to sue for waste; since his interest may never perhaps come into possession, and then he hath suffered no injury.(7) Yet a parson, vicar, archdeacon, prebendary, and the like, who are seised in right of their churches of any remainder or reversion may have an action of waste; for they, in many cases, have for the benefit of the church and of the successor a fee-simple qualified; and yet, as they are not seised in their own right, the writ of waste shall not say, *ad exhæredationem ipsius*,(8) as for other tenants in fee-simple; but *ad exhæredationem ecclesiæ*,(9) in whose right the fee-simple is holden.(g)(10)

II. The redress for this injury of waste is of two kinds; preventive and corrective: the former of which is by writ of *estrepement*, the latter by that of *waste*.

1. Estrepement is an old French word, signifying the same as waste or extirpation: and the writ of *estrepement* lay at the common law, *after* judgment obtained in any action real,(h) and before possession was delivered by the sheriff, to stop any waste which the vanquished party might be tempted to commit in lands which were determined to be no longer his. But as in some cases the demandant may be justly apprehensive that the tenant may make waste or *estrepement* pending the suit, well knowing the weakness of his title, therefore the statute of Glocester(i) gave another writ of

(b) F. N. B. 59.   9 Rep. 112.
(c) 2 Inst. 299.
(d) 52 Hen. III. c. 23.
(e) 6 Edw. I. c. 5.

(f) Co. Litt. 53.
(g) Co. Litt. 341.
(h) 2 Inst. 328.
(i) 6 Edw. I. c. 13.

(7) No person is entitled to an action of waste against a tenant for life but he who has the immediate estate of *inheritance* in remainder or reversion, expectant upon the estate for life. If between the estate of the tenant for life who commits waste, and the subsequent estate of inheritance, there is interposed an estate of freehold to any person *in esse*, [in being,] then, during the continuance of such interposed estate, the action of waste is suspended; and if the first tenant for life dies during the continuance of such interposed estate, the action is gone forever. Co. Litt. 218 b. 2 Saund. 252, note 7. See further, as to the persons who may maintain a writ or action for waste, id. ibid.—CHRISTIAN. See Rotan v. Fletcher, 15 Johns (N. Y.) 204, 206 (1818). So likewise with respect to a mortgagor, especially when the mortgage is not forfeited, his interest in the land is contingent, and may be defeated by the payment of the money secured by the mortgage. The doctrine of the courts of New York has always been that a mortgage upon real estate is but a chattel interest, and that the freehold remains in the mortgagor. Southworth v. Van Pelt, 8 Barb. (N. Y.) 347, 349 (1848).
(8) [To his disherison.]
(9) [To the disherison of the church.]
(10) Sheppard's Touchstone, 126 n. (1 Am. ed. 1808).

estrepement pendente placito,(11) commanding the sheriff firmly *to   [*226 inhibit the tenant "*ne faciat vastum vel estrepementum pendente placito dicto indiscusso.*"(*k*)(12) And by virtue of either of these writs the sheriff may resist them that do, or offer to do, waste; and, if otherwise he cannot prevent them, he may lawfully imprison the wasters, or make a warrant to others to imprison them: or, if necessity require, he may take the *posse comitatus* to his assistance. So odious in the sight of the law is waste and destruction.(*l*) In suing out these two writs this difference was formerly observed; that in actions merely possessory, where no damages are recovered, a writ of *estrepement* might be had at any time *pendente lite*, nay, even at the time of suing out the original writ, or first process: but, in an action where damages were recovered, the demandant could only have a writ of *estrepement*, if he was apprehensive of waste after verdict had;(*m*) for, with regard to waste done before the verdict was given, it was presumed the jury would consider that in assessing the *quantum* of damages. But now it seems to be held, by an equitable construction of the statute of Glocester, and in advancement of the remedy, that a writ of *estrepement*, to prevent waste, may be had in every stage, as well of such actions wherein damages are recovered, as of those wherein only possession is had of the lands; for peradventure, saith the law, the tenant may not be of ability to satisfy the demandant his full damages.(*n*) And therefore now, in an action of waste itself, to recover the place wasted and also damages, a writ of *estrepement* will lie, as well before as after judgment. For the plaintiff cannot recover damages for more waste than is contained in his original complaint; neither is he at liberty to assign or give in evidence any waste made after the suing out of the writ: it is therefore reasonable that he should have this writ of *preventive* justice, since he is in his present suit debarred of any further *remedial.*(*o*) If a writ of *estrepement*, forbidding waste, be directed and delivered to the tenant himself, as it may be, and he afterwards proceeds to commit waste, an action may be carried on upon the *foundation of this writ; wherein the only   [*227 plea of the tenant can be, *non fecit vastum contra prohibitionem:*(13) and, if upon verdict it be found that he did, the plaintiff may recover costs and damages,(*p*) or the party may proceed to punish the defendant for the contempt: for if, after the writ directed and delivered to the tenant or his servants, they proceed to commit waste, the court will imprison them for this contempt of the writ.(*q*) But not so, if it be directed to the sheriff, for then it is incumbent upon him to prevent the *estrepement* absolutely, even by raising the *posse comitatus*, if it can be done no other way.

Besides this preventive redress at common law, the courts of equity, upon bill exhibited therein, complaining of waste and destruction, will grant an injunction in order to stay waste, until the defendant shall have put in his answer, and the court shall thereupon make further order. Which is now become the most usual way of preventing waste.(14)

2. A writ of *waste*(15) is also an action, partly founded upon the common law, and partly upon the statute of Glocester;(*r*) and may be brought by

(*k*) Registr. 77.
(*l*) 2 Inst. 329.
(*m*) F. N. B. 60, 61.
(*n*) Ibid. 61.

(*o*) 5 Rep. 115.
(*p*) Moor. 100.
(*q*) Hob. 85.
(*r*) 6 Edw. I. c. 5.

---

(11) [Waste pending the suit.]

(12) ["That he do not commit waste or devastation during the continuance of the suit."] [*Posse comitatus*—The power of the county.] [*Pendente lite*—Pending suit.]

(13) [That he did not commit waste against prohibition.]

(14) The writ of *estrepement* was abolished by statute 3 & 4 Wm. IV. c. 27, s. 36.

(15) The action or writ of waste is now very seldom brought. Owing to usage and legislation the more expeditious and easy remedy by an action on the case in the nature

him who hath the immediate estate of inheritance in reversion or remainder, against the tenant for life, tenant in dower, tenant by curtesy, or tenant for years. This action is also maintainable in pursuance of statute(s) Westm. 2, by one tenant in common of the inheritance against another, who makes waste in the estate holden in common. The equity of which statute extends to joint-tenants, but not to coparceners; because by the old law coparceners might make partition, whenever either of them thought proper, and thereby prevent future waste, but tenants in common and joint-tenants could not; and therefore the statute gave them this remedy, compelling the defendant either to make partition, and take the place wasted to his own share, or to give security not to commit any further waste.(t) But these tenants *228] in common and joint-tenants are *not liable to the penalties of the statutes of Glocester, which extends only to such as have life-estates, and do waste to the prejudice of the inheritance. The waste, however, must be something considerable; for if it amount only to twelve pence, or some such petty sum, the plaintiff shall not recover in an action of waste; *nam de minimis non curat lex.*(u)(16)

(s) 13 Edw. I. c. 22.
(t) 2 Inst. 403, 404.

(u) Finch, L. 29.

of waste has been substituted quite generally for it, although under the statutes of some states both remedies exist. See 28 Am. & Eng. Ency. of Law, 908 (1895.)

The plaintiff derives the same benefit from it as from an action of waste in the *tenuit*, where the term is expired and he has got possession of his estate, and consequently can only recover damages for the waste; and though the plaintiff cannot in an action on the case recover the place wasted, where the tenant is still in possession, as he may do in an action of waste in the *tenet*, yet this latter action was found by experience to be so imperfect and defective a mode of recovering seisin of the place wasted that the plaintiff obtained little or no advantage from it; and therefore, where the demise was by deed, care was taken to give the lessor power of re-entry in case the lessee committed any waste or destruction; and an action on the case was then found to be much better adapted for the recovery of mere damages than an action of waste in the *tenuit*. It has also this further advantage over an action of waste, that it may be brought by him in the reversion or remainder for *life* or *years*, as well as in fee or in tail; and the plaintiff is entitled to costs in this action, which he cannot have in an action of waste. However, this action on the case prevailed at first with some difficulty. 3 Lev. 130. 4 Burr. 2141.

But now it is become the usual action as well for permissive as voluntary waste. Some recent decisions have made it doubtful whether an action on the case for permissive waste can be maintained against any tenant for years. See 1 New Rep. 290. 4 Taunt. 764. 7 Taunt. 392. 1 Moore, 100, S. C. See also 1 Saund. 323, a., n. (i.) Where the lessee even covenants not to do waste, the lessor has his election to bring either an action on the case, or of covenant against the lessee, for waste done by him during the term. 2 Black. Rep. 1111. See, further, 2 Saund. 252, and 1 Chitty on Pl. 4 ed. 132, 133. —CHITTY.

Where one purchased real estate at a mortgage sale, thereby acquiring an inchoate title which might be defeated by redemption, and after such sale waste was committed; the purchaser, when his title became absolute by failure to redeem, might recover for such waste as his title related back to the time of the purchase. Stout *v.* Keyes, 2 Doug. 184, 188 (Mich. 1845). So also where land was sold on execution, and a junior judgment creditor redeemed the same, he could recover for waste committed between the time of the sale and the sheriff's deed to him, though such waste was committed with the consent of the judgment debtor who was in possession. Thomas *v.* Croft, 14 N. Y. (4 Kern.) 474, 477 (1856). Where a mortgagee of a reversion of an estate in dower entered after condition broken, but not before, it was held that he might maintain an action against the tenant for life for waste committed before the breach of the condition. Fay *v.* Brewer, 3 Pick. 203, 205 (Mass. 1825).

(16) [For the law does not recognize trifles.] See 2 Bos. & Pul. 86. But the doctrine that the smallness of the damages given by the jury shall defeat the action does not extend to other actions. See 1 Dowl. Rep. 209.—CHITTY. Thus a commoner may maintain an action on the case for an injury done to the common by taking away the manure which was dropped on it by the cattle; though his proportion of the damages be found only to the amount of a farthing. The smallness of the damages is not reason for entering a non-suit. Pindar *v.* Wadsworth, 2 East, 154 (pp. 405, 409 of vol. 12 Am. ed.) (1802). See Cook *v.* Champlain Trans. Co., 1 Denio (N. Y.) 91, 104 (1845). Parker *et al. v.*

This action of waste is a mixed action; partly real, so far as it recovers land, and partly personal, so far as it recovers damages. For it is brought for both those purposes; and, if the waste be proved, the plaintiff shall recover the thing or place wasted, and also treble damages by the statute of Glocester. The writ of waste calls upon the tenant to appear and show cause why he hath committed waste and destruction in the place named, *ad exhæredationem*, to the disinhersion, of the plaintiff. (*w*) And if the defendant makes default, or does not appear at the day assigned him, then the sheriff is to take him a jury of twelve men, and go in person to the place alleged to be wasted, and there inquire of the waste done, and the damages; and make a return or report of the same to the court, upon which report the judgment is founded. (*x*) For the law will not suffer so heavy a judgment, as the forfeiture and treble damages, to be passed upon a mere default, without full assurance that the fact is according as it is stated in the writ. But if the defendant appears to the writ, and *afterwards* suffers judgment to go against him by default, or upon a *nihil dicit*, (when he makes no answer, puts in no plea, in defence,) this amounts to a confession of the waste; since, having once appeared, he cannot now pretend ignorance of the charge. Now, therefore, the sheriff shall not go to the place to inquire of the fact whether any waste has, or has not, been committed; for this is already ascertained by the silent confession of the defendant; but he shall only, as in defaults upon other actions, make inquiry of the *quantum* of *damages. (*y*) The defendant, on the trial, may give in evidence   [*229 any thing that proves there was no waste committed, as that the destruction happened by lightning, tempest, the king's enemies, or other inevitable accident. (*z*) (17) But it is no defence to say that a stranger did

(*w*) F. N. B. 55.
(*x*) Poph. 24.

(*y*) Cro. Eliz. 18, 290.
(*z*) Co. Litt. 53.

Charnbliss, 12 Ga. 235, 237 (1852). In Duvall *v.* Waters, 1 Bland ch. 573 (1835). It is said: No one could maintain this action unless he had the estate of inheritance in him at the time the waste was committed; nor could it be sustained against an executor, for waste committed by the testator, it being a wrong which died with the person; nor could one coparcener bring an action of waste against another, although one joint tenant or tenant in common might have a writ of waste against his co-tenant compelling him either to make partition, and take the place wasted, or to give security not to commit further waste.

(17) Action on the case doth not lie for permissive waste. 5 Rep. 13. Hale MSS. The case cited by lord Hale is that of the countess of Salop, who brought an action on the case against her tenant at will for negligently keeping his fire so that the house was burned; and the whole court held that neither action on the case nor any other action lay, because at common law, and before the statute of Glocester, action did not lie for waste against tenant for life or years, or any other tenant coming in by agreement of parties, and tenant at will is not within the statute. But if tenant at will stipulates with his lessor to be responsible for fire by negligence or for other permissive waste, without doubt an action will lie on such express agreement. The same observation holds with respect to tenants for life or years before the statute of Glocester; for though the law did not make them liable to any action; yet it did not restrain them from making themselves liable by agreement. At the common law lessees were not answerable to landlords for accidental or negligent burning, for as to fires by accident, it is expressed in Fleta that *fortuna ignis vel hujusmodi eventûs inopinati omnes tenentes excusant;* [The accident of fire, or unexpected events of that kind, excuse all tenants;] and lady Shrewsbury's case is a direct authority to prove that tenants are equally excusable for fires by negligence. Fleta, lib. i. c. 12. Then came the statute of Glocester, which, by making tenants for life and years liable to waste without exception, consequently rendered them answerable for destruction by fire; but now, by the 6 Anne, c. 31, the ancient law is restored, for the statute of Anne exempts all persons from actions for accidental fire in any house, except in the case of special agreements between landlord and tenant. See 14 Geo. III. c. 78, s. 86. It was doubted under this statute whether a covenant to repair generally extends to the case of fire, and so becomes an agreement within the statute; and therefore, where it is intended that the tenant shall not be liable, it has been usual in

the waste, for against him the plaintiff hath no remedy; though the defendant is entitled to sue such stranger in an action of trespass *vi et armis*, and shall recover the damages he has suffered in consequence of such unlawful act.(*a*)(18)

When the waste and damages are thus ascertained, either by confession, verdict, or inquiry of the sheriff, judgment is given in pursuance of the statute of Glocester, c. 5, that the plaintiff shall recover the place wasted,(19) for which he has immediately a writ of *scisin*, provided the particular estate be still subsisting, (for, if it be expired, there can be no forfeiture of the land,) and also that the plaintiff shall recover treble the damages assessed by the jury, which he must obtain in the same manner as all other damages, in actions personal and mixed, are obtained, whether the particular estate be expired, or still in being.(20)

- - -

CHAPTER XV.

OF SUBTRACTION.

*230]   *SUBTRACTION,(1) which is the fifth species of injuries affecting a man's real property, happens when any person who owes any suit, duty, custom, or service to another withdraws or neglects to perform it. It differs from a disseisin, in that *this* is committed without any denial of the right, consisting merely of non-performance; *that* strikes at the very title of the party injured, and amounts to an ouster or actual dispossession. Subtraction, however, being clearly an injury, is remediable by due course of law; but the remedy differs according to the nature of the services, whether they be due by virtue of any tenure, or by custom only.

I. Fealty, suit of court, and rent are duties and services usually issuing and arising *ratione tenuræ*,(2) being the conditions upon which the ancient lords granted out their lands to their feudatories, whereby it was stipulated that they and their heirs should take the oath of fealty or fidelity to their lord, which was the feodal bond, or *commune vinculum*,(3) between lord and

(*a*) Law of *Nisi Prius*, 112.

- - -

the covenant for repairing expressly to except accidents by fire. See Harg. Co. Litt. 57, a.—CHRISTIAN.

But it is now settled that a general unqualified covenant to repair subjects the tenant to the expense of rebuilding. 6 T. R. 650. The tenant at all events continues liable to pay rent. 3 Anst. 687. 3 Dowl. 233. 1 T. R. 310. 4 Taunt. 45. 18 Ves. Jr. 115.—CHITTY. See Wade *v.* Malloy, 28 Hun. (N. Y.) 226, 229 (1879).

(18) [With force and arms.] The reversioner of a freehold can maintain an action on the case against a stranger who commits waste on the property. Elliott *v.* Smith, 2 N. H. 430, 431 (1822). Randall *v.* Cleaveland, 6 Conn. 328, 332 (1827). Ripka *v.* Sergeant, 7 W. & S. 9, 14 (Pa. 1844). Though an action of waste would not lie. Chase *v.* Hazelton, 7 N. H. 171, 175 (1834). A tenant for life is answerable for waste committed by a trespasser. Fay *v.* Brewer, 3 Pick. 203, 205 (Mass. 1825).

(19) The verdict for the plaintiff in a writ of waste ought to find the place wasted. 2 Bingh. R. 262.—CHITTY.

(20) But this writ of waste has also been abolished, by 3 & 4 W. IV. c. 27, s. 36; and there now only remain therefore the two remedies already referred to: the first, to restrain waste by obtaining an injunction in a court of equity; and the second, to obtain damages for the waste after it has been committed, by an action on the case in a court of law, which action lies not only against the tenant, but against any stranger by whom an act of waste has been committed.—STEWART.

(1) The subject-matter of this and the succeeding chapter is obsolete.

(2) [By reason of the tenure.]

(3) [Common bond.]

tenant; that they should do suit or duly attend and follow the lord's courts, and there from time to time give their assistance, by serving on juries, either to decide the property of their neighbors in the court-baron or correct their misdemeanors in the court-leet; and, lastly, that they should yield to the lord certain annual stated returns, in military attendance, in provisions, in arms, in matters of ornament or pleasure, in rustic employments or *prædial labors, or (which is *instar omnium*)(4) in money, which   [*231 will provide all the rest; all which are comprised under the one general name of *reditus*, return, or rent.   And the subtraction or non-observance of any of these conditions, by neglecting to swear fealty, to do suit of court, or to render the rent or service reserved, is an injury to the freehold of the lord, by diminishing and depreciating the value of his seignory.

The general remedy for all these is by *distress;* and it is the only remedy at the common law for the two first of them.   The nature of distresses, their incidents and consequences, we have before more than once explained:(a) it may here suffice to remember that they are a taking of beasts or other personal property by way of pledge to enforce the performance of something due from the party distrained upon.   And, for the most part, it is provided that distresses be reasonable and moderate; but in the case of distress for fealty or suit of court, no distress can be unreasonable, immoderate, or too large:(b) for this is the only remedy to which the party aggrieved is entitled, and therefore it ought to be such as is sufficiently compulsory; and, be it of what value it will, there is no harm done, especially as it cannot be sold or made away with, but must be restored immediately on satisfaction made.   A distress of this nature, that has no bounds with regard to its quantity and may be repeated from time to time until the stubbornness of the party is conquered, is called a *distress infinite;* which is also used for some other purposes, as in summoning jurors, and the like.

Other remedies for subtraction of rents or services are, 1. By action of *debt*, for the breach of this express contract, of which enough has been formerly said.   This is the most usual remedy when recourse is had to any action at all for the recovery of pecuniary rents, to which species of render almost all free services are now reduced since the abolition of the military tenures.   But for a freehold rent, reserved on *a lease for   [*232 life, etc., no action of *debt* lay by the common law during the continuance of the freehold out of which it issued;(c) for the law would not suffer a *real* injury to be remedied by an action that was merely *personal*. However, by the statutes 8 Anne, c. 14, and 5 Geo. III. c. 17, actions of debt may now be brought at any time to recover such freehold rents.   2. An assize of *mort d'ancestor*(5) or *novel disseisin* will lie of rents as well as of lands,(d) if the lord, for the sake of trying the possessory right, will make it his election to suppose himself ousted or disseised thereof.   This is now seldom heard of; and all other real actions to recover rents, being in the nature of writs of right, and therefore more dilatory in their progress, are entirely disused, though not formally abolished by law.(6)   Of this species, however, is, 3. The writ *de consuetudinibus et servitiis*,(7) which lies for the lord against his tenant who withholds from him the rents and services due by custom or tenure for his land.(e)   This compels a specific payment or per-

(a) See pages 6, 148.   (d) F. N. B. 195.
(b) Finch, L. 285.   (e) Ibid. 151.
(c) 1 Roll. Abr. 595.

(4) [Equal to all.]
(5) [Death of an ancestor.]
(6) It is now abolished by statute 3 & 4 Wm. IV. c. 27, s. 36.
(7) [Of customs and services.]

formance of the rent or service; and there are also others, whereby the lord shall recover the land itself in lieu of the duty withheld. As, 4. The writ of *cessavit,*(8) which lies by the statutes of Glocester, 6 Edward I. c. 4, and of Westm. 2, 13 Edw. I. c. 21 and 41, when a man who holds lands of a lord by rent or other services neglects or *ceases* to perform his services for two years together; or where a religious house hath lands given it on condition of performing some certain spiritual service, as reading prayers or giving alms, and neglects it; in either of which cases, if the *cesser* or neglect have continued for two years, the lord or donor and his heirs shall have a writ of *cessavit* to recover the land itself, *eo quod tenens in faciendis servitiis per biennium jam cessavit.*(f)(9) In like manner, by the civil law, if a tenant who held lands upon payment of rent or services, or "*jure emphyteutico,*" neglected to pay or perform them *per totum triennium,*(10) he might be ejected from such emphyteutic lands.(g) But, by the statute of Glocester, the *cessavit* does not lie for lands let upon fee-farm rents, unless they have lain fresh

*233] and uncultivated for two years, and there be *not sufficient distress upon the premises; or unless the tenant hath so enclosed the land that the lord cannot come upon it to distrain.(h) For the law prefers the simple and ordinary remedies by distress or by the actions just now mentioned to this extraordinary one of forfeiture for a *cessavit:* and therefore the same statute of Glocester has provided further, that upon tender of arrears and damages before judgment, and giving security for the future performance of the services, the process shall be at an end, and the tenant shall retain his land; to which the statute of Westm. 2 conforms so far as may stand with convenience and reason of law.(i) It is easy to observe that the statute(k) 4 Geo. II. c. 28 (which permits landlords who have a right of re-entry for non-payment of rent to serve an ejectment on their tenants when half a year's rent is due and there is no sufficient distress on the premises) is in some measure copied from the ancient writ of *cessavit:* especially as it may be satisfied and put an end to in a similar manner, by tender of the rent and costs within six months after. And the same remedy is, in substance, adopted by statute 11 Geo. II. c. 19, § 16,(11) which enacts that where any tenant at rack-rent shall be one year's rent in arrear, and shall desert the demised premises, leaving the same uncultivated or unoccupied, so that no sufficient distress can be had; two justices of the peace (after notice affixed on the premises for fourteen days without effect) may give the landlord possession thereof, and thenceforth the lease shall be void. 5. There is also another very effectual remedy, which takes place when the tenant upon a writ of assize for rent, or on a replevin, disowns or disclaims his tenure, whereby the lord loses his verdict; in which case the lord may have a writ of right, *sur disclaimer,*(12) grounded on this denial of tenure; and shall upon proof of the tenure recover back the land itself so holden, as a punishment to the tenant for such his false disclaimer.(l) This piece of retaliating justice, whereby the tenant who endeavors to defraud his lord is himself deprived of the estate, as it evidently proceeds upon feudal principles,

(f) F. N. B. 208.
(g) Cod. 4, 66, 2.
(h) F. N. B. 209. 2 Inst. 298.

(i) 2 Inst. 401, 460.
(k) See page 206.
(l) Finch, L. 270, 271.

---

(8) [He hath ceased.]

(9) [Because the tenant has already ceased to do service for two years.]

(10) [For three whole years.]

(11) And see by 57 Geo. III. c. 52, which gives similar power though only half a year's rent is in arrear, and although no right of re-entry be reserved.—CHITTY.

(12) [On disclaimer.]

*so it is expressly to be met with in the feodal constitutions:(m)   [*234
"*vasallus, qui abnegavit fendum ejusve conditionem exspoliabitur.*"
(13)

And, as on the one hand the ancient law provided these several remedies
to obviate the knavery and punish the ingratitude of the tenant, so on the
other hand it was equally careful to redress the oppression of the lord; by
furnishing, 1. The writ of *ne injuste vexes;*(n)(14) which is an ancient
writ founded on that chapter(o) of *magna carta*,(15) which prohibits distresses for greater services than are really due to the lord; being itself of the
prohibitory kind, and yet in the nature of a writ of right.(p)(16)   It lies,
where the tenant in fee-simple and his ancestors have held of the lord by
certain services, and the lord hath obtained seisin of more or greater services, by the inadvertent payment or performance of them by the tenant
himself.   Here the tenant cannot in an avowry avoid the lord's possessory
right, because of the seisin given by his own hands; but is driven to this
writ, to devest the lord's possession, and establish the mere right of property,
by ascertaining the services, and reducing them to their proper standard.
But this writ does not lie for tenant in tail; for he may avoid such seisin of
the lord, obtained from the payment of his ancestors, by plea to an avowry
in replevin.(q)   2. The writ of *mesne, de medio;* which is also in the nature
of a writ of right,(r) and lies, when upon a subinfeudation the *mesne*, or
middle lord,(s) suffers his under-tenant, or tenant *paravail*, to be distrained
upon by the lord *paramount*, for the rent due to him from the mesne lord.(t)
And in such case the tenant shall have judgment to be acquitted (or in-
demnified) by the mesne lord; and if he makes default therein, or does not appear originally to the tenant's writ, he shall be forejudged of his mesnalty,
and the tenant shall hold immediately of the lord paramount himself.
(u)(17)

(m) Feud. l. 2, t. 26.	(r) Booth, 136.
(n) F. N. B. 10.	(s) See book ii. ch. 5, pages 59, 60.
(o) C. 10.	(t) F. N. B. 135.
(p) Booth, 126.	(u) 2 Inst. 374.
(q) F. N. B. 11. 2 Inst. 21.	

(13) ["The vassal who has denied either his fee, or the condition by which he held it,
shall be deprived of it."]

(14) [Do not unjustly oppress.]

(15) Lord Coke (2 Inst. p. 21) expressly denies this, and cites the writ from Glanville,
and says it is mentioned in the Mirror.—COLERIDGE.

(16) At common law an action on the case may be supported by a tenant, or third person, against a landlord for distraining for more rent than is due; and that is now the usual
remedy. 2 Chitty on Pl. (4 ed.) 719.—CHITTY.

(17) But these several writs have long been obsolete and are now abolished. 3 & 4 W.
IV. c. 27, s. 36.—STEWART. A tenant may maintain case against his landlord if the landlord distrains irregularly, or takes goods which are not subject to distress, or distrains for
more rent than is due. Taylor's Landlord and Tenant (7 ed. 1879), § 729; even though
the distress taken was not sufficient to pay the rent due, for, in such case, though there
is no real damage, there is legal damage. Ibid. § 735. Where the tenant has overpaid
the landlord in ignorance of the facts, the money so overpaid is considered by the law to
be money received for the use of the tenant, and the tenant may accordingly, provided
there have been no laches on his part, recover it in an action. Marriott *v.* Hampton, 2
Smith's Lead. Cases, (4 ed.) p. 325, notes. The true ground of recovery in all cases of
money paid by mistake is that the money has been paid without any consideration.
Little *v.* Derby, 3 Cooley, 325, 327 (Mich. 1859). In the second case stated,—that of an
under-tenant paying the landlord in default of the mesne tenant's doing so,—the payment
by the under-tenant is considered a payment *pro tanto* of the rent due to his immediate
landlord, the mesne tenant, and may either be deducted from the rent accruing due to
the mesne landlord, (Carter *v.* Carter, 5 Bingh. 406,) or sued for in an action as money
paid to his use. Exall *v.* Partridge, 8 T. R. 308. Bandy *v.* Cartwright, 8 Exc. 913. For
where a tenant underlets the premises, the law implies a duty on his part to indemnify
the under-tenant against all his covenants with the superior landlord; and the under-
tenant may have an action on the case against him for any injury he may sustain, by

*235]   *II. Thus far of the remedies for subtraction of rents or other services due by *tenure*. There are also other services due by ancient *custom* and *prescription* only. Such is that of doing suit to another's mill: where the persons, resident in a particular place, by usage time out of mind have been accustomed to grind their corn at a certain mill; and afterwards any of them go to another mill, and withdraw their suit (their *secta, a sequendo*)(18) from the ancient mill. This is not only a damage, but an injury, to the owner; because this prescription might have a very reasonable foundation; viz., upon the erection of such mill by the ancestors of the owner for the convenience of the inhabitants, on condition that, when erected, they should all grind their corn there only. And for this injury the owner shall have a writ *de secta ad molendinum,*(w)(19) commanding the defendant to do his suit at that mill, *quam ad illud facere debet, et solet,*(20) or show good cause to the contrary: in which action the validity of the prescription may be tried, and if it be found for the owner, he shall recover damages against the defendant.(x) In like manner, and for like reasons, the register (y) will inform us, that a man may have a writ of *secta ad furnum, secta ad torrale, et ad omnia alia hujusmodi;*(21) for suit due to his *furnum*, his public oven or bake-house; or to his *torrale*, his kiln, or malt-house; when a person's ancestors have erected a convenience of that sort for the benefit of the neighborhood, upon an agreement (proved by immemorial custom) that all the inhabitants should use and resort to it when erected. But besides these special remedies for subtractions, to compel the specific performance of the service due by custom, an action *on the case* will also lie for all of them, to repair the party injured in damages.(22) And thus much for the injury of subtraction.

CHAPTER XVI.

OF DISTURBANCE.

*236]   *THE sixth and last species of real injuries is that of *disturbance;* which is usually a wrong done to some incorporeal hereditament, by hindering or disquieting the owners in their regular and lawful enjoyment of it.(a) I shall consider five sorts of this injury: viz., 1. Disturbance of *franchises.* 2. Disturbance of *common.* 3. Disturbance of *ways.* 4. Disturbance of *tenure.* 5. Disturbance of *patronage.*

I. Disturbance of *franchises* happens when a man has the franchise of holding a court-leet, of keeping a fair or market, of free-warren, of taking toll, of seizing waifs or estrays, or (in short) any other species of franchise whatsoever, and he is disturbed or incommoded in the lawful exercise thereof. As if another, by distress, menaces, or persuasions, prevails upon the

(m) F. N. B. 123.   (y) Fol. 153.
(x) Co. Entr. 461.   (a) Finch, L. 187.

---

reason of any such breach of covenant. Taylor's Landlord and Tenant (7 ed. 1879) ? 738.

(18) [From following.]
(19) [For suit at his mill.]
(20) [Which he ought, and was used to do at it.]
(21) [His suit at the oven, his suit at the kiln, and all others of the same kind.]
(22) This is now the only action in use for most of the injuries specified in this chapter the ancient appropriate writs having become so obsolete that few special pleaders, if any, would know how to proceed in them. See, further, 2 Saund. 113, b.—CHRISTIAN.

suitors not to appear at my court; or obstructs the passage to my fair or market; or hunts in my free-warren; or refuses to pay me the accustomed toll; or hinders me from seizing the waif or estray, whereby it escapes or is carried out of my liberty; in every case of this kind, all which it is impossible here to recite or suggest, there is an injury done to the legal owner; his property is damnified; and the profits arising from such his franchise are diminished. To remedy which, as the law has given no other writ, he is *therefore entitled to sue for damages by a special action [*237 *on the case;* or, in case of toll, may take a distress if he pleases.(b)

II. The disturbance of *common* comes next to be considered; where any act is done, by which the right of another to his common is incommoded or diminished. This may happen, in the first place, where one who hath no right of common puts his cattle into the land; and thereby robs the cattle of the commoners of their respective shares of the pasture. Or if one, who hath a right of common, puts in cattle which are not commonable, as hogs and goats; which amounts to the same inconvenience. But the lord of the soil may (by custom or prescription, but not without) put a stranger's cattle into the common;(c) and also, by a like prescription for common appurtenant, cattle that are not commonable may be put into the common.(d) The lord also of the soil may justify making burrows therein, and putting in rabbits, so as they do not increase to so large a number as totally to destroy the common.(e) But in general in case the beasts of a stranger, or the uncommonable cattle of a commoner, be found upon the land, the lord or any of the commoners may distrain them damage-feasant:(f) or the commoner may bring an action on the case to recover damages, provided the injury done be any thing considerable: so that he may lay his action with a *per quod*, or allege that *thereby* he was deprived of his common. But for a trivial trespass the commoner has no action; but the lord of the soil only, for the entry and trespass committed.(g)(1)

(b) Cro. Eliz. 558.	(e) Cro. Eliz. 876. Cro. Jac. 195. Lutw. 108.
(c) 1 Roll. Abr. 396.	(f) 9 Rep. 112.
(d) Co. Litt. 122.	(g) Ibid.

(1) If cattle escape into the common, and are driven out by the owner as soon as he has notice, though the lord may have his action of trespass, yet the commoner cannot bring his action upon the case, because sufficient feeding still remains for him. But if cattle are permitted to depasture the common, whether they belong to a stranger or are the supernumerary cattle of a commoner, an action lies; and it is not necessary to prove specific injury, for the *right* of the commoner is injured by such an act, and, if permitted, the wrong-doer might gain a right by repeated acts of encroachment. 2 Bla. Rep. 1233. 4 T. R. 71. 2 East, 154. 1 Saund. 346, b. And where A., being possessed of a portion of a lammas-field over which a right of common existed part of the year, took down the customary post-and-rail fence, containing gaps through which the commoner's cattle might pass, and built a *wall* with a single doorway, at which they might enter and return, it was held that this was a disturbance of the common right, and an action was maintainable, though the abridgment of the right was inconsiderable. 1 McCleland's Rep. 373. One farthing damages will sustain the verdict in such case. Ib.; and 2 East, 154. It has been held that a claim of common for all the plaintiff's cattle *levant* [lying down] and *couchant* [resting] on his land was supported by evidence of a custom for all the occupiers of a large common field to turn cattle into the whole field when the corn was taken off, the number of cattle being regulated by the extent, and not the produce of each man's land in the field, although the cattle were not actually maintained on such land during the winter. 1 B. & A. 706. In an action for disturbance of common, where the plaintiff stated that he was possessed of a *messuage and land*, by reason whereof he was entitled to the right of common, and it appeared on the trial that he was possessed of land only, it was held that the allegation was divisible, and the plaintiff entitled to damages *pro tanto* [For so much]. 2 B. & A. 360. See 15 East, 115. The declaration must in all cases allege that the plaintiff thereby could not use his common in so ample a manner as he ought to have done. 9 Co. 113, a.—CHITTY.

The passage referred to in the Reports is this:—"If the trespass be so small that the commoner has not any loss, but sufficient in ample manner remains for him, no action

Another disturbance of common is by *surcharging* it; or putting more cattle therein than the pasture and herbage will sustain, or the party hath a right to do. In this case he that surcharges does an injury to the rest of the owners, by depriving them of their respective portions, or at least

*238] *contracting them into a smaller compass. This injury by surcharging can, properly speaking, only happen where the common is *appendant* or *appurtenant*,(h) and of course limitable by law; or where, when *in gross*, it is expressly limited and certain; for where a man hath common *in gross*, *sans nombre* or *without stint*, he cannot be a surcharger. However, even where a man is said to have common without stint, still there must be left sufficient for the lord's own beasts;(i) for the law will not suppose that, at the original grant of the common, the lord meant to exclude himself.(2)

The usual remedies, for surcharging the common, are either by distraining so many of the beasts as are above the number allowed, or else by an action of trespass, both which may be had by the lord: or lastly, by a special action on the case for damages; in which any commoner may be plaintiff.(j) But the ancient and most effectual method of proceeding is by writ of *admeasurement* of *pasture*. This lies either where a common appurtenant or in gross is certain as to number, or where a man has common appendant or appurtenant to his land, the quantity of which common has never yet been ascertained. In either of these cases, as well the lord,(3) as any of the commoners,

(h) See book ii. ch. 3.
(i) 1 Roll. Abr. 399.

(j) Freem. 273.

lies for it." Mr. Sergeant Williams observes that this must be understood with some restriction. Undoubtedly if cattle escape into the common and are driven out by the owner as soon as he has notice, though the lord may have an action of trespass for the injury to his soil, the commoner cannot bring an action upon the case; for this seems to fall directly within the rule. But if cattle are permitted to depasture the common, whether they are a stranger's or the supernumerary cattle of a commoner, whether they are driven or escape there, a commoner may have an action upon the case, in which it does not seem necessary for him to prove any *specific injury* sustained. The consumption of the grass by the other cattle is of itself a diminution of the right and profit of the commoner, and considered as a sufficient proof of the damage alleged in the declaration; for if the other cattle had not been there, the commoner's cattle might have eaten every blade of grass which was consumed by the other. Besides, the law considers that the *right* of the commoner is injured by such an act, and therefore allows him to bring an action for it to prevent the wrong-doer from gaining a right by repeated acts of encroachment. For wherever any act injures another's right, and would also be evidence in favor of the wrong-doer claiming the right on any future occasion, an action may be maintained for such act without proof of any specific injury. Mellor v. Spateman, 1 Saund. Rep. 546, a., n. 2, citing Wells v. Watling, 2 Bla. Rep. 1233. Hobson v. Todd, 4 T. R. 71.—COLERIDGE.

(2) The modern doctrine upon this subject is somewhat different; for it is now held that a prescription for a sole and several pasture, etc. in exclusion of the owner of the soil *for the whole year* is good, (2 Lev. 2. Pollexf. 13. 1 Mod. 74;) for it does not exclude the lord from all the profits of the soil, as he is entitled to the mines, trees, and quarries. And though a man cannot prescribe to have common *eo nomine* [Under that name] for the *whole* year in exclusion of the lord, (1 Lev. 268. 1 Ventr. 395,) still, the lord may by custom be restrained to a qualified right of common during a *part* of the year, (Yelv. 129;) and it is said the lord may be restrained, together with the commoners, from using the common at all during a part of the year. 1 Saund. 353, n. (2.) See also 2 H. Bl. 4. And it is said to have been clearly held that the commoners may prescribe to have common in exclusion of the lord for a part of the year. 2 Roll. Abr. 267, L. pl. 1.—CHITTY.

This seems to be too generally expressed; for the lord's right may be narrowed down to any thing short of absolute exclusion for the whole year. He may, together with the commoners, be entirely excluded for a part of the year, his right may be limited to the feeding of a limited number for a part of the year, or the commoner may have the pasture entirely to his exclusion for a part of the year. Potter v. North, 1 Saund. Rep. 353, n. 2.—COLERIDGE.

(3) Finch, in the passage cited, expressly says that "the lord cannot have the writ of admeasurement against his tenants surcharging; for he may distrain the surplusage for

is entitled to this writ of admeasurement; which is one of those writs that are called *viconticl*, (*k*) being directed to the sheriff, (*vicecomiti*,) and not to be returned to any superior court till finally executed by him.   It recites a complaint, that the defendant hath surcharged, *superoneravit*, the common; and therefore commands the sheriff to admeasure and apportion it; that the defendant may not have more than belongs to him, and that the plaintiff may have his rightful share.   And upon this suit all the commoners shall be admeasured, as well those who have not as those who have surcharged the common; as well the plaintiff as the defendant.(*l*)   The execution of this writ must be by a jury of twelve men, who are upon their *oaths to ascertain, under the superintendence of the sheriff, what   [*239 and how many cattle each commoner is entitled to feed.   And the rule for this admeasurement is generally understood to be, that the commoner shall not turn more cattle upon the common than are sufficient to manure and stock the land to which his right of common is annexed; or, as our ancient law expressed it, such cattle only as are *levant* and *couchant*(4) upon his tenement;(*m*) which, being a thing uncertain before admeasurement, has frequently, though erroneously, occasioned this unmeasured right of common to be called a common *without stint* or *sans nombre;*(*n*) a thing which, though possible in law,(*o*) does in fact very rarely exist.(5)

If, after the admeasurement has thus ascertained the right, the same defendant surcharges the common again, the plaintiff may have a writ of *second surcharge, de secunda superoneratione,* which is given by the statute Westm. 2, 13 Edw. I. c. 8, and thereby the sheriff is directed to inquire by a jury whether the defendant has in fact again surcharged the common contrary to the tenure of the last admeasurement; and, if he has, he shall then forfeit to the king the supernumerary cattle put in, and also shall pay damages to the plaintiff. (*p*)   This process seems highly equitable: for the first offence is held to be committed through mere inadvertence, and therefore there are no damages or forfeiture on the first writ, which was only to ascertain the right which was disputed; but the second offence is a wilful contempt and injustice, and therefore punished very properly with not only damages but also forfeiture.   And herein the right, being once settled, is never again

---

(*k*) 2 Inst. 369. Finch, L. 314.
(*l*) F. N. B. 125.
(*m*) Bro. Abr. tit. *prescription*, 28.

(*n*) Hardr. 117.
(*o*) Lord Raym. 407.
(*p*) F. N. B. 126. 2 Inst. 370.

---

damage-feasant.''   And Fitz. N. B. 125, D. is an authority to the same effect. Lord Hale, citing several cases from the year-books, is of a different opinion. But all these seem agreed that the commoner cannot have it against the lord. - COLERIDGE.

(4) [Rising up and lying down, *i. e.*, when cattle have been long enough on a man's ground to lie down and rise up again to feed.]

(5) The lord may distrain not only the cattle of a stranger, but also so many of a commoner's cattle as surcharge the common. 2 Bla. R. 818. Willes, 638. A commoner can only distrain the cattle of a stranger, (1 Roll. Abr. 320, 405, pl. 5. Yelv. 104,) and not of the lord, (2 Buls. 117,) nor where a commoner overcharges the common, by putting in cattle that are not *levant* and *couchant*, can another commoner distrain the surplus, at least before admeasurement. 3 Wils. 287. 2 Lutw. 1238. 4 Burr. 2426. But where the right of common is limited to a *certain number* of cattle, without any relation to the quantity of land which the commoner possesses, and he puts in a greater number, perhaps another commoner may distrain the supernumerary cattle. 4 Burr. 2431. It seems clear that a claim of common *pleaded* by an inhabitant, as an inhabitant merely, is bad: it must be pleaded either in the name of a corporation for the benefit of the inhabitants, or in a que estate. 6 Co. 69, b. 4 T. R. 717. 1 Saund. 346, f., n. (g.) But if the defendant be lord of the manor, or one who puts his cattle on the common with the lord's license, the commoner cannot maintain an action unless he has sustained a specific injury; for the lord is entitled to what remains of the grass, and therefore may consume it himself, or license another to depasture it. 4 T. R. 73. 2 Mod. 6. 6 Willes, 619.— CHITTY.

disputed; but only the fact is tried, whether there be any second surcharge or no: which gives this neglected proceeding(6) a great advantage over the modern method by action on the case, wherein the *quantum* of common belonging to the defendant must be proved upon every fresh trial for every repeated offence.

*240]   *There is yet another disturbance of common, when the owner of the land, or other person, so encloses or otherwise obstructs it that the commoner is precluded from enjoying the benefit to which he is by law entitled.

This may be done either by erecting fences, or by driving the cattle off the land, or by ploughing up the soil of the common.(*q*) Or it may be done by erecting a warren therein, and stocking it with rabbits in such quantities that they devour the whole herbage and thereby destroy the common. For, in such case, though the commoner may not destroy the rabbits, yet the law looks upon this as an injurious disturbance of his right, and has given him his remedy by action against the owner.(*r*)(7) This kind of disturbance does indeed amount to a disseisin, and, if the commoner chooses to consider it in that light, the law has given him an assize of *novel disseisin*, against the lord, to recover the possession of his common.(*s*) Or it has given a writ of *quod permittat*,(8) against any stranger, as well as the owner of the land, in case of such a disturbance to the plaintiff as amounts to a total deprivation of his common; whereby the defendant shall be compelled to permit the plaintiff to enjoy his common as he ought.(*t*) But if the commoner does not choose to bring a *real* action to recover seisin, or to try the right, he may (which is the easier and more usual way) bring an action on the case for his damages, instead of an assize or a *quod permittat*.(*u*)(9)

There are cases, indeed, in which the lord may enclose and abridge the common; for which, as they are no injury to any one, so no one is entitled to any remedy. For it is provided by the statute of Merton, 20 Hen. III. c. 4, that the lord may *approve*, that is, enclose and convert to the uses of husbandry, (which is a melioration or approvement,) any waste grounds, woods, or pastures, in which his tenants have common *appendant* to their estates, provided he leaves *sufficient common to his tenants, accord-
*241] ing to the proportion of their land. And this is extremely reasonable; for it would be very hard if the lord, whose ancestors granted out these estates to which the commons are appendant, should be precluded from making what advantage he can of the rest of his manor, provided such advantage and improvement be no way derogatory from the former grants. The statute Westm. 2, 13 Edw. I. c. 46 extends this liberty of approving, in like manner, against *all others* that have common *appurtenant*, or *in gross*, as well as against the tenants of the lord who have their common *appendant;* and further enacts that no assize of *novel disseisin* for common shall lie against a lord for erecting on the common any windmill, sheep-house, or other necessary buildings therein specified: which, Sir Edward Coke says,(*w*) are only

---

(*q*) Cro. Eliz. 198.
(*r*) Cro. Jac. 195.
(*s*) F. N. B. 179.

(*t*) Finch. L. 275.   F. N. B. 123.
(*u*) Cro. Jac 195.
(*w*) 2 Inst. 476.

---

(6) Now abolished, 3 & 4 W. IV. c. 27, s. 36.
(7) It is the policy of the law not to allow commoners to abate, except only in a few cases; for an action will best ascertain the just measure of the damage sustained. But if the lord erect a wall, gate, hedge, or fence round the common, to prevent the commoner's cattle from going into the common, the commoner may abate the erection, because it is inconsistent with the grant. 1 Burr. 259. 6 T. R. 484.—Chitty.
(8) [That he permit.]
(9) This is now the only remedy, these real actions having been abolished. 3 & 4 W. IV. c. 27, s. 36.—Stewart.

put as examples; and that any other necessary improvements may be made by the lord, though in reality they abridge the common and make it less sufficient for the commoners. And lastly, by statute 29 Geo. II. c. 36, and 31 Geo. II. c. 41, it is particularly enacted that any lords of wastes and commons, with the consent of the major part in number and value of the commoners, may enclose any part thereof for the growth of timber and underwood.(10)

III. The third species of disturbance, that of *ways*, is very similar in its nature to the last; it principally happening when a person who hath a right to a way over another's grounds, by grant or prescription, is obstructed by enclosures or other obstacles, or by ploughing across it; by which means he cannot enjoy his right of way, or at least not in so commodious a manner as he might have done. If this be a way annexed to his estate, and the obstruction is made by the tenant of the land, this brings it to another species of injury; for it is then a *nuisance*, for which an assize will lie, as mentioned in a former chapter.(x) But if the right of way thus obstructed by the tenant be only in *gross*, (that is, annexed to a man's person and unconnected with any lands or *tenements,) or if the obstruction of a way [*242 belonging to a house or land is made by a stranger, it is then in either case merely a disturbance; for the obstruction of a way in gross is no detriment to any lands or tenements, and therefore does not fall under the legal notion of a nuisance, which must be laid *ad nocumentum liberi tenementi;*(y)(11) and the obstruction of it by a stranger can never tend to put the *right* of way in dispute; the remedy, therefore, for these disturbances is not by assize or any real action, but by the universal remedy of action on the case to recover damages.(z)

IV. The fourth species of disturbance is that of disturbance of *tenure*, or breaking that connection which subsists between the lord and his tenant, and to which the law pays so high a regard, that it will not suffer it to be wantonly dissolved by the act of a third person. To have an estate well tenanted is an advantage that every landlord must be very sensible of; and therefore the driving away of a tenant from off his estate is an injury of no small consequence. So that if there be a tenant at will of any lands or tenements, and a stranger, either by menaces and threats, or by unlawful distresses, or by

---

(x) C. 13, p. 218.   (z) Hale on F. N. B. 185.   Lutw. 111, 119.
(y) F. N. B. 183.

---

(10) As the lord may approve, leaving a sufficiency of common, the commoner abates an erection at the peril of an action. A person seised in fee of the waste may approve, although he be not lord. 3 T. R. 445. But there can be no approvement against the tenants of a manor, who have a right to dig gravel in the wastes and take estovers, (2 T. R. 391,) nor against common of turbary, (1 Taunt, 435;) and although the lord may approve against common of pastures, by 20 Hen. III. c. 4, 5 T. R. 411, yet there may be other rights of common against which he cannot approve. 6 T. R. 741. A custom for tenants to approve by the lord's consent and by presentment of the homage does not restrain the lord's right to approve. 2 T. R. 392, n. The lord may, with consent of the homage, grant part of the soil for building, if the exercise of the right be immemorial, (5 T. R. 417, n.;) but a custom for the lord to grant leases of the waste without restriction is bad in point of law. 3 B. & A. 153.

The cultivation of common lands, and the enclosure and management of them, are now carried on under private acts of parliament, subject to and adopting the regulations laid down in the 13 Geo. III. c. 81 and 41 Geo. III. c. 109, which are incorporated into all special enclosure acts.—CHITTY.

By the general enclosure acts, (41 Geo. III. c. 109, amended by 1 & 2 Geo. IV. c. 23, 6 & 7 W. IV. c. 115, and 3 & 4 Vict. c. 31,) it is particularly enacted that any lords of wastes and commons, with the consent of two-third parts in number and value of the commoners, may enclose any part thereof for the growth of timber and underwood.—STEWART.

(11) [To the detriment of his free tenement.]

fraud and circumvention, or other means, contrives to drive him away, or inveigle him to leave his tenancy, this the law very justly construes to be a wrong and injury to the lord, (a) and gives him a reparation in damages against the offender by a special action on the case.

V. The fifth and last species of disturbance, but by far the most considerable, is that of disturbance of *patronage;* which is a hindrance or obstruction of a patron to present his clerk to a benefice.

This injury was distinguished at common law from another species of injury, called *usurpation;* which is an absolute ouster or dispossession of the patron, and happens when a stranger, that hath no right, presenteth *243]   a clerk, and he is thereupon *admitted and instituted. (b)   In which case of usurpation, the patron lost by the common law not only his turn of presenting *pro hac vice,* (12) but also the absolute and perpetual inheritance of the advowson, so that he could not present again upon the next avoidance, unless in the meantime he recovered his right by a real action, viz., a writ of *right of advowson.* (c)   The reason given for his losing the present turn, and not ejecting the usurper's clerk, was that, the final intent of the law in creating this species of property being to have a fit person to celebrate divine service, it preferred the peace of the church (provided a clerk were once admitted and instituted) to the right of any patron whatever. (13)   And the patron also lost the inheritance of his advowson, unless he recovered it in a writ of right, because by such usurpation he was put out of possession of his advowson, as much as when by actual entry and ouster he is disseised of lands or houses; since the only possession of which an advowson is capable is by actual presentation and admission of one's clerk. As, therefore, when the clerk was once instituted (except in the case of the king, where he must also be inducted)(d) the church became absolutely *full;* so the usurper by such plenarty, arising from his own presentation, became in fact *seised* of the advowson: which seisin it was impossible for the true patron to remove by any possessory action, or other means, during the plenarty or fulness of the church; and when it became void afresh, he could not then present, since another had the right of possession.   The only remedy, therefore, which the patron had left, was to try the mere right in a writ of *right of advowson;* which is a peculiar writ of right, framed for this special purpose, but in every other respect corresponding with other writs of right:(e) and if a man recovered therein, he regained the possession of his advowson, and was entitled to present at the next avoidance. (f)   But in order to such recovery he must allege a presentation in himself or some of his ancestors, which proves him or them to have been once in possession: for, as a grant of the advowson, during the fulness of church, conveys *244]   *no manner of possession for the present, therefore a purchaser, until he hath presented, hath no actual seisin whereon to ground a writ of right. (g)   Thus stood the common law.

(a) Hal. Anal. c. 40.   1 Roll. Abr. 108.
(b) Co. Litt. 257.
(c) 6 Rep. 49.
(d) Ibid.

(e) F. N. B. 30.
(f) Ibid. 36.
(g) 2 Ins. 357.

(12) [For this turn.]
(13) And this preference of the peace of the church to the litigated rights of patrons was held to prevail in all cases, without any regard to infancy, coverture, or any such like disability of the patron; for it was a maxim of the common law "that he who came in by admission and institution came in by a judicial act; and the law presumes that the bishop who has the care of the souls of all within his diocese, for which he shall answer at his fearful and final account, (in respect of which he ought to keep and defend them against all heretics and schismatics and other ministers of the devil,) will not do or assent to any wrong to be done to their patronages, which is of their earthly possession, but, if the church be litigious, that he will inform himself of the truth by a *de jure patronatus* [Concerning the right of a patron], and so do right." 6 Coke, 49.—CHITTY.

But, bishops in ancient times, either by carelessness or collusion, frequently instituting clerks upon the presentation of usurpers, and thereby defrauding the real patrons of their right of possession, it was in substance enacted by statute Westm. 2, 13 Edw. I. c. 5, § 2, that if a possessory action be brought within six months after the avoidance, the patrons shall (notwithstanding such usurpation and institution) recover that very presentation; which gives back to him the seisin of the advowson. Yet still, if the true patron omitted to bring his action within six months, the seisin was gained by the usurper, and the patron, to recover it, was driven to the long and hazardous process of a writ of right.(14) To remedy which, it was further enacted, by statute 7 Anne, c. 18, that no usurpation shall displace the estate or interest of the patron, or turn it to a mere right; but that the true patron may present upon the next avoidance, as if no such usurpation had happened. So that the title of usurpation is now much narrowed, and the law stands upon this reasonable foundation: that if a stranger usurps my presentation, and I do not pursue my right within six months, I shall lose that turn without remedy, for the peace of the church and as a punishment for my own negligence; but that turn is the only one I shall lose thereby. Usurpation now gains no right to the usurper with regard to any future avoidance, but only to the present vacancy: it cannot indeed be remedied after six months are past; but during those six months it is only a species of disturbance.

Disturbers of a right of advowson may therefore be these three persons: the pseudo-patron, his clerk, and the ordinary; the pretended patron, by presenting to a church to which he has no right, and thereby making it litigious or disputable; the clerk, by demanding or obtaining institution, *which tends to and promotes the same inconvenience; and the   [*245 ordinary, by refusing to admit the real patron's clerk, or admitting the clerk of the pretender. These disturbances are vexatious and injurious to him who hath the right: and therefore, if he be not wanting to himself, the law (besides the writ of *right of advowson*, which is a final and conclusive remedy) hath given him two inferior possessory actions for his relief; an assize of *darrein presentment*,(15) and a writ of *quare impedit;*(16) in which the patron is always the plaintiff, and not the clerk. For the law supposes the injury to be offered to him only, by obstructing or refusing the admission of his nominee; and not to the clerk, who hath no right in him till institution, and of course can suffer no injury.

1. An assize of *darrein presentment*, or last presentation, lies when a man, or his ancestors, under whom he claims, have presented a clerk to a benefice, who is instituted, and afterwards upon the next avoidance a stranger presents a clerk, and thereby disturbs him that is the real patron. In which case the patron shall have this writ(h) directed to the sheriff to summon an assize or jury, to inquire who was the last patron that presented to the church now vacant, of which the plaintiff complains that he is deforced by the defendant: and, according as the assize determines that question, a writ shall issue to the bishop; to institute the clerk of that patron, in whose favor the determination is made, and also to give damages, in pursuance of statute Westm. 2, 13 Edw. I. c. 5. This question, it is to be observed, was before the statute 7 Anne before mentioned, entirely conclusive as between the patron or his heirs and a stranger: for, till then, the full possession of the advowson was in him who presented last and his heirs: unless, since that presentation,

(h) F. N. B. 31.

(14) Down to Queen Anne's day, a usurpation followed by inaction for more than six months would utterly destroy the patron's right. 2 Pollock and Maitland's History of English Law, 138.
(15) [Last presentation.]
(16) [Wherefore he has hindered.]

the clerk had been evicted within six months, or the rightful patron had recovered the advowson in a writ of right; which is a title superior to all others. But that statute having given a right to any person to bring a *quare impedit*, and to recover (if his title be good) notwithstanding *246] the last presentation, by whomsoever *made; assizes of *darrein presentment*, now not being in any wise conclusive, have been totally disused, as indeed they began to be before,(17) a *quare impedit* being more general, and therefore a more usual action. For the assize of *darrein presentment* lies only where a man has an advowson by descent from his ancestors; but the writ of *quare impedit* is equally remediable whether a man claims title by descent or by purchase.(*i*)

2. I proceed therefore secondly, to inquire into the nature(*k*) of a writ of *quare impedit*, now the only action used in case of the disturbance of patronage; and shall first premise the usual proceedings previous to the bringing of the writ.

Upon the vacancy of a living, the patron, we know, is bound to present within six calendar months,(*l*) otherwise it will lapse to the bishop. But if the presentation be made within that time, the bishop is bound to admit and institute the clerk, if found sufficient;(*m*) unless the church be full, or there be notice of any litigation. For, if any opposition be intended, it is usual for each party to enter a *caveat*(18) with the bishop, to prevent his institution of his antagonist's clerk. An institution after a *caveat* entered is void by the ecclesiastical law;(*n*) but this the temporal courts pay no regard to, and look upon a *caveat* as a mere nullity.(*o*) But if two presentations be offered to the bishop upon the same avoidance, the church is then said to become *litigious;* and, if nothing further be done, the bishop may suspend the admission of either, and suffer a lapse to incur. Yet if the patron or clerk on either side request him to award a *jus patronatus;*(19) he is bound to do it. A *jus patronatus* is a commission from the bishop, directed usually to his chancellor and others of competent learning: who are to summon a jury of six clergymen and six laymen, to inquire into and examine who is the *247]   *rightful patron;(*p*) and if, upon such inquiry made and certificate thereof returned to the commissioners, he admits and institutes the clerk of that patron whom they return as the true one, the bishop secures himself at all events from being a disturber, whatever proceedings may be had afterwards in the temporal courts.

The clerk refused by the bishop may also have a remedy against him in the spiritual court, denominated a *duplex querela:*(*q*)(20) which is a complaint in the nature of an appeal from the ordinary to his next immediate superior; as from a bishop to the archbishop, or from an archbishop to the delegates;(21) and if the superior court adjudges the cause of refusal to be insufficient, it will grant institution to the appellant.

Thus far matters may go on in the mere ecclesiastical course; but in contested presentations they seldom go so far; for, upon the first delay or refusal of the bishop to admit his clerk, the patron usually brings his writ of *quare impedit* against the bishop, for the temporal injury done to his property in

(f) 2 Inst. 355.
(k) See Boswell's case, 6 Rep. 48.
(l) See book ii. ch. 18.
(m) See book i. ch. 11.

(n) 1 Burn. 207.
(o) 1 Roll. Rep. 191.
(p) 1 Burn. 16, 17.
(q) Ibid. 113.

(17) Now abolished, 3 & 4 W. IV. c. 27, s. 36. [*Quare empedit*—Wherefore did he hinder.]
(18) [That he take care.]   [*Darrein presentment*—The last presentation.]
(19) [Right of advowson.]
(20) [Double complaint.]
(21) Now to the Judicial Committee of the Privy Council.—STEWART.

disturbing him in his presentation. And, if the delay arises from the bishop alone, as upon pretence of incapacity, or the like, then he only is named in the writ; but if there be another presentation set up, then the pretended patron and his clerk are also joined in the action; or it may be brought against the patron and clerk, leaving out the bishop; or against the patron only. But it is most advisable to bring it against all three: for if the bishop be left out, and the suit be not determined till the six months are past, the bishop is entitled to present by lapse; for he is not party to the suit;(r) but, if he be named, no lapse can possibly accrue till the right is determined. If the patron be left out, and the writ be brought only against the bishop and the clerk, the suit is of no effect, and the writ shall abate;(s) for the right of the patron is the principal question in the cause.(t) If the *clerk be left out, and has received institution before the action [*248 brought, (as is sometimes the case,) the patron by this suit may recover his right of patronage, but not the present turn; for he cannot have judgment to remove the clerk, unless he be made a defendant, and party to the suit, to hear what he can allege against it. For which reason it is the safer way to insert all three in the writ.

The writ of *quare impedit*(u) commands the disturbers, the bishop, the pseudo-patron, and his clerk, to permit the plaintiff to present a proper person (without specifying the particular clerk) to such a vacant church, which pertains to his patronage; and which the defendants, as he alleges, do obstruct; and unless they so do, then that they appear in court to show the reason why they hinder him.

Immediately on the suing out of the *quare impedit*, if the plaintiff suspects that the bishop will admit the defendant's or any other clerk, pending the suit, he may have a prohibitory writ, called a *ne admittas*,(w)(22) which recites the contention begun in the king's courts, and forbids the bishop to admit any clerk whatsoever till such contention be determined. And if the bishop doth, after the receipt of this writ, admit any person, even though the patron's right may have been found in a *jure patronatûs*, then the plaintiff, after he has obtained judgment in the *quare impedit*, may remove the incumbent, if the clerk of a stranger, by writ of *scire facias*;(x) and shall have a special action against the bishop, called a *quare incumbravit*,(23) to recover the presentation, and also satisfaction in damages for the injury done him by encumbering the church with a clerk pending the suit and after the *ne admittas* received.(y) But if the bishop has encumbered the church by instituting the clerk before the *ne admittas* issued, no *quare incumbravit* lies; for the bishop hath no legal notice till the writ of *ne admittas* is served upon *him. The patron is therefore left to his *quare impedit* [*249 merely, which, as was before observed, now lies (since the statute of Westm. 2) as well upon a recent usurpation within six months past, as upon a disturbance without any usurpation had.

In the proceedings upon a *quare impedit*, the plaintiff must set out his title at length, and prove at least one presentation in himself, his ancestors, or those under whom he claims; for he must recover by the strength of his own right, and not by the weakness of the defendant's;(z) and he must also show a disturbance before the action brought.(a) Upon this the bishop and

(r) Cro. Jac. 98.
(s) Hob. 316.
(t) 7 Rep. 25.
(u) F. N. B. 32.
(w) F. N. B. 37.

(x) 2 Sid. 94.
(y) F. N. B. 43.
(z) Vaugh. 7, 8.
(a) Hob. 199.

(22) [Do not admit.] [*Quare impedit*—Wherefore did he hinder.]
(23) [Wherefore he has encumbered.] This writ is now abolished, by 3 & 4 W. IV. c. 27, s. 36. [*Jure patronatus*—The right of patronage.]

the clerk usually disclaim all title: save only the one as ordinary, to admit and institute, and the other as presentee of the patron, who is left to defend his own right.   And upon failure of the plaintiff in making out his own title, the defendant is put upon the proof of his, in order to obtain judgment for himself, if needful.   But if the right be found for the plaintiff on the trial, three further points are also to be inquired: 1. If the church be full; and, if full, then of whose presentation: for if it be of the defendant's presentation, then the clerk is removable by writ brought in due time.   2. Of what value the living is: and this in order to assess the damages which are directed to be given by the statute of Westm. 2.   3.   In case of plenarty upon a usurpation, whether six calendar(b) months have passed between the avoidance and the time of bringing the action, for then it would not be within the statute, which permits a usurpation to be devested by a *quare impedit* brought *infra tempus semestre*.(24)   So that plenarty is still a sufficient bar in an action of *quare impedit* brought above six months after the vacancy happens; as it was universally by the common law, however early the action was commenced.

If it be found that the plaintiff hath the right and hath commenced
*250]   his action in due time, then he shall have *judgment to recover the presentation, and if the church be full by institution of any clerk, to remove him; unless it were filled *pendente lite*(25) by lapse to the ordinary, he not being a party to the suit; in which case the plaintiff loses his presentation *pro hac vice*, (26) but shall recover two years' full value of the church from the defendant, the pretended patron, as a satisfaction for the turn lost by his disturbance; or in case of insolvency the defendant shall be imprisoned for two years.(c)   But if the church remains still void at the end of the suit, then which ever party the presentation is found to belong to, whether plaintiff or defendant, shall have a writ directed to the bishop *ad admittendum clericum*,(d)(27) reciting the judgment of the court, and ordering him to admit and institute the clerk of the prevailing party; and if upon this order he does not admit him, the patron may sue the bishop in a writ of *quare non admisit*,(e)(28) and recover ample satisfaction in damages.

Besides these possessory actions, there may be also had (as hath before been incidentally mentioned) a writ of *right of advowson*,(29) which resembles other writs of right; the only distinguishing advantage now attending it being that it is more conclusive than a *quare impedit*, since to an action of *quare impedit*(30) a recovery had in a writ of right may be pleaded in bar.

There is no limitation with regard to the time within which any actions touching advowsons are to be brought; at least, none later than the times of Richard I. and Henry III.: for by statute 1 Mar. st. 2, c. 5, the statute of limitations, 32 Hen. VIII. c. 2 is declared not to extend to any writ of right of advowson, *quare impedit*, or assize of *darrein presentment*, or *jus patronatus*.(31)   And this upon very good reason: because it may very easily happen that the title to an advowson may not come in question, nor the right have opportunity to be tried, within sixty years, which is the longest period of
*251]   limitation assigned by the statute of Henry VIII.   For Sir Edward Coke(f) tells us that there was a parson of one of his *churches that

(b) 2 Inst. 361.   (e) Ibid. 47.
(c) Stat. Westm. 5, 13 Edw. I. c. 5, § 3.   (f) 1 Inst. 115.
(d) F. N. B. 38.

(24) [Within half a year.]
(25) [Pending the suit.]
(26) [For this turn.]
(27) [For admitting the clerk.]
(28) [Why he has not admitted.]
(29) The writ of right of advowson has been abolished, 3 & 4 W. IV. c. 27, s. 36.
(30) [Wherefore did he disturb.]
(31) [The last presentation or right of patronage.]

had been incumbent there above fifty years; nor are instances wanting wherein two successive incumbents have continued for upwards of a hundred years. (*g*)   Had therefore the last of these incumbents been the clerk of
a usurper, or had he been presented by lapse, it would have been necessary
and unavoidable for the patron, in case of a dispute, to have recurred back
above a century in order to have shown a clear title and seisin by presentation and admission of the prior incumbent.   But though, for these reasons,
a limitation is highly improbable with respect only to the length of time, yet,
as the title of advowson is, for want of some limitation, rendered more precarious than that of any other hereditament, (especially since the statute of
queen Anne hath allowed possessory actions to be brought upon any prior
presentation, however distant,) it might not perhaps be amiss if a limitation
were established with respect to the number of avoidances, or, rather, if a
limitation were compounded of the length of time and the number of avoidances together: for instance, if no seisin were admitted to be alleged in any of
these writs of patronage after sixty years and three avoidances were past.(32)

In a writ of *quare impedit*,(33) which is almost the only real action that
remains in common use, and also in the assize of *darrein presentment*, (34)
and writ of right, the patron only, and not the clerk, is allowed to sue the
disturber.   But, by virtue of several acts of parliament,(*h*) there is one

(*g*) Two successive incumbents of the rectory of
Cholsfield-*cum*-Farnborough, in Kent, continued one
hundred and one years, of whom the former was

admitted in 1650, the latter in 1700, and died in 1751.
(*h*) Stat. 3 Jac. I. c. 5. 1 W. and M. c. 26. 12 Anne,
st. 2, c. 14. 11 Geo. II. c. 17.

(32) A *quare impedit* lies for a church, an hospital, and a donative; and, by the equity
of the statute of Westminster, it lies for prebends, chapels, vicarages. 3 T. R. 650.
Willes' Rep. 608. 2 Roll. Abr. 380. This action may be brought by the king in right of
his crown, or on a title by lapse by a common parson, or by several who have the same
title, by an executor or administrator. To maintain the action, there must be a disturbance; as, if brought by a purchaser, he may allege a presentation in him from whom
he purchased the same. Stra. 1007. 1 Hen. Bla. 376, 530. If there are distinct patrons
of an advowson in one and the same church, as where one has the first portion and
another the second, he who is disturbed may have a *quare impedit*, (3 T. R. 646;) and if
there are distinct patrons and incumbents, so that the church is divided into moieties, he
who is disturbed shall have the writ. 10 Rep. 136. 5 Rep. 102. 1 Inst. 18, a. 4 Rep.
75. And if the right of nomination is in one, and that of presentation in another, the
quare impedit will lie by the person having the nomination against the person who has
the presentation and obstructs the right. 3 T. R. 651. Rast. 506, b. If there are two
or more tenants in common, or joint-tenants, they must join in a *quare impedit* of an
advowson, for it is an entire thing; and one of them cannot have a *quare impedit* of a
moiety or of a third or fourth part of an advowson of a church, but they must all join;
though it is otherwise of coparceners, for if they do not agree the eldest shall have the
presentation. Bro. Joinder in Action, 103. But where A. and B. were the grantees of
the next avoidance of a church, and before any avoidance A. released his interest to B.,
and then the church became void, it was holden that B. alone should present to the
church, and if he be disturbed might bring a *quare impedit* in his own name only. Cro.
Eliz. 600. If the suit be by an executor or administrator, upon an avoidance in the life
of the testator, an allegation of the disturbance in the life of the testator is sufficient.
R. Sav. 95. Lutw. 2. See also, as to the right of the executor to bring this action, Vin.
Abr. Executors, P. pl. 7. Latch, 168, 169. Sir W. Jones, 175. Poph. 190. 1 Ventr. 30.
As the defendant is considered an actor in a *quare impedit*, he may make up the issues,
(Tidd. Prac. 793,) and may have a trial by proviso, although the plaintiff has not committed any laches in proceeding to trial. Ib. 820.—CHITTY.
And this alteration in the law recommended by the learned commentator has recently
been carried into effect by stat. 3 & 4 W. IV. c. 27, by which (s. 30) it is enacted that no
advowson shall be recovered after three incumbencies occupying a period of sixty years'
adverse possession: incumbencies after lapse are to be reckoned within the period, but
not incumbencies after promotion to bishoprics, (s. 31;) and no advowson shall be recovered after one hundred years' adverse possession, although three incumbencies have not
elapsed. S. 33.—STEWART.
By the statute 6 & 7 Vic. c. 54, the same period of limitations is applied to a *quare
impedit* or any other action or suit to enforce a right in a bishop as patron to collate to
or bestow any ecclesiastical benefice.
(33) [Wherefore did he disturb.]
(34) [The last presentation.]

species of presentations, in which a remedy, to be sued in the temporal courts, is put into the hands of the clerks presented, as well as of the owners of the advowson. I mean the presentation to such benefices as belong to Roman Catholic patrons; which, according to their several counties, are vested in and secured to the two universities of this kingdom. And particularly by the statute of 12 Anne, st. 2, c. 14, s. 4, a new method of proceeding is provided; viz., that, besides the writs of *quare impedit*,(35) which the universities as patrons are entitled to bring, they, or their clerks, may
*252] be at liberty to file a bill *in equity against any person presenting to such livings, and disturbing their right of patronage, or his *cestuy que trust*(36), or any other person whom they have cause to suspect; in order to compel a discovery of any secret trusts, for the benefit of papists, in evasion of those laws whereby this right of advowson is vested in those learned bodies; and also (by the statute 11 Geo. II. c. 17) to compel a discovery whether any grant or conveyance, said to be made of such advowson, were made *bona fide* to a protestant purchaser, for the benefit of protestants, and for a full consideration; without which requisites every such grant and conveyance of any advowson or avoidance is absolutely null and void. This is a particular law, and calculated for a particular purpose: but in no instance but this does the common law permit the clerk himself to interfere in recovering a presentation of which he is afterwards to have the advantage. For besides that he has (as was before observed) no temporal right in him till after institution and induction, and, as he therefore can suffer no wrong, is consequently entitled to no remedy; this exclusion of the clerk from being plaintiff seems also to arise from the very great honor and regard which the law pays to his sacred function. For it looks upon the cure of souls as too arduous and important a task to be eagerly sought for by any serious clergyman; and therefore will not permit him to contend openly at law for a charge and trust which it presumes he undertakes with diffidence.

But when the clerk is in full possession of the benefice, the law gives him the same possessory remedies to recover his glebe, his rents, his tithes, and other ecclesiastical dues, by writ of entry, assize, ejectment, debt, or trespass, (as the case may happen,) which it furnishes to the owners of lay property. Yet he shall not have a writ of right, nor such other similar writs as are grounded upon the mere right; because he hath not in him the entire fee and right,(i) but he is entitled to a special remedy called a writ of *juris utrum*,(37) which it sometimes styled the parson's writ of right,(k)
*253] *being the highest writ which he can have.(l) This lies for a parson or prebendary at common law, and for a vicar by statute 14 Edw. III. c. 17, and is in the nature of an assize, to inquire whether the tenements in question are frankalmoign belonging to the church of the demandant, or else the lay fee of the tenant.(m) And thereby the demandant may recover lands and tenements, belonging to the church, which were alienated by the predecessor; or of which he was disseised; or which were recovered against him by verdict, confession, or default, without praying in aid of the patron and ordinary; or on which any person has intruded since the predecessor's death.(n) But since the restraining statute of 13 Eliz. c. 10, whereby the alienation of the predecessor, or a recovery suffered by him of the lands of the church, is declared to be absolutely void, this remedy is of very little use, unless where the parson himself has been deforced for more than twenty

(i) F. N. B. 49. (m) Registrar, 32.
(k) Booth, 221. (n) F. N. B. 48, 49.
(l) F. N. B. 48.

(35) [Wherefore did he disturb.]
(36) [Beneficiary's trust.]
(37) [Whether of right.]

years;(o) for the successor, at any competent time after his accession to the benefice, may enter, or bring an ejectment.(38)

CHAPTER XVII.

OF INJURIES PROCEEDING FROM, OR AFFECTING, THE CROWN.

*HAVING in the nine preceding chapters considered the injuries,   [*254 or private wrongs, that may be offered by one subject to another, all of which are redressed by the command and authority of the king, signified by his original writs returnable in the several courts of justice, which thence derive a jurisdiction of examining and determining the complaint; I proceed now to inquire into the mode of redressing those injuries to which the crown itself is a party: which injuries are either where the crown is the aggressor, and which therefore cannot without a solecism admit of the same kind of remedy;(a) or else is the sufferer, and which then are usually remedied by peculiar forms of process, appropriated to the royal prerogative. In treating therefore of these, we will consider first the manner of redressing those wrongs or injuries which a subject may suffer from the crown, and then of redressing those which the crown may receive from a subject.

I. That the king can do no wrong, is a necessary and fundamental principle of the English constitution; meaning only, as has formerly been observed,(b) that, in the first place, whatever may be amiss in the conduct of public affairs is not *chargeable personally on the king;   [*255 nor is he, but his ministers, accountable for it to the people; and, secondly, that the prerogative of the crown extends not to do any injury; for, being created for the benefit of the people, it cannot be exerted to their prejudice.(c) Whenever therefore it happens that, by misinformation, or inadvertence, the crown hath been induced to invade the private rights of any of its subjects, though no action will lie against the sovereign,(d) (for who shall command the king?)(e) yet the law hath furnished the subject with a decent and respectful mode of removing that invasion, by informing the king of the true state of the matter in dispute: and, as it presumes that to *know of* any injury and to *redress* it are inseparable in the royal breast, it then issues as of course, in the king's own name, his orders to his judges to do justice to the party aggrieved.(1)

(o) Booth, 221.
(a) Bro. Abr. tit. *petition*, 12; tit. *prerogative*, 2.
(b) Book i. ch. 7, pp. 243-246.

(c) Plowd. 437.
(d) Jenkins, 78.
(e) Finch, L. 83.

---

(38) It is now formally abolished, 3 & 4 W. IV. c. 27, s. 36. Until recently, defendants in actions of *quare impedit* [Wherefore did he disturb] were not liable for the payment of costs, and the patrons were thereby sometimes deterred from prosecuting their rights, (Edwards *v.* Bishop of Exeter, 6 Bingh. N. C. 146;) but now, by stat. 4 & 5 W. IV. c. 39, plaintiffs are enabled to recover their full costs.—STEWART.

(1) This maxim has, of course, no place in the American law. If an individual be injured by a public officer, he shall have his redress the same as if the injury was done by a private person. If property is taken or injured by the state or those acting under its authority the owner is entitled to compensation. See Hooker *v.* N. H. & N. Co., 14 Conn. 146 (1841). Such taking or injury is generally under the right of eminent domain. The government is not liable to be sued, except by its own consent given by law. Hill *v.* U. S., 9 How. 386 (U. S. 1850). And the same is true of the several states. The right of a debtor of the United States government, when sued by it to interpose a counter-claim or counter-credits, rests in all cases upon the provisions of the act of Congress granting and regulating it (Act of March 3, 1797, §§ 3 and 4); and while, under said act, a defendant, upon complying with its conditions, may give in evidence any counter-claim he may have in his own right, which is a proper subject of set off, such counter-claim is available only to the extent necessary to defeat the claim of the government, and no affirmative judgment for any excess can be rendered against it. People *v.* Dennison, 84 N. Y. (39 Sickels) 272 (1881). By statutes 23 and 24 Vic. c. 34, proceedings on behalf of

The distance between the sovereign and his subjects is such, that it rarely can happen that any *personal* injury can immediately and directly proceed from the prince to any private man; and, as it can so seldom happen, the law in decency supposes that it never will or can happen at all; because it feels itself incapable of furnishing any adequate remedy, without infringing the dignity and destroying the sovereignty of the royal person, by setting up some superior power with authority to call him to account. The inconveniency therefore of a mischief that is barely possible is (as Mr. Locke has observed)(*f*) well recompensed by the peace of the public and security of the government, in the person of the chief magistrate being set out of the reach of coercion. But injuries to the rights of *property* can scarcely be committed by the crown without the intervention of its officers; for whom the law in matters of right entertains no respect or delicacy, but furnishes various methods of detecting the errors or misconduct of those agents, by whom the king has been deceived and induced to do a temporary injustice.(2)

*256]   *The common-law methods of obtaining possession or restitution from the crown, of either real or personal property, are, 1. By *petition de droit*, or petition of right: which is said to owe its original to king Edward the First.(*g*) 2. By *monstrans de droit*, manifestation or plea of right: both of which may be preferred or prosecuted either in the chancery or exchequer.(*h*) The former is of use, where the king is in full possession of any hereditaments or chattels, and the petitioner suggests such a right as controverts the title of the crown, grounded on facts disclosed in the petition itself; in which case he must be careful to state truly the whole title of the crown, otherwise the petition shall abate;(*i*) and then, upon this answer being endorsed or underwritten by the king, *soit droit fait al partie*, (let right be done to the party,)(*j*) a commission shall issue to inquire of the truth of this suggestion:(*k*) after the return of which, the king's attorney is at liberty to plead in bar; and the merits shall be determined upon issue or demurrer, as in suits between subject and subject. Thus, if a disseisor of lands which are holden of the crown dies seised without any heir, whereby the king is *prima facie* entitled to the lands, and the possession is cast on him either by inquest of office, or by act of law without any office found; now the disseisee shall have remedy by petition of right, suggesting the title of the crown, and his own superior right before the disseisin made.(*l*)(3) But where the right of the party, as well as the right of the crown, appears upon record, there the party shall have *monstrans de droit*, which is putting in a claim of right grounded on facts already acknowledged and established, and praying the judgment of the court, whether upon those facts the king or the subject hath the right. As if, in the case before supposed, the whole special matter is found by an inquest of office, (as well the disseisin, as the dying without an heir,) the party grieved shall have *monstrans de*
*257]   *droit* at the common law.(*m*) But as this seldom happens, and *the remedy by *petition* was extremely tedious and expensive, that by *monstrans* was much enlarged and rendered almost universal by several

(*f*) On Govt. p. 2, § 205.
(*g*) Bro. Abr. tit. *prerogative*, 2. Fitz. Abr. tit. *error*, 8.
(*h*) Skin. 609.
(*i*) Finch, L. 256.

(*j*) Stat. Tr. vii. 134.
(*k*) Skin. 608. East. Entr. 461.
(*l*) Bro. Abr. tit. *petition*, 20. 4 Rep. 58.
(*m*) 4 Rep. 55.

a subject to obtain redress from the crown are simplified and made more effective. The party is given a trial in the proper court of law or equity, upon an issue made up substantially as in a suit between individuals.

(2) See The Banker's Case, 14 St. Tr. 1, (1690-1696-1700) S. C. Skin. 601, 5 Mod. 29, 1 Free. 331; and notes thereto. Broom's Const. Law, 225-244 (2 ed. 1885).

(3) A petition of right will lie for damages resulting from a breach of contract by the crown. Windsor etc. Ry. Co. *v.* Queen etc. Ry. Co., 11 App. Cas. 607 (1886). See Hepburn's case, 3 Bland ch. (Md.) 95, 100 (1830).

statutes, particularly 36 Edw. III. c. 13, and 2 & 3 Edw. VI. c. 8, which also allow inquisitions of office to be traversed or denied wherever the right of a subject is concerned, except in a very few cases.(*n*) These proceedings are had in the petty-bag office in the court of chancery; and, if upon either of them the right be determined against the crown, the judgment is, *quod manus domini regis amoveantur et possessio restituatur petenti, salvo jure domini regis;*(*o*)(4) which last clause is always added to judgment against the king,(*p*) to whom no *laches* is ever imputed, and whose right (till some late statutes)(*q*) was never defeated by any limitation or length of time. And by such judgment the crown is instantly out of possession:(*r*) so that there needs not the indecent interposition of his own officers to transfer the seisin from the king to the party aggrieved.

II. The methods of redressing such injuries as the crown may receive from the subject are,—

1. By such usual common-law actions as are consistent with the royal prerogative and dignity. As therefore the king, by reason of his legal ubiquity, cannot be disseised or dispossessed of any real property which is once vested in him, he can maintain no action which supposes a dispossession of the plaintiff; such as an assize or an ejectment;(*s*)(5) but he may bring a *quare impedit,*(*t*) which always supposes the complainant to be seised or possessed of the advowson; and he may prosecute this writ, like every other by him brought, as well in the king's bench(*u*) as the common pleas, or in whatever court he pleases. So, too, he may bring an action of trespass for taking away his goods; but such actions are not usual (though in strictness maintainable) for breaking his close, or other injury done upon his soil or possession.(*w*) It would be equally tedious *and difficult,   [*258 to run through every minute distinction that might be gleaned from our ancient books with regard to this matter; nor is it in any degree necessary, as much easier and more effectual remedies are usually obtained by such prerogative modes of process as are peculiarly confined to the crown.

Such is that of *inquisition,* or *inquest of office;* which is an inquiry made by the king's officer, his sheriff, coroner, or escheator, *virtute officii,*(6) or by writ to them sent for that purpose, or by commissioners specially appointed, concerning any matter that entitles the king to the possession of lands or tenements, goods or chattels.(*x*) This is done by a jury of no determinate number, being either twelve, or less, or more. As, to inquire whether the king's tenant for life died seised, whereby the reversion accrues to the king; whether A., who held immediately of the crown, died without heirs, in which case the lands belong to the king by escheat; whether B. be attainted of

(*n*) Skin. 608.
(*o*) 2 Inst. 695.   Rast. Entr. 463.
(*p*) Finch, L. 460.
(*q*) 21 Jac. I. c. 2.   9 Geo. III. c. 16.
(*r*) Finch. L. 459.
(*s*) Bro. Abr. tit. *prerogative,* 89.

(*t*) F. N. B. 32.   [Wherefore did he hinder.]
(*u*) *Dyversyti des courtes, c. bank le roy.*
(*w*) Bro. Abr. tit. *prerog.* 130.   F. N. B. 90.   Year-book.   4 Hen. IV. 4.
(*x*) Finch, L. 323, 324, 325.

(4) [That the hand of the king be removed, and possession restored to the petitioner, saving the right of the king.]

(5) But this objection to an ejectment does not seem to apply where the king is *lessor of the plaintiff;* for it is the *lessee,* and not the lessor, who is supposed by the legal fiction to be ousted; and it is held that where the possession is not *actually* in the king, but in lease to another, then, if a stranger enter on the lessee, he gains possession without taking the reversion out of the crown, and may have his ejectment to recover the possession if he be afterwards ousted, because there is a possession in *pais,* and not in the king, and that possession is not privileged by prerogative. Hence it follows that the king's *lessee* may likewise have an ejectment to punish the trespasser and to recover the possession which was taken from him. 2 Leon. 206.   Cro. Eliz. 331.   Adams on Ejectm. 72.—CHITTY. See Sedgwick and Wait on Trial of Title to Land (2 ed.) 118 and authorities there cited.

(6) [By virtue of their office.] See Cunningham *v.* Browning, 1 Bland's Ch. 299, 303

treason, whereby his estate is forfeited to the crown; whether C. who has purchased lands, be an alien, which is another cause of forfeiture; whether D. be an idiot *a nativitate*,(7) and therefore, together with his lands, appertains to the custody of the king; and other questions of like import, concerning both the circumstances of the tenant and the value or identity of the lands. These inquests of office were more frequently in practice than at present during the continuance of the military tenures among us; when, upon the death of every one of the king's tenants, an inquest of office was held, called an *inquisitio post mortem*,(8) to inquire of what lands he died seised, who was his heir, and of what age, in order to entitle the king to his marriage, wardship, relief, *primer-seisin*, or other advantages, as the circumstances of the case might turn out. To superintend and regulate these inquiries, the court of wards and liveries was instituted by statute 32 Hen. VIII. c. 46, which was abolished at the restoration of king Charles the Second, together with the oppressive tenures upon which it was founded.

*259]   *With regard to other matters, the inquests of office still remain in force, and are taken upon proper occasions; being extended not only to lands, but also to goods and chattels personal, as in the case of wreck, treasure-trove, and the like; and especially as to forfeitures for offences. For every jury which tries a man for treason or felony, every coroner's inquest that sits upon a *felo de se* or one killed by chance-medley, is, not only with regard to chattels, but also to real interests in all respects, an inquest of office; and if they find the treason or felony, or even the flight, of the party accused, (though innocent,) the king is thereupon, by virtue of this *office found*, entitled to have his forfeitures; and also, in case of chance-medley, he or his grantees are entitled to such things, by way of deodand, as have moved to the death of the party.

These inquests of office were devised by law, as an authentic means to give the king his right by solemn matter of record,(9) without which he, in general, can neither take nor part from any thing.(*y*) For it is a part of the liberties of England, and greatly for the safety of the subject, that the king may not enter upon and seize any man's possession upon bare surmises without the intervention of a jury.(*z*) It is, however, particularly enacted by the statute of 33 Hen. VIII. c. 20, that in case of attainder for high treason the king shall have the forfeiture instantly, without any inquisition of office. And as the king hath (in general) no title at all to any property of this sort before office found, therefore, by the statute 18 Hen. VI. c. 6, it was enacted, that all letters-patent or grants of lands and tenements before office found, or returned into the exchequer, shall be void. And, by the bill of rights at the revolution, 1 W. and M. st. 2, c. 2, it is declared that all grants and promises of fines and forfeitures of particular persons before conviction

(*y*) Finch, L. 82.   (*z*) Gilb. Hist. Exch. 132. Hob. 347.

(1835). If the grantee of the commonwealth fail to perform the condition of his grant, the remedy at common law, whereby the commonwealth should take advantage of the forfeiture, or in other words resume her rights over the thing granted, would be by inquest of office. White *v.* King, 5 Leigh. (Va.) 726, 733 (1835).

(7) [From his birth.]

(8) [An inquest after death.]

(9) State *v.* Stark, 3 Brevard (S. C.) 245, 247 (1812). Kenney *v.* Beverly, 2 Va. (Hen.) 313, 333 (1808). Alexander *v.* Greenup, 1 Va. (M.) 134, 149 (1810). Hughes *v.* Jones, 116 N. Y. 67, 75 (1889). An alien may hold real estate against anyone and even against the government until office found. It has been the policy of the government of the U. S. to encourage the immigration of foreigners; hence, a system of pre-emption has been adopted in all the territories and new states, in which there has been no discrimination between foreigners and native citizens. People *v.* Folsom, 5 Cal. 373, 378 (1855). See Com. *v.* Hite, 6 Va. (Leigh.) 588, 595 (1835).

(which is here the inquest of office) are illegal and void; which, indeed, was the law of the land in the reign of Edward the Third.(a)

*With regard to real property, if an office be found for the king,   [*260 it puts him in immediate possession, without the trouble of a formal entry, provided a subject in the like case would have had a right to enter; and the king shall receive all the mesne or intermediate profits from the time his title accrued.(b)   As, on the other hand, by the *articuli super cartas*,(c)(10) if the king's escheator or sheriff seize lands into the king's hand without cause, upon taking them out of the king's hand again the party shall have the mesne profits restored to him.

In order to avoid the possession of the crown, acquired by the finding of such office, the subject may not only have his *petition of right*, which discloses new facts not found by the office,(11) and his *monstrans de droit*,(12) which relies on the facts as found; but also he may (for the most part) *traverse* or deny the matter of fact itself, and put it in a course of trial by the common-law process of the court of chancery: yet still, in some special cases, he hath no remedy left but a mere petition of right.(d)   These *traverses*, as well as the *monstrans de droit*, were greatly enlarged and regulated for the benefit of the subject by the statutes before mentioned, and others.(e)   And in the traverses thus given by statute, which came in the place of the old petition of right, the party traversing is considered as the plaintiff,(f) and must therefore make out his own title, as well as impeach that of the crown, and then shall have judgment *quod manus domini regis amoveantur, etc.*(13)

3. Where the crown hath unadvisedly granted any thing by letters-patent which ought not to be granted,(g) or where the patentee hath done an act that amounts to a forfeiture of *the grant,(h) the remedy to   [*261 repeal the patent is by a writ of *scire facias* in chancery.(i)   This may be brought, either on the part of the king, in order to resume the thing granted; or, if the grant be injurious to the subject, the king is bound of right to permit him (upon his petition) to use his royal name for repealing the patent in a *scire facias*.(k)   And so also, if upon office untruly found for the king he grants the land over to another, he who is grieved thereby and traverses the office itself is entitled, before issue joined, to a *scire facias* against the patentee in order to avoid the grant.(l)(14)

4. An *information* on behalf of the crown, filed in the exchequer by the king's attorney-general, is a method of suit for recovering money or other chattels, or for obtaining satisfaction in damages for any personal wrong (m) committed in the lands or other possessions of the crown.(15)   It differs

---

(a) 2 Inst. 48.
(b) Finch, L. 325, 326.
(c) 28 Edw. I. st. 3, c. 19.
(d) Finch, L. 324.
(e) Stat. 34 Edw. III. c. 13. 36 Edw. III. c. 13. 2 & 3 Edw. VI. c. 8.
(f) Law of Nisi Prius, 201, 202.

(g) See book ii. ch. 21.
(h) Dyer, 198.
(i) 3 Lev. 220. 2 Inst. 88.
(k) 2 Ventr. 344.
(l) Bro. Abr. tit. *scire facias*, 69, 185.
(m) Moor. 375.

Mr. Justice Story in Fairfax *v.* Hunter, 7 Cranch, 621, says: "Even after office found, the king is not adjudged in possession, unless the possession were then vacant; for if the possession were then in another, the king must enter or seize by his officer, before the possession in deed shall be adjudged to him."   Commonwealth *v.* Hite, 41 Leigh. (Va.) 588, 594 (1835).

(10) [Articles upon the charters.]
(11) See Com. *v.* Hite, 6 Va. (Leigh.) 588, 596 (1835).
(12) [Showing the right.]
(13) See *supra.* p. 257.]
(14) See generally as to writ of *scire facias*.   Tidd's Practice, pp. 1090 to 1133 (4 Am. ed. 1856).   Taylor *v.* Fletcher, 7 B. Monroe (Ky.) 80, 84 (1846).
(15) The State *v.* Ashley, 1 Ark, 279, 304 (1840).   The People *v.* Van Ranssellar, 7 Barb.

from an information filed in the court of king's bench, of which we shall treat in the next book, in that *this* is instituted to redress a private wrong, by which the property of the crown is affected; *that* is calculated to punish some public wrong, or heinous misdemeanor in the defendant. It is grounded on no writ under seal, but merely on the intimation of the king's officer, the attorney-general, who " gives the court to understand and be informed of " the matter in question: upon which the party is put to answer, and trial is had, as in suits between subject and subject. The most usual informations are those of *intrusion* and *debt: intrusion*, for any trespass committed on the lands of the crown, (*n*) as by entering thereon without title, holding over after a lease is determined, taking the profits, cutting down timber, or the like; and *debt*, upon any contract for moneys due to the king, or for any forfeiture due to the crown upon the breach of a penal statute. This is most commonly used

*262]   to recover forfeitures occasioned by transgressing those laws which are enacted for the establishment *and support of the revenue; others, which regard mere matters of police and public convenience, being usually left to be enforced by common informers, the *qui tam* informations or actions, of which we have formerly spoken. (*o*) But after the attorney-general has informed upon the breach of a penal law, no other information can be received. (*p*) There is also an information *in rem*, when any goods are supposed to become the property of the crown, and no man appears to claim them, or to dispute the title of the king. As anciently in the case of treasure-trove, wrecks, waifs, and estrays, seized by the king's officer for his use. Upon such seizure an information was usually filed in the king's exchequer, and thereupon a proclamation was made for the owner (if any) to come in and claim the effects; and at the same time there issued a commission of *appraisement* to value the goods in the officer's hands; after the return of which, and a second proclamation had, if no claimant appeared, the goods were supposed derelict, and condemned to the use of the crown. (*q*) And when, in later times, forfeitures of the goods themselves, as well as personal penalties on the parties, were inflicted by act of parliament for transgressions against the laws of the customs and excise, the same process was adopted in order to secure such forfeited goods for the public use, though the offender himself had escaped the reach of justice.

5. A writ of *quo warranto* (16) is in the nature of a writ of right for the king, against him who claims or usurps any office, franchise, or liberty, to inquire by what authority he supports his claim, in order to determine the right. (*r*) It lies also in case of non-user or long neglect of a franchise, or mis-user or abuse of it; being a writ commanding the defendant to show by what warrant he exercises such a franchise, having never had any grant of it, or having forfeited it by neglect or abuse. (17) This was originally return-

(*n*) Cro Jac. 212. 1 Leon. 48. Savil. 46.
(*o*) See page 162.
(*p*) Hardr. 201.

(*q*) Gilb. Hist. of Exch. c. 13.
(*r*) Finch, L. 322. 2 Inst. 282.

(N. Y.) 189, 195 (1850). State *v.* Stark, 3 Brevard (S. C.) 101, 103 (1812). It is only where the letters patent are void on their face, by reason of being issued contrary to law, as against the prohibition of the statute, that such grant will be held void in a collateral proceeding. Jackson *v.* Lawton, 10 Johns. 23. Parmelee *v.* Oswego and Syracuse R. R. Co., 7 Barb. 599, 622 (1850). [*In rem*—Against the property.]

(16) [By what warrant.] Grier *v.* Schackleford, 2 Constn'l Rep. (Treadway) 642, 649 (1819). The issuing of a writ of *quo warranto* is not a proceeding on the equity side of the court, but is a common-law proceeding. Fulgham *v.* Johnson, 40 Ga. 164, 166 (1869).

(17) People *v.* Dashaway, Ass'n, 114, 118 (1890). State *v.* Brown, 5 R. I. 1, 7 (1859). State *v.* Hequembourg, 38 Mo. 529, 538 (1866). Derr *v.* Foy and Bishop, 1 N. C. (Murphey) 58, 85 (1805). The People *v.* Pease, 30 Barb. (N. Y.) 588, 591 (1860). Thompson *v.* The People, 23 Wend. (N. Y.) 538, 577 (1840).

It must not be forgotten that, although it is said the writ of quo warranto lies against

able before the king's justices at Westminster;(s) but afterwards only
*before the justices in eyre, by virtue of the statutes of *quo warranto*,　　[*263
(18) 6 Edw. I. c. 1, and 18 Edw. I. st. 2;(t) but since those justices
have given place to the king's temporary commissioners of assize, the judges
on the several circuits, this branch of the statutes has lost its effect;(u) and
writs of *quo warranto* (if brought at all) must now be prosecuted and determined before the king's justices at Westminster. And in case of judgment for
the defendant, he shall have an allowance of his franchise; but in case of
judgment for the king, for that the party is entitled to no such franchise, or
hath disused or abused it, the franchise is either seised into the king's hands,
to be granted out again to whomever he shall please; or, if it be not such a
franchise as may subsist in the hands of the crown, there is merely judgment
of *ouster*, to turn out the party who usurped it.(w)

The judgment on a writ of *quo warranto* (being in the nature of a writ of
right) is final and conclusive even against the crown.(x) Which, together
with the length of its process, probably occasioned that disuse into which it
is now fallen, and introduced a more modern method of prosecution, by
information filed in the court of king's bench by the attorney-general, in the
nature of a writ of *quo warranto;* wherein the process is speedier, and the
judgment not quite so decisive. This is properly a criminal method of
prosecution, as well to punish the usurper by a fine for the usurpation of the
franchise, as to oust him, or seise it for the crown; but hath long been applied
to the mere purposes of trying the civil right, seising the franchise, or oust-
ing the wrongful possessor; the fine being nominal only.(19)

During the violent proceedings that took place in the latter end of the reign
of king Charles the Second, it was, among other things, thought expedient
to new-model most of the corporation-towns in the kingdom; for
which purpose many of those *bodies were persuaded to surrender　　[*264
their charters, and informations in the nature of *quo warranto* were
brought against others, upon a supposed, or frequently a real, forfeiture of
their franchises by neglect or abuse of them. And the consequence was, that
the liberties of most of them were seised into the hands of the king, who

---

(s) Old Nat. Brev. fol. 107, edit. 1534..
(t) 2 Inst. 498. Rast. Entr. 540.
(u) 2 Inst. 498.

(w) Cro. Jac. 259. 1 Show. 280.
(x) 1 Sid. 86. 2 Show. 47. 12 Mod. 225.

---

him who claims or usurps *any* office, a limitation is implied by the fact that it is in the
nature of a writ of right *for the king.* Upon this principle, when an application was
made for a quo warranto information to try the validity of an election to the office of
church-warden, lord Kenyon said that this was not a usurpation on the rights or prerogatives of the crown, for which only the old writ of quo warranto lay; and that an information in nature of a quo warranto could only be granted in such cases. 4 T. R. 381. See
also 2 Stra. 1196. Bott. pl. 107. And the writ was also refused in a case of forfeiture of
a recorder's place. 2 Stra. 819,—CHITTY.

State *v.* Graham, 13 Kan. 137, 143 (1874). Under the New York statutes an action will
not lie against a mere claimant to an office. Lindsay *v.* People, 1 Idaho, 452 (1872).
An information in the nature of a quo warranto will not lie against a municipal corporation to enforce the performance of a duty imposed upon it by law. Atty.-Gen. *v.* Salem,
103 Mass. 138, 139 (1869). Sec. 6, ch. 160, R. S. of Wisconsin gives a new proceeding by
private parties in the name of the state without use of the attorney-general's name or
office, in cases of local office and in all cases in which that officer refuses to act. State *v.*
Baker. State *v.* Kromer, 38 Wis. 71, 82 (1875).

(18) [By what warrant.]

(19) Minck *v.* People, 6 Ill. App. 127, 128 (1880). Donnelly *v.* People, 11 Ill. 552, 553
(1850). State *v.* Gleason, 12 Fla. 190, 219 (1869). Atty. Gen. *v.* Delaware and Bound
Brook R. R. Co., 9 N. J. 282, 286 (1876). State *v.* Hardie, 1 N. C. (Ire.) 42, 48 (1840).
A suit by information in the nature of a *quo warranto* prosecuted in the name of the
state of Texas against a person charged with unlawfully holding the office of mayor of
Austin is a civil proceeding. Texas *v.* De Gress, 53 Tex. 387, 396 (1880).

granted them fresh charters, with such alterations as were thought expedient; and, during their state of anarchy, the crown named all their magistrates. This exertion of power, though perhaps *in summo jure*(20) it was for the most part strictly legal, gave a great and just alarm; the new-modeling of all corporations being a very large stride towards establishing arbitrary power; and therefore it was thought necessary at the revolution to bridle this branch of the prerogative, at least so far as regarded the metropolis, by statute 2 W. and M. c. 8, which enacts, that the franchises of the city of London shall never hereafter be seised or forejudged for any forfeiture or misdemeanor whatsoever.(21)

This proceeding is, however, now applied to the decision of corporation disputes between party and party, without any intervention of the prerogative, by virtue of the statute 9 Anne, c. 20, which permits an information in nature of *quo warranto* to be brought with leave of the court, at the relation of any person desiring to prosecute the same, (who is then styled the *relator*,) against any person usurping, intruding into, or unlawfully holding any franchise or office in any city, borough, or town corporate; provides for its speedy determination; and directs that, if the defendant be convicted, judgment of ouster (as well as a fine) may be given against him, and that the relator shall pay or receive costs according to the event of the suit.(22.)·

6. The writ of *mandamus*(*y*)(23) is also made, by the same statute 9 Anne, c. 20, a most full and effectual remedy, in the first place, for refusal of admission where a person is entitled to an office or place in any such corporation;

(*y*) See page 110.

---

(20) [In strict right.]

(21) Farrington *v*. Tennessee, 95 U. S. 679, 684 (1877.) Myers on Vested Rights, 865.

(22) This statute, with regard to costs, extends only to cases where the title of a person to be a corporate officer—as mayor, bailiff, or freeman—is in question; but an information to try the right of holding a court is not within it, but stands upon the common law only, and, being a prosecution in the name of the king, no costs are given. 1 Burr. 402. The court of King's Bench, having a discretionary power of granting information in the nature of quo warranto, had long ago established a general rule to guide their discretion,—viz, not to allow in any case an information in the nature of quo warranto against any person who had been twenty years in the possession of his franchise, (see 4 Burr. 1962;) but, having reason to consider this too extensive a limit, they resolved upon a new rule,—viz, not to allow such an information against any person who had been six years in possession. 4 T. R. 284. The legislature, however, thinking this too sudden a change in the practice of the court, and because it did not extend to informations filed by the attorney-general, enacted, by 32 Geo. III. c. 58, that to any information in the nature of quo warranto, for the exercise of any corporate office or franchise, the defendant might plead that he had been in possession of, or had executed, the office for six years or more. And, by s. 3, no defendant shall be affected by any defect in the title of the person from whom he derived his right and title, if that person had been in the undisturbed exercise of his office or franchise six years previous to the filing of the information. A title to one office which is a qualification to hold another is not within this clause. 2 M. & S. 71.—CHITTY.

But, by statute 32 Geo. III. c. 58, no member or officer of any town corporate shall be disturbed in the enjoyment of his office or franchise which he has enjoyed for six years, whether the information in the nature of a quo warranto is exhibited by leave of the court or on behalf of the crown by virtue of the royal prerogative. And, by the recent statutes 7 W. IV. and 1 Vict. c. 78 and 6 & 7 Vict. c. 89, the application to the court for the purpose of calling upon any person to show by what warrant he claims to exercise the office of mayor, alderman, or burgess, in any borough within the Municipal Corporation Act, must be made within twelve months after the election of the defendant, or the time at which he became disqualified.—STEWART.

See Paris *v*. Conture etc., 10 Quebec L. Rep. 1, 13 (1883). Dew *v*. The Judges of Sweet Springs, 3 Va. (H. & M.) 1, 36 (1808). Bissell *v*. M. S. & N. R. R. Co., 22 N. Y. App. 258, 268 (1860). Butler *v*. Callahan, 4 N. Dak. 481, 487 (1895). The proceeding by information in the nature of a *quo warranto* is essentially a civil proceeding, and the pleadings in it are as much subject to amendment as they are in other civil actions. It is criminal only in form. Florida *v*. Gleason, 12 Fla. 190 (1868-9).

(23) [We command.]

and, secondly, for wrongful removal, when a person is legally possessed. *These are injuries, for which though redress for the party [*265 interested may be had by assize, or other means, yet as the franchises concern the public, and may affect the administration of justice, this prerogative writ also issues from the court of king's bench; commanding, upon good cause shown to the court, the party complaining to be admitted or restored to his office. And the statute requires, that a return be immediately made to the first writ of *mandamus;* which return may be pleaded to or traversed by the prosecutor, and his antagonist may reply, take issue, or demur, and the same proceedings may be had, as if an action on the case had been brought, for making a false return; and, after judgment obtained for the prosecutor, he shall have a peremptory writ of *mandamus* to compel his admission or restitution; which latter (in case of an action) is effected by a writ of restitution.(*z*)   So that now the writ of *mandamus*, in cases within this statute, is in the nature of an action; whereupon the party applying and succeeding may be entitled to costs, in case it be the franchise of a citizen, burgess, or freeman;(*a*) and also, in general, a writ of error may be had thereupon.(*b*)(24)

(*z*) 11 Rep. 79.
(*a*) Stat. 12 Geo. III. c. 21.

(*b*) 1 P. Wms. 351.

---

(24) Besides the cases arising in corporations, writs of mandamus have been granted to admit prebendaries, (Stra. 159,) an apparitor-general, (Stra. 897,) parish clerks, (Say, R. 159.   Cowp. 371,) and sextons. 2 Lev. 18.   1 Ventr. 143.   So to admit scavengers, etc., (ib. 2 T. R. 181;) to restore a schoolmaster of a grammar-school founded by the crown. Stra. 58.   So to restore a member of a university who had been improperly suspended from his degrees.   In like manner, a mandamus will lie to compel a dean and chapter to fill up a vacancy among canons-residentiary, (1 T. R. 652;) so to the ecclesiastical court, (1 Ventr. 115;) so to grant the probate of a will to an executor. 1 Ventr. 335. So a mandamus lies to the judge of the prerogative court of Canterbury to grant administration to the husband of the wife's estate when the husband has done nothing to depart from his right.   Stra. 891, 1118.   A mandamus will lie to justices to nominate overseers of the poor, although the time mentioned in the 43 Eliz. has expired.   Stra. 1123.   So to appoint a surveyor of the highways where the justices had not appointed at the time mentioned in the statute 13 Geo. III. c. 78, (4 East, 132;) so to sign and allow a poor's rate, absolute in the first instance, (Say, R. 160;) so to admit a copyholder, directed to the lord of the manor, (2 T. R. 197, 484.   6 East, 431;) so also to the lord to hold and the burgesses to attend a court, to present the conveyances of burgage-tenements. 1 Wils. 283.   1 Bla. Rep. 60.   Bull. N. P. 200.
Where it does not lie.—It is a general rule that a mandamus does not lie unless the party applying has no other specific legal remedy. 1 T. R. 404. 3 T. R. 652. See Doug. 526. Thus, it does not lie to a bishop to license a curate of a curacy which had been twice augmented by queen Anne's bounty, where the right of appointing was claimed by two several parties and there had been cross-nominations, because the party had another specific remedy by *quare impedit* [Wherefore did he hinder].   So a mandamus does not lie to the governor and company of the Bank of England to transfer stock, because the party has his remedy by assumpsit, (Doug. 523;) nor to insert certain persons in a poor's rate, although the omission is alleged to have been, to prevent their having votes for members of parliament.   Stra. 1259.   The court will not award a mandamus for the licensing of a public house, (Stra. 881.   Stra. R. 217;) nor to compel admission to the degree of a barrister (Doug. 353) or doctor of civil law as an advocate of the court of arches, (8 East, 213,) (the only mode of appeal is to the twelve judges;) nor to compel any of the inns of court to admit a person as a student, or to assign reasons for refusing to admit him, (Wooler *v.* Society of Lincoln's Inn, King's Bench, Mich. T, 1825, 4 B. & C.   5 Dowl. & Ryl.;) nor for a fellow of a college, where there is a visitor; nor to the mayor and corporation of the city of London, to admit a person to the office of auditor who had served it three years successively, because contrary to the custom of the city, (1 T. R. 423;) nor to the college of physicians, to examine a doctor of physic who had been licensed in order to his being admitted a fellow of the college, (7 T. R. 282:) nor to a visitor where he is clearly acting under a visitatorial authority, (2 T. R. 345:) nor to *restore* a minister of an endowed dissenting meeting-house, for if he has been before regularly admitted he may try his right in an action for money had and received. 2 T. R. 198.   A mandamus is granted only for public persons and to compel the performance of public duties. Hence the court will not grant it to a trading-corporation at the instance of one of its members, to

This writ of *mandamus* may also be issued, in pursuance of the statute 11 Geo. I. c. 4, in case within the regular time no election shall be made of the mayor or other chief officer of any city, borough, or town corporate, or (being made) it shall afterwards become void; requiring the electors to proceed to election, and proper courts to be held for admitting and swearing in the magistrates so respectively chosen.(25)

We have now gone through the whole circle of civil injuries, and the redress which the laws of England have anxiously provided for each. In which the student cannot but observe that the main difficulty which attends their discussion arises from their great variety, which is apt at our first acquaintance to breed a confusion of ideas, and a kind of distraction

*266] in the memory: a difficulty not a little increased *by the very unmethodical arrangement in which they are delivered to us by our ancient writers, and the numerous terms of art in which the language of our ancestors has obscured them. Terms of art there will unavoidably be in all sciences; the easy conception and thorough comprehension of which must depend upon frequent and familiar use; and the more subdivided any branch of science is, the more terms must be used to express the nature of these several subdivisions, and mark out with sufficient precision the ideas they are meant to convey. But I trust that this difficulty, however great it may appear at first view, will shrink to nothing upon a nearer and more frequent approach, and indeed be rather advantageous than of any disservice, by imprinting on the student's mind a clear and distinct notion of the nature of these several remedies. And, such as it is, it arises principally from the excellence of our English laws; which adapt their redress exactly to the circumstances of the injury, and do not furnish one and the same action for different wrongs, which are impossible to be brought within one and the same description; whereby every man knows what satisfaction he is entitled to expect from the courts of justice, and as little as possible is left in the breast of the judges, whom the law appoints to administer and not to prescribe the remedy. And I may venture to affirm that there is hardly a possible injury, that can be offered either to the person or property of another, for which the party injured may not find a remedial writ, conceived in such terms as are properly and singularly adapted to his own particular grievance.

In the several personal actions which we have cursorily explained, as debt, trespass, detinue, action on the case, and the like, it is easy to observe how plain, perspicuous, and simple the remedy is, as chalked out by the ancient common law. In the methods prescribed for the recovery of landed and

---

compel the production of accounts to declare a dividend. 2 B. & A. 620. 5 B. & A. 899. The mode of burying the dead is a matter of ecclesiastical cognizance, and therefore, where the question was whether a parishioner had a right to be buried in a churchyard in an iron coffin, which was a new and unusual mode, the court refused a mandamus. 2 B. & A. 806 The court have no power to grant a mandamus to justices to compel them to come to a particular decision, as, to made an order of maintenance on a particular parish. The admission under a mandamus gives no right, but only a legal possession, to enable the party to assert his right, if he has any. Hence *non fuit electus* [He has not been chosen] has been holden not to be a good return to a mandamus to swear in a church-warden, (Stra. 894. 895,) because it is directed only to a ministerial officer, who is to do his duty, and no inconvenience can follow; for if the party has a right, he ought to be admitted; if he has not, the admission will do him no good. Wherever the officer is but ministerial, he is to execute his part, let the consequence be what it will. Stra. 895.—CHITTY. But the case of Collins v. The State, 8 Ind. 344, which is approved in Gulick v. New, 14 Ind. 93, is inconsistent with the proposition stated, and inaugurates a different practice, to this extent, that the courts will not aid, by mandamus, an officer illegally elected to get possession of the office to which he claims to be elected. Beal v. Ray, 17 Ind. 554, 558 (1861).

(25) Chumasero v. Potts, 2 Mass. 242, 262 (1875).

other permanent property, as the right is more intricate, the feodal or rather Norman remedy by real actions is somewhat more complex and difficult, and attended with some delays. And since, in order to obviate those difficulties and retrench those *delays, we have permitted the rights   [*267 of real property to be drawn into question in mixed or personal suits, we are (it must be owned) obliged to have recourse to such arbitrary fictions and expedients, that unless we had developed their principles, and traced out their progress and history, our present system of remedial jurisprudence (in respect of landed property) would appear the most intricate and unnatural that ever was adopted by a free and enlightened people.

But this intricacy of our legal process will be found, when attentively considered, to be one of those troublesome, but not dangerous, evils, which have their root in the frame of our constitution, and which therefore can never be cured without hazarding every thing that is dear to us. In absolute governments, when new arrangements of property and a gradual change of manners have destroyed the original ideas on which the laws were devised and established, the prince by his edict may promulge a new code, more suited to the present emergencies. But when laws are to be framed by popular assemblies, even of the representative kind, it is too herculean a task to begin the work of legislation afresh, and extract a new system from the discordant opinions of more than five hundred counsellors. A single legislator or an enterprising sovereign, a Solon or Lycurgus, a Justinian or a Frederick, may at any time form a concise, and perhaps a uniform, plan of justice: and evil betide that presumptuous subject who questions its wisdom or utility. But who that is acquainted with the difficulty of new-modeling any branch of our statute laws (though relating but to roads or to parish settlements) will conceive it ever feasible to alter any fundamental point of the common law, with all its appendages and consequents, and set up another rule in its stead? When therefore, by the gradual influence of foreign trade and domestic tranquillity, the spirit of our military tenures began to decay, and at length the whole structure was removed, the judges quickly perceived that the forms and delays of the old feodal actions (guarded with their several outworks of essoins, vouchers, aid-prayers, and a hundred other formidable intrenchments) were ill suited to that *more simple and commercial mode of   [*268 property which succeeded the former, and required a more speedy decision of right, to facilitate exchange and alienation. Yet they wisely avoided soliciting any great legislative revolution in the old-established forms, which might have been productive of consequences more numerous and extensive than the most penetrating genius could foresee; but left them as they were, to languish in obscurity and oblivion, and endeavored by a series of minute contrivances to accommodate such personal actions, as were then in use, to all the most useful purposes of remedial justice: and where, through the dread of innovation, they hesitated at going so far as perhaps their good sense would have prompted them, they left an opening for the more liberal and enterprising judges, who have sat in our courts of equity, to show them their error by supplying the omissions of the courts of law. And, since the new expedients have been refined by the practice of more than a century, and are sufficiently known and understood, they in general answer the purpose of doing speedy and substantial justice, much better than could now be effected by any great fundamental alterations. The only difficulty that attends them arises from their fictions and circuities: but, when once we have discovered the proper clew, that labyrinth is easily pervaded. Our system of remedial law resembles an old Gothic castle, erected in the days of chivalry, but fitted up for a modern inhabitant. The moated ramparts, the embattled towers, and the trophied halls, are magnificent and venerable, but useless, and therefore neglected. The inferior apartments, now accommodated to daily use, are cheerful and commodious, though their approaches may be winding and difficult.

In this part of our disquisitions I however thought it my duty to unfold, as far as intelligibly I could, the nature of these real actions, as well as of personal remedies. And this not only because they are still in force, still the law of the land, though obsolete and disused, and may perhaps, in their turn, *269] be hereafter, with some necessary corrections, called out again into common use; but also because, as a sensible *writer has well observed,(c) "whoever considers how great a coherence there is between the several parts of the law, and how much the reason of one case opens and depends upon that of another, will, I presume, be far from thinking any of the old learning useless, which will so much conduce to the perfect understanding of the modern." And, besides, I should have done great injustice to the founders of our legal constitution, had I led the student to imagine that the remedial instruments of our law were originally contrived in so complicated a form as we now present them to his view; had I, for instance, entirely passed over the direct and obvious remedies by assizes and writs of entry, and only laid before him the modern method of prosecuting a writ of ejectment.

CHAPTER XVIII.

OF THE PURSUIT OF REMEDIES BY ACTION; AND FIRST OF THE ORIGINAL WRIT.

*270]   *HAVING, under the head of *redress by suit in courts*, pointed out in the preceding pages, in the first place, the *nature* and several *species* of courts of justice, wherein remedies are administered for all sorts of private wrongs; and, in the second place, shown to which of these courts in particular application must be made for redress, according to the distinction of injuries, or, in other words, what wrongs are *cognizable* by one court, and what by another; I proceeded, under the title of *injuries cognizable by the courts of common law*, to define and explain the specific remedies by action provided for every possible degree of wrong or injury, as well such remedies as are dormant and out of use as those which are in every day's practice, apprehending that the reason of the one could never be clearly comprehended without some acquaintance with the other; and I am now, in the last place, to examine the *manner* in which these several remedies are *pursued* and applied by action in the courts of common law; to which I shall afterwards subjoin a brief account of the proceedings in courts of equity.

In treating of remedies by action at common law, I shall confine myself to the *modern* method of practice in our courts of judicature. For though I *271] thought it necessary to throw out a few observations on the nature of real actions, however *at present disused, in order to demonstrate the coherence and uniformity of our legal constitution, and that there was no injury so obstinate and inveterate but which might in the end be eradicated by some or other of those remedial writs; yet it would be too irksome a task to perplex both my readers and myself with explaining all the rules of proceeding in those obsolete actions, which are frequently mere positive establishments, *forma et figura judicii*,(1) and conduce very little to

(c) Hawk. Abr. Co. Litt. pref.

(1) [The form and appearance of judgment.]

1242

illustrate the reason and fundamental grounds of the law. Wherever I apprehend they may at all conduce to this end, I shall endeavor to hint at them incidentally.

What, therefore, the student may expect in this and the succeeding chapters is, an account of the method of proceeding in and prosecuting a suit upon any of the personal writs we have before spoken of, in the court of *common pleas* at Westminster, that being the court originally constituted for the prosecution of all civil actions. It is true that the courts of king's bench and exchequer, in order, without entrenching upon ancient forms, to extend their remedial influence to the necessities of modern times, have now obtained a concurrent jurisdiction and cognizance of very many civil suits; but as causes are therein conducted by much the same advocates and attorneys, and the several courts and their judges have an entire communication with each other, the methods and forms of proceeding are in all material respects the same in all of them. So that in giving an abstract or history(a) of the progress of a suit through the court of common pleas, we *shall   [*272 at the same time give a general account of the proceedings of the other two courts, taking notice, however, of any considerable difference in the local practice of each. And the same abstract will moreover afford us some general idea of the conduct of a cause in the inferior courts of common law, those in cities and boroughs, or in the court-baron, or hundred or county court; all which conform (as near as *may* be) to the example of the superior tribunals, to which their causes may probably be, in some stage or other, removed.

The most natural and perspicuous way of considering the subject before us will be (I apprehend) to pursue it in the order and method wherein the proceedings themselves follow each other, rather than to distract and subdivide it by any more logical analysis. The general, therefore, and orderly parts of a suit are these: 1. The original writ; 2. The process; 3. The pleadings; 4. The issue or demurrer; 5. The trial; 6. The judgment, and its incidents; 7. The proceeding in nature of appeals; 8. The execution.

First, then, of the *original*, or original writ;(3) which is the beginning or foundation of the suit. When a person hath received an injury, and thinks

---

(a) In deducing this history the student must not expect authorities to be constantly cited, as practical knowledge is not so much to be learned from any books of law as from experience and attendance on the courts. The compiler must therefore be frequently obliged to rely upon his own observations,—which in general he hath been studious to avoid where those of any other might be had. To accompany and illustrate these remarks, such gentlemen as are designed for the profession will find it necessary to peruse the books of *entries*, ancient and modern, which are transcripts of proceedings that have been had in some particular actions. A book or two of technical learning will also be found very convenient, from which a man of liberal education and tolerable understanding may glean *pro re nata* [For this business] as much as is sufficient for his purpose. These *books of practice*, as they are called, are all pretty much on a level in point of composition and solid instruction, so that that which bears the latest edition is usually the best. But Gilbert's History and Practice of the Court of Common Pleas is a book of a very different stamp; and though (like the rest of his posthumous works) it has suffered most grossly by ignorant or careless transcribers, yet it has traced out the reason of many parts of our modern practice, from the feodal institutions and the primitive construction of our courts, in a most clear and ingenious manner. (2)

---

(2) The more recent publications of Mr. Sergt. Sellon and Mr. Tidd, and those of Mr. Impey and Mr. Lee, now afford still more explicit information on the subject of Practice.—CHITTY.

(3) Before the passing the 6 Geo. IV. c. 96, one great object of proceeding by special original was to compel the defendant to bring a writ of error in parliament, if he intended to delay; but that act having restrained writs of error upon judgments, even before verdict, unless the defendant finds bail in error, proceedings are now more frequently by capias in the court of Common Pleas and by latitat in the King's Bench.—CHITTY.

Although a *scire facias* is in the nature of an original writ, in that the defendant may plead to it, yet otherwise it is considered to be a judicial, not an original writ, and, therefore, is not the commencement of the suit. Hopkins *v.* Howard, 12 Tex. 7–9 (1854). But this writ is not used now; the proceeding by summons has superseded it.

it worth his while to demand a satisfaction for it, he is to consider with himself, or take advice, what redress the law has given for that injury; and thereupon is to make application or suit to the crown, the fountain of all justice, for that particular specific remedy which he is determined or advised to pursue. As, for money due on bond, an action of *debt;* for goods detained without force, an action of *detinue* or *trover;* or, if taken with force, *273] an action of *trespass vi *et armis;* or to try the title of lands, a *writ of entry,* or action of trespass in *ejectment;* or for any consequential injury received, a special action *on the case.* To this end he is to sue out, or purchase by paying the stated fees, an *original,* or original writ, from the court of chancery, which is the *officina justitiæ,* the shop or mint of justice, wherein all the king's writs are framed.(4) It is a mandatory letter from the king, in parchment, sealed with his great seal,(b) and directed to the sheriff of the county wherein the injury is committed, or supposed so to be, requiring him to command the wrong-doer or party accused either to do justice to the complainant, or else to appear in court and answer the accusation against him. Whatever the sheriff does in pursuance of this writ, he must *return* or certify to the court of common pleas, together with the writ itself; which is the foundation of the jurisdiction of that court, being the king's warrant for the judges to proceed to the determination of the cause. For it was a maxim introduced by the Normans, that there should be no proceedings in common pleas before the king's justices without his original writ; because they held it unfit that those justices, being only the substitutes of the crown, should take cognizance of any thing but what was thus expressly referred to their judgment.(c) However, in small actions below the value of forty shillings, which are brought in the court-baron or county-court, no royal writ is necessary; but the foundation of such suits continues to be (as in the times of the Saxons) not by original *writ,* but by *plaint;*(d) that is, by a private memorial tendered in open court to the judge, wherein the party injured sets forth his cause of action; and the judge is bound of common right to administer justice therein, without any special mandate from the king. Now, indeed, even the royal writs are held to be demandable of common right, on paying the usual fees; for any delay in the granting them, or setting an unusual or exorbitant price upon them, would be a breach of *magna carta* c. 29, "*nulli vendemus, nulli negabimus aut differemus, justitiam vel rectum.*"(5)

*274]   *Original writs are either *optional* or *peremptory;* or, in the language of our lawyers, they are either a *præcipe,* or a *si te fecerit securum.*(e)(6) The *præcipe* is in the alternative, commanding the defendant to do the thing required, or show the reason wherefore he hath not done it.(f) The use of this writ is where something certain is demanded by the

(b) Finch, L. 237.
(c) Flet. *l.* 2, c. 34.
(d) Mirr. c. 2, § 3.

(e) Finch, L. 257.
(f) Append. No. III. § 1.

(4) But in personal actions the use of the original writ is abolished, by the statute 2 W. IV. c. 39, although, as it is still necessary in real actions, some account of it may be useful. In the old action of ejectment, which has been before described, but which is now also abolished, although its existence was supposed, it was in fact never sued out — STEWART. See Society for Propagating the Gospel *v.* Whitcomb, 2 N. H. 227, 230 (1820). This writ has been succeeded in practice by proceedings by summons. The substitution of a bankrupt's assignee as plaintiff in a suit is not to be regarded as the commencement of the suit, under the U. S. statute limiting the bringing of such suits to two years. C. & N. W. R. R. Co. *v.* Jenkins, 103 Ill. (Freeman) 588, 594 (1882).

(5) ["To no one will we sell, to none deny, to none delay either right or justice."] Show *v.* Dutcher, 19 Wend. (N. Y.) 216, 219 (1838). Yager *v.* Hannah, 6 Hill (N. Y.) 631, 634 (1844). See Womsley *v.* Cummins, 1 Ark. 125, 129 (1838), concerning the time when a plaintiff may terminate his suit.

(6) [If he gives you security.]

plaintiff, which it is incumbent on the defendant himself to perform; as, to restore the possession of land, to pay a certain liquidated debt, to perform a specific covenant, to render an account, and the like: in all which cases the writ is drawn up in the form of a *præcipe* or command, to do thus or show cause to the contrary; giving the defendant his choice, to redress the injury or stand the suit. The other species of original writs is called a *si fecerit te securum*, from the words of the writ; which directs the sheriff to cause the defendant to appear in court, without any option given him, provided the plaintiff gives the sheriff security effectually to prosecute his claim.(*g*) This writ is in use where nothing is specifically demanded, but only a satisfaction in general: to obtain which, and minister complete redress, the intervention of some judicature is necessary. Such are writs of trespass, or on the case, wherein no debt, or other specific thing is sued for in certain, but only damages to be assessed by a jury. For this end the defendant is immediately called upon to appear in court, provided the plaintiff gives good security of prosecuting his claim. Both species of writs are *tested*, or witnessed in the king's own name; "witness ourselves at Westminster," or wherever the chancery may be held.

The security here spoken of, to be given by the plaintiff for prosecuting his claim, is common to both writs, though it gives denomination only to the latter. The whole of it is at present become a mere matter of form; and John Doe and Richard Roe are always returned as the standing pledges for this purpose. The ancient use of them was to answer for the *plain- [*275 tiff, who in case he brought an action without cause, or failed in the prosecution of it when brought, was liable to an amercement from the crown for raising a false accusation; and so the form of judgment still is.(*h*) In like manner, as by the Gothic constitutions no person was permitted to lay a complaint against another "*nisi sub scriptura aut specificatione trium testium, quod actionem vellet persequi;*"(*i*)(7) and as by the laws of Sancho I., king of Portugal, damages were given against a plaintiff who prosecuted a groundless action.(*k*)

The day on which the defendant is ordered to appear in court, and on which the sheriff is to bring in the writ and report how far he has obeyed it, is called the *return* of the writ: it being then returned by him to the king's justices at Westminster. And it is always made returnable at the distance of at least fifteen days from the date or *teste*, that the defendant may have time to come up to Westminster, even from the most remote parts of the kingdom; and upon some day in one of the four *terms*, in which the court sits for the despatch of business.(8)

These terms are supposed by Mr. Selden(*l*) to have been instituted by William the Conqueror; but Sir Henry Spelman hath clearly and learnedly shown, that they were gradually formed from the canonical constitutions of the church; being indeed no other than those leisure seasons of the year which were not occupied by the great festivals or fasts, or which were not liable to the general avocations of rural business. Throughout all Christendom, in very early times, the whole year was one continual term for hearing and deciding causes. For the Christian magistrates, to distinguish themselves from the heathens, who were extremely superstitious in the observation of their *dies fasti et nefasti*,(9) went into a contrary extreme,

(*g*) Append. No. II. § 1.
(*h*) Finch. L. 189, 252.
(*i*) Stiernhook *de jure Goth. l.* 3, c. 7.

(*k*) Mod. Un. Hist. xxii. 45.
(*l*) Jan. Angl. l. 2, § 9.

---

(7) ["Unless under writing or the specification of three witnesses that he will prosecute the action."]
(8) See Dunbar and Vass *v.* Long's Adm'rs, 4 Va. (H. & M.) 212, 219 (1809).
(9) [Lawful and unlawful days.]

*276] and administered justice upon all days alike. *Till at length the church interposed and exempted certain holy seasons from being profaned by the tumult of forensic litigations. As, particularly, the time of Advent and Christmas, which gave rise to the winter vacation; the time of Lent and Easter, which created that in the spring; the time of Pentecost, which produced the third; and the long vacation between Midsummer and Michaelmas, which was allowed for the hay-time and harvest. All Sundays also, and some particular festivals, as the days of the purification, ascension, and some others, were included in the same prohibition; which was established by a canon of the church, A. D. 517, and was fortified by an imperial constitution of the younger Theodosius, comprised in the Theodosian code.(m)

Afterwards, when our own legal constitution came to be settled, the commencement and duration of our law-terms were appointed with an eye to those canonical prohibitions; and it was ordered by the laws of king Edward the Confessor,(n) that from advent to the octave of the epiphany, from *septuagesima* to the octave of Easter, from the ascension to the octave of Pentecost, and from three in the afternoon of all Saturdays till Monday morning, the peace of God and of holy church shall be kept throughout all the kingdom. And so extravagant was afterwards the regard that was paid to these holy times, that though the author of the Mirror(o) mentions only one vacation of any considerable length, containing the months of August and September, yet Britton is express,(p) that in the reign of king Edward the First no secular plea could be held, nor any man sworn on the evangelists,(q) in the times of Advent, Lent, Pentecost, harvest, and vintage, the days of the great litanies, and all solemn festivals. But he adds, that the bishops did nevertheless grant dispensations, (of which many are preserved in Rymer's *Fœdera*,)(r) that assizes and juries might be taken in some *277] of these holy seasons. And soon afterwards a general *dispensation was established by statute Westm. 1, 3 Edw. I. c. 51, which declares, that "by the assent of all the prelates, assizes of *novel disseisin*, *mort d'ancestor*, and *darrein presentment*(10) shall be taken in advent, septuagesima, and Lent; and that at the special request of the king to the bishops." The portions of time, that were not included within these prohibited seasons, fell naturally into a fourfold division, and, from some festival day that immediately preceded their commencement, were denominated the terms of St. Hilary, of Easter, of the Holy Trinity, and of St. Michael: which terms have been since regulated and abbreviated by several acts of parliament; particularly Trinity term by statute 32 Hen. VIII. c. 21, and Michaelmas term by statute 16 Car. I. c. 6, and again by statute 24 Geo. II. c. 48.(11)

There are in each of these terms stated days called *days in bank, dies in banco:* that is, days of appearance in the court of common bench. They are generally at the distance of about a week from each other, and have reference to some festival of the church.(12) On some one of these days in bank all original writs must be made returnable; and therefore they are generally called the *returns* of that term: whereof every term has more or less said by the Mirror(s) to have been originally fixed by king Alfred, but certainly

(m) Spelman of the Terms.
(n) C. 3, *de temporibus et diebus pacis.*
(o) C. 3, § 8.
(p) C. 53.

(q) See page 59.
(r) *Temp. Hen. III. passim.*
(s) C. 5, § 108.

(10) [Death of the ancestor, and the last presentation.]
(11) Michaelmas and Hilary are fixed terms, and invariably begin on the same day every year; but Easter and Trinity are movable, their commencement being regulated by the Feast of Easter. Hilary and Trinity are called *issuable* terms, being the terms after which the judges go their circuits for the trial of causes wherein issues have been previously joined.—CHITTY.
(12) Easter term has five return-days, the rest four. These are called *general* or *common*

settled as early as the statute of 51 Hen. III. st. 2. But though many of the return-days are fixed upon Sundays, yet the court never sits to receive these returns till the Monday after:(t) and therefore no proceedings can be held, or judgment can be given, or supposed to be given, on the Sunday.(u)

The first return in every term is, properly speaking, the first day in that term; as, for instance, the octave of St. Hilary, or the eighth day inclusive after the feast of that saint: which falling on the thirteenth of January, the octave therefore or first day of Hilary term is the twentieth of January. And thereon the court sits to take *essoigns*, or excuses, for such as *do not appear according to the summons of the writ: wherefore this 　[*278 is usually called the *essoign day* of the term.(13) But on every return-day in the term, the person summoned has three days of grace, beyond the day named in the writ, in which to make his appearance; and if he appears on the fourth day inclusive, *quarto die post*, it is sufficient.(14) For our sturdy ancestors held it beneath the condition of a freeman to appear, or to do any other act, at the precise time appointed. The feodal law therefore always allowed three distinct days of citation, before the defendant was adjudged contumacious for not appearing;(v) preserving in this respect the German custom, of which Tacitus thus speaks:(w) "*illud ex libertate vitium, quod non simul nec jussi conveniunt; sed et alter et tertius dies cunctatione coëuntium absumitur.*"(15) And a similar indulgence prevailed in the Gothic constitution: "*illud enim nimiæ libertatis indicium, concessa toties impunitas non parendi; nec enim trinis judicii concessibus pænam perditæ causæ contumax meruit.*"(x)(16) Therefore, at the beginning of each term, the court does not usually(y) sit for despatch of business till the *fourth* or *appearance* day, as in Hilary term on the twenty-third of January;(17) and in Trinity term, by statute 32 Hen. VIII. c. 21, not till the *fifth* day, the *fourth* happening on the great popish festival of *Corpus Christi*;(z) which

<hr/>

(t) Registr. 19. Salk. 627. 6 Mod. 250.
(u) 1 Jon. 156. Swann & Broome, B. R. Mich. 5 Geo. III. *et in Dom Proc.* 1766.
(v) Feud. *l.* 2, *t.* 22.
(w) *De Mor. Germ.* c. 11.
(x) Stiernhook *de jure Goth. l.* 1, c. 6.
(y) See 1 Bulstr. 35.
(z) See Spelman on the Terms, ch. 17. Note, that if the Feast of St. John the Baptist, or midsummer-day, falls on the morrow of *Corpus Christi* day, (as it

did A. D. 1614, 1698, and 1709, and will again A. D. 1791,) Trinity full term then *commences*, and the courts sit on that day, though in other years it is no juridical day. Yet in 1702, 1713, and 1724, when midsummer-day fell upon what was regularly the *last* day of the term, the courts did not then sit, but it was regarded like a Sunday, and the term was prolonged to the twenty-fifth of June. Rot. C. B. Bunb. 176.

<hr/>

return-days; all the others are *particular* or *special* return-days.—CHITTY. See McAvoy v. Trustees, 38 N. J. Eq. 420, 421 (1884).

(13) At the present day, no essoign is allowed in any personal action whatever, even though the defendant be a peer or member of parliament. See 2 Term R. 16. 16 East, 7 (a.)—CHITTY.

(14) But the appearance need not be entered until eight days after the *quarto die post* [The fourth day after]. 3 Bar. & Cres. 110.—CHITTY.

(15) ["There is this fault resulting from their liberty that they come not together at the time appointed, but a second and a third day are lost by the delay of those who are to assemble."]

(16) ["For the impunity with which they so often neglected to appear was a sign of their excessive liberty; nor were the contumacious punished by losing their cause, as three days' grace was allowed."]

(17) Michaelmas Term always begins on the 6th of November and ends on the 28th of the same month. Hilary Term always begins on the 23d of January and ends on the 12th of February,—unless either of those four days falls on a Sunday, and then the term begins or ends on the day following. Easter Term begins always on the Wednesday fortnight after Easter Sunday, and ends on the Monday three weeks afterwards. Trinity Term begins always on the Friday after Trinity Sunday, and ends on the Wednesday fortnight after it begins. 1 Cromp. Prac. 1. Tidd, 8th ed. 101, 102.—CHRISTIAN.

By the 11 Geo. IV. and 1 W. IV. c. 70, s. 6, amended by 1 W. IV. sess. 2, c. 3, s. 2, it is enacted that Hilary Term shall begin on the 11th and end on the 31st day of January; Easter Term shall begin on the 15th day of April and end on the 8th day of May; Trinity Term shall begin on the 22d day of May and end on the 12th day of June; and

days are therefore called and set down in the almanacs as the first days of the term, and the court also sits till the *quarto die post* or appearance-day of the last return, which is therefore the end, of each of them.(18)

CHAPTER XIX.

OF PROCESS.

*279]   *THE next step for carrying on the suit, after suing out the original, is called the *process;* being the means of compelling the defendant to appear in court. This is sometimes called *original* process, being founded upon the original writ; and also to distinguish it from *mesne* or intermediate process which issues, pending the suit, upon some collateral interlocutory matter; as to summon juries, witnesses, and the like.(*a*) *Mesne* process is also sometimes put in contradistinction to *final* process, or process *of execution;* and then it signifies all such process as intervenes between the beginning and end of a suit.

But process, as we are now to consider it, is the method taken by the law to compel a compliance with the original writ, of which the primary step is by giving the party notice to obey it.(1) This notice is given upon all real *præcipes,* and also upon all personal writs for injuries not against the peace, by *summons,* which is a warning to appear in court at the return of the original writ, given to the defendant by two of the sheriff's messengers, called *summoners,* either in person or left at his house or land(*b*) in like manner as in the civil law the first process is by personal citation, *in jus vocando.*(*c*)(2) This warning on the land is given, in real actions, by erecting a white stick or wand on the defendant's ground,(*d*) (which *280] stick or wand among the northern nations is called the *baculus *nunciatorius;*)(*e*)(3) and by statute 31 Eliz. c. 3., the notice must also be proclaimed on some Sunday before the door of the parish church.

(*a*) Finch. L. 436.
(*b*) Ibid. 344, 352.
(*c*) Ff. 2, 4, 1.

(*d*) Dalt. of Sher. c. 31.
(*e*) Stiernh. *de jure Sueon. l.* 1, c. 6.

Michaelmas Term shall begin on the 2d and end on the 25th day of November; so that there is now no uncertainty in this matter.—STEWART.

(18) [Fourth day after.] But these rules are now altered, and the whole law on this subject much simplified, by the statute 11 Geo. IV., and 1 W. IV. c. 70, s. 6, by which it is enacted that the first *essoign* or general return-day, for every term, shall be the fourth day before the day of the commencement of the term, both days being included in the computation; the second *essoign* day shall be the fifth day of the term; the third shall be the fifteenth day of the term,—the first day of the term being already included in the computation.

Until lately, matters of law were disposed of in the courts during term,—only the judges, indeed, in their chambers exercise an ancillary jurisdiction; but their orders are not acts of the court, and if disobeyed can only be enforced by turning them into rules of court, and then obtaining an attachment, which can only be had during term. It is true that great part of the vacation is occupied in the trial of causes at the sittings and assizes; but these trials are not supposed to take place before the court, but before the individual judge who tries them. In consequence, however, of the press of business during term, the courts have now received the power of appointing sittings in banc, to be held during the vacation. 1 & 2 Vict. c. 32.—STEWART.

But *essoigns* have been practically abolished, (Price *v.* Hayes, 1 Dowl. 418;) and the sittings of the courts are now exclusively on the days of the term, or on such days after term as may be fixed for sittings *in banco* [In banc].—KERR.

(1) Dorman *v.* Bayley, 10 Minn. 383, 384 (1865). Hanna *v.* Russell, 12 Minn. 80, 86 (1868). See also Regina *v.* O'Rourke, 32 Upp. Can. C. P. 388, 405 (1882). Alderson on Judicial Writs and Process, 12.

(2) [By citing to justice.] See Baldwin *v.* McClelland, 50 Ill. App. 645, 660 (1893).

(3) [The nontiatory staff.]

If the defendant disobeys this verbal monition, the next process is by writ of *attachment* or *pone*, so called from the words of the writ,(*f*) "*pone per vadium et salvos plegios*, put by gage and safe pledges A. B. the defendant, etc.'' This is a writ not issuing out of chancery, but out of the court of common pleas, being grounded on the non-appearance of the defendant at the return of the original writ; and thereby the sheriff is commanded to attach him, by taking *gage*, that is, certain of his goods, which he shall forfeit if he doth not appear;(*g*) or by making him find *safe pledges* or sureties who shall be amerced in case of his non-appearance.(*h*) This is also the first and immediate process, without any previous summons, upon actions of trespass *vi et armis*, or for other injuries, which, though not forcible, are yet trespasses against the peace, as *deceit* and *conspiracy;*(*i*) where the violence of the wrong requires a more speedy remedy, and therefore the original writ commands the defendant to be at once attached, without any precedent warning.(*j*)(4)

If, after *attachment*, the defendant neglects to appear, he not only forfeits this security, but is moreover to be further compelled by writ of *distringas*(*k*) or *distress infinite;* which is a subsequent process issuing from the court of common pleas, commanding the sheriff to distrain the defendant from time to time, and continually afterwards by taking his goods and the profits of his lands, which are called *issues*, and which by the common law be forfeits to the king if he doth not appear.(*l*) But now the issues may be sold, if the court shall so direct, in order to defray the reasonable costs of the plaintiff.(*m*)(5) In like *manner, by the civil law, if the defendant   [*281

(*f*) Appendix, No. III. § 2.   (*j*) Appendix, No. II. § 1.
(*g*) Finch, L. 345. Lord Raym. 278.   (*k*) Append. No. III. § 2.
(*h*) Dalt. of Sher. c. 32.   (*l*) Finch, L. 325.
(*i*) Finch, L. 305, 352.   (*m*) Stat. 10 Geo. III. c. 50.

(4) Upon this writ the sheriff cannot justify entering the defendant's house and continuing there till the defendant pay him a sum of money for surety for his appearance. 6 T. R. 137.—CHITTY. See Fife & Co. *v.* Clark, 3 S. C. 347, 358 (1825).

A considerable change was made by stat. 2 W. IV. c. 39 in the mode of commencing personal actions. In these the use of the original writ was abolished, and the process in all such actions, in cases where it was not intended to hold the defendant to bail or to proceed against a member of parliament, according to the provisions of the bankrupt-laws, it was enacted, should be according to the form contained in a schedule to the act, and which process was thenceforth to issue from either of the superior courts, and to be called a writ of summons. In every such writ and copy thereof the place and county of the residence or supposed residence of the party defendant was to be mentioned, and every such writ was to be served in the manner heretofore and in the county therein mentioned; and the person serving the same was required to endorse on the writ the day of the month and week of the service thereof. The provisions as to writs of summons of the statute 2 W. IV. c. 39 were extended, by stat. 1 & 2 Vict. c. 110, to all personal actions in her majesty's superior courts of law at Westminster; but the process or writ of summons in personal actions is now regulated by "The Common-Law Procedure Act, 1852," which provides a form of writ similar to that given by the statute 2 W. IV. c. 49, except that no *county* need be mentioned therein, while it is specially provided that the defendant may be served in any county. The writ is directed to the defendant, whom it commands that within eight days after the service of the writ on him, inclusive of the day of such service, he do cause an appearance to be entered for him in the court in which the action is brought, in an action at the suit of the plaintiff, and requires the defendant to take notice that in default of his so doing the plaintiff may proceed to judgment and execution. The writ is *teste'd, i. e.*, witnessed in the name of the chief-justice or chief-baron, or, in case of vacancy, of a senior puisne judge of the court out of which it issues, and dated on the day on which it issued. A memorandum is subscribed to it, directing its execution within six months from the day of its date, after which period it ceases to be of force unless renewed. The defendant may apply to set it aside if served after the six months; if it cannot be served within that period, the plaintiff may have it renewed from time to time, until service be effected.—STEWART.

(5) Now, by 51 Geo. III. c. 124, s. 2, continued by 57 Geo. III. c. 101, a *distringas* cannot be issued; but at the foot of the summons or attachment notice as therein directed is to be given to defendant to appear, or, in default of an appearance, that plaintiff will enter one for him, and proceed thereon as if he had appeared. If, however, the summons

absconds, so that the citation is of no effect, "*mittitur adversarius in posses-sionem bonorum ejus.*"(*n*)(6)

And here, by the common as well as the civil law, the process ended in case of injuries without force; the defendant, if he had any substance, being gradually stripped of it all by repeated distresses, till he rendered obedience to the king's writ; and, if he had no substance, the law held him incapable of making satisfaction, and therefore looked upon all further process as nugatory. And besides, upon feodal principles, the person of a feudatory was not liable to be attached for injuries merely civil, lest thereby his lord should be deprived of his personal services. But, in case of injury accompanied with force, the law, to punish the breach of the peace, and prevent its disturbance for the future, provided also a process against the defendant's *person* in case he neglected to appear upon the former process of attachment, or had no substance whereby to be attached; subjecting his body to imprisonment by the writ of *capias ad respondendum.*(*o*)(7) But this immunity of the defendant's person, in case of peaceable though fraudulent injuries, producing great contempt of the law in indigent wrong-doers, a *capias* was also allowed to arrest the person, in actions of *account*, though no breach of the peace be suggested, by the statutes of Marlberge, 52 Hen. III. c. 23, and Westm. 2, 13 Edw. I. c. 11, in actions of *debt* and *detinue*, by statute 25 Edw. III. c. 17, and in all actions *on the case*, by statute 19 Hen. VII. c. 9. Before which last statute a practice had been introduced of commencing the suit by bringing an original writ of trespass *quare clausum fregit*,(8) for breaking the plaintiff's close *vi et armis;* which by the old common law subjected the defendant's person to be arrested by writ of *capias:* and then, afterwards, by connivance of the court, the plaintiff might proceed to prosecute for any other less forcible injury. This practice (through custom rather than necessity, and for saving some trouble and expense, in suing out a special *282] original *adapted to the particular injury) still continues in almost all cases, except in actions of debt; though now, by virtue of the statutes above cited and others, a *capias* might be had upon almost every species of complaint.

If therefore the defendant being summoned or attached makes default, and neglects to appear; or if the sheriff returns a *nihil*, or that the defendant

(*n*) *FJ.* 2, 4, 19.　　　　　(*o*) 3 Rep. 12.

---

or attachment cannot be personally served on defendant, and it be left for him at his house or place of abode, the court or a judge in vacation may grant leave to sue out a *distringas*, with a notice thereon as pointed out in the act, and plaintiff may levy 40s.; and if defendant still make default in appearing, an appearance may be entered for him, and plaintiff may proceed as usual. These acts have expired.

These provisions seem to extend to the process by *distringas* in the exchequer. 5 Taunt. 71, a.; but see 3 Price, 263, 266. 5 Price, 522, 639. They do not extend to persons having privilege of parliament, nor to the process by attachment on a *justicies* in a county palatine. 5 Taunt. 69.—CHITTY.

The proceeding by *distringas* and outlawry is abolished by the "Common-Law Procedure Act, 1852;" and now, if the defendant keeps out of the way, or personal service of the writ cannot be effected, the plaintiff must still use reasonable efforts to serve the defendant; and upon an affidavit showing such efforts to have been made, and either that the writ has come to the defendant's knowledge, or that he wilfully evades service of it, and that he has not appeared to the writ, the plaintiff may obtain an order from the court or a judge authorizing him to proceed as if personal service had been effected. —STEWART. See Ward *v.* Vance, 3 Pr. Cas. Canada, 130, 132 (1863). In the New England states, property attached remains in the custody of the law until after an appearance and until final judgment. Beardsley *v.* Beecher, 47 Conn. 408, 414 (1879).

(6) ["His adversary is put into possession of his goods."] See Poll. and Mait. Hist. of Eng. Law, vol. II, p. 592.

(7) [That you take him to answer.]

(8) [Why he hath broken his close with force and arms.]

hath nothing whereby he may be summoned, attached, or distrained; the *capias* now usually issues:(*p*) being a writ commanding the sheriff to *take* the body of the defendant if he may be found in his bailiwick or county, and him safely to keep, so that he may have him in court on the day of the return, to answer to the plaintiff of a plea of debt or trespass, etc., as the case may be. This writ, and all others subsequent to the original writ, not issuing out of chancery, but from the court into which the original was returnable, and being grounded on what has passed in that court in consequence of the sheriff's return, are called *judicial*, not *original* writs; they issue under the private seal of that court, and not under the great seal of England; and are *teste'd*, not in the king's name, but in that of the chief (or, if there be no chief, of the senior) justice only. And these several writs, being grounded on the sheriff's return, must respectively bear date the same day on which the writ immediately preceding was returnable.(*q*)

This is the regular and ordinary method of process. But it is now usual in practice to sue out the *capias* in the first instance, upon a supposed return of the sheriff; especially if it be suspected that the defendant, upon notice of the action, will abscond; and afterwards a fictitious original is drawn up, if the party is called upon so to do, with a proper return thereupon, in order to give the proceedings a color of regularity. When this *capias* is delivered to the sheriff, he by his under-sheriff grants a warrant to his inferior officers or bailiffs, to execute it on the defendant. And, if the sheriff of Oxfordshire (in which county the injury is supposed to be committed and the action is laid) cannot find the defendant in his jurisdiction, *he returns that   [*283 he is not found, *non est inventus*,(10) in his bailiwick; whereupon another writ issues, called a *testatum capias*,(*q*) directed to the sheriff of the county where the defendant is supposed to reside, as of Berkshire, reciting the former writ, and that it is *testified*, *testatum est*, that the defendant lurks or wanders in *his* bailiwick, wherefore he is commanded to take him, as in the former *capias*. But here also, when the action is brought in one county and the defendant lives in another, it is usual, for saving trouble, time, and expense, to make out a *testatum capias* at the first; supposing not only an original, but also a former *capias*, to have been granted, which in fact never was. And this fiction, being beneficial to all parties, is readily acquiesced in and is now become the settled practice; being one among many instances to illustrate that maxim of law, that *in fictione juris consistit æquitas*.(11)

But where a defendant absconds, and the plaintiff would proceed to an outlawry against him, an original writ must then be sued out regularly, and after that a *capias*.(12) And if the sheriff cannot find the defendant upon the first

<hr>

(*p*) Append. No. III. § 2.   (*q*) Ibid.

<hr>

(9) Or rather on the quarto die post [Fourth day after], and then only where the plaintiff means to proceed to outlawry, in which case there must be fifteen days at least between the *teste* and the return of each writ, (Trye, 60. 2 Wils. 117;) but the cursitor will expedite the process. Dyer, 175. Tidd, 8 ed. 103. Unless the plaintiff mean to proceed to outlawry, the *capias* may be *teste'd* before the original, and even before the cause of action accrued, provided it be actually taken out afterwards. See Tidd, 8 ed. 125. 3 Wils. 454.—CHITTY.

(10) [That he is not found.] See Chickering v. Failes, 26 Ill. 507, 517 (1861). Blackburn v. Sweet, 38 Wisc. 578, 582 (1875).

(11) [All fiction of law is founded in equity.] By stat. 1 & 2 Vict. c. 110, arrest on mesne process in civil actions is almost entirely abolished. Where it can be shown to the satisfaction of a judge of one of the superior courts that a plaintiff has a cause of action against a defendant to the amount of 20*l*. or upwards, or has sustained damage to that amount, and that there is probable cause for believing that the defendant is about to quit England unless he shall be apprehended, the judge may direct that such defendant may be held to bail, and that a writ or writs of *capias* may be sued out.—STEWART. See U. S. *v.* Mundell, 6 Call. (Va.) 245, 250 (1795). [*Testatum capias*—That you take the person testified (or to have been proceeded) against elsewhere.]

(12) And if in a joint action against several defendants one of them keep out of the way, the plaintiff may have a writ of *exigi facias* [That you cause to be exacted or de-

writ of *capias*, and return a *non est inventus*, there issues out an *alias* writ, and after that a *pluries*, to the same effect as the former;(*r*) only after these words, "we command you," this clause is inserted, "as we have *formerly*," or, "as we have *often* commanded you:"—"*sicut* alias," or "*sicut* pluries, *præcepimus*." And, if a *non est inventus* is returned upon all of them, then a writ of *exigent* or *exigi facias*(13) may be sued out,(*s*) which requires the sheriff to cause the defendant to be proclaimed, required, or exacted, in five county courts successively, to render himself; and if he does, then to take him as in a *capias;* but if he does not appear, and is returned *quinto exactus*,(14) he shall then be outlawed by the coroners of the county. Also by statutes 6 Hen. VIII. c. 4, and 31 Eliz. c. 3, whether the defendant dwells within the same or another county than that wherein the *exigent* is sued out, *a *writ of proclamation*(*t*) shall issue out at the same time with

*284]

the *exigent*, commanding the sheriff of the county, wherein the defendant dwells, to make three proclamations thereof in places the most notorious, and most likely to come to his knowledge, a month before the outlawry shall take place. Such *outlawry* is putting a man out of the protection of the law, so that he is incapable to bring an action for redress of injuries; and it is also attended with a forfeiture of all one's goods and chattels to the king. And therefore, till some time after the conquest, no man could be outlawed but for felony; but in Bracton's time, and somewhat earlier, process of outlawry was ordained to lie in all actions for trespasses *vi et armis*.(*u*)(15) And since his days, by a variety of statutes, (the same which allow the writ of *capias* before mentioned,) process of outlawry doth lie in divers actions that are merely civil; provided they be commenced by original and not by bill.(*v*) If after outlawry the defendant appears publicly, he may be arrested by a writ of *capias utlagatum*,(*w*)(16) and committed till the outlawry be

(*r*) Append. No. III. § 2.
(*s*) Ibid.
(*t*) Ibid.

(*u*) Co. Litt. 128.
(*v*) 1 Sid. 159.
(*w*) Append. No. III. § 2.

manded] against that defendant, (Trye, 155,) and must proceed to outlawry against him before he can go on against the others. 1 Stra. 473. 1 Wils. 78. 1 Bla. Rep. 20. Tidd, 8 ed. 126.

If the defendant be a woman, the proceeding is called a waiver. Litt. 186. Co. Litt. 122, b. An infant under twelve years cannot be outlawed. Co. Litt. 128, a.—CHITTY. See 1 Treadway Const. Rep. (S. C.) 157, 159 (1812).

(13) [That you cause to be required.]

(14) [Required for the fifth time.] See Hahn *v.* Kelly, 34 Cal. 391, 418 (1868). It is not given for equitable relief against a judgment by default on publication in an action for taxes in arrears, that the defendant, a non-resident, had not actual notice of the action. Stevenson *v.* Howard, 14 Mo. App. 252 (1883). As to notice by proclamation not being of statutory origin see Essig *v.* Lower, 120 Ind. 239, 246 (1889).

(15) [With force and arms.] Mason *v.* Massinger & May, 17 Ia. 261, 267 (1864). In Pennsylvania there has never been any process of outlawry in civil cases. Coleman's Appeal, 75 Pa. 441, 456 (1874).

(16) [That you take the outlaw.] Upon a special *capias utlagatum*, the sheriff is commanded to summon a jury to appraise the chattels and value the lands, etc., of the outlaw. The sheriff then takes possession of the chattels and of the profits of the land, etc., and returns the writ. Upon a transcript of the proceedings being returned to the exchequer, there issues to the sheriff a *venditioni exponas* [That you expose for sale] to all the goods, a *scire facias* [That you make known] to recover the debts, and a *levari facias* [That you cause to be levied] to levy the issues and profits of the lands extended. The money raised under these writs belongs to the crown; but the plaintiff, either by application to the court of exchequer or by petition to the lords of the treasury, according to circumstances, may have it paid to him, and may obtain a grant of the king's right to levy the profits of the land extended. See Tidd's Practice, 137, 138. Should the outlawry, however, be reversed, the property of the outlaw, if in the king's hands, shall be restored to him by writ of *amoveas manus* [That you remove the hand], etc.—ARCHBOLD. Outlawry is a judicial proceeding and cannot be consummated by legislative enactment. Ibid. In Alabama the term outlaw as used in the act of December 28, 1868, signifies a person who belongs to a secret organization, the members of which disguise themselves to avoid identification in their commission of crime. Dale County *v.* Gunter, 46 Ala. 118, 138 (1871).

reversed. Which reversal may be had by the defendant's appearing personally in court or by attorney,(x) (though in the king's bench he could not appear by attorney,(y) till permitted by statute 4 & 5 W. and M. c. 18;) and any plausible cause, however slight, will in general be sufficient to reverse it, it being considered only as a process to compel an appearance. But then the defendant must pay full costs, and put the plaintiff in the same condition as if he had appeared before the writ of *exigi facias* was awarded.(17)

Such is the first process in the court of *common pleas*. In the *king's bench* they *may* also (and frequently *do*) proceed in certain causes, particularly in actions of ejectment and trespass, by *original* writ, with *attachment* and *capias* thereon;(z) returnable, not at Westminster, where the common pleas are now fixed in consequence of *magna carta*, but "*ubicunque fuerimus in Anglia*," wheresoever the king shall then be in *England;   [*285 the king's bench being removable into any part of England at the pleasure and discretion of the crown. But the more usual method of proceeding therein is without any original, but by a peculiar species of process entitled a *bill of Middlesex:* and therefore so entitled, because the court now sits in that county; for if it sat in *Kent*, it would then be a *bill of Kent*.(a) For though, as the justices of this court have, by its fundamental constitution, power to determine all offences and trespasses, by the common law and custom of the realm,(b) it needed no original writ from the crown to give it cognizance of any misdemeanor in the county wherein it resides; yet, as by this court's coming into any county it immediately superseded the ordinary administration of justice by the general commissions of *eyre* and of *oyer and terminer*,(c)(18) a process of its own became necessary within the county where it sat, to bring in such persons as were accused of committing any *forcible injury*. The bill of Middlesex(d) (which was formerly always founded on a *plaint* of trespass *quare clausum fregit*,(19) entered on the records of the court)(e) is a kind of *capias*, directed to the sheriff of that county, and commanding him to take the defendant and have him before our lord the king at Westminster on a day prefixed, to answer to the plaintiff of a plea of trespass. For this accusation of trespass it is, that gives the court of king's bench jurisdiction in other civil causes, as was formerly observed; since when once the defendant is taken into custody of the marshal, or prison-keeper, of this court, for the supposed trespass, he being then a prisoner of this court, may here be prosecuted for any other species of injury. Yet, in order to found this jurisdiction, it is not necessary that the defendant be actually the marshal's prisoner; for, as soon as he appears, or puts in bail, to the process, he is deemed by so doing to be in such custody of the marshal as will give the court a jurisdiction to proceed.(f) And, upon these accounts, *in   [*286 the bill or process a complaint of trespass is always suggested, what-

(x) 2 Roll. Rep. 490. Regul. C. B. A. D. 1654, c. 13.
(y) Cro. Jac. 616. Salk. 496.
(z) Append. No. II. § 1.
(a) Thus, when the court sat at Oxford by reason of the plague, Mich. 1665, the process was by *bill of Oxfordshire*. Trye's *Jus Filizar*. 101.

(b) Bro. Abr. tit, *Oyer and Terminer*, 8.
(c) Bro. Abr. tit. *Jurisdiction*, 66. 3 Inst. 27.
(d) Append. No. III. § 8.
(e) Trye's *Jus Filizar*. 98.
(f) 4 Inst. 72.

(17) Unless where the outlawry was obtained for the purpose of oppression, as where defendant was already in prison at plaintiff's suit, etc. 2 Ventr. 46. 2 Salk. 495. The absence of the defendant beyond sea at the time the exigent is promulgated is, at common law, ground for a writ of error to reverse the outlawry; but if defendant went abroad purposely for delay, that fact may effectually be replied. 2 Roll. R. 11. 12 East, 625.— CHITTY. In some of our older states process of outlawry was permitted and regulated by statute; but it never had much practical existence in this country, and is now wholly disused. 1 Pars. on Cont. (8 ed.) 422.

(18) [To hear and determine.]

(19) [Why he broke the close.]

ever else may be the real cause of action. This bill of Middlesex must be served on the defendant by the sheriff, if he finds him in that county; but, if he returns " *non est inventus,*" then there issues out a writ of *latitat(g)*(20) to the sheriff of another county, as Berks; which is similar to the *testatum capias* in the common pleas, and recites the bill of Middlesex and the proceedings thereon, and that it is testified that the defendant *latitat et discurrit,*" lurks and wanders about in Berks; and therefore commands the sheriff to take him, and have his body in court on the day of the return.(21) But, as in the common pleas the *testatum capias* may be sued out upon only a supposed, and not an actual, preceding *capias;*(22) so in the king's bench a *latitat* is usually sued out upon only a supposed, and not an actual, *bill of Middlesex.* So that, in fact, a *latitat* may be called the first process in the court of king's bench, as the *testatum capias* is in the common pleas. Yet, as in the common pleas, if the defendant lives in the county wherein the action is laid, a common *capias* suffices; so in the king's bench, likewise, if he lives in Middlesex, the process must still be by *bill of Middlesex* only.(23)

In the exchequer the first process is by writ of *quo minus,* in order to give the court a jurisdiction over pleas between party and party. In which writ(h) the plaintiff is alleged to be the king's farmer or debtor, and that the defendant hath done him the injury complained of, *quo minus sufficiens existit,* by which he is the less able to pay the king his rent, or debt. And upon this the defendant may be arrested as upon a *capias* from the common pleas(24)

Thus differently do the three courts set out at first, in the commencement of a suit, in order to entitle the two courts of king's bench and exchequer to hold plea in causes between subject and subject, which by the original constitution of Westminster hall they were not empowered to do. Afterwards, when the cause is once drawn into the respective courts, the method of pursuing it is pretty much the same in all of them.

*287]   *If the sheriff has found the defendant upon any of the former writs, the *capias, latitat,* etc., he was anciently obliged to take him

(g) Append. No. III. ? 3.   (h) Append. No. III. ? 4.

(20) [He is not found. He lies hidden.]
(21) If the *latitat* prove ineffectual, an *alias* [As formerly] and after that a *pluries latitat,* [As more than once,] or, more properly speaking, an *alias* or *pluries capias,* may be sued out. Tidd, 8th ed. 145. When it is doubtful in what county the defendant is to be found, there may be several writs at the same time into different counties. Id. 1 Chitt. Rep. 514. In any of these writs there may be a clause of *non omittas;* commanding the sheriff that he do not *omit* on account of any liberty in his county, but that he enter the same, etc., and take the defendant, etc., which *non omittas* writ may be issued in the first instance. Tidd, 8th ed. 145, 146.—CHITTY.
(22) [*Testatum capias*—That you take the person testified.]
(23) And a *latitat* cannot be served out of the proper county, though when a person has been served on the confines of a county, though out of it, the court will not in general set aside the service. 4 M. & S. 412. 1 Chitty's R. 15; and see id. 233.—CHITTY. See also Sherman v. Barnes, 8 Conn. 138, 141 (1830).
(24) In the Exchequer an action may also be commenced by a *venire facias ad respondendum,* [That you cause to come to answer,] which is in the nature of an original writ, and is the process used in this court against peers and members of the house of commons. On this writ the defendant is summoned; and if he do not appear, a *distringas* [That you distrain] issues, and after that, if necessary, an *alias, pluries,* or *testatum distringas.* Tidd's Practice, 67. An action *by* an attorney or officer of this court is commenced by a *capias* of privilege, and *against* attorneys, officers, or prisoners by bill. Ibid. 68.—ARCHBOLD.
But in this court the defendant cannot be outlawed, as the plaintiff cannot proceed therein by original writ. 1 Price, 309. Besides, the writ of *quo minus* [By which the less] is a *venire facias* [That you cause to come] and subpœna *ad respondendum* [To respond]. For the process in this court, see Tidd, 8th ed. 154 to 157.—CHITTY.

into custody, in order to produce him in court upon the return, however small and minute the cause of action might be. For, not having obeyed the original summons, he had shown a contempt of the court, and was no longer to be trusted at large. But when the summons fell into disuse, and the *capias* became in fact the first process, it was thought hard to imprison a man for a contempt which was only supposed: and therefore in common cases, by the gradual indulgence of the courts, (at length authorized by statute 12 Geo. I. c. 29, which was amended by 5 Geo. II. c. 27, made perpetual by 21 Geo. II. c. 3, and extended to all inferior courts by 19 Geo. III. c. 70,) the sheriff or proper officer can now only personally serve the defendant with the copy of the writ or process, and with notice in writing to appear by his attorney in court to defend this action; which in effect reduces it to a mere summons. (25) And if the defendant thinks proper to appear upon this notice, his appearance is recorded, and he puts in sureties for his future attendance and obedience; which sureties are called *common bail*, being the same two imaginary persons that were pledges for the plaintiff's prosecution, John Doe and Richard Roe. Or, if the defendant does not appear upon the return of the writ, or within four (or in some cases, eight) days after, (26) the plaintiff

---

(25) As to the form of the notice, see Tidd, 8th ed. 166. If there be no notice to appear, when necessary, or the notice be not properly directed, etc., the defendant may move the court to set aside the proceedings; but any trifling informality in the notice, as setting down the day of the month on which the defendant is to appear, without saying *instant, next,* or specifying the *year*, or mentioning an impossible day, will not invalidate it. Tidd, 8th ed. 167. As to the service of the process, see id. 167 to 169.

If there be no process, or if it be defective in point of form, or in its direction, *teste*, or return, or the attorney's name be not endorsed upon it, the defendant may move the court to set aside the proceedings for irregularity; and a writ having a wrong return will not be aided by a correct day being mentioned in the notice (to appear. But he cannot take advantage of any error or defect in the process after he has appeared to it or taken the declaration out of the office; for it is the universal practice of the courts that the application to set aside proceedings for irregularity should be made as early as possible, or, as it is commonly said, in the first instance; and where there has been an irregularity, if the party overlook it and take subsequent steps in the cause, he cannot afterwards revert back and object to it. In the Common Pleas the court will not quash a writ on the ground of its having been served in a wrong county. And it is said that a mistake in the process is cured by the plaintiff's entering an appearance for the defendant, which has been always looked upon as effectual for that purpose as if he had done it himself; but it is otherwise where the defendant has not been served with a copy of the process, or the notice subscribed thereto is defective. It is also said that no advantage can be taken of the irregularity of process without having it returned, and before the court; and where the irregularity complained of is not in the process, but in the notice to appear thereto, or in the service of it, the rule should be to set aside such service, and not the process itself. See Tidd, 8th ed. 159, and the various cases there collected.

The process may in general be amended where there is any thing to amend by; and it has been amended in the name of the defendant where he was a prisoner in custody under it. But the court of King's Bench would not grant a rule for amending the writ, under which the defendant had been arrested by a wrong name, after actions of false imprisonment had been brought for such arrest; so an amendment cannot be made of mesne process by adding the name of another person as plaintiff. A writ returnable on a *dies non* [Not a court day] is altogether void, and cannot be amended by the court; and the courts, we have seen, will not in general allow a writ to be amended to the prejudice of the bail. Tidd, 8th ed. 160, and cases there collected.—CHITTY.

(26) In all cases where the defendant is served with a copy of the process, he has eight days to file common bail in the King's Bench, or to enter a common appearance in the Common Pleas, exclusive of the return-day; and if the last of the eight days be a Sunday, he has all the next day. 1 Cromp. Prac. 48. 1 Burr. 56.

As to what *cause of action* will justify an arrest, it is a rule that where a debt is certain, or damages may be reduced to a certainty, as in assumpsit or covenant for the payment of money, (Barnes, 79, 80, 108,) the defendant may be arrested as a matter of course, on an affidavit stating the cause of action. Tidd, 170. But where damages are altogether uncertain, as in assumpsit, or covenant, to indemnify, etc., or in actions for a tort or

may enter an appearance for him, as if he had really appeared; and may file common bail in the defendant's name, and proceed thereupon as if the defendant had done it himself.

But if the plaintiff will make *affidavit*, or assert upon oath, that the cause of action amounts to ten pounds or upwards, (27) then he may arrest the defendant, and make him put in substantial sureties for his appearance, called *special bail*. In order to which, it is required by statute 13 Car. II. st. 2, c. 2, that the true cause of action should be expressed in the body of the writ or process: else no security can be taken in a greater sum than 40*l*. This statute (without any such intention in the makers) had like to have

*288]   ousted the king's bench of *all its jurisdiction over civil injuries without force; for, as the bill of Middlesex was framed only for actions of trespass, a defendant could not be arrested and held to bail thereupon for breaches of civil contracts. But to remedy this inconvenience, the officers of the king's bench devised a method of adding what is called a clause of *ac etiam*(28) to the usual complaint of trespass: the bill of Middlesex commanding the defendant to be brought in to answer the plaintiff of a plea of trespass, *and also* to a bill of debt;(*i*) the complaint of trespass giving cognizance to the court, and that of debt authorizing the arrest. In imitation of which, lord chief justice North, a few years afterwards, in order to save the suitors of his court the trouble and expense of suing out special originals, directed that in the common pleas, besides the usual complaint of breaking the plaintiff's close, a clause of *ac etiam* might be also added to the writ of *capias*, containing the true cause of action; as, "that the said Charles, the defendant, may answer to the plaintiff of a plea of trespass in breaking his close; and also, *ac etiam*, may answer him, according to the custom of the court, in a certain plea of trespass upon the case, upon promises, to the value of twenty pounds, etc."(*j*) The sum sworn to by the plaintiff is marked upon the back of the writ, and the sheriff, or his officer the bailiff, is then obliged actually to arrest or take into custody the body of the defendant,

---

(*i*) Trye's *Jus Filizar*. 102. Append. No. III. § 3.   of Lord Guildford, 99. This work is strongly recom-
(*j*) Lilly's Pract. Reg. tit. *ac etiam*. North's Life   mended to the student's perusal.

---

trespass, there can be no arrest without a special order of the court, or a judge, on a full affidavit of the circumstances, (id. 171;) and, by rule of H. T. 48 Geo. III., a person cannot be held to special bail in trover or detinue without an order. And there are other cases where an arrest is not allowed, even though the action be brought for a sum certain. Thus, a defendant cannot be arrested on a penal statute, (Yelv. 53,) though he may on a remedial one, (7 T. R. 259,) or where the act expressly authorizes an arrest. The defendant cannot be arrested on a bail-bond, (R. M. 8 Anne,) or replevin-bond, (1 Salk. 99. 6 T. R. 336. 8 T. R. 450,) or on a recognizance of bail, (Tidd, 8 ed. 172;) nor for goods bargained and sold, or sold without stating a delivery, (12 East, 398. 1 Bingh. 357;) nor on a policy of insurance without an adjustment, or an express promise to pay the amount, (5 Taunt. 201. 1 Marsh. 19, S. C.;) but he may be on a guarantee. 9 Price, 155. So defendant cannot be arrested for more than is equitably due. Thus, he cannot be arrested on the penalty of a bond, (6 T. R. 217. 2 East, 409;) but he may if the sum is agreed to be for liquidated damages. Tidd, 8 ed. 173. He cannot be arrested for more than the balance due where there is a set-off. 3 B. & C. 139. 5 B. & A. 513. 1 D. & R. 67, S. C.—CHITTY.

(27) Now, by stat. 7 & 8 Geo. IV. c. 71, the debt must amount to 20*l*., and in Wales and the counties palatine to 50*l*. Intermediate statutes—viz., 51 Geo. III. c. 124, and 27 Geo. III. c. 171—extended the sum from 10*l*. to 15*l*., except upon bills of exchange and promissory-notes. The statute of the present king contains no such exemption.—CHITTY.

This affidavit must be certain and positive; for an affidavit made upon belief, or with a reference to something else,—as where the plaintiff swears the defendant is indebted to him in ten pounds or upwards, as appears by his books or by a bill delivered,—will not be sufficient unless the plaintiff is an executor, administrator, or assignee; for then, from the nature of his situation, he cannot swear more positively than from belief or from a reference to the accounts of others. 1 Sellon's Practice, 112.—CHRISTIAN.

(28) [And also.]

and, having so done, to return the writ with a *cepi corpus*(29) endorsed thereon.

An *arrest* must be by corporal seizing or touching the defendant's body,(30) after which the bailiff may justify breaking open the house in which he is(31) to take him; otherwise he has no such power, but must watch his opportunity to arrest him; for every man's house is looked upon by the law to be his castle of defence and asylum, wherein he should suffer no violence:(32) which principle is carried so far in the civil law, that, for the most part, not so much as a common citation or summons, much less an arrest, can be executed upon a man within his own walls.(*k*) Peers of the realm, members *of parliament, and corporations, are privileged from arrests; and [*289 of course from outlawries.(*l*) And against them the process to enforce an appearance must be by summons and distress infinite,(*m*) instead of a *capias*. Also clerks, attorneys, and all other persons attending the courts of justice, (for attorneys, being officers of the court, are always supposed to be there attending,) are not liable to be arrested by the ordinary process of the court, but must be sued by *bill*, (called usually a *bill of privilege*,) as being personally present in court.(*n*)(33) Clergymen performing divine service, and not merely staying in the church with a fraudulent design, are for the time privileged from arrests, by stat. 50 Edw. III, c. 5, and 1 Ric. II. c. 16,

---

(*k*) *Ff.* 2, 4, 18–21.
(*l*) Whitelock of Parl. 206, 207.

(*m*) See page 280.
(*n*) Bro. Abr. tit. *bille*, 29.　12 Mod. 163.

---

(29) [I have taken the body.]

(30) But this does not seem to be absolutely necessary; for if a bailiff come into a room and tell the defendant he arrests him, and lock the door, it is sufficient. C. T. Hardw. 301.　2 New Rep. 211.　Bull. N. P. 82.　Bare words, however, will not constitute an arrest.　1 Ry. & M. C. N. P. 26.　It is sufficient that the officer have the authority, be near, and acting in the arrest, without being the person who actually arrests.　Cowp. 65. If the defendant be wrongfully taken without process, (2 Anst. 461.　1 N. R. 135,) or after it is returnable, (2 H. Bla. 29,) he cannot be lawfully detained in custody under subsequent process at the suit of the same plaintiff, though he may at the suit of third persons.　2 B. & A. 743.　1 Chit. Rep. 579, S. C.—CHITTY.

It is not necessary that the arrest should be made by the hand of the bailiff, nor that he should be actually in sight; yet when an arrest is made by his assistant or follower, the bailiff ought to be so near as to be considered as acting in it. Cowp. 65.—CHRISTIAN. See also Genner *v.* Sparks, 6 Mod. 173 (3 Anne).　Emery *v.* Chesley, 18 N. H. 198 (1846). Whitehead *v.* Keys, 3 Allen (Mass.) 495 (1862).

(31) This appears to be stated too extensively: it is the defendant's own dwelling which by law is said to be his castle; for if he be in the house of another, the bailiff or sheriff may break and enter it to effect his purpose, but he ought to be very certain that the defendant be, at the time of such forcible entry, in the house. See Johnson *v.* Leigh, 6 Taunt. 246.—CHITTY. See Semayne's case, 5 Coke, 91.

(32) A bailiff, before he has made the arrest, cannot break open an outer door of a house; but if he enter the outer door peaceably, he may then break open the inner door. though it be the apartment of a lodger, if the owner himself occupies part of the house, Cowp. 1.　2 Moore, 207.　8 Taunt. 250, S. C. And where a house is let to lodgers, the owner retaining one room thereof for himself, an officer may break open an inner door which leads to a lodger's room for the purpose of arresting him. Williams *v.* Spencer, 5 Johns. 352 (1810). But if the whole house be let in lodgings, as each lodging is then considered a dwelling-house, in which burglary may be stated to have been committed, it has been supposed that the door of each apartment would be considered an outer door, which could not be legally broken open to execute an arrest. Oystead *v.* Shed *et al.*, 13 Mass. 519 (1816). If, however, a person who has been arrested escapes, the officer may break into such person's house to retake him. Genner *v.* Sparks, 6 Mod. 173 (3 Anne). Allen *v.* Martin, 25 Am. Dec. 564.

But to justify breaking open an inner door belonging to a lodger, admittance must be first demanded, unless defendant is in the room.　3 B. & P. 223.　4 Taunt. 619. And the breaking open an inner door of a stranger cannot be justified on a suspicion that defendant is in the room.　5 Taunt. 765, 6 ed. 246.—CHITTY.

(33) These privileges are allowed not so much for the benefit of attorneys as their clients, (2 Wils. 44.　4 Burr. 211.　3 Doug. 381,) and are therefore confined to attorneys

as likewise members of convocation actually attending thereon, by statute 8 Hen. VI. c. 1. Suitors, witnesses, and other persons, necessarily attending any courts of record on business, are not to be arrested during their actual attendance, which includes their necessary coming and returning.(34) And no arrest can be made in the king's presence, nor within the verge of his royal palace,(o)(35) nor in any place where the king's justices are actually sitting.(36) The king hath moreover a special prerogative, (which, indeed, is very seldom exerted,)(p) that he may by his *writ of protection* privilege a defendant from all personal, and many real, suits for one year at a time, and no longer; in respect of his being engaged in his service out of the realm.(q) And the king also, by the common law, might take his debtor into his protection, so that no one might sue or arrest him till the king's debt be paid;(r)

(o) See book iv. 276. The verge of the palace of Westminster extends, by stat. 28 Hen. VIII. c. 12, from Charing Cross to Westminster hall.

(p) Sir Edward Coke informs us (1 Inst. 131) that herein "he could say nothing of his own experience: for albeit queen Elizabeth maintained many wars, yet she granted few or no protections: and her reason was that he was no fit subject to be em-

ployed in her service, that was subject to other men's actions, lest she might be thought to delay justice." But king William, in 1692, granted one to lord Cutts, to protect him from being outlawed by his tailor, (3 Lev. 882:) which is the last that appears upon our books.

(q) Finch, L. 454. 3 Lev. 332.

(r) F. N. B. 28. Co. Litt. 131.

---

who practice, (2 Wils. 232. 4 Burr. 2113. 2 Bla. Rep. 1086. 1 Bos. & Pul. 4. 2 Lutw. 1667, *contra*,) or at least have practiced within a year; for it is a rule that such attorneys as have not been attending their employment in the King's Bench for the space of a year, unless hindered by sickness, be not allowed their privilege of attorneys. R. M. 1654, S. 1, K. B. & C. P. 2 M. & S. 605.—CHITTY.

(34) See, further as to the privileges from arrest, Tidd, 8 ed. 193–214. Lee's Dict. tit. Arrest, 90, 92. In addition to those named in the text are the following, viz.: *Administrator*, as such, (Yelv. 53;) but not if he has personally promised to pay. 1 T. R. 716. *Aliens* for debt beyond seas. 38 Geo. III. c. 50, s. 9. *Ambassadors and servants*. 7 Anne, c. 12. 1 B. & C. 554. 3 D. & R. 833, 25. *Bail*, being about to justify, or otherwise attending court as bail. 1 H. Bla. 636. 1 M. & S. 638. *Bankrupt* for forty-two days, unless before in prison, and after forty-two days, if the time for surrender be enlarged, (8 T. R. 475;) also if summoned before the commissioners relative to his estate, though several years after his last examination. Id. 534. See the 6 Geo. IV. c. 16, ss. 117, 118. *Barristers* attending court or on circuit. 1 H. Bla. 636. *Bishops*. *Consul-general*. 9 East, 447; *sed vid*. 1 Taunt. 106. 3 M. & S. 284. *Executor*, as such, *Feme-covert*, (1 T. R. 486. 2 H. B. 17;) but if she obtain credit, pretending to be single, she may be arrested, (1 N. R. 54; and see 1 Bing. 344. 2 Marsh. 40. 7 Taunt. 55. Tidd, 8 ed. 197;) though if a foreigner and her husband be abroad, she is liable for her debts, though neither separated by deed nor having a separate maintenance, (2 N. R. 380;) but if plaintiff knew her to be married, she will be discharged, (6 T. R. 451. 1 East, 17, n. 7 East, 582;) and in such case plaintiff will be ruled to pay costs of motion, (3 Taunt. 307;) but if she cohabit with another man, and trade on her own account, she will not be discharged, (1 B. & P. 8;) if she, by mistake, misrepresent her husband to be dead, she will be discharged. 1 East, 16. *Heir*, sued as such. *Hundredors*, as such. *Insolvent debtor* discharged, (3 M. & S. 595,) unless on a subsequent express promise. 6 Taunt. 563; *sed vid*. 1 Chit. R. 274, n. *Irish peer*, whether a representative or not. 39 & 40 Geo. III. c. 67, art. 4. *Marshal* of King's Bench. *Officers*, non-commissioned, (4 Taunt. 557;) but volunteer drill sergeants are not exempt. 8 T. R. 105. *Plaintiff* attending execution of inquiry, etc. 4 Moore, 34. *Sailors*, under 20l. 1 Geo. II. st. 2, c. 14, s. 15. 32 Geo. III. c. 33, s. 22. *Sergeants* at law. 6 T. R. 686. *Suitors* attending court, (11 East, 439,) and insolvent court is such a court, 2 Marsh. 57. 6 Taunt. 336. *Warden* of the Fleet. *Witnesses* subpoenaed, or summoned before commissioners under great seal, or attending an arbitrator appointed by the court. 1 Chit. Rep. 679. 3 B. & A. 252, S. C. 3 Anst. 941. 3 East, 189. A creditor attending commissioners of bankrupt to prove a debt. 7 Ves. 312. 1 Ves. & B. 316. 2 Rose, 24. By mutiny act, witnesses attending court-martial are privileged. But witnesses are not privileged if they delay by the way. 1 Chit. Rep. 679. 3 B. & A, 252, S. C.; *sed vid*. 7 Price, 699. A reasonable time is allowed for going and returning. 2 Bla. Rep. 1113. 2 Marsh. 57.—CHITTY.

(35) Except by an order of the board of green cloth, or unless the process issue out of the palace court. 3 T. R. 735. But an arrest within the verge of the palace has been holden in the Common Pleas to be no ground for discharging the defendant out of custody. 7 Taunt. 311; and see 1 Chit. Rep. 375. 3 B. & A. 502.—CHITTY.

(36) *Sed vide* 1 Lev. 106. Process cannot be executed in Kensington palace, (10 East, 578. 1 Camp. 475,) or within the Tower without leave from the governor. 2 Chit. Rep. 48, 51.—CHITTY.

but by the statute 25 Edw. III. st. 5, c. 19, notwithstanding such protection, another creditor may proceed to judgment against *him,   [*290 with a stay of execution, till the king's debt be paid; unless such creditor will undertake for the king's debt, and then he shall have execution for both.   And lastly, by statute 29 Car. II. c. 7, no arrest can be made, nor process served, upon a Sunday, except for treason, felony, or breach of the peace.(37)

When the defendant is regularly arrested he must either go to prison for safe custody, or put in *special bail* to the sheriff.(38) For, the intent of the arrest being only to compel an appearance in court at the return of the writ, that purpose is equally answered whether the sheriff detains his person, or takes sufficient security for his appearance, called *bail*, (from the French word *bailler*, to deliver,) because the defendant is bailed or delivered to his sureties, upon their giving security for his appearance, and is supposed to continue in their friendly custody instead of going to gaol.   The method of putting in bail to the sheriff is by entering into a bond or obligation, with one or more sureties, not fictitious persons, as in the former case of common bail, but real, substantial, responsible bondsmen, to insure the defendant's appearance at the return of the writ; which obligation is called the *bail-bond.(s)(39)*   The sheriff, if he pleases, *may* let the defendant go without any sureties; but that is at his own peril: for, after once taking him, the sheriff is bound to keep him safely, so as to be forthcoming in court; otherwise an action lies against him for an escape.(40)   But, on the other hand, he is obliged, by statute 23 Hen. VI. c. 10, to take (if it be tendered) a sufficient bail-bond(41) and by statute 12 Geo. I. c. 29, the sheriff shall take bail for no other sum than such as is sworn to by the plaintiff and endorsed on the back of the writ.

Upon the return of the writ, or within four days after, the defendant must *appear* according to the exigency of the writ.   This *appearance* is effected by putting in and justifying bail *to the action;* which is   [*291

(s) Append. No. III. § 5.

---

(37) See construction of this act, Tidd, 8 ed. 216. After a negligent escape, the defendant may be taken on a Sunday. 2 Lord Raym. 1028.

The arrest must be made in the county into which the process is issued; an arrest on the verge of a county into which the writ is issued is bad, unless there be a dispute as to boundaries. 3 B. & A. 408.—CHITTY.

(38) Or, by 43 Geo. III. c. 46, deposit in the sheriff's hands the sum endorsed on the writ, with 10*l*. in addition to answer costs, etc., and the fine paid, if proceeding by original; and this deposit is paid into court, and repaid to the defendant on his perfecting bail, or rendering himself to prison, (4 Taunt. 669. 1 Bing. 103. Chitty R. 145. 3 M. & S. 283;) but, if neither of these measures be taken, it is to be paid over to the plaintiff by order of the court. See cases on construction of this act, Tidd, 8 ed. 226, 227. Quære if depositing goods instead of money will do. 7 Moore, 432.—CHITTY.

(39) An agreement by a third person with a sheriff's officer to put in good bail, etc., (1 T. R. 418,) or an attorney's undertaking to the office for defendant's appearance (7 T. R. 109) or to give bail-bond in due time, are void, and no action lies on it; but if given to the plaintiff in the action, it is valid. 4 East, 568.—CHITTY.

(40) But the action may be defeated by putting in bail in the original action, of the term in which the writ is returnable, though after the expiration of the time allowed for putting it in, and even after the action for the escape is brought. 1 Esp. Rep. 87. 2 B. & P. 35, 246. 1 Taunt. 25. 1 Chit. Rep. 575, a.; *sed vide* 7 T. R. 109. 4 East, 568. To prevent this, plaintiff should oppose justification of bail, (Tidd, 8 ed. 235,) or render. 7 T. R. 109. 2 Marsh. 261. 1 Price, 103. 4 M. & S. 397.

Sheriff cannot sue defendant for money paid when he has discharged him out of custody on mesne process without a bail-bond, and has, in consequence of his non-appearance, been obliged to pay debt and costs. 8 East, 171.—CHITTY.

(41) If he so refuse, he is liable to a special action on the case, (Gilb. C. P. 20. Cro. Car. 196. 6 T. R. 355;) but, to maintain such action, the parties offered as bail must have had sufficient property in the county where the arrest was made. 15 East, 320.—CHITTY.

commonly called putting in bail *above*.(42) If this be not done, and the bail that were taken by the sheriff *below* are responsible persons, the plaintiff may take an assignment from the sheriff of the bail-bond (under the statute 4 & 5 Anne, c. 16) and bring an action thereupon against the sheriff's bail. But if the bail so accepted by the sheriff be insolvent persons, the plaintiff may proceed against the sheriff himself by calling upon him, first to return the writ, (if not already done,) and afterwards to bring in the body of the defendant. And, if the sheriff does not then cause sufficient bail to be put in and perfected *above*, he will himself be responsible to the plaintiff.

The bail *above*, or bail *to the action*, must be put in either in open court or before one of the judges thereof, or else, in the country, before a commissioner appointed for that purpose by virtue of the statute 4 W. and M. c. 4, which must be transmitted to the court. These bail, who must at least be two in number, must enter into a recognizance(*t*) in court or before the judge or commissioner in a sum equal (or in some cases double) to that which the plaintiff hath sworn to, whereby they do jointly and severally undertake that if the defendant be condemned in the action he shall pay the costs and condemnation or render himself a prisoner, or that they will pay it for him; which recognizance is transmitted to the court in a slip of parchment entitled a *bail-piece*.(*u*) And, if excepted to, the bail must be *perfected;* that is, they must *justify* themselves in court, or before the commissioner in the country, by swearing themselves housekeepers,(43) and each of them to be worth the full sum for which they are bail, after payment of all their debts.(44) This answers in some measure to the *stipulatio* or *satisdatio*

(*t*) Append. No. III. § 5.   (*u*) Ibid.

(42) In proceedings in the King's Bench by *bill*, whenever *special bail is not necessary* or has been dispensed with by the court, *common bail* (which are merely nominal) must be filed, or in proceedings in the *common pleas* of King's Bench by *original*, a common appearance must be entered. In the King's Bench, where defendant has been served with a copy of a bill of Middlesex, or other process therein, common bail should be filed at the return, or in eight days, exclusive (not including Sunday, if the last) after it. 5 Geo. II. c. 27, s. 1. 1 Burr. 56. Tidd, 8th ed. 240.

In proceedings by original in the King's Bench, the appearance must be entered with the filacer of the county in which the action is laid, within eight days after appearance-day or *quarto die post* [The fourth day after] of return of process. 3 B. & C. 110. 4 D. & R. 713, S. C. In the Common Pleas the eight days are reckoned from the return-day, and not from the quarto die post of the return of the writ. Id. Ibid. Impey, C. P. 216, 217.

By 5 Geo. II. c. 27, to expedite the plaintiff's proceedings, if the defendant, having been served with process, shall not appear at the return thereof or within eight days after such return, the plaintiff, upon affidavit of the service of such process, may enter a common appearance or file common bail for the defendant, and proceed therein as if such defendant had entered his appearance or filed common bail. The plaintiff cannot enter such appearance or file common bail till the ninth day. Tidd, 242.—CHITTY.

(43) Or a freeholder, or copyholder, or a long leaseholder. 8 Taunt. 148. 1 Chitty, R. 7, 88, 144. 2 Chitty, R. 96, 97.—CHITTY.

(44) Upon special bail being put in, a *notice* thereof must be given to the plaintiff's attorney or agent, whereupon the latter may *except* to the bail within twenty days after notice given, by entering such exception, (4 D. & R. 365;) and *notice of the exception* must be given to the defendant's attorney before the sheriff is ruled. Alexander *v.* Miller, 24 Nov., 1825, K. B. But where bail is not put in, at the time of ruling the sheriff to return the writ or bring in the body, he must put in and perfect bail at his peril, or render the defendant within *four* days in a town cause, or six days in a country cause, without any exception. 2 Bla. R. 1206. 2 Chit. R. 82, 108. Tidd, 8th ed. 256.

Within a particular time (in general, four days) after the exception entered and notice given, the bail must *justify*. See Tidd, 257, 258, 259. If they do not mean to do so, others should be added.

Previous to the bail justifying, there should be a *notice* setting forth that the bail already put in will on a certain day justify themselves in open court, (2 Chit. R. 103, Tidd, 259;) or that one or more persons will be added, and justify themselves as good bail for the defendant. Id.

(45) of the Roman laws, (*v*) which is mutually given by each litigant party to the other: by the plaintiff that he will prosecute his suit, and pay the costs if he loses his cause; in like manner as our law still requires nominal pledges of prosecution from the plaintiff: by the defendant, that he shall continue in court and abide the sentence of the judge, much like our special bail, but with this difference, that the *fidejussores* were there absolutely bound *judicatum solvere*, to see the costs and condemnation *paid at all   [*292 events; whereas our special bail may be discharged, by surrendering the defendant into custody within the time allowed by law; for which purpose they are at all times entitled to a warrant to apprehend him. (*w*) (46)

(*v*) Inst. *l.* 4, t. 11. *Ff. l.* 2, *t.* 8.   (*w*) Show. 202. 6 Mod. 231.

In the King's Bench, bail are added and *justified* before one of the judges sitting in the bail court, by virtue of the 57 Geo. III. c. 11. The bail must be in Westminster hall by half-past nine in the morning; and if the bail are not ready, and the papers delivered to counsel, before ten o'clock, they cannot be taken after that hour. Rul. H. T. 59 Geo. III. K. B. When there are but few bail, it is necessary that they should be very punctual in the time of their attendance, for if they are not ready when the judge takes his seat, he will not wait for them till ten o'clock; but when the bail are numerous, the exact time of their attendance is not so material; and on the last day of term they are still allowed to justify, as formerly, in full court, at its rising. Tidd, 262.

In the Common Pleas the bail must justify at the sitting of the court only, except on the last day of term, when bail who may have been prevented from attending at the sitting of the court shall be permitted to justify at the *rising* of the court. R. M. 51 Geo. III. C. P. 3 Taunt. 569; *sed vide* 8 Taunt. 56. In the Exchequer, the junior baron attends in court alone, a few minutes before ten o'clock every morning during term; and it is expected justifications of bail be then made; and no justification can take place after half-past ten o'clock. 8 Price, 612, R. E. 56 Geo. III. 2 Chit. 381. 9 Price, 57. Tidd, 263.

To justify themselves, each must swear that he is worth double the amount of the debt, *after payment* of his own debts. But if the sum exceed 1000*l.*, each is only required to justify himself in 1000*l.* more than that sum. M. 51 Geo. III. It is not sufficient for bail to swear they are worth a certain sum *exclusive* of their debts. 4 Taunt. 704. There must also be an affidavit made of the service of the notice of justification, which must state the mode of service of such notice. Tidd, 264.—CHITTY.

(45) [A stipulation and putting in sufficient security.]

(46) And the bail may render the defendant in their discharge, even after judgment; and they may take him on a Sunday, (6 Mod. 231; but see 2 Bla. R. 1273,) or during his examination before commissioners of bankrupt, (1 Atk. 238. 5 T. R. 210;) or going into a court of justice, (1 Selw. Prac. 180. 3 Stark. 132. 1 D. & R. M. P. C. 20;) and they may justify entering the house of a stranger (the outer door being open) to take the defendant, though he be not in the house, (2 Hen. Bla. 220;) and if the defendant is in custody, either in a civil action or upon a criminal charge, they may in King's Bench have a writ of *habeas corpus* to bring him up to the court, to be surrendered in their discharge. 7 T. R. 226. When the principal is taken, one of the bail, it is said, must always remain with him, (1 Selw. Pr. 180;) but a third person may assist in the taking and detaining defendant, though the bail do not continue present. 3 Taunt. 425.

Besides the mode of discharging the bail by rendering their principal, there are various other causes for discharging them, such as the death of the defendant, (Tidd, 293, 1183;) his bankruptcy and certificate, (1 Burr. 244. Cowp. 824;) his being made a peer, or member of parliament, (Dougl. 45. Tidd, 293;) or being sent abroad under the alien act, (6 T. R. 50, 52. 7 T. R. 517,) or under sentence of transportation, (6 T. R. 247;) or his being impressed or discharged on the 48 Geo. III. c. 123; or by the act of the plaintiff in not declaring in due time; by making a material variance in the declaration from the process or affidavit in the cause of action, (2 East, 305. 2 B. & P. 358. 6 T. R. 363;) or a variance between the affidavit and judgment in Common Pleas; or in declaring in a different county by original in King's Bench; or recovering under a bailable amount; or in giving time to the defendant on a cognovit, etc.; or removing the cause from an inferior court, or referring to arbitration, or taking principal in execution, (Cro. Jac. 320,) or any other irregularity in proceeding against the principal. Tidd, 1182. See the various cases on these points and other qualifications in Tidd's Prac. 8th ed. 290 to 295, 403, 1147, 1182, 1187.—CHITTY. The bail may take their principal wherever he may be found, although he be without the jurisdiction of the court where bail was taken. Parker *v.* Bidwell, 3 Conn. 84 (1819). Harp *v.* Osgood, 2 Hill, 216 (1842). An agent may exer-

Special bail is required (as of course) only upon actions of debt, or actions on the case in trover or for money due, where the plaintiff can swear that the cause of action amounts to ten pounds:(47) but in actions where the damages are precarious, being to be assessed *ad libitum*(48) by a jury, as in actions for words, ejectment, or trespass, it is very seldom possible for a plaintiff to swear to the amount of his cause of action; and therefore no special bail is taken thereon, unless by a judge's order or the particular directions of the court, in some peculiar species of injuries, as in cases of mayhem or atrocious battery; or upon such special circumstances as make it absolutely necessary that the defendant should be kept within the reach of justice. Also in actions against heirs, executors, and administrators, for debts of the deceased, special bail is not demandable; for the action is not so properly against them in person, as against the effects of the deceased in their possession. But special bail is required even of them, in actions for a *devastavit*, or wasting the goods of the deceased; that wrong being of their own committing.

Thus much for *process;* which is only meant to bring the defendant into court, in order to contest the suit and abide the determination of the law. When he appears either in person as a prisoner, or out upon bail, then follow the *pleadings* between the parties, which we shall consider at large in the next chapter.

CHAPTER XX.

OF PLEADING.

*293]   *PLEADINGS are the mutual altercations between the plaintiff and defendant;(1) which at present are set down and delivered into the proper office in writing, though formerly they were usually put in by their counsel *ore tenus*, or *viva voce*,(2) in court, and then minuted down by the chief clerks, or prothonotaries; whence in our old law-French the pleadings are frequently denominated the *parol*.(3)

---

cise such right. Parker *v.* Bidwell, 3 Conn. 84; and doors may be broken to make such arrest. Read *v.* Case, 166 (1821).

(47) Several extensions of the sum have taken place; and now, by the last statute, viz., 7 & 8 Geo. IV. c. 71, the cause of action must amount to 20*l.*—CHITTY.

(48) [At pleasure.]

(1) See Brainard *v.* Simmons, 58 Hights (Ia.) 467 (1882).

(2) [By word of mouth.]

(3) By stat. 3 & 4 W. IV. c. 42, power was given to the judges of the superior courts to make such alterations in the mode of pleading then in use in the said courts as they might deem expedient. By stat. 13 & 14 Vict. c. 16, this power was extended; and by "The Common-Law Procedure Act, 1852," renewed powers were again given to the judges for this purpose. The rules of pleading framed under the first statute have been repealed under the powers given by the last, but to a great extent also re-enacted, and many alterations have been made in the forms of pleadings.—STEWART.

Pleading is the statement in a logical and *legal form* of the *facts* which constitute the plaintiff's cause of action or the defendant's ground of defence; it is the formal mode of alleging on the record that which would be the support or the defence of the party in evidence. Per Buller, J., 3 T. R. 159. Dougl. 278. "It is [as also observed by the same learned judge, in Dougl. Rep. 159] one of the first principles of pleading, that there is only occasion to state *facts*, which must be done for the purpose of informing the court, whose duty it is to declare the *law* arising upon those facts, and of apprizing the opposite party of what is meant to be proved, in order to give him an opportunity to answer or traverse it." And see the observations of lord C. J. DeGrey, Cowp. 682. From this it

The first of these is the *declaration, narratio,* or *count;* anciently called the *tale;*(a) in which the plaintiff sets forth his cause of complaint at length; being, indeed, only an amplification or exposition of the original writ upon which his action is founded, with the additional circumstances of time and place when and where the injury was committed.   But we may remember,(b)

(a) Append. No. II. § 2; No. III. § 6.   (b) See pages 285, 288.

will be seen that the science of special pleading may be considered under two heads: 1st. The facts necessary to be stated. 2d. The mode of stating them. In these considerations, the reader must be contented with a general outline of the law upon the subject.

1st. THE FACTS NECESSARY TO BE STATED.—No more should be stated than is essential to constitute the cause of complaint or the ground of defence. Cowp. 683.   1 Lord Raym. 171. And facts only should be stated, and not arguments or inferences, or matter of law. Cowp. 684. 5 East, 275. The party can only succeed on the facts as they are alleged and proved.

There are various facts which need not be stated, though it may be essential that they should be established in evidence, to entitle the party pleading to succeed.

Thus, there are facts of which the court will, from the nature of its *office,* take notice without their being stated: as when the king came to the throne, (2 Lord Raym. 794,) his privileges, (id. 980,) proclamations, etc., (1 Lord Raym. 282. 2 Camp. 44. 4 M. & S. 532;) but private orders of council, pardons, and declarations of war, etc., must be stated. 2 Litt. Bac. Reg. 303. 3 M. & S. 67. 11 Ves. 292. 3 Camp. 61, 67. The time and place of holding parliaments, and their course of proceedings, need not be stated, (1 Lord Raym. 343, 210. 1 Saund. 131;) but their journals must. Lord Raym. 15. Cowp. 17. *Public* statutes, and the facts they ascertain, (1 T. R. 145. Com. Dig. Pleader, c. 76,) the ecclesiastical, civil, and marine laws, (Bro. Quare Impedit, pl. 12. Lord Raym. 338,) need not be stated; but *private* acts, (Lord Raym. 381. 2 Dougl. 97,) and foreign (2 Carth. 273. Cowp. 174) and plantation and forest (2 Leon. 209) laws, must. Common-law rights, duties, and *general* customs, customs of gavelkind, and borough-English, (Doug. 150. Lord Raym. 175, 1542. Carth. 83. Co. Litt. 175. Lord Raym. 1025. Cro. Car. 561,) need not be stated; but particular local customs must. 1 Roll. Rep. 509. 9 East, 185. Stra. 187. 1287. Dougl. 387. The almanac is part of the law of the land, and the courts take notice thereof, and the days of the week, and of the movable feasts and terms. Dougl. 380. Salk. 269. 1 Roll. Abr. 524, c. pl. 4. 6 Mod. 81. Salk. 626. So the division of *England* into *counties* will be noticed without pleading, (2 Inst. 557. Marsh, 124,) but not so of a less division (id.) nor of Ireland. 1 Chitt. Rep. 28, 32. 3 B. & A. 301, S. C. 2 D. & R. 15. 1 B. & C. 16, S. C. The court will take judicial notice of the incorporated towns, of the extent of ports, and the river Thames. Stra. 469. 1 H. Bla. 356. So it will take notice of the meaning of English words and terms of art, according to their ordinary acceptation, (1 Roll. Abr. 86, 525;) also of the names and quantities of legal weights and measures, (1 Roll. Abr. 525;) also courts will take notice of their own course of proceedings, (1 T. R. 118.   2 Lev. 176,) and of those of the superior courts, (2 Co. Rep. 18. Cro. Jac. 67,) the privileges they confer on their officers, (Lord Raym. 869, 898,) of courts of general jurisdiction, and the course of proceedings therein; as the court of Exchequer in Wales and the counties palatine, (1 Lord Raym. 154. 1 Saund. 73;) but the courts are not bound, ex officio, to take notice who were or are the judges of another court at Westminster, (2 Andr. 74.   Stra. 1226;) nor are the superior courts, ex officio, bound to notice the customs, laws, or proceedings of inferior courts of limited jurisdiction, (1 Roll. Rep. 105. Lord Raym. 1334. Cro. Eliz. 502,) unless indeed in courts of error. Cro. Car. 179.

Where the law presumes a fact, as that a person is innocent of a fraud or crime, or that a transaction is illegal, it need not be stated. 4 M. & S. 105.   2 Wils. 147. Co. Litt. 78, b.   1 B. & A. 463.

Matter which should come more properly from the other side, as it is presumed to lie more in the knowledge of the other party, or is an answer to the charge of the party pleading, need not be stated, unless in pleas of estoppel and alien enemy; but this rule must be acted upon with caution; for if the fact in any way constitutes a condition precedent, to enable the party to avail himself of the charge stated in his pleading, such fact should be stated. Com. Dig. Pleader, c. 81.   1 Leon. 18. 2 Saund. 62, b. 4 Camp. 20. 11 East, 638; and see cases, 1 Chit. on Pl. 206. Stephen, 354.

Though the facts of a case must be stated in pleading, it is not necessary to state that which is a mere matter of evidence of such fact. 9 Rep. 9, b. 9 Edw. III. 5, b., 6, a. Willes, 130. Raym. 8.

And though the general rule is that facts only are to be stated, yet there are some instances in which the statement in the pleading is proper, though it does not accord

that in the king's bench, when the defendant is brought into court by bill of Middlesex, upon a supposed trespass, in order to give the court a jurisdiction, the plaintiff may declare in whatever action, or charge him with whatever injury, he thinks proper; unless he has held him to bail by a special *ac etiam*,(4) which the plaintiff is then bound to pursue. And so also, in order to have the benefit of a *capias*(5) to secure the defendant's person, it was the ancient practice, and is therefore still warrantable in the common pleas, to sue out a writ of trespass *quare clausum fregit*,(6) for breaking the plaintiff's close: and when the defendant is once brought in upon this *writ, the plaintiff declares in whatever action the nature of his true injury may require; as in an action of covenant, or on the case for breach of contract, or other less forcible transgression:(c) unless, by holding the defendant to bail on a special *ac etiam*, he has bound himself to declare accordingly.(7)

*294]

(c) 2 Ventr. 259.

---

with the real facts, the law allowing a fiction, as in ejectment, trover, detinue, etc. Burr. 667. 1 N. R. 140.

No fact that is not essential to substantiate the pleading should be stated. The statement of immaterial or irrelevant matter is not only censurable on the ground of expense, but frequently affords an advantage to the opposite party, either as the ground of a variance, or as rendering it incumbent on the party pleading to adduce more evidence than would otherwise have been necessary; though, indeed, if the matter unnecessarily stated be wholly foreign and impertinent to the cause, so that no allegation whatever on the subject was necessary, it will be rejected as surplusage, it being a maxim that *utile per inutile non vitiatur* [The useful shall not be vitiated by the unuseful]. See cases, etc., in Chit. on Pl. 208, 209, 210. Besides this, the pleading must not state two or more facts either of which would of itself, independently of the other, constitute a sufficient ground of action or defence. Co. Litt. 304, a. Com. Dig. Pleader. C. 33, E. 2. 1 Chit. on Pl. 208.

2d. The Mode of stating Facts.—The facts should be stated logically, in their natural order; as, on the part of the plaintiff, his right, the injury and consequent damage; and these with certainty, precision, and brevity. The facts, as stated, must not be insensible or repugnant, nor ambiguous or doubtful in meaning, nor argumentative, nor in the alternative, nor by way of recital, but positive, and according to their legal effect and operation. Dougl. 666, 667. 1 Chit. on Pl. 211. Stephen, 378 to 405.

Certainty signifies a clear and distinct statement, so that it may be understood by the opposite party, by the jury, who are to ascertain the truth of such statement, and by the court, who are to give judgment. Cowp. 682. Com. Dig. Pleader, C. 17. Less certainty is requisite when the law presumes that the knowledge of the facts is peculiarly in the opposite party; and so when it is to be presumed that the party pleading is not acquainted with minute circumstances. 13 East, 112. Com. Dig. Pleader, C. 26. 8 East, 85. General statements of facts admitting of almost any proof are objectionable, (1 M. & S. 441. 3 M. & S. 114;) but where a subject comprehends multiplicity of matter, there, in order to avoid prolixity, general pleading is allowed. 2 Saund. 411, n 4. 8 T. R. 462.

In the *construction* of facts stated in pleading, it is a general rule that every thing shall be taken most strongly against the party pleading, (1 Saund. 259, n. 8;) or rather, if the meaning of the words be equivocal, they shall be construed most strongly against the party pleading them, (2 H. Bla. 530;) for it is to be intended that every person states his case as favorably to himself as possible, (Co. Litt. 30, 36;) but the language is to have a reasonable intendment and construction, (Com. Dig. Pleader, C. 25;) and if the sense be clear, mere exceptions ought not to be regarded, (5 East, 529;) and where an expression is *capable* of different meanings, that shall be taken which will support the averment, and not the other which would defeat it. 4 Taunt. 492. 5 East, 257. After verdict, an expression should be construed in such sense as would sustain the verdict. 1 B. & C. 297.—Chitty.

(4) [And also.]

(5) [That you take.]

(6) [Wherefore he broke the close.]

(7) And even then the plaintiff will only lose the benefit of the bail, and the court will not set aside the proceedings. 7 T. R. 80. 8 T. R. 27. 5 Moore, 483. 6 T. R. 363. So in the King's Bench, where the proceedings are by original, the venue must be laid in the county into which the original was issued; or in bailable cases the defendant will be

In *local* actions, where possession of land is to be recovered, or damages for an actual trespass, or for waste, etc., affecting land, the plaintiff must lay his declaration or declare his injury to have happened in the very county and place that it really did happen;(8) but in *transitory* actions, for injuries that might have happened anywhere, as debt, detinue, slander, and the like, the plaintiff may declare in what county he pleases, and then the trial must be had in that county in which the declaration is laid.(9) Though if the defendant will make affidavit that the cause of action, if any, arose not in that but in another county, the court will direct a change of the *venue* or *visne*, (that is, the *vicinia* or neighborhood in which the injury is declared to be done,) and will oblige the plaintiff to declare in the other county; unless he will undertake to give material evidence in the first. For the statutes 6 Ric. II. c. 2, and 4 Hen. IV. c. 18, having ordered *all* writs to be

---

discharged; but it would be otherwise in Common Pleas, (Imp. C. P. 159;) and this would be the only advantage gained by the defendant.

The declaration should in other respects correspond with the process, as in the names and numbers of the parties, the character or right in which they sue or are sued; but as, according to the present practice of the courts, oyer of the writ cannot be craved, and a variance between the writ and declaration cannot in any case be pleaded in abatement, (1 Saund. 318. 3 B. & P. 395,) and as there are several instances in which the court will not set aside the proceedings on account of a variance between the writ and declaration, (6 T. R, 364,) many of the older decisions are no longer applicable in practice. But if the defect appear on the face of the declaration, the plaintiff may plead in abatement, or demur accordingly. As to these general requisites, see 1 Chit. on Pl. 222 to 229.—CHITTY. In declaring upon a judgment it is necessary to set forth the place where was held the court at which the judgment was obtained. Duyckink *v.* Ins. Co., 3 N. J. 279 (1852).

(8) Actions for every kind of injury to real p roperty are local, as for nuisances, waste, etc., unless there be some contract between the parties, on which to ground the action. 1 Taunt. 379. 11 East, 226. And if the land be out of this kingdom, the plaintiff has no remedy in the English courts, if there be a court of justice to resort to where the land is situate. 4 T. R. 503. 1 Stra. 646. Cowp. 180. 6 East, 598. Where an injury has been caused in one county, to land, etc. in another, or when the action is founded upon two or more material facts which took place in different counties, the venue may be laid in either. 2 Taunt. 252, overruling 2 Camp. 266. 7 Co. 1. 3 Leon. 141. 7 T. R. 583. 1 Chitty on Pl. 242.

In an action upon a lease for the non-payment of rent, or other breach of covenant, when the action is founded on the *privity of contract*, it is *transitory;* but not so when the action is founded on the *privity of estate*. 3 T. R. 394. 3 Co. 23. 1 Saund. 237. Tidd, 431. 1 Chit. 244 to 246.

In some cases the action, though of a transitory nature, must, by act of parliament, be brought in a particular county, as by 31 Eliz. c. 5, s. 2. 21 Jac. I. c 4, s. 2. In actions or informations on penal statutes, the venue must be laid where the offence was committed. Tidd, 432. 1 Chit. 246. So actions of case or trespass are local when against justices of the peace, mayors, bailiffs of cities or towns corporate, headboroughs, portreves, constables, tithing-men, church-wardens, etc., or other persons acting in their aid and assistance or by their command, for any thing done in their official capacity, (21 Jac. I. c. 12, s. 5,) or against any person or persons for any thing done by an officer of the excise, (23 Geo. III. c. 70, s. 34,) or customs, (24 Geo. III. sess. 2, c. 47, s. 35, 39; and see 28 Geo. III. c. 37, s. 23,) or others acting in his aid, in execution or by reason of his office or for anything done in pursuance of the act relating to taxes, etc. 43 Geo. III. c. 99, s. 70. And the 42 Geo. III. c. 85, s. 6 extends the above provisions of the 21 Jac. I. to all persons in any public employment, or any office, station, or capacity, anywhere with a proviso that the action may be brought in Westminster, or where the defendant resides. There are also various other provisions in other acts, requiring that the venue shall be local, as in the highway, turnpike, militia acts, etc. Attorneys may lay and retain the venue in Middlesex.—CHITTY. See Pilgrim *v.* Mellor, 1 Brad. (Ill.) 450 (1877).

(9) Ambler and wife *v.* Norton, 4 Va. (H. & M.) 23, 50 (1809). An action for personal injuries arising under a statute of one state may be enforced in another if the statute of the state where the cause of action arises be not inconsistent with the known policy, or prejudicial to the interest of the state in which the suit is brought. Nelson *v.* Chesapeake & Ohio R. R. Co., 88 Va. 971, 974 (1892).

laid in their proper counties, this, as the judges conceived, empowered them to change the *venue*, if required, and not to insist rigidly on abating the writ: which practice began in the reign of James the First.(*d*) And this power is discretionally exercised, so as to prevent and not to cause a defect of justice.(10) Therefore the court will not change the *venue* to any of the four northern counties, previous to the spring circuit; because there the assizes are holden only once a year, at the time of the summer circuit. And it will sometimes remove the *venue* from the proper jurisdiction, (especially of a narrow and limited kind,) upon a suggestion, duly supported, that a fair and impartial trial cannot be had therein.(*e*)

*295]   *It is generally usual in actions upon the case to set forth several cases by different *counts* in the same declaration; so that if the plaintiff fails in the proof of one, he may succeed in another. As, in an action on the case upon an *assumpsit* for goods sold and delivered, the plaintiff usually counts or declares, first, upon a settled and agreed price between him and the defendant; as that they bargained for twenty pounds: and lest he should fail in the proof of this, he counts likewise upon a *quantum valebant;*(11) that the defendant bought other goods, and agreed to pay him so much as they were reasonably worth; and then avers that they were worth other twenty pounds; and so on, in three or four different shapes,(12) and at last concludes with declaring that the defendant had refused to fulfil any of these agreements, whereby he is endamaged to such a value. And if he proves the case laid in any one of his counts, though he fails in the rest, he shall recover proportionable damages. This declaration always concludes with these words, "and thereupon he brings *suit*, etc.," "*inde producit sectam, etc.*"(13) By which words *suit* or *secta* (*a sequendo*) were anciently under-

(*d*) Rastall, tit. *Dette*, 184, b. Fitz. Abr. tit. *Briefe*, 18. Salk. 670. Trye's *Jus. Filiz.* 251. Styl. Pract. Reg. (edit. 1657) 331.

(*e*) Stra. 874, Mylock *v.* Saladine. Trin. 4 Geo. III. B. R.

---

(10) This power of changing the *venue* was extended, by stat. 3 & 4 W. IV. c. 42, s. 22, to local actions.—STEWART. In Wisconsin under the act of 1839, entitled "An act concerning the supreme and district courts," the number of changes is not limited, and the change is limited only when the legal cause therefor ceases to exist. U. S. *ex rel.* Smith *v.* Dist. Court, 1 Wisconsin (Pinney) 571 (1845).

(11) [As much as they were worth.]

(12) The variations should be substantial; for if the different counts be so similar that the same evidence would support each of them, and be of any considerable length, and vexatiously inserted, the court would on application refer it to the master for examination and to strike out the redundant counts, and in gross cases direct the costs to be paid by the attorney. 1 N. R. 289. Rep. T. Hardw. 129. And as to striking out superfluous counts, see Tidd, 8 ed. 667, 648. In Bingh. 412, nine counts were allowed in an action for slander, though the words used were very few. See 1 Chitt. on Pl. 350, 351, 352, as to the insertion of several counts. There must be no misjoinder of different counts; and, in order to prevent the confusion which might ensue if different forms of action, requiring different pleas and different judgments, were allowed to be found in one action, it is a general rule that actions in form *ex contractu* [Arising from a contract] cannot be joined with those in form *ex delicto* [Arising from offence or misdeed]. Thus, assumpsit and debt, (2 Smith, 618, 3 ib. 114,) or assumpsit and an action on the case, as for a tort, cannot be joined, (1 T. R. 276, 277. 1 Ventr. 366. Carth. 189;) nor assumpsit with trover, (2 Lev. 101. 3 Lev. 99. 1 Salk. 10. 3 Wils. 354. 6 East, 335. 2 Chitty R. 343;) nor trover with detinue. Willes, 118. 1 Chitty on Plead. 182. Debt and detinue may, however, be joined, although the judgments be different. 2 Saund. 117. And see further, as to what is a misjoinder, 1 Chitty on Pl. 199. Unless the subsequent count expressly refers to the preceding, no defect therein will be aided by such preceding count. Bac. Abr. Pleas and Pleader, 16, I.—CHITTY.

(13) It does not so conclude in actions against attorneys and other officers of the court, but thus:—"and therefore he prays relief, etc." Andr. 247. Barnes, 3, 167.

In actions at the suit of an executor or administrator, immediately after the conclusion to the damage, etc., and before the pledges, a profert of the letters testamentary, or let-

stood the witnesses or followers of the plaintiff.(*f*)(14) For in former times the law would not put the defendant to the trouble of answering the charge till the plaintiff had made out at least a probable case.(*g*) But the actual production of the *suit*, the *secta*, or *followers*, is now antiquated, and hath been totally disused, at least ever since the reign of Edward the Third, though the form of it still continues.(15)

At the end of the declaration are added also the plaintiff's common pledges of prosecution, John Doe and Richard Roe,(16) which as we before observed,(*h*) are now mere names of form, though formerly they were of use to answer to the king for the amercement of the plaintiff in case he were nonsuited, barred of his action, or had a verdict or judgment against him.(*i*) For if the plaintiff neglects to deliver a declaration for two terms after the defendant appears, or is guilty of other delays or defaults against the rules of law in any subsequent *stage of the action, he is   [*296 adjudged *not to follow* or pursue his remedy as he ought to do, and thereupon a *nonsuit* or *non prosequitur* is entered, and he is said to be *non-pros'd*.(17) And for thus deserting his complaint, after making a false claim or complaint, (*pro falso clamore suo*,) he shall not only pay costs to the defendant, but is liable to be amerced to the king. A *retraxit* differs from a nonsuit in that the one is negative and the other positive; the nonsuit is a mere default and neglect of the plaintiff, and therefore he is allowed to begin his suit again upon payment of costs; but a *retraxit*,(18) is an open and voluntary renunciation of his suit in court, and by this he forever loses his action.(19) A *discontinuance* is somewhat similar to a

---

(*f*) Seld. on Fortesc. c. 21.
(*g*) Bract. 400. Flet. *l*, 2, c. 6.

(*h*) See page 274.
(*i*) 3 Bulstr. 275. 4 Inst. 189.

---

ters of administration, should be made. Bac. Abr. Executor, C. Doug. 5, in notes. But omission is added unless defendant demur specially. 4 Anne, c. 16, s. 1.—CHITTY.

(14) Harlin's Heirs *v.* Eastland, 1 Ky. 311, Hardin (1808). Howes *v.* Austin, 35 Ill. 413, Freeman (1864).

(15) In this wide sense a writ is pending, and undetermined in court until the plaintiff has fully recovered and realized his just demand. Ulshafer *v.* Stewart, 71 Pa. 174 Smith (1872).

(16) But these pledges need not be stated in proceedings by original, or in the Common Pleas, unless in proceedings against attorneys, etc. Summary on Pl. 42. Barnes, 163. Nor are they necessary in an action at the suit of the king or queen. 8 Co. 61. Cro. Car. 161. And no advantage can be taken of the omission in any case, even on special demurrer. 3 T. R. 157, 158.—CHITTY.

(17) But unless the defendant take advantage of the plaintiff's neglect, by signing such judgment, the plaintiff may deliver his declaration at any time within a year next after the return of the writ. 3 T. R. 123. 5 id. 35. 7 id. 7; *sed vide* 2 N. R. 404. As to when the defendant is entitled to, and how he should sign a judgment of, and the costs on, a non pros., see Tidd, 8 ed. Index, tit. Non Pros.—CHITTY. Holmes *v.* C. & A. R. R. Co. 94 Ill. 443, Freeman (1880). A nonsuit is not a judgment nor a cause's final determination. Under § 379 of the civil code of Wyoming, a district court thereof cannot enter a peremptory nonsuit against the plaintiff's will. Mulhern *v.* The Union Pacific R. R. Co. 3 Wyoming, 446 (1881).

(18) [He hath withdrawn.]

(19) Thomason *v.* Odum, 31 Ala. 113 Shepherd (1857). Hodges *v.* Council, 86 N. C. 180 Kenan (1882). An agreement to dismiss an action is not equivalent to retraxit. A retraxit is a voluntary acknowledgment on record by a plaintiff present in court that he has no cause of action. Olcot *v.* Banfil *et al.* 7 N. H. 474 (1835). If a party commence a suit before a justice, and takes an appeal from the judgment of the justice, and afterwards pays the costs in settlement of the suit, twelve days before the sitting of the county court, and neglects to prosecute the appeal in the appellate court, it will operate as a retraxit. Small *v.* Hoskins *et al.* 26 Vermont, 217, Dean (1855). Evans *v.* McMahon, 1 Ala. 47, Judges (1840). Although defence may mean literally a denial of the truth or validity of the complaint, an assertion that the plaintiff has no cause of action, it has ceased to mean a justification, and as now used by courts and judges it is applied to the matters which go to the partial as well as to the total extinction of the plaintiff's claim. Bush *v.* Prosser, 1 Kernan, N. Y. 352 (1854). Black on Judgments, 838. It is

nonsuit;(20) for when a plaintiff leaves a chasm in the proceedings of his cause, as by not continuing the process regularly from day to day and time to time bound, as he ought to do, the suit is discontinued, and the defendant is no longer to attend;(21) but the plaintiff must begin again by suing out a new original, usually paying costs to his antagonist. Anciently, by the demise of the king, all suits depending in his courts were at once discontinued, and the plaintiff was obliged to renew the process by suing out a fresh writ from the successor, the virtue of the former writ being totally gone, and the defendant no longer bound to attend in consequence thereof ; but, to prevent the expense as well as delay attending this rule of law, the statute 1 Edw. VI. c. 7, enacts that by the death of the king no action shall be discontinued, but all proceedings shall stand good as if the same king had been living.

When the plaintiff hath stated his case in the declaration, it is incumbent on the defendant within a reasonable time to make his *defence* and to put in a *plea;* else the plaintiff will at once recover judgment by *default* or *nihil dicit* of the defendant.

Defence, in its true legal sense, signifies not a justification, protection, or guard, which is now its popular signification, but merely an *opposing* or *denial*, (from the French verb *defender*) of the truth or validity of the complaint.(22) It is the *contestatio litis*(23) of the civilians, a general assertion that the plaintiff hath no ground of action, which assertion is afterwards extended *and maintained in his plea. For it would be ridiculous to suppose that the defendant comes and *defends* (or, in the vulgar acceptation, justifies) the force and injury in one line, and pleads that he is *not guilty* of the trespass complained of, in the next. And therefore, in actions of dower, where the demandant doth not count of any injury done, but merely demands her endowment,(*k*) and in assizes of land, where also there is no injury alleged, but merely a question of right stated for the determination of the recognitors or jury, the tenant makes no such defence.(*l*) In writs of entry,(*m*) where no injury is stated in the count, but merely the right of the demandant and the defective title of the tenant, the tenant comes and defends or denies *his* right, *jus suum;* that is, (as I understand it, though

*297]

(*k*) Rastal. Ent. 131.
(*l*) Booth of Real Actions, 118.

(*m*) Book II. Append. No. V. § 2.

improper to enter a retraxit or a judgment in the nature of a retraxit and having the effect of a judgment upon the merits without the personal consent of the plaintiff in the action; such is the rule of the English common law, and in the absence of statute, such is the rule in this country. Hatlock *v.* Loft, 19 Col. 80, Robinson (1893). Where there is a question as to whether the report of referees covers certain matters stated in the complaint, the plaintiff's attorney, under the first clause of section 772 of the practice act 2 R. S. 1876, p. 305, has power to make and file a written retraxit of such matters and bind his client thereby, and such retraxit will cure the omission or defect in such report and the court ought thereupon to render judgment in the defendant's favor for the matter so released. Barnard *v.* Daggett, 68 Ind. 305, 310 (1879).

(20) Kahn *v.* Herman, 3 Kelly (Ga.) 272 (1847).

(21) Curtis *v.* Gaines, 46 Ala. (Jones) 459 (1871). Drinkard *v.* The State, 20 Ala. (Sheperd) 12 (1852). Miller *v.* Martin, 3 N. J. (Halstead) 204 (1825). Exchange Bank of Va. *v.* Hall, 6 W. Va. 450 (1873). The word is also frequently used to indicate that the plaintiff discontinues his action. The judgment in such case is no more than an agreement not to proceed farther in that suit against that particular defendant, and is not a bar to any future action against the same party. Black on Judgments, 839 (1891). An appearance after a discontinuance waives it; and taking a final judgment for the unanswered part of a cause of action, at any time during the term, will prevent a discontinuance, if such judgment be taken before the entry of a discontinuance. McDougle *v.* Gates, 21 Ind. 66 (1863).

(22) It now means that which is offered by a defendant as sufficient to defeat the complaint by denying, justifying or confessing and avoiding the action. Brower *v.* Nellis, 6 Ind. 326 (1892). King *v.* Bell, 13 Neb. 414 (1882).

(23) [The opening of a case before witnesses.]

with a small grammatical inaccuracy,) the right of the demandant, the only one expressly mentioned in the pleadings, or else denies his own right to be such as is suggested by the count of the demandant.   And in writs of right (*n*) the tenant always comes and defends the right of the demandant and his seisin, *jus prædicti S. et seisinam ipsius*, (*o*)(24) (or else the seisin of his ancestor upon which he counts, as the case may be,) and the demandant may reply that the tenant unjustly defends his, the demandant's, right, and the seisin on which he counts. (*p*)   All which is extremely clear if we understand by *defence* an *opposition* or *denial*, but it is otherwise inexplicably difficult. (*q*)

The courts were formerly very nice and curious with respect to the nature of the defence; so that if no defence was made, though a sufficient plea was pleaded, the plaintiff should recover judgment; (*r*) and therefore the book entitled *novæ narrationes* or the *new talys*, (*s*) at the end of almost every count, *narratio*, or tale, subjoins such defence as is proper for the defendant to make.   For a general defence or denial was not prudent in every situation, since thereby the propriety of the writ, the competency of the plaintiff, and the cognizance of the court, were allowed.   By defending the force and injury, *the defendant waived all pleas of misnomer;(*t*)   by   [*298 defending the damages, all exceptions to the person of the plaintiff; and by defending either one or the other *when and where* it should behoove him, he acknowledged the jurisdiction of the court. (*u*)   But of late years these niceties have been very deservedly discountenanced, (*w*) though they still seem to be law, if insisted on. (*x*)

Before defence made, if at all, *cognizance* of the suit must be *claimed* or demanded; when any person or body corporate hath the franchise, not only of *holding pleas* within a particular limited jurisdiction, but also of the *cognizance of pleas:* and that, either *without* any words exclusive of other courts, which entitles the lord of the franchise, whenever any suit that belongs to his jurisdiction is commenced in the courts at Westminster, to demand the cognizance thereof; or *with* such exclusive words, which also entitle the defendant to plead to the jurisdiction of the court. (*y*)   Upon this claim of cognizance, if allowed, all proceedings shall cease in the superior court, and the plaintiff is left at liberty to pursue his remedy in the special jurisdiction.   As when a scholar, or other privileged person, of the universities of Oxford or Cambridge, is impleaded in the courts at Westminster for any cause of action whatsoever, unless upon a question of freehold.(*z*)(25) In these cases, by the charter of those learned bodies, confirmed by act of parliament, the chancellor or vice-chancellor may put in a claim of cognizance; which, if made in due time and form and with due proof of the facts alleged, is regularly allowed by the courts.(*a*)(26)   It must be demanded before full defence is made(*b*) or imparlance prayed; for these are a submission to the jurisdiction of the superior court, and the delay is a *laches* in the

(*n*) Append. No. I. § 5.
(*o*) Co. Entr. 182.
(*p*) *Nov. Nar.* 230, edit. 1534.
(*q*) The true reason of this, says Booth, (on Real Actions, 94, 112,) I could never yet find ; so little did he understand of principles !
(*r*) Co. Litt. 127.
(*s*) Edit. 1534.
(*t*) Theloal. *dig. l.* 14, c. 1, pag. 357.
(*u*) *En la defence sont iij choses entendantz; per tant quil defende tort et force, home doyt entendre quil se excuse de tort a luy surmys per counte, et fait se partie al ple; et per tant quil defende les damages, il affirm le parte able destre respondu; et per tant quil defende ou et quant il devera, il accepte la poiar de court de conustre ou trier lour ple.* Mod tenend. cur. 408, edit. 1534. See also Co. Litt. 127. [Translated in the text.]
(*w*) Salk. 217. Lord Raym. 282.
(*x*) Carth. 230. Lord Raym. 217.
(*y*) 2 Lord Raym. 836. 10 Mod. 126.
(*z*) See page 83.
(*a*) Hardr. 505.
(*b*) Rast. 128, etc. 1 Chitty on Pl. 364.

(24) [The right and seisin of the aforesaid S.]
(25) But only *resident* members of either university are entitled to this privilege, it being local as well as personal. 2 Wils. 310.—CHITTY.
(26) Ginnett *v.* Whittingham, L. R. 16 Q. B. Div. 770 (1886).

*299]   lord of the franchise, and it will not be allowed if it occasions a
failure of justice,(c) or if an action be brought against the person
himself who claims the franchise, unless he hath also a power in such cases
of making another judge.(d)(27)

After defence made, the defendant must put in his *plea*. But before he
defends, if the suit is commenced by *capias* or *latitat*, without any special
original, he is entitled to demand one *imparlance*,(e) or *licentia loquendi*,(28)
and may before he pleads have more time granted by consent of the court, to
see if he can end the matter amicably without further suit, by talking with
the plaintiff; a practice which is(f) supposed to have arisen from a principle
of religion in obedience to that precept of the gospel, "Agree with thine
adversary quickly, whilst thou art *in the way* with him."(g) And it may
be observed that this gospel precept has a plain reference to the Roman law
of the twelve tables, which expressly directed the plaintiff and defendant to
make up the matter while they were *in the way*, or going to the prætor, —
tu via, rem uti pacunt orato. There are also many other previous steps which
may be taken by a defendant before he puts in his plea. He may, in real
actions, demand a *view* of the thing in question, in order to ascertain its
identity and other circumstances. He may crave *oyer*(h) of the writ, or of
the bond, or other specialty upon which the action is brought; that is, to
hear it read to him; the generality of defendants in the times of ancient simplicity being supposed incapable to read it themselves, whereupon the whole
is entered *verbatim* upon the record, and the defendant may take advantage
of any condition or other part of it, not stated in the plaintiff's
*300]   declaration.(29) *In real actions also the tenant may pray in *aid*, or

(c) 2 Ventr. 363.
(d). Hob. 87. Year-book, M. 8 Hen. VI. 20. In this
latter case the chancellor of Oxford claimed cognizance of an action of trespass brought against himself, which was disallowed, because he should not
be judge in his own cause. The argument used by
serjeant Rolfe on behalf of the cognizance is curious
and worth transcribing;—*leo vous dirai un fable.
En ascun temps fuit un pape, et avoit fait un grand
offence, et le cardinals vindrent a luy et disoyent a luy,
"peccasti;" et il dit, "judica me;" et ils disoyent, "non
possumus, quia caput es ecclesie: judica teipsum;" et
l'apostol dit, "justica me crenari;" et fuit combustus;
et apres fuit un seinct. Et in ceo cas il fuit son juge
demene, et issint n'est pas inconvenient que un home soit*

*juge demene. [I will tell you a story. There was
formerly a pope and he committed a great crime,
and the cardinals came to him and said: "Thou
hast sinned;" and he said: "Judge me;" and they
answered, "We cannot, for thou art the head of the
church; judge thyself." And the apostle said: "I
sentence myself to be burned;" and burned he
was, and afterwards he was made a saint. And in
that case he was his own judge, and therefore it is
not improper that a man should judge himself.]
(e). Append. No. III. § 6.
(f) Gilb. Hist. Com. Pl. 35.
(g) Matt. v. 25.
(h) Append. No. III. § 6.

(27) But a party may waive and preclude himself from taking any objection to a decision on this account; for if a defendant agree to refer the matter to the plaintiff, he cannot object to the award that the plaintiff was a judge in his own cause. Thus, in
Matthew *v.* Ollerton, (4 Mod. 226. Comb. 218   Hardr. 44.) which was an action of debt
upon an award, and a verdict for the plaintiff; and, upon its being moved in arrest of judgment, the exception taken was that the matter in difference was referred to the plaintiff
himself, who made an award. *Sed non allocatur* [But is not discussed]. And the case
of serjeant Hards was remembered by Dolben, Justice,—viz:—The serjeant took a horse
from my lord of Canterbury's bailiff for a deodand, and the archbishop brought his action;
and, it coming to a trial at the assizes in Kent, the serjeant, by rule of court, referred it
to the archbishop, to set the price of the horse, which was done accordingly; and the
serjeant afterwards moved the court to set aside the award for the reason now offered;
but it was denied by lord Hale and *per totam curiam* [By the whole court].—CHITTY.
Where the judge granting an order in a case to which he is a party, as well as judge, and
joins in the application for the order, even though he be a party merely in an official
capacity, the order is void. Nor is the defendant estopped because the order was entered
by consent of his counsel. Converse *v.* McArthur, 17 N. Y. (Barbour) 413 (1854).
(28) [Liberty of speaking.]
(29) But now a defendant is not allowed oyer of the *writ*. 1 B. & P. 646. 3 B. & P.
395. 7 East, 383. As to the demand and giving of oyer, and the manner of setting out
deeds, etc. therein, see 1 Saund. 9, (1,) 289, (2.) 2 Saund. 9, (12,) (13,) 46,(7,) 366, (1,)
405, (1,) 410, (2.) Tidd, 8 ed. 635 to 638, and Index, tit. Oyer. 1 Chitt. on Pl. 369 to
375.—CHITTY. If the defendant demand oyer of the writ, the plaintiff might proceed
as if no such demand had been made. Wilson *et al. v.* Moore *et al.*, 72 N. C. 560 (1875).

call for assistance of another, to help him to plead, because of the feebleness or imbecility of his own estate. Thus, a tenant for life may pray in aid of him that hath the inheritance in remainder or reversion; and an incumbent may pray in aid of the patron and ordinary; that is, that they shall be joined in the action and help to defend the title.(30) *Voucher* also is the calling in of some person to answer the action that hath warranted the title to the tenant or defendant. This we still make use of in the form of common recoveries,(*i*) which are grounded on a writ of entry; a species of action that we may remember relies chiefly on the weakness of the tenant's title, who therefore vouches another person to warrant it. If the vouchee appears, he is made defendant instead of the voucher; but if he afterwards makes default, recovery shall be had against the original defendant, and he shall recover over an equivalent in value against the deficient vouchee. In assizes, indeed, where the principal question is, whether the demandant or his ancestors were or were not in possession till the ouster happened, and the title of the tenant is little (if at all) discussed, there no voucher is allowed; but the tenant may bring a writ of *warrantia chartæ* against the warrantor, to compel him to assist him with a good plea or defence, or else to render damages and the value of the land, if recovered against the tenant.(*k*)(31) In many real actions also,(*l*) brought by or against an infant under the age of twenty-one years, and also in actions of debt brought against him, as heir to any deceased ancestor, either party may suggest the nonage of the infant, and pray that the proceedings may be deferred till his full age; or (in our legal phrase) that the infant may have his age, and that the *parol may demur*, that is, that the pleadings may be stayed; and that they shall not proceed till his full age, unless it be apparent that he cannot be prejudiced thereby.(*m*)(32) But, by the statutes of Westm. 1, 3 Edw. I. c. 46, and of Glocester, 6 Edw. I. c. 2, in writs of entry *sur disseisin* in some particular cases, and in actions ancestral brought by *an infant, the   [*301 parol shall not demur: otherwise he might be deforced of his whole property, and even want a maintenance till he came of age. So likewise in a writ of dower the heir shall not have his age, for it is necessary that the widow's claim be immediately determined, else she may want a present subsistence.(*n*) Nor shall an infant patron have it in a *quare impedit*,(*o*) since the law holds it necessary and expedient that the church be immediately filled.(33)

When these proceedings are over, the defendant must then put in his excuse or plea. Pleas are of two sorts; *dilatory* pleas, and pleas *to the action*. Dilatory pleas are such as tend merely to delay or put off the suit, by questioning the propriety of the remedy, rather than by denying the injury: pleas to the action are such as dispute the very cause of suit. The former cannot be pleaded after a general imparlance,(34) which is an acknowledgment of

---

(*i*) Book II. Append. No. V. § 2.
(*k*) F. N. B. 135.
(*l*) Dyer, 137.

(*m*) Finch, L. 360.
(*n*) 1 Roll. Abr. 137.
(*o*) Ibid. 138.

---

(30) De Lancey *v.* Ganong, 5 Seld. 9, 16 (1853).
(31) Chapman *v.* Holmes, 5 N. J. Hals. 31 (1828).
(32) Or unless his guardian or next friend satisfy the court that it will be for his benefit. Tessier *v.* Wise, 3 Bland (Md) 43 (1825).
    The general assembly of Maryland have made a material alteration in the pre-existing law in relation to the sale of real estate descended, or devised to infants, by virtually abolishing the infant's privilege of having the parol to demur in a creditor's suit. Tessier *v.* Wise, 3 Bland (Md.) 43 (1825).
(33) And now, indeed, by statute 11 Geo. IV. and 1 W. IV. c. 47, s. 10, the parol shall not demur in any action.—KERR.
(34) If the defendant wish to preserve his right to such a plea he must vary his form of

the propriety of the action. For imparlances are either *general*, of which we have before spoken, and which are granted of course; or *special*, with a saving of all exceptions to the writ or count, which may be granted by the prothonotary; or they may be still *more special*, with a saving of all exceptions whatsoever which are granted at the discretion of the court.(*p*)

I. Dilatory pleas are,(35) 1. To the *jurisdiction* of the court: alleging, that it ought not to hold plea of this injury, it arising in Wales or beyond sea; or because the land in question is of ancient demesne, and ought only to be demanded in the lord's court, etc. 2. To the *disability* of the plaintiff, by reason whereof he is incapable to commence or continue the suit; as, that he is an alien enemy, outlawed, excommunicated, attainted of treason or felony, under a *præmunire*, not *in rerum natura*, (36) (being only a fictitious person,) an infant, a feme-covert, or a monk professed.(37) 3. In *abatement*,
*302] which abatement is either of the *writ or the count, for some defect in one of them; as by misnaming the defendant, which is called a *misnomer;* giving him a wrong addition, as *esquire* instead of *knight;* or other want of form in any material respect.(38) Or it may be that the

(*p*) 12 Mod. 529.

prayer, by making it with the reservation of his right, and asking a special imparlance, which must be entered on the record. Chamberlin *v.* Hite, 5 Watts (Pa.) 374 (1837).

(35) These pleas are not favored by the courts; and they must be filed within four days after the day upon which the declaration is delivered, both days being inclusive. 1 T. R. 277. 5 T. R. 210.—CHITTY.

(36) [In the nature of things, or in the world]

(37) As to this plea, see 1 Chit. 387, 388. Whenever the subject-matter of the plea or defence is that the plaintiff cannot maintain *any* action *at any time*, in respect of the supposed cause of action, it may, and usually should, be pleaded in *bar;* but matter which merely defeats the present proceeding and does not show that the plaintiff is forever precluded should in general be pleaded in *abatement*. 4 T. R. 227. Some matters may be pleaded either in abatement or bar; as outlawry for felony, alien enemy, or attainder, etc. Bac. Abr. Abatement, N. Com. Dig. Abatement, K.

The defendant may also plead in abatement his or her own personal disability; as in case of coverture, when the husband ought to have been joined. 3 T. R. 627. Bac. Abr. Abatement, G.—CHITTY. Binns' Justice, (Brightly 10 ed.) 72 (1895).

(38) Pleas in abatement to the writ are so termed rather from their *effects* than from their being strictly such pleas; for, as oyer of the writ can no longer be craved, no objection can be taken by plea to matter which is merely contained in the *writ*. 3 B. & P. 399. 1 B. & P. 645. But if the mistake in the writ be carried also into the declaration, or, rather, if the declaration, which is presumed to correspond with the writ or bill, be incorrect in respect of some extrinsic matter, it is then open to the defendant to plead in abatement to the writ or bill, (1 B. & P. 648;) and as to such pleas, see 1 Chit. on Pl. 390 to 394. Consequently, a misnomer of the defendant, or giving him a wrong addition, or other want of form, in the *writ*, unless it be contained in the declaration, is not now pleadable in abatement. See 1 Saund. 318, n. 3. 3 B. & P. 395. And the defendant, to take advantage of any defect in the writ, should, in general, before appearance move to set it aside for irregularity. 1 B. & P. 647. 5 Moore, 168.—CHITTY.

But now the writ itself may be amended; and further restrictions have, by the Common Law Procedure Act, 1852, been imposed on pleas in abatement in addition to those previously imposed by statute 3 & 4 W. IV. c. 42. By that statute (s. 8) no plea in abatement for the non-joinder of any person as a co-defendant shall be allowed unless it shall be stated in such plea that such person is resident within the jurisdiction of the court, and unless the place of residence of such person shall be stated with certainty in an affidavit verifying the plea. And, by s. 11, no plea in abatement for a misnomer shall be allowed in any personal action; but, in all cases in which a misnomer would but for that act have been pleadable, the defendant may cause the declaration to be amended at the cost of the plaintiff, by inserting the right name upon a judge's summons founded on an affidavit of the right name. And, by s. 12, in all actions upon bills of exchange or promissory notes or other written instruments, the parties to which are designated by the initials or some contraction of the Christian or first name, it is sufficient in every affidavit to hold to bail, and in the process or declaration to designate such persons by the same initial letter or contraction of the Christian or first name.—STEWART. See McKenna *v.* Fisk, 1 How. (U. S.) 241-247 (1843).

plaintiff is dead; for the death of either party is at once an abatement of the suit.(39) And in actions merely personal, arising *ex delicto,*(40) for wrongs actually done or committed by the defendant, as trespass, battery, and slander, the rule is that *actio personalis moritur cum persona;*(q)(41) and it never shall be revived either by or against the executors or other representatives. For neither the executors of the plaintiff have received, nor those of the defendant have committed, in their own personal capacity, any manner of wrong or injury.(42) But in actions arising *ex contractu,*(43) by breach of promise, and the like, where the right descends to the representatives of the plaintiff, and those of the defendant have assets to answer the demand, though the suits shall abate by the death of the parties, yet they may be revived against or by the executors:(r)(44) being indeed rather actions against the property than the person, in which the executors have now the same interest that their testator had before.(45)

These pleas to the jurisdiction, to the disability, or in abatement, were formerly very often used as mere dilatory pleas, without any foundation of truth, and calculated only for delay; but now, by statute 4 & 5 Anne, c. 16, no dilatory plea is to be admitted without affidavit made of the truth thereof, or some probable matter shown to the court to induce them to believe it

(q) 4 Inst. 315.   (r) March. 14.

---

(39) But, now, by the Common-Law Procedure Act, 1852, an action shall no longer abate by the death of either party, but may be continued by the legal representative of sole plaintiff on his entering (by leave of the court) a suggestion of the plaintiff's death on the record; or by a surviving plaintiff when the cause of action survives; or against the legal representative of a defendant.—STEWART.

(40) [From wrong done.]

(41) [A personal action dies with the person.] An exception to this rule is the statutory provision, giving the right of action to the representatives against any party who wrongfully causes the death of the decedent. Curry *v.* Mannington, 23 Watts (W. Va.) 18 (1883). Hadley *v.* Bryars Adm'rs, 58 Ala. 186 (Clark, 1877). Watson *v.* Loop, 12 Tex. (Hartley) 14 (1854). Wilson *v.* Knox, 12 N. H. 350 (1845). Where the plaintiff in an action—the cause of which does not by law survive obtains a judgment, and the defendant institutes a review of the action, the death of the original plaintiff will not defeat the action of review. Knox *v.* Knox, 12 N. H. 353 (1845). Broom's Parties to Actions, 287.

(42) By statute 3 & 4 W. IV. c. 42, s. 2, an action of trespass, or trespass on the case, may be maintained by the executors or administrators of any deceased person for injury to his real estate in his lifetime, if such injury were committed within six calendar months before death and the action brought within one year after the time of the death; and an action of trespass, or trespass on the case, may also be maintained against executors or administrators for wrongs committed by the deceased to another's property, real or personal, such injury having been committed within six months of the death and the action brought within six months after administration taken.—STEWART. See Bigelow on Fraud, vol. 1. 350, 471. By statutes in England and in this country, representatives of the deceased party may bring an action for any injury done to the personal estate of the deceased in his lifetime, whereby it has become less beneficial. Curry *v.* Mannington, 23 W. Va. (Watts) 18 (1883). Petts *v.* Ison, 11 Ga. (Cobb) 153 (1852). Under the statute laws of Iowa (laws of 1862, p. 229) no cause of action either *ex contractu* [From contract] or *ex delicto* [From tort] abates by the death of either party, if from the legal nature of the case it can survive. Hence, an action of seduction commenced by the injured party who died during its pendency, survived to her administrator. Shafer *v.* Grimes, 23 Iowa, 553 (Stiles, 1867). Action against a town for personal injury caused by defect in a highway will not, under the statutes of Maine, (c. 87, sec. 8, of the R. S. of 1857,) abate by the death of the plaintiff, but may be prosecuted by the administrator or executor of the deceased. Hooper *v.* Gorham, 45 Hubbard (Me.) 214 (1858). Some mistakes in a declaration, such as would be amendable on motion, should be pleaded in abatement. Kempton *v.* Saving's Inst., 53 N. H. 589 (Shirley, 1873).

(43) [From contract.]

(44) An action of trespass for mesne profits may be brought against an administrator to recover profits received by the intestate in his life time. Molton *v.* Miller, 3 Hawke (N. C.) 497 (1825). Ela *v.* Rand, 4 N. H. 56 (1827).

(45) Browne's Actions of Law, 261.

true.(46) And with respect to the pleas themselves, it is a rule, that no exception shall be admitted against a declaration or writ, unless the defendant will in the same plea give the plaintiff a better;(s)(47) that is, show him how it might be amended, that there may not be two objections upon the same account. Neither, by statute 8 & 9 W. III. c. 31, shall any plea in abatement be admitted in any suit for partition of lands; nor shall the same be abated by reason of the death of any tenant.

*303] *All pleas to the jurisdiction conclude to the cognizance of the court: praying "judgment, whether the court will have further cognizance of the suit:" pleas to the disability conclude to the person; by praying "judgment, if the said A. the plaintiff ought to be answered:" and pleas in abatement (when the suit is by original) conclude to the writ or declaration; by praying "judgment of the writ, or declaration, and that the same may be quashed," *cassetur*, made void, or abated; but, if the action be by bill, the plea must pray "judgment of the bill," and not of the declaration; the bill being here the original, and the declaration only a copy of the bill.

When these dilatory pleas are allowed, the cause is either dismissed from that jurisdiction; or the plaintiff is stayed till his disability be removed; or he is obliged to sue out a new writ, by leave obtained from the court:(t) or to amend and new-frame his declaration. But when on the other hand they are overruled as frivolous, the defendant has judgment of *respondeat ouster*, or to *answer over* in some better manner.(48) It is then incumbent on him to plead.

2. A plea *to the action;* that is, to answer to the merits of the complaint. This is done by confessing or denying it.

A confession of the whole complaint is not very usual, for then the defendant would probably end the matter sooner, or not plead at all, but suffer judgment to go by default. Yet sometimes, after tender and refusal of a debt, if the creditor harasses his debtor with an action, it then becomes necessary for the defendant to acknowledge the debt, and plead the tender; adding, that he has always been ready, *tout temps prist*, and still is ready, *uncore prist*, to discharge it: for a tender by the debtor and refusal by the creditor will in all cases discharge the costs,(u) but not the debt itself;(49)

*304] though in some particular cases the creditor will totally lose his money.(v)(50) *But frequently the defendant confesses one *part of*

(s) Brownl. 139.
(t) Co. Entr. 271.

(u) 1 Ventr. 21.
(v) Litt. § 338. Co. Litt. 209.

(46) Sham pleas are not dilatory pleas within the statute, and an affidavit is not necessary in all cases: thus, a plea of privilege as an attorney of the same court, to be sued by bill, it is supposed does not require an affidavit. 3 B. & P. 397. 1 Chit. on Pl. 401. As to the form of the affidavit, see 1 Chit. on Pl. 402. Tidd, 8 ed. 693.—CHITTY.

(47) Iron Co. *v.* Rutherford, 3 N. J. 161 (Harrison, 1840).

(48) Straus *v.* Weil, 5 Coldwell (Tenn.) 126 (1867).

(49) The tender is a production and manual offer of the money, and regularly it should be counted down. A bag for the money will do, but not a pocket. Bakeman *v.* Pooler, 15 N. Y. 638 (Wendall, 1836).

(50) That is to say, if the only right which A. has to the money arise from the offer which B. makes to him of it, and he once refuse to accept that offer, he thereby loses all right, and of course can bring no action. The case put by lord Coke is, "If A., *without any loane, debt, or dutie preceding*, infeoff B. of land, upon condition for the payment of a hundred pounds to B., *in nature of a gratuitie or gift*, in that case if he (A.) tender the hundred pounds to him (B.) according to the condition, and he refuseth it, B. hath no remedie therefor." Here B. had primarily no title to the land or the money: if he does not accept it, therefore, when offered, no debt is due to him, but A. by the offer has discharged his land from that burden which he had voluntarily imposed on it. But supposing the land to have been mortgaged by A. to B. for money lent, which A. is to repay on a certain day, then if the money is duly tendered on the day and refused, A. shall have his land again, because he has performed the condition; but still B. may bring an action for his money.

the complaint, (by a *cognovit actionem*(51) in respect thereof,) and traverses or denies the rest: in order to avoid the expense of carrying that part

---

(51) [He hath acknowledged the action.]

The plea of tender must always, except in the case above supposed, be accompanied by a bringing of the sum tendered into court, or the plea is a mere nullity; and though the plaintiff denies that the tender was made before he commenced the action, or disputes the sufficiency of the sum tendered, and therefore goes on with the action, still he is entitled to take that sum out of court at once, which the defendant by the tender has admitted to be his due. If, however, he neglects to do so, and a verdict on either point should pass for the defendant, the court will then lay hold of the money as a security for the defendant's costs. Le Grew *v.* Cook, 1 B. & P. 332. See also Birks *v.* Trippet, 1 Saund. Rep. 33, a., note.—COLERIDGE.

As to the form and requisites of this plea in assumpsit, see 3 Chit. on Pl. 4th ed. 992; in debt, id. 955, and Lee, Prac. Dict. tit. "Tender;" and as to the payment of money into court on, see Tidd, 8th ed. Index, tit. "Money;" Lee, Dict. tit. "Payment of Money into Court." As to the replication, etc., see also 3 Chit. on Pl. 1151 to 1156, and Lee, Dict. tit. "Tender."

While the general rule is, that it is essential to the validity of a tender that the money be actually produced and proffered to the plaintiff, yet it is well settled that the production of the money is dispensed with if the party is ready and willing to pay the same, and is about to produce it, but is prevented by the creditor's declaring that he will not receive it.

Rudolph *v.* Wagner, 36 Ala. (Shepherd) 703 (1860).

Tender of the whole amount, principal and interest, at any time after the debt falls due, but before suit brought, stops the interest, and discharges the party from costs of a subsequent suit. Idem. Raymond *v.* Bernard, 12 Johns. 274 (1815).

If suit is brought on the obligation, the obligor must keep his tender good by having the money before the court on the trial. St. L. K. & N. W. Ry. Co. *v.* Clark, 119 Mo. (Brown) 372 (1893).

The usual tender should not be conditioned. Cothray *v.* Scanlon, 34 Ga. 555. The refusal of an absolute tender of the amount due on a mortgage operates as a discharge of the lien, although the tender be not afterwards kept good. Potts *v.* Plaisted, 30 Mich. 149 (1874); if the refusal be not absolute nor unreasonable, the security is not necessarily discharged. Waldron *v.* Murphy, 40 Mich. 668 (1879). The money should be at hand and capable of immediate delivery. 5 Esp. 47 (1803). If a place be not fixed for the payment of the debt, it is the duty of the debtor to offer to pay the creditor wherever he may be, in order that the tender be good. King *v.* Finch, 60 Ind. 420 (1878).

An actual production of the money is not necessary if, in making the offer, the creditor refuse to receive it. Hazard *v.* Loring, 10 Cash. (Mass.) 267.

As questions relative to the *tender* of a debt or money are of so frequent occurrence, we will consider the respective rules and decisions under the following heads: 1st. What is a good tender. 2d. In what cases it may be made. And *lastly*, the effect and advantages gained by it, and how these may be superseded.

1. WHAT IS A GOOD TENDER.—It is a general rule, that, in order to constitute a good legal tender, the party should not only be ready to pay, and make an *actual* offer of the sum due, but actually produce the same, unless such production be dispensed with by the express declaration of the creditor that he will not accept it, or by some equivalent act. 10 East, 101. 5 Esp. R. 48. 3 T. R. 684. Peake, C. N. P. 88. 1 Cromp. 152. 2 M. & S. 86. 7 Moore, 59. If the plaintiff do not object to receive the money, it is not sufficient for the defendant to prove that he had the money with him and held it in a bag under his arm: he ought to have laid it down for him. Id. ibid. Bull. N. P. 157. 6 Esp. 46. If A. says, "I am not aware of the exact balance, but if any be due I am ready to pay it," this is no tender. 15 East, 428.

With respect to the *nature* of the money tendered, it should be in the current coin of the realm, and not in bank-notes; and see the 56 Geo. III. c. 68, s. 11, by which gold coin is declared to be the only legal tender. But a tender in bank-notes is good unless particularly objected to on that account at the time. 3 T. R. 554. 2 B. & P. 526. So is a tender of foreign coin made current here by royal proclamation. 5 Rep. 114, b. So is a tender of provincial bank-notes, or a draft on a banker, unless so objected to. Peake N. P. 3d ed. 239. Tidd, 8th ed. 187, n. f. It seems that as any money coined at the mint upon which there is the king's stamp is good, and that all such money is good in proportion to its value, without a proclamation, such money would be a good tender. 2 Salk. 446.

With respect to the *amount* of the sum tendered, it should in general be *an offer of the specific sum due, unqualified by any circumstance whatever;* and therefore tendering a larger sum, and making cross-demand, is insufficient. 2 D. & R. 305. A tender of 20*l.* in bank-notes, with a request to pay over the difference of fifteen guineas, is not a good

to a formal trial, which he has no ground to litigate. A species of this sort of confession is the *payment of money into court:*(w) which is for the most

tender as to the fifteen guineas, though it would have been otherwise if the tender had been in guineas. 3 Camp. 70. 1 Camp. 181. 6 Taunt. 336. But a tender of a larger sum generally is good. 5 Rep. 114. 8 T. R. 683; *sed vide* 2 Esp. 711. And a tender of a larger sum, and asking change, is good, provided the creditor do not object to it on that account, but only demands a larger sum. 6 Taunt. 336. Peake C. N. P. 88. 2 Esp. C. 711. 3 Camp. 70; and see 1 Gow. C. N. P. 121. A tender of a sum to A., including both a debt due to A., B., and C. and also a debt due to C., is a good tender of the debt due to the three, (3 T. R. 683;) and if several creditors, to whom money is due in the same right, assemble for the purpose of demanding payment, a tender of the gross sum, which they all refuse on account of the insufficiency of the amount, is good. Peake C. 88. 2 T. R. 414.

To constitute a good tender, it must be an unconditional one in payment of the debt; and therefore where a tender of payment was made, accompanied with a protestation against the right of the party to receive it, it was held insufficient. 3 Esp. C. 91. So is a tender accompanied with the demand of a receipt in full, (5 Esp. Rep. 48. 2 Camp. 21; *sed vide* Peake C. 179. Stark. on Evid. part 4, 1392, n. (g),) or upon condition that it shall be received as the whole of the balance due, (4 Camp. 156,) or that a particular document shall be given up to be cancelled. 2 Camp. 21. To constitute a good tender of stock, the buyer must be called on opening the books, (1 Stra 533,) and the defendant must do all in his power to make it good. 1 Stra. 504.

With respect to the *time* of the tender, it should be observed that, in order to avoid the defendant's liability to damages for the non-performance of the contract, it should be made in the very time agreed upon for the performance of such contract: a tender after such time only goes in mitigation of damages for the breach of the contract, and not even then if the tender be not made before the writ sued out. 7 Taunt. 487. See 21 Jac. I. c. 16, s. 5. It is said to have been decided by Buller, J., that a tender on the day the bill is filed is not available, there being no fraction of a day, (Imp. K. B. 324;) consequently, if payment of a bill has been demanded on the day it was due, and the acceptor plead a subsequent tender, it will not avail. 8 East, 168. 5 Taunt. 240. 1 Marsh, Rep. 36. 1 Saund. 33, a., note 2. But that doctrine is not law; and it is no answer to a plea of tender that the plaintiff had, before the tender, instructed his attorney to sue out the writ, and that the attorney had applied before the tender for the writ which was afterwards sued out, (8 T. R. 629;) and if the plaintiff brings his action, and discontinues it and commences another, a tender before the latter action is good. 1 Moore, 200. To constitute a good tender of stock, it should be made on the very day, (1 Stra. 579;) and at the last part of the day it can be accepted. 2 id. 777, 832. Any party, being an agent of the debtor, may tender the money. 2 M. & S. 86.

With respect to the persons to *whom* the tender should be made, it will suffice if it be to the creditor or any authorized agent. 1 Camp. 477. Tender to an attorney, authorized to issue out a writ, etc., is good. Dougl. 625. And a tender to an agent has been held good although the principal had previously prohibited the agent from receiving the money if offered, the principal having put his business into the hands of his attorney. 5 Taunt. 307. 1 Marsh. 55, S. C. A bailiff, who makes a distress, cannot delegate his authority: therefore a tender to his agent is insufficient, (6 Esp. 95;) and a tender to one of several creditors is a tender to all. 3 T. R. 683.

2dly. IN WHAT CASES A TENDER MAY BE MADE WITH EFFECT.—In general, a tender can only be made with effect in cases where the demand is of a liquidated sum, or of a sum capable of liquidation by computation. See 2 Burr. 1120. Therefore a tender cannot be pleaded to an action for general damages upon a contract, (1 Vent. 356. 2 Bla. Rep. 837. 2 B. & P. 234. 3 B. & P. 14;) or in covenant, unless for the payment of money, (7 Taunt. 486. 1 Moore, 200, S. C. 5 Mod. 18. 1 Lord Raym. 566. 12 Mod. 376. 2 H. Bla. 837;) or for a tort, (2 Stra. 787, 906. 7 T. R. 335,) or trespass. 2 Wils. 115. It cannot be pleaded in an action for dilapidations, (8 T. R. 47. Stra. 906;) or for not repairing, (2 Salk. 596;) or against a carrier for goods spoiled, though the tender should be of the invoice-price, (2 B. & P. 234;) or for not delivering goods at a certain price per ton, (3 B. & P. 14;) or in an action for a false return, (7 T. R. 335;) or for mesne profits. 2 Wils. 115. But in assumpsit against a carrier for not delivering goods, the defendant having advertised that he would not be answerable for any goods beyond the value of 20l. unless they were entered and paid for accordingly, a tender of the 20l. would, it seems, be available. 1 H. Bla. 299. So a tender may be made with effect to a demand for navigation calls, (7 T. R. 36. 1 Stra. 142,) or in an action for principal and interest due on bonds for payment of moneys by instalments. 3 Burr. 1370. So the penalty of a bond may with effect be tendered. 2 Bla. 1190. So the arrears of a bond for 40l. payable by 5l. per annum. 2 Stra. 814. So a tender may with effect be made in covenant for rent, or for the advanced rent of 5l. per acre for ploughing meadow-grounds. 2 H. Bla. 837. 7 Taunt. 486. 1 Moore, 200, S. C.; and *vide* 2 Salk. 596. So also on a

part necessary upon pleading a tender, and is itself a kind of tender to the plaintiff, (52) by paying into the hands of the proper officer of the court

(52) The allowing the defendant to pay money into court was introduced for the purpose of avoiding the hazard of proving a tender; and in all cases where there has been no tender, or the tender cannot be proved, it should not be pleaded, but the defendant should merely pay the admitted claim into court. The cases in which the proceeding is allowed are similar to those in which a tender may be pleaded, and which will be found *supra*, note (50). One case, however, should be noticed, viz., where the goods have been taken under a mistake without any loss to the owner, the court, upon motion, will stay the proceedings in an action of trespass against a public officer, upon the defendant's undertaking to restore them or to pay their full value with the costs of the action. 7 T. R. 53.—CHITTY.

policy of insurance, (19 Geo. II. c. 37, s. 7. 2 Taunt. 317;) or in debt for penalty for exercising trade contrary to 5 Eliz. c. 4, (1 Burr. 431;) or for penalty on game-laws, being actions popular, and not *qui tam.* 2 H. Bla. 1052. 2 Stra. 1217. Where a party has wrongfully possessed himself of goods, no tender of freight is necessary in order to enable the party to maintain the action. 2 T. R. 285. Justices of the peace, and in like manner excise and custom-house officers, and surveyors of highways, are enabled by several statutes to tender amends for any thing done by them in the execution of their offices. See *ante*, 1 book, 354, n. 37, *et seq.* Also by the 21 Jac. I. c. 16, s. 5, in case of involuntary trespasses, tender of amends may be made. See *ante*, 16.

Lastly, AS TO THE EFFECT OF A TENDER, AND THE ADVANTAGES ACQUIRED BY IT.— It should in the first place be observed that the debtor is liable for the non-performance of his contract if the money be not paid at the time agreed upon: the mere tendering the money afterwards is not sufficient to discharge him from such liability; it goes only *in mitigation of damages;* though, indeed, if a jury should find that no damages were sustained by reason of the defendant not tendering the money at the time agreed upon, the defendant would defeat the action by the tender afterwards. See Salk. 622. 8 East, 168. 1 Lord Raym. 254. 7 Taunt. 486. The tender of money due on a promissory note, accompanied with a demand of the note, stops the running of interest. 3 Camp. 296. 8 East, 168. 4 Leon. 209. The tender, if pleaded, admits the contract and facts stated in the declaration. 3 Taunt. 95. Peake, 15. 2 T. R. 275. 4 T. R. 579. If, therefore, the defendant's liability is to be disputed, a tender should not be pleaded. So if there be a special count, and the defendant mean to deny it, the tender should be pleaded to the other counts only, (and see Tidd, 8 ed. 676;) and if there be any doubt as to the sufficiency of the tender, it is not advisable to plead it, but more expedient to pay the amount into court upon the common rule: for if the defendant should not succeed in proving the tender he will have to pay all the costs of the trial; whereas, if the money be paid into court, and the plaintiff cannot prove more due, he will be liable to pay all costs subsequent to the time of paying the money into court. If the sum tendered be not sufficient, and the plaintiff should succeed on the general issue, the plaintiff would still be entitled to the costs of the issue on the plea of tender. 5 East, 282. 5 Taunt. 660. If the defendant bring money into court on a plea of tender, the plaintiff may take it out, though he deny the tender. 1 B. & P. 332. The plaintiff, it seems, can gain no advantage by not taking the money out of court; and it has been said that if the plaintiff will not take the money, but takes issue on the tender and it is found against him, the defendant shall have it. 1 B. & P. 334, note a. Lord Raym. 642. 2 Stra. 1027. If the plaintiff should succeed on the trial in proving a larger sum to be due than that tendered, though that sum be below 40s., yet the plaintiff will be entitled to costs. Doug. 448. But where the debt originally was under 5l. the defendant is, it seems, entitled to the benefit of the Court of Requests' Act for London, though he has pleaded a tender (5 M. & S. 196) or paid money into court. 5 East, 194.

A tender not being equivalent to payment itself, and only suspending the plaintiff's remedy, 2 T. R. 27,) its effect may be superseded by prior or a *subsequent* demand and refusal to pay the *precise* sum tendered. 1 Camp. 181. 5 B. & A. 630. A subsequent demand of a larger sum will not suffice, (id.,) nor a subsequent demand accompanied by another demand of another sum not due. 1 Esp. 115. 7 Taunt. 213. Such demand should be made by a person authorized to give the debtor a discharge. 1 Camp. 478, n. 1 Esp. 115. A demand made by the clerk of the plaintiff's attorney, who was an entire stranger to defendant, is insufficient. 1 Camp. 478. A subsequent application to one of two joint debtors, and a refusal, is sufficient. 1 Stark. 323. 4 Esp. 93. Noy, 135. Vin. Abr. Evid. T. b. 97. Delivering a letter at defendant's house to a clerk, who returned with an answer that the debt should be settled, is *prima facie* evidence of a demand. 1 Stark. 323. A *prior* demand, and refusal, is an answer to the plea of tender. 8 East, 168. 1 Saund. 33, n. 2. Bull. N. P. 156. 1 Camp. 478.—CHITTY. A tender of a sum less than is due is made at the debtor's peril although he believe that the amount offered is as much as is due. Helphrey *v.* Railroad Company, 29 Ia. 480 (1870).

as much as the defendant acknowledges to be due, together with the costs hitherto incurred, in order to prevent the expense of any further proceedings. This may be done upon what is called a *motion;*(53) which is an occasional application to the court by the parties or their counsel, in order to obtain some rule or order of court, which becomes necessary in the progress of a cause; and it is usually grounded upon an *affidavit*, (the perfect tense of the verb *affido*,) being a voluntary oath before some judge or officer of the court, to evince the truth of certain facts, upon which the motion is grounded:(54) though no such *affidavit* is necessary for payment of money into court.(55) If, after the money paid in, the plaintiff proceeds in his suit, it is at his own peril: for, if he does not prove more due than is so paid into court, he shall be non-suited and pay the defendant costs;(56) but he shall still have the money so paid in; for that the defendant has acknowledged to be his due.(57) In the French law the rule of practice is grounded upon principles somewhat similar to this; for there, if a person be sued for more than he owes, yet he loses his cause if he doth not tender so much as he really does owe.(*w*) To this head may also be referred the practice of what is called a *set-off:* whereby the defendant acknowledges the justice of the plaintiff's demand on the one hand, but on the other sets up a demand of his own, to counterbalance that of the plaintiff, either in the whole or in part: as, if the plaintiff sues for ten pounds due on a note of hand, the defendant may set off nine pounds due to himself for merchandise sold to the plaintiff,(58) and,

in case he *pleads* such set-off, must pay the remaining balance into *305] court.(59) This answers *very nearly to the *compensatio*, or *stoppage*, of the civil law,(*x*) and depends on the statutes 2 Geo. II. c. 22, and 8 Geo. II. c. 24, which enact, that where there are mutual debts between the plaintiff and defendant, one debt may be set against the other,(60) and either pleaded in bar or given in evidence upon the general issue at the trial; which shall operate as payment, and extinguish so much of the plaintiff's demand.(61)

(*w*) Sp. L. b. 6, c. 4.   (*x*) *Ff*. 16, 2, 1.

---

(53) A paper purporting to be a motion, filed with the clerk of the court, without notice to anybody interested, and which, so far as the record shows, may never have come to the knowledge of the court or opposing counsel, is not such a motion as may thereafter be exhumed and held sufficient cause for undoing all that has been regularly done. Washington Park Club *v.* Baldwin, 59 Newell (Ill. App.) 64 (1895).

(54) Williams *et al. v.* Stevenson, 103 Ind. 248 (1885). Hood *v.* Pearson, 67 Ind. 374 (1879). It is not necessary that an affidavit be signed by the party swearing to it. Hitsman *et al. v.* Ganard, 1 N. J. (Harr.) 125 (1837). Binns' Justice (Brightley, 10 ed.) 67 (1895). Signing, though not essential, is better practice. Crist *v.* Parks, 19 Tex. 235 (Hartley, 1857).

(55) By statute 3 & 4 W. IV. c. 42, s. 21, and now by the Common-Law Procedure Act, 1852, the defendant in all actions (except actions for assault and battery, and false imprisonment, libel, slander, malicious arrest or prosecution, crim. con., or debauching the plaintiff's daughter or servant) may, by leave of the court or a judge, pay into court a sum of money by way of compensation or amends.—STEWART. The payment of money into court, is payment to the plaintiff. Sowle *v.* Holdridge, 20 Indiana, 209 (1863).

(56) Voss *v.* Maguire, 26 Berry (Mo.) 456 (1887). Binns' Justice (Brightley, 10 ed.) 79 (1895).

(57) The effect of the payment of money into court is nearly similar to that of a tender. See *supra*, note (50). Lee's P. Dict. 2 ed. 1013. Tidd, 8 ed. 676. This is the only case where a party is bound by the payment of money, (2 T. R. 645;) and, though paid in by mistake, the court will not order it to be restored to defendant, though perhaps in a case of fraud they would. 2 B. & P. 392.—CHITTY.

(58) Binns' Justice (Brightley, 10 ed.) 81 (1895).

(59) Steck *v.* C. F. & I. Co., 142 N. Y. 257 (1894).

(60) A defendant may set off their claims, but this is a privilege and not an imperative duty. Browne *v.* Rowe, 10 Texas, 185 (1853).

(61) But in such case notice must be given at the time of pleading the general issue; and as to the mode of setting off, see 1 Chitt. on Pl. 4 ed. 494 to 497.

Pleas that totally deny the cause of complaint are either the *general* issue, or a *special* plea, in bar.

1. The *general* issue, or general plea, is what traverses, thwarts, and denies at once the whole declaration; without offering any special matter

---

In some cases this plea or notice is unnecessary, as where the defendant's demand is more in the nature of a *deduction* than a set-off. Thus, a defendant is in all cases entitled to retain or claim by way of deduction all just allowances or demands accruing to him, or payments made by him, in respect of the *same* transaction or account which forms the ground of action: this is not a set-off, but rather a deduction. See 1 Bla. Rep. 651. 4 Burr. 2133, 2221. And where demands originally cross, and not arising out of the same transaction, have by subsequent express agreement been connected and stipulated to be deducted or set off against each other, the balance is the debt, and the only sum recoverable by suit without any special plea of set-off, though it is advisable in most cases, and necessary when the action is on a specialty, to plead it. 5 T. R. 135. 3 T. R. 599. 3 Taunt. 76. 2 Taunt. 170. In actions at the suit of assignees of bankrupts, a set-off need not be pleaded or given notice of, (1 T. R. 115, 116. 6 T. R. 58, 59,) though the practice is so to plead, or give notice of such set-off.

It may be important here also to observe that these acts were passed more for the benefit of the defendants than the plaintiffs, and are not imperative; so that a defendant may have his right to set off and bring a cross-action for the debt due to him from the plaintiff, (2 Camp. 594. 5 Taunt. 148,) though he cannot safely arrest. 3 B. & Cres. 139. And where the defendant is not prepared at the time the plaintiff sues him to prove the set-off, it is best not to avail himself of it, for if the defendant should attempt but not succeed on the trial in proving the set-off, he could not afterwards sue for the amount; and a party cannot bring an action for what he has succeeded in setting off in a former suit against him; though if the set-off were more than sufficient to cover the plaintiff's demand in the former action, the defendant therein might then maintain an action for the surplus. 3 Esp. Rep. 104. Though the defendant does not avail himself of the set-off, intending to bring a cross-action, the plaintiff may defeat it by taking a verdict for the whole sum he proves to be due to him, subject to be reduced to the sum really due on the balance of accounts, if the defendant will afterwards enter into a rule not to sue for the debt intended to be set off; or he may take a verdict for the smaller sum, with a special endorsement on the postea, as a foundation for the court to order a stay of proceedings, if an action should be brought for the amount of the set-off. 1 Camp. 252.

The demand, as well of the plaintiff as of the defendant, must be a *debt*. A set-off is not allowed in an action for uncertain damages, whether in assumpsit, covenant, or for a tort, trover, detinue, replevin, or trespass. Bull. N. P. 181. 3 Camp. 329. 4 T. R. 512. 1 Bla. Rep. 594. 2 Bla. Rep. 910.

The only cases in which a set-off is allowed are in assumpsit, debt, and covenant for the non-payment of money, and for which an action of debt or indebitatus might be sustained, (2 Bla. Rep. 911;) or where a bond in a penalty is given for securing the payment of money on an annuity, (2 Burr. 820;) or at least stipulated damages. 2 T. R. 32. The demand to be set off, also, must not be for unliquidated damages, although incurred by a penalty. 1 Bla. Rep. 394. 6 T. R. 488. 1 Taunt. 137. 2 Burr. 1024. 2 Bla. Rep. 910. 1 Taunt. 137. 5 B. & A. 92. 3 Camp. 329. Peake's Rep. 41. 6 Taunt. 162. 1 Marsh. 514, S. C. 2 Brod. & B. 89. 1 M. & S. 499. 5 M. & S. 539, etc. See cases in 1 Chitt. on Pl. 4th ed. 486, 487. Stark. on Evid. 1312, part 4. The defendant's bringing an action or obtaining a verdict for a debt is no waiver of the right to set-off the debt. 2 Burr. 1229. 3 T. R. 186. And a judgment may be pleaded by way of set-off, though a writ of error be depending upon it, (3 T. R. 188, in notes;) but not so after plaintiff be taken in execution. 5 M. & S. 103. The debt to be set off must be a *legal* and *subsisting* demand: an equitable debt will not suffice. See 16 East, 36. 136. 7 East, 173. A demand barred by the statute of limitations cannot be set off. 2 Stra. 1271. Peake's Rep. 121. Bull. N. P. 180. An attorney cannot set off his bill for business done in court unless he has previously, and in a reasonable time to be taxed, delivered a bill signed. 1 Esp. C. 449. But it is not necessary that a month should intervene between the delivery of the bill and the trial. Id.

The debt sought to be recovered and that to be set off must be mutual and due in the same right: therefore a joint debt cannot be set off against a separate demand, nor a separate debt against a joint one, (2 Taunt. 173. Montague, 23. 5 M. & S. 439,) unless it be so expressly agreed between all the parties, (2 Taunt. 170;) and a debt on a joint and several bond of several persons may be set off to an action brought by only one of the obligors. 2 T. R. 32. A defendant sued for his own debt may set off a debt due to him as surviving partner, (5 T. R. 493. 6 T. R. 582;) and in an action brought by an ostensible and a dormant partner, the defendant may set off a debt due from the ostensi-

whereby to evade it.(62) As in trespass either *vi et armis*, or on the case, *non culpabilis:*(63) not guilty:(*y*) in debt upon contract, *nihil debet*, he owes nothing; in debt on bond, *non est factum*, it is not his deed; on an *assumpsit*, *non assumpsit*, he made no such promise.(64) Or in real actions, *nul tort*, no wrong done; *nul disseisin*, no disseisin; and in a writ of right, the mise or issue is, that the tenant has more right to hold than the demandant has to demand.   These pleas are called the general issue, because, by importing an absolute and general denial of what is alleged in the declaration, they amount at once to an issue: by which we mean a fact affirmed on one side and denied on the other.

Formerly the general issue was seldom pleaded, except when the party meant wholly to deny the charge alleged against him. But when he meant to distinguish away or palliate the charge, it was always usual to set forth the particular facts in what is called a *special* plea; which was originally intended to apprise the court and the adverse party of the nature and cir-

(*y*) Appendix, No. II. § 4.

---

ble partner alone. 2 Esp. C. 469. 7 T. R. 361, n. c., S. C. See Peake, 197. 12 Ves. 346. 11 Ves. 27. Id. 517. 16 East, 130. A debt due to a man in right of his wife cannot be set off in an action against him on his own bond. Bull. N. P. 179. A debt due from a wife *dum sola* [While single] cannot be set off in an action brought by the husband alone, unless the defendant has himself individually liable. 2 Esp. C. 594. A debt from an executor in his own right cannot be set off against a debt to the testator, (3 Atk. 691,) though the executor is residuary legatee. Id. So a debt which accrued to the defendant in the life-time of the testator cannot be set off against a debt that accrued to the executor even in that character after the testator's death. Bull. N. P. 180. Willes, 103, 106.

Questions of difficulty frequently arise in cases of set-off, where the agent of a party deals as principal. The rule in these cases is, that if an agent dealing for a principal, but concealing that principal, delivers goods in his own name, the person contracting with him has a right to consider him as the principal; and though the real principal may appear and sue, yet the purchaser may in such case set off any claim he has against the agent. 7 T. R. 360. 1 M. & S. 576. 2 Marsh. 501. Holt. C. N. P. 124. But a debt due from a *broker* cannot be set off in an action by the principal against the purchaser to recover the price of goods sold by the broker, not disclosing his name. 2 B. & A. 137. And if an agent sells goods as his own, or has a lien upon them, and does not part with the goods unless the purchaser expressly agrees to pay him, the purchaser in an action brought against him by such agent for the price of the goods cannot set off a debt due from the owner to the purchaser. 2 Chitt. R. 387. 7 T. R. 359. But if an agent deliver goods without payment, and thereby parts with his lien, the purchaser may, in an action by the agent, set off a debt due from the principal. 7 Taunt. 243. And where an auctioneer had sold to the defendant the goods of A. as the goods of B., it was held that this was such a fraud that defendant might set off a debt due to him from B. against the price of the goods of A. Id. ibid. 1 J. B. Moore, 178. As to set-off in actions, by or against assignees of bankrupts, see 1 Chitt. on Pl. 492 to 494. Stark. on Evid. part 4, 106, *ante*, 2 book, 472, k., (n.) And 6 Geo. IV. c. 16, § 50.—CHITTY.

(62) The party who must allege a fact which is traversed, has the affirmative of the issue, and the burden of proof—a traverse being in law, not an assertion but a denial of the truth of an assertion. The plea of the general issue is not, in form or in substance, and does not include, an affirmative allegation of any fact; it is a mere denial of every fact alleged in the declaration material to the plaintiff's case. Kendall v. Brownson, 47 N. H. 196 (Hadley) (1866).

(63) On a joint plea of "not guilty" in trespass *vi et armis* [With force and arms] against two defendants for breaking the plaintiff's close and beating his slaves, the defendants ought not to be permitted to give in evidence by way of mitigation of damages, a license from the plaintiff to *one of them* to visit his negro quarters, and chastise any of them he might find acting improperly—the battery being committed by the *other* defendant—and no proof appearing that the slaves were acting improperly. Brown v. May, 1 Munford (Va.) 291 (1810).

(64) A plea of payment before breach of contract, and before, or upon actual demand, is not a plea in confession and avoidance, but a negative of the plaintiff's cause of action. The burden of proof is upon the plaintiff. Defendant's evidence of payment is admissible under the general issue. A decision that it was not thus admissible would be a decision that there is no general issue in assumpsit. Kendall v. Brownson, 47 N. H. 202 (Hadley) (1866).

cumstances of the defence, and to keep the law and the fact distinct. And it is an invariable rule, that every defence which cannot be thus specially pleaded may be given in evidence upon the general issue at the trial. But the science *of special pleading having been frequently perverted [*306 to the purposes of chicane and delay, the courts have of late in some instances, and the legislature in many more, permitted the general issue to be pleaded, which leaves every thing open, the fact, the law, and the equity of the case, and have allowed special matter to be given in evidence at the trial. And, though it should seem as if much confusion and uncertainty would follow from so great a relaxation of the strictness anciently observed, yet experience has shown it to be otherwise; especially with the aid of a new trial, in case either party be unfairly surprised by the other.

2. Special pleas, *in bar* of the plaintiff's demand, are very various, according to the circumstances of the defendant's case. As, in real actions, a general release or a fine, both of which may destroy and bar the plaintiff's title. Or, in personal actions, an accord, arbitration, conditions performed, nonage of the defendant, or some other fact which precludes the plaintiff from his action.(z) A *justification* is likewise a special plea in bar; as in actions of assault and battery, *son assault demesne*, that it was the plaintiff's own original assault; in trespass, that the defendant did the thing complained of in right of some office which warranted him so to do; or, in an action of slander, that the plaintiff is really as bad a man as the defendant said he was.

Also a man may plead the statutes of limitation(a) in bar;(65) or the time

(z) Appendix, No. III. § 6.   (a) See pages 188, 196.

---

(65) 2 Barb. Rights Pers. and Prop. 985. The statute of limitations must be pleaded, when a party would take advantage of it. It cannot be given in evidence under the general issue. Alston v. Alston, 3 Brevard (S. C.) 537 (1814). As questions on the statute of limitations (21 Jac. I. c. 16) so frequently occur, we will consider this subject more fully in the following order, viz., First, as to what cases the statute extends, and herein in what cases payment of a debt may be presumed at common law. Secondly, when the statute begins to take effect; and herein of the exceptions contained in the statute. Thirdly, what is a good commencement of an action to take the case out of the statute; and, Lastly, what acts or admissions will revive the claim.

First. To WHAT CASES THE STATUTE EXTENDS.—The statute does not extend to actions of account, or of covenant, or debt on specialty, or other matter of a higher nature, but only to actions of debt upon alending, or contract without specialty, or for arrearages of rent reserved on parol leases. Hut. 109. 1 Saund. 38. 2 Saund. 66. Tidd, Pr. 3 ed. 15. It does not extend to warrants of attorney. 2 Stark. 234. It extends to bills of exchange, (Carth. 3,) attorneys' fees, (3 Lev. 367,) and to a demand for rent on a parol demise. 1 B. & A. 625.

It does not extend to *debt* on a bond, (Cowp. 109;) but where the bond has been given more than twenty years before the commencement of the action, and no interest has been paid upon it, nor any acknowledgment by the obligor of the existence of the debt during that period, the law will in general presume it to have been satisfied, (6 Mod. 22. 1 Bla. Rep. 532. 1 T. R. 270. 3 P. Wms. 395,) particularly if the debt be large and the obligor has been all along in good circumstances, (1 T. R. 271;) and in some cases, where a bond has been given and interest paid on it within twenty years, the law will presume it to have been satisfied; as where it has been given eighteen or nineteen years, and in the mean time an account has been settled between the parties without taking any notice of the demand, (1 Burr. 434. 1 T. R. 271;) but in such case the presumption must be fortified by evidence of some auxiliary circumstances. Cowp. 214. 1 T. R. 271. 1 Camp. 27. After a considerable length of time, slight evidence is sufficient. 1 T. R. 271; and see Tidd, 8 ed. 17, 18. In *assumpsit*, though the statute be not pleaded, the jury may presume, from the length of time and other circumstances, that the debt has been satisfied. 2 Stark. C. N. P. 497; and see 5 Esp. 52. 3 Camp. 13. 1 Taunt. 572; *sed vide* 1 D. & R. 16.

This presumption may be repelled by proof of the recent admission of the debt, or of the payment of interest on the bond within twenty years, (1 T. R. 270;) or that the obligee has resided abroad for the last twenty years, (1 Stark. 101; *sed vide* 1 D. & R. 16;) or that the obligor was in insolvent circumstances, and had not the means of payment, (19 Ves. 196. Cowp. 109. 1 Stark. 101;) or that the demand was trifling, (Cowp.

limited by certain acts of parliament, beyond which no plaintiff can lay his

---

214;) or other circumstances, explaining satisfactorily why an earlier demand has not been made. 1 Stark. 101. The fluctuation of credit, together with the circumstance of the security remaining with the obligee, is of great weight to rebut presumption of payment thereof, (19 Ves. 199. 1 Stark. 374;) an endorsement by the obligee, purporting that part of the principal sum has been received, if made after the presumption of payment has arisen, is inadmissible. 2 Stra. 827. 2 Ves. 42; *sed vide* 1 Barnard, 432. And further, if the defendant produce direct evidence of the payment of the principal sum and interest at a certain time within twenty years, the plaintiff will not be allowed to encounter that evidence by an endorsement in the handwriting of the obligee, purporting that interest was paid at a subsequent time. 2 Camp. 322.

Secondly. WHEN THE STATUTE BEGINS TO TAKE EFFECT.—It does not do so till the cause of action is complete and the party is capable of suing on it. Cro. Car. 139. 1 Lev. 48. Salk. 442. 1 Bla. Rep. 354. No action lies against a consignee of goods for sale, for not accounting and returning the goods undisposed of until demand; and therefore the statute does not begin to run until the time when demand is made. 1 Taunt. 572. The statute begins to operate only from the time when a bill of exchange or promissory note, etc. is due, and not from the date, (1 H. B. 631. 5 B. & A. 212;) and no debt accrues on a bill payable at *sight* until it be presented for payment. 2 Taunt. 323. The statute of limitations begins to run from the date of a note payable on demand. 1 Ves. 344. 2 Selw. 4 ed. 131, 339. Cro. Eliz. 548; and see Chitty on Bills, 6 ed. 373; *sed quære*, see Hard. 36. 14 East. 500. 1 Taunt. 575, 576. Sir W. Jones, 194. 12 Mod. 444. 15 Ves. 487. Where a payee of a bill of exchange was dead at the time the bill became due, it was held that the statute did not begin to run until letters of administration were taken out, (5 B. & A. 212. Skin. 555;) but where the cause of action is complete in the lifetime of the testator, then the statute begins to run from that time, and not from the granting of the probate. Willes, 27. Where a breach of a contract is attended with special damage, the statute runs from the time of the breach, which is the gist of the action, and not from the time it was discovered (3 B. & A. 628, 288. 4 Moore, 508. 2 Brod. & B. 73, S. C.) or the damage arose. 5 B. & A. 204. If there is mutual credit between two parties, though the items on both sides are above six years old, with the exception of one item on each side, which are just within the period, this is sufficient to take the whole out of the statute; for every new item and credit in an account given by one party to the other is an admission of there being some unsettled account between them. 6 T. R. 189. 2 Saund. 127, a., n. (6). But where all the items are on one side, so that the account is not mutual, as, for instance, in an account between a tradesman and his customer, the last item which happens to be within six years will not draw after it those which are of a longer standing. Bull. N. P. 149.

The exception in the statute respecting merchants' accounts extends only to those cases where there are mutual and reciprocal accounts and demands between two persons, and where such accounts are current and open, and not to accounts stated between them, (2 Ves. 400. Bull. N. P. 149. Sir W. Jones, 401. 1 Sid. 465. 1 Ventr. 89;) for no other actions are excepted but actions of account. Carth. 226. 1 Show. 341, S. C. 2 Saund. 127, a. 2 Mod. 312, and 1 Mod. 70. 1 Lev. 298. 4 Mod. 105. Peake, 121. 1 Vern. 456. 2 Vern. 276. It has been considered that by the effect of the above exception there can be no limitation to a merchant's open and unsettled account. This opinion, however, appears erroneous; and if there is no item in the account or acknowledgment of the debt within six years, the statute will take effect; but, as we have before seen, if even the last item of the account is within six years, that preserves all the preceding items of debt and credit from the operation of the statute, (6 Ves. 580. 15 Ves. 198. 18 Ves. 286. 2 Ves. 200, acc.; *sed vide* opinion of lord Hardwicke mentioned in 19 Ves. 185. 6 T. R. 189, 192, *cont.*;) and from these decisions it appears that merchants' accounts stand not upon better grounds in regard to the statute than other parties. The exception extends to all merchants, as well inland as to those trading beyond sea, (Peake, C. N. P. 121. 2 Saund. 127. B. acc. Chanc. Ca. 152, *cont.*;) and the effect of the exception has also been extended to other tradesmen and persons having mutual dealings. 6 T. R. 189. Peake, N. P. 127, overruling; *sed vide* 7 Mod. 270, *cont.* But in all these cases the accounts must be mutual, together with reciprocal demands on each side, and not, as in the case of a tradesman and his customer, where the items of credit are all on one side. Bull. N. P. 149.

The exception in the act respecting infants, etc. only extends to plaintiffs. (Carth. 136, 226. 6 Show. 99. Salk. 420. 2 Stra. 836;) but, by 4 & 5 Anne, c. 16, s. 19, it is extended to defendants beyond seas at the time of the cause of action accruing. If the plaintiff be in England when the cause of action accrues, though he afterwards go abroad, the time of limitation begins to run from the accruing of the action, (1 Wils. 134;) and so though one of several plaintiffs be abroad when the cause of action accrues. 4 T. R. 516.

cause of action. This, by the statute 32 Hen. VIII. c. 2, in a writ of right, is *sixty* years; in assizes, writs of entry, or other possessory actions

---

It extends to persons absent in Scotland, (1 Bla. R. 286. 1 D. & R. 16,) and the plaintiff, though absent there, must sue within the limited time; but it does not extend to persons in Ireland, (1 Show. 91,) the latter being considered as beyond the sea, within themeaning of the above provision. Foreigners living beyond the sea have the same advantage of the proviso as natives residing here. 2 Bla. R. 723. 3 Wils. 145, S. C. Though the demand be on a bill of exchange, the plaintiff's absence beyond sea saves the statute. Strange, 836. Where the cause of action accrues within the jurisdiction of the supreme court at Bengal, whilst the parties are resident there, the statute of limitations, as far as respects a suit in this country, begins to run only from the time of their concurrent presence here. 13 East, 439.

When once the statute has begun to run, nothing stops its course; as where a tenant in tail leaves two sons infants, and the eldest, having attained the age of twenty-one, dies without issue, the statute begins to run against his brother, though a minor. 4 Taunt. 826. And see the cases (1 Wils. 134. 4 T. R. 516) just cited.

Thirdly, WHAT IS A GOOD COMMENCEMENT OF AN ACTION TO TAKE THE CASE OUT OF THE STATUTE. See Tidd, 8 ed. 24, 25, 144, 152, 161.

If the plaintiff, having commenced a suit in due time, die, or, being a feme-sole at the commencement of the action, marry, the representative in the one case, or husband and wife in the other, if they commence a new action within a reasonable time afterwards, it will suffice. See Willes, 259, N. E. 2 Salk. 425. Bull. N. P. 150. A year seems to be a reasonable time within this rule, (1 Lord Raym. 434. 1 Lutw. 256, S. C. 2 Stra. 907. Cro. Car. 294; *sed vide* 1 Lord Raym. 283. 1 Salk. 393, S. C.:) at all events, half a year would be. Cowp. 738, 740.

Lastly, WHAT ACTS OR ADMISSIONS WILL REVIVE THE CLAIM.—The object of this statute was to protect individuals against forgotten claims of so obsolete a nature that the evidence relating to the contract might probably be no longer to be found, and thereby might lead to perjury. It proceeds, also, upon the supposition that the debtor has paid but after a lapse of time may have lost his voucher. See 5 M. & S. 76, *per* Bayley, J. 3 B. & A. 142, *per* Abbott, J. In cases, therefore, where there is an acknowledgment of the debtor or contractor to prove the existence of the debt or obligation, or an express promise to pay or perform the same, the statute will not operate to protect him notwithstanding the lapse of six years or more since the cause of the action may have accrued. But if a cause of action arising from the breach of a contract to do an act at a specific time be once barred by the statute, a subsequent acknowledgment by the party that he broke the contract will not, it seems, take the case out of the statute, (2 Camp. 160: and see Peake's Evid. 205. 5 Moore, 105. 2 B. & C. 372, S. C. 5 B. & A. 204. 3 B. & A. 288;) and a subsequent acknowledgment of a trespass will not take the case out of the act. 1 B. & A. 92. 2 Chit. Rep. 249, S. C. The sufficiency of an acknowledgment to take the case out of the statute will be considered, *first*, where it directly acknowledges the debt; *secondly*, where it acknowledges the debt having existed, but is accompanied by a declaration of its being discharged; and *thirdly*, with reference to the party making the admission.

In the *first* case, the slightest acknowledgment has been held sufficient, (2 Burr. 1099. Bull. N. P. 149. Cowp. 548;) as where the debtor exclaimed to the plaintiff, "What an extravagant bill you have delivered me!" Peake N. P. 93. So, where the defendant met a man in a fair and said that he went there to avoid the plaintiff, to whom he was indebted, this was held to save the statute. Loft, 86. In an action by an administrator, an agreement for a compromise executed between intestate and defendant, wherein the existence of the debt sued for was admitted, was deemed sufficient to take the case out of the statute. 9 Price, 122. It is sufficient to prove that, a demand being made by a seaman on the owner of a ship for wages which had accrued during an embargo, he said, "if others paid, he should do the same." 4 Camp. 185. A promise, "if there should be any mistake it should be rectified," referring to payments actually made, is sufficient. 2 B. & C. 149. 3 D. & R. 522, S. C.; *sed quære* [But why]. And it makes no difference whether the acknowledgment be accompanied with a promise or refusal to pay: a bare acknowledgment is sufficient. 16 East, 420. 2 Burr. 1099. 5 M. & S. 75. 2 B. & Cres. 154. The construction of an ambiguous letter or declaration of a defendant on being served with a writ or requested to pay a debt, neither admitting or denying it, is strong intimation that it is an acknowledgment; since if the defendant knew he owed nothing he would have declared so. 2 T. R. 760. 1 Bing. 266. A conditional promise to pay when able, or by instalments, etc., is sufficient, without proof of ability or waiting till instalment become due. 16 East, 420. 2 Stark. 98, 99. 5 M. & S. 75; *sed vide* 3 D. & R. 267. Where the original agreement is in writing, in order to take the case out of the statute of frauds, a subsequent promise, or admission of the liability to perform such agreement need not be in writing to take the case out of the statute of limitations. 1 B.

real, of the seisin of one's ancestors, in lands; and either of their seisin, or one's own, in rents, suits, and services, *fifty* years: and in actions real for

---

& A. 690. An acknowledgment after action brought is good. Selw. N. P. tit. Limitations. Burr. 1099. The admission to a third person is sufficient. 3 B. & A. 141. Loft., 86. 2 B. & C. 154.

On the other hand, where the defendant said, "The testator always promised not to distress me," this was held no evidence of a promise to the testator to take the case out of the statute, (6 Taunt. 210;) so a declaration, "I cannot afford to pay my new debts, much more my old ones," is insufficient, (4 D. & R. 179;) and so where, in assumpsit by an attorney to recover his charges relative to the grant of an annuity, evidence that the defendant said "he thought it had been settled when the annuity was granted, but that he had been in so much trouble since that he could not recollect any thing about it," is not a sufficient acknowledgment of the debt to save the statute, notwithstanding proof that plaintiff's bill was not paid when the annuity was granted. 1 J. B. Moore, 340. 7 Taunt. 608, S. C. The referring plaintiff to the defendant's attorney, who, he added, was in possession of his determination and ability, is not an admission that any thing is due, (1 New Rep. 20;) and where a defendant, on being applied to by the plaintiff's attorney for the payment of the debt, wrote in answer "that he would wait on the plaintiff when he should be able to satisfy him respecting the misunderstanding which had occurred between them," this was holden not sufficient to take the case out of the statute. Holt, C. N. P. 380; and see 4 Esp. 184. 5 Esp. 81. A declaration, "I will see my attorney and tell him to do what is right," is insufficient. 3 D. & R. 267. Payment of money into court on a special count will not save the operation of the statute, (3 B. & C. 10. 4 D. & R. 632, S. C.:) it only admits the debt to the amount paid in. Id. Bunb. 100.

In the *second* place, where the defendant makes no express acknowledgment of the debt, but says he is not liable, because it is more than six years since, this will not take the case out of the statute. 3 Taunt. 380. 5 Esp. 81. 4 M. & S. 457. 5 Price, 636. But an acknowledgment that the defendant had been liable, but was not at the time of acknowledgment, because the demand was out of date, and that he would not then pay, as it was not then due, takes the case out of the act. 16 East, 420. 2 Stark. 98, 99.

If a debtor admit that he was once liable, but that he was discharged by a particular mode of performance, to which he with precision referred himself, and where he has designated that time and mode of performance so strictly that he can say it is impossible it had been discharged in any other mode, there the courts have said, that if the plaintiff can disprove that mode, he lets himself in to recover, by striking from under the defendant the only ground on which he professes to rely. 7 Taunt. 608. 4 B. & A. 568. 1 Salk. 29. Cowp. 548. Peake, N. P. C. 93. So where a party acknowledges but refuses to pay the debt, relying on the deficiency of his legal liability to pay, this will take the case out of the statute, upon proof of liability. 5 M. & S. 75. 6 Rep. 66. But a qualified admission by a party who relies on an objection which would at any time have been a good defence to the action does not take the case out of the statute, as if the defendant had said, "If you had presented the protest the same as the rest, it would have been paid: I had then funds in the acceptor's hands," (1 Stark. 7; see 3 Esp. N. P. C. 155. 2 Camp. 161. 2 B. & A. 759. 4 B. & A. 568. 4 East, 599, and cases there cited:) this was held no sufficient acknowledgment. Where the defendant, an executor,—who was sued for money had and received from his testator, was proved to have said, "I acknowledge the receipt of the money, but the testatrix gave it me," it was held insufficient, (Bull. N. P. 148;) and so where the defendant, on being applied to for payment of a debt, said, "You owe me more money: I have a set-off against it." 2 B. & A. 759. Where a party, on being asked for the payment of his attorney's bill, admitted that there had been such a bill, but stated that it had been paid to the deceased partner of the attorney, who had retained the amount out of the floating balance in his hands, it seems that, in order to take the case out of the statute, evidence is inadmissible to show that the bill had never, in fact, been paid in this manner. 4 B. & A. 568. In all cases, unless the defendant actually acknowledge that the debt or obligation did originally exist, the statute will not be avoided. 4 Maule & S. 457. 2 Camp. 160.

In the *third* case, with respect to the party from whom the acknowledgment should come to render it sufficient, an acknowledgment by an agent or servant intrusted by the defendant to transact his business for him will suffice, (5 Esp. 145;) and so will the admission of the wife who was accustomed to conduct her husband's business. Holt's Ca. Ni. Pri. 591. In an action against a husband for goods supplied to his wife for her accommodation while he occasionally visited her, a letter written by the wife, acknowledging the debt within six years, is admissible evidence to take the case out of the statute. 1 Camp. 394; and see 2 Esp. N. P. C. 511. 5 Esp. N. P. C. 145. If a demand is owing from two parties, an acknowledgment by one will avoid the statute. 4 T. R. 516. So an acknowledgment by one of several makers of a joint and several promissory-note

lands grounded upon one's own seisin or possession, such possession must have been within *thirty* years.(66)   By statute 1 Mar. st. 2, c. 5, this

---

will take the case out of the statute, as against any one of the other makers, in a separate action on the note against him, (Doug. 652:) and this though against a surety, (2 Bingh. 306;) and in an action against A. on the joint and several promissory-note of himself and B. to take case out of the statute, it is enough to give in evidence a letter written by A. to B. within six years, desiring him to settle the debt. 3 Camp. 32; and see 11 East, 585. 1 Stark. 81. But the acknowledgment of one partner to bind the other must in such case be clear and explicit; and therefore it is not sufficient in order to take a case out of the statute, in an action on a promissory-note, to show a payment by a joint maker of a note to the payee within six years, so as to throw it upon the defendant, to show that the payment was not made on account of the note. 1 Stark. 488. It has been held that when, one of two drawers of a joint and several promissory-note having become bankrupt, the payee received a dividend under the commission on account of the note, this will prevent the other drawer from availing himself of the statute in an action brought against him for the remainder of the money due on the note, the dividend having been received within six years before the action brought. 2 H. Bla. 340. But in a more recent case, where one of two joint drawers of a bill of exchange became bankrupt, and under his commission the endorsees proved a debt (beyond the amount of the bill) for goods sold, etc., and they exhibited the bill as a security, they then held for their debt, and afterwards received a dividend: it was held that in an action by the endorsees of the bill against the solvent partner, the statute of limitations was a good defence, although the dividend had been paid by the assignees of the bankrupt partner within six years. 1 B. & A. 463; and see 1 B. & C. 248. 2 D. & R. 363, S. C. So where A. & B. made a joint and several promissory-note, and A. died, and ten years after his death B. paid interest on the note, it was holden, in an action thereon against the executors of A., that the payment of interest by B. did not take the case out of the statute, so as to make the executors liable. 2 B. & C. 23. 3 D. & R. 200, S. C. An acknowledgment by an accommodation acceptor, within six years, of his liability to the payee, is not sufficient to take the case out of the statute for the drawer. 3 Stark. 186.

It is enacted, by 9 Geo. IV, c. 14, that in actions of debt or upon the case, grounded upon any simple contract, no acknowledgments or promise by words only should be deemed sufficient evidence of a new or continuing contract, whereby to take any case out of the operation of the enactments of the statutes of limitations, or to deprive any party of the benefit thereof, unless such acknowledgment or promise shall be made or contained by or in some writing to be signed by the party chargeable thereby. And that where there shall be two or more joint contractors, or executors or administrators of any contractor, no such joint contractor, executor, or administrator shall lose the benefit of the said enactments, or either of them, so as to be chargeable in respect or by reason only of any written acknowledgment or promise made and signed by any other or others of them. The act not to alter the effect of any payment of any principal or interest made by any person whatsoever. And in actions to be commenced against two or more such joint contractors, or executors or administrators, if it shall appear at the trial, or otherwise, that the plaintiff, though barred by either of the said recited acts, or this act, as to one or more of such joint contractors, or executors or administrators, shall nevertheless be entitled to recover against any other or others of the defendants by virtue of a new acknowledgment or promise, or otherwise, judgment may be given and costs allowed for the plaintiff as to such defendant or defendants against whom he shall recover, and for the other defendant or defendants against the plaintiff.

By sect. 2, that if defendant in action on simple contract shall plead an abatement to the effect that any other person ought to be jointly sued, and issue be joined on such plea, and it should appear at the trial that the action could not, by reason of the said recited acts, or the present act, be maintained against the other person named in such plea, the issue joined on such plea should be found against the party pleading the same.

By sect. 3, no endorsement or memorandum of payment made after the first of January, 1829, upon any promissory-note, bill of exchange, or other writing, by or on behalf of the party to whom such payment shall be made, shall be deemed sufficient proof of such payment, so as to take the case out of the operation of either of the said statutes.

By sect. 4, said recited acts and the present act shall apply to the case of any debt on simple contracts by way of set-off on the part of any defendant, either by plea, notice, or otherwise.

By sect. 8, no memorandum or other writing made necessary by the act shall be deemed to be an agreement within the meaning of the Stamp Acts.—CHITTY.

(66) In actions of ejectment the defendant cannot show as a defence that he and his grantors have been in uninterrupted adverse possession of the land for twenty-one years

*307] limitation does not extend to *any suit for advowsons, upon reasons given in a former chapter.(b) But by the statute 21 Jac. I. c 2, a time of limitation was extended to the case of the king, viz., *sixty* years precedent to 19 Feb. 1623;(c) but, this becoming ineffectual by efflux of time, the same date of limitation was fixed by statute 9 Geo. III. c. 16, to commence and be reckoned backwards, from the time of bringing any suit or other process, to recover the thing in question; so that a possession for *sixty* years is now a bar even against the prerogative, in derogation of the ancient maxim "*nullum tempus occurrit regi.*"(67) By another statute, 21 Jac. I. c. 16, *twenty* years is the time of limitation in any writ of formedon; and, by a consequence, *twenty* years is also the limitation in every action of ejectment; for no ejectment can be brought unless where the lessor of the plaintiff is entitled to enter on the lands,(d) and by the statute 21 Jac. I. c. 26, no entry can be made by any man, unless within twenty years after his right shall accrue.(68) Also all actions of trespass, (*quare clausum fregit*, or otherwise,) detinue, trover, replevin, account, and case, (except upon accounts between merchants,) debt on simple contract, or for arrears of rent, are limited by the statute last mentioned to *six* years after the cause of action commenced, and actions of assault, menace, battery, mayhem, and imprisonment, must be brought within *four* years, and actions for words within *two* years, after the injury committed.(69) And by the statute 31 Eliz. c. 5, all suits,

(b) See page 250.
(c) Inst. 189.

(d) See page 206.

next preceding the commencement of the action, unless he has set up such adverse possession as a defence in his answer. Hansel *v.* Mead. 27 Hun. (N. Y.) 164 (1882).

(67) ["No time runs against the king."] In Maryland, the lord proprietary was always held to be bound by the statute of limitations, and ever since the revolution the republic has expressly subjected her rights to its operation. Hepburn's case, 3 Bland (Md.) 111 (1830).

(68) Some important alterations have been made by two recent statutes as to the limitation of actions and suits. By one of these statutes, (3 & 4 W. IV. c. 27, s. 2,) one period of limitation is established for bringing suits and actions relating to lands and rents, it being enacted that after the thirty-first day of December, 1833, no person shall bring an action to recover any land or rent but within *twenty* years next after the time at which the right to bring such action shall have first accrued, except in cases of disability, when *ten* years longer is allowed, (s. 16;) but no action or suit shall be brought beyond *forty* years after the right of action accrued. S. 17. By s. 41, no arrears of dower shall be recovered for more than six years; and (s. 42) no arrears of rent or interest are to be recovered for more than six years. By the other of these statutes, (3 & 4 W. IV. c. 42, s. 3,) an action of debt for rent upon an indenture, actions of covenant or debt upon bond or other specialty, action of debt or *scire facias* upon recognizance, action of debt upon awards, where the submission is not by specialty or for fines in respect of copyhold estates, or for an escape, or for money levied on *fieri facias*, and actions for penalties, damages, or sums of money given to the party grieved by any statute, shall be commenced within the following times:—Actions of debt for rent or covenant, or debt upon bond or other specialty, actions of debt or *scire facias* upon recognizance, within *twenty* years after the cause of action; actions by the party grieved, two years after the cause of such actions; and other actions within six years after the cause of action. But it is provided that nothing herein enacted shall extend to any action by statute specially limited. —STEWART.

(69) The statute makes an exception for all persons who shall be under age, *femecoverts, non compos mentis,* [Married women, not of sound mind,] in prison, or abroad, when the cause of action accrues; and the limitations of the statute shall only commence from the time when their respective impediments or disabilities are removed. (s. 7;) and the 4 Anne, c. 16, s. 19 extends this provision to defendants beyond seas at the time the cause of action accrues.—CHITTY.

By the statute 9 Geo. IV. c. 14, usually called Lord Tenterden's Act, in actions upon any simple contract, no acknowledgment or promise by *words* only shall be sufficient evidence of a new or continuing contract, whereby to take the case out of the operation of the statute 21 Jac. I. c. 16; but any such *acknowledgment* or promise must be *in writing*, signed by the party chargeable thereby. That statute also enacts that, when there are several joint contractors or executors or administrators of a contractor, one of them

indictments, and informations, upon any penal statutes, where any forfeiture is to the crown alone, shall be sued within *two* years; and where the forfeiture is to a subject, or to the crown and a subject, within *one* year, after the offence committed,(70) unless where any other time is specially limited by the statute. Lastly, by statute 10 W. III. c. 14, no writ of error, *scire facias*, or other suit, shall be brought to reverse any judgment, fine, or recovery, for error, unless it be prosecuted within *twenty* years.(71)   The use of these statutes of limitation is to preserve the peace of the kingdom, and to prevent those innumerable perjuries which might ensue if a man were allowed to bring an action for any injury committed at any distance of time.(72)

*Upon both these accounts the law therefore holds, that "*interest*   [*308 *reipublicæ ut sit finis litium:*"(73) and upon the same principle the Athenian laws in general prohibited all actions where the injury was committed *five* years before the complaint was made.(e)(74)   If therefore in any suit the injury or cause of action happened earlier than the period expressly limited by law, the defendant may plead the statutes of limitations in bar: as upon an *assumpsit*, or promise to pay money to the plaintiff, the defendant may plead *non assumpsit infra sex annos;* he made no such promise within six years; which is an effectual bar to the complaint.(75)

An *estoppel* is likewise a special plea in bar; which happens where a man hath done some act or executed some deed which estops or precludes him from averring any thing to the contrary.(76)   As if tenant for years (who hath no freehold) levies a fine to another person.   Though this is void as to strangers, yet it shall work as an estoppel to the cognizor; for if he afterwards brings an action to recover these lands, and his fine is pleaded against him, he shall thereby be estopped from saying that he had no freehold at the time and therefore was incapable of levying it.

The conditions and qualities of a plea (which, as well as the doctrine of estoppels, will also hold equally, *mutatis mutandis*,(77) with regard to other parts of pleading) are—1. That it be single and containing only one matter;

(e) Pott. Ant. b. i. c. 21.

---

shall not lose the benefit of the statute by reason of a *written acknowledgment* or promise made by another; and the statute 19 & 20 Vict. c. 97 contains an enactment to the same effect with respect to a *payment* by any joint contractor or joint debtor, or the executor or administrator of any contractor.—KERR.

(70) Where the forfeiture is to the crown and a subject, a common informer must sue within one year, and the crown may prosecute for the whole penalty at any time within two years after that year ended.—CHITTY.

(71) But now, by the Common-Law Procedure Act, 1852, s. 146, error must be brought within *six* years.—STEWART.

(72) 1 Barb. Rights Pers. and Prop. 564.   Brown on the Law of Liens.

(73) ["It is for the public good that there be an end to contention."]

(74) Newburn *v.* Street, 21 Upp. Can. O. B. 498, 509 (1862).

(75) Besides these statutes of limitations pointed out by the learned commentator, there are various others, as the 4 Anne, c. 16, s. 17, relating to seamen's wages; and the 24 Geo. II. c. 44, s. 8, *ante*, 1 book, 354, n. (60), as to actions against justices, constables, etc.; and the 28 Geo. III. c. 37, s. 23, as to actions against persons in the customs and excise; and the 43 Geo. III. c. 99, s. 70, as to actions against tax-collectors, etc., etc.—CHITTY.

(76) Grant *et al. v.* The Savannah etc. Co., 57 Ga. (Jackson) 355 (1874).   A verbal promise not to plead the statute of limitations, in case a promissory note shall be suffered to outlaw, will not avail by way of estoppel, if the statute be pleaded, because both parties are equally informed of all the facts.   Shapley *v.* Abbott, 42 N. Y. 457 (Hand, 1870).   A grantee of land, to whom it was conveyed with a covenant against incumbrances, is not estopped in an action against the grantor for breach of covenant, because he had reconveyed to the grantor, by way of mortgage to secure the purchase money, under a similar covenant.   Haynes *v.* Stevens, 11 N. H. 31 (1840).

(77) [The necessary changes being made.]

for duplicity begets confusion. But by statute 4 & 5 Anne, c. 16, a man with leave of the court may plead two or more distinct matters or single pleas; as, in an action of assault and battery, these three, not guilty, *son assault demesne*,(78) and the statute of limitations. 2. That it be direct and positive, and not argumentative. 3. That it have convenient certainty of time, place, and persons.(79) 4. That it answer the plaintiff's allegations in every material point. 5. That it be so pleaded as to be capable of trial.(80)

*309]   *Special pleas are usually in the affirmative, sometimes in the negative;(81) but they always advance some new fact not mentioned in the declaration; and then they must be averred to be true in the common form,—"and this he is ready to verify."(82) This is not necessary in pleas of the general issue; those always containing a total denial of the facts before advanced by the other party, and therefore putting him upon the proof of them.

It is a rule in pleading that no man be allowed to plead specially such a plea as amounts only to the general issue, or a total denial of the charge; but in such case he shall be driven to plead the general issue in terms, whereby the whole question is referred to a jury. But if the defendant, in an assize or action of trespass, be desirous to refer the validity of his title to the court rather than the jury, he may state his title specially, and at the same time *give color* to the plaintiff, or suppose him to have an appearance or color of title, bad, indeed, in point of law, but of which the jury are not competent judges. As, if his own true title be, that he claims by feoffment, with livery from A., by force of which he entered on the lands in question, he cannot plead this by itself, as it amounts to no more than the general issue, *nul tort, nul disseisin*, in assize, or *not guilty* in an issue of trespass. But he may allege this specially, provided he goes further, and says, that the plaintiff claiming by *color* of a prior deed of feoffment without livery, entered; upon whom he entered; and may then refer himself to the judgment of the court which of these two titles is the best in point of law.(*f*)(83)

When the plea of the defendant is thus put in, if it does not amount to an

(*f*) Dr. & Stud. 2, c. 53.

---

(78) [His own assault.]

(79) Less particularity is necessary in relation to matters which equally lie within the knowledge of the adverse party, than in relation to such as are only within the knowledge of the party pleading. Ambler and wife, *v.* Norton, 4 H. & R. (Va.) 49 (1809).

(80) In addition to these qualities, it should be observed that every plea in bar must be adapted to the nature of the action and conformable to the count, (Co. Litt. 303, a., 285, b. Bac. Abr. Pleas, I. *per tot.* 1 Roll. Rep. 216;) must answer the whole declaration or count, or rather all that it assumes in the introductory part to answer, and no more, (Co. Litt. 303, b. Com. Dig. Pleader, E. 1, 36. 1 Saund. 28. 2 B. & P. 427. 3 B. & P. 174;) must admit or confess the fact it justifies, (3 T. R. 298. 1 Salk. 394. Carth. 380. 1 Saund. 28;) must be certain, (Com. Dig. tit. Pleader, E. 5, etc.;) and must be true, and not too large. Hob. 295. Bac. Abr. tit. Pleas, G. 4. For more particular information as to these qualities, see 1 Chitt. on Pl. 451 to 463; as to their forms and particular parts, see id. 467 to 477.

The same rules which prevail in the *construction* and allowance of a declaration do so in the case of pleas in bar. See *ante*, 289, notes 1, 2, 3. If the plea be bad in part, it is so for the whole. Com. Dig. Pleader, E. 36. 3 T. R. 376. 3 B. & P. 174. 1 Saund. 337. The rules as to surplusage in a declaration here also prevail. *Ante*, 293, notes 1, 2, 3.—CHITTY. See Rumberger *v.* Stiver, 6 Hammond (Ohio) 100 (1833).

(81) Ralston *v.* Bullitts, 3 Bibb. (Ky.) 264 (1814).

(82) Chambers *v.* Hunt, 3 Harr. (N. J.) 350 (1841).

(83) But this form of pleading is now abolished, and other facilities for referring questions of title directly to the court are given by the Common-Law Procedure Act, 1852.—STEWART.

issue or total contradiction of the declaration, but only evades it, the plaintiff may plead again, and *reply* to the defendant's plea; either traversing it; that is, totally denying it; as if in an action of debt upon bond the defendant pleads *solvit ad diem*, that he paid the money when *due; [*310 here the plaintiff in. his *replication* may totally traverse this plea by denying that the defendant paid it; or he may allege new matter in contradiction to the defendant's plea; as when the defendant pleads *no award made*, the plaintiff may reply and set forth an actual award, and assign a breach;(*g*) or the replication may *confess and avoid* the plea, by some new matter or distinction consistent with the plaintiff's former declaration; as, in an action for trespassing upon land whereof the plaintiff is seised, if the defendant shows a title to the land by descent, and that therefore he had a right to enter, and gives color to the plaintiff, the plaintiff may either traverse and totally deny the fact of the descent; or he may confess and avoid it by replying, that true it is that such descent happened, but that since the descent the defendant himself demised the lands to the plaintiff for a term of life.(84) To the replication the defendant may *rejoin*, or put in an answer, called a *rejoinder*. The plaintiff may answer the rejoinder by a *sur-rejoinder;* upon which the defendant may *rebut;* and the plaintiff may answer him by a *sur-rebutter.* Which pleas, replications, rejoinders, sur-rejoinders, rebutters, and sur-rebutters answer to the *exceptio, replicatio, duplicatio, triplicatio,* and *quadruplicatio* of the Roman laws.(*h*)(85)

The whole of this process is denominated the *pleading;* in the several stages of which it must be carefully observed not to depart or vary from the title or defence which the party has once insisted on. For this (which is called a *departure* in pleading) might occasion endless altercation. Therefore the replication must support the declaration, and the rejoinder must support the plea, without departing out of it. As in the case of pleading no award made, in consequence of a bond of arbitration, to which the plaintiff replies, setting forth an actual award; now the defendant cannot rejoin that he hath performed this award, for such rejoinder would be an entire departure from his original plea, which alleged that no such award was made: therefore he has now no other *choice but to traverse the fact of the replica- [*311 tion, or else to demur upon the law of it.

Yet in many actions the plaintiff who has alleged in his declaration a general wrong may in his replication, after an evasive plea by the defendant, reduce that general wrong to a more particular certainty, by assigning the injury afresh, with all its specific circumstances, in such manner as clearly to

---

(*g*) Append. No. III. § 6. (*h*) Inst. 4, 14. Bract. *l.* 5, *tr.* 5 c. 1.

---

(84) As to the several replications in general, see 1 Chitt. on Pl. 4th ed. 500 to 518; and as to their forms and parts in particular, id. 518 to 555. The general *qualities* of a replication are that it must answer the plea, and answer so much of it as it professes to answer, or it will be a discontinuance, (Com. Dig. tit. Pleader, F. 4, W. 2. 1 Saund. 338;) and it must answer the plea directly, not argumentatively, (10 East, 205;) it must not depart from the declaration. 2 Saund. 84, a., n. 1. Co. Litt. 304, a. 2 Wils. 98. See 1 Chitt. on Pl. 556 to 560. It must be certain; and it is said that more certainty is requisite in a replication than a declaration, though certainty to a common intent is in general sufficient, (Com. Dig. Pleader, F. 17. 12 East, 263;) and, lastly, it must not be double, or, in other words, contain two answers to the same plea, (10 East, 73. 2 Camp. 176, 177. Com. Dig. Pleader, F. 16;) and the plaintiff cannot reply double, under the 4 Anne, c. 16, (Fortes. 335,) unless in replevin, (2 B. & P. 368, 376;) and more particularly as to these qualities, see 1 Chitt. on Pl. 556 to 562. An entire replication bad in part is bad for the whole. Com. Dig. Pleader, F. 25. 3 T. R. 376. 1 Saund. 28, n. 3.—CHITTY.

(85) [Exception, replication, duplication, triplication, and quadruplication.] Formerly but one replication and but one rejoinder were allowed; but the rule has been altered by the Common-Law Procedure Act, 1852. A party, however, can only have several replications, rejoinders, etc. by leave of the court or a judge.—STEWART.

ascertain and identify it, consistently with his general complaint; which is called a *new* or *novel assignment*.(86)   As, if the plaintiff in trespass declares on a breach of his close in D., and the defendant pleads that the place where the injury is said to have happened is a certain close of pasture in D., which descended to him from B. his father, and so is his own freehold; the plaintiff may reply and assign another close in D., specifying the abuttals and boundaries, as the real place of the injury.(*i*)

It hath previously been observed(*k*) that *duplicity* in pleading must be avoided.   Every plea must be simple, entire, connected, and confined to one single point: it must never be entangled with a variety of distinct, independent answers to the same matter; which must require as many different replies, and introduce a multitude of issues upon one and the same dispute. For this would often embarrass a jury, and sometimes the court itself, and at all events would greatly enhance the expense of the parties.   Yet it frequently is expedient to plead in such a manner as to avoid any implied admission of a fact which cannot with propriety or safety be positively affirmed or denied. And this may be done by what is called a *protestation;* whereby the party interposes an oblique allegation or denial of some fact, protesting (by the gerund *protestando*) that such a matter does or does not exist; and at the same time avoiding a direct affirmation or denial.   Sir Edward Coke hath defined(*l*) a protestation (in the pithy dialect of that age) to be "an *312]   exclusion of a conclusion."   *For the use of it is, to save the party from being concluded with respect to some fact or circumstance, which cannot be directly affirmed or denied without falling into duplicity of pleading; and which yet, if he did not thus enter his protest, he might be deemed to have tacitly waived or admitted.   Thus, while tenure in villenage subsisted, if a villein had brought an action against his lord, and the lord was inclined to try the merits of the demand, and at the same time to prevent any conclusion against himself that he had waived his seignory; he could not in this case both plead affirmatively that the plaintiff was his villein, and also take issue upon the demand; for then his plea would have been *double*, as the former alone would have been a good bar to the action; but he might have alleged the villenage of the plaintiff, by way of protestation, and then have denied the demand.   By this means the future vassalage of the plaintiff was saved to the defendant in case the issue was found in his (the defendant's) favor;(*m*) for the protestation prevented that conclusion, which would otherwise have resulted from the rest of his defence, that he had enfranchised the plaintiff,(*n*) since no villein could maintain a civil action against his lord. So also, if a defendant, by way of inducement to the point of his defence, alleges (among other matters) a particular mode of seisin or tenure, which the plaintiff is unwilling to admit, and yet desires to take issue on the principal point of the defence, he must deny the seisin or tenure by way of protestation, and then traverse the defensive matter.   So, lastly, if an award be set forth by the plaintiff, and he can assign a breach in one part of it, (viz., the non-payment of a sum of money,) and yet is afraid to admit the performance of the rest of the award, or to aver in general a non-performance of any part of it, lest something should appear to have been performed; he may save to himself any advantage he might hereafter make of the general non-perform-

(*i*) Bro. Abr. tit. *trespass*, 205, 218.
(*k*) P. 308.
(*l*) 1 Inst. 124.

(*m*) Co. Litt. 126.
(*n*) See book ii. ch. 6, p. 94.

(86) The office and design of a novel assignment is to avoid an evasive plea.   Berry *v.* Vreeland, 1 N. J. (Zabriskie) 189 (1847).

ance, by alleging *that* by protestation, and plead only the non-payment of the money.(*o*)(87)

*In any stage of the pleadings, when either side advances or [*313 affirms any new matter, he usually (as we said) avers it to be true; "and this he is ready to verify." On the other hand, when either side traverses or denies the facts pleaded by his antagonist, he usually tenders an issue, as it is called; the language of which is different according to the party by whom the issue is tendered; for if the traverse or denial comes from the defendant, the issue is tendered in this manner, "and of this he puts himself upon the country,"¹ thereby submitting himself to the judgment of his peers;(*p*) but if the traverse lies upon the plaintiff he tenders the issue, or prays the judgment of the peers against the defendant in another form; thus: "and this he prays may be inquired of by the country."

But if either side (as, for instance, the defendant) pleads a special negative plea; not traversing or denying any thing that was before alleged, but disclosing some new negative matter; as, where the suit is on a bond, conditioned to perform an award, and the defendant pleads, negatively, that no award was made, he tenders no issue upon this plea; because it does not appear whether the fact will be disputed, the plaintiff not having yet asserted the existence of any award; but when the plaintiff replies, and sets forth an actual specific award, if then the defendant traverses the replication, and denies the making of any such award, he then, and not before, tenders an issue to the plaintiff. For when in the course of pleading they come to a point which is affirmed on one side, and denied on the other, they are then said to be at issue; all their debates being at last contracted into a single point, which must now be determined either in favor of the plaintiff or of the defendant.

CHAPTER XXI.

OF ISSUE AND DEMURRER.

*ISSUE, *exitus*, being the end of all the pleadings, is the fourth [*314 part or stage of an action, and is either upon matter of *law*, or matter of *fact*.(1)

An issue upon matter of law is called a *demurrer:* and it confesses the facts to be true, as stated by the opposite party; but denies that, by the law arising upon those facts, any injury is done to the plaintiff, or that the defendant has made out a legitimate excuse; according to the party which first demurs, *demoratur*, rests or abides upon the point in question. As, if the matter of the plaintiff's complaint or declaration be insufficient in law, as by not assigning any sufficient trespass, then the defendant demurs to the declaration: if, on the other hand, the defendant's excuse or plea be invalid, as if he pleads that he committed the trespass by authority from a stranger, without making out the stranger's right; here the plaintiff may demur in law to the plea: and so on in every other part of the proceedings, where either side perceives any material objection in point of law, upon which he may rest his case.

(*o*) Append. No. III. § 6.　　　　　　　(*p*) Ibid. No. II. § 4.

---

(87) No protestation is now required—or allowed, indeed—in any pleading; but either party is entitled to the same advantage as if protestation had been made.—KERR.
(1) Keener *et al. v.* Finger *et al.*, 70 Hargrave (N. C.) 48 (1874).

The form of such demurrer is by averring the declaration or plea, the
replication or rejoinder, to be insufficient in law to maintain the
*315]   action or the defence; and therefore praying *judgment for want of
sufficient matter alleged.(a)   Sometimes demurrers are merely for
want of sufficient *form* in the writ or declaration.   But in cases of exceptions to the form or manner of pleading, the party demurring must, by statute
27 Eliz. c. 5, and 4 & 5 Anne, c. 16, set forth the causes of his demurrer,
or wherein he apprehends the deficiency to consist.(2)   And upon either a
general or such a *special* demurrer, the opposite party must aver it to be sufficient, which is called a joinder in demurrer,(b) and then the parties are at
issue in point of law.(3)   Which issue in law, or demurrer, the judges of
the court before which the action is brought must determine.

An issue of fact is where the fact only, and not the law, is disputed.   And
when he that denies or traverses the fact pleaded by his antagonist has tendered the issue, thus, " and this he prays may be inquired of by the country;"
or, " and of this he puts himself upon the country;" it may immediately be
subjoined by the other party, " and the said A. B. doth the like."   Which
done, the issue is said to be joined, both parties having agreed to rest the fate
of the cause upon the truth of the fact in question.(c)   And this issue of
fact must, generally speaking, be determined, not by the judges of the court,
but by some other method; the principal of which methods is that by the
country, *per pais*, (in Latin *per patriam*,) that is, by jury.   Which establishment of different tribunals for determining these different issues is in
some measure agreeable to the course of justice in the Roman republic,
where the *judices ordinarii*(4) determined only questions of fact, but questions of law were referred to the decisions of the *centumviri*.(d)(5)

(a) Append. No. III. § 6.   (c) Ibid. No. II. § 4.
(b) Ibid.   (d) Cic. de Orator l. 1, c. 38.

---

(2) Either party may demur when the preceding pleadings of his adversary are defective.
A demurrer has been defined to be a declaration that the party demurring will go no
further, because the other has not shown sufficient matter against him. 5 Mod. 132. Co.
Litt. 71, b.   When the pleading is defective in substance, a general demurrer will suffice;
but where the objection is to the *form*, the demurrer must be special. Bac. Abr. Pleas,
N. 5.   A special demurrer must not merely show the kind of fault, but the specific fault
complained of.—CHITTY.

(3) A party holding the negative of the issue, after introducing repellant testimony,
cannot compel his adversary to join in a demurrer to evidence. Hart *v.* Calloaway, 2
Bibb (Ky.) 463 (1810).

There is, in the state of Indiana, no special demurrer under the code, its place being
occupied by the controlling power of the court to amend, render more certain, or strike
out pleadings, or parts thereof.   Graham *v.* Martin, 64 Ind. 571 (1878).

Since the enactment of the Common Law Procedure Act of 1852, special demurrers
have not been in use in England.   Now, the court or judge, upon application, may strike
out such pleadings as are made to interfere with a fair trial of the cause.   Useless and
fictitious pleadings are abolished.

(4) [Ordinary judges.]

(5) Formerly a party could not in any case demur and plead, by way of traverse or
otherwise, to the same pleading at the same time.   A defendant could not, for instance,
answer a declaration, *first*, by a demurrer, for that it showed no cause of action; and,
secondly, by pleading in confession and avoidance that the plaintiff had released the suit;
for the objection in point of law could not be raised with an issue in fact, the demurrer
being considered to admit the facts, although in reality this was only for the sake of argument.   Now, however, a party may plead and demur to the same pleading at the same
time, if he can satisfy a judge or the court that he ought to be allowed to do so.   He
may—as is but reasonable—be required to make an affidavit of the truth of the facts
stated in the pleas, and of his belief that the objections raised by the demurrer are valid
in law, before such leave will be granted.   And the court or judge, in granting leave,
may direct which shall be first determined, the issue in law or the issue in fact.—KERR.

But here it will be proper to observe, that during the whole of these proceedings, from the time of the defendant's appearance in obedience to the king's writ, it is necessary *that both the parties be kept or   [*316 *continued* in court from day to day, till the final determination of the suit. For the court can determine nothing unless in the presence of both the parties,(6) in person or by their attorneys, or upon default of one of them, after his original appearance and a time prefixed for his appearance in court again. Therefore, in the course of pleading, if either party neglects to put in his declaration, plea, replication, rejoinder, and the like, within the times allotted by the standing rules of the court, the plaintiff, if the omission be his, is said to be *non-suit*, or not to follow and pursue his complaint, and shall lose the benefit of his writ: or, if the negligence be on the side of the defendant, judgment may be had against him for such his default. And, after issue or demurrer joined, as well as in some of the previous stages of proceeding, a day is continually given and entered upon the record, for the parties to appear on from time to time, as the exigence of the case may require. The giving of this day is called the *continuance*, because thereby the proceedings are continued without interruption from one adjournment to another. If these continuances are omitted, the cause is thereby discontinued, and the defendant is discharged *sine die*,(7) without a day, for this turn: for by his appearance in court, he has obeyed the command of the king's writ; and, unless he be adjourned over to a certain day, he is no longer bound to attend upon that summons; but he must be warned afresh, and the whole must begin *de novo*.(8)

Now, it may sometimes happen, that after the defendant has pleaded, nay, even after issue or demurrer joined, there may have arisen some new matter, which it is proper for the defendant to plead; as that the plaintiff, being a feme-sole, is since married, or that she has given the defendant a release, and the like: here, if the defendant takes advantage of this new matter as early as he possibly can, viz., at the day given for his next appearance, he is permitted to plead it in what is called a plea of *puis darrein continuance*, or since the last adjournment.(9)   *For it would be unjust to exclude   [*317 him from the benefit of this new defence, which it was not in his power to make when he pleaded the former.(10)   But it is dangerous to rely on such a plea, without due consideration; for it confesses the matter which was before in dispute between the parties.(*e*)   And it is not allowed to be put in, if any continuance has intervened between the arising of this fresh

(*e*) Cro. Eliz. 49.

---

(6) Gordon's Executors, 1 Munford (Va.) 12 (1810).

(7) Yet notwithstanding this, it is well settled that where a suit has been commenced, and no order continuing it has been entered for many terms, the party may still keep it alive by filing a continuance roll, (Blair *v.* Cary, 9 Wis. 543;) this is allowed for the furtherance of justice where the right might otherwise be barred by the statute of limitations. Pierce *v.* Kneeland *et al.*, 14 Wis. 344 (Spooner, 1861).

(8) But these continuances are now become mere matter of form, and may be entered at any time to make the record complete.—COLERIDGE. Not now the law in Indiana. The spirit of the code practice is that a suit once in the proper court need never go out until it is decided upon its merits. Bayless *v.* Tonsey, 20 Ind. 153 (1863).

(9) This plea, though treated in some respects as a dilatory plea, the court cannot refuse to receive, (2 Wils. 157. 3 T. R. 554. 1 Marsh. 280. 5 Taunt. 333. 1 Stark. 62;) but it must be verified on oath before it is filed. Freem. 252. 1 Stra. 493. 2 Smith's Rep. 396. It may be pleaded at nisi prius as well as in banc, but cannot be amended after the assizes are over. Yelv. 181. Freem. 252. Bull. N. P. 309. See further, 1 Chitty on Pl. 4th ed. 569 to 573.—CHITTY.

(10) It cannot be relied on, in connection with answers to the original merits. The attempt to do so should be met by a motion to compel election. Collins *v.* Karatopsky, 36 Turner (Ark.) 331 (1880).

matter and the pleading of it: for then the defendant is guilty of neglect, or laches, and is supposed to rely on the merits of his former plea. Also it is not allowed after a demurrer is determined, or verdict given; because the relief may be had in another way, namely, by writ of *audita querela*,(11) of which hereafter. And these pleas *puis darrein continuance*, when brought to a demurrer in law or issue of fact, shall be determined in like manner as other pleas.

We have said that demurrers, or questions concerning the *sufficiency* of the matters alleged in the pleadings, are to be determined by the judges of the court, upon solemn argument by counsel on both sides, and to that end a demurrer-book is made up, containing all the proceedings at length, which are afterwards entered on *record;* and copies thereof, called *paper-books*, are delivered to the judges to peruse.(12) The *record*(f) is a history of the most material proceedings in the cause, entered on a parchment roll, and continued down to the present time; in which must be stated the original writ and summons, all the pleadings, the declaration, view, or *oyer* prayed, the imparlances, plea, replication, rejoinder, continuances, and whatever further proceedings have been had; all entered *verbatim* on the roll, and also the issue or demurrer, and joinder therein.(13)

These were formerly all written, as indeed all public proceedings were, in Norman or law French,(14) and even the arguments of the counsel and decisions of the court were in the same barbarous dialect. An evident and shameful badge, it must be owned, of tyranny and foreign servitude; *318] being *introduced under the auspices of William the Norman, and his sons: whereby the ironical observation of the Roman satirist came to be literally verified, that "*Gallia causidicos docuit facunda Britannos.*"(g)(15) This continued till the reign of Edward III.; who, having employed his arms successfully in subduing the *crown* of France, thought it unbeseeming the dignity of the victors to use any longer the *language* of a vanquished country. By a statute, therefore, passed in the thirty-sixth year of his reign,(h) it was enacted, that for the future all pleas should be pleaded, shown, defended, answered, debated, and judged in the English tongue; but be entered and enrolled in Latin.(16) In like manner as Don Alonso X., king of Castile, (the great-grandfather of our Edward III.,) obliged his subjects to use the Castilian tongue in all legal proceedings;(i) and as, in 1286, the German language was established in the courts of the empire.(k) And perhaps if our legislature had then directed that the writs themselves, which are mandates from the king to his subjects to perform certain acts or to appear at certain places, should have been framed in the English language, according to the rule of our ancient law,(l) it had not been very improper. But the record or enrollment of those writs and the proceedings thereon, which was calculated for the benefit of

(f) Append. No. II. § 4. No. III. § 6.
(g) Jur. xv. 111.
(h) C. 15.
(i) Mod. Un. Hist. xx. 211.
(k) Ibid. xxix. 235.
(l) Mirr. c. 4, § 3.

---

(11) [The complaint has been heard.]
(12) The plaintiff, or his attorney, must deliver paper-books to the chief justice and senior judge, and the defendant, or his attorney, to the two other judges. R. M. 17 Car. I.—CHITTY.
(13) Atkinson v. Bank, 85 Maine, 371 (Hamlin, 1885).
(14) This is disputed, with great reason, by Mr. Sergeant Stephen, *Pleading*, Appendix, p. 22, who thinks that the record was always in Latin.—STEWART.
(15) ["Eloquent Gaul hath instructed British lawyers."]
(16) Helm v. Franciscous, 2 Bland (Md.) 552 (1830). Blackstone and some others have fallen into what is now understood to be the error of supposing, that, previous to this statute, even the records were in French. Actual inspection has shown that they were in Latin. See on this general matter 1 Bish. on Crim. Proc. sec. 341, and authorities there cited.

posterity, was more serviceable (because more durable) in a dead and immutable language than in any flux or living one. The practicers, however, being used to the Norman language, and therefore imagining they could express their thoughts more aptly and more concisely in that than in any other, still continued to take their notes in law-French; and of course, when those notes came to be published, under the denomination of reports, they were printed in that barbarous dialect; which, joined to the additional terrors of Gothic black letter, has occasioned many a student to throw away his Plowden and Littleton, without venturing to attack a page of them. And yet, in reality, upon a nearer acquaintance, they would have found nothing very formidable in the language; which differs in its grammar *and orthography as much from the modern French, as the diction　[*319 of Chaucer and Gower does from that of Addison and Pope. Besides, as the English and Norman languages were concurrently used by our ancestors for several centuries together, the two idioms have naturally assimilated, and mutually borrowed from each other: for which reason the grammatical construction of each is so very much the same, that I apprehend an Englishman (with a week's preparation) would understand the laws of Normandy, collected in their *grand coustumier*, as well, if not better, than a Frenchman bred within the walls of Paris.

The Latin, which succeeded the French for the entry and enrollment of pleas, and which continued in use for four centuries, answers so nearly to the English (oftentimes word for word) that it is not at all surprising it should generally be imagined to be totally fabricated at home, with little more art or trouble than by adding Roman terminations to English words. Whereas in reality it is a very universal dialect, spread throughout all Europe at the irruption of the northern nations, and particularly accommodated and moulded to answer all the purposes of the lawyers with a peculiar exactness and precision. This is principally owing to the simplicity, or (if the reader pleases) the poverty and baldness, of its texture, calculated to express the ideas of mankind just as they arise in the human mind, without any rhetorical flourishes or perplexed ornaments of style; for it may be observed, that those laws and ordinances, of public as well as private communities, are generally the most easily understood, where strength and perspicuity, not harmony or elegance of expression, have been principally consulted in compiling them. These northern nations, or rather their legislators, though they resolved to make use of the Latin tongue in promulging their laws, as being more durable and more generally known to their conquered subjects than their own Teutonic dialects, yet (either through choice or necessity) have frequently intermixed therein some words of a Gothic original, which is more or less the case in every country *of Europe, and　[*320 therefore not to be imputed as any peculiar blemish in our English legal Latinity.(*m*) The truth is, what is generally denominated law-Latin is in reality a mere technical language, calculated for eternal duration, and easy to be apprehended both in present and future times; and on those accounts best suited to preserve those memorials which are intended for perpetual rules of action. The rude pyramids of Egypt have endured from the earliest ages, while the more•modern and more elegant structures of Attica, Rome, and Palmyra have sunk beneath the stroke of time.

As to the objection of locking up the law in a strange and unknown tongue, that is of little weight with regard to records, which few have occasion to read, but such as do, or ought to, understand the rudiments of Latin. And, besides, it may be observed of the law-Latin, as the very ingenious Sir

(*m*) The following sentence, " *Si quis ad battalia curte sua exierit,* if any one goes out of his own court to fight," etc., may raise a smile in the student as a flaming modern Anglicism; but he may meet with it, among others of the same stamp, in the laws of the Burgundians on the continent, before the end of the fifth century. Add. 1, c. 5, § 2.

John Davis(*n*) observes of the law-French, "that it is so very easy to be learned, that the meanest wit that ever came to the study of the law doth come to understand it almost perfectly in ten days without a reader."

It is true indeed that the many terms of art, with which the law abounds, are sufficiently harsh when Latinized, (yet not more so than those of other sciences,) and may, as Mr. Selden observes,(*o*) give offence "to some grammarians of squeamish stomachs, who would rather choose to live in ignorance of things the most useful and important, than to have their delicate ears wounded by the use of a word unknown to Cicero, Sallust, or the other writers of the Augustan age." Yet this is no more than must unavoidably happen when things of modern use, of which the Romans had no idea and

*321]   consequently no phrases to express them, come to be delivered in the Latin tongue. It would puzzle *the most classical scholar to find an appellation, in his pure Latinity, for a constable, a record, or a deed of feoffment; it is therefore to be imputed as much to necessity, as ignorance, that they were styled in our forensic dialect *constabularius*, *recordum*, and *feoffamentum*. Thus, again, another uncouth word of our *ancient* laws, (for I defend not the ridiculous barbarisms sometimes introduced by the ignorance of *modern* practicers,) the substantive *murdrum*, of the verb *murdrare*, however harsh and unclassical it may seem, was necessarily framed to express a particular offence; since no other word in being, *occidere*, *interficere*, *necare*,(17) or the like, was sufficient to express the *intention* of the criminal, or *quo animo* the act was perpetrated; and therefore by no means came up to the notion of murder at present entertained by our law; viz., a killing *with malice aforethought*.

A similar necessity to this produced a similar effect at Byzantium, when the Roman laws were turned into Greek for the use of the Oriental empire: for, without any regard to Attic elegance, the lawyers of the imperial courts made no scruple to translate *fidei commissarios*, φιδεϊκομμισσαριους;(*p*) *cubiculum*, κουβουκλειον;(*q*) *filium-familias*, παιδα-φαμιλιας;(*r*) *repudium*, ρεπουδιον;(*s*) *compromissum*, κομπρομισσον;(*t*) *reverentia et obsequium*, ρευερεντια και οβσεκωνιον;(*u*)(18) and the like. They studied more the exact and precise import of the words than the neatness and delicacy of their cadence. And many academical readers will excuse me for suggesting that the terms of the law are not more numerous, more uncouth, or more difficult to be explained by a teacher, than those of logic, physics, and the whole circle of Aristotle's philosophy, nay, even of the politer arts of architecture and its kindred studies, or the science

*322]   of rhetoric itself. Sir Thomas More's famous legal question(*w*) contains in it nothing more difficult than the *definition which in his time the philosophers currently gave of their *materia prima*,(19) the groundwork of all natural knowledge; that it is "*neque quid*, *neque quantum*, *neque quale*, *neque aliquid eorum quibus ens determinatur;*"(20) or its subsequent explanation by Adrian Heereboord, who assures us(*x*) that "*materia prima non est corpus*, *neque per formam corporeitatis*, *neque per simplicem essentiam: est tamen ens*, *et quidem substantia*, *licet incompleta; habet-*

(*n*) Pref. Rep.
(*o*) Pref. ad Eadmer.
(*p*) Nov. 1, c. 1.
(*q*) Nov. 8, edict. Constantinop.
(*r*) Nov. 117, c. 1.

(*s*) Ibid. c. 8.
(*t*) Ibid. 82, c. 11.
(*u*) Ibid. 78, c. 2.
(*w*) See page 149.
(*x*) Philosoph. Natural, c. 1, § 23, etc.

(17) [To kill, to put to death, to slay.]

(18) [Trustees, a bed chamber, the son of a family, a divorce, a bond or engagement wherein two parties oblige themselves to stand to the arbitration or award of the umpire, reverence and compliance.]

(19) [The primary matter.]

(20) ["Neither that nor as much as, nor such as, nor any part of those things by which being is determined."]

que actum ex se entitativum, et simul est potentia subjectiva."(21) The law therefore, with regard to its technical phrases, stands upon the same footing with other studies, and requests only the same indulgence.

This technical Latin continued in use from the time of its first introduction till the subversion of our ancient constitution under Cromwell; when, among many other innovations in the law, some for the better and some for the worse, the language of our records was altered and turned into English. But, at the restoration of king Charles, this novelty was no longer countenanced; the practicers finding it very difficult to express themselves so concisely or significantly in any other language but the Latin. And thus it continued without any sensible inconvenience till about the year 1730, when it was again thought proper that the proceedings at law should be done into English; and it was accordingly so ordered by statute 4 Geo. II. c. 26.(22) This provision was made, according to the preamble of the statute, that the common people might have knowledge and understanding of what was alleged or done for and against them in the process and pleadings, the judgment and entries, in a cause. Which purpose has, I fear, not been answered; being apt to suspect that the people are now, after many years' experience, altogether as ignorant in matters of law as before.   On the other hand, these inconveniences have already arisen from the alteration; that now many clerks and attorneys are hardly able to read, much less to understand, a record even of so modern a date as the reign of George the First.   And it has much enhanced the expense of all legal proceedings; for since the practicers are confined (for *the sake of the stamp-duties, which are   [*323 thereby considerably increased) to write only a stated number of words in a sheet; and as the English language, through the multitude of its particles, is much more verbose than the Latin, it follows that the number of sheets must be very much augmented by the change.(*y*)   The translation also of technical phrases, and the names of writs and other process, were found to be so very ridiculous (a writ of *nisi prius, quare impedit, fieri facias, habeas corpus,* and the rest, not being capable of an English dress with any degree of seriousness) that in two years' time it was found necessary to make a new act, 6 Geo. II. c. 14; which allows all technical words to continue in the usual language, and has thereby almost defeated every beneficial purpose of the former statute.

What is said of the alteration of language by the statute 4 Geo. II. c. 26 will hold equally strong with respect to the prohibition of using the ancient immutable *court-hand* in writing the records or other legal proceedings; whereby the reading of any record that is fifty years old is now become the object of science, and calls for the help of an antiquarian.   But that branch of it, which forbids the use of abbreviations, seems to be of more solid advantage, in delivering such proceedings from obscurity: according to the precept of Justinian;(*z*) "*ne per scripturam aliqua fiat in posterum dubitatio, jubemus non per siglorum captiones et compendiosa enigmata ejusdem codicis textum conscribi, sed per literarum consequentiam explanari concedimus.*"(23)   But to return to our demurrer.

(*y*) For instance, these three words, "*secundum formam statuti,*" are now converted into seven,   "according to the form of the statute."
(*z*) *De concept. digest. § 13.*

---

(21) ["Primary matter is not form, neither by form of corporeity nor by simple essence; nevertheless it is a being and certain substance, although incomplete; and has an entitative action from itself, and is at the same time a subjective power."]
(22) Berrian *v.* State, 2 N. J. 32 (Zabriskie, 1849).
(23) [" Lest through the method of writing the meaning of this code be rendered doubtful to posterity, we command that it be not written in abbreviation or ciphers; but that it be rendered plain by the regular succession of letters."]

When the substance of the record is completed, and copies are delivered to the judges, the matter of law upon which the demurrer is grounded is upon solemn argument determined by the court, and not by any trial by jury; and judgment is thereupon accordingly given. As, in an action of

*324]   trespass, if the defendant in his plea confesses the fact, but *justifies

it *causa venationis*, for that he was hunting; and to this the plaintiff demurs, that is, he admits the truth of the plea, but denies the justification to be legal: now, on arguing this demurrer, if the court be of opinion that a man may not justify trespass in hunting, they will give judgment for the plaintiff; if they think that he may, then judgment is given for the defendant. Thus is an issue in law, or demurrer, disposed of.

An issue of fact takes up more form and preparation to settle it; for here the truth of the matters alleged must be solemnly examined and established by proper evidence in the channel prescribed by law. To which examination of facts, the name of trial is usually confined, which will be treated of at large in the two succeeding chapters.

CHAPTER XXII.

OF THE SEVERAL SPECIES OF TRIAL.

*325]   *THE uncertainty of legal proceedings is a notion so generally adopted, and has so long been the standing theme of wit and good humor, that he who should attempt to refute it would be looked upon as a man who was either incapable of discernment himself, or else meant to impose upon others. Yet it may not be amiss, before we enter upon the several modes whereby certainty is meant to be obtained in our courts of justice, to inquire a little wherein this uncertainty, so frequently complained of, consists; and to what causes it owes its original.

It hath sometimes been said to owe its original to the number of our municipal constitutions, and the multitude of our judicial decisions;(a) which occasion, it is alleged, abundance of rules that militate and thwart with each other, as the sentiments or caprice of successive legislatures and judges have happened to vary. The fact of multiplicity is allowed; and that thereby the researches of the student are rendered more difficult and laborious; but that, with proper industry, the result of those inquiries will be doubt and indecision, is a consequence that cannot be admitted.   People are apt to be angry at the want of simplicity in our laws: they mistake variety for con-

*326]   fusion, and complicated cases for contradictory. *They bring us the example of arbitrary governments, of Denmark, Muscovy, and Prussia; of wild and uncultivated nations, the savages of Africa and America; or of narrow domestic republics, in ancient Greece and modern Switzerland; and unreasonably require the same paucity of laws, the same conciseness of practice, in a nation of freemen, a polite and commercial people, and a populous extent of territory.

In an arbitrary despotic government, where the lands are at the disposal of the prince, the rules of succession, or the mode of enjoyment, must depend upon his will and pleasure. Hence there can be but few legal determinations relating to the property, the descent, or the conveyance of real estate; and the same holds in a stronger degree with regard to goods and chattels, and

(a) See the preface to Sir John Davies's Reports,   more at large.
wherein many of the following topics are discussed

the contracts relating thereto. Under a tyrannical sway, trade must be continually in jeopardy, and of consequence can never be extensive: this therefore puts an end to the necessity of an infinite number of rules, which the English merchant daily recurs to for adjusting commercial differences. Marriages are there usually contracted with slaves; or at least women are treated as such: no laws can be therefore expected to regulate the rights of dower, jointures, and marriage settlements. Few also are the persons who can claim the privileges of any laws; the bulk of those nations, viz., the commonalty, boors, or peasants, being merely villeins and bondmen. Those are therefore left to the private coercion of their lords, are esteemed (in the contemplation of these boasted legislators) incapable of either right or injury, and of consequence are entitled to no redress. We may see, in these arbitrary states, how large a field of legal contests is already rooted up and destroyed.

Again: were we a poor and naked people, as the savages of America are, strangers to science, to commerce, and the arts as well of convenience as of luxury, we might perhaps be content, as some of them are said to be, to refer all disputes to the next man we meet upon the road, and so put a short end *to every controversy. For in a state of nature there is no   [*327 room for municipal laws; and the nearer any nation approaches to that state, the fewer they will have occasion for. When the people of Rome were little better than sturdy shepherds or herdsmen, all their laws were contained in ten or twelve tables; but as luxury, politeness, and dominion increased, the civil law increased in the same proportion, and swelled to that amazing bulk which it now occupies, though successively pruned and retrenched by the emperors Theodosius and Justinian.

In like manner we may lastly observe, that, in petty states and narrow territories, much fewer laws will suffice than in large ones, because there are fewer objects upon which the laws can operate. The regulations of a private family are short and well known; those of a prince's household are necessarily more various and diffuse.

The causes therefore of the multiplicity of the English laws are, the extent of the country which they govern, the commerce and refinement of its inhabitants, but, above all, the liberty and property of the subject. These will naturally produce an infinite fund of disputes which must be terminated in a judicial way; and it is essential to a free people, that these determinations be published and adhered to; that their property may be as certain and fixed as the very constitution of their state. For though in many other countries every thing is left in the breast of the judge to determine, yet with us he is only to *declare* and *pronounce*, not to *make* or *new-model*, the law. Hence a multitude of decisions, or cases adjudged, will arise; for seldom will it happen that any one rule will exactly suit with many cases. And in proportion as the decisions of courts of judicature are multiplied, the law will be loaded with decrees, that may sometimes (though rarely) interfere with each other: either because succeeding judges may not be apprised of the prior adjudication; or because they may think differently from their predecessors; or because the same arguments did not occur formerly as at *present; or, in fine, because of the natural imbecility and imper-   [*328 fection that attends all human proceedings. But wherever this happens to be the case in any material point, the legislature is ready, and from time to time both may, and frequently does, intervene to remove the doubt; and, upon due deliberation had, determines by a declaratory statute how the law shall be held for the future.

Whatever instances therefore of contradiction or uncertainty may have been gleaned from our records, or reports, must be imputed to the defects of human laws in general, and are not owing to any particular ill construction of the English system. Indeed, the reverse is most strictly true. The English law is less embarrassed with inconsistent resolutions and doubtful questions, than any other known system of the same extent and the same duration. I may instance in the civil law: the text whereof, as collected by Justinian and his agents, is extremely voluminous and diffuse; but the idle comments, obscure glosses, and jarring interpretations grafted thereupon by the learned jurists are literally without number. And these glosses, which are mere private opinions of scholastic doctors, (and not, like our books of reports, judicial determinations of the court,) are all of authority sufficient to be vouched and relied on: which must needs breed great distraction and confusion in their tribunals. The same may be said of the canon law; though the text thereof is not of half the antiquity with the common law of England; and though the more ancient any system of law is, the more it is liable to be perplexed with the multitude of judicial decrees. When therefore a body of laws, of so high antiquity as the English, is in general so clear and perspicuous, it argues deep wisdom and foresight in such as laid the foundations, and great care and circumspection in such as have built the superstructure.

But is not (it will be asked) the multitude of law-suits, which we daily see and experience, an argument against the clearness and certainty of *329]   the law itself? By no means: for *among the various disputes and controversies which are daily to be met with in the course of legal proceedings, it is obvious to observe how very few arise from obscurity in the rules or maxims of law. An action shall seldom be heard of, to determine a question of inheritance, unless the fact of the descent be controverted. But the dubious points which are usually agitated in our courts arise chiefly from the difficulty there is of ascertaining the intentions of individuals, in their solemn dispositions of property; in their contracts, conveyances, and testaments. It is an object indeed of the utmost importance, in this free and commercial country, to lay as few restraints as possible upon the transfer of possessions from hand to hand, or their various designations marked out by the prudence, convenience, necessities, or even by the caprice, of their owners: yet to investigate the *intention* of the owner is frequently matter of difficulty, among heaps of entangled conveyances or wills of a various obscurity. The law rarely hesitates in declaring its own meaning; but the judges are frequently puzzled to find out the meaning of others. Thus the powers, the interest, the privileges and properties of a tenant for life, and a tenant in tail, are clearly distinguished and precisely settled by law: but, what words in a will shall constitute this or that estate, has occasionally been disputed for more than two centuries past, and will continue to be disputed as long as the carelessness, the ignorance or singularity of testators shall continue to clothe their intentions in dark or new-fangled expressions.

But, notwithstanding so vast an accession of legal controversies, arising from so fertile a fund as the ignorance and wilfulness of individuals, these will bear no comparison in point of number to those which are founded upon the dishonesty and disingenuity of the parties: by either their suggesting complaints that are also false in fact, and thereupon bringing groundless actions; or by their denying such facts as are true, in setting up unwarrantable defences. *Ex facto oritur jus:*(1) if therefore the fact be perverted or misrepresented, the law which arises from thence will unavoidably be unjust *330]   or partial. *And, in order to prevent this, it is necessary to set right the fact, and establish the truth contended for, by appealing to some mode of *probation* or *trial*, which the law of the country has ordained for a criterion of truth and falsehood.

---

(1) [Law arises from fact.]

These modes of probation or trial form in every civilized country the great object of judicial decisions. And experience will abundantly show, that above a hundred of our law-suits arise from disputed facts, for one where the law is doubted of. About twenty days in the year are sufficient in Westminster hall, to settle (upon solemn argument) every demurrer, or other special point of law, that arises throughout the nation: but two months are annually spent in deciding the truth of facts, before six distinct tribunals, in the several circuits of England: exclusive of Middlesex and London, which afford a supply of causes much more than equivalent to any two of the largest circuits.

Trial, then, is the examination of the matter of fact in issue:(2) of which there are many different species, according to the difference of the subject, or thing to be tried: of all which we will take a cursory view in this and the subsequent chapter. For the law of England so industriously endeavors to investigate truth at any rate, that it will not confine itself to one, or to a few, manners of trial; but varies its examination of facts according to the nature of the facts themselves: this being the one invariable principle pursued, that as well the best method of trial, as the best evidence upon that trial which the nature of the case affords, and no other, shall be admitted in the English courts of justice.

The species of trials in civil cases are seven. By *record;* by *inspection,* or *examination;* by *certificate;* by *witnesses;* by *wager of battel;* by *wager of law;* and by *jury.*

I. First, then, of the trial by *record.* This is only used in one particular instance: and that is where a matter of record *is pleaded in any action, as a fine, a judgment, or the like; and the opposite party   [*331 pleads, "*nul tiel record,*" that there is no such matter of record existing: upon this, issue is tendered and joined in the following form, "and this he prays may be inquired of by *the record,* and the other doth the like;" and hereupon the party pleading the record has a day given him to bring it in, and proclamation is made in court for him to "bring forth the record by him in pleading alleged, or else he shall be condemned;" and, on his failure, his antagonist shall have judgment to recover. The trial therefore of this issue is merely by the record; for, as Sir Edward Coke(b) observes, a record or enrollment is a monument of so high a nature, and importeth in itself such absolute verity, that if it be pleaded that there is no such record, it shall not receive any trial by witness,(3) jury, or otherwise, but only by itself. Thus

(b) 1 Inst. 117, 260.

---

(2) Cruce *v.* The State, 59 Ga. 97 (1877). Hickman *v.* R. R. Co., 30 W. Va. 296, 299 (1887). Under the code of Idaho, trial also means the determination of issues of law. Lamkin *v.* Sterling, 1 Idaho, 120, 127 (1867); but the civil code of Oregon, sec. 175, adopts the definition in the text. Oregon *v.* Spores, 4 Ore. 198, 199 (1871). A trial is an examination before a competent tribunal, according to the law of the land, of the facts, or law, or both, put in issue in a cause, for the purpose of determining such issue; and, by a court, we understand a permanent organization for the administration of justice. Bassett's Cr. Pl. 327.

(3) Adams *v.* Betz, 1 Watts (Pa.) 427 (1834). Simpson *v.* Watson, 15 Mo. App. 431 (1884). Crocket *v.* Routen, 1 Dudley (Ga.) 255 (1833). Books of entries are records,—they must be received in the condition in which they are found, nor is the court permitted to presume that any improper alterations have been made and parol evidence thereof will not be received. Kerr *v.* Porter, 1 Tenn. (Overton) 16 (1802). There can be no averment in pleading against a record, though there may be against its operation, —therefore no matter of defence can be pleaded, which existed anterior to the judgment. Share *v.* Becker, 8 S. & R. (Pa.) 240 (1822). An act of the legislature, enrolled in the proper office, is a record. Commonwealth *v.* Martin, 107 Pa. 190 (1884). The judgment of a domestic court of general jurisdiction cannot be impeached. unless the record shows that the court did not have jurisdiction of the subject matter of the action or of the person of the defendant. Crim *v.* Kessing, 89 Cal. 485 (Pomroy) (1891). If it

titles of nobility, as whether earl or no earl, baron or no baron, shall be tried by the king's writ or patent only, which is matter of record.(c) Also in case of an alien, whether alien friend or enemy, shall be tried by the league or treaty between his sovereign and ours; for every league or treaty is of record.(d) And also, whether a manor be to be held in ancient demesne or not, shall be tried by the record of *domesday* in the king's exchequer.

II. Trial by *inspection*, or *examination*, is when, for the greater expedition of a cause, in some point or issue being either the principal question or arising collaterally out of it, but being evidently the object of senses, the judges of the court, upon the testimony of their own sense, shall decide the point in dispute. For, where the affirmative or negative of a question is matter of such obvious determination, it is not thought necessary to summon a jury to decide it; who are properly called in to inform the conscience of the court in respect of *dubious* facts: and therefore when the fact, from its nature, must be evident to the court either from ocular demonstration or other *332] irrefragable proof, there the law departs *from its usual resort, the verdict of twelve men, and relies on the judgment of the court alone. As in case of a suit to reverse a fine for non-age of the cognizor, or to set aside a statute or recognizance entered into by an infant; here, and in other cases of the like sort, a writ shall issue to the sheriff;(e) commanding him that he constrain the said party to appear, that it may be ascertained, by the view of his body by the king's justices, whether he be of full age or not; "*ut per aspectum corporis sui constare poterit justiciariis nostris, si prædictus A. sit plenæ ætatis necne.*"(f)(4) If however the court has, upon inspection, any doubt of the age of the party, (as may frequently be the case,) it may proceed to take proofs of the fact; and, particularly, may examine the infant himself upon an oath of *voire dire, veritatem dicere*, that is, to make true answer to such questions as the court shall demand of him: or the court may examine his mother, his godfather, or the like.(g)(5)

In like manner, if a defendant pleads in abatement of the suit that the plaintiff is *dead*, and one appears and calls himself the plaintiff, which the defendant denies: in this case the judges shall determine by inspection and examination whether he be the plaintiff or not.(h) Also, if a man be found by a jury an idiot *a nativitate*, he may come in person into the chancery before the chancellor, or be brought there by his friends, to be inspected and examined, whether idiot or not: and if upon such view and inquiry it appears that he is not so, the verdict of the jury and all the proceedings thereon are utterly void and instantly of no effect.(i)

Another instance in which the trial by inspection may be used is when, upon an appeal of mayhem, the issue joined is whether it be mayhem or no

(c) 6 Rep. 53.
(d) 9 Rep. 31.
(e) Ibid.
(f) This question of non-age was formerly, according to Glanvil, (l. 13, c. 15,) tried by a jury of eight

men, though now it is tried by inspection.
(g) 2 Roll. Abr. 573.
(h) 9 Rep. 30.
(i) Ibid. 31.

---

is claimed that a statute is not correctly published, or if the fact of its passage is denied, the question is to be tried and determined by the court as one of law. If it be properly enrolled, authenticated and deposited with the secretary of state, it is a record which is conclusive evidence of its passage, and that the act passed as enrolled. Sherman *v.* Story, 30 Cal. 253 (Tuttle) (1866).

(4) ["That on a view of his person it may appear to our Justices whether the aforesaid A. be of full age or not."] 1 Sheppard's Touchstone, Prest. 7. It is not known that this mode of trial was ever adopted in the United States. Metcalf on Contracts, 50 Heard's ed. (1888). Smith *v.* The State, 42 Tex. (Ter. & Walk.) 449 (1875). The existence or non-existence of a seal is to be determined upon inspection by the court. Cromwell *v.* Tates, Exr., 7 Leigh. (Va.) 305 (1836).

(5) The jury may infer the minority of a witness examined before them. Snodgrass *v.* Bradley, 2 Grant (Pa.) 43 (1860). [*A nativitate*—From birth.]

mayhem; this shall be decided by the court upon inspection, for which purpose they may *call in the assistance of surgeons.(j)(6)   And,   [*333 by analogy to this, in an action of trespass for mayhem, the court (upon view of such mayhem as the plaintiff has laid in his declaration, or which is certified by the judges who tried the cause to be the same as was given in evidence to the jury) may increase the damages at their own discretion,(k) as may also be the case upon view of an atrocious battery.(l) But then the battery must likewise be alleged so certainly in the declaration that it may appear to be the same with the battery inspected.

Also, to ascertain any circumstances relative to a particular day past, it hath been tried by an inspection of the almanac by the court.   Thus, upon a writ of error from an inferior court, that of Lynn, the error assigned was that the judgment was given on a Sunday, it appearing to be on 26 February, 26 Eliz., and upon inspection of the almanacs of that year it was found that the 26th of February in that year actually fell upon a Sunday: this was held to be a sufficient trial, and that a trial by a jury was not necessary, although it was an error in fact; and so the judgment was reversed.(m) But in all these cases the judges, if they conceive a doubt, may order it to be tried by jury.

III. The trial by *certificate* is allowed in such cases where the evidence of the person certifying is the only proper criterion of the point in dispute. For, when the fact in question lies out of the cognizance of the court, the judges must rely on the solemn averment or information of persons in such a station as affords them the most clear and competent knowledge of the truth.   As therefore such evidence (if given to a jury) must have been conclusive, the law, to save trouble and circuity, permits the fact to be determined upon such certificate merely.   Thus, 1. If the issue be, whether A. was absent with the king in his army out of the realm in time of war; this shall be tried(n) by the certificate of the mareschal of *the   [*334 king's host in writing under his seal, which shall be sent to the justices.   2. If, in order to avoid an outlawry or the like, it was alleged that the defendant was in prison, *ultra mare*,(7) at Bordeaux, or in the service of the mayor of Bordeaux, this should have been tried by the certificate of the mayor; and the like of the captain of Calais.(o)   But when this was law(p) those towns were under the dominion of the crown of England. And therefore, by parity of reason, it should now hold that in similar cases arising at Jamaica or Minorca, the trial should be by certificate from the governor of those islands.   We also find(q) that the certificate of the queen's messenger, sent to summon home a peeress of the realm, was formerly held a sufficient trial of the contempt in refusing to obey such summons.   3. For matters within the realm, the customs of the city of London shall be tried by the certificate of the mayor and aldermen, certified by the mouth of their recorder;(r) upon a surmise from the party alleging it, that the custom ought to be thus tried: else it must be tried by the country.(s)   As, the custom of distributing the effects of freemen deceased, of enrolling apprentices, or that he who is free of one trade may use another; if any of these or other similar points come in issue.   But this rule admits of an exception where the corporation of London is party or interested in the suit; as in an

---

(j) 2 Roll. Abr. 578.
(k) 1 Sid. 108.
(l) Hardr. 408.
(m) Cro. Eliz. 227.
(n) Litt. § 102.

(o) 9 Rep. 31.
(p) 2 Roll. Abr. 583.
(q) Dyer. 176, 177.
(r) Co. Litt. 74. 4 Burr. 248.
(s) Bro. Abr. tit. *trial*, pl. 96.

---

(6) All appeals of mayhem are now abolished.   59 Geo. III. c. 46.—Stewart.
(7) [Beyond sea.]

action brought for a penalty inflicted by the custom; for there the reason of the law will not endure so partial a trial; but this custom shall be determined by a jury, and not by the mayor and aldermen certifying by the mouth of their recorder.(*t*) 4. In some cases the sheriff of London's certificate shall be the final trial; as, if the issue be whether the defendant be a citizen of London or a foreigner,(*u*) in case of privilege pleaded to be sued only in the city courts. Of a nature somewhat similar to which is the trial of the privi- lege of the university, when the chancellor claims cognizance of the
*335] cause because one of the parties is a *privileged person. In this case, the charters confirmed by act of parliament direct the trial of the question, whether a privileged person or no, to be determined by the certificate and notification of the chancellor under seal, to which it hath also been usual to add an *affidavit* of the fact; but if the parties be at issue between themselves, whether A. is a member of the university or no, on a plea of privilege, the trial shall be then by jury and not by the chancellor's certi- ficate;(*v*) because the charters direct only that the privilege be allowed on the chancellor's certificate when the claim of cognizance is made by him, and not where the defendant himself pleads his privilege; so that this must be left to the ordinary course of determination. 5. In matters of ecclesiastical juris- diction, as *marriage*, and of course *general bastardy;* and also *excommu- nications* and *orders*, these and other like matters shall be tried by the bishop's certificate.(*w*) As, if it be pleaded in abatement that the plaintiff is excommunicated, and issue is joined thereon; or, if a man claims an estate by descent, and the tenant alleges the demandant to be a bastard; or, if on a writ of dower the heir pleads no marriage; or, if the issue in a *quare im- pedit*(8) be whether or no the church be full by institution; all these, being matters of mere ecclesiastical cognizance, shall be tried by certificate from the ordinary. But, in an action on the case for calling a man bastard, the defendant having pleaded in justification that the plaintiff was really so, this was directed to be tried by a jury:(*x*) because, whether the plaintiff be found either a general or special bastard, the justification will be good; and no ques- tion of special bastardy shall be tried by the bishop's certificate, but by a jury.(*y*) For a special bastard is one born before marriage of parents who afterwards intermarry; which is bastardy by our law, though not by the ecclesiastical. It would therefore be improper to refer the trial of that ques- tion to the bishop, who, whether the child be born before or after
*336] marriage, will be *sure to return or certify him legitimate.(*z*) *Ability* of a clerk presented,(*a*) *admission*, *institution*, and *deprivation* of a clerk, shall also be tried by certificate from the ordinary or metropolitan, because of these he is the most competent judge;(*b*) but *induction* shall be tried by a jury, because it is a matter of public notoriety,(*c*) and is likewise the corporal investiture of the temporal profits. *Resignation* of a benefice may be tried in either way;(*d*) but it seems most properly to fall within the bishop's cognizance. 6. The trial of all customs and practice of the courts shall be by certificate from the proper officers of those courts respectively; and what return was made on a writ by the sheriff or under-sheriff shall be only tried by his own certificate.(*e*) And thus much for those several issues or matters of fact which are proper to be tried by certificate.

(*t*) Hob. 85.
(*u*) Co. Litt. 74.
(*v*) 2 Roll. Abr. 588.
(*w*) Co. Litt. 74. 2 Lev. 250.
(*x*) Hob. 179.
(*y*) Dyer, 79.
(*z*) See Introd. to the Great Charter, *edit. Oxon. sub*

anno 1233.
(*a*) See book i. ch. 11.
(*b*) 2 Inst. 632. Show.* Parl. c. 88. 2 Roll. Abr. 583, etc.
(*c*) Dyer, 228.
(*d*) 2 Roll. Abr. 583.
(*e*) 9 Rep. 31.

(8) [Wherefore he impedes.]

IV. A fourth species of trial is that by *witnesses, per testes*, without the intervention of a jury. This is the only method of trial known to the civil law in which the judge is left to form in his own breast his sentence upon the credit of the witnesses examined; but it is very rarely used in our law, which prefers the trial by jury before it in almost every instance.(9) Save only that when a widow brings a writ of dower, and the tenant pleads that the husband is not dead; this, being looked upon as a dilatory plea, is in favor of the widow, and for greater expedition allowed to be tried by witnesses examined before the judges; and so, saith Finch,(f) shall no other case in *our* law. But Sir Edward Coke(g) mentions some others; as to try whether the tenant in a real action was duly summoned, or the validity of a challenge to a juror: so that Finch's observation must be confined to the trial of direct and not collateral issues. And in every case Sir Edward Coke lays it down that the affirmative must be proved by two witnesses at the least.(10)

*V. The next species of trial is of great antiquity, but much dis- [*337 used; though still in force if the parties choose to abide by it: I mean the trial by *wager of battel*.(11) This seems to have owed its original to the military spirit of our ancestors, joined to a superstitious frame of mind; it being in the nature of an appeal to Providence under an apprehension and hope (however presumptuous and unwarrantable) that Heaven would give the victory to him who had the right. The decision of suits by this appeal to the God of battles is by some said to have been invented by the Burgundi, one of the northern or German clans that planted themselves in Gaul. And it is true that the first written injunction of judiciary combats that we meet with is in the laws of Gundebald, A. D. 501, which are preserved in the Burgundian code. Yet it does not seem to have been merely a local custom of this or that particular tribe, but to have been the common usage of all those warlike people from the earliest times.(h) And it may also seem, from a passage in Velleius Paterculus,(i) that the Germans, when first they became known to the Romans, were wont to decide all contests of right by the sword; for when Quintilius Varus endeavored to introduce among them the Roman laws and method of trial, it was looked upon (says the historian) as a "*novitas incognitæ disciplinæ, ut solita armis decerni jure terminarentur*."(12) And among the ancient Goths in Sweden we find the practice of judiciary duels established upon much the same footing as they formerly were in our own country.(j)

This trial was introduced into England, among other Norman customs, by

(f) L. 423.
(g) Inst. 6.
(h) Seld. of Duels, c. 5.

(i) L. 2, c. 118.
(j) Stiernh. *de jure Sueon l.* 1, c. 7.

---

(9) By numerous local acts for the recovery of small debts, the claim of a creditor may be sustained by his own oath without the intervention of a jury.—CHITTY. By statute 52 & 53 Vict. c. 49, § 14, in any cause of action other than a criminal proceeding by the crown, if all the parties interested not under disability consent, in case of any matter requiring a prolonged, scientific or local investigation, which cannot, in the courts or judge's opinion, be conveniently made before a jury, or conducted by the court through its ordinary officers, or in case the dispute wholly or partly concerns this account, the court or judge may at any time cause the whole matter to be submitted to an arbitrator or referee, especially agreed upon by the parties, or before an official referee or officer of the court.

(10) In courts of law in general, it suffices to prove a fact by one witness. In courts of equity it is sometimes otherwise, and two witnesses are required. *Vide post*, ch. 27 and note.—CHITTY.

(11) Now abolished, by 59 Geo. III. c. 46, passed in consequence of a defendant having waged his battel in Ashford *v.* Thornton, 1 B. & Ald. 405.—STEWART.

(12) ["The introduction of a custom never before heard of, that matters which had always been decided by arms should be determined by law."]

William the Conqueror; but was only used in three cases, one military, one criminal, and the third civil. The first in the court martial, or court of chivalry and honor;(*k*) the second in appeals of felony,(*l*) of which we shall speak in the next book; and the third upon issue joined in a *338] *writ of right, the last and most solemn decision of real property.

For in writs of right the *jus proprietatis*,(13) which is frequently a matter of difficulty, is in question; but other real actions being merely questions of the *jus possessionis*,(14) which are usually more plain and obvious, our ancestors did not in them appeal to the decision of Providence. Another pretext for allowing it upon these final writs of right was also for the sake of such claimants as might have the true right, but yet, by the death of witnesses, or other defect of evidence, be unable to prove it to a jury. But the most curious reason of all is given in the Mirror,(*m*) that it is allowable upon warrant of the combat between David for the people of Israel of the one party, and Goliath for the Philistines of the other party; a reason which pope Nicholas I. very seriously decides to be inconclusive.(*n*) Of battle, therefore, on a writ of right,(*o*) we are now to speak; and although the writ of right itself, and of course this trial thereof, be at present much disused, yet, as it is law at this day, it may be matter of curiosity, at least to inquire into the forms of this proceeding as we may gather them from ancient authors.(*p*)

The last trial by battle that was waged in the court of common pleas at Westminster (though there was afterwards(*q*) one in the court of chivalry in 1631, and another in the county palatine of *Durham*(*r*) in 1638) was in the thirteenth year of queen Elizabeth, A. D. 1571, as reported by Sir James Dyer,(*s*) and was held in Tothill fields, Westminster, "*non sine magna juris consultorum perturbatione,*"(15) saith Sir Henry Spelman,(*t*) who was himself a witness of the ceremony. The form, as appears from the authors before cited, is as follows:

When the tenant in a writ of right pleads the general issue, viz., *339] that he hath more right to hold than the *demandant hath to recover, and offers to prove it by the body of his champion, which tender is accepted by the demandant; the tenant in the first place must produce his champion, who by throwing down his glove as a gage or pledge thus *wages* or stipulates battle with the champion of the demandant; who, by taking up the gage or glove, stipulates on his part to accept the challenge. The reason why it is waged by champions and not by the parties themselves in civil actions is, because if any party to the suit dies, the suit must abate and be at an end for the present, and therefore no judgment could be given for the lands in question if either of the parties were slain in battle:(*u*) and also that no person might claim an exemption from this trial, as was allowed in criminal cases where the battle was waged in person.

A piece of ground is then in due time set out of sixty feet square, enclosed with lists, and on one side a court erected for the judges of the court of common pleas, who attend there in their scarlet robes; and also a bar is prepared for the learned sergeants-at-law. When the court sits, which ought to

(*k*) Co. Litt. 261.
(*l*) 2 Hawk. P. C. 45.
(*m*) C. 3, ? 23.
(*n*) *Decret. parl*. 2, *caus.* 2. *qu.* 5, c. 22.
(*o*) Append. No. I. ? 5.
(*p*) Glanvil. *l.* 2, c. 3. *Vet. Nat. Brev.* fol. 2. *Nov Nar.* tit. *Droit, patent,* fol. 221, (edit. 1534,) Year-book. 29 Edw. III. c. 12. Finch. L. 421. Dyer, 301, 2 Inst. 247.

(*q*) Rushw. Coll. Vol. 2, part 2, fol. 112. 19 Rym. 322.
(*r*) Cro. Car. 512.
(*s*) Dyer, 801.
(*t*) Gloss. 102.
(*u*) Co, Litt. 294. *Dyversyte des courtes,* 304.

(13) [Right of property.]
(14) [Right of possession.]
(15) [" Not without great disturbance of the lawyers."]

be by sunrising, proclamation is made for the parties and their champions, who are introduced by two knights and are dressed in a coat of armor, with red sandals, bare-legged from the knee downwards, bare-headed, and with bare arms to the elbows. The weapons allowed them are only batons or staves of an ell long, and a four-cornered leathern target; so that death very seldom ensued this civil combat. In the court military, indeed, they fought with sword and lance, according to Spelman and Rushworth; as likewise in France only villeins fought with the buckler and baton, gentlemen armed at all points. And upon this and other circumstances, the president Montesquieu(*v*) hath with great ingenuity not only deduced the impious custom of private duels upon imaginary points of honor, but hath also traced the heroic madness of knight errantry from the same original of judicial combats. But to proceed.

*When the champions thus armed with batons arrive within the   [*340 lists or place of combat, the champion of the tenant then takes his adversary by the hand and makes oath that the tenements in dispute are not the right of the demandant; and the champion of the demandant then, taking the other by the hand, swears in the same manner that they are; so that each champion is, or ought to be, thoroughly persuaded of the truth of the cause he fights for. Next, an oath against sorcery and enchantment is to be taken by both the champions, in this or similar form:—" Hear this, ye justices, that I have this day neither eat, drank, nor have upon me, neither bone, stone, nor grass, nor any enchantment, sorcery, or witchcraft, whereby the law of God may be abased or the law of the devil exalted. So help me God and his saints."

The battle is thus begun, and the combatants are bound to fight till the stars appear in the evening; and if the champion of the tenant can defend himself till the stars appear, the tenant shall prevail in his cause; for it is sufficient for him to maintain his ground and make it a drawn battle, he being already in possession; but if victory declares itself for either party, for him is judgment finally given. This victory may arise from the death of either of the champions; which, indeed, hath rarely happened; the whole ceremony, to say the truth, bearing a near resemblance to certain rude athletic diversions, which are probably derived from this original. Or, victory is obtained if either champion proves *recreant*, that is, yields, and pronounces the horrible word of *craven;* a word of disgrace and obloquy rather than of any determinate meaning.(16) But a horrible word it indeed is to the vanquished champion; since, as a punishment to him for forfeiting the land of his principal by prouncing that shameful word, he is condemned as a recreant *amittere liberam legem*,(17) that is, to become infamous, and not to be accounted *liber et legalis homo;* (18) being supposed by the event to

(*v*) Sp. L. b. 28, c. 20, 22.

---

(16) The word "*craven*" has an obvious and intelligible meaning from the occasion on which it is employed. It is of Anglo-Saxon derivation, (crafian,) and means to *crave*, to beg, or to implore,—which to do of an adversary in combat was held to be cowardly and dishonorable, however hopeless the conflict, in the age of chivalry. See Kendall's Argument on Trial by Battle, 143, n.—CHITTY.

(17) [To lose his free law.]

(18) [A free and lawful man.] One who was drafted into the military service of the United States, failed to report for duty, and was registered by the provostmarshal of his district as a deserter, without due trial and conviction, (under act of 1866, June 4, for disfranchising deserters,) was not thereby deprived of any civil right or privilege. The said act was held to be unconstitutional. McCafferty *v.* Guyer *et al.* 59 Pa. 117 (1868).

be proved foresworn, and therefore never to be put upon a jury or admitted as a witness in any cause.

*341]   *This is the form of a trial by battle; a trial which the tenant or defendant in a writ of right has it in his election at this day to demand, and which was the only decision of such writ of right after the Conquest, till Henry the Second by consent of parliament introduced the *grand assize,* (w) a peculiar species of trial by jury in concurrence therewith, giving the tenant his choice of either the one or the other. Which example of discountenancing these judicial combats was imitated about a century afterwards in France, by an edict of Louis the Pious, A. D. 1260, and soon after by the rest of Europe. The establishment of this alternative, Glanvil, chief justice to Henry the Second, and probably his adviser herein, considers as a most noble improvement, as in fact it was, of the law.(x)

VI. A sixth species of trial is by *wager of law,* (19) *vadiatio legis,* as the foregoing is called *wager of battle, vadiatio duelli;* because, as in the former case, the defendant gave a pledge, gage, or *vadium,* to try the cause by battle; so here he was to put in sureties or *vadios* that at such a day he will make his law, that is, to take the benefit which the law has allowed him.(y) For our ancestors considered that there were many cases where an innocent man of good credit might be overborne by a multitude of false witnesses, and therefore established this species of trial, by the oath of the defendant himself; for if he will absolutely swear himself not chargeable, and appears to be a person of reputation, he shall go free and forever acquitted of the debt or other cause of action.

*342]   *This method of trial is not only to be found in the codes of almost all the northern nations that broke in upon the Roman Empire and established petty kingdoms upon its ruins;(z) but its original may also be traced as far back as the Mosaical law. " If a man deliver unto his neighbor an ass, or an ox, or a sheep, or any beast, to keep; and it die, or be hurt, or driven away, no man seeing it; then shall an oath of the Lord be between them both, that he hath not put his hand unto his neighbor's goods; and the owner of it shall accept thereof, and he shall not make it good."(a)   We

---

(w) Append. No. I. § 6.

(x) Est autem magna assisa regale quoddam beneficium, clementia principis, de concilio procerum, populis indultum; quo vitæ hominum, et status integritati tam salubriter consulitur, ut, retinendo quod quis possidet in libero tenemento suo, duelli casum declinare possint homines ambiguum. Ac per hoc contingit, inseperatæ et prematuræ mortis ultimum credere supplicium, vel saltem perennis infamiæ opprobrium illius infesti et inverecundi verbi, quod in ore victi turpiter sonat, consecutivum. Ex expilate item maxima profita est legalis ista institutio. Jus enim, quod post multas et longas dilationes vix eruitur per duellum, per beneficium istius constitutionis commodius et acceleratius expeditur. [The grand assize is a certain royal favor granted to the people by the clemency of the king, in counsel with his nobles; by which the lives and es-

tates of men are so effectually consulted that, every one retaining what he possesses in fee, may decline the doubtful event of the trial by battle; and by this means avoid the greatest of all punishments, an unexpected and premature death or at least the disgrace and perpetual infamy attached to that base and odious word pronounced to the vanquished. This legal institution proceeds also from the highest equity; for the right which after many and long delays can scarcely be ascertained by battle, is by this means more commodiously and expeditiously determined.] L. 2, c. 7.

(y) Co. Litt. 295.

(z) Sp. L. b. 28, c. 13. Stiernh. de jure Succon. l. 1, c. 9. Feud. l 1, t. 4, 10, 28.

(a) Exod. xxii. 10.

---

(19) The right to wage law in an action of debt on simple contract still exists. See Barry v. Robinson, 1 Bos. & Pul. New Rep. 297. In the case of King v. Williams, (2 B. & C. 538,) the defendant having waged his law, and the master assigned a day for him to come in and perfect it, he applied by his counsel, to the court to assign the number of compurgators with whom he should come to perfect it, on the ground that, the number being uncertain, it was the duty of the court to say how many were necessary; but the court, being disinclined to assist the revival of this obsolete mode of trial, refused the application, and left the defendant to bring such number as he should be advised were sufficient; and observed, that if the plaintiff were not satisfied with the number brought, the objection would be open to him, and then the court would hear both sides. The defendant afterwards prepared to bring eleven compurgators; but the plaintiff abandoned the action. 2 B. & C. 538   4 Dowl. & Ryl. 3.—CHITTY.

Abolished by 3 & 4 W. IV. c. 42, s. 13.—STEWART.

shall likewise be able to discern a manifest resemblance between this species of trial, and the canonical purgation of the popish clergy when accused of any capital crime. The defendant or person accused was in both cases to make oath of his own innocence, and to produce a certain number of compurgators, who swore they believed his oath.(20) Somewhat similar also to this is the *sacramentum decisionis*, or the voluntary and decisive oath of the civil law;(*b*) where one of the parties to the suit, not being able to prove his charge, offers to refer the decision of the cause to the oath of his adversary; which the adversary was bound to accept, or tender the same proposal back again; otherwise the whole was taken as confessed by him. But, though a custom somewhat similar to this prevailed formerly in the city of London,(*c*) yet in general the English law does not thus, like the civil, reduce the defendant, in case he is in the wrong, to the dilemma of either confession or perjury: but is indeed so tender of permitting the oath to be taken, even upon the defendant's own request, that it allows it only in a very few cases, and in those it has also devised other collateral remedies for the party injured, in which the defendant is excluded from his wager of law.

*The manner of waging and making law is this. He that has [*343 waged, or given security, to make his law, brings with him into court eleven of his neighbors: a custom which we find particularly described so early as in the league between Alfred and Guthrun the Dane;(*d*) for by the old Saxon constitution every man's credit in courts of law depended upon the opinion which his neighbors had of his veracity. The defendant, then standing at the end of the bar, is admonished by the judges of the nature and danger of a false oath.(*e*) And if he still persists, he is to repeat this or the like oath:—"Hear this, ye justices, that I do not owe unto Richard Jones the sum of ten pounds, nor any penny thereof, in manner and form as the said Richard hath declared against me. So help me God." And thereupon his eleven neighbors, or compurgators, shall avow upon their oaths that they believe in their consciences that he saith truth; so that himself must be sworn *de fidelitate*,(21) and the eleven *de credulitate*.(*f*)(22) It is held indeed by later authorities,(*g*) that fewer than eleven compurgators will do: but Sir Edward Coke is positive that there must be this number; and his opinion not only seems founded upon better authority, but also upon better reason: for as wager of law is equivalent to a verdict in the defendant's favor, it ought to be established by the same or equal testimony, namely, by the oath of *twelve* men. And so indeed Glanvil expresses it,(*h*) "*jurabit duodecima manu:*"(23) and in 9 Henry III., when a defendant in an action of debt waged his law, it was adjudged by the court "*quod defendat se duodecima manu.*"(*i*)(24) Thus, too, in an author of the age of Edward the First,(*k*) we read, "*adjudicabitu reus ad legem suam duodecima manu.*"(25) And the ancient treatise, entitled, *Dyversite des courts*, expressly confirm Sir Edward Coke's opinion.(*l*)

(*b*) Cod. 1, 4, 12.
(*c*) Bro. Abr. tit. *ley gager*. 77.
(*d*) Cap. 3. Wilk. *L. L. Angl. Sax.*
(*e*) Salk. 682.
(*f*) Co. Litt. 295.
(*g*) 2 Ventr. 171.
(*h*) L. 1, c. 9.

(*i*) Fitz. Abr. tit. *ley*, 78.
(*k*) Hengham magna, c. 5.
(*l*) Il covint aver' one luy xi maymz de jurer one luy, sc. que ilz entendre en lour consciens que il disoyt voier. [He shall have eleven men to swear for him—that is, that they believe in their conscience that he spoke the truth.] Fol. 305, edit. 1534.

(20) Anson on Contracts, 2 Am. ed. 477 (b.). Chase & Another *v*. Breed, 5 Gray (Mass.) 440, 450 (1855).
(21) [Of his fidelity.]
(22) [Of their belief.]
(23) ["He shall swear by twelve men."]
(24) ["That he defend himself by twelve men."]
(25) ["The defendant shall be adjudged to make his law by twelve men."]

*344]   *It must be however observed, that so long as the custom con-
tinued of producing the *secta*, the *suit*, or witnesses to give probability to the plaintiff's demand, (of which we spoke in a former chapter,)
the defendant was not put to wage his law unless the *secta* was first produced
and their testimony was found consistent.   To this purpose speaks *magna
carta*, c. 28.   "*Nullus ballivus de cætero ponat aliquem ad legem mani-
festam*," (that is, wager of battle,) "*nec ad juramentum*," (that is,
wager of law,) "*simplici loquela sua*," (that is, merely by his count or
declaration,) "*sine testibus fidelibus ad hoc inductis*."(26)   Which Fleta thus
explains:(m) "*si petens sectam produxerit, et concordes inveniantur, tunc reus
poterit vadiare legem suam contra petentem et contra sectam suam prolatam;
sed si secta variabilis inveniatur, extunc non tenebitur legem vadiare contra
sectum illum*."(27)   It is true, indeed, that Fleta expressly limits the number
of compurgators to be only double to that of the *secta* produced; "*ut si duos
vel tres testes produxerit ad probandum, oportet quod defensio fiat per quatuor
vel per sex; ita quod pro quolibet teste duos producat juratores, usque ad
duodecim*;"(28)   so that according to this doctrine the eleven compurgators
were only to be *produced*, but not all of them *sworn*, unless the *secta* consisted of *six*.   But though this might possibly be the rule till the production
of the *secta* was generally disused, since that time the *duodecima manus* seems
to have been generally required.(n)

In the old Swedish or Gothic constitution, wager of law was not only permitted, as it still is in *criminal* cases, unless the fact be extremely clear
against the prisoner,(o) but was also absolutely required, in many *civil* cases:
which an author of their own(p) very justly charges as being the source of
frequent perjury.   This, he tells us, was owing to the popish ecclesiastics,
who introduced this method of purgation from their canon law, and,
*345]   having sown a plentiful crop of oaths *in all judicial proceedings,
reaped afterwards an ample harvest of perjuries: for perjuries were
punished in part by pecuniary fines, payable to the coffers of the church.
But with us in England wager of law is never *required;* and is then only
admitted where an action is brought upon such matters as may be supposed
to be privately transacted between the parties, and wherein the defendant
may be presumed to have made satisfaction without being able to prove it.
Therefore it is only in actions of debt upon simple contract, or for amercement,(29) in actions of detinue, and of account, where the debt may have
been paid, the goods restored, or the account balanced, without any evidence
of either; it is only in these actions, I say, that the defendant is admitted to
wage his law:(q)(30) so that wager of law lieth not, when there is any specialty (as a bond or deed) to charge the defendant, for that would be cancelled, if satisfied; but when the debt groweth by word only: nor doth it lie
in an action of debt, for arrears of an account settled by auditors in a former

---

(m) L. 2. c. 63.
(n) Bro. Abr. tit. *ley gager*, 9.   [Twelve men.]
(o) Mod. Un.]Hist. xxxiii. 22.

(p) Stiernhook, *de jure sueon. l.* 1, c. 9.
(q) Co. Litt. 295.

---

(26) ["No bailiff shall put anyone to his wager of battle or to his wager of law, on his
simple declaration, without faithful witnesses brought for that purpose."]

(27) ["If the plaintiff bring his witnesses and they agree in their testimony, then the
defendant may wage his law against him, and against his suit; but if the suit vary in
their testimony, he will thenceforward not be bound to wage his law against that suit."]

(28) ["That if he bring two or three witnesses to prove the fact, the defence must be
made by four or six, so that for every witness he must bring two jurors up to twelve."]

(29) In a court not of record; for if the amercement were imposed by a court of record,
the defendant could not wage his law. Co. Litt. 295, a.—COLERIDGE.

(30) McMurray v. Rawson, 3 Hill (N. Y.) 69 (1842).

action.(r) And by such wager of law (when admitted) the plaintiff is perpetually barred; for the law, in the simplicity of the ancient times, presumed that no one would forswear himself for any·worldly thing.(s) Wager of law, however, lieth in a real action, where the tenant alleges he was not legally summoned to appear, as well as in mere personal contracts.(t)

A man outlawed, attainted for false verdict, or for conspiracy or perjury, or otherwise become infamous, as by pronouncing the horrible word in a trial by battle, shall not be permitted to wage his law. Neither shall an infant under the age of twenty-one, for he cannot be admitted to his oath; and therefore, on the other hand, the course of justice shall flow equally, and the defendant, where an infant is plaintiff, shall not wager his law. But a feme-covert, when joined with her husband, may be admitted to wage her law, and an alien shall do it in his own language.(u)

*It is moreover a rule, that where a man is compellable by law to   [*346 do any thing whereby he becomes creditor to another, the defendant in that case shall not be permitted to wage his law; for then it would be in the power of any bad man to run in debt first against the inclinations of his creditor, and afterwards to swear it away. But where the plaintiff hath given voluntary credit to the defendant, there he may wage his law; for by giving him such credit the plaintiff has himself borne testimony that he is one whose character may be trusted. Upon this principle it is that in an action of debt against a prisoner by a gaoler for his victuals, the defendant shall not wage his law; for the gaoler cannot refuse the prisoner, and ought not to suffer him to perish for want of sustenance. But otherwise it is for the board or diet of a man at liberty. In an action of debt brought by an attorney for his fees, the defendant cannot wage his law, because the plaintiff is compellable to be his attorney. And so, if a servant be retained according to the statute of laborers, 5 Eliz. c. 4, which obliges all single persons of a certain age, and not having other visible·means of livelihood, to go out to service; in an action of debt for the wages of such a servant the master shall not wage his law, because the plaintiff was compellable to serve. But it had been otherwise had the hiring been by special contract, and not according to the statute.(w)

In no case where a contempt, trespass, deceit, or any injury *with force* is alleged against the defendant, is he permitted to wage his law:(x) for it is impossible to presume he has satisfied the plaintiff his demand in such cases where damages are uncertain and left to be assessed by a jury. Nor will the law trust the defendant with an oath to discharge himself where the private injury is coupled as it were with a public crime, that of force and violence; which would be equivalent to the purgation-oath of the civil-law, which ours has so justly rejected.

*Executors and administrators, when charged for the debt of the   [*347 deceased, shall not be admitted to wage their law:(y) for no man can with a safe conscience wage law of another man's contract; that is, swear that he never entered into it, or at least that he privately discharged it. The king also has his prerogative; for as all wager of law imports a reflection on the plaintiff for dishonesty, therefore there shall be no such wager on actions brought by him.(z) And this prerogative extends and is communicated to his debtor and acomptant, for on a writ of *quo minus* in the exchequer for a debt on simple contract, the defendant is not allowed to wager his law.(a)

Thus the wager of law was never permitted but where the defendant bore a fair and unreproachable character: and it also was confined to such cases

(r) 10 Rep. 103.
(s) Co. Litt. 295.
(t) Finch, L. 423.
(u) Co. Litt. 295.
(w) Co. Litt. 295.

(x) Ibid. Raym. 286.
(y) Finch, L. 424.
(z) Finch, L. 523.
(a) Co. Litt. 295.

where a debt might be supposed to be discharged, or satisfaction made in private, without any witnesses to attest it; and many other prudential restrictions accompanied this indulgence. But at length it was considered that (even under all its restrictions) it threw too great a temptation in the way of indigent or profligate men; and therefore, by degrees, new remedies were devised, and new forms of action were introduced, wherein no defendant is at liberty to wage his law. So that now no plaintiff need at all apprehend any danger from the hardiness of his debtor's conscience, unless he voluntarily chooses to rely on his adversary's veracity by bringing on obsolete instead of a modern action. Therefore, one shall hardly hear at present of an action of *debt* brought upon a simple contract; that being supplied by an action of *trespass on the case* for the breach of a promise, or *assumpsit;* wherein, though the specific debt cannot be recovered, yet damages may, equivalent to the specific debt. And, this being an action of trespass, no law can be waged therein. So, instead of an action of *detinue* to recover the very thing detained, an action of trespass on the case in *trover* and *conversion*
*348] is usually brought:(31) *wherein, though the horse or other specific chattel cannot be had, yet the defendant shall pay damages for the conversion equal to the value of the chattel; and for this trespass also no wager of law is allowed. In the room of actions of *account*, a bill in equity is usually filed, wherein, though the defendant answers upon his oath, yet such oath is not conclusive to the plaintiff, but he may prove every article by other evidence, in contradiction to what the defendant has sworn. So that wager of law is quite out of use, being avoided by the mode of bringing the action; but still it is not out of force. And therefore, when a new statute inflicts a penalty, and gives an action of debt for recovering it, it is usual to add. in which no wager of law shall be allowed: otherwise a hardy delinquent might escape any penalty of the law, by swearing he had never incurred, or else had discharged it.

These six species of trials that we have considered in the present chapter are only had in certain special and eccentrical cases; where the trial by the country, *per pais*, or by jury would not be so proper or effectual. In the next chapter we shall consider at large the nature of that principal criterion of truth in the law of England.

CHAPTER XXIII.

OF THE TRIAL BY JURY.

*349]   *THE subject of our next inquiries will be the nature and method of the trial *by jury;* called also the trial *per pais*, or *by the country:* a trial that hath been used time out of mind in this nation, and seems to have been coeval with the first civil government thereof. Some authors have endeavored to trace the original of juries up as high as the Britons themselves, the first inhabitants of our island; but certain it is that they were in use among the earliest Saxon colonies, their institution being ascribed by Bishop Nicholson(a) to Woden himself, their great legislator and captain. Hence it is, that we may find traces of juries in the laws of all those nations which adopted the feodal system, as in Germany, France, and Italy; who had

(a) *De jure Saxonum*, p. 12.

---

(31) Angel on Limitation of Actions (6 ed.) 13.

all of them a tribunal composed of twelve good men and true, "*boni homines*," usually the vassals or tenants of the lord, being the equals or peers of the parties litigant; and, as the lord's vassals judged each other in the lord's courts, so the king's vassals, or the lords themselves, judged each other in the king's court.(*b*)   In England we find actual mention of them so early as the laws of king Ethelred, and that not as a new invention.(*c*)   Stiernhook(*d*) ascribes the invention of the jury, which in the Teutonic language is denominated *nembda*, to Regner, king of Sweden and Denmark, who was contemporary with our king Egbert.   Just as we are apt to impute the invention of this, and some *other pieces of juridical polity, to the   [*350 superior genius of Alfred the Great; to whom, on account of his having done much, it is usual to attribute everything; and as the tradition of ancient Greece placed to the account of their own Hercules whatever achievement was performed superior to the ordinary prowess of mankind.   Whereas the truth seems to be, that this tribunal was universally established among all the northern nations, and so interwoven in their very constitution, that the earliest accounts of the one give us also some traces of the other.(1)   Its establishment however and use, in this island, of what date soever it be, though for a time greatly impaired and shaken by the introduction of the Norman trial by battle, was always so highly esteemed and valued by the people, that no conquest, no change of government, could ever prevail to abolish it.   In *magna carta* it is more than once insisted on as the principal bulwark of our liberties; but especially by chap. 29, that no freeman shall be hurt in either his person or property; "*nisi per legale judicium parium suorum vel per legem terræ.*"(2)   A privilege which is couched in almost the same words with that of the emperor Conrad, two hundred years before:(*e*) "*nemo beneficium suum perdat, nisi secundum consuetudinem antecessorum nostrorum et per judicium parium suorum.*"(3)   And it was ever esteemed, in all countries, a privilege of the highest and most beneficial nature.

But I will not misspend the reader's time in fruitless encomiums on this method of trial; but shall proceed to the dissection and examination of it in all its parts, from whence indeed its highest encomium will arise; since, the more it is searched into and understood, the more it is sure to be valued. And this is a species of knowledge most absolutely necessary for every gentleman in the kingdom: as well because he may be frequently called upon to determine in this capacity the rights of others, his fellow-subjects, as because his own property, his liberty, and his life, depend upon maintaining, in its legal force, the constitutional trial by jury.(4)

(*b*) Sp. L. b. 30, c. 18.   *Capitul. Lud. pii.* A. D. 819, c. 2.
   (*c*) Wilk. *LL. Angl. Sax.* 117.

(*d*) *De jure Sueonum, l.* 1, c. 4.
(*e*) *LL. Longob. l.* 3, *t.* 8, *l.* 4.

---

(1) The Athenians, according to Sir Wm. Jones, had trials by jury.   Sir Wm. Jones on Bailment, 74.—CHITTY.   See Forsyth's History of Trial by Jury for a narrative of such method of trial among the nations of the north.
(2) ["Unless by the lawful judgment of his peers, or by the law of the land."]   State *v.* Keeran, 5 R. I. (Ames) 497-506 (1859).
(3) ["No man shall be deprived of his property but according to the custom of our predecessors, and by the judgment of his peers."]
(4) State *v.* Keeran, 5 R. I. 497 (1858).   Cregier *v.* Bunton, 2 Strab. (S. Car.) 487-500 (1848).   Cruce *v.* The State, 59 Ga. 83-97 (1877).   The right to a trial by jury, is by no means so extensive as is commonly supposed: in many cases a person may be deprived of property and may be subjected to imprisonment without the intervention of a jury; but he can never be subject to capital punishment or to any punishment which would render him infamous and deprive him of his political rights as a citizen without a trial by jury.   In civil proceedings, in all suits at common law, above a fixed sum deemed relatively small, the jurisdiction of which is given to inferior courts, a person may claim the right to trial by a jury.   But this right may be *regulated* by the legislature in certain

*351]　　*Trials by jury in civil causes are of two kinds; *extraordinary* and *ordinary.* The extraordinary I shall only briefly hint at, and confine the main of my observations to that which is more usual and ordinary.

The first species of extraordinary trial by jury is that of the *grand assize,* which was instituted by king Henry the Second in parliament, as was mentioned in the preceding chapter, by way of alternative offered to the choice of the tenant or defendant in a writ of right, instead of the barbarous and unchristian custom of dueling. For this purpose a writ *de magna assisa eligenda*(5) is directed to the sheriff,(*f*)(6) to return four knights, who are to elect and choose twelve others to be joined with them, in the manner mentioned by Glanvil;(*g*) who, having probably advised the measure itself, is more than usually copious in describing it; and these, all together, form the grand assize, or great jury, which is to try the matter of right, and must now consist of sixteen jurors.(*h*)(7)

Another species of extraordinary juries is the jury to try an *attaint;* which is a process commenced against a former jury, for bringing in a false verdict; of which we shall speak more largely in a subsequent chapter. At present I shall only observe, that this jury is to consist of twenty-four of the best men in the county, who are called the *grand* jury in the attaint, to distinguish them from the first or *petit* jury; and these are to hear and try the goodness of the former verdict.(8)

With regard to the *ordinary* trial by jury in civil cases, I shall pursue the same method in considering it, that I set out with in explaining the nature of prosecuting actions in general, viz., by following the order and course of the proceedings themselves, as the most clear and perspicuous way of treating it.

*352]　　*When therefore an issue is joined, by these words, "and this the said A. prays may be inquired of by the country," or, "and of this he puts himself upon the country,—and the said B. does the like," the court awards a writ of *venire facias* upon the roll or record, commanding the sheriff "that he cause to come *here,* on such a day, twelve free and lawful men, *liberos et legales homines,*(9) of the body of his county, by whom the truth of the matter may be better known, and who are neither of kin to the aforesaid A. nor the aforesaid B., to recognize the truth of the issue between the said parties."(*i*) And such writ was accordingly issued to the sheriff.

Thus the cause stands ready for a trial *at the bar* of the court itself; for all trials were there anciently had, in actions which there first commenced; which then never happened but in matters of weight and consequence, all trifling suits being ended in the court-baron, hundred, or county courts: and

---

(*f*) F. N. B. 4.
(*g*) L. 2, c. 11, 12.

(*h*) Finch, L. 412. 1 Leon. 303.
(*i*) Append. No. III. § 4.

---

ways, provided its fundamental requisites are not impaired; that is, provided its number, unanimity, and impartiality are not violated. Proffatt on Jury Trials, 149.

(5) [Of choosing the grand assize.]

(6) Bailey's Onus Probandi, 576 (1886).

(7) It seems not to be ascertained that any specific number above twelve is absolutely necessary to constitute the grand assize; but it is the usual course to swear upon it the four knights and twelve others. Viner, Trial, Xc.

See the proceedings upon a writ of right before the sixteen recognitors of the grand assize, in 3 Wils. 541.—CHITTY.

As the writ of right has been abolished, this mode of trial can no longer be resorted to.—STEWART.

(8) But, by stat. 6 Geo. IV. c. 50, s. 60, this kind of trial by jury is abolished, and a juror for such an offence may be proceeded against by way of indictment or information.—STEWART.

(9) State *v.* Albee, 61 N. H. 423–5 (1881).

indeed all causes of great importance or difficulty are still usually retained upon motion, to be tried at the bar in the superior courts. But when the usage began to bring actions of any trifling value in the courts of Westminster hall, it was found to be an intolerable burden to compel the parties, witnesses, and jurors to come from Westmoreland perhaps or Cornwall, to try an action of assault at Westminster. A practice therefore very early obtained, of *continuing* the cause from term to term, in the court above, provided the justices in eyre did not previously come into the county where the cause of action arose;(*j*) and if it happened that they arrived there within that interval, then the cause was removed from the jurisdiction of the justices at Westminster to that of the justices in eyre. Afterwards, when the justices in eyre were superseded by the modern justices of assize, (who came twice or thrice in the year into the several counties, *ad capiendas assisas*, to take or try writs of assize, of *mort d'ancestor*,(10) *novel disseisin, nuisance*, *and   [*353 the like,) a power was superadded by statute Westm. 2, 13 Edw. I. c. 30, to these justices of assize to try common issues in trespass, and other less important suits, with direction to return them (when tried) into the court above, where alone the judgment should be given. And as only the trial, and not the determination, of the cause, was now intended to be had in the court below, therefore the clause, of *nisi prius* (11) was left out of the conditional *continuances* before mentioned, and was directed by the statute to be inserted in the writs of *venire facias;*(12) that is, "that the sheriff should cause the jurors to come to Westminster (or wherever the king's court should be held,) on such a day in Easter and Michaelmas Terms; *nisi prius*, unless before that day the justices assigned to take assizes shall come into his said county." By virtue of which the sheriff returned his jurors to the court of the justices of assize, which was sure to be held in the vacation before Easter and Michaelmas Terms; and there the trial was had.

An inconvenience attended this provision: principally because, as the sheriff made no return of the jury to the court at Westminster, the parties were ignorant who they were till they came upon the trial, and therefore were not ready with their challenges or exceptions. For this reason, by the statute 42 Edw. III. c. 11, the method of trials by *nisi prius* was altered; and it was enacted that no inquests (except of assize and gaol-delivery) should be taken by writ of *nisi prius*, till after the sheriff had returned the names of the jurors to the court above. So that now in almost every civil cause the clause of *nisi prius* is left out of the writ of *venire facias*, which is the sheriff's warrant to warn the jury; and is inserted in another part of the proceedings, as we shall see presently.

For now the course is, to make the sheriff's *venire* returnable on the last return of the same term wherein issue is joined, viz., Hilary or Trinity Terms; which, from the making up of the issues therein, are usually called *issuable* terms. And he returns the names of the jurors in a *panel* (a little pane, or oblong piece of parchment) annexed to the writ. This jury *is not summoned, and therefore, not appearing at the day, must   [*354 unavoidably make default. For which reason a compulsive process is now awarded against the jurors, called in the common pleas a writ of

---

(*j*) *Semper dabitur dies partibus ab justiciariis de banco, sub tali conditione, "nisi justiciarii itinerantes*   *prius venerint ad partes illas."* Bract. *l.* 3, *tr.* 1, c. 11, § 8.

---

(10) [Death of the ancestor.]
(11) [Unless before.]
(12) [That you make to come.]

habeas corpora juratorum,(13) and in the king's bench a *distringas,*(14) commanding the sheriff to have their bodies or to distrain them by their lands and goods, that they may appear upon the day appointed. The entry therefore on the roll or record is,(k) "that the jury is respited, through defect of the jurors, till the first day of the next term, then to appear at Westminster, unless before that time, viz., on Wednesday the fourth of March, the justices of our lord the king, appointed to take assizes in that county, shall have come to Oxford, that is, to the place assigned for holding the assizes." And thereupon the writ commands the sheriff to have their bodies at Westminster on the said first day of next term, or before the said justices of assize, if before that time they come to Oxford; viz., on the fourth of March aforesaid. And, as the judges are sure to come and open the circuit commissions on the day mentioned in the writ, the sheriff returns and summons the jury to appear at the assizes, and there the trial is had before the justices of *assize* and *nisi prius:* among whom (as hath been said)(l) are usually two of the judges of the courts of Westminster, the whole kingdom being divided into six(15) circuits for this purpose.(16) And thus we may observe that the trial of common issues, at *nisi prius,* which was in its original only a collateral incident to the original business of the justices of assize, is now, by the various revolutions of practice, become their principal civil employment: hardly any thing remaining in use of the real *assizes* but the name.

If the sheriff be not an indifferent person; as if he be a party in the suit, or be related by either blood or affinity to either of the parties, he is not then trusted to return the jury, but the *venire* shall be directed to the coroners, who in this, as in many other instances, are the substitutes of the sheriff, to execute process when he is deemed an improper person. If any exception lies to the coroners, the *venire* shall be directed to two clerks of the court, or two persons of the county *named by the court, and sworn.(m) And these two, who are called *elisors,* or electors, shall indifferently name the jury, and their return is final; no challenge being allowed to their array.

*355]

Let us now pause a while, and observe (with Sir Matthew Hale)(n) in these first preparatory stages of the trial, how admirably this constitution is adapted and framed for the investigation of truth beyond any other method of trial in the world. For, first, the *person returning* the jurors is a man of some fortune and consequence; that so he may be not only the less tempted to commit wilful errors, but likewise be responsible for the faults of either himself or his officers: and he is also bound by the obligation of an oath faithfully to execute his duty. Next, as to the *time of their return:* the panel is returned to the court upon the original *venire,* and the jurors are to be summoned and brought in many weeks afterwards to the trial, whereby the parties may have notice of the jurors, and of their sufficiency or insufficiency, characters, connections, and relations, that so they may be challenged upon just cause; while at the same time by means of the compulsory process

(k) Append. No. II. § 4.　　　　　　　(m) Fortesc. *de Laud. LL.* c. 25.　Co. Litt. 158.
(l) See page 59.　　　　　　　　　　　(n) Hist. C. L. c. 12.

(13) [That you have the bodies of the jurors.]
(14) [That you distrain.]
(15) Now seven.—STEWART.
(16) These several writs, generally called the "Jury Process," are now, however, abolished, and the jurors are summoned by the sheriff for the commission-day, in virtue of a precept issued to him for that purpose by the judges of assize, a panel of the jurors so summoned being made and kept in the sheriff's office for inspection seven days before the commission-day, and a copy of it annexed to the record. Com. Law Proc. Act, 1852, B. 105-109.—STEWART.
This is not the present law.

(of *distringas*, or *habeas corpora*) the cause is not like to be retarded through defect of jurors. Thirdly, as to the *place* of their appearance: which in causes of weight and consequence is at the bar of the court, but in ordinary cases at the assizes, held in the county where the cause of action arises, and the witnesses and jurors live: a provision most excellently calculated for the saving of expense to the parties. For though the preparation of the causes in point of pleading is transacted at Westminster, whereby the order and uniformity of proceeding is preserved throughout the kingdom, and multiplicity of forms is prevented; yet this is no great charge or trouble, one attorney being able to transact the business of forty clients. But the troublesome and most expensive attendance is that of jurors and witnesses at the trial; which therefore is brought home to them, in the country, where most of them inhabit. Fourthly, the *persons before* *whom [*356 they are to appear, and before whom the trial is to be held, are the judges of the superior court, if it be a trial at bar; or the judges of assize, delegated from the courts at Westminster by the king, if the trial be held in the country: persons whose learning and dignity secure their jurisdiction from contempt, and the novelty and very parade of whose appearance have no small influence upon the multitude. The very point of their being strangers in the county is of infinite service, in preventing those factions and parties, which would intrude in every cause of moment, were it tried only before persons resident on the spot, as justices of the peace, and the like. And, the better to remove all suspicion of partiality, it was wisely provided by the statutes 4 Edw. III. c. 2, 8 Ric. II. c. 2, and 32 Hen. VIII. c. 24, that no judge of assize should hold pleas in any county wherein he was born or inhabits. (17) And, as this constitution prevents party and faction from intermingling in the trial of right, so it keeps both the rule and the administration of the laws uniform. These justices, though thus varied and shifted at every assizes, are all sworn to the same laws, have had the same education, have pursued the same studies, converse and consult together, communicate their decisions and resolutions, and preside in those courts which are mutually connected and their judgments blended together, as they are interchangeably courts of appeal or advice to each other. And hence their administration of justice and conduct of trials are consonant and uniform; whereby that confusion and contrariety are avoided, which would naturally arise from a variety of uncommunicating judges, or from any provincial establishment. (18) But let us now return to the assizes.

When the general day of trials is fixed, the plaintiff or his attorney must bring down the record to the assizes and enter it with the proper officer in order to its being called on in course. If it be not so entered, it cannot be tried; therefore it is in the plaintiff's breast to delay any trial by not carrying down the record: unless the defendant, being fearful of such neglect in the

---

(17) At the present day relationship of judge or juror to a party to an action before them disqualifies them in law from sitting in the cause. Bayard *v.* McLane, 3 Harrington (Del.) 139 (1844).

(18) On the 22d of June, 1825, the 6 Geo. IV. c. 50 was passed for consolidating and amending the laws relative to jurors and juries, and came into complete operation the 1st of January, 1826.—CHITTY.

Besides the trial at bar and that at nisi prius, there is another mode of trial by jury, which is given by stat. 3 & 4 W. IV. c. 42, s. 17, and is applicable only to causes where the debt or demand does not exceed 20*l.* In such cases, if the court or one of the judges be satisfied that the trial will involve no difficult question of law or fact, they will make a rule or order that the issue be tried by the sheriff of the county where the action is brought, or any judge of a court of record for the recovery of debts in such county. In pursuance of the rule or order, a writ of trial is directed to such judge or sheriff, commanding him to try the issue and return the proceedings to the court, that judgment may be given accordingly.—STEWART.

plaintiff, and willing to discharge himself from the action, will him-
*357] self undertake to bring on *the trial, giving proper notice to the
plaintiff. Which proceeding is called the trial by *proviso;* by reason
of the clause then inserted in the sheriff's *venire,* viz., "*proviso,* provided
that if two writs come to your hands, (that is, one from the plaintiff and
another from the defendant,) you shall execute only one of them." But this
practice hath begun to be disused since the statute of 14 Geo. II. c. 17, which
enacts that if, after issue joined, the cause is not carried down to be tried
according to the course of the court, the plaintiff shall be esteemed to be
non-suited, and judgment shall be given for the defendant as in case of a
non-suit. In case the plaintiff intends to try the cause, he is bound to give
the defendant (if he lives within forty miles of London) eight days' notice
of trial, and if he lives at a greater distance, then fourteen day's notice, in
order to prevent surprise;(19) and if the plaintiff then changes his mind and
does not countermand the notice six days before the trial, he shall be liable
to pay costs to the defendant for not proceeding to trial, by the same last-
mentioned statute.(20) The defendant, however, or plaintiff, may, upon
good cause shown to the court above, as upon absence or sickness of a material
witness, obtain leave upon motion to defer the trial of the cause to the next
assizes.(21)

But we will now suppose all previous steps to be regularly settled, and
the cause to be called on in court. The record is then handed to the
judge, to peruse and observe the pleadings, and what issues the parties are
to maintain and prove, while the jury is called and sworn. To this end the
sheriff returns his compulsive process, the writ of *habeas corpora,*(22) or
distringas,(23) with the panel of jurors annexed, to the judge's officer in
court. The jurors contained in the panel are either *special* or *common* jurors.
Special juries were originally introduced in trials at bar when the causes were
of too great nicety for the discussion of ordinary freeholders, or where the
sheriff was suspected of partiality, though not upon such apparent cause as

---

(19) This practice is confined to causes tried in London and Middlesex. Tidd, 8 ed.
814. In all causes tried at an assizes, ten days' notice suffice. Tidd, 8 ed. 815.—CHITTY.

(20) At the sittings in London or Westminster, when defendant resides within forty
miles from London, two days' notice of countermand before it is to be tried is sufficient.
Tidd, 8 ed. 81, n.—CHRISTIAN.

(21) Where there have been no proceedings within four terms, a full term's notice of
trial must be given previous to the assizes or sittings; unless the cause has been delayed
by the defendant himself, by an injunction or other means. 2 Bla. Rep. 784. 3 T. R.
530. If the defendant proceeds to trial by *proviso,* he must give the same notice as would
have been required from the plaintiff. 1 Cromp. Prac. 219. Sometimes the courts impose
it as a condition upon the defendant that he shall accept *short-notice* of trial, which in
country causes shall be given at the least four days before the commission-day,—one day
being exclusive, and the other inclusive. 3 T. R. 600. But in town causes, two days'
notice seems to be sufficient in such a case. Tidd, 250.—CHRISTIAN.

This statute, so far as it relates to judgment, as in case of a non-suit, is repealed by the
Common-Law Procedure Act, 1852, which, however, enables a defendant after the plaintiff has neglected to bring on the cause for trial within a certain period after issue has
been joined, to give the plaintiff twenty days' notice to bring the cause on for trial at
the next sittings or assizes. If the plaintiff again neglects to try the cause, the defendant
may obtain judgment for his costs of suit. In case the plaintiff intends to try the cause,
he is bound to give the defendant ten days' notice of trial, in order to prevent surprise,
and if the plaintiff then changes his mind and does not countermand the notice four
days before the trial, he shall be liable to pay costs to the defendant for not proceeding
to trial, by the same last-mentioned statute. The defendant, however, or plaintiff, may,
upon good cause shown to the court above, as upon absence or sickness of a material
witness, obtain leave, upon motion, to defer the trial of the cause till the next assizes.—
STEWART.

(22) [That you have the bodies.]
(23) [That you distrain.]

to warrant an exception to him.   He is in such cases, upon motion in court and a rule granted thereupon, to attend the prothonotary or other proper officer with his freeholders' book: and the officer is to take *indifferently forty-eight of the principal freeholders in the presence   [*358 of the attorneys on both sides; who are each of them to strike off twelve, and the remaining twenty-four are returned upon the panel.(24) By the statute 3 Geo. II. c. 25, either party is entitled, upon motion, to have a special jury struck upon the trial of any issue, as well at the assizes as at bar; he paying the extraordinary expense, unless the judge will certify (in pursuance of the statute 24 Geo. II. c. 18) that the cause required such special jury.(25)

A common jury is one returned by the sheriff according to the direction of the statute 3 Geo. II. c. 25, which appoints that the sheriff or officer shall not return a separate panel for every separate cause, as formerly; but one and the same panel for every cause to be tried at the same assizes,(26) containing not less than forty-eight nor more than seventy-two jurors: and that their names, being written on tickets, shall be put into a box or glass; and when each cause is called, twelve of these persons, whose names shall be first drawn out of the box, shall be sworn upon the jury, unless absent, challenged, or excused; or unless a previous view of the messuages, lands, or place in question shall have been thought necessary by the court:(o) in which case six or more of the jurors returned, to be agreed on by the parties, or named by a judge or other proper officer of the court, shall be appointed by special writ of *habeas corpora* or *distringas* to have the matters in question shown to them by two persons named in the writ; and then such of the jury as have had the view, or so many of them as appear, shall be sworn on the inquest previous to any other jurors.   These acts are well calculated to restrain any suspicion of partiality in the sheriff, or any tampering with the jurors when returned.(27)

As the jurors appear, when called, they shall be sworn, unless *challenged* by either party.   Challenges are of two sorts: challenges to the *array*, and challenges to the *polls*.

*Challenges to the array are at once an exception to the whole   [*359 panel, in which the jury are arrayed or set in order by the sheriff in his return; and they may be made upon account of partiality or some default in the sheriff or his under-officer who arrayed the panel.(28)   And, generally speaking, the same reasons that before the awarding the *venire* were sufficient to have directed it to the coroners or elisors will be also sufficient to quash the array when made by a person or officer of whose partiality there is any

(o) Stat. 4 Anne, c. 16.

---

(24) Proffatt on Jury Trials, § 73.
(25) Lessee of Bayard *v.* McInnes, 1 Addison (Pa.) 292-296 (1800).
(26) State *v.* Potter, 18 Conn. 166-175 (1846).
(27) The qualification of both common and special jurymen is now regulated by stat. 6, Geo. IV. c. 50, by which all other acts are repealed.—STEWART.
(28) Quinebaug Bank *v.* Tarbox, 20 Conn. 510-517 (1850). People *v.* McKay, 18 Johns. N. Y. 211-218 (1820). Conkey *v.* Bank, 6 Wis. 447-449 (1858). By our law a sheriff is a mere ministerial officer. The clerk arrays the panel and a challenge to the array may be taken to the mode in which the jury were summoned, or the manner in which the jury list was made up and the manner in which they were drawn or selected and also to any default on the part of the clerk, who is for many purposes substituted for the sheriff. The challenge must be in writing and the person challenging must be prepared to prove the cause alleged then and there, and if he omit to challenge the array before the full jury have appeared, he cannot take advantage of it afterwards. The Law of Self Defence; Anthony, 315 and authorities there cited. Also 1 Archbold Crim. Pr. and Pl. 512 and authorities there cited; and State *v.* Knight, 43 Me. 111 (1857). State *v.* Cartwright, 20 W. Va. 32-36 (1882).

tolerable ground of suspicion.(29) Also, though there be no personal objection against the sheriff, yet if he arrays the panel at the nomination or under the direction of either party, this is good cause of challenge to the array. Formerly, if a lord of parliament had a cause to be tried, and no knight was returned upon the jury, it was a cause of challenge to the array:(*p*) but, an unexpected use having been made of this dormant privilege by a spiritual lord,(*q*) it was abolished by statute 24 Geo. II. c. 18. But still, in an attaint, a knight must be returned on the jury.(*r*)(30) Also, by the policy of the ancient law, the jury was to come *de vicineto*, from the neighborhood of the vill or place where the cause of action was laid in the declaration: and therefore some of the jury were obliged to be returned from the hundred in which such vill lay; and, if none were returned, the array might be challenged for defect of hundredors. Thus the Gothic jury, or *nembda*, was also collected out of every quarter of the country: "*binos, trinos, vel etiam senos, ex singulis territorii quadrantibus.*"(*s*)(31) For, living in the neighborhood, they were properly the very country, or *pais*, to which both parties had appealed, and were supposed to know beforehand the characters of the parties and witnesses, and therefore they better knew what credit to give to the facts alleged in evidence. But this convenience was overbalanced by another very natural and almost unavoidable inconvenience: that jurors coming out of the immediate neighborhood *360] would be apt *to intermix their prejudices and partialities in the trial of right. And this our law was so sensible of that it for a long time has been gradually relinquishing this practice; the number of necessary hundredors in the whole panel, which in the reign of Edward III. were constantly *six*,(*t*) being in the time of Fortescue(*u*) reduced to *four*. Afterwards, indeed, the statute 35 Hen. VIII. c. 6 restored the ancient number of *six*: but that clause was soon virtually repealed by statute 27 Eliz. c. 6, which required only *two*. And Sir Edward Coke(*v*) also gives us such a variety of circumstances whereby the courts permitted this necessary number to be evaded, that it appears they were heartily tired of it. At length, by statute 4 & 5 Anne, c. 6, it was entirely abolished upon all civil actions, except upon penal statutes; and upon those also by the 24 Geo. II. c. 18, the jury being now only to come *de corpore comitatus*, from the body of the county at large, and not *de vicineto*, or from the particular neighborhood.(32) The array, by the ancient law, may also be challenged if an alien be party to the suit, and, upon a rule obtained by his motion to the court for a jury *de medietate linguæ*,(33) such a one be not returned by the sheriff, pursuant to the statute 28 Edw. III. c. 13, enforced by 8 Hen. VI. c. 29, which enact, that where either party is an alien born, the jury shall be one half denizens and the other aliens, (if so many be forthcoming in the place,) for the more impartial trial; a privilege indulged to strangers in no other country in the world, but which is as ancient with us as the time of king Ethelred, in whose statute *de monticolis Walliæ*,(34) (then aliens to the crown of England,) *cap.* 3, it is ordained that "*duodeni legales homines, quorum sex Walli et sex*

(*p*) Co. Litt. 156. Seld. on Baronage. ii. 11.
(*q*) K. vs. Bishop of Worcester, M. 28 Geo. II. B R.
(*r*) Co. Litt. 156.
(*s*) Stiernhook *de jure Goth. l.* 1, c. 4.

(*t*) Gilb. Hist. C. P. c. 8.
(*u*) De Land. LL. c. 25.
(*v*) 1 Inst. 157.

(29) The People *v.* Felker, 61 Mich. 114-116 (1886).
(30) Prince *v.* The State, 3 Ala. 253, 262 (Stewart & Porter, 1833).
(31) ["Two, three, or even six, from every quarter of the country."]
(32) See an excellent note, Co. Litt. 125, a. b. (n.).—CHITTY. See also, State *v.* Albee, 61 N. H. 423-425 (1881). State *v.* Kemp., 34 Minn. 61-63 (1886).
(33) [Consisting of half foreigners and half natives.]
(34) [Of the mountaineers of Wales.]

Angli erunt, Angli et Wallis jus dicunto."(35)   But where both parties are aliens, no partiality is to be presumed to one more than another; and therefore it was resolved soon after the statute 8 Hen. VI.(*w*) that where the issue is joined between two aliens (unless the plea be had before the mayor of the staple, and thereby subject to the restrictions of statute 27 Edw. III. st. 2, c. 8) the jury shall all be denizens.   And it now might be a question how far the *statute 3 Geo. II. c. 25 (before referred to) hath in civil   [*361 causes undesignedly abridged this privilege of foreigners by the positive directions therein given concerning the manner of impaneling jurors, and the persons to be returned in such panel.(36)   So that (unless this statute is to be construed by the same equity which the statute 8 Hen. VI. c. 29 declared to be the rule of interpreting the statute 2 Hen. V. st. 2, c. 3 concerning the landed qualifications of jurors in suits to which aliens were parties) a court might perhaps hesitate whether it has now a power to direct a panel to be returned *de medietate linguæ*, and thereby alter the method prescribed for striking a special jury or balloting for common jurors.(37)

Challenges to the polls, *in capita*, are exceptions to particular jurors,(38) and seem to answer the *recusatio judicis*(39) in the civil and canon laws; by the constitutions of which a judge might be refused upon any suspicion of partiality.(*x*)   By the laws of England also, in the times of Bracton(*y*) and Fleta,(*z*) a judge might be refused for good cause; but now the law is otherwise, and it is held that judges and justices cannot be challenged.(*a*)   For the law will not suppose a possibility of bias or favor in a judge, who is already sworn to administer impartial justice, and whose authority greatly depends upon that presumption and idea.(40)   And should the fact at any time prove flagrantly such, as the delicacy of the law will not presume beforehand, there is no doubt but that such misbehavior would draw down a heavy censure from those to whom the judge is accountable for his conduct.

But challenges to the polls of the jury (who are judges of fact) are reduced to four heads by Sir Edward Coke:(*b*) *propter honoris respectum; propter defectum; propter affectum;* and *propter delictum.*(41)

1. *Propter honoris respectum;* as, if a lord of parliament be impaneled on a jury, he may be challenged by either party, or he may challenge himself.

*2. *Propter defectum;* as if a juryman be an alien born,(42) this is   [*362 defect of birth; if he be a slave or bondman, this is defect of liberty, and he cannot be *liber et legalis homo*.(43)   Under the word *homo* also, though

---

(*w*) Year-book. 21 Hen. VI. 4.
(*x*) Cod. 3, 1, 16. *Decretal. l. 2, t. 28.   c, 36.
(*y*) L. 5, c. 15.

(*z*) L. 6, c. 37.
(*a*) Co. Litt. 294.
(*b*) 1 Inst. 156.

---

(35) ["Let twelve lawful men, of whom six shall be Welsh and six English, give their verdict for English and Welsh."]

(36) Richard's Case, 11 Leigh. (Va.) 690-700 (1841).

(37) From the enactments of the statute 6 Geo. IV. c. 50, and especially section 47 thereof, it would seem that a jury *de medietate linguæ* [Consisting half of foreigners and half of natives] is now allowed only upon trials for felony or misdemeanor.—KERR.

(38) It is within the province of the legislature to fix the number of jurors a party may challenge, provided it does not interfere with the constitutional right to trial by an impartial jury.   Proffatt on Jury Trial, 149.   Cruce *v.* State, 57 Ga. 83, (1877).   Dowling *v.* The State, 5 Miss. 664-685 (1846).

(39) [Objection to the judge.]

(40) Bowyer's Com. on Const. Law of Eng. 302.

(41) [On account of dignity, on account of incompetency, on account of partiality, on account of the commission of some offence.]

(42) Bailey's Onus Probandi, 576 (1886).   Shumacker *v.* The State, 5 Wis. 324-328 (1855).

(43) [A free and lawful man.]

a name common to both sexes, the female is however excluded *propter defectum sexus;*(44) except when a widow feigns herself with child, in order to exclude the next heir, and a supposititious birth is suspected to be intended; then upon the writ *de ventre inspiciendo,*(45) a jury of women is to be impaneled to try the question whether with child or not.(c)(46)　But the principal deficiency is defect of estate sufficient to qualify him to be a juror. This depends upon a variety of statutes. And, first, by the statute of Westm. 2, 13 Edw. I. c. 38, none shall pass on juries in assizes within the county, but such as may dispend 20s. by the year at the least; which is increased to 40s. by the statutes 21 Edw. I. st. 1, and 2 Hen. V. st. 2, c. 3.　This was doubled by the statute 27 Eliz. c. 6, which requires in every such case the jurors to have estate of freehold to the yearly value of 4l. at the least.　But, the value of money at that time decreasing very considerably, this qualification was raised by the statute 16 & 17 Car. II. c. 3 to 20l. *per annum,* which being only a temporary act, for three years, was suffered to expire without renewal, to the great debasement of juries.　However, by the statute 4 & 5 W. & M. c. 24, it was again raised to 10l. *per annum* in England and 6l. in Wales, of freehold lands *or copyhold;* which is the first time that copyholders (as such) were admitted to serve upon juries in any of the king's courts, though they had before been admitted to serve in some of the sheriff's courts, by statute 1 Ric. III. c. 4, and 9 Hen. VII. c. 13.　And, lastly, by statute 3 Geo. II. c. 25, any leaseholder for the term of five hundred years absolute, or for any term determinable upon life or lives, of the clear yearly value of 20l. *per annum* over and above the rent reserved, is qualified to serve upon juries.(47) When the jury is *de medietate linguæ,*(48) that is, one moiety of the English tongue or nation, and the other of any foreign one, no want of lands *363] shall be *cause of challenge to the alien; for, as he is incapable to hold any, this would totally defeat the privilege.(d)(49)

3. Jurors may be challenged *propter affectum,*(50) for suspicion of bias or partiality. This may be either a *principal* challenge, or *to the favor.*(51)　A *principal* challenge is such where the cause assigned carries with it *prima facie* evident marks of suspicion either of malice or favor: as, that a juror is of kin to either party within the ninth degree:(e)(52) that he has been arbi-

(c) Cro. Eliz. 566.
(d) See stat. 2 Hen. V. st. 2, c. 3.　8 Hen. VI. c. 29.

(e) Finch, L. 401.

---

(44) [Because not of the male sex.]

(45) [Of inspecting pregnancy.]

(46) Robinson's Case, 131 Mass. 376–377 (1881).

(47) A juror must be twenty-one years; and, if above sixty, he is exempted, though not disqualified, from serving. He must also possess freehold or copyhold property of the clear yearly value of ten pounds, or have leasehold property, held by lease for twenty-one years or longer, of the annual value of twenty pounds, or occupy a house containing not less than fifteen windows. In London, the occupation of a house, shop, or place of business within the city, or the possession of real or personal property of the value of 100l., constitutes a qualification.　6 & 7 Geo. IV. c. 50.—KERR.

In the United States a juror's qualifications are usually such as the law of the individual state requires of one of its electors.

(48) [*Vide supra,* p. 360.]

(49) Inability upon the part of persons called to serve as jurors, to speak the English language, and to understand it when spoken, does not *necessarily* disqualify them from serving as jurors under the statutes of Colorado.　Town of Trinidad *v.* Simpson, 5 Colo. 63–67 (1879).

(50) Robinson *v.* The State, 1 Ga. 563–571 (1846).　State *v.* Baldwin, 3 S. Car. Law (Brevard) 309–312 (1813).

(51) State *v.* Baldwin, 1 Const. Rep. (S. Car.) 289, 296 (1813).

(52) Bayard *v.* McLane, 3 Harrington (Del.) 139–150 (1844).　Coleman *v.* Lukens, 3 W. & S. (Pa.) 39–43 (1842).　Abbott's Trial Brief, Crim. Causes, 136.

trator on either side;(53) that he has an interest in the cause; that there is an action depending between him and the party; that he has taken money for his verdict; that he has formerly been a juror in the same cause;(54) that he is the party's master, servant,(55) counsellor, steward, or attorney, or of the same society or corporation with him;(56) all these are principal causes of challenge, which, if true, cannot be overruled, for jurors must be *omni exceptione majores.*(57) Challenges *to the favor* are where the party hath no principal challenge, but objects only some probable circumstances of suspicion, as acquaintance and the like;(*f*) the validity of which must be left to the determination of *triers*, whose office it is to decide whether the juror be favorable or unfavorable.(58) The triers, in case the first man called be challenged, are two indifferent persons named by the court; and if they try one man and find him indifferent, he shall be sworn; and then he and the two triers shall try the next; and when another is found indifferent and sworn, the two triers shall be superseded, and the two first sworn on the jury shall try the rest.(*g*)(59)

4. Challenges *propter delictum* are for some crime or misdemeanor that affects the juror's credit and renders him infamous. As for a conviction of treason, felony, perjury, or conspiracy; or if for some infamous offence he hath received judgment of the pillory, tumbrel, or the like; or to be branded, *whipt, or stigmatized; or if he be outlawed or excommu- [*364 nicated, or hath been attainted of false verdict, *præmunire*, or forgery; or lastly, if he hath proved recreant when champion in the trial by battle, and thereby hath lost his *liberam legem*. A juror may himself be examined on oath of *voir dire veritatem dicere*,(60) with regard to such causes of chal-

---

(*f*) In the *nembda*, or jury of the ancient Goths, three challenges only were allowed to the favor, but the principal challenges were indefinite. "*Licebat palam excipere, et semper ex probabili causa tres repudiari: etiam plures ex causa prægnanti et mani-*

festa." ["They might openly object to and always refuse three for a probable cause; and even more for a cause that was pregnant and manifest."] Stiernhook, *l.* 1, c. 4.

(*g*) Co, Litt. 153.

---

(53) Hasceig *v.* Tripp, 20 Mich. 216-218 (1870). O'Connor *v.* The State, 9 Fla. 215-222 (1860). In this matter relation by affinity is the same as by consanguinity, but the affinity ceases with a dissolution, by the death of one of the married parties, of the marriage by which it was created. Proffatt on Jury Trials, ? 174. Fox *v.* Hills, 1 Conn. 295-309 (1814). It is not a principal cause of challenge to a juror that the plaintiff has had against the juror a suit like the one about to be tried, and involving like issues, it not appearing that the suit is still pending. At most it is only cause of challenge to the favor. Austin & Ellis *v.* Cox *et al.*, 60 Ga. 520 (1877).

(54) Hawkins *v.* Andrews, 39 Ga. 118-119 (1869).

(55) Central R. R. Co. *v.* Mitchell, 63 Ga. 113-180 (1879).

(56) In the case of the City of Boston *v.* Baldwin, 139 Mass. 317 (1885), it was held that a member of the common council of the city was not competent to sit as a juror, the city being a party to the suit.

(57) [Above all exception.] The People *v.* Bodine, 1 Denio (N. Y.) 281-305 (1845).

(58) Bailey's Onus Probandi, 577 (1886). In some states of this union this office is now exercised by the judge. The State *v.* Potter, 18 Conn. 166-171 (1846).

(59) The question of challenge to the array, and incidentally to the polls and triers, underwent much discussion in The King *v.* Edmonds, 4 B. & A. 476; and in that case it was determined that no challenge, either to the array or to the polls, can be taken until a full jury shall have appeared; that the disallowing a challenge is not a ground for a new trial, but for a *venire de novo* [To come anew]; that every challenge, either to the array or to the polls, ought to be propounded in such a way that it may be put at the time upon the *nisi prius* record, so that when a challenge is made the adverse party may either demur or counterplead, or he may deny what is alleged for matter of challenge; and it is then only that triers can be appointed. It was also thereby determined that the whole special jury-panel cannot be challenged for the supposed unindifferency of the Master of the Crown Office, he being the officer of the court appointed to nominate the jury. And a material point was also ruled in the same case,—namely, that it is not competent to ask jurymen, whether special or talesmen, whether they have not, previously to the trial, expressed opinions hostile to the defendants and their cause, in order to found a challenge to the polls on that ground; but such expressions must be proved by extrinsic evidence. But see now stat. 6 Geo. IV. c. 50, ss. 27, 89.—CHITTY.

(60) [Free law.] [To speak the truth.]

lenge as are not to his dishonor or discredit; but not with regard to any crime, or any thing which tends to his disgrace or disadvantage. (*h*)(61)

Besides these challenges, which are exceptions against the fitness of jurors, and whereby they may be *excluded* from serving, there are also other causes to be made use of by the jurors themselves, which are matter of exemption; whereby their service is *excused*, and not *excluded*. As by statute Westm. 2, 13 Edw. 1, c. 38, sick and decrepit persons, persons not commorant in the county, and men above seventy years old; and by the statute 7 & 8 W. III. c. 32, infants under twenty-one. This exemption is also extended, by divers statutes, customs, and charters, to physicians and other medical persons, counsel, attorneys, officers of the courts, and the like; all of whom, if impaneled, must show their special exemption. Clergymen are also usually excused, out of favor and respect to their function: but, if they are seised of lands and tenements, they are in strictness liable to be impaneled in respect of their lay-fees, unless they be in the service of the king or of some bishop: "*in obsequio domini regis, vel alicujus episcopi.*" (*i*)(62)

If by means of challenges, or other cause, a sufficient number of unexceptionable jurors doth not appear at the trial, either party may pray a *tales*. A *tales* is a supply of *such* men as are summoned upon the first panel, in order to make up the deficiency.(63) For this purpose, a writ of *decem tales*, *octo tales*,(64) and the like, was used to be issued to the sheriff at common law, and must be still so done at a trial at bar, if the jurors make default.

But at the assizes or *nisi prius*, by virtue of the statute 35 Hen. VIII. *365]* c. 6, and other subsequent *statutes, the judge is empowered at the prayer of either party to award a *tales de circumstantibus*, (*j*)(65) of persons present in court, to be joined to the other jurors to try the cause; who are liable, however, to the same challenges as the principal jurors. This is usually done, till the legal number of twelve be completed; in which patriarchal and apostolical number Sir Edward Coke(*k*) hath discovered abundance of mystery. (*l*)

When a sufficient number of persons impaneled, or *tales*-men, appear, they are then separately sworn, well and truly to try the issue between the parties, and a true verdict to give according to the evidence; and hence they are denominated the jury, *jurata*, and jurors, *se. juratores*.(66)

We may here again observe, and observing we cannot but admire, how scrupulously delicate, and how impartially just, the law of England approves itself, in the constitution and frame of a tribunal, thus excellently contrived for the test and investigation of truth; which appears most remarkably, 1. In the avoiding of frauds and secret management, by electing the twelve jurors out of the whole panel by lot. 2. In its caution against all partiality and bias, by quashing the whole panel or array, if the officer returning is suspected to be other than indifferent; and repelling particular jurors, if

(*h*) Co. Litt. 158, b.
(*i*) F. N. B. 166, *Reg. Brev.* 179.
(*j*) Append. No. 11. § 4.
(*k*) 1 Inst. 155.
(*l*) Pausanias relates that at the trial of Mars, for murder, in the court denominated *Areopagus* from that incident, he was acquitted by a jury composed of *twelve* pagan deities. And Dr. Hicks, who attributes the introduction of this *number* to the Nor-

mans, tells us that among the inhabitants of Norway, from whom the Normans as well as the Danes were descended, a great veneration was paid to the number *twelve*: "*nihil sanctius, nihil antiquius fuit; perinde ac si in ipso hoc numero sancta quædam inesset religio.*" [* Nothing was more sacred, nothing more venerable than this number, as though it contained within itself something sacred."] *Dissert. Epistolar.* 49. Spelm. Gloss. 329.

(61) Abbott's Trial Brief, Crim. Causes, 127. Bailey's Onus Probandi, 577 (1886). State *v.* Baldwin, 3 S. Car. Law (Brevard) 309-311 (1813).
(62) They are now excused, by 6 Geo. IV. c. 50.—CHITTY.
(63) [A tales of ten; a tales of eight.]
(64) Proffatt on Jury Trials, 191, § 141.
(65) [A tales from the by-standers.] Anthony on Self-Defence, 200. In the United States an order of court is made, but no writ issued.
(66) Mix *v.* Woodward, 12 Connecticut, 263 (1837).

probable cause be shown of malice or favor to either party.(67) The prodigious multitude of exceptions or challenges allowed to jurors, who are the judges of fact, amounts nearly to the same thing as was practiced in the Roman republic, before she lost her liberty: that the select judges should be appointed by the prætor with the mutual consent of the parties.
*Or, as Tully(*m*) expresses it: "*neminem voluerunt majores nostri,*   [*366 *non modo de existimatione cujusquam, sed ne pecuniaria quidem de re minima, esse judicem: nisi qui inter adversarios convenisset.*"(68)

Indeed, these *selecti judices*(69) bore in many respects a remarkable resemblance to our juries: for they were first returned by the prætor; *de decuria senatoria conscribuntur:* then their names were drawn by lot, till a certain number was completed; *in urnam sortito mittuntur, ut de pluribus necessarius numerus confici posset;* then the parties were allowed their challenges; *post urnam permittitur accusatori, ac reo, ut ex illo numero rejiciant quos putaverint sibi, aut inimicos, aut ex aliqua re incommodos fore:*(70) next they struck what we call a *tales; rejectione celebrata, in eorum locum qui rejecti fuerunt subsortiebatur prætor alios, quibus ille judicum legitimus numerus compleretur;*(71) lastly, the judges, like our jury, were sworn; *his perfectis, jurabant in leges judices, ut obstricti religione judicarent.*(*n*)

The jury are now ready to hear the merits; and, to fix their attention the closer to the facts which they are impaneled and sworn to try, the pleadings are opened to them by counsel on that side, which holds the affirmative of the question in issue.   For the issue is said to lie, and proof is always first required, upon that side which affirms the matter in question: in which our law agrees with the civil;(*o*) "*ei incumbit probatio, qui dicit, non qui negat; cum per rerum naturam factum-negantis probatio nulla sit.*"(72)   The opening counsel briefly informs them what has been transacted in the court above; the parties, the nature of the action, the declaration, the plea, replication, and other proceedings, and, lastly, upon what point the issue is joined, which is there set down to be determined.   Instead of which,(*p*) formerly the whole record and process of the pleadings was read to *them in English by the court, and the matter in issue clearly   [*367 explained to their capacities.   The nature of the case, and the

---

(*m*) *Pro Cluentio*, 43.
(*n*) Ascon. in *Cic. Ver.* 1, 6. A learned writer of our own, Dr. Pettingal, hath shown in an elaborate work (published A. D. 1796) so many resemblances between the δικασται [Judges] of the Greeks, the *judices selecti* of the Romans, and the juries of the English, that he is tempted to conclude that the latter are derived from the former.
(*o*) *Ff.* 22, 3, 2. Cod. 4, 19, 23.
(*p*) Fortesc. c. 20.

---

(67) The rejection of a competent juror is ground of error, although the jurors who actually try the case are competent; it is a right of a party to require that the range of selection shall not be limited by excluding without cause a competent juror from the panel. Hildreth *v.* City of Troy, 101 N. Y. (Sickles) 234 (1886). But where the trial judge excused two jurors, one of whom, summoned under the general venire, lived at a distance from the court-house, and in his stead was called a juror from that vicinity; but the prisoner, afterwards put upon his trial for murder committed at the court-house, did not exhaust his peremptory challenges. *Held*, that there was no ground for arresting the judgment. State *v.* Gill, 14 S. C. (Shand.) 410 (1880).

(68) ["Our ancestors would have no judge concerning the reputation of a man, or even concerning the smallest pecuniary matter, unless he was agreed upon by the contending parties."]

(69) [Chosen judges.]

(70) [After the names were drawn, both the prosecutor and the defendant were allowed to reject all those from the number whom they thought might from any cause be unfriendly or ill-disposed toward them.]

(71) [These being rejected, the prætor drew others to supply their place, by whom the lawful number of judges was completed.]

(72) ["The proof lies on him who asserts the fact, not on him who denies it, as from the nature of things a negative is no proof."]

evidence intended to be produced, are next laid before them by counsel also on the same side: and when their evidence is gone through, the advocate on the other side opens the adverse case, and supports it by evidence; and then the party which began is heard by way of reply.

The nature of my present design will not permit me to enter into the numberless niceties and distinctions of what is, or is not, legal *evidence* to a jury.*(q)* I shall only therefore select a few of the general heads and leading maxims relative to this point, together with some observations on the manner of giving evidence.

And, first, evidence signifies that which demonstrates, makes clear, or ascertains the truth of the very fact or point in issue, either on the one side or on the other; and no evidence ought to be admitted to any other point. Therefore upon an action of debt, when the defendant denies his bond by the plea of *non est factum*,(73) and the issue is, whether it be the defendant's deed or no; he cannot give a release of this bond in evidence: for that does not destroy the bond, and therefore does not prove the issue which he has chosen to rely upon, viz., that the bond has no existence. (74)

Again: evidence in the trial by jury is of two kinds, either that which is given in proof, or that which the jury may receive by their own private knowledge.(75) The former, or *proofs*, (to which in common speech the name of evidence is usually confined,) are either written, or *parol*, that is, by word of mouth. Written proofs or evidence are,—1. Records, and 2. Ancient deeds of thirty years' standing, which prove themselves;(76)
*368] but, 3. Modern deeds, and 4. Other *writings, must be attested and verified by parol evidence of witnesses. And the one general rule that runs through all the doctrine of trials is this,—that the best evidence the nature of the case will admit of shall always be required, if possible to be had; but, if not possible, then the best evidence that can be had shall be allowed.(77) For if it be found that there is any better evidence existing

---

(*q*) This is admirably well performed in lord chief-baron Gilbert's excellent treatise of evidence—a work which it is impossible to abstract or abridge without losing some beauty and destroying the chain of the whole, and which hath lately been engrafted into a very useful work, The Introduction of the Law of Nisi Prius, 4to, 1767.

---

(73) [It is not his deed.]

(74) Binns' Justice (Brightly, 10 ed.) 414. Stegar *v.* Eggleston, 5 Calls (Va.) 449 (1885).

(75) Smith *v.* The State, 42 Tex. 444 (1875).

(76) The same rule applies to wills thirty years old. 4 T. R. 709, note. This rule is laid down in books of evidence without sufficient explanation of its principle, or of the extent of its application. There seems to be danger in permitting a deed to be read merely because it bears date above thirty years before its production, and in requiring no evidence, where a forgery may be committed with the least probability of detection. Chief-Baron Gilbert lays down, that where possession has gone agreeably to the limitations of a deed bearing date thirty years ago, it may be read without any evidence of its execution, though the subscribing witnesses be still living. Law of Ev. 94. For such possession affords so strong a presumption in favor of the authenticity of the deed as to supersede the necessity of any other proof of the validity of its origin, or of its due execution. The court of King's Bench have determined that the mere production of a parish certificate dated above thirty years ago was sufficient to make it evidence, without giving any account of the custody from which it was extracted. 5 T. R. 259—CHRISTIAN.

(77) No rule of law is more frequently cited and more generally misconceived than this. It is certainly true when rightly understood; but it is very limited in its extent and application. It signifies nothing more than that, if the best *legal* evidence cannot possibly be produced, the next best *legal* evidence shall be admitted. Evidence may be divided into primary and secondary; and the secondary evidence is as accurately defined by the law as the primary. But in general the want of better evidence can never justify the admission of hearsay, interested witnesses, or the copies of copies, etc. Where there are exceptions to general rules, these exceptions are as much recognized by the law as the general rule; and, where boundaries and limits are established by the law for every

than is produced, the very not producing it is a presumption that it would have detected some falsehood that at present is concealed. Thus, in order to prove a lease for years, nothing else shall be admitted but the very deed of lease itself, if in being; but if that be positively proved to be burned or destroyed, (not relying on any loose negative, as that it cannot be found, or the like,) then an attested copy may be produced; or *parol* evidence be given of its contents.(78) So, no evidence of a discourse with another will be admitted, but the man himself must be produced; yet in some cases (as in proof of any general customs, or matters of common tradition or repute) the courts admit of *hearsay* evidence, or an account of what persons deceased have declared in their lifetime; but such evidence will not be received of any particular facts.(79) So, too, books of account or shop-books are not allowed of themselves to be given in evidence for the owner; but a servant who made the entry may have recourse to them to refresh his memory; and if such servant (who was accustomed to make those entries) be dead, and his hand be proved, the book may be read in evidence;(*r*) for as tradesmen are often under a necessity of giving credit without any note or writing, this is therefore, when accompanied with such other collateral proofs of fairness and regularity,(*s*) the best evidence that can then be produced. However, this dangerous species of evidence is not carried so far in England as abroad;(*t*) where a man's own books of accounts, by a distortion of the civil law, (which seems to have meant the same thing as is practiced with us,)(*u*) with

(*r*) Law of Nisi Prius, 266.
(*s*) Salk. 285.
(*t*) Gail. *observat.* 2, 20, 23.
(*u*) *Instrumenta domestica, seu adnotatio, si non aliis quoque adminiculis adjuventur, ad probationem sola non sufficiunt.* Cod. 4, 19, 5. *Nam exemplo perniciosum est, ut ei scripturæ credatur, qua unusquisque sibi adnotatione propria debitorem constituit.* [Private instruments, or memoranda, unless supported by other evidence, are not alone sufficient proof. For it is a dangerous precedent to give credit to any memorandum by which the writer makes another man his debtor.] Ibid. *l.* 7.

case that can possibly occur, it is immaterial what we call the rule and what the exception.—CHRISTIAN.

Some of the numerous cases which are found even in modern books may be cited for illustration and in confirmation of the text and note.

If the subscribing witness be living and within the jurisdiction of the court, he must be called to prove the execution; or if he cannot be found, and that fact be satisfactorily explained, proof of his handwriting will be sufficient evidence of the execution. Barnes *v.* Trompowsky, 7 T. R. 266. And the witness of the execution is necessary; acknowledgment of the party who executed the deed cannot be received. Johnson *v.* Mason, 1 Esp. 89. At least only as secondary evidence. Call, Bart *v.* Dunning, 4 East, 53. And acknowledgment to a subscribing witness by an obligor of a bond that he has executed it is sufficient. Powell *v.* Blackett, 9 Esp. 87; and see Grellier *v.* Neale, Peake, 146. But a mere bystander may not be received to supply the absence of the subscribing witness, (McCraw *v.* Gentry, 3 Camp. 232,) or only as secondary evidence. See the next case. If the apparent attesting witness deny that he saw the execution, secondary evidence is admissible; that is to say, the handwriting of the obligor, etc., may be proved. Lev *v.* Ballard, 3 Esp. 173, n. And, as a general rule, it seems that wherever a subscribing witness appears to an instrument, note, etc., he must be called, or his absence explained. See Higgs *v.* Dixon, 2 Stark. 180. Breton *v.* Cope, Peake, 31.—CHITTY. See also 1 Arch. Crim. Pr. & Pl. 415.

(78) Carpenter *v.* Dawe, 10 Indiana, 125 (1858).

(79) It is a general rule that the mere recital of a fact—that is, the mere oral assertion or written entry by an individual that a particular fact is true - cannot be received in evidence. But the objection does not apply to any public documents made under lawful authority, such as gazettes, proclamations, public surveys, records, and other memorials of a similar description, and whenever the declaration or entry is in itself a fact and is part of the *res gestæ.* Stark. on Evid. p. 1, 46, 47. But it is to be carefully observed that neither the declarations nor any other acts of those who are mere strangers, or, as it is usually termed, any *res inter alios acta* [A transaction between other parties], is admissible in evidence against any one, as affording a presumption against him in the way of admission, or otherwise. Ib. 51.—CHITTY.

In cases of customs and prescriptive rights, hearsay or traditional evidence is not admitted until some instances of the custom or exercise of the right claimed are first proved. The declarations of parents respecting their marriage, and the legitimacy of

*369]   the suppletory oath of *the merchant, amount at all times to full proof.(80)   But as this kind of evidence, even thus regulated, would

---

their children, are admitted after their decease as evidence. And hearsay is also received respecting pedigrees and the death of relations abroad. Bull. N. P. 294. 2 Esp. 784. What has been said in conversation in the hearing of any party, if not contradicted by him, may be given in evidence; for, not being denied, it amounts to a species of confession. But it can only be received where it must be presumed to have been heard by the party; and therefore in one case the court stopped the witness from repeating a conversation which had passed in a room where the prisoner was, but at the time while she had fainted away. It has been the practice of the quarter-sessions to admit the declarations of paupers respecting their settlements, to be received as evidence after their death, or, if living, where they could not be produced. See 3 T. R. 707, where the judges of the King's Bench were divided upon the legality of this practice, and where the subject of hearsay evidence is much discussed. For many years, whilst lord Mansfield presided in the court of King's Bench, the court were unanimously of opinion that the declarations of a pauper respecting his settlement might after his death be proved and given in evidence. When lord Kenyon and another judge were introduced, the court were divided, and the former practice prevailed; but when the court were entirely changed, they determined that this hearsay evidence was not founded on any principles of law, and that the evidence at the quarter-sessions in the cases of settlement ought to be the same as that in all other courts, in the trials which could respectively be brought before them. 2 East, 54, 63. The court of King's Bench has decided that a father's declaration of the place of the birth of his son is not evidence after the father's death. 8 East, 539. But it would not, probably, be difficult to prove that this is of the nature of pedigree, and ought to be admitted, as the father's declaration of the time of his son's birth, which has always been legal evidence. In criminal cases, the declarations of a person who relates *in extremis*, [In his last moments,] or under an apprehension of dying, the cause of his death, or any other material circumstance, may be admitted in evidence; for the mind in that awful state is presumed to be under as great a religious obligation to disclose the truth as is created by the administration of an oath. But declarations of a deceased person ought not to be received unless the court is satisfied from the circumstances of the case that they were made under the impression of approaching dissolution. Leach's Cases, 400. But the declarations of a felon at the place of execution cannot be received, as he is incompetent to give evidence upon oath, and the situation of a dying man is only thought equivalent to that of a competent witness when he is sworn. Ibid. 276. By the 1 & 2 Ph. & Mar c. 13, depositions taken before a justice of peace in cases of felony may be read in evidence at the trial, if the witness dies before the trial. But as the statute confines this to felony, and as it is an innovation upon the common law, it cannot be extended to any misdemeanor. 1 Salk. 281.—CHRISTIAN.

(80) Although in England the shop-book of a tradesman is not evidence without the oath of the clerk who made the entry, yet in the United States, in the early periods of settlement, as business was generally carried on by the principal, and few shop-keepers kept clerks, the book of original entries, proved by the oath of the plaintiff, has, from the necessity of the case, generally, if not universally, been admitted. It has been confined, however, to the case of goods sold and delivered and work and labor done. It is necessary, however, that the book should appear to be the book in which the first entry was made contemporaneously with the original transaction which it professes to record. It is not necessary, indeed, that it should be in the form of a journal or day-book. Entries in ledger-form have been admitted, or in a pocket memorandum-book. Still, the entry must have been made within a reasonable time after the transaction,—not further than twenty-four, or at most forty-eight, hours. It should not be made until the contract is complete, the work done, the goods delivered, or, at least, so far set aside and distinguished as that the property has passed. Where, however, entries are first made on a slate or a blotter, which is afterwards destroyed and the transfer made in due time to the regular book, it is sufficient. The credibility of such a book may be attacked by any circumstances which would go to show that it is not a regular and reliable record of daily transactions. Poultney *et al. v.* Ross, 1 Dall. 239. Curren *v.* Crawford, 4 Serg. & Rawle, 5. Ingraham *v* Bockius, 9 Serg. & R. 285. Hartley *v.* Brookes, 6 Whart. 189. Patton *v.* Ryan, 4 Rawle, 408. Rhoads *v.* Gaul, 4 Rawle, 404. Parker *v.* Donaldson, 2 Watts & Serg. 20. Coggswell *v.* Dolliver, 2 Mass. 217. Case *v.* Potter, 8 Johns. 211. Linnell *v.* Sutherland, 11 Wend. 568. It would encumber this note to go further in the citation of cases from every state in the Union in support of this species of evidence. Since the parties themselves are now competent witnesses in England, the original entry may evidently be effectually used as a memorandum to refresh the memory.—SHARSWOOD. Parol evidence cannot be given as to the contents of a libelous publication, although the court refused to issue *a subpœna duces tecum* [A subpœna that you bring with (books or papers)]. Gray *v.* Pentland, 3 Rawle (Pa.) 33 (1815).

be much too hard upon the buyer at any long distance of time, the statute 7 Jac. I. c. 12, (the penners of which seem to have imagined that the books themselves were evidence at common law) confines this species of proof to such transactions as have happened within one year before the action brought; unless between merchant and merchant in the usual intercourse of trade. For accounts of so recent a date, if erroneous, may more easily be unraveled and adjusted.

With regard to *parol* evidence, or *witnesses;* it must first be remembered, that there is a process to bring them in by writ of *subpœna ad testificandum:*(81) which commands them, laying aside all pretences and excuses, to appear at the trial on pain of 100*l.* to be forfeited to the king; to which the statute 5 Eliz. c. 9, has added a penalty of 20*l.* to the party aggrieved, and damages equivalent to the loss sustained by want of his evidence. But no witness, unless his reasonable expenses be tendered him, is bound to appear at all; nor, if he appears, is he bound to give evidence till such charges are actually paid him;(82) except he resides within the bills of mortality, and is summoned to give evidence within the same. This compulsory process, to bring in unwilling witnesses, and the additional terrors of an attachment in case of disobedience, are of excellent use in the thorough investigation of truth: and, upon the same principle, in the Athenian courts, the witnesses who were summoned to attend the trial had the choice of three things: either to swear to the truth of the fact in question, to deny or abjure it, or else to pay a fine of a thousand drachmas.(*v*)

All witnesses, of whatever religion or country, that have the use of their reason,(83) are to be received and examined, except such as are *infamous,*

(*v*) Pott. Antiq. b. i. c. 21.

---

(81) [A subpœna to give evidence.] Binn's Justice (Bright.) (10 ed.) 82.

(82) Ogden *v.* Gibbons, 2 N. J. (South.) 518–533 (1819). In some states it is held that an expert cannot be required to testify as such by giving his professional opinion unless compensated therefor, by a professional fee. Buchman *v.* The State, 59 Ind. 1 (1877). Dills *v.* The State, 59 Ind. 15 (1877). In Ala. and Tex. the rule is otherwise. *Ex parte* Dement, 53 Ala. 389. Sumner *v.* The State, 5 Tex. App. 365.

(83) A Mohammedan may be sworn upon the Alcoran, and a Gentoo according to the custom of India; and their evidence may be received even in a criminal case. Leach's Cases, 52. 1 Atk. 21. But an atheist, or a person who has no belief or notion of a God or a future state of rewards and punishments, ought not in any instance to be admitted as a witness. 1 Atk. 45. B. N. P. 202. See Peake, Rep. 11, where Buller, J., held that the proper question to be asked of a witness is, whether he believes in God, the obligation of an oath, and in a future state of rewards and punishments.—CHITTY.

I have known a witness rejected and hissed out of court who declared that he doubted of the existence of a God and a future state. But I have since heard a learned judge declare at nisi prius that the judges had resolved not to permit adult witnesses to be interrogated respecting their belief of a Deity and a future state. It is probably more conducive to the course of justice that this should be presumed till the contrary is proved; and the most religious witness may be scandalized by the imputation which the very question conveys.

Quakers, who refuse to take an oath under any form, by the 7 & 8 W. III. c. 34 are permitted in judicial proceedings to make a solemn affirmation; and if such affirmation, like an oath, is proved to be false, they are subject to the penalties of perjury. But this does not extend to criminal cases. 8 Geo. I. c. 6. 22 Geo. II. c. 30 and c. 46.

Their affirmations are received in penal actions, as for bribery. See Atcheson *v.* Everitt, Cowp. 382, where this subject is largely discussed.

Lord Mansfield lays down generally that an affirmation is not refused where the action, though in form of a criminal action, in substance is a mere action between party and party. Lord Mansfield there laments that such an exception had been made by the legislature.—CHRISTIAN. In Maden *et ux. v.* Catanach, 5 Law Times (N. S.) 288 (1861), it was held that every witness must be sworn according to some religious form, and the witness having declared herself destitute of any religious belief, could not be so sworn, and so could not be received as a witness; and where it was proved that a person offered as a witness, had, within three months before the trial, often deliberately and publicly declared his disbelief in the existence of a God and a future state of rewards and punish-

or such as are *interested* in the event of the cause. All others are *competent*
                witnesses; though the jury from other circumstances will judge of their
*370]   *credibility.*(84)   *Infamous persons are such as may be challenged
                as jurors *propter delictum,*(85) and therefore never shall be admitted
to give evidence to inform that jury with whom they were too scandalous to
associate.(86)   Interested witnesses may be examined upon a *voir dire,*(87)
if suspected to be secretly concerned in the event; or their interest may be
proved in court.   Which last is the only method of supporting an objection
to the former class: for no man is to be examined to prove his own infamy.(88)

---

ments, it was held that he could not, on being called to be sworn, and objected to, be
admitted to deny those declarations, or to state his recantation of them, and his present
belief in a God.   But that he might be restored to competency on giving satisfactory evidence of a change of mind some time before the trial, so as to repel the presumption
arising from his former declarations of his infidelity, existing at the time he is called to
be sworn.   Jackson *v.* Gridley, 18 Johns. (N. Y.) 99 (1820).   A person who does not
believe in any punishment in a future state, though he believes in the existence of a
Supreme Being, and that men are punished in this life for their sins, is not a competent
witness.   Atwood *v.* Welton, 7 Conn. 66 (1828).   But generally in the United States
a belief in God and punishment for a wrongful act, either during life or after its termination, is sufficient to qualify a witness who is objected to on the ground of lack of
religious belief.

(84) McCafferty *v.* Guger, 59 Pennsylvania, 109 (1868).

(85) [On account of incompetency.]

(86) "The old cases upon the competency of witnesses have gone upon very subtle
grounds; but of late years the courts have endeavored as far as possible, consistent with
authorities, to let the objection go to the credit rather than to the competency of a witness." Lord Mansfield, 1 T. R. 300.

It is now established that if a witness does not immediately gain or lose by the event
of the cause, and if the verdict in the cause cannot be evidence either for or against him
in any other suit, he shall be admitted as a competent witness, though the circumstances
of the case may in some degree lessen his credibility.   3 T. R. 27.   The interest must be
a present, certain, vested interest, and not uncertain or contingent, (Doug. 134. 1 T. R.
163.   1 P. Wms. 287;) therefore the heir-apparent is competent in support of the claim
of the ancestor, though the remainderman, having a *vested* interest, is incompetent.
Salk. 283.   Ld. Raym. 724.   A clerk of the company of wire-drawers is competent in an
action against a person for acting as an assistant, although the verdict might cause the
defendant to be sworn, upon which the clerk would obtain a fee.   See Stark. on Evid.
p. 4, 745.

A servant of a tradesman from necessity is permitted in an action by his master to
prove the delivery of goods, though he himself may have purloined them; but in an
action brought against the master for the negligence of his servant, the servant cannot
be a witness for his master without a release; for his master may afterwards have his
action against the servant, and the verdict recovered against him may be given in
evidence in that action to prove the damage which the master has sustained.   4 T. R. 589.

By the 46 Geo. III. c. 37, it is enacted that a witness cannot refuse to answer a question relevant to the matter in issue, the answering of which has no tendency to accuse
himself or to expose him to a penalty or forfeiture, by reason only that the answer to
such question may establish, or tend to establish, that he owes a debt or is subject to a
civil suit.

This statute was passed because upon a point which arose at lord Melville's impeachment the high living authorities of the law were nearly divided, whether a witness was
compellable to answer such a question.   But surely it was agreeably to the law of England that a man should be compelled to be honest, and where, if he avoided the question,
injustice would be done both between the parties before the court and afterwards between
the witness and some other party.—CHRISTIAN.

(87) [To speak the truth.]

(88) A witness may be examined with regard to his own infamy, if the confession of it
does not subject him to any future punishment; as a witness may be asked if he has not
stood in the pillory for perjury, (4 T. R. 440;) but he cannot be entirely rejected as a
witness without the production of the record of conviction, by which he is rendered incompetent.   8 East, 77.—CHRISTIAN.

Though it has been held in some other cases that a witness is not *bound to answer* such
questions.   4 St. Tri. 748.   1 Salk. 153.   4 Esp. 225, 242.   It is quite clear that a man is
not bound to answer any questions, either in a court of law or equity, which may tend to
criminate himself, or which may render him liable to a penalty.   Stra. 444.   3 Taunt. 424.

And no counsel, attorney, or other person, intrusted with the secrets of the cause by the party himself, shall be compelled, or perhaps allowed, to give evidence of such conversation or matters of privacy, as came to his knowledge by virtue of such trust and confidence:(w)(89) but he may be examined as to mere matters of fact, as the execution of a deed or the like, which might have come to his knowledge without being intrusted in the cause.

One witness (if credible) is *sufficient* evidence to a jury of any single facts, though undoubtedly the concurrence of two or more corroborates the proof. Yet our law considers that there are many transactions to which only one person is privy; and therefore does not *always* demand the testimony of two, as the civil law universally requires. "*Unius responsio testis omnino non*

(w) Law of Nisi Prius, 267.

4 St. Tri. 6.   6 ib. 649.   16 Ves. 242.   2 Ld. Raym. 1088.   Mitford's Ch. Pl. 157.   As to questions which *merely* disgrace the witness, there is some difficulty.   See Stark. on Evid. pt. 2, 139.   Still, a witness is in no case legally *incompetent* to allege his own turpitude, or give evidence which involves his own infamy (2 Stark. Rep. 116.   8 East, 78.   11 East, 309) or impeaches his own solemn acts, (5 M. & S. 244.   7 T. R. 604,) unless he be rendered incompetent by a legal interest in the event of the cause, or in the record.   It seems to be a universal rule that a *particeps criminis* [Participator in the crime] may be examined as a witness in both civil and criminal cases, provided he has not been incapacitated by a conviction of crime.   As a clerk who had laid out money which he had embezzled in illegal insurances was held to be a competent witness for the master against the insurer.   Cowp. 197.   So a man who has pretended to convey lands to another may prove that he had no title.   Ld. Raym. 1008.   A co-assignee of a ship may prove that he had no interest in the vessel.   Cited in 1 T. R. 301.   The parents may give evidence to bastardize their issue, (6 T. R. 330, 331,) or to prove the legitimacy, (ib.;) though it is said that the sole evidence of the mother, a married woman, shall not be sufficient to bastardize her child.   B. R. H. 79.   1 Wils. 340.—CHITTY.
The first inroad on the systematic exclusion of evidence, which was the result of the former state of the law, was made by the statute 3 & 4 W. IV. c. 42, s. 96, which enacted that "in order to render the rejection of witnesses on the ground of interest less frequent, if any witness should be objected to as incompetent, on the ground that the verdict or judgment in the action would be admissible in evidence for or against him, he should nevertheless be examined; but in that case the verdict or judgment should not be admissible for or against him or any one claiming under him."   A much greater improvement was, however, effected by the statute 6 & 7 Vict. c. 85, which removed incompetency by reason of incapacity from crime or on the ground of *interest* in all persons, *except the parties to the suit*, or the persons whose rights were involved therein, such as the real plaintiff in the fictitious action of ejectment, or any person in whose immediate and individual behalf any action was brought or defended, or the husband or wife of such persons.   The advantages found to flow from this alteration in the law led to the statute 14 & 15 Vict. c. 99, by the first section of which the proviso in the statute 6 & 7 Vict. c. 85 (which excluded all persons directly interested in the suit) was repealed.   By the second section, the parties and the persons in whose behalf any action, suit, or other proceeding is brought or defended are made (except as therein excepted) *competent* and *compellable* to give evidence on behalf of either or any of the parties to the suit in any court of justice.   The third section of the statute provides that it shall not render any person charged with an offence competent or compellable to give evidence against himself, nor shall it render any person compellable to answer any question tending to criminate himself, nor shall it in any criminal proceeding render any husband competent or compellable to give evidence for or against his wife, or any wife competent or compellable to give evidence for or against her husband.   The fourth section of the statute further provides that it shall not apply to any proceeding instituted in consequence of adultery, or to any action for breach of promise of marriage.   It was decided soon after it had become law that the *second* section of the statute did not render a wife admissible as a witness for or against her husband; and accordingly the statute 16 & 17 Vict. c. 83 was passed, enacting that the husbands and wives of the parties to any suit, or of the persons on whose behalf any such proceeding is brought or defended, shall thereafter be competent and compellable to give evidence on behalf of either party or any of the parties.   Neither husband nor wife is compellable, however, to disclose any communication made or received during marriage; and neither party is a competent witness in a criminal proceeding, or in any proceeding instituted in consequence of adultery.—KERR.
(89) But the principles and policy of this rule restrain it to that confidence only which is placed in a counsel or solicitor, and which must necessarily be inviolable where the

audiatur. (*x*)(90) To extricate itself out of which absurdity, the modern practice of the civil-law courts has plunged itself into another. For, as they do not allow a less number than two witnesses to be *plena probatio*,(91) they call the testimony of one, though never so clear and positive, *semi-plena probatio*(92) only, on which no sentence can be founded. To make up therefore the necessary complement of witnesses, when they have one only to a single fact, they admit the party himself (plaintiff or defendant) to be examined in his own behalf, and administer to him what is called the *suppletory* oath; and, if his evidence happens to be in his own favor, this immediately converts the half proof into a whole one.(93) By this ingenious device satisfying at once the forms of the Roman law, and acknowledging the superior reasonableness of the law of England: which permits one witness to be sufficient where no more are to be had: and, to avoid all temptations of perjury, lays it down as an invariable rule, that *nemo testis esse debet in propria causa.* (94)

*371]   *Positive proof is always required, where from the nature of the case it appears it might possibly have been had.(95) But next to *positive* proof, *circumstantial* evidence or the doctrine of *presumptions* must take place; for when the fact itself cannot be demonstratively evinced, that which comes nearest to the proof of the fact is the proof of such circumstances which either *necessarily*, or *usually*, attend such facts; and these are called presumptions, which are only to be relied upon till the contrary be actually proved. *Stabitur præsumptioni donec probetur in contrarium.* (*y*) *Violent* presumption is many times equal to full proof;(*z*) for there those circumstances appear, which *necessarily* attend the fact.(96) As if a landlord sues for rent due at Michaelmas, 1754, and the tenant cannot prove the payment, but produces an acquittance for rent due at a subsequent time, in full of all demands, this is a violent presumption of his having paid the former rent, and is equivalent to full proof; for though the actual payment is not proved,

---

(*x*) Cod. 4, 20, 9.   (*z*) Ibid. 6.
(*y*) Co. Litt. 373.

---

use of advocates and legal assistants is admitted. But the purposes of public justice supersede the delicacy of every other species of confidential communication. In the trial of the duchess of Kingston, it was determined that a friend might be bound to disclose, if necessary in a court of justice, secrets of the most sacred nature which one sex could repose in the other; and that a surgeon was bound to communicate any information whatever which he was possessed of in consequence of his professional attendance. 11 St. Tr. 243, 246. And those secrets only communicated to a counsel or attorney are inviolable in a court of justice which have been intrusted to them whilst acting in their respective characters to the party as their client. 4 T. R. 431, 753.—CHRISTIAN.

(90) [The evidence of one witness may not be admitted.]
(91) [Full proof.]
(92) [Half proof.]
(93) Gillett *et al. v.* Sweat, 1 Gilman (Ill.) 475.
(94) [No one should be a witness in his own behalf.] Law of Witnesses, Rapalje, 29. Gilmore *v.* Bowden, 12 Me. 412 (1835). In equity no decree can be made on the oath of one witness against the defendant's answer on oath, (Ventr. 161. 3 Ch. C. 123, 69;) and one witness is not sufficient against the husband, although it be supported by the answer of the wife, for she cannot be a witness against her husband. 2 ib. 30. 3 P. Wms. 238. But a decree may be made on the evidence of a single witness, where the evidence of the other party is falsified or discredited by strong circumstances. 2 Vern. 554. 2 Atk. 19. 3 ib. 419. 1 Bro. Ch. C. 52. In high treason, when it works corruption of blood, two witnesses are necessary, by 7 W. III. c. 3. So two are necessary in perjury. 10 Mod. 195; *post*, 4 book, 150. In all other cases the effect of admissible evidence, whether given by one or more witnesses, is solely for the consideration of the jury. See Stark. on Evid. pp. 3, 398, 399.—CHITTY.
(95) Scott *v.* State, 19 Tex. App. 325 (1885).
(96) Rowan *v.* Lamb, 4 Green. (Iowa) 418 (1854).

yet the acquittance in full of all demands is proved, which could not be without such payment; and it therefore induces so forcible a presumption, that no proof shall be admitted to the contrary. (a)(97) *Probable* presumption, arising from such circumstances as *usually* attend the fact, hath also its due weight: as if, in a suit for rent due in 1754, the tenant proves the payment of the rent due in 1755; this will prevail to exonerate the tenant,(b) unless it be clearly shown that the rent of 1754 was retained for some special reason, or that there was some fraud or mistake; for otherwise it will be presumed to have been paid before that in 1755, as it is most usual to receive first the

(a) Gilb. Evid. 161.   (b) Co. Litt. 373.

---

(97) The author does not, perhaps, literally mean here that no evidence would be *received*, if in fact it could be produced, to rebut even the most violent presumption, for the maxim which he has cited above implies the contrary; but I suppose him to mean that such a presumption is so weighty that no evidence will countervail it. Even in this light it is too strongly expressed; for the acquittance might undoubtedly be shown to have been given by mistake, or extorted by menace, or drawn from the party by fraud. So in lord Coke's instance:—"If one be runne throw the bodie with a sword in a house, whereof he instantly dieth, and a man is seene to come out of that house with a bloody sword, and no other man was at that time in the house." The party here might have run himself through the body, in spite of the endeavors of the other to the contrary; and if a witness had seen that from an opposite window, undoubtedly he would be received to destroy the violent presumption arising from the apparent circumstances. Indeed, if witnesses are receivable, as they daily are, to contradict or explain away *positive* proof, of course they must, *a fortiori* [By a stranger reason], be so to rebut presumptive proof.

But there are presumptions in law which are not controvertible; that is, where the law has declared that such a consequence *always* follows such a fact, and therefore withdraws that consequence from the decision of the jury. These, therefore, are not the proper subject of evidence as we understand the word here; and therefore when the causing fact is proved, as no evidence *aliunde* [Of another kind] is required, so none will be admitted to rebut the consequence. Thus, if a conspiracy to imprison the king's person be proved, the law presumes an intention to kill him. Fost. 196. See Fearne *v.* Hutchinson, 9 Ad. & Ell. 641.—COLERIDGE.

Presumptions are of three kinds: 1st, Legal presumptions, made by the law itself, 2d, Legal presumptions, to be made by a jury, of law and fact; 3d, Natural presumptions, or presumptions of *mere* fact.

1st. Legal presumptions are in some cases absolute, as that a bond or other specialty was executed upon a good consideration, (4 Burr. 2225,) so long as the deed or bond remains unimpeached; but it may be impeached on the ground of fraud, and then the consideration becomes the subject of inquiry. But in the case of bills of exchange, the presumption that it was accepted for a good consideration may be rebutted by evidence. So where a fine has been levied, it will be implied that it has been levied with proclamations, (3 Co. 86, b.,) unless rebutted, (Bull. N. P. 229,) and some other like instances; but the presumption in favor of innocence is, it has been held, too strong to be overcome by any artificial intendment of law. 2 B. & A. 386. 2d. Presumptions of law and fact, as that adverse enjoyment, unquestioned for twenty years, of an incorporeal hereditament, presumes a grant; that a bond has been satisfied upon which no interest has been paid, nor other acknowledgment made of its existence, for a like period, (2 Stra. 826. 2 Ld. Raym. 1370;) that there has been a conversion in the case of trover where the defendant refuses to deliver them up. 3d. Natural presumptions. It is the peculiar province of the jury to deal with presumptions of this class; yet, where the particular facts are inseparably connected according to the usual course of nature, the courts themselves will draw the inference; as when a child has been born within a few weeks after access of the husband, its bastardy will be inferred, without the aid of a jury. 8 East, 193. All cases of circumstantial evidence may be more or less within this class. And it is obvious that the case put in the text belongs to this division, upon which Mr. Christian has made the following remark:—

"This can scarcely be correct. I should conceive that proof may be admitted to repel all presumptions whatever; and even if a receipt should be produced expressly for the rent of the year 1754, still, the landlord might show that it had been obtained by mistake or fraud, and that no rent had been received at the time." In a case of a similar nature tried before Abbott, C. J., at Guildhall, A. D. 1824, the landlord adduced evidence to show the mistake, and recovered.—CHITTY.

rents of longest standing. *Light*, or rash, presumptions have no weight or validity at all.(98)

*372]   *The oath administered to the witness is not only that what he deposes shall be true, but that he shall also depose the *whole* truth; so that he is not to conceal any part of what he knows, whether interrogated particularly to that point or not.(99) And all this evidence is to be given in open court, in the presence of the parties, their attorneys, the counsel, and all bystanders, and before the judge and jury; each party having liberty to except to its competency, which exceptions are publicly stated, and by the judge are openly and publicly allowed or disallowed, in the face of the country; which must curb any secret bias or partiality that might arise in his own breast. And if, either in his directions or decisions, he mistakes the law by ignorance, inadvertence, or design, the counsel on either side may require him publicly to seal a *bill of exceptions*, stating the point in which he is supposed to err; and this he is obliged to seal, by statute Westm. 2, 13 Edw. I. c. 31,(100) or, if he refuse so to do, the party may have a compulsory writ against him,(c) commanding him to seal it, if the fact alleged be truly stated:(101) and if he returns that the fact is untruly stated, when the case is otherwise, an action will lie against him for making a false return. This bill of exceptions is in the nature of an appeal, examinable, not in the court out of which the record issues for the trial at *nisi prius*,(102) but in the next immediate superior court, upon a writ of error, after judgment given in the court below. But a *demurrer* to evidence shall be determined by the court out of which the record is sent.(103) This happens where a record or other matter is produced in evidence, concerning the legal consequences of which there arises a doubt in law;(104) in which case the adverse party may if he pleases demur to the whole evidence;(105) which admits the truth of every fact that has been alleged, but denies the sufficiency of them all in point of law to maintain or overthrow the issue;(d) which draws the question of law from the cognizance of the jury to be decided (as it ought) by the court.

But neither these demurrers to evidence, nor the bills of exceptions,
*373]   are at present so much *in use as formerly; since the more frequent extension of the discretionary powers of the court in granting a new

(c) Reg. Br. 182. 2 Inst. 487.   (d) Co. Litt. 72. 5 Rep. 104.

---

(98) It is difficult to say what is a light and rash presumption, if it is any presumption at all. Any circumstance may be proved from which a fair inference can be drawn, though alone it would be too slight to support the verdict of the jury; yet it may corroborate other testimony, and a number of such presumptions may become of importance.—CHRISTIAN. See also Arch. Crim. Pr. & Pl. 412.

(99) Dickson *v.* Pinch, 11 Upp. Can. C. P. 146, 157 (1862).

(100) State *v.* Drake, 11 Ore. 396-398 (1884). Wheeler *v.* Fick, 4 New Mex. 36-39 (1887). It must be sealed during the term at which the trial is had. Kirby *v.* Bowland, 69 Ind. 290 (1879). Onandaga Co. M. Ins. Co. *v.* Minard, 2 Comstock (N. Y.) 98-100 (1848). Doddridge *v.* Gaines, 1 McArthur (Dist. C.) 335-339 (1874).

(101) Webb's Pollock on Torts, enlarged Am. ed. 140. The Supreme Court of the United States has power to issue a mandamus directed to a circuit court, commanding the court to sign a bill of exceptions in a case tried before such court. *Ex parte* Crane, 5 Pet. 189 (1831).

(102) [Unless before.]

(103) Belton *v.* Gibbon, 7 N. J. (Hals.) 76-78 (1830). Thomas *v.* Ruddell, 66 Ind. 326-327 (1879). Hyers *v.* Green, 2 Call. (Va.) 555 (1801).

(104) Nelson *v.* State, 47 Miss. 624 (1873).

(105) A demurrer to the evidence is sufficient if it sets out in full the oral testimony of witnesses, making the written portions of the evidence parts of the demurrer by identifying them as in a bill of exceptions without writing them out in full. Baker *v.* Baker, 69 Indiana, 399 (1879).

trial, which is now very commonly had for the misdirection of the judge at *nisi prius.*(106)

This open examination of witnesses *viva voce,* in the presence of all mankind, is much more conducive to the clearing up of truth(*e*) than the private and secret examination taken down in writing before an officer or his clerk in the ecclesiastical courts and all others that have borrowed their practice from the civil law, where a witness may frequently depose that in private which he will be ashamed to testify in a public and solemn tribunal. There an artful or careless scribe may make a witness speak what he never meant, by dressing up his depositions in his own forms and language; but he is here at liberty to correct and explain his meaning, if misunderstood, which he can never do after a written deposition is once taken.(107) Besides, the occasional questions of the judge, the jury, and the counsel, propounded to the witnesses on a sudden, will sift out the truth much better than a formal set of interrogatories previously penned and settled; and the confronting of adverse witnesses is also another opportunity of obtaining a clear discovery, which can never be had upon any other method of trial. Nor is the presence of the judge during the examination a matter of small importance; for, besides the respect and awe with which his presence will naturally inspire the witness, he is able by use and experience to keep the evidence from wandering from the point in issue. In short, by this method of examination, and this only, the persons who are to decide upon the evidence have an opportunity of observing the quality, age, education, understanding, behavior, and

(*e*) Hale's Hist. C. L. 254, 255, 256.

---

(106) The matter which the jury has to try is the issue joined upon the pleadings which are copied on the nisi prius record, and at which alone the judge is permitted to look for the question to be tried. Although, therefore, the plaintiff may be able to prove a good cause of action, or the defendant a good defence, that is not sufficient to entitle either to a verdict, unless the proof of it establishes that side of the issue which it is his duty to maintain. When there was no power to amend the pleadings at nisi prius, it accordingly often happened that a party failed on the trial, by reason of some minute discrepancy between the statement of his cause of action or defence and the evidence produced to support it; for though as a rule it is sufficient that the issue shall be *substantially* proved, it is necessary that it be *completely* proved. This strictness consequently produced great injustice; for parties perfectly aware of the true nature of the dispute came to trial relying upon some slight misstatement in his adversary's pleadings not material to the merits of the case, and which, had it been discovered in time, would have been corrected. To obviate hardships of this kind, the statute 9 Geo. IV. c. 15 enacted that it should be lawful for any court or any judge sitting at nisi prius, when any variance appeared between any matter in writing or in print produced in evidence and the recital thereof on the record, to cause the record to be forthwith amended in such particular on payment of such costs, if any, to the other party, as such judge or court thought reasonable; the trial thenceforth to proceed as if no such variance had appeared. The statute 3 & 4 W. IV. c. 42, ss. 23, 24 extended this power of amendment to all cases where any variance appeared between the proof and the recital or setting forth thereof on the record, the trial to proceed as if no variance had happened.

The powers of amendment given by these statutes have been still further extended, if not superseded, by the provisions of the Common-Law Procedure Act, 1852. Thus, a *non-joinder* or *misjoinder* may be amended at the trial; so the evidence of the plaintiff may show a contract or cause of action varying somewhat from that alleged in his declaration; or the defendant's witnesses may make out a defence which has not been pleaded with technical exactness. In either case the declaration or plea may be amended; and this must be done by the presiding judge, so that the real question in controversy between the parties to the cause may be determined in the existing suit. Amendments are generally granted on payment of the costs previously incurred, and which by the amendment have been rendered unnecessary or without result. The defendant may be allowed, if necessary, to plead *de novo,* [Anew,] in which latter case the further trial of the action is at once stopped and the jury discharged from giving any verdict. If either party is dissatisfied with the decision of the judge, he may apply for a new trial; and if the court think that the amendment was improper, a new trial will be granted.—KERR.

(107) Carver *v.* Louthain, 38 Indiana, 549 (1872).

inclinations of the witness; in which points all persons must appear alike when their depositions are reduced to writing and read to the judge in the absence of those who made them; and yet as much may be frequently collected from the manner in which the evidence is delivered as from the
*374] matter of *it. These are a few of the advantages attending this the English way of giving testimony *ore tenus.*(108) Which was also, indeed, familiar among the *ancient* Romans, as may be collected from Quintilian,(*f*) who lays down very good instructions for examining and crossexamining witnesses *viva voce.*(109) And this, or somewhat like it, was continued as low as the time of Hadrian;(*g*) but the civil law, as it is now modeled, rejects all public examination of witnesses.

As to such evidence as the jury may have in their own consciences by their private knowledge of facts, it was an ancient doctrine that this had as much right to sway their judgment as the written or parol evidence which is delivered in court. And therefore, it hath been often held(*h*) that though no proofs be produced on either side, yet the jury might bring in a verdict. For the oath of the jurors to find according to their evidence was construed(*i*) to be, to do it according to the best of their own knowledge. This seems to have arisen from the ancient practice of taking recognitions of assize at the first introduction of that remedy; the sheriff being bound to return such recognitors as knew the truth of the fact, and the recognitors when sworn being to retire immediately from the bar, and bring in their verdict according to their own personal knowledge, without hearing extrinsic evidence or receiving any direction from the judge.(*j*) And the same doctrine (when attaints came to be extended to trials by jury as well as to recognitions of assize) was also applied to the case of common jurors, that they might escape the heavy penalties of the *attaint* in case they could show by any additional proof that their verdict was agreeable to the truth, though not according to the evidence produced, with which additional proof the law presumed
*375] they were privately acquainted, though it did not appear in *court. But this doctrine was again gradually exploded, when *attaints* began to be disused and *new trials* introduced in their stead. For it is quite incompatible with the grounds upon which such new trials are every day awarded, viz., that the verdict was given *without*, or *contrary to*, evidence.(110) And therefore, together with new trials, the practice seems to have been first introduced(*k*) which now universally obtains, that if a juror knows any thing of the matter in issue he may be sworn as a witness and give his evidence publicly in court.

(*f*) *Institut. Orat. l.* 5, c. 7.
(*g*) See his epistle to Varus, the legate or judge of Cilicia: " *Tu magis scire potes, quanta jides sit habenda testibus; qui, et cujus dignitatis, et cujus æstimationis sint; et, qui simpliciter visi sint dicere: utrum unum eandemque meditatum sermonem attulerint, an ad ea quæ interrogaveris extempore verisimilia responderint.*" ["You are better able to judge what faith is to be placed in witnesses; who they are, and in what credit and estimation they are held; whether they appear to speak ingenuously, and whether their answers to your questions be preconcerted, or the expressions of the moment."] *Ff.* 22, 5, 3.
(*h*) Year-book, 14 Hen. VII. 29. Plowd. 12 Hob. 227. 1 Lev. 87.
(*i*) Vaugh. 148, 149.
(*j*) Bract. *l.* 4, *tr.* 1, c. 19, § 3. Flet. *l.* 4, c. 9, § 2.
(*k*) Styl. 233. 1 Sid. 133.

(108) [By word of mouth.]
(109) [Orally.]
(110) Nelson *v.* State, 47 Mississippi, 621 (1873). Smith *v.* The State, 42 Tex. 444-449 (1875). Daggett *v.* Jordan, 2 Fla. 541 (1849). Where in a prosecution for felony the evidence was conflicting, and the jury, after leaving the bar to consult and determine their verdict, one of them disclosed his knowledge of the particular point at issue, which knowledge he failed to disclose at the trial, and upon the disclosure of which the jury were induced to render a verdict against the defendant, it was held that under such circumstances it should not be permitted to stand. Sarn *v.* State, 1 Swan. (Tenn.) 61 (1851). Fisher *v.* Concord R. R. Co., 50 New Hampshire, 200 (1870). Writs of attaint and assize are now abolished.

When the evidence is gone through on both sides, the judge, in the presence of the parties, the counsel, and all others, sums up the whole to the jury; omitting all superfluous circumstances, observing wherein the main question and principal issue lies, stating what evidence has been given to support it, with such remarks as he thinks necessary for their direction, and giving them his opinion in matters of law arising upon that evidence.(111)

The jury, after the proofs are summed up, unless the case be very clear, withdraw from the bar to consider of their verdict; and, in order to avoid intemperance and causeless delay, are to be kept without meat, drink, fire, or candle, unless by permission of the judge, till they are all unanimously agreed. A method of accelerating unanimity not wholly unknown in other constitutions of Europe, and in matters of greater concern. For by the golden bull of the empire,(*l*) if, after the congress is opened, the electors delay the election of a king of the Romans for thirty days, they shall be fed only with bread and water, till the same is accomplished. But if our juries eat or drink at all, or have any eatables about them, without consent of the court, and before verdict, it is finable; and if they do so at his charge for whom they afterwards find, it will set aside the verdict.(112) Also if they speak with either of the parties or their agents, after they are gone *from   [*376 the bar; or if they receive any fresh evidence in private; or if to prevent disputes they cast lots for whom they shall find;(113) any of these circumstances will entirely vitiate the verdict. And it has been held, that if the jurors do not agree in their verdict before the judges are about to leave the town, though they are not to be threatened or imprisoned,(*m*) the judges are not bound to wait for them, but may carry them round the circuit from town to town in a cart.(*n*)(114) This necessity of a total unanimity

(*l*) C. 2.
(*m*) Mirr. c. 4, § 24.

(*n*) *Lib. Ass.* fol. 40, pl. 11.

---

(111) Walker *v.* Windsor Nat. Bank, 56 Fed. Rep. 76 (1893). Johnson *v.* Kinsey, 7 Cobb (Ga.) 428 (1849).

(112) Where the jurors procured liquor at their own expense, and the testimony showed that none of them were affected by drinking it, and were perfectly sober during the entire trial, and that neither their deliberations nor verdict was influenced or affected by the use of the liquor, the court refused to set aside the verdict. Jones *v.* People, 6 Colorado, 452 (1882). And where a juror dined with the plaintiff, but the verdict was not influenced thereby, a motion to set aside the verdict was denied. Vaughn *v.* Dotson, 2 Swan. Tenn. 348 (1852).

(113) Smith *v.* Cheetman, 3 Caines (N. Y.) 56 (1805). Cluggage *v.* Swan, 4 Binney (Pa.) 150 (1811). A verdict is not vitiated because published on Sunday. Heller *v.* English, 4 Strat. (S. Car.) 486 (1848).

(114) Anthony on Self Defence, 280. Pending a trial of long duration, the jury may be adjourned, and in civil cases and criminal cases, not capital, may separate, under a proper charge; but after the judge has summed up the evidence, they cannot separate. 2 Bar. & Ald. 462. Grace *v.* McKissack, 49 Ala. 163 (1873). State *v.* Baldy, 17 Iowa, 39 (1864). People *v.* Ransom, 7 Wend. (N. Y.) 417 (1831). Francis *v.* The State, 6 Fla. 306 (1855). Authorities differ as to the right of a judge to discharge a jury, after the case has been committed to them, on account of their being unable to agree. In N. Y. it has been held (People *v.* Goodwin, 18 Johns. 187) that the right does exist in cases of extreme necessity. In Penn. (Comm. *v.* Cook, 6 S. & R. 577) it was decided, after great consideration and a review of all the cases, that a jury could not be discharged because they were unable to agree, and the same doctrine obtains in N. C., where it was held (*Ex parte* Spear, 1 Div. 491; and State *v.* Garrigues, 2 Hayw. 241) that when the jury did not agree within the time during which the court was authorized to sit, the omission to return a verdict was equivalent to an acquittal, as the prisoner could never be legally tried by another jury. The doctrine in Alabama is the same as that in N. Y., and in Ned *v.* The State, 7 Porter, 187, the court laid down the following rules after an exhaustive review of ancient and modern authorities: (1) That courts have not, in capital cases, a discretionary authority to discharge a jury after evidence given. (2) That a jury is *ipso facto*, discharged, by the termination of the authority of the court to which it is

seems to be peculiar to our own constitution:(o) or, at least, in the *nembda* or *jury of the ancient Goths*, there was required (even in criminal cases) only the consent of the major part; and, in case of an equality, the defendant was held to be acquitted.(*p*)(115)

When they are all unanimously agreed, the jury return back to the bar; and, before they deliver their verdict, the plaintiff is bound to appear in court, by himself, attorney, or counsel, in order to answer the amercement to which by the old law he is liable, as has been formerly mentioned,(*q*) in case he fails in his suit, as a punishment for his false claim.(116) To be *amerced*, or *à mercie*, is to be at the king's mercy with regard to the fine to be imposed; *in misericordia domini regis pro falso clamore suo.*(117) The amercement is disused, but the form still continues; and if the plaintiff does not appear, no verdict can be given, but the plaintiff is said to be *non-suit*, *non sequitur clamorem suum*.(118) Therefore it is usual for a plaintiff,

(o) See Barrington on the Statutes, 19, 20, 21.
(p) Stiern. l. 1, c. 4.

(q) Page 275. See also book iv. 379.

attached. (3) That a court does possess the power to discharge a jury, in any case of pressing necessity. (4) That a court does not possess the power, in a capital case, to discharge a jury because it cannot agree. Where the parties agree to a sealed verdict, the rendition of the verdict does not operate as a discharge to the jury; they must assemble again, that they may be polled, should either party desire it. Riggs *v.* Beas, 44 Randolph, Va. 148 (1890).

(115) The learned judge has displayed much erudition in the beginning of this chapter to prove the antiquity of the trial by jury; but the trials referred to by the authors there cited, and even the *judicium parium*, [The judgment of peers] mentioned in the celebrated chapter of *magna charta*, are trials which were something similar to that by a jury, rather than instances of a trial by jury according to the present established form. The *judicium parium* seems strictly the judgment of a subject's equals in the feudal courts of the king and barons. And so little appears to be ascertained by antiquarians respecting the introduction of the trial in criminal cases by two juries, that although it is one of the most important, it is certainly one of the most obscure and inexplicable, parts of the law of England.

The unanimity of twelve men, so repugnant to all experience of human conduct, passions, and understandings, could hardly in any age have been introduced into practice by a deliberate act of the legislature.

But that the life, and perhaps the liberty and property, of a subject should not be affected by the concurring judgment of a less number than twelve, where more were present, was a law founded in reason and caution, and seems to be transmitted to us by the common law, or from immemorial antiquity. The grand assize might have consisted of more than twelve, yet the verdict might have been given by twelve or more; and if twelve did not agree, the assize was afforced,—that is, others were added till twelve did concur. See 1 Reeve's Hist. of Eng. Law, 241, 480. This was a majority, and not unanimity. A grand jury may consist of any number from twelve to twenty-three inclusive, but a presentment ought not to be made by less than twelve. 2 Hale. P. C. 161. The same is true also of an inquisition before the coroner. In the high court of parliament and the court of the lord high steward a peer may be convicted by the greater number; yet there can be no conviction unless the greater number consists at least of twelve. 3 Inst. 30. Kelyng. 56. Moore, 622. Under a commission of lunacy the jury was seventeen, but twelve joined in the verdict. 7 Ves. Jr. 450. A jury upon a writ of inquiry may be more than twelve. In all these cases, if twelve only appeared, it followed as a necessary consequence that to act with effect they must have been unanimous.

Hence this may be suggested as a conjecture respecting the origin of the unanimity of juries, that, as less than twelve—if twelve or more were present—could pronounce no effective verdict, when twelve only were sworn, their unanimity became indispensable. —CHRISTIAN.

(116) This fine or amercement is not at the present day imposed for any cause, and the costs to which the plaintiff is liable, if he fail in his suit, may be adjudged against him, although he be not present in court at the time the verdict is rendered. It would seem, therefore, that the reason assigned by Blackstone for requiring the plaintiff to attend to receive the verdict no longer exists. Stiles *v.* Ford, 2 Colo. 128-129 (1873).

(117) [At the king's mercy for his false claim.]

(118) [He does not pursue his claim.]

when he or his counsel perceives that he has not given evidence sufficient to maintain his issue, to be voluntarily non-suited, or withdraw himself: whereupon the crier is ordered to *call the plaintiff:* and if neither he, nor anybody for him, appears, he is non-suited, the jurors are discharged, the action is at an end, and the defendant shall recover his costs.(119) The reason of this practice is, that a non-suit is more eligible for the plaintiff than a verdict against him: for after a non-suit, which is only a default, he may commence the same suit *again for the same cause of   [*377 action; but after a verdict had, and judgment consequent thereupon, he is forever barred from attacking the defendant upon the same ground of complaint. But, in case the plaintiff appears, the jury by their foreman deliver in their verdict.(120)

A verdict, *vere dictum*, is either *privy*, or *public*. A *privy* verdict is when the judge hath left or adjourned the court: and the jury, being agreed, in order to be delivered from their confinement, obtain leave to give their verdict privily to the judge out of court:(r)(121) which privy verdict is of no force unless afterwards affirmed by a public verdict given openly in court; wherein the jury may, if they please, vary from the privy verdict.(122) So that the privy verdict is indeed a mere nullity; and yet it is a dangerous practice, allowing time for the parties to tamper with the jury, and therefore very seldom indulged.(123) But the only effectual and legal verdict is the *public* verdict: in which they openly declare to have found the issue for the plaintiff, or for the defendant; and if for the plaintiff, they assess the damages also sustained by the plaintiff in consequence of the injury upon which the action is brought.

Sometimes, if there arises in the case any difficult matter of law, the jury, for the sake of better information, and to avoid the danger of having their verdict attainted, will find a *special* verdict; which is grounded on the statute

(r) If the judge hath adjourned the court to his own lodgings and there receives the verdict, it is a   *public* and not a *privy* verdict.

---

(119) Schmidt *v.* Halle, 15 Missouri App. 36 (1884). Washburn *v.* Allen, 77 Maine, 344 (1885). In the United States the practice as to non-suits is not uniform. In some of the states it is the practice to grant non-suits against the will of the plaintiff. The Supreme Court of the United States and many of the states follow the common law rule that an involuntary non-suit cannot be granted. Bove *v.* Davis, 5 Blackf. (Ind.) 115 (1839).

(120) When a verdict will carry all the costs, and it is doubtful from the evidence for which party it will be given, it is a common practice for the judge to recommend, and the parties to consent, that a juror should be withdrawn; and thus no verdict is given, and each party pays his own costs.

Where there is a doubt at the trial whether the evidence produced by the plaintiff is sufficient to support the verdict given in his favor by the jury, the judge will give leave to apply to the court above to set aside the verdict and to enter a non-suit; but if such liberty is not reserved at the trial, the court above can only grant the defendant a new trial, if they think the plaintiff's evidence insufficient to support his case. 6 T. R. 67. —CHRISTIAN.

Until the verdict is received and recorded the jury may alter it; and if one juror dissents from the verdict after it is sealed and before it is received the court cannot accept it. Devereux *v.* Champion Cotton Press Co., 14 Shand. (S. Car.) 396 (1880). Young *v.* Seymour, 4 Neb. 86 (1875). But the dissent of a juror cannot be shown except by his own declaration publicly made in open court when the verdict is read by the clerk. Nichols *v.* Suncook Manuf. Co., 24 N. H. (4 Foster) 438 (1852); see also Hickman *v.* R. R. Co., 30 W. Va. 296-320 (1887).

(121) Campbell *v.* Linton, 27 Upp. Can. Q. B. Rep. 563, 566, 567 (1867).

(122) Hilliard on New Trials (2 ed.) 241.

(123) A privy verdict cannot be given in treason and felony. 2 H. P. C. 300.—CHITTY. See also Comm. *v.* Tobin, 125 Mass. 203 (1878). Lawrence *v.* Stearns, 11 Pick. (Mass.) 501-2 (1831).

of Westm. 2, 13 Edw. I. c. 30, § 2. And herein they state the naked facts, as they find them to be proved, and pray the advice of the court thereon; concluding conditionally, that if upon the whole matter the court should be of opinion that the plaintiff had cause of action, they then find for the plaintiff; if otherwise, then for the defendant.(124) This is entered at length on the record and afterwards argued and determined in the court at Westminster, from whence the issue came to be tried.

*378]   *Another method of finding a species of special verdict is when the jury find a verdict generally for the plaintiff, but subject nevertheless to the opinion of the judge or the court above, on a *special case* stated by the counsel on both sides with regard to a matter of law; which has this advantage over a special verdict, that it is attended with much less expense, and obtains a much speedier decision; the *postea* (of which in the next chapter) being stayed in the hands of the officer of *nisi prius*,(125) till the question is determined, and the verdict is then entered for the plaintiff or defendant, as the case may happen. But, as nothing appears upon the record but the general verdict, the parties are precluded hereby from the benefit of a writ of error, if dissatisfied with the judgment of the court, or judge, upon the point of law. Which makes it a thing to be wished, that a method could be devised of either lessening the expense of special verdicts, or else of entering the cause at length upon the *postea*. But in both these instances the jury may, if they think proper, take upon themselves to determine, at their own hazard, the complicated question of fact and law, and, without either special verdict or special case, may find a verdict absolutely either for the plaintiff or defendant.(s)(126)

When the jury have delivered in their verdict, and it is recorded in court, they are then discharged. And so ends the trial by jury: a trial which, besides the other vast advantages which we have occasionally observed in its progress, is also as expeditious and cheap, as it is convenient, equitable, and certain; for a commission out of chancery, or the civil-law courts, for examining witnesses in one cause will frequently last as long, and of course be full as expensive, as the trial of a hundred issues at *nisi prius*: and yet the fact cannot be determined by such commissioners at all; no, not till the depositions are published, and read at the hearing of the cause in court.

*379]   *Upon these accounts the trial by jury ever has been, and I trust ever will be, looked upon as the glory of the English law. And if it has so great an advantage over others in regulating civil property, how much must that advantage be heightened when it is applied to criminal cases!(127) But this we must refer to the ensuing book of these commentaries: only observing for the present, that it is the most transcendent privilege which any subject can enjoy, or wish for, that he cannot be affected either in his property, his liberty, or his person, but by the unanimous consent of twelve of his neighbors and equals.(128) A constitution that I may venture to affirm has, under Providence, secured the just liberties of this nation for a long succession of ages. And therefore a celebrated French

(s) Litt § 386.

---

(124) Wallington *v.* Dunlap, 14 Pa. 31 (1850). Mumford *v.* Wardwell, 6 Wall. 423 (1867). Abat *v.* Rion, 1 Cond. La. Rep. (Martin) 598-9 (1820). The parties may also waive a trial by jury and then the finding of facts by the court whether general or special, has the same effect as the verdict of a jury and cannot be reviewed on writ of error. Ins. Co. *v.* Boon, 95 U. S. 117 (1877).

(125) [Unless before.]

(126) C. & N. W. Ry. Co. *v.* Dunleavy, 27 Ill. App. 438-440 (1880). Cook *v.* Wilson, 3 Hen. & Mun. (Va.) 483-498 (1809). Robinson *v.* Adkins, 19 Cobb (Ga.) 398 (1856).

(127) Criminal Briefs, Malone. 3.

(128) State *v.* Gill, 14 S. C. (Shand.) 410-412 (1880).

writer,(*t*) who concludes that because Rome, Sparta, and Carthage have lost their liberties, therefore those of England in time must perish, should have recollected that Rome, Sparta, and Carthage, at the time when their liberties were lost, were strangers to the trial by jury.(129)

Great as this eulogium may seem, it is no more than this admirable constitution, when traced to its principles, will be found in sober reason to deserve. The impartial administration of justice, which secures both our persons and our properties, is the great end of civil society. But if that be entirely intrusted to the magistracy, a select body of men, and those generally selected by the prince, or such as enjoy the highest offices in the state, their decisions, in spite of their own natural integrity, will have frequently an involuntary bias towards those of their own rank and dignity; it is not to be expected from human nature, that *the few* should be always attentive to the interests and good of *the many*. On the other hand, if the power of judicature were placed at random in the hands of the multitude, their decisions would be wild and capricious, and a new rule of action would be every day established in our courts. It is wisely therefore ordered, that the principles and axioms of law, which are general propositions, flowing from abstracted reason, and not *accommodated to times or to men,   [*380 should be deposited in the breasts of the judges, to be occasionally applied to such facts as come properly ascertained before them. For here partiality can have little scope: the law is well known, and is the same for all ranks and degrees; it follows as a regular conclusion from the premises of fact pre-established.(130) But in settling and adjusting a question of fact, when intrusted to any single magistrate, partiality and injustice have an ample field to range in; either by boldly asserting that to be proved which is not so, or by more artfully suppressing some circumstances, stretching and warping others, and distinguishing away the remainder. Here therefore a competent number of sensible and upright jurymen, chosen by lot from among those of the middle rank, will be found the best investigators of truth and the surest guardians of public justice. For the most powerful individual in the state will be cautious of committing any flagrant invasion of another's right, when he knows that the fact of his oppression must be examined and decided by twelve indifferent men, not appointed till the hour of trial; and that, when once the fact is ascertained, the law must of course redress it. This therefore preserves in the hands of the people that share which they ought to have in the administration of public justice, and prevents the encroachments of the more powerful and wealthy citizens. Every new tribunal, erected for the decision of·facts, without the intervention of a jury, (whether composed of justices of the peace, commissioners of the revenue, judges of a court of conscience, or any other standing magistrates,) is a step towards establishing aristocracy, the most oppressive of absolute governments. The feudal system, which, for the sake of military subordination, pursued an aristocratical plan in all its arrangements of property, had been intolerable in times of peace, had it not been wisely counterpoised by that privilege, so universally diffused through every part of it, the trial by the feudal peers. And in every country on the continent, as the trial by the peers has been gradually disused, so the nobles have increased in power, till the state has been torn to pieces by rival factions, and oligarchy in effect has been established, though under the shadow of regal government;

(*t*) Montesq. Sp. L. xi. 6.

---

(129) Perkins *v.* Scott, 57 N. H. 55-79 (1876).
(130) Ruckersville Bank *v.* Hemphill, 7 Ga. (Cobb.) 396, 417 (1849).

*381]   *unless where the miserable commons have taken shelter under abso-
lute monarchy, as the lighter evil of the two. And, particularly, it
is a circumstance well worthy an Englishman's observation, that in Sweden
the trial by jury, that bulwark of northern liberty, which continued in its
full vigor so lately as the middle of the last century,(u) is now fallen into
disuse:(w) and that there, though the regal power is in no country so closely
limited, yet the liberties of the commons are extinguished, and the government is degenerated into a mere aristocracy.(x) It is therefore, upon the
whole, a duty which every man owes to his country, his friends, his posterity,
and himself, to maintain to the utmost of his power this valuable constitution
in all its rights; to restore it to its ancient dignity, if at all impaired by the
different value of property, or otherwise deviated from its first institution; to
amend it, wherever it is defective; and, above all, to guard with the most
jealous circumspection against the introduction of new and arbitrary methods
of trial, which, under a variety of plausible pretences, may in time imperceptibly undermine this best preservative of English liberty.

Yet, after all, it must be owned, that the best and most effectual method to
preserve and extend the trial by jury in practice, would be by endeavoring to
remove all the defects, as well as to improve the advantages, incident to this
mode of inquiry. If justice is not done to the entire satisfaction of the
people in this method of deciding facts, in spite of all encomiums and pane-
gyrics on trials at the common law, they will resort in search of that justice
to another tribunal; though more dilatory, though more expensive, though
more arbitrary in its frame and constitution. If justice is not done to the
crown by the verdict of a jury, the necessities of the public revenue will call
for the erection of summary tribunals. The principal defects seem to be,—

1. The want of a complete discovery by the oath of the parties.
*382]   This each of them is now entitled to have, by *going through the
expense and circuity of a court of equity; and therefore it is sometimes had by consent, even in the courts of law. How far such a mode of
compulsive examination is agreeable to the rights of mankind, and ought to
be introduced in any country, may be matter of curious discussion, but is
foreign to our present inquiries. It has long been introduced and established
in our courts of equity, not to mention the civil-law courts; and it seems the
height of judicial absurdity, that in the same cause, between the same parties, in the examination of the same facts, a discovery by the oath of the
parties should be permitted on one side of Westminster hall, and denied on
the other; or that the judges of one and the same court should be bound by
law to reject such a species of evidence, if attempted on a trial at bar, but,
when sitting the next day as a court of equity; should be obliged to hear
such examination read, and to found their decrees upon it. In short, within
the same country, governed by the same laws, such a mode of inquiry should
be universally admitted, or else universally rejected.(131)

2. A second defect is of a nature somewhat similar to the first: the want
of a compulsive power for the production of books and papers belonging to
the parties. In the hands of third persons they can generally be obtained
by rule of court, or by adding a clause of requisition to the writ of *subpœna*,

(u) 2 Whitelocke of Parl. 427.   (x) Ibid. 17.
(w) Mod. Un. Hist. xxxiii. 22.

---

(131) The Common-Law Procedure Act, 1854, now, however, enables either party, by
leave of the court or a judge, to *interrogate* his opponent upon any matter as to which
discovery may be sought, and to require such party to answer the questions within ten
days, by affidavit sworn and filed in court in the ordinary way. Any person omitting,
without just cause, to answer all questions as to which a discovery is sought, is guilty of a
contempt, and liable to be proceeded against accordingly.—KERR.

which is then called a *subpœna duces tecum*.(132)　But, in mercantile transactions especially, the sight of the party's own books is frequently decisive; as the day-book of a trader, where the transaction was recently entered, as really understood at the time; though subsequent events may tempt him to give it a different color.　And, as this evidence may be finally obtained, and produced on a trial at law, by the circuitous course of filing a bill in equity, the want of an original power for the same purposes in the courts of law is liable to the same _observations as were made on the preceding article.(133)

3. *Another want is that of powers to examine witnesses abroad, ·[*383 and to receive their depositions in writing, where the witnesses reside, and especially when the cause of action arises, in a foreign country.(134) To which may be added the power of examining witnesses that are aged, or going abroad, upon interrogatories *de bene esse;*(135) to be read in evidence if the trial should be deferred till after their death or departure, but otherwise to be totally suppressed.　Both these are now very frequently effected by mutual consent, if the parties are open and candid; and they may also be done indirectly at any time, through the channel of a court of equity; but

---

(132) *In re* Storror, 63 Fed. Rep. 564, 566 (1894).　Binns' Justice, p. 82.　Where a deposition has been taken, but at the time of trial the witness was in court, it was held that the deposition should be excluded and the witness should be called upon the stand. Hayward *v.* Barron, 38 N. H. 366 (1857).

(133) Where one party is in possession of papers or any species of written evidence material to the other, if notice is given him to produce them at the trial, upon his refusal copies of them will be admitted; or, if no copy has been made, parol evidence of their contents will be received.　The court and jury presume in favor of such evidence, because, if it were not agreeable to the strict truth, it would be corrected by the production of the originals.　There is no difference with respect to this species of evidence between criminal and civil cases.　2 T. R. 201.—CHRISTIAN.

The statute 14 & 15 Vict. c. 99, s. 6, enacts that, on any action or other legal proceeding in the superior courts of common law, the court or any judge thereof may, on application by either of the litigants, compel the opposite party to allow the party applying to *inspect* all documents in his custody or under his control relating to such action or other legal proceeding, in all cases in which a discovery may be obtained by filing a bill or other proceeding in a court of equity.—KERR.

(134) But now, by stat. 1 W. IV. c. 22, the courts of law at Westminster are empowered, in any action depending in such courts, upon the application of any of the parties to such action, to order the examination, upon oath, upon interrogatories, or otherwise, of any witnesses, and, if any of such witnesses are out of the jurisdiction of the court when the action is pending, to order a commission to issue for their examination, and to give all such directions touching the time, place, and manner of the examination as may appear reasonable and just; but no examination or deposition taken by virtue of the act can be read in evidence at any trial without the consent of the party against whom the same may be offered, unless it shall appear to the satisfaction of the judge that the examinant is then beyond the jurisdiction of the court, or dead, or unable, from permanent sickness, to attend the trial.　And now, by stat. 6 & 7 Vict. c. 82, s. 5, power is given to compel the attendance of persons to be examined under any commission.—STEWART.

(135) [To be accepted for the present subject to future circumstances.]

In the United States courts the procedure in equity and admiralty causes, is regulated by the rules adopted by the supreme court and R. S. title, 14, chap. 17.　On the law side, technically taken *de bene esse* [Conditionally] there must be proof of the death of the witness, or that he has left the United States, or that he has gone a greater distance than one hundred miles from the place where the court is sitting, or by reason of age, sickness, bodily infirmity or imprisonment, he is unable to appear in person.　Rev. Stat. sec. 865. Bailey's Onus Probandi, 575.　As to depositions taken *in perpetuam rei memoriam* [In perpetuation of the fact] the practice is assimilated to that of the state courts.　(Rev. Stats. sec. 867.)　According to the English chancery practice there must be a publication of the depositions by the clerks either by consent or on rule.　The mode of publication is regulated by the different statutes.　Bailey's Onus Probandi, 276.　Minnis *v.* Echols, 3 Henning & Munford's, 31 (1808).

such a practice has never yet been directly adopted(*y*) as the rule of a court of law.(136) Yet where the cause of action arises in India, and a suit is brought thereupon in any of the king's courts at Westminster, the court may issue a commission to examine witnesses upon the spot and transmit the depositions to England.(*z*)

4. The administration of justice should not only be chaste, but should not even be suspected. A jury coming from the neighborhood has in some respects a great advantage, but is often liable to strong objections; especially in small jurisdictions, as in cities which are counties of themselves, and where such assizes are but seldom holden; or where the question in dispute has an extensive local tendency; where a cry has been raised, and the passions of the multitude been inflamed; or where one of the parties is popular, and the other a stranger or obnoxious. It is true that, if a whole county is interested in the question to be tried, the trial by the rule of law(*a*) must be in some adjoining county; but, as there may be a strict interest so minute as not to occasion any bias, so there may be the strongest bias without any pecuniary interest. In all these cases, to summon a jury, laboring under local prejudices, is laying a snare for their consciences; and, though they should have virtue and vigor of mind sufficient to keep them upright, the parties will grow suspicious, and resort under various pretences to another mode of trial. The courts of law will therefore, in *transitory* actions, very often change the *venue*, or county wherein the cause is to be *384]   *tried:(*b*)(137) but in *local* actions, though they sometimes do it indirectly and by mutual consent, yet to effect it directly and absolutely, the parties are driven to a court of equity; where, upon making out a proper case, it is done upon the ground of being necessary to a fair, impartial, and satisfactory trial.(*c*)(138)

The locality of trial required by the common law seems a consequence of the ancient locality of jurisdiction. All over the world, actions transitory follow the person of the defendant, territorial suits must be discussed in the territorial tribunal. I may sue a Frenchman here for a debt contracted abroad; but lands lying in France must be sued for there, and English lands must be sued for in the kingdom of England. Formerly they were usually demanded only in the court-baron of the manor, where the steward could summon no jurors but such as were the tenants of the lord. When the cause was removed to the hundred court, (as seems to have been the course in the Saxon times,)(*d*) the lord of the hundred had a further power, to convoke the inhabitants of different vills to form a jury; observing probably always to intermix among them a stated number of tenants of that manor wherein the dispute arose. When afterwards it came to the county-court, the great tribunal of Saxon justice, the sheriff had wider authority, and could impanel a jury from the men of his county at large: but was obliged (as a mark of the original locality of the cause) to return a competent number of hundredors;

(*y*) See page 73.
(*z*) Stat. 13 Geo. III. c. 63.
(*a*) Stra. 177.
(*b*) See page 294.
(*c*) This, among a number of other instances, was

the case of the issues directed by the house of lords in the cause between the duke of Devonshire and the miners of the county of Derby, A. D. 1762.
(*d*) LL. Edw. Conf. c. 32   Wilk. 203.

---

(136) A court can compel the plaintiff to consent to have a witness going abroad examined upon interrogatories, or to have an absent witness examined under a commission, by the power the judges have of putting off the trial; but they have no control in these instances over the defendant.—CHRISTIAN.

(137) Titus *v.* Frankfort, 15 Maine, 89 (1838). Executors of Lynch *v.* Horry, 1 Bay (S. C.) 229 (1792). The venue may be changed after the issue is joined where strong prejudices existed which were unknown until after the issue was joined. Darmsdatt *v.* Wolfe, 4 Henning & Munford (Va.) 246 (1809).

(138) This may now be done in a court of law. Tidd, 8 ed. 655.—CHITTY.

omitting the inferior distinction, if indeed it ever existed.   And when at length, after the conquest, the king's justiciars drew the cognizance of the cause from the county-court, though they could have summoned a jury from any part of the kingdom, yet they chose to take the cause as they found it, with all its local appendages; triable by a stated number of hundredors, mixed with other freeholders of the county.   The restriction as to hundredors hath gradually worn away, and at length entirely vanished;(*e*) that of *counties still remains, for many beneficial purposes: but, as the   [*385 king's courts have a jurisdiction coextensive with the kingdom, there surely can be no impropriety in sometimes departing from the general rule, when the great ends of justice warrant and require an exception.

I have ventured to mark these defects, that the just panegyric, which I have given on the trial by jury, might appear to be the result of sober reflection, and not of enthusiasm or prejudice.   But should they, after all, continue unremedied and unsupplied, still (with all its imperfections) I trust that this mode of decision will be found the best criterion, for investigating the truth of facts, that was ever established in any country.

CHAPTER XXIV.

OF JUDGMENT AND ITS INCIDENTS.

*In the present chapter we are to consider the transactions in a   [*386 cause, next immediately subsequent to arguing the demurrer, or trial of the issue.

If the issue be an issue of fact, and, upon trial by any of the methods mentioned in the two preceding chapters, it be found for either the plaintiff or defendant, or specially; or if the plaintiff makes default, or is non-suit; or whatever, in short, is done subsequent to the joining of issue and awarding the trial, it is entered on record, and is called a *postea*.(*a*)   The substance of which is, that *postea, afterwards*, the said plaintiff and defendant appeared by their attorneys at the place of trial; and a jury, being sworn, found such a verdict; or, that the plaintiff, after the jury sworn, made default, and did not prosecute his suit; or, as the case may happen.   This is added to the roll, which is now returned to the court from which it was sent; and the history of the cause, from the time it was carried out, is thus continued by the *postea*.(1)

(*e*) See page 360.   (*a*) Append. No. II. § 6.

---

(1) As to the *postea* in general, see Tidd, 8 ed. 931 to 934. The verdict is entered on the back of the record of nisi prius, which entry, from the Latin word it began with, is called the *postea*. When the cause is tried in the King's Bench in London or Middlesex, the record is delivered to the attorney of the successful party, and he afterwards endorses the *postea* from the associate's minute on the panel; but in country causes the associate keeps the record till the next term, and then delivers it, with the *postea* endorsed, to the party obtaining the verdict. The practice is in some respects different in the Common Pleas, where in town causes also the record remains with the associate till the *quarto die post* [Fourth day after] of the return of the *habeas corpora juratorum* [That you have the bodies of the jury], who endorses the *postea* upon the record, but, by a recent order, it is not to be delivered till the morning of the fifth day of the term. See 1 Brod. & B. 298. 3 Moore. 643. If the *postea* be lost, a new one may, in some cases, be made out from the record above and the associate's notes, (2 Stra. 1264;) if wrong, it may be amended by the plea-roll, (1 Ld. Raym. 133,) by the memory or notes of the judge, (Cro. Car. 338. Bull. N. P. 320. 2 Stra. 1197. 6 T. R. 694. 1 Bar. & Ald. 161. 2 Cha. R. 352,) or the notes of the associate or clerk of assize. 2 Chitt. R. 352. 1 Bos. & Pul.

Next follows, *sixthly*, the judgment of the court upon what has previously passed; both the matter of law and matter of fact being now fully *387] weighed and adjusted. Judgment *may, however, for certain causes be *suspended*, or finally *arrested:* for it cannot be entered till the next term after trial had, and that upon notice to the other party. So that if any defect of justice happened at the trial, by surprise, inadvertence, or misconduct, the party may have relief in the court above, by obtaining a new trial; or if, notwithstanding the issue of fact be regularly decided, it appears that the complaint was either not actionable in itself, or not made with sufficient precision and accuracy, the party may supersede it by arresting or staying the judgment.

1. Causes of *suspending* the judgment, by granting a *new* trial, (2) are at present wholly *extrinsic*, arising from matter foreign to, or *dehors* the

---

329. The application to amend by the judge's notes must be made to the judge who tried the cause. 1 Chitt. R. 283. The court will not alter a verdict unless it appear on the face of it that the alteration would be according to the intention of the jury, (1 H. Bla. 78;) but not after a considerable lapse of time to increase damages, although the jury join in an affidavit stating their intention to have been to give the increased sum, and thought they had in effect done so. 2 T. R. 281; *sed vide* 1 Burr. 383, where a verdict was rectified which had been mistakenly delivered by the foreman. Where the jury had found the treble value in an action of debt on the statute for not setting out tithes, on a writ of inquiry, the inquisition was amended by the insertion of nominal damages. 1 Bingh. R. 182. In an action by one defendant in assumpsit against a co-defendant for contribution, the *postea* is evidence to prove the amount of the damages. 2 Stark, R. 364. See 9 Price, 359. Tidd, 8 ed. 932, 933. The production of the *postea* is not sufficient evidence of a judgment: a copy of the judgment founded thereon must also be produced. Bull. N. P. 234. Willes, 367. But the nisi prius record, with the *postea* endorsed, is sufficient to prove that the cause came on to be tried, (1 Stra. 162. Willes, 368,) or the day of trial. 6 Esp. R. 80, 83. See 9 Price, 359. Tidd, 8 ed. 977.—CHITTY.

(2) As to new trials in general, see Tidd, 8 ed. 934 to 949. When there are two contrary verdicts, it is not of course, but in the discretion of the court, to grant a new trial. 2 Bla. R. 963. In an inferior court it is said a new trial cannot be had upon the merits, but only for irregularity, (1 Salk. 201. 2 Salk. 650. 1 Stra. 113. 499. 1 Burr. 572. Doug. 380. 2 Chitty's R. 250;) but it may set aside a regular interlocutory judgment to let in a trial of the merits. 1 Burr. 571. The principal grounds for setting aside a verdict or non-suit, and granting a new trial, besides those mentioned in the text, are—1st. The discovery of new and material evidence since the trial. 2 Bla. Rep. 955. 2d. If the witnesses on whose testimony the verdict was obtained have been since convicted of perjury in giving their evidence, (M. 22 Geo. III. K. B.;) or if probable ground be laid to induce the court to believe that the witnesses are perjured, they will stay the proceedings on the finding of a bill of indictment against them for perjury, till the indictment is tried, (ib.;) but the circumstance of an indictment for perjury having been found against a witness is no ground of motion for new trial. 4 M. & S. 140. 8 Taunt. 182. 3d. For excessive damages, indicating passion or partiality in the jury. 1 Stra. 692. 1 Burr. 609. 3 Wils. 18. 2 Bl. Rep. 929. Cowp. 230. 5 T. R. 257. 7 ib. 529. 11 East, 23. It is not usual to grant a new trial for smallness of damages, (2 Salk. 647. 2 Stra. 940. Doug. 509. Barnes, 455, 456;) in which latter case it is said, if the demand is certain, as on a promissory-note, the court will set aside a verdict for too small damages, but not where the damages are uncertain. Lastly, it is a general rule not to grant a new trial, except for the misdirection of the judge, (4 T. R. 753. 5 ib. 19. 6 East, 316, (b). 1 Marsh. 555;) or where a point has been saved at the trial, (1 B. & P. 338;) in a penal, (2 Stra. 899. 10 East, 268. 4 M. & S. 338. 2 Chitty's R. 273,) hard, or trifling action, (2 Salk. 653. 3 Burr. 1306;) and an action is considered trifling in this respect when the sum to be recovered is under 20*l.* (5 Taunt. 537. 1 Chitty's R. 265, (a.),) unless the trial is to settle a right of a permanent nature. Ib. In all these cases, if the verdict be agreeable to equity and justice, the court will not grant a new trial, though there may have been an error in the admission or rejection of evidence, or in the direction of the judge, if it appear to the court on the whole matter disclosed by the report that the verdict ought to be confirmed. 4 T. R. 468.

A new trial cannot be granted in civil cases at the instance of *one* of several defendants, (12 Mod. 275. 2 Stra. 814,) nor for a *part* only of the cause of action. 2 Burr. 1224. 3 Wils. 47. But there may be cases in which the new trial is restricted to a particular part of the record, as if the judge give leave to move on one part or point only, on a stipula-

record.(3) Of this sort are want of notice of trial; or any flagrant misbehavior of the party prevailing towards the jury, which may have influenced their verdict; or any gross misbehavior of the jury among themselves:(4) also if it appears by the judge's report, certified by the court, that the jury have brought in a verdict without or contrary to evidence, so that he is reasonably dissatisfied therewith;(b) or if they have given exorbitant damages;(c) or if the judge himself has misdirected the jury, so that they found an unjustifiable verdict: for these, and other reasons of the like kind, it is the practice of the court to award a *new*, or second, *trial*.(5) But if two juries agree in the same or a similar verdict, a third trial is seldom awarded:(d) for the law will not readily suppose that the verdict of any one subsequent jury can countervail the oaths of the two preceding ones.

The exertion of these superintendent powers of the king's courts, in setting aside the verdict of a jury and granting a new trial, on account of misbehavior in the jurors, is of a date extremely ancient. There are instances, in the year-books of the reigns of Edward III., (e) Henry IV.,(f) and Henry VII.,(g) of judgments being stayed (even after a trial at bar) and *new *venires* awarded, because the jury had eat and drank without   [*388 consent of the judge, and because the plaintiff had privately given a paper to a juryman before he was sworn. And upon these the chief justice Glynn, in 1655, grounded the first precedent that is reported in our books(h) for granting a new trial upon account of *excessive damages* given by the jury: apprehending, with reason, that notorious partiality in the jurors was a principal species of misbehavior. A few years before, a practice took rise in the common pleas,(i) of granting new trials upon the mere certificate of the judge (unfortified by any report of the evidence) that the verdict had passed against his opinion; though chief justice Rolle (who allowed of new trials in case of misbehavior, surprise, or fraud, or if the verdict was notoriously contrary to evidence)(k) refused to adopt that practice in the court of king's bench. And

(b) Law of Nisi Prius, 303, 304.
(c) Comb. 357.
(d) 6 Mod. 22.   Salk. 649.
(e) 24 Edw. III. 24.   Bro. Abr. tit. *verdite*, 17.
(f) 11 Hen. IV. 18.   Bro. Abr. tit. *enquest*, 75.

(g) 14 Hen. VII. 1.   Bro. Abr. tit. *verdite*, 18.
(h) Styl. 466.
(i) Ibid. 238.
(k) 1 Sid. 235.   Styl. Pract. Reg. 310, 311, edit. 1657.

tion that counsel shall not move for any thing else; or if the court think injustice may be done by setting the whole matter at large again, they may restrict the second trial to certain particular points. 4 Taunt. 566.

In *criminal* cases no new trial can be granted where the defendant has been acquitted. 6 East, 315.   4 M. & S. 337.   1 B. & A. 64. Where several defendants are tried at the same time for a misdemeanor, and some are acquitted and others convicted, the court may grant a new trial to those convicted, if they think the conviction improper. 6 East, 619. See further, on this subject, Tidd, 8 ed. 934. In civil cases a motion for a new trial cannot be made after an unsuccessful motion in arrest of judgment. 4 Bar. & Cres. 160. The granting of a new trial is either without or upon payment of the costs of the former trial; or such costs are directed to abide the event of the suit. The general rule seems to be, that if the new trial be granted for the misbehavior of the jury or the misdirection of the judge, the costs are not required to be paid by the party applying for a new trial; but where the mere error of the jury, or the discovery of fresh evidence, is the ground, the costs must be paid by the party moving to set aside the former verdict. See Tidd, 8 ed. 945.—CHITTY. See People *v.* Comstock, 8 Wend. (N. Y.) 549 (1832). And in misdemeanors it seems a new trial may be granted where the defendant has been improperly *convicted*, but not where he has been acquitted. Ib.

(3) Bowie *v.* The State, 19 Ga. 1–6 (1855).

(4) Where, during the hearing of the evidence on the trial, and while the jury was temporarily separated, A., one of the jurors, asked B., a stranger, how he thought the case would go. B. replied that from the appearance of the jury he thought it would find for the plaintiff, and A. replied, "Yes, by God, I know it will," it was held that this was not such misconduct as would justify a court of error in reversing the judgment of the trial court sustaining the verdict. Harrison *v.* Price, 22 Ind. 165 (1864).

(5) In some special cases where justice requires it, a motion for a new trial may be made after a motion for arrest of judgment. Candler *v.* Hammond, 23 Ga. 493 (1857).

at that time it was clearly held for law,(*l*) that whatever matter was of force to avoid a verdict ought to be returned upon the *postea*,(6) and not merely surmised by the court; lest posterity should wonder why a new *venire* was awarded, without any sufficient reason appearing upon the record.(7) But very early in the reign of Charles the Second new trials were granted upon *affidavits;*(*m*) and the former strictness of the courts of law, in respect of new trials, having driven many parties into courts of equity to be relieved from oppressive verdicts,(8) they are now more liberal in granting them: the maxim at present adopted being this, that (in all cases of moment) where justice is not done upon one trial, the injured party is entitled to another.(*n*)(9)

Formerly the principal remedy, for reversal of a verdict unduly given, was by writ of *attaint;* of which we shall speak in the next chapter, and which is at least as old as the institution of the grand assize by Henry II.,(*o*) in lieu

of the Norman trial by battle. Such a sanction was probably thought
*necessary when, instead of appealing to Providence for the decision of a dubious right, it was referred to the oath of fallible or perhaps corrupted men. Our ancestors saw that a jury might give an erroneous verdict, and, if they did, that it ought not finally to conclude the question in the first instance: but the remedy, which they provided, shows the ignorance and ferocity of the times, and the simplicity of the points then usually litigated in the courts of justice. They supposed that, the law being told to the jury by the judge, the proof of fact must be always so clear, that, if they found a wrong verdict, they must be wilfully and corruptly perjured. Whereas a juror may find a just verdict from unrighteous motives, which can only be known to the great Searcher of hearts: and he may, on the contrary, find a verdict very manifestly wrong, without any bad motive at all; from inexperience in business, incapacity, misapprehension, inattention to circumstances, and a thousand other innocent causes. But such a remedy as this laid the injured party under an insuperable hardship, by making a conviction of the jurors for perjury the condition of his redress.

The judges saw this; and therefore very early, even upon writs of assize, they devised a great variety of distinctions, by which an attaint might be avoided, and the verdict set to rights in a more temperate and dispassionate method.(*p*) Thus, if excessive damages were given, they were moderated by the discretion of the justices.(*q*) And if, either in that or in any other instance, justice was not completely done, through the error of either the judge or the recognitors, it was remedied by *certificate of assize,* which was neither more nor less than a second trial of the same cause by the same jury.(*r*) And, in mixed or personal actions, as trespass and the like, (wherein no attaint originally lay,) if the jury gave a wrong verdict, the judges did not think themselves warranted thereby to pronounce an iniquitous judgment; but amended it, if possible, by subsequent inquiries of their own; and, *390] if that *could not be, they referred it to another examination.(*s*) When

*389]

(*l*) Cro. Eliz. 616. Palm. 325, 1 Brownl. 207.
(*m*) 1 Sid. 235. 2 Lev. 140.
(*n*) 4 Burr. 395.
(*o*) *Ipsi regni institutioni eleganter inserta.* [Dexterously inserted in that royal institution.] Glanv. *l.* 2, c. 19.
(*p*) Bract. *l.* 4, tr. 5, c. 4.
(*q*) Ibid. tr. 1, c. 19, § 8.

(*r*) Ibid. *l.* 4, tr. 5, c. 6, § 2. F. N. B. 181. 2 Inst. 415.
(*s*) *Si juratores erraverint, et justiciarii secundum eorum dictum judicium pronuntiaverint, falsum faciunt pronuntiationem: et ideo sequi non debent eorum dictum, sed illud emendare tenentur per diligentem examinationem. Si autem dijudicare nesciant, recurrendum erit ad majus judicium.* [If the jury shall have erred,

---

(6) [*Vide supra*, p. 386.]
(7) The People *v.* The Judges of Dutchess Oyer & Terminer, 2 Barb. (N. Y.) 282-286 (1847).
(8) Wells, Fargo & Co. *v.* Wall., 1 Ore. 295-299 (1860).
(9) Hilliard on New Trials (2 ed.) 2.

afterwards attaints, by several statutes, were more universally extended, the judges frequently, even for the misbehavior of jurymen, instead of prosecuting the writ of attaint, awarded a second trial; and subsequent resolutions for more than a century past have so amplified the benefit of this remedy that the attaint is now as obsolete as the trial by battle which it succeeded: and we shall probably see the revival of the one as soon as the revival of the other. And here I cannot but again admire(*t*) the wisdom of suffering time to bring to perfection new remedies, more easy and beneficial to the subject, which by degrees, from the experience and approbation of the people, supersede the necessity or desire of using or continuing the old.

If every verdict was final in the first instance, it would tend to destroy this valuable method of trial, and would drive away all causes of consequence to be decided according to the forms of the imperial law, upon depositions in writing, which might be reviewed in a course of appeal. Causes of great importance, titles to land, and large questions of commercial property come often to be tried by a jury, merely upon the general issue, where the facts are complicated and intricate, the evidence of great length and variety, and sometimes contradicting each other, and where the nature of the dispute very frequently introduces nice questions and subtleties of law. Either party may be surprised by a piece of evidence which, had he known of its production, he could have explained or answered; or he may be puzzled by a legal doubt which a little recollection would have solved.(10) In the hurry of a trial, the ablest judge may mistake the law and misdirect the jury; he may not be able so to state and range the evidence as to lay it clearly before them, nor to take off the artful impressions which have been made on their minds by learned and experienced advocates. The jury are to give their *opinion *instanter;* that is, before they separate, eat, or drink. And [*391 under these circumstances the most intelligent and best-intentioned men may bring in a verdict which they themselves upon cool deliberation would wish to reverse.

Next to doing right, the great object in the administration of public justice should be to give public satisfaction.(11) If the verdict be liable to many objections and doubts in the opinion of his counsel, or even in the opinion of bystanders, no party would go away satisfied unless he had a prospect of reviewing it. Such doubts would with him be decisive: he would arraign the determination as manifestly unjust, and abhor a tribunal which he imagined had done him an injury without a possibility of redress.

Granting a new trial, under proper regulations, cures all these inconveniences, and at the same time preserves entire and renders perfect that most excellent method of decision which is the glory of the English law.(12) A new trial is a rehearing of the cause before another jury, but with as little prejudice to either party as if it had never been heard before. No advantage is taken of the former verdict on the one side, or the rule of court for awarding such second trial on the other:(13) and the subsequent verdict, though

---

and the justices have pronounced judgment according to their verdict, they pronounce a false judgment;
and therefore ought not to follow up the verdict
but should amend it by a careful examination,—but

if they cannot decide it, it shall be referred to a
higher tribunal.] Bract. *l.* 4, *tr.* 5, c. 4, § 2.
(*t*) See page 268.

---

(10) Wellborn *v.* Younger, 3 N. C. (Hawks) 205 (1824). Lippincott *et al. v.* Souders, 3 Halstead (N. J.) 161 (1825).

(11) Fraser *v.* Willey, 2 Fla. 116-124 (1848).

(12) Horn *v.* Queen, 4 Neb. 108-112 (1875). Halley *v.* M'Cargo, 4 Ky. (Bibb.) 349-353 (1816).

(13) The State *v.* Hornsby, 8 La. 583-587 (1844).

contrary to the first, imports no tittle of blame upon the former jury, who, had they possessed the same lights and advantages, would probably have altered their own opinion. The parties come better informed, the counsel better prepared, the law is more fully understood, the judge is more master of the subject; and nothing is now tried but the real merits of the case.

A sufficient ground must, however, be laid before the court, to satisfy them that it is necessary to justice that the cause should be further considered.(14) If the matter be such as did not or could not appear to the judge who presided at *nisi prius*, it is disclosed to the court by *affidavit:* if it arises from what passed at the trial, it is taken from the judge's information, who usually

*392] makes a special and minute report of the evidence. Counsel are heard on both sides to impeach *or establish the verdict and the court give their reasons at large why a new examination ought or ought not to be allowed. The true import of the evidence is duly weighed, false colors are taken off, and all points of law which arose at the trial are upon full deliberation clearly explained and settled.

Nor do the courts lend too easy an ear to every application for a review of the former verdict. They must be satisfied that there are strong probable grounds to suppose that the merits have not been fairly and fully discussed, and that the decision is not agreeable to the justice and truth of the case. (15) A new trial is not granted where the value is too inconsiderable to merit a second examination. It is not granted upon nice and formal objections, which do not go to the real merits. It is not granted in cases of strict right or *summum jus*, where the rigorous exaction of extreme legal justice is hardly reconcilable to conscience. Nor is it granted where the scales of evidence hang nearly equal:(16) that which leans against the former verdict ought always very strongly to preponderate.

In granting such further trial (which is matter of sound discretion)(17) the court has also an opportunity, which it seldom fails to improve, of supplying those defects in this mode of trial which were stated in the preceding chapter; by laying the party applying under all such equitable terms as his antagonist shall desire and mutually offer to comply with: such as the discovery of some facts upon oath; the admission of others not intended to be litigated; the production of deeds, books, and papers; the examination of witnesses, infirm or going beyond sea; and the like. And the delay and expense of this proceeding are so small and trifling, that it seldom can be moved for to gain time or to gratify humor. The motion must be made within the first four days of the next succeeding term, within which term it is usually heard and decided. And it is worthy observation, how infinitely superior to all others the trial by jury approves itself, even in the very mode

*393] of its revision. In every other country of Europe, and in those of our own tribunals which conform themselves to the *process of the civil law, the parties are at liberty, whenever they please, to appeal from day to day, and from court to court, upon questions merely of fact; which is a perpetual source of obstinate chicane, delay, and expensive litigation.(u) With us no new trial is allowed unless there be a manifest mistake,

---

(u) Not many years ago an appeal was brought to the house of lords from the court of session in Scotland, in a cause between Napier and Macfarlane. It was instituted in March, 1745, and (after many interlocutory orders and sentences below, appealed from and reheard as far as the course of proceedings would admit) was finally determined in April, 1749,—the question being only on the property in an ox, adjudged to be of the value of three guineas. No pique or spirit could have made such a cause, in the court of King's Bench or Common Pleas, have lasted a tenth of that time, or have cost a twentieth part of the expense.

---

(14) Handley *v.* Call, 27 Me. 35-47 (1847). Sumner *v.* Lyman, 1 Kirby (Conn.) 241-244 (1787).
(15) Hipp *v.* Bissell, 3 Tex. 18-20 (1848).
(16) Horn *v.* Queen, 4 Neb. 108-112 (1875). Tingley *v.* Dolby, 13 Neb. 371-374 (1882).
(17) Lester *v.* The State, 11 Conn. 415-418 (1836).

and the subject-matter be worthy of interposition. The party who thinks himself aggrieved may still, if he pleases, have recourse to his writ of attaint(18) after judgment; in the course of the trial he may d mur to the evidence, or tender a bill of exceptions. And, if the first is totally laid aside, and the other two very seldom put in practice, it is because long experience has shown that a motion for a second trial is the shortest, cheapest, and most effectual cure for all imperfections in the verdict; whether they arise from the mistakes of the parties themselves, of their counsel, or attorneys, or even of the judge or jury.(19)

2. Arrests of judgment(20) arise from *intrinsic* causes, appearing upon the face of the record.(21) Of this kind are, first, where the declaration varies totally from the original writ;(22) as where the writ is in debt or detinue, and the plaintiff declares in an. action on the case for an *assumpsit;* for, the original writ out of chancery being the foundation and warrant of the whole proceedings in the common pleas, if the declaration does not pursue the nature of the writ, the court's authority totally fails.(23) Also, secondly, where the verdict materially differs from the pleadings and issue thereon;(24) as if, in an action for words, it is laid in the declaration that the defendant said, "the plaintiff *is* a bankrupt;" and the verdict finds specially that he said, "the plaintiff *will be* a bankrupt." Or, thirdly, if the case laid in the declaration is not sufficient in point of law to found an action upon.(25) And this is an invariable *rule with regard to arrests of judgment [*394 upon matter of law, "that whatever is alleged in arrest of judgment must be such matter as would upon demurrer have been sufficient to overturn the action or plea."(26) As if, on an action for slander in calling the plaintiff a Jew, the defendant denies the words, and issue is joined thereon; now if a

----

(18) This writ is now abolished.

(19) Where it would be proper for a court of law to grant a new trial, if the application had been made while that court had the power, it is equally proper for a court of equity to do so, if the application be made when the court of law has no means of granting such trial; but it will only interfere in case of newly discovered evidence, surprise or fraud, or where a party is deprived of the means of defence by circumstances beyond his control. Horn *v.* Queen, 4 Neb. 108 (1875).

(20) The parties cannot move in arrest of judgment for any thing that is aided after verdict at common law, or by the statute of amendments, or cured, as matter of form, by the statute of jeofails. See 1 Saund. 228, n. (1.) It is a general rule that a verdict will aid a title imperfectly set out, but not an imperfect title. 2 Burr. 1159. 3 Wils. 275. 4 T. R. 472. The defendant cannot move in arrest of judgment for anything which he might have pleaded in abatement. 2 Bla. R. 1120. Surplusage will not vitiate after verdict; as in trover stating the possession of the goods in plaintiff on the 3d of March, and the conversion by defendant "afterwards *to wit on the 1st of March,*" it was held that afterwards might stand, and the other words be treated as surplusage. Cro. C. 428. The motion in arrest of judgment, etc. may be made in the King's Bench at any time before judgment is given, (5 T. R. 445. 2 Stra. 845,) though a new trial has been previously moved for. Doug. 745, 746. In the Common Pleas, the motion must be made before or on the appearance-day of the return of the *habeas corpora juratorum* [That you have the bodies of the jurymen]. Barnes, 445. In the Exchequer, the motion must be made within the first four days of the next term after the trial, and it may be made after an unsuccessful motion for a new trial. See Manning's Ex. Prac. 353. Tidd, 960, 961; but see 7 Price, 566.

If the judgment be arrested in consequence of mistake of the form of action, or otherwise, the plaintiff is at liberty to proceed *de novo* [Anew] in a fresh action. 1 Mod. 207. Vin. Abr. tit. Judgment, Q. 4. Bla. R. 831. Each party pays his own costs upon the judgment being arrested. Cowp. 407.—CHITTY.

(21) Westfield Gas, etc. Co. *v.* Abernathy, 8 Ind. 73–83 (1893).

(22) Robinson *v.* Hartrigde, 13 Fla. 501-8 (1871). Hanly & Scott *v.* Holmes, 1 Mo. 84-85 (1821).

(23) Now no form of action is stated in the writ. Com. Law Proc. Act. (1853) s. 3.—STEWART.

(24) Bower's Com. on Const. Law of Eng. 306.

(25) Smith *v.* Dodds, 35 Ind. 452–459 (1871). Lee *v.* Emery, 10 Minn. 187-190 (1865).

(26) Sedgwick *v.* Dawkins, 18 Fla. 335–339 (1881).

verdict be found for the plaintiff, that the words were actually spoken, whereby the fact is established, still the defendant may move in arrest of judgment, that to call a man a Jew is not actionable: and, if the court be of that opinion, the judgment shall be arrested and never entered for the plaintiff. But the rule will not hold *e converso*, "that every thing that may be alleged as cause of demurrer will be good in arrest of judgment;" for if a declaration or plea omits to state some particular circumstance, without proving of which at the trial it is impossible to support the action or defence, this omission shall be aided by a verdict. As if, in an action of trespass, the declaration doth not allege that the tresspass was committed on any certain day;(*w*) or if the defendant justifies, by prescribing for a right of common for his cattle, and does not plead that his cattle were *levant* and *couchant* on the land;(*x*)(27) though either of these defects might be good cause to demur to the declaration or plea, yet if the adverse party omits to take advantage of such omission in due time, but takes issue, and has a verdict against him, these exceptions cannot after verdict be moved in arrest of judgment.(28) For the verdict ascertains those facts, which before from the inaccuracy of the pleadings might be dubious; since the law will not suppose, that a jury under the inspection of a judge would find a verdict for the plaintiff or defendant, unless he had proved those circumstances, without which his general allegation is defective.(*y*)(29) Exceptions therefore that are moved in arrest of judgment must be much more material and glaring than such as will maintain a demurrer: or, in other words, many inaccuracies and omissions, which would be fatal if early observed, are cured by a subsequent verdict; and not suffered, in the last stage of a cause, to unravel
*395]   the whole proceedings.(30)   *But if the thing omitted be essential to the action or defence, as if the plaintiff does not merely state his title in a defective manner, but sets forth a title that is totally defective in itself,(*z*) or if to an action of debt the defendant pleads *not guilty* instead of *nil debet*,(*a*)(31) these cannot be cured by a verdict for the plaintiff in the first case, or for the defendant in the second.(32)

(*w*) Carth. 389.
(*x*) Cro. Jac. 44.
(*y*) 1 Mod. 292.

(*z*) Salk. 365.
(*a*) Cro. Eliz. 778.

(27) See, however, 1 Saund. 228, note 1.—CHITTY.
(28) Thompson *v.* Musser, 1 Dall. (Pa.) 480-484 (1789).
(29) It is correctly observed, upon this passage, that though Sir W. Blackstone has stated with correctness the principle upon which defects are aided by a verdict at common law, yet his two examples are instances of defects aided after verdict by the statute of jeofails. See *post*, 408. Stewart *v.* Hogg, 1 Saund. 228, n. (1.) In the first case the trespass was alleged to *have been* committed on a day not yet come, this was clearly no omission of any circumstance necessary in the proof, but a formal misstatement. So again, where the party stated a prescriptive right of common, but neglected to bring his case formally within it by averring the levancy and couchancy of the cattle, which was one condition of the prescription, the issue being taken on the prescription itself, no proof was necessary that the particular cattle were levant and couchant in fact; the omission of that fact therefore was not the omission of a circumstance necessary in the proof: in other words, the verdict in neither case raises a presumption that the fact omitted was proved to the jury. But an instance in point may be put thus: if a man states the grant of a reversion, which can only be conveyed by deed, without alleging it to have been by deed, here if the fact of the grant be put in issue and found by the jury, the verdict covers the omission; for without proof of the deed the presumption is that it could not have been so found.—COLERIDGE.
(30) Gander *v.* The State, 50 Ind. 539-541 (1875). Flanders *v.* Stewartstown, 47 N. H. 549-550 (1867).
(31) [He does not owe.]
(32) Wilbridge *et al. v.* Case, 2 Ind. (Carter) 36-37 (1850). Beale *et al. v.* Commonwealth, 16 S. & R. (Pa.) 150-153 (1827).

If, by the misconduct or inadvertence of the pleaders,(33) the issue be joined on a fact totally immaterial, or insufficient to determine the right, so that the court upon the finding cannot know for whom judgment ought to be given; as if, in an action on the case in *assumpsit* against an executor, he pleads that he himself (instead of the testator) made no such promise:(*b*) or if, in an action of debt on bond conditioned to pay money *on* or *before* a certain day, the defendant pleads payment *on* the day:(*c*) (which issue, if found for the plaintiff, would be inconclusive, as the money might have been paid *before;*) in these cases the court will after verdict award a *repleader quod partes replacitent;*(34) unless it appears from the whole record that nothing material can possibly be pleaded in any shape whatsoever, and then a repleader would be fruitless.(*d*) And, whenever a repleader is granted, the pleadings must begin *de novo*(35) at that stage of them, whether it be the plea, replication, or rejoinder, etc., wherein there appears to have been the first defect, or deviation from the regular course.(*e*)

If judgment is not by some of these means arrested within the first four days of the next term after the trial, it is then to be entered on the roll or record.(36) Judgments are the sentence of the law, pronounced by the court upon the matter contained in the record;(37) and are of four sorts. First, where the facts are confessed by the parties, and the law determined by the court; as in case of judgment upon *demurrer:* secondly, where the law is admitted by the parties and the facts disputed; as in case of judgment on a *verdict:* thirdly, where *both the fact and the law arising thereon　[*396 are admitted by the defendant; which is the case of judgments by *confession* or *default:*(38) or, lastly, where the plaintiff is convinced that either fact, or law, or both, are insufficient to support his action, and therefore abandons or withdraws his prosecution; which is the case in judgments upon a *non-suit* or *retratrix.*

(*b*) 2 Ventr. 190.
(*c*) Stra. 994.

(*d*) 4 Burr. 301, 302.
(*e*) Raym. 458.　Salk. 579.

---

(33) The following rules have been laid down on this subject. A repleader ought never to be allowed till trial, because the fault of the issue may be helped after the verdict by the statute of jeofails. 2dly. If a repleader be denied where it should be granted, or granted where it should be denied, it is error. 3dly. The judgment of repleader is general, and the parties must begin again at the first fault which occasioned the immaterial issue. 1 Lord Raym. 169. Thus, if the declaration be ill, and the bar and replication are also ill, the parties must begin *de novo* [Anew]; but if the bar be good and the replication ill, at the replication. 3 Keb. 664. 4thly. No costs are allowed on either side. 6 T. R. 131. 2 B. & P. 376. 5thly. That a repleader cannot be awarded after a default at nisi prius; to which may be added, that it can never be awarded after a demurrer or writ of error, but only after issue joined, (3 Salk. 306,) nor where the court can give judgment on the whole record, (Willes, 532;) and it is not grantable in favor of the person who made the first fault in pleading. Doug. 396. See 2 Saund. 319, b.—CHITTY.

(34) [That the parties may replead.] Carmichael *v.* Browder's Adm'rs, 4 Howard (Miss.) 431-434 (1840).

(35) [Anew.]

(36) If a verdict is taken generally, with entire damages, judgment may be arrested if any one count in the declaration is bad; but if there is a general verdict of guilty upon an indictment consisting of several counts, and any one count is good, that is held to be sufficient. Doug. 730.—CHITTY.

(37) Lawson's Rights, Rem. & Prac. 5387. Binns' Justice (Brightly) 10 ed. 1895. Whittem *v.* The State, 36 Ind. 196-204 (1871). Gifford *v.* Livingstone, 2 Denio (N. Y.) 380-391 (1845). Humboldt M. & M. Co. *v.* Terry, 11 Nev. 237-243 (1876). Williams *v.* McGrade, 13 Minn. 46-48 (1868). Blaikie *v.* Griswold, 10 Wis. 293-300 (1860). Ludlow *v.* City of Norfolk, 87 Va. 319-322 (1891). McDonald *v.* Bunn, 3 Denio (N. Y.) 45-49 (1846). Lockwood *v.* Saffold, 1 Kelly (Ga.) 72-74 (1846). But the adjustment and liquidation of a conservator's account by the county court is not a judgment. Spalding *v.* Butts, 5 Conn. 427 (1824).

(38) Thompson *v.* Gilmore, 50 Me. 428-430 (1861).

The judgment, though pronounced or awarded by the judges, is not their determination or sentence, but the determination and sentence of *the law*. It is the conclusion that naturally and regularly follows from the premises of law and fact, which stand thus: against him, who hath rode over my corn, I may recover damages by law: but A. hath rode over my corn; therefore I shall recover damages against A. If the major proposition be denied, this is a demurrer in law: if the minor, it is then an issue of fact: but if both be confessed (or determined) to be right, the conclusion or judgment of the court cannot but follow. Which judgment or conclusion depends not therefore on the arbitrary caprice of the judge, but on the settled and invariable principles of justice. The judgment, in short, is the remedy prescribed by law for the redress of injuries; and the suit or action is the vehicle or means of administering it. What that remedy may be, is indeed the result of deliberation and study to point out; and therefore the style of the judgment is, not that it is decreed or resolved by the court, for then the judgment might appear to be their own; but, "it is considered," *consideratum est per curiam*,(39) that the plaintiff do recover his damages, his debt, his possession, and the like: which implies that the judgment is none of their own; but the act of law, pronounced and declared by the court, after due deliberation and inquiry.(40)

All these species of judgments are either *interlocutory* or *final*. *Interlocutory* judgments are such as are given in the middle of a cause, upon some plea proceeding, or default which is only intermediate, and does not finally determine or complete the suit.(41) Of this nature are all judgments for the plaintiff upon pleas in abatement of the suit or action: in *which

[*397

it is considered by the court, that the defendant do answer over, *respondeat ouster;* that is, put in a more substantial plea.(*f*)(42) It is easy to observe, that the judgment here given is not final, but merely interlocutory; for there are afterwards further proceedings to be had, when the defendant has put in a better answer.

But the interlocutory judgments, most usually spoken of, are those incomplete judgments, whereby the *right* of the plaintiff is indeed established, but the *quantum* of damages sustained by him is not ascertained: which is a matter that cannot be done without the intervention of a jury. As by the old Gothic constitution the cause was not completely finished, till the *nembda* or jurors were called in " *ad executionem decretorum judicii, ad æstimationem pretii, damni lucri, etc.*"(*g*)(43) This can only happen where the plaintiff recovers; for, when judgment is given for the defendant, it is always complete as well as final. And this happens, in the first place, where the defendant suffers judgment to go against him by default, or *nihil dicit;* as if he puts in no plea at all to the plaintiff's declaration: by confession or *cognovit actionem,* where he acknowledges the plaintiff's demand to be just: or by *non sum informatus,*(44) when the defendant's attorney declares he has no instruction to say any thing in answer to the plaintiff, or in defence of his client; which is a species of judgment by default.(45) If these, or any of

---

(*f*) 2 Saund. 30.   (*g*) Stiernhook, *de jure Goth. l.* 1, c. 4.

(39) [It is considered by the court.]
(40) Nuckolls *v.* Irwin, 2 Neb. 60–64 (1873). Ensworth *v.* Davenport, 9 Conn. 390–393 (1832). Low *v.* Commissioners of Pilotage, 1 Charlton (Ga.) 302–309 (1830).
(41) Lockwood *v.* Jones, 7 Conn. 431–446 (1829). Ward *v.* Ward, 37 Tex. 389–390 (1872).
(42) Jenks *v.* The State, 16 Wis. 332 (1863).
(43) ["To execute the decrees of court, to estimate the price, damage, gain, etc."]
(44) [I am not instructed.]
(45) 1 Sch. Pers. Prop. 2 ed. 421. Williams on Pers. Prop. 4 ed. 98.

them, happen in action where the specific thing sued for is recovered, as in actions of debt for a sum certain, the judgment is absolutely complete. And therefore it is very usual, in order to strengthen a creditor's security, for the debtor to execute a warrant of attorney to some attorney named by the creditor, empowering him to confess a judgment by either of the ways just now mentioned (by *nihil dicit*, *cognovit actionem*, or *non sum informatus*) in an action of debt to be brought by the creditor against the debtor for the specific sum due:(46) which judgment, when confessed, is absolutely complete and binding; provided the same (as is also required in all other judgments) be regularly *docquetted*, that is, abstracted and entered in a book, *according to the directions of statute 4 & 5 W. and M. c. 20.(47)   [*398 But, where damages are to be recovered, a jury must be called in to assess them; unless the defendant, to save charges, will confess the whole damages laid in the declaration: otherwise the entry of the judgment is, "that the plaintiff ought to recover his damages, (indefinitely,) but, because the court know not what damages the said plaintiff hath sustained, therefore the sheriff is commanded, that by the oaths of twelve honest and lawful men he inquire into the said damages, and return such inquisition into court." This process is called a *writ of inquiry:* in the execution of which the sheriff sits as judge, and tries by a jury, subject to nearly the same laws and conditions as the trial by jury at *nisi prius*,(48) what damages the plaintiff hath really sustained; and when their verdict is given, which must assess *some* damages, the sheriff returns the inquisition, which is entered upon the roll in manner of a *postea;*(49) and thereupon it is considered, that the plaintiff do recover the exact sum of the damages so assessed. In like manner, when a demurrer is determined for the plaintiff upon an action wherein damages are recovered, the judgment is also incomplete, without the aid of a writ of inquiry.(50)

---

(46) For the purpose of preventing frauds upon creditors by secret warrants of attorney to confess judgment, it is enacted, by statute 3 Geo. IV. c. 39, enlarged by 6 & 7 Vict. c. 66, that the clerk of the dockets of the court of Queen's Bench shall cause a book in which the particulars of every warrant of attorney and *cognovit actionem* shall be entered; and also a book or index shall be kept of names of persons to whom warrants of attorney are given, which shall be open to inspection. And by the Bankrupt-Law Consolidation Act, 1849, s. 137, every judge's order given by a trader defendant, whereby the plaintiff is authorized to sign judgment or issue execution, (or a copy of this order,) must be filed with the clerk of the docquets in the Queen's Bench within twenty-one days after the making of such order: otherwise judgment signed thereon, or execution issued, shall be null and void. And by stat. 1 & 2 Vict. c. 110, a more important alteration has been made in the same respecting warrants of attorney and cognovits. By s. 9, after reciting that it is expedient that provision should be made for giving every person executing such instruments due information of the nature thereof, it is enacted that no warrant of attorney or cognovit shall be of any force unless an attorney of one of the superior courts shall be present on behalf of the person executing it and shall subscribe his name as a witness. And by s. 10, a warrant of attorney or cognovit not formally executed shall be invalid.—STEWART.

(47) The judgment must be re-registered every five years, in order to remain in force and preserve its priority of subsequent judgment-creditors. 1 & 2 Vict. c. 110. 3 & 4 Vict. c. 82, s. 2. 2 Vict. c. 11, s. 1. 18 & 19 Vict. c. 15, s. 4. Freer *v.* Hesse, 22 L. F. Chanc. 597.—KERR.

(48) [Unless before.]

(49) [*Vide supra*, p. 386.]

(50) It has been said by C. J. Wilmot that "this is an inquest of office to inform the conscience of the court, who, if they please, may themselves assess the damages." 3 Wils. 62. Hence a practice is now established in the courts of King's Bench and Common Pleas, in actions where judgment is recovered by default upon a bill of exchange or a promissory-note, to refer it to the master or prothonotary to ascertain what is due for principal, interest, and costs, whose report supersedes the necessity of a writ of inquiry. 4 T. R. 275. 1 H. Bla. 541. And this practice is now adopted by the court of exchequer. 4 Price, 134. See, further, Tidd, 8 ed. 817, 818, 819. In cases of difficulty

Final judgments are such as at once put an end to the action by declaring that the plaintiff has either entitled himself, or has not, to recover the remedy he sues for.(51) In which case, if the judgment be for the plaintiff, it is also considered that the defendant be either amerced, for his wilful delay of justice in not immediately obeying the king's writ by rendering the plaintiff his due;(h) or be taken up, *capiatur*, till he pays a fine to the king for the public misdemeanor which is coupled with the private injury in all cases of force,(i) of falsehood in denying his own deed,(k) or unjustly claiming property in replevin, or of contempt by disobeying the command of the king's writ or the express prohibition of any statute.(l) But now in case of trespass, ejectment, assault, and false imprisonment, it is provided, by the statute 5 & 6 W. and M. c. 12, *that no writ of *capias* shall issue for this fine, nor any fine be paid; but the plaintiff shall pay 6s. 8d. to the proper officer, and be allowed it against the defendant among his other costs. And therefore upon such judgments in the common pleas they used to enter that the fine was remitted; and now in both courts they take no notice of any fine or *capias* at all.(m) But if judgment be for the defendant, then, in case of fraud and deceit to the court or malicious or vexatious suits, the plaintiff may also be fined;(n) but in most cases it is only considered that he and his pledges of prosecuting be (nominally) amerced for his false claim, *pro falso clamore suo*, and that the defendant may go thereof without a day, *eat inde sine die*, that is, without any further continuance or adjournment; the king's writ, commanding his attendance, being now fully satisfied, and his innocence publicly cleared.(o)(52)

*399]

(h) 8 Rep. 40, 61.
(i) 8 Rep. 59. 11 Rep. 43. 5 Mod. 285. See Append. No. II. § 4.
(k) F. N. B. 121. Co. Litt. 131. 8 Rep. 60. 1 Roll. Abr. 219. Lill. Entr. 379, C. B. Hil. 4 Ann. rot. 430.

(l) 8 Rep. 60.
(m) Salk. 54. Carth. 390.
(n) 8 Rep. 59, 60.
(o) Append. No. III. § 6.

and importance, the court will give leave to have the writ of inquiry executed before a judge at sittings or nisi prius; and then the judge acts only as an assistant to the sheriff. The number of the jurors sworn upon this inquest need not be confined to twelve; for when a writ of inquiry was executed at the bar of the court of King's Bench, in an action of *scandalum magnatum* [Scandal against the peerage] brought by the duke of York (afterwards James the Second) against Titus Oates, who had called him a traitor, fifteen were sworn upon the jury, who gave all the damages laid in the declaration,—viz., 100,000l. In that case the sheriffs of Middlesex sat in court, covered, at the table below the judges. 3 St. Tr. 987. CHRISTIAN.

Before the 8 & 9 W. III. c. 11, the penalty in a bond for the performance of covenants became forfeited upon a single breach thereof; but now, by the 8th section of that statute, though the plaintiff is permitted to enter up judgment for the whole penalty, it can only stand as a security for the damages actually sustained. The plaintiff must then proceed by suggesting breaches on the roll, of which it is usual to give a copy to the defendant, with notice of inquiry for the sittings or assizes; and the damages are assessed upon the writ in the usual way by a jury; and, upon payment of them, execution upon the judgment entered up is stayed, the judgment itself remaining as a security against further breaches. See Tidd, 8 ed. 632. This statute does not extend to a bond conditioned for the payment of a sum certain at a day certain, as a post-obit bond, (2 B. & C. 82,) nor a common money bond, (4 Anne, c. 16, s. 13. 1 Saund. 58.) nor a warrant of attorney payable by instalments, (3 Taunt. 74. 5 Taunt. 264,) though a bond be also given, (2 Taunt. 195,) nor to a bail-bond, (2 B. & P. 446,) nor a petitioning creditor's bond. 3 East, 22. 7 T. R. 300. But all other bonds, either for payment of money by instalments, or of annuities, or for the performance of any covenants or agreements, are within the statute. See 8 T. R. 126. 6 East, 550. 2 Saund. 187, n. (c.) 3 M. & S. 156. 1 Chitty on Pl. 507, where the parties in a bond agree that the sum mentioned to be paid on a breach of any of its covenants shall be taken to be, and be considered as, *stipulated damages*, the case is not then within the statute, and the whole sum becomes at once payable, according to the terms of the agreement; for, where the precise sum is the ascertained damage, the jury are confined to it. See 4 Burr. 2225. 2 B. & P. 346. 1 Camp. 78. 2 T. R. 32. Holt. Rep. 43.—CHITTY.

(51) Hardeman v. Downer, 39 Ga. 425-451 (1869). Lockwood v. Jones, 7 Conn. 431-446 (1829). Taylor v. Towner, 8 Ohio (O. S.) 136-141 (1837).

(52) At common law the *death* of a sole plaintiff or sole defendant at any time before

Thus much for judgments; to which costs are a necessary appendage; it being now as well the maxim of ours as of the civil law that "*victus victori in expensis condemnandus est:*" (*p*)(53) though the common law did not professedly allow any, the amercement of the vanquished party being his only punishment. The first statute which gave costs, *eo nomine*,(54) to the demandant in a real action was the statute of Gloucester, 6 Edw. I. c. 1, as did the statute of Marlberge, 52 Hen. III. c. 6, to the defendant in one particular case, relative to wardship in chivalry; though in reality costs were always considered and included in the *quantum* of damages in such actions where damages are given; and even now costs for the plaintiff are always entered on the roll as increase of damages by the court.(*q*)(55) But because those damages were frequently inadequate to the plaintiff's expenses, the statute of Gloucester orders costs to be also added; and further directs that the same rule shall hold place in all cases where the party is to recover damages. And therefore, in such actions where no damages were then recoverable, (as in *quare impedit*,(56) in which *damages were   [*400 not given till the statute of Westm. 2, 13 Edw. I.,) no costs are now allowed,(*r*) unless they have been expressly given by some subsequent statute.(57) The statute 3 Hen. VII. c. 10 was the first which allowed any costs on a writ of error. But no costs were allowed the *defendant* in any shape till •the statutes 23 Hen. VIII. c. 15, 4 Jac. I. c. 3, 8 & 9 W. III. c. 11, 4 & 5 Anne, c. 16, which very equitably gave the defendant, if he prevailed, the same costs as the plaintiff would have had in case he had

(*p*) Cod. 3, 1, 13.
(*q*) Append. No. II. ? 4.

(*r*) 10 Rep. 116.

---

final judgment abated the suit; but now, by 17 Car. II. c. 8, where either party dies between *verdict* and judgment, it may still be entered up within two terms after the verdict. This statute does not apply where either party dies after *interlocutory* judgment and before the return of the inquiry. 4 Taunt. 884. There must be a *scire facias* to revive the judgment thus entered up before execution. 1 Wils. 302. By the 8 & 9 W. III. c. 11, the *casus omissus* [Case omitted] in the statute of Charles II. is supplied. It provides that in case of either party dying between interlocutory and final judgment in any action which might have been maintained by or against the personal representative of the party dying; or in case of one or more of the plaintiffs or defendants dying, in an action the cause of which would by law survive to the survivors, the action shall not abate by reason thereof, but, the death being suggested on the record, the action shall proceed. The death of either party in the interval of hearing and deciding upon motions in arrest of judgment, special verdicts, and the like, does not deprive the party of the right to enter up judgment, though the delay thus occasioned by the court may exceed two terms after verdict. See Tidd, 8 ed. 966, 967, 1168, 1169. It has been held that if the party die after the assizes begin, though before the trial of the cause, it is within the statute, which, being remedial, must be construed favorably, the assizes being considered but as one day in law. 1 Salk. 8. 7 T. R. 31. See 2 Ld. Raym. 1415, n. But, in the Common Pleas, a verdict and judgment were set aside when the defendant died the night before trial at the sittings in term. 3 B. & P. 549. And where the verdict has been taken subject to a reference, the death of a party before an award revokes the authority of the arbitrator. 1 Marsh. 366. 2 B. & A. 394. 2 Chitt. R. 432.—Chitty.

(53) ["He who loses the suit pays the costs thereof to the successful party."] Robinson *v*. Roberts, 16 Fla. 156–157 (1877).

(54) [By that name.]

(55) McRea *v*. Brown, 2 Mun. 46, 48 (Va. 1811). Douglas *v*. McCoy, 24 W. Va. 722, 727 (1884).

(56) [Why he impedes.]

(57) Wherever a party has sustained damage, and a new act gives another than the common-law remedy, such party may recover costs as well as damages; for the statute of Gloucester extends to give costs in all cases where damages are given to any plaintiff, in any action, by any statute after that parliament. 2 Inst. 289. 6 T. R. 355.—Chitty.

recovered.(58)   These costs, on both sides, are taxed and moderated by the prothonotary, or other proper officer of the court.(59)

The king (and any person suing to his use)(s) shall neither pay nor receive costs; for, besides that he is not included under the general words of these statutes, as it is his prerogative not to pay them to a subject, so it is beneath his dignity to receive them.(60)   And it seems reasonable to suppose that the queen-consort participates of the same privilege; for in actions brought by her she was not at the common law obliged to find pledges of prosecution, nor could be amerced in case there was judgment against her.(t)   In two other cases an exemption also lies from paying costs. Executors and administrators, when suing in the right of the deceased, shall pay none;(u) for the statute 23 Hen. VIII. c. 15 doth not give costs to the defendants unless where the action supposeth the contract to be made with, or the wrong to be done to, the plaintiff himself.(61)   And paupers, that is, such as will

(s) Stat. 24 Hen. VIII. c. 8.   (u) Cro. Jac. 229. 1 Ventr. 92.
(t) F. N. B. 101. Co. Litt. 133.

(58) It is by virtue of statute law alone that judgment for costs *eo nomine* [By that name] can be rendered in favor of either party.   West *v.* Ferguson, 16 Gratt. 270, 271 (Va. 1861).   Wilkinson *v.* Hoke, 39 W. Va. 403, 405 (1894).

(59) By the Louisiana code, costs are due and may be collected on execution, even although the decree is silent with regard to them.   Borgstede *v.* Clark, 5 La. Ann. 733, 734 (1850).

(60) There are some exceptions to the rule that the king neither pays nor receives costs.   Thus, by 33 Hen. VIII. c. 39, s. 54, the king in all suits, upon any obligations or specialties made to himself or to his use, shall have and recover his just debts, *costs*, and damages, as other common persons used to do.   By the 25 Geo III. c. 35, if the goods and chattels are insufficient, (3 Price, 40,) and the lands are sold towards discharging the debt due to the crown in such case, "all *costs* and expenses incurred by the crown in enforcing the payment of such debt are to be paid."   By 43 Geo. III. c. 99, s. 41, *costs* may be levied against collectors of taxes in certain cases.   See 3 Price 280.   In equity, the attorney-general receives costs where he is made a defendant in respect of legacies given to charities, or in respect of the immediate rights of the crown in cases of intestacy. And see 1 S. & S. 394.—CHITTY.

This principle, so far as it applies to the payment of costs by the state, has been adopted as a general principle of American law; so, in criminal cases, county officers are not entitled to recover any costs against the state or county where the defendants are either acquitted, or discharged upon *nolle prosequi* [An unwillingness to prosecute], and in cases of conviction they can only recover of the persons convicted.   Commissioners *v.* Blake, 21 Ind. 32, 35 (1863).   See also Comm. *v.* Johnson, 5 S. & R. 195, 199 (Pa. 1819).   It will not be questioned that generally costs may now be awarded to the United States when it is the prevailing party.   On the other hand, there are a number of statutes in which the liability of the United States to respond for costs is recognized, and methods of procuring payment thereof are provided.   U. S. *v.* Davis, 54 Fed. Rep. 147, 153 (U. S. 1893).

(61) If executors sue as executors for money paid to their use after the testator's death, they shall pay costs.   5 T. R. 234.   Tidd, 1014.   When executors and administrators are defendants, they pay costs like other persons.   Tidd, 8 ed. 1016.   Or wherever the cause of action arises in the time of the executor, as the conversion in the case of trover, the executor shall pay costs, because it is not necessary to bring the action in the character of executor.   7 T. R. 358.   So an executor or administrator is liable to pay the costs of a *non-pros.* [An abandonment of a suit].   6 T. R. 654.   See, in general, Tidd, 8 ed. 1014.— CHRISTIAN.

"In England, executors and administrators were not, until a very recent statute, personally liable for costs when they sued *at law* on contracts alleged to have been made with the deceased, though they were non-suited or had a verdict against them; but the estate was liable in such cases."   Baker *v.* Tyrwhitt, 4 Campb. 27.   If the declaration alleged the contract to have been made with the plaintiff, though in his representative character, and he failed as mentioned above, he was then *personally* responsible for the costs.   Jobson *v.* Forster, 1 Burn. & Adol. 6.   Slater *v.* Lawson, id. 893.   *In equity*, an executor, whether plaintiff or defendant, who incurred costs in performance of his duty, was allowed them out of the estate.   2 Williams on Ex'rs. 1252-3.   The *English* statute now enacts: "That in every action brought by an executor or administrator, in right of the testator or intestate, such executor or administrator shall, unless the court

swear themselves not worth five pounds, are, by statute 11 Hen. VII. c. 12, to have original writs and *subpœnas gratis*,(62) and counsel and attorney assigned them without fee; and are excused from paying costs when plaintiffs, by the statute 23 Hen. VIII. c. 15, but shall suffer other punishment at the discretion of the judges.(63) And it was formerly usual to give such paupers, if non-suited, their election either to be whipped or pay the costs:(*w*) though that practice is now disused.(*x*)(64) It seems, *however, [*401 agreed, that a pauper may recover costs, though he pays none;(65) for the counsel and clerks are bound to give their labor to *him*, but not to his antagonist.(*y*) To prevent also trifling and malicious actions for words, for assault and battery, and for trespass, it is enacted, by statutes 43 Eliz. c. 6,(66) 21 Jac. I. c. 16, and 22 & 23 Car. II. c. 9, § 136, that where the jury who try any of these actions shall give less damages than 40*s.* the plaintiff shall be allowed no more costs than damages, unless the judge before whom the cause is tried shall certify under his hand on the back of the record that an actual battery (and not an assault only) was proved, or that in trespass the freehold or title of the land came chiefly in question.(67) Also, by

(*w*) 1 Sid. 261.   7 Mod. 114.   (*y*) 1 Eq. Ca. Abr. 125.
(*x*) Salk. 506.

in which such action is brought, or a judge of any of the superior courts shall otherwise order, be liable to pay costs to the defendant in case of being non-suited, or a verdict passing against the plaintiff, and in all other cases in which he would be liable if such plaintiff were suing in his own right, upon a cause of action accruing to himself; and the defendant shall have judgment for such costs, and they shall be recovered in like manner." Stat. 3 & 4 Wm. IV. [c. 42], see 2 Chitt. Gen. Pr. Supp. 105. Since this statute it has been decided—that on a declaration, containing an account stated with the plaintiffs as executors, though it also contains counts on promises to the testator, the defendant is entitled to costs as of course, in case of a non-suit; and that the executors cannot be relieved, in such a case, under the statute of 3 & 4 Wm. IV., which extends only to cases in which executors were before exempted from the payment of costs. Spence v. Albert, 4 Nev. & Mun. 385. Note to Cooper v. Thatcher, 3 Blackf. 59, 60 (Ind. 1832).

(62) [Free subpœnas.]

(63) Bailey's Onus Probandi, 567.

(64) But, as observed in Tidd Prac. 8 ed. 94, it does not appear that so disgraceful a proceeding was ever adopted by inflicting the punishment.—CHITTY

(65) 1 Bos. & P. 39. The pauper in such case can only recover as costs the sum he *is actually* out of pocket, not such sums as would have been so paid in an ordinary suit by any other plaintiff; and it seems that he and his solicitor may be required to state on oath the amount thus expended in equity. Hullock on Costs, 228.—CHITTY.

(66) The 43 Eliz. c. 6 enacts that where the plaintiff in any personal action, except for any title or interest in lands, or for a battery, recovers less than 40*s.*, he shall have no more costs than damages, if the judge certifies that the debt or damages were under 40*s.* But if the judge does not grant such a certificate to the defendant, the plaintiff recovers full costs. Actions of trespass *vi et armis* [With force and arms], as for beating a dog, are within the statute. 3 T. R. 38. The certificate under the statute may be granted after the trial. This certificate, it will be remarked, is to restrain the costs; but a certificate under the 22 & 23 Car. II. c. 9 is given in favor of the plaintiff to extend them from a sum under 40*s.* to full costs. If the defendant justifies the battery, the plaintiff shall have full costs without the judge's certificate, though the damages are under 40*s.*, for it is held the admission of the defendant precludes the necessity of the certificate. But a justification of the assault only will not be sufficient for this purpose; for the judge must certify an actual battery. 3 T. R. 391. This certificate also may be granted a reasonable time after the trial. 2 Bar. & Cres. 621 & 580.

In declarations for assault and battery there is sometimes a count for tearing the plaintiff's clothes; and if this is stated as a substantive injury, and the jury find it to have been such and not to have happened in consequence of the beating, the plaintiff will be entitled to full costs, (1 T. R. 656;) unless the judge should assist the defendant under the 43 Eliz. c. 6. So in a trespass upon land, the carrying away, or *asportavit*, of any independent personal property will entitle the plaintiff to full costs, unless the asportation, as by digging and carrying away turves, is a mode or qualification of the trespass upon the land. Doug. 780. See these acts and the cases upon them fully collected, Tidd, 987, 988, 996 to 1005.—CHRISTIAN.

(67) The account given of the 43 Eliz. c. 6 is not quite correct. That statute is not confined to the causes of action specified in the text, (indeed, it specifically excludes one

statute 4 & 5 W. and M. c. 23, and 8 & 9 W. III. c. 11, if the trespass were committed in hunting or sporting by an inferior tradesman, or if it appear to be wilfully and maliciously committed, the plaintiff shall have full costs,(z) though his damages as assessed by the jury amount to less than 40s.

After *judgment* is entered, *execution* will immediately follow, unless the party condemned thinks himself unjustly aggrieved by any of these proceedings; and then he has his remedy to reverse them by several writs in the nature of appeals, which we shall consider in the succeeding chapter.

CHAPTER XXV.

OF PROCEEDINGS IN THE NATURE OF APPEALS.

*402]   *PROCEEDINGS, in the nature of *appeals* from the proceedings of the king's courts of law, are of various kinds: according to the subject-matter in which they are concerned. They are principally four.

I. A writ of *attaint*,(1) which lieth to inquire whether a jury of *twelve* men gave a false verdict;(a) that so the judgment following thereupon may be reversed: and this must be brought in the lifetime of him for whom the verdict was given; and of two at least of the jurors who gave it. This lay at the common law only upon writs of *assize;* and seems to have been coeval with that institution by king Henry II., at the instance of his chief justice Glanvil: being probably meant as a check upon the vast power then reposed in the recognitors of assize, of finding a verdict according to their own personal knowledge, without the examination of witnesses. And even
*403]   here it extended no further than to such instances *where the issue was joined upon the very point of assize, (the heirship, disseisin, etc.,) and not on any collateral matter; as villenage, bastardy, or any other disputed fact. In these cases the *assize* was said to be turned into an *inquest* or a *jury*, (*assisa vertitur in juratum*,) or that the assize should be taken *in modum juratæ et non in modum assisæ;* that is, that the issue should be tried by a common jury or inquest, and not by recognitors of assize:(b) and then I apprehend that no attaint lay against the inquest or jury that determined such collateral issue.(c)   Neither do I find any mention made by our ancient writers, of such a process obtaining after the trial by inquest or jury, in the old Norman or feodal actions prosecuted by writ of *entry*.   Nor did any attaint lie in *trespass*, *debt*, or other action personal, by the old common law: because those were always determined by common inquests or juries.(d) At length the statute of Westm. 1, 3 Edw. I. c. 38, allowed an attaint to be sued upon *inquests*, as well as *assizes*, which were taken upon any plea of *land* or of *freehold*. But this was at the king's discretion, and is so understood by the author of Fleta,(e) a writer contemporary with the statute; though Sir Edward Coke (f) seems to hold a different opinion. Other sub-

(z) See pages 214, 215.
(a) Finch, L. 484.
(b) Bract. *l.* 4, *tr.* 1, c. 34, ₴₴ 2, 3, 4 ; *tr.* 3, c. 17; *tr.* 5, c. 4, ₴₴ 1, 2.   Flet. *l.* 5, c. 22, ₴ 8. Co. Entr. 61, b. Booth, 213.

(c) Bract. 4, 1, 34, 2.   Flet. ibid.
(d) Year-book, 28 Edw. III. 15, 17. Ass. pl. 15. Flet. 5, 22, 16.
(e) *L.* 5, c. 22, ₴₴ 8, 16.
(f) 2 Inst. 130, 237.

---

of them, battery,) but extends generally to all personal actions; and its object was to confine suits for trifling matters to inferior courts. It does not require a certificate to *give* full costs, but to take them away; and it was the unwillingness of the judges to interpose under this statute which induced the legislature to pass the statutes of James and Charles upon a different system, these last restraining *generally* the costs in certain cases, unless the judge by his certificate deemed it proper to grant them.—COLERIDGE.

(1) Abolished by stat. 6 Geo. IV. c. 60, *ante*.

sequent statutes(*g*) introduced the same remedy in all pleas of *trespass*, and the statute 34 Edw. III. c. 7 extended it to *all* pleas whatsoever, personal as well as real; except only the writ of *right*, in such cases where the mise or issue is joined on the *mere right*, and not on any *collateral* question. For though the attaint seems to have been generally allowed in the reign of Henry the Second, (*h*) at the first introduction of the grand assize, (which at that time might consist of only *twelve* recognitors, in case they were all unanimous,) yet subsequent *authorities have holden that no   [*404 attaint lies on a false verdict given upon the mere right, either at common law or by statute; because that is determined by the grand assize, appealed to by the party himself, and now consisting of *sixteen* jurors.(*i*)

The jury who are to try this false verdict must be twenty-four, and are called the grand jury; for the law wills not that the oath of one jury of twelve men should be attainted or set aside by an equal number, nor by less indeed than double the former.(*k*) If the matter in dispute be of forty pounds' value in personals, or of forty shillings a year in lands and tenements, then, by statute 15 Hen. VI. c. 5, each grand juror must have freehold to the annual value of twenty pounds. And he that brings the attaint can give no other evidence to the grand jury, than what was originally given to the petit. For as their verdict is now trying, and the question is, whether or no they did right upon the evidence that appeared to them, the law adjudged it the highest absurdity to produce any subsequent proof upon such trial, and to condemn the prior jurisdiction for not believing evidence which they never knew. But those against whom it is brought are allowed, in affirmance of the first verdict, to produce new matter;(*l*) because the petit jury may have formed their verdict upon evidence of their own knowledge, which never appeared in court. If the grand jury found the verdict a false one, the judgment by the common law was, that the jurors should lose their *liberam legem*(2) and become forever infamous;(3) should forfeit their goods and the profits of their lands; should themselves be imprisoned, and their wives and children thrown out of doors; should have their houses razed, their trees extirpated, and their meadows ploughed; and that the plaintiff should be restored to all that he lost by reason of the unjust verdict. But as the severity of this punishment had its usual effect, in preventing the law from being executed, therefore by the *statute 11 Hen. VII. c. 24, revived   [*405 by 23 Hen. VIII. c. 3, and made perpetual by 13 Eliz. c. 25, an attaint is allowed to be brought after the death of the party, and a more moderate punishment was inflicted upon attainted jurors; viz., perpetual infamy, and, if the cause of action were above 40*l*. value, a forfeiture of 20*l*. apiece by the jurors, or, if under 40*l*., then 5*l*. apiece: to be divided between the king and the party injured.(4) So that a man may now bring an attaint either upon the statute or at common law, at his election;(*m*) and in both of them may reverse the former judgment. But the practice of setting aside verdicts upon motion, and granting *new trials*, has so superseded the use of both sorts of attaints, that I have observed very few instances of an attaint in our books later than the sixteenth century.(*n*)(5) By the old Gothic

(*g*) Stat. 1 Edw. III. st. 1, c. 6, 5 Edw. III. c. 7. 25 Edw. III. c. 8.

(*h*) See page 389.

(*i*) Bract. 290. Flet. 5,22, 7. Britt. 212, b. 12 Hen. VI. 6 Bro. Abr. tit. *atteint*, 42. 1 Roll. Abr. 289.

(*k*) Bract. *l*. 4, *tr*. 5, c. 4, § 1. Flet. *l*. 5, c. 22 § 7.

(*l*) Finch, L. 486.

(*m*) 3 Inst. 164.

(*n*) Cro. Eliz. 309. Cro. Jac. 90.

(2) [Free law.]

(3) Lawrence *v*. Dickey, 7 Hals. 370 (N. J. 1831). McCafferty *v*. Guyer, 59 Pa. 109, 116 (1868). Lawson's Insanity as a Defence, 319.

(4) Emeric *v*. Alvarado, 64 Cal. 529, 604 (1884).

(5) But it was not abolished until the statute 6 Geo. IV. c. 50. Wendell *v*. Safford, 12 N. H. 171, 175 (1845). Griffis *v*. Stoddard, 2 Mich. (N. P.) 35, 37 (1870).

constitution, indeed, no certificate of a judge was allowed, in matters of evidence, to countervail the oath of the jury; but their verdict, however erroneous, was absolutely final and conclusive. Yet there was a proceeding from whence our attaint may be derived.—If, upon a lawful trial before a superior tribunal, the jury were found to have given a false verdict, they were fined, and rendered infamous for the future.(o)

II. The writ of *deceit*, or action on the case in nature of it, may be brought in the court of common pleas, to reverse a judgment there had by fraud or collusion in a real action, whereby lands and tenements have been recovered to the prejudice of him that hath right.(6)   But of this enough hath been observed in a former chapter.(*p*)

III. An *audita querela* is where a defendant, against whom judg-
*406]   ment is recovered, and who is therefore in danger of execution, *or
perhaps actually in execution, may be relieved upon good matter of discharge, which has happened since the judgment: as if the plaintiff hath given him a general release; or if the defendant hath paid the debt to the plaintiff without procuring satisfaction to be entered on the record.   In these and the like cases, wherein the defendant hath good matter to plead, but hath had no opportunity of pleading it, (either at the beginning of the suit, or *puis darrein continuance*, (7) which, as was shown in a former chapter,(*q*) must always be before judgment,) an *audita querela* lies, in the nature of a bill in equity, to be relieved against the oppression of the plaintiff.(8)   It is a writ directed to the court, stating that the complaint of the defendant hath been heard, *audita querela defendentis*, and then, setting out the matter of the complaint, it at length enjoins the court to call the parties before them, and, having heard their allegations and proofs, to cause justice to be done between them.(*r*)   It also lies for bail, when judgment is obtained against them by *scire facias* to answer the debt of their principal, and it happens afterwards that the original judgment against their principal is reversed: for here the bail, after judgment had against them, have no opportunity to *plead* this special matter, and therefore they shall have redress by *audita querela;*(*s*) which is a writ of a most remedial nature, and seems to have been invented lest in any case there should be an oppressive defect of justice, where a party who hath a good defence is too late to make it in the ordinary forms of law.(9)

<hr>

(o) "*Si tamen evidenti argumento falsum jurasse convincuntur (id quod superius judicium cognoscere debet) mulctentur in bonis, de cetero perjuri et intestabiles.*" [Translated in the text.] Stiernh. *de jure Goth. l. 1, c. 4.*

(*p*) See page *165.
(*q*) See page 810.
(*r*) Finch, L. 488.   F. N. B. 102.
(*s*) 1 Roll. Abr. 308.

<hr>

(6) The writ has been abolished, by 3 & 4 W. IV. c. 27, s. 36.—STEWART.

By stat. 9 Geo. IV. c. 14, s. 6, no action shall be brought whereby to charge any person upon or by reason of any representation or assurance made or given concerning or relating to the character, conduct, credit, liability, trade or dealings of any other person, to the intent or purpose that such other person may obtain credit, money, or goods, unless such representation or assurance be made in writing signed by the party to be charged therewith.   Statute not to take effect till the 1st of January, 1829.—CHITTY.

(7) [Since the last continuance.]

(8) Longworth *v.* Dupont, 2 Hill Law, *298, *300 (S. C. 1834).   Driscoll *v.* Blake, 9 Irish Ch. Rep. 356, 361 (1859).

(9) A judgment debtor, who is arrested on execution and voluntarily permitted by the officer to escape, and is afterwards arrested by the officer and committed to jail on the same execution, cannot maintain a writ of *audita querela* against the officer to recover damages for false imprisonment.   Coffin *v.* Ewer, 46 Mass. 228 (1842).   McRoberts *v.* Nesbit, 2 Mich. Nisi Prius, 37.   Injury or danger of injury is essential to the maintenance of the action.   Bryant *v.* Johnson, 26 Me. 304–307 (1844).   When a judgment of fiat is rendered under circumstances which give an insolvent debtor no opportunity of pleading his defence, he is entitled to an *audita querela* at common law.   Starr *v.* Heckert, 32 Md. 272 (1869).   Foss *v.* Witham, 91 Allen (Mass.) 572 (1865).   Under a writ of *audita querela*, brought to reverse a judgment erroneously rendered in favor of the plaintiff in

But the indulgence now shown by the courts in granting a summary relief upon motion, in cases of such evident oppression,(*t*) has almost rendered useless the writ of *audita querela*, and driven it quite out of practice (10)

IV. But, fourthly, the principal method of redress for erroneous judgments in the king's court of record is by *writ of error* to some superior court of appeal.

*A writ of error(*u*) lies for some supposed mistake in the proceed-   [*407 ings of a court of record; for to amend errors in a base court, not of record, a writ of *false judgment* lies.(*v*) The writ of error only lies upon matter of *law* arising upon the face of the proceedings; so that no evidence is required to substantiate or support it; there being no method of reversing an error in the determination of *facts*, but by an attaint, or a new trial, to correct the mistakes of the former verdict.(11)

Formerly, the suitors were much perplexed by writs of error brought upon very slight and trivial grounds, as mis-spellings and other mistakes of the clerks, all which might be amended at the common law, while all the proceedings were in *paper*,(*w*) for they were then considered as only in *fieri*, and therefore subject to the control of the courts. But, when once the record was made up, it was formerly held that by the common law no amendment could be permitted, unless within the very terms in which the judicial act so recorded was done: for during the term the record is in the breast of the court, but afterwards it admitted of no alteration.(*x*) But now the courts are become more liberal, and, where justice requires it, will allow of amendments at any time while the suit is depending, notwithstanding the record be made up, and the term be past. For they at present consider the proceed-

(*t*) Lord Raym. 489.
(*u*) Append. No. III. § 6.
(*v*) Finch. L. 484.

(*w*) 4 Burr. 1099.
(*x*) Co. Litt. 260.

an action, and to supersede an execution which has been improvidently issued thereon, no order can be passed to bring forward the original action upon the docket. Foss *v.* Witham, 9 Allen, 572, 573 (Mass. 1865).

(10) Harper *v.* Kean, 11 S. & R. 280, 297 (Pa. 1824). Lawrence *v.* Dickey, 7 Hals. 368, 370 (N. J. 1831). Job *v.* Walker, 3 Md. 129, 132 (1852). The writ, though seldom used, is not abolished in Massachusetts and New York. Coffin *v.* Ewer, 5 Metc. 228, 230 (Mass. 1842). Mallory *v.* Norton, 21 Barb. 424, 435 (N. Y. 1856). The modern practice is to interpose in a summary way in all cases where the party would be entitled to relief on an *audita querela*. Lister *v.* Mundell, 1 Bos. & Pull. 427, 428 (Eng. 1799). Steele *v.* Boyd, 6 Leigh, 547, 553 (Va. 1835). Longworth *v.* Screven, 2 Hill Law, *298, *299 (S. C. 1834). Job *v.* Walker, 3 Md. 129, 132 (1852). The same relief is granted on motion. Brown *v.* Branch Bank of Montgomery, 20 Ala. 420, 423 (1852). It often happens that complete justice cannot be administered in this summary manner, and the courts are compelled to frame an issue, or to direct an action to be brought, in order to determine the rights of the parties. Clark *v.* Rowling, 3 Coms. 216, 222 (N. Y. 1850).

(11) For the purpose of reversing or annulling a judgment in an action at law a writ of error issued out of the court above to bring up the record for examination. This was considered a new action to annul and set aside the judgment of the court below; and if the writ was seasonably sued out and bail put into the action, it was a *supersedeas*, so far as to prevent an execution from issuing on the judgment, pending the writ of error, but left it otherwise in full force between the parties, either as a ground of action, a bar, or an estoppel. But in the equity and admiralty courts the remedy for an erroneous decree is an appeal, which removes the whole case into the court above for trial *de novo* [Anew]. There is no decree left in the lower court, and pending the hearing on appeal there is no decree in the case, and there can be no estoppel by reason thereof. The tendency during the past half century has been to assimilate proceedings in equity and law cases, and in the states where the modern code prevails, the proceeding by which a judgment is reviewed in the appellate court is generally known as an appeal, although in effect it is more like a writ of error than an appeal. Sharon *v.* Hill, 26 Fed. Rep. 337, 345 (U. S. 1885). Day *v.* Holland, 15 Ore. 464, 471 (1887). See also Gibson *v.* Rogers, 2 Ark. 334, 335 (1839). Harris *v.* Cole, 2 Fla. 400 (1848). Huff *v.* Miller, 2 Swan, 85, 87 (Tenn. 1852). *Ex parte* Scott, 47 Ala. 609, 610 (1872). Buttrick *v.* Roy, 72 Wis. 164, 165 (1888). Crocker *v.* State, 60 Wis. 553. Wiscart *v.* D'Auchy, 3 Dall. (Pa.) 321. U. S. *v.* Goodison, 7 Cranch (U. S.) 111. Day *v.* Holland, 15 Ore. 470 (1887). [*In fieri*—In making.]

ings as in *fieri*, till judgment is given; and therefore, that till then they have power to permit amendments by the common law;(12) but when judgment is once given and enrolled, no amendment is permitted in any subsequent term.(*y*)(13) Mistakes are also effectually helped by the statutes of amendment and *jeofails:* so called because when a pleader perceives any slip in the form of his proceedings and acknowledges such error,(*jeo faile,*) he is at liberty by those statutes to amend it; which amendment is seldom

*408]   actually made, but the benefit of the *acts is attained by the court's overlooking the exception.(*z*)(14) These statutes are many in number, and the provisions in them too minute to be here taken notice of otherwise than by referring to the statutes themselves;(*a*)(15) by which all trifling exceptions are so thoroughly guarded against that writs of error cannot now be maintained but for some material mistake assigned.(16)

This is at present the general doctrine of amendments; and its rise and history are somewhat curious. In the early ages of our jurisprudence, when all pleadings were *ore tenus,*(17) if a slip was perceived and objected to by

---

(*y*) Stat. 11 Hen. IV. c. 3.
(*z*) Stra. 1011.
(*a*) Stat. 14 Edw. III. c. 6. 9 Hen. V. c. 4. 4 Hen. VI. c. 3. 8 Hen. VI. c. 12 and 15. 32 Hen. VIII. c.

30. 18 Eliz. c. 14. 21 Jac. I. c. 13. 16 & 17 Car. II. c. 8. (styled in 1 Ventr. 100 an omnipotent act.) 4 & 5 Anne, c. 16. 9 Anne, c. 20. 5 Geo.I. c. 13.

---

(12) See Bachus *v.* Mickle, 45 Ala. 415, 446 (1871). *Ex parte* Lange, 18 Wallace 163, 199 (U. S. 1873). Adams *v.* Main, 3 Ind. App. Ct. 232, 240 (1891). The Law of Self-Defence, Anthony 361. 1 Elliott's General Practice, p. 184. When the court below permitted the declaration to be amended by the writ, after the jury had been sworn; and then had the jury sworn again, and received their verdict without the consent of the defendant, and without giving him liberty to plead anew, and without an imparlance or awarding payment of costs by the plaintiff, it was held that the proceeding was erroneous. Thompson *v.* Musser, 1 Dall. 480. 487, 488 (Pa. 1789).

(13) Wilkie *v.* Hall, 15 Conn. 32, 37 (1842). Servatius *v.* Pickel, 30 Wis. 507, 509 (1872). This rule is applicable alike to criminal and civil causes. People *v.* Zane, 105 Ill. 662. 669 (1883). But a mistake or clerical error in entering the judgment may be corrected so as to make the judgment conform to what it was intended by the court to be. Harrison *v.* State, 10 Mo. 686, 689 (1847). Sanford *v.* Sanford, 28 Conn. 6, 27 (1859). Moore *v.* Hinnant, 90 N. C. 163, 166 (1884). See Short *v.* Kellogg, 10 Ga. 180, 182 (1851), for discussion of the doctrine of amendments to records and judicial proceedings.

After the term of court at which a judgment is rendered, the sheriff cannot amend a defective return of service of the citation, on which a judgment by default was taken. Thomason *v.* Bishop, 24 Tex. 302, 303 (1859).

See Hyde *v.* Cushing, 18 Mo. 359 (1847). Jenkins *v.* Long, 23 Ind. 460, 462 (1864). Schoonover *v.* Reed, 65 Ind. 313, 315 (1879). Knight *v.* State. 70 Ind. 375, 378 (1880). as to *nunc pro tunc* [Now for then] entries after the close of the term at which judgment was rendered. See Turner *v.* Lane's Adm'r, 9 Leigh. 262, 278 *et seq.* (Va. 1838) for discussion as to power of supreme court to allow a rehearing at a subsequent term upon the ground that its decree was founded on a mistake in point of fact.

(14) Eakin *v.* Burger, 1 Sneed, 417, 425 (Tenn. 1853). Beeler *v.* Huddleston, 3 Coldw. 201, 203 (Tenn. 1866).

(15) They are of force in this country. Porteous *v.* Givens, 2 McCord 48, 51 (S. C. 1822).

(16) And now, by stat. 9 Geo. IV. c. 15. every court of record holding plea in civil actions, any judge sitting at nisi prius, and any court of oyer and terminer and general gaol-delivery in England, etc. and Ireland, if any such court or judge shall see fit to do so, may cause the record on which any trial may be pending before any such judge or court, in any civil action, or in any indictment or information for any misdemeanor, when any variance shall appear between any matter in writing or in print produced in evidence, and the recital or setting forth thereof upon the record, wherein the trial is pending, to be forthwith amended in such particular by some officer of the court, on payment of such costs, if any, to the other party as such judge or court shall think reasonable, and thereupon the trial shall proceed as if no such variance had appeared; and in case such trial shall be had at nisi prius, the order for the amendment shall be endorsed on the *postea*, and returned together with the record; and thereupon the papers, rolls, and other records of the court from which such record issued shall be awarded accordingly.—CHITTY. See statutes 3 & 4 Wm. IV. c. 42, and 36 & 37 Vict. c. 66.

(17) [By word of mouth.]

the opposite party or the court, the pleader instantly acknowledged his error and rectified his plea; which gave occasion to that length of dialogue reported in the ancient year-books. So liberal were then the sentiments of the crown as well as the judges, that in the statute of Wales, made at Rothelan, 12 Edw. I., the pleadings are directed to be carried on in that principality, "*sine calumpnia verborum, non observata illa dura consuetudine, qui cadit a syllaba cadit a tota causa.*"(18) The judgments were entered up immediately by the clerks and officers of the court; and if any mis-entry was made, it was rectified by the minutes, or by the remembrance of the court itself.

When the treatise by Britton was published, in the name and by authority of the king, (probably about the 13 Edw. I., because the last statutes therein referred to are those of Winchester and Westminster the second,) a check seems intended to be given to the unwarrantable practices of some judges, who had made false entries on the rolls to cover their own misbehavior, and had taken upon them by amendments and rasures to falsify their own records. The king therefore declares,(b) that "although we have granted to our justices to *make record of pleas pleaded before them, yet we   [*409 will not that their own record shall be a warranty for their own wrong, nor that they may rase their rolls, nor amend them, nor record them contrary to their original enrollment." The whole of which, taken together, amounts to this, that a record surreptitiously or erroneously made up, to stifle or pervert the truth, should not be a sanction for error; and that a record, originally made up according to the truth of the case, should not afterwards by an private rasure or amendment be altered to any sinister purpose.

But when afterwards king Edward, on his return from his French dominions in the seventeenth year of his reign, after upwards of three years' absence, found it necessary (or convenient, in order to replenish his exchequer) to prosecute his judges for their corruption and other malpractices, the perversion of judgments and other manifold errors,(c) occasioned by their erasing and altering records, were among the causes assigned for the heavy punishments inflicted upon almost all the king's justices, even the most able and upright.(d)   The severity of which proceedings seems to have alarmed the *succeeding judges, that through a fear of being said to   [*410 do wrong, they hesitated at doing what was right. As it was so

(b) Brit. proem. 2, 3.
(c) *Judicia perverterunt, et in aliis erraverunt.* Matth. West. A. D. 1289.
(d) Among the other judges, Sir Ralph Hengham, chief-justice of the King's Bench, is said to have been fined 7000 marks; Sir Adam Stratton, chief-baron of the exchequer, 34,000 marks: and Thomas Wayland, chief-justice of the Common Pleas, to have been attainted of felony, and to have abjured the realm, with a forfeiture of all his estates: the whole amount of the forfeitures being upwards of 100,000 marks, or 70,000 pounds (3 Pryn. Rec. 401, 402.)—an incredible sum in those days, before paper credit was in use, and when the annual salary of a chief-justice was only sixty marks. *Claus.* 6 *Edw.* I. m. 6. Dugd. *Chron. Ser.* 26. The charge against Sir Ralph Hengham (a very learned judge, to whom we are obliged for two excellent treatises of practice) was only, according to a tradition that was current in Richard the Third's time, (Year-book. M. 2 Ric. III. 10,) his altering, out of mere compassion, a fine which was set upon a very poor man from 13s. 4d. to 6s. 8d., for which he was fined 800 marks,—a more probable sum than 7000. It is true the book calls the judge so punished *Ingham*, and not *Hengham*; but I find no judge of the name of *Ingham* in Dugdale's Series, and Sir Edward Coke (4 Inst. 955) and

Sir Matthew Hale (1 P. C. 646) understand it to have been the chief-justice. And certainly his offence (whatever it was) was nothing very atrocious or disgraceful; for though removed from the King's Bench at this time, (together with the rest of the judges,) we find him, about eleven years afterwards, one of the justices in eyre for the general perambulation of the forest, (Rot. perambul. forest. in turri Lond., 29 Edw. I. m. 8,) and the next year made chief-justice of the Common Pleas. (Pat. 29 Edw. I. m. 7. Dugd. *Chron. Ser.* 32.) in which office he continued till his death, in 2 Edw. II. *Claus.*1 Edw. II. m. 19. Pat. 2 Edw. II. p. 1, m. 9. Dugd. 31. Selden, pref. to Hengham. There is an appendix to this tradition, remembered by justice Southcote in the reign of queen Elizabeth, (3 Inst. 72. 4 Inst. 255,) that with this fine of chief-justice Hengham a clock-house was built at Westminster, and furnished with a clock, to be heard into Westminster hall. Upon which story I shall only remark that (whatever early instances may be found of the private exertion of mechanical genius in constructing horological machines) clocks came not into common use till a hundred years afterwards, about the end of the fourteenth century. *Encyclopedie*, tit. *Horloge*, 6 Rym. Fœd. 590. Derham's Artif. Clockmaker, 91.

(18) [" Without that strictness to the letter; that rigid custom not being observed, that he who fails in one syllable loses the whole cause."]

hazardous to alter a record duly made up, even from compassionate motives, (as happened in Hengham's case, which in strictness was certainly indefensible,) they resolved not to touch a record any more; but held that even palpable errors, when enrolled and the term at an end, were too sacred to be rectified or called in question: and, because Britton had forbidden all criminal and clandestine alterations, to make a record speak a falsity, they conceived that they might not judicially and publicly amend it, to make it agreeable to truth. In Edward the Third's time, indeed, they once ventured (upon the certificate of the justice in eyre) to estreat a larger fine than had been recorded by the clerk of the court below:(e) but instead of amending the clerk's erroneous record, they made a second enrollment of what the justice had declared *ore tenus;* and left it to be settled by posterity in which of the two rolls that absolute verity resides which every record is said to import in itself.(f) And, in the reign of Richard the Second, there are instances(g) of their refusing to amend the most palpable errors and misentries, unless by the authority of parliament.

To this real sullenness, but affected timidity, of the judges, such a narrowness of thinking was added, that every slip (even of a syllable or
*411] letter)(h) was now held to be fatal to the *pleader, and overturned his client's cause.(i) If they durst not, or would not, set right mere formal mistakes at any time, upon equitable terms and conditions, they at least should have held, that trifling objections were at all times inadmissible, and that more solid exceptions in point of form came too late when the merits had been tried. They might, through a decent degree of tenderness, have excused themselves from amending in criminal, and especially in capital, cases. They needed not have granted an amendment, where it would work an injustice to either party; or where he could not be put in as good a condition as if his adversary had made no mistake. And, if it was feared that an amendment after trial might subject the jury to an attaint, how easy was it to make waiving the attaint the condition of allowing the amendment!(19) And yet these were among the absurd reasons alleged for never suffering amendments at all.(k)

The precedents then set were afterwards most religiously followed,(l) to the great obstruction of justice, and ruin of the suitors: who have formerly suffered as much by this scrupulous obstinacy and literal strictness of the courts, as they could have done even by their iniquity. After verdicts and judgments upon the merits, they were frequently reversed for slips of the pen or mis-spellings; and justice was perpetually entangled in a net of mere technical jargon. The legislature hath therefore been forced to interpose, by no less than twelve statutes, to remedy these opprobrious niceties: and its endeavors have been of late so well seconded by judges of a more liberal cast, that this unseemly degree of strictness is almost entirely eradicated,(20) and will probably in a few years be no more remembered than the learning of essoigns and defaults, or the counterpleas of voucher, are at present.(21)

But to return to our writs of error.
**410] **If a writ of error be brought to reverse any judgment of an

---

(e) 1 Hal. P. C. 647.
(f) 1 Leon. 183. Co. Litt 117. See page 331.
(g) 1 Hal. P. C. 648.
(h) Stat. 14 Edw. III. c. 6.
(i) In those days it was strictly true, what Ruggle (in his *Ignoramus*) has humorously applied to more modern pleadings:—"*in nostra lege unum comma evertit totum placitum.*" ["In our law, one comma overturns the whole plea."]
(k) Styl. 207.
(l) 8 Rep. 156, etc.

---

(19) Lisbon *v.* Lyman, 49 N. H. 553, 598 (1870). [*Ore tenus*—verbally.]
(20) Porteous *v.* Givens, 2 McCord, 48, 51, 52 (S. C. 1822). King *v.* Lacey, 8 Conn. 498, 500 (1831).
(21) Shaw *v.* Redmond, 11 S. & R. 27, 34 (Pa. 1824).

inferior court of record, where the damages are less than ten pounds; or if it is brought to reverse the judgment of any superior court after verdict, he that brings the writ, or that is plaintiff in error, must (except in some peculiar cases) find substantial pledges of prosecution, or bail:(*m*) to prevent delays by frivolous pretences to appeal; and for securing payment of costs and damages, which are now payable by the vanquished party in all except in a few particular instances, by virtue of the several statutes recited in the margin.(*n*)(22)

A writ of error lies from the inferior courts of record in England into the king's bench,(*o*) and not into the common pleas.(*p*)(23) Also from the king's bench in Ireland to the king's bench in England.(24) It likewise may be brought from the common pleas at Westminster to the king's bench; and then from the king's bench the cause is removable to the house of lords. From proceedings on the law side of the exchequer a writ of error lies into the court of exchequer chamber before the lord chancellor, lord treasurer, and the judges of the court of king's bench and common pleas;(25) and from

---

(*m*) Stat. 3 Jac. I. c. 8. 13 Car. II. c. 2. 16 & 17 Car. II. c. 8. 19 Geo. III. c. 70.
(*n*) 3 Hen. VII. c. 10. 13 Car. II. c. 2. 8 & 9 W. III.
c. 11. 4 & 5 Anne, c. 16.
(*o*) See ch. 4.
(*p*) Finch, L. 480. Dyer, 250.

---

(22) By the 3 Jac. I. c. 8, (made perpetual by 3 Car. I. c. 4, s. 4,) to restrain unnecessary delays of execution, it was provided "that in the actions therein specified no writ of error should be allowed, unless the party bringing the same, with *two sufficient sureties*, shall first be bound unto the party for whom the judgment is given, by recognizance to be acknowledged in the same court, in double the sum, to be recovered by the former judgment, to prosecute the said writ of error with effect, and also to satisfy and pay if the said judgment be affirmed or the writ of error nonprossed, all and singular the debts, damages, and costs adjudged upon the former judgment, and all costs and damages to be awarded for the delaying of the execution." And now, by the 6 Geo. IV. c. 96, for further preventing the delays occasioned by frivolous writs of error, it is enacted that upon *any* judgment hereafter to be given in any of the courts of record at Westminster, in the counties palatine, and in the courts of great session in Wales, in *any* personal action, execution shall not be stayed or delayed by any writ of error, or supersedeas thereupon, without the special order of the court, or some judge thereof, unless a recognizance, with a condition according to the 3 Jac. I. c. 8, (above noticed,) be first acknowledged in the same court. After final judgment, and before execution executed, a writ of error is, generally speaking, a supersedeas of execution from the time of its allowance, (1 Vent. 31. 1 Salk. 321. 1 T. R. 280. 2 B. & P. 370. 2 East, 439. 5 Taunt. 204. 1 Gow. 66. 1 Chitty R. 238, 241. 3 Moore, 89;) but it is no supersedeas unless bail in error be put in, and notice thereof given within the time limited by the rules of the court. 2 Dowl. & Ry. 85. And when it is apparent to the court that a writ of error is brought against good faith, (2 T. R. 183. 8 Taunt. 434,) or for the mere purpose of delay, (4 T. R. 436. 2 M. & S. 474, 476. 1 Bar. & Cres. 287,) or it is returnable of a term previous to the signing of final judgment, (Barnes, 197,) it is not a supersedeas. Tidd, 8th ed. 1202. In Tidd, 1199, 8th ed. it is said that there must be fifteen days between the teste and return of a writ of error; but it was said in Laidler *v.* Foster, where there was an interval of twelve days only, that there is a distinction between writs of error and those which are the commencement of a suit; and the usual course of practice was followed in this case, (viz., not to pass over more than one return between the teste and return:) the court therefore refused to quash the writ. 4 Bar. & Cres. 116. And in another case the court of King's Bench held that the court could not quash a writ of error upon a judgment of the Common Pleas of Durham, nor award execution upon the judgment of an inferior court. 4 Dowl. & Ry. 153.—CHITTY.

(23) It is not correct that a writ of error does not lie from an inferior court into the court of Common Pleas. There is a modern instance of such a proceeding in Bower *v.* Wait, 1 M. & G. 1, in a learned note to which (p. 2, note a.) the opinion in the text is controverted.—COUCH.

(24) This appeal is taken away by 23 Geo. III. c. 21. Since the union, however, a writ of error lies from the superior courts in Ireland to the house of lords. Before the union with Scotland, a writ of error lay not in this country upon any judgment in Scotland; but it is since given, by statute 6 Anne, c. 26, s. 12, from the court of Exchequer in Scotland, returnable in parliament. And see the 48 Geo. III. c. 151, concerning appeals to the house of lords from the court of session in Scotland.—CHITTY.

(25) The 31 Edw. III. c. 12 directs that the chancellor and treasurer shall take to their

thence it lies to the house of peers.(26)　From proceedings in the king's bench, in debt, detinue, covenant, account, case, ejectment, or trespass, originally begun therein by bill, (except where the king is party,) it lies to the exchequer chamber, before the justices of the common pleas, and barons of the exchequer; and from thence also to the house of lords;(q) but where the proceedings in the king's bench do not first commence therein by bill, but

＊＊411]　　　by original writ sued out of chancery,(r) this takes the case out of the general rule ＊＊laid down by the statute;(s) so that the writ of error then lies, without any intermediate state of appeal, directly to the house of lords, the dernier resort for the ultimate decision of every civil action.(27)　Each court of appeal, in their respective stages, may, upon hearing the matter of law in which the error is assigned, reverse or affirm the judgment of the inferior courts; but none of them are final, save only the house of peers, to whose judicial decisions all other tribunals must therefore submit, and conform their own.　And thus much for the reversal or affirmance of judgments at law by writs in the nature of appeals.(28)

CHAPTER XXVI.

OF EXECUTION.

＊412]　＊If the regular judgment of the court, after the decision of the suit, be not suspended, superseded, or reversed by one or other of the

(q) Stat. 27 Eliz. c. 8.
(r) See page 43.

(s) 1 Roll. Rep. 264. 1 Sid. 424. 1 Saund. 340. Carth. 180. Comb. 295.

assistance the judges of the other courts, and *autres sages come lour semblera*, [Such other skillful men as they shall think fit.]　But the 20 Car. II. c. 4 has dispensed with the presence of the lord treasurer when the office is vacant; and it is the practice for the two chief justices alone to sit in this court of error, who report their opinion to the chancellor, and the judgment is pronounced by him.—CHITTY.

(26) Gibson *v.* Rogers, 2 Ark. 334, 335 (1849).

(27) But now, by statute 1 Will. IV. c. 70, and the Common-Law Procedure Act, 1852, error upon any judgment of the Queen's Bench, Common Pleas, or Exchequer must be brought in the Exchequer chamber before the judges, or judges and barons, as the case may be, of the other two courts, whence it again lies to the house of lords.—STEWART.

(28) In this chapter Sir W. Blackstone has considered only the modes by which a judgment may be reversed by writ of error brought in a court of appeal, and has stated that this can only be done for error in law.　There is, however, a proceeding to reverse a judgment by writ of error in the same court, where the error complained of is *in fact* and not in law, and where of course no fault is imputed to the court in pronouncing its judgment.　This writ is called the writ *coram nobis* [Before us] or *coram vobis*, [Before you,] according as the proceedings are in the King's Bench or Common Pleas, because the record is stated to *remain* before us (the king) if in the former, and before you (the judges) if in the latter, and is not removed to another court.　In this proceeding it is of course necessary to suggest a new fact upon the record, from which the error in the first judgment will appear; thus, supposing the defendant, being an infant, has appeared by attorney instead of guardian, it will be necessary to suggest the fact of his infancy of which the court was not before informed.　There is therefore no inconsistency in bringing this writ of error before the same judges who pronounced the judgment in the first instance; because they are required to pronounce upon a new state of facts, without impeachment of the former judgment on the facts as they then stood.—COLERIDGE.

These writs are also used in the United States.　Jones *v.* Pearce, 12 Heisk. 281, 286 (Tenn. 1873).　By the statute 36 & 37 Vict. c. 66, the high court of chancery of England, the court of Queen's Bench, the court of Common Pleas at Westminster, the court of exchequer, the high court of admiralty, the court of probate, the court of divorce and matrimonial causes, and the London court of bankruptcy are united, and made to constitute the supreme court of judicature in England.　By the statute 39 and 40 Vict. c. 59, an appeal lies to the house of lords from any order or judgment of court of appeal in England of any Scotch or Irish court from which a writ of error lay before the passage of that act.

methods mentioned in the two preceding chapters, the next and last step is the *execution* of that judgment; or putting the sentence of the law in force. This is performed in different manners, according to the nature of the action upon which it is founded, and of the judgment which is had or recovered.

If the plaintiff recovers in an action real or mixed, whereby the seisin or possession of land is awarded to him, the writ of execution shall be an *habere facias seisinam,*(1) or writ of seisin, of a freehold; or an *habere facias possessionem,*(2) or writ of possession,(*a*) of a chattel interest.(*b*) These are writs directed to the sheriff of the county, commanding him to give actual possession to the plaintiff of the land so recovered: in the execution of which the sheriff may take with him the *posse comitatus,* or power of the county; and may justify breaking open doors, if the possession be not quietly delivered. But, if it be peaceably yielded up, the delivery of a twig, a turf, or the ring of the door, in the name of seisin, is sufficient execution of the writ. Upon a presentation to a benefice recovered in a *quare impedit,*(3) or assize of *darrein presentment,*(4) *the execution is by a writ *de clerico admit-*   [*413 *tendo;*(5)directed, not to the sheriff, but to the bishop or archbishop, and requiring him to admit and institute the clerk of the plaintiff.(6)

In other actions, where the judgment is that something in special be done or rendered by the defendant, then, in order to compel him so to do, and to see the judgment executed, a special writ of execution issues to the sheriff according to the nature of the case. As, upon an assize of nuisance, or *quod permittat prosternere,*(7) where one part of the judgment is *quod nocumentum amoveatur,*(8) a writ goes to the sheriff to abate it at the charge of the party, which likewise issues even in case of an indictment.(*c*)(9) Upon a replevin, the writ of execution is the writ *de retorno habendo:*(*d*)(10) and, if the distress be eloigned, the defendant shall have a *capias in withernam;*(*e*)(11) but on the plaintiff's tendering the damages and submitting to a fine, the process *in withernam* shall be stayed.(*f*) In detinue, after judgment, the plaintiff shall have a *distringas,* to compel the defendant to deliver the goods, by repeated distresses of his chattels:(*g*)or else a *scire facias*(12) against any third person in whose hands they may happen to be, to show cause why they should not be delivered: and if the defendant still continues obstinate, then (if the judgment hath been by default or on demurrer) the sheriff shall summon an inquest to ascertain the value of the goods, and the plaintiff's damages; which (being either so assessed, or by the verdict in case of an issue)(*h*) shall be levied on the person or goods of the defendant. So that, after all,

---

(*a*) Apend. No. II. § 4.
(*b*) Finch, L. 470.
(*c*) Comb. 10.
(*d*) See page 150.

(*e*) See page 149.
(*f*) 2 Leon. 174.
(*g*) 1 Roll. Abr. 737. Rast. Ent. 215.
(*h*) Bro. Abr. tit. *damages,* 29.

---

(1) [That you give him seisin.]
(2) [That you give him possession.]
(3) [Wherefore he impedes.]
(4) [The last presentment.]
(5) [On admitting the clerk.]
(6) The writ recites the judgment of the court and orders him to admit a fit person to the rectory and parish church at the presentation of the plaintiff; and if upon this order he refuse to admit accordingly, the patron may sue the bishop in a *quare non admisit* [Why he does not admit him], and recover ample satisfaction in damages. 2 Selw. Prac. 330. —CHITTY.
(7) [That he permit to put down.]
(8) [That he abate the nuisance.]
(9) That is, if it be stated in the indictment that the nuisance is still existing. If it does not appear in the indictment that the nuisance was then in existence, it would be absurd to give judgment to abate a nuisance which does not exist. 8 T. R. 144.—CHITTY.
(10) [To have returned.]
(11) [That you take in withernam.]
(12) [That you cause to know.]

in replevin and detinue, (the only actions for recovering the specific possession of personal chattels,) if the wrong-doer be very perverse, he cannot be compelled to a restitution of the identical thing taken or detained; but he still has his election, to deliver the goods, or their value:(*i*) an imperfection in the law, that results from the nature of personal property, which is easily concealed or conveyed out of the reach of justice, and not always amenable to the magistrate.

*414]　　*Executions in actions where money only is recovered, as a debt or damages, (and not any specific chattel,) are of five sorts: either against the body of the defendant; or against his goods and chattels; or against his goods and the *profits* of his lands; or against his goods and the *possession* of his lands; or against all three, his body, lands, and goods.

1. The first of these species of execution is by writ of *capias ad satisfaciendum;*(*j*)(13) which addition distinguishes it from the former *capias ad respondendum,*(14) which lies to compel an appearance at the beginning of a suit. And, properly speaking, this cannot be sued out against any but such as were liable to be taken upon the former *capias.*(*k*) The intent of it is, to imprison the body of the debtor till satisfaction be made for the debt, costs, and damages; it therefore doth not lie against any privileged persons, peers, or members of parliament, nor against executors or administrators, nor against such other persons as could not be originally held to bail. And Sir Edward Coke also gives us a singular instance,(*l*) where a defendant in 14 Edw. III. was discharged from a *capias,* because he was of so advanced an age *quod pœnam imprisonamenti subire non potest.*(15) If an action be brought against a husband and wife for the debt of the wife, when sole, and the plaintiff recovers judgment, the *capias* shall issue to take both husband and wife in execution:(*m*) but, if the action was originally brought against herself, when sole, and pending the suit she marries, the *capias* shall be awarded against her only, and not against her husband.(*n*) Yet, if judgment be recovered against a husband and wife for the contract, nay, even for the personal misbehavior(*o*) of the wife during her coverture, the *capias* shall issue against the husband only: which is one of the many great privileges of English wives.(16)

*415]　　*The writ of *capias ad satisfaciendum* is an execution of the highest nature inasmuch as it deprives a man of his liberty, till he

(*i*) Keilw. 64.
(*j*) Append. No. III. ? 7.
(*k*) 3 Rep. 12. Moor. 767.
(*l*) 1 Inst. 289.

(*m*) Moor. 704.
(*n*) Cro. Jac. 323.
(*o*) Cro. Car. 513.

---

(13) [That you take to satisfy.]
(14) [That you take to answer.]
(15) [That he is not able to undergo the punishment of imprisonment.]
(16) There are many cases in which the defendant may be taken in execution after judgment, though he could not be arrested at the commencement of the suit; but it is an universal rule that whenever a capias is allowed on *mesne* process before judgment, it may be had upon the judgment itself. 3 Salk. 286. 3 Co. 12. It lies against peers, or members of parliament, upon a statute merchant, or staple, or recognizance in nature thereof. 2 Leon. 173. 1 Cromp. 345. But, by 57 Geo. III. c. 99, s. 47, no penalty or costs incurred by any spiritual person, by reason of non-residence on his benefice, shall be levied by execution against his body, whilst he holds the same or any other benefice, out of which the same can be levied by sequestration within the term of three years. An infant seems liable to this process. 2 Stra. 1217; see id. 708. 1 B. & P. 480. Husband and wife may be taken in execution in an action against both, and she shall not be discharged unless it appear she has no separate property out of which the demand can be satisfied, (T. 2 Geo. IV. C. P.; see 5 B. & A. 759,) or that there is fraud and collusion between the plaintiff and her husband to keep her in prison. 2 Stra. 1167, 1237. 1 Wils. 149. 2 Bla. R. 720. Volunteer soldiers and seamen are protected by several statutes from being taken in execution unless the original debt, in the case of soldiers, amounted

makes the satisfaction awarded; and therefore, when a man is once taken in execution upon this writ, no other process can be sued out against his lands or goods.(17)   Only, by statute 21 Jac. I. c. 24, if the defendant dies while charged in execution upon this writ, the plaintiff may, after his death, sue out a new execution against his lands, goods, or chattels.   The writ is directed to the sheriff, commanding him to take the body of the defendant and have him at Westminster on a day therein named, to make the plaintiff satisfaction for his demand.   And, if he does not then make satisfaction, he must remain in custody till he does.   This writ may be sued out, as may all other executory process, for costs, against a plaintiff as well as a defendant, when judgment is had against him.

When a defendant is once in custody upon this process, he is to be kept in *arcta et salva custodia:*(18) and if he be afterwards seen at large, it is an *escape;* and the plaintiff may have an action thereupon against the sheriff for his whole debt.   For though, upon arrests, and what is called *mesne* process, being such as intervenes between the commencement and end of a suit,(*p*) the sheriff, till the statute 8 & 9 W. III. c. 27, might have indulged the defendant as he pleased, so as he produced him in court to answer the plaintiff at the return of the writ; yet, upon a taking in execution, he could never give any indulgence; for, in that case, confinement is the whole of the debtor's punishment, and of the satisfaction made to the creditor.(19) Escapes are either voluntary, or negligent.   Voluntary are such as are by the express consent of the keeper; after which he never can retake his prisoner again,(*q*) (though the plaintiff may retake him at any time,)(*r*) but the sheriff must answer for the debt.   Negligent escapes are where the prisoner escapes without his keeper's knowledge or consent; and then upon fresh pursuit the defendant may *be retaken, and the sheriff   [*416 shall be excused, if he has him again before any action brought against himself for the escape.(*s*)   A rescue of a prisoner *in execution*, either going to gaol or in gaol, or a breach of prison, will not excuse the sheriff from being guilty of and answering for the escape; for he ought to have sufficient force to keep him, since he may command the power of the county.(*t*)   But by statute 32 Geo. II. c. 28, if a defendant charged in execution for any debt not exceeding 100*l*. will surrender all his effects to his creditors, (except his apparel, bedding, and tools of his trade, not amounting in the whole to the value of 10*l*.,) and will make oath of his punctual compliance with the statute, the prisoner may be discharged,(20) unless the

(*p*) See page 279.
(*q*) 3 Rep. 52. 1 Sid. 330.
(*r*) Stat. 8 & 9 W. III. c. 27.

(*s*) F. N. B. 130.
(*t*) Cro. Jac. 419.

---

to 20*l*., or in the case of seamen the debt and costs, etc., are of that amount, and that the debt was contracted when the defendant did not belong to any ship in his majesty's service.   See 11 East, 25.   Nor can parties be taken in execution at the time or place when and where they are privileged from arrest.   Tidd, 1065, 1066, 1067.—CHITTY.

See statute 32 & 33 Vict. c. 60, for further changes in the law on this subject.

(17) Snead *v.* M'Caull, 12 Hew. 407, 416 (U. S. 1851).

(18) [In close and safe custody.]

(19) But execution by imprisonment is considered so far a satisfaction of the debt, that if the creditor release the debtor from confinement he cannot afterwards have recourse to any other remedy, though the discharge be on terms which are not afterwards complied with, (4 Burr. 2482.   6 T. R. 526.   7 ib. 420;) or upon giving a fresh security which afterwards becomes ineffectual, (1 T. R. 557;) the execution being considered *quoad* [As to] the defendant as a satisfaction of the debt.   Hob. 59.   But the plaintiff may take out execution against other persons liable to the same debt or damages.   Ib.; and see 5 Taunt. 614.   1 Marsh. 250, S. C.   If, however, the plaintiff consent to discharge the only one of several defendants taken on a *joint* capias, he cannot afterwards retake either him or take any of the other defendants.   6 T. R. 525.—CHITTY.

(20) In Maine, where a debtor was arrested in accordance with the provisions of law, and, while in custody, filed his voluntary petition in insolvency, he was not thereby

creditor insists on detaining him; in which case he shall allow him 2*s.* 4*d.* per week, to be paid on the first day of every week, and on failure of regular payment the prisoner shall be discharged.(21)   Yet the creditor may at any future time have execution against the lands and goods of such defendant, though never more against his person.(22)   And, on the other hand, the creditors may, as in case of bankruptcy, compel (under pain of transportation for seven years) such debtor charged in execution for any debt under 100*l.* to make a discovery and surrender of all his effects for their benefit, where-upon he is also entitled to the like discharge of his person.(23)

---

entitled to be released from arrest.   The provision of the insolvent act of 1878 (R. S. c. 70, § 51), that "no debtor against whom a warrant of insolvency has been issued shall be liable to arrest on *mesne* process, etc.," did not apply in such a case.   Hussey *v.* Dan-forth, 77 Me. 17, 20 (1884).

(21) The statutes of Massachusetts allowed the debtor to obtain his discharge by taking the poor debtor's oath, unless he had been guilty of some fraud or wasteful misuse of his property.   Stockwell *v.* Silloway, 100 Mass. 287, 297 (1868).

(22) The statute mentioned in the text is that which is commonly known by the appel-lation of the Lords' Act, from the circumstances of its originating in the upper house of parliament.   By the 33 Geo. III. c. 5, made perpetual by 39 Geo. III. c. 50, the regula-tions of the former act are extended to debts amounting to 300*l.*   And by other statutes, (see Tidd, 379,) persons in custody for contempt by the non-payment of money or costs ordered by courts of equity (49 Geo. III. c. 6) or common law, are declared within the provisions for the relief of prisoners in custody for debt only.   But a defendant in a *qui tam* action is not entitled to the benefit of the lords' act, (3 Burr. 1322.   1 Bla. R. 372;) nor a defendant in custody under a writ *de excommunicato capiendo* [For taking the excommunicated], for contumacy in not paying a sum for alimony, and also for costs in the ecclesiastical court.   11 East, 231.   When the prisoner is charged in execution above twenty miles from Westminster hall, or the court out of which the execution issued, he must be brought up to the next assizes, or, by 52 Geo. III. c. 34, before the justices at quarter sessions, to be examined and discharged.   The application is directed to be made by the prisoner before the end of the first term after his arrest; but ignorance or mistake will excuse a delay beyond that period.   When the debt recovered does not exceed 20*l.*, exclusive of costs, the 48 Geo. III. c. 123 provides for the discharge of the debtor's person after he has lain in prison twelve months.   But, this statute being confined to persons in execution upon a judgment, it has been holden that one in custody on an attachment for non-payment of a sum under 20*l.* found due upon an award made a rule of court is not entitled to his discharge under it.   10 East, 408.   2 B. & A. 61.

The 1 Geo. IV. c 119 established a new court of record, called the Court for the Relief of Insolvent Debtors, which is held twice a week in London throughout the year, with a short vacation in the summer, and by the 5 Geo. IV. c. 16 it is provided that the judges of this court, who are four in number, shall make three circuits in the year for the dis-charge of insolvents.   A prisoner discharged under these acts becomes personally free, having first delivered a schedule on oath of all his debts, etc., and assigned all his pro-perty in possession or expectancy for the benefit of his creditors, to whose demands all property which he may afterwards acquire is made liable.   If upon his examination it appear that he has been guilty of bad practices or fraud, in contracting debts, or have opposed a vexatious defence to any action brought against him for the recovery of any debt, concealed credits, or debts, given a voluntary preference to any creditor, or made away with his property, or his imprisonment be for damages recovered in an action of crim. con., seduction, or malicious injury, or does not answer satisfactorily to the court, he may be sent back to prison for two or three years, at the discretion of the court.   A fraudulent concealment of property in his schedule subjects him to the additional punish-ment of hard labor.   If a voluntary preference be given by him within three months before filing his petition for discharge, it is void.—CHITTY.

(23) The creditors who can compel the surrender of the debtor's effects, and who are to have the benefit of it, are only those who have charged him in execution.   This statute— the 32 Geo. II. c. 28—is generally called the lords' act.   By the 26 Geo. III. c. 44, the provisions of it were extended to 200*l.*, and by the 33 Geo. III. c. 5, they have been still further enlarged to 300*l.*   By the 37 Geo. III. c. 85, one creditor shall agree in writing, in order to detain such a debtor, to make him a weekly allowance of 3*s.* 6*d.*; and where two or more shall agree to detain him, they shall pay him what the court shall direct, not exceeding 2*s.* a week each.   See the clauses of the act in 2 Burn, tit. Gaol.   The prisoner shall never afterwards be liable to be arrested on any action for the same debt, unless convicted of perjury.   But a prisoner to have the benefit of this act must petition the court from which the process issued upon which he shall be in custody, before the

If a *capias ad satisfaciendum*(24) is sued out, and a *non est inventus*(25) is returned thereon, the plaintiff may sue out a process against the bail, if any were given: who, we may remember, stipulated in this triple alternative, that the defendant should, if condemned in the suit, satisfy the plaintiff his debt and costs; or that he should surrender himself a prisoner; or, that they would pay it for him: as therefore the two former branches of the alternative are neither of them complied with, the latter must immediately take place.(*u*) In order to which, a writ of *scire facias*(26) may be sued out against the bail, commanding them to show cause why the plaintiff should not have execution against them for his *debt and damages: and on such　　[*417 writ, if they show no sufficient cause, or the defendant does not surrender himself on the day of the return, or of showing cause, (for afterwards is not sufficient,) the plaintiff may have judgment against the bail, and take out a writ of *capias ad satisfaciendum*, or other process of execution against them.(27)

2. The next species of execution is against the goods and chattels of the defendant, and is called a writ of *fieri facias*,(*w*)(28) from the words in it where the sheriff is commanded, *quod fieri faciat de bonis*, that he cause to be made of the goods and chattels of the defendant the sum or debt recovered.(29)　　This lies as well against privileged persons, peers, etc., as other common persons; and against executors or administrators with regard to the goods of the deceased.　　The sheriff may not break open any outer doors,(*x*) (30) to execute either this or the former writ, but must enter peaceably; and may then break open any inner door, belonging to the defendant, in order to take the goods.(*y*)(31)　　And he may sell the goods and chattels (even an estate for years, which is the chattel real)(*z*)(32) of the defendant, till

---

(*u*) Lutw. 1269–1273.
(*w*) Append. No. III. § 7.
(*x*) 5 Rep. 92.

(*y*) Palm. 54.
(*z*) 8 Rep. 171.

---

end of the first term after he is arrested, unless he afterwards shows his neglect arose from ignorance or mistake.—CHRISTIAN.

Although the prisoner cannot avail himself of the benefit of the lords' act if his debts exceed 300*l.*, yet he is liable to the compulsory clause upon any debt within that amount, whatever may be the amount of all his debts for which he is in execution.　5 B. & A. 537.

The judges of King's Bench have decided that an insolvent brought up under the compulsory clause in the lords' act is not bound to answer questions as to the disposition of his property *during* his imprisonment, but merely as to the amount and condition of it at the time of making his schedule; and that the form of the oath must be altered conformably with this construction of the statute.　Per Holroyd, J., in re. Askew, 24th Nov. 1825.—CHITTY.

(24) *Vide supra*, p. 414.

(25) [He is not forthcoming.]

(26) *Vide supra*, p. 412.

(27) In *scire facias* against bail, where no plea has been filed, judgment may be rendered upon motion, without the intervention of a jury.　Reed *v.* Sullivan, 1 Kelly, 292, 294 (Ga. 1846).　But the undertaking of the bail does not subject them to execution against the body in the Common Pleas.—CHITTY.

(28) [That you cause to be made.]

(29) If, upon a judgment in tort against two or more, execution be levied for the whole damages upon one only, (1 Camp. 343,) that one cannot recover a moiety against the other for his contribution; but he may maintain an action for the moiety, if the original action were founded upon contract.　8 T. R. 186.　See also 2 Camp. 452.—CHITTY.

(30) Alderson on Jud. Writs and Proc. 489, 490.

(31) This is believed to be true of all civil process.　Snydacker *v.* Brosse, 51 Ill. 357, 360 (1869).

(32) A leasehold interest might be sold as a chattel at common law.　But the leased lands and water power of the state of Ohio, upon the canals and rivers, are not subject to judgment liens.　Buckingham's Ex'rs *v.* Reeve, 19 Grisw. 399, 405 (1850).

he has raised enough to satisfy the judgment, and costs:(33) first paying the landlord of the premises, upon which the goods are found, the arrears of rent then due, not exceeding one year's rent in the whole.(a)(34)   If part only of the debt be levied on a *fieri facias*(35) the plaintiff may have a *capias ad satisfaciendum* for the residue.(b)

3. A third species of execution is by writ of *levari facias;*(36) which affects a man's goods and the *profits* of his lands, by commanding the sheriff to levy the plaintiff's debt on the lands and goods of the defendant; whereby the sheriff may seize all his goods, and receive the rents and profits of his *418] lands, till satisfaction be made to the plaintiff.(c)(37)   Little use *is now made of this writ; the remedy by *elegit*, which takes possession of the lands themselves, being much more effectual.   But of this species is a writ of execution proper only to ecclesiastics; which is given when the sheriff, upon a common writ of execution sued, returns that the defendant is a bene-ficed clerk, not having any lay fee.   In this case a writ goes to the bishop of the diocese, in the nature of a *levari* or *fieri facias,*(d)(38) to levy the debt and damage *de bonis ecclesiasticis,*(39) which are not to be touched by lay hands: and thereupon the bishop sends out a *sequestration* of the profits of the clerk's benefice, directed to the church-wardens, to collect the same and pay them to the plaintiff, till the full sum be raised.(e)

4. The fourth species of execution is by the writ of *elegit;*(40) which is a judicial writ given by the statute Westm. 2, 13 Edw. I. c. 18, either upon a

---

(a) Stat. 8 Anne, c. 14.
(b) 1 Roll. Abr. 904. Cro. Eliz. 344.
(c) Finch, L. 471.

(d) *Registr. Orig.* 300, *juris.* 22. 2 Inst. 4.
(e) 2 Burn, Eccl. Law, 329.

---

(33) And, by a late statute,—viz., 43 Geo. III. c. 46,—to satisfy also the costs of the writ of execution, together with the sheriff's fees, poundage, etc.   But the statute does not extend to give the like costs, fees, poundages, etc. to the defendant.   But *query* whether "expenses of execution" include expenses of levying?   Ramsey *v.* Tuffnell, 9 J. B. Moore, 425.—CHITTY.

(34) The statute enacts that such payment shall be made out of the proceeds, provided the sheriff have notice of the landlord's claim at any time while the goods or the pro-ceeds remain in his hands.   See Arnitt *v.* Garnett, 3 B. & A. 440.   In this case the goods had been removed from the premises previously to the notice.   And where the sheriff takes corn in the blade under a *fi. fa.*, and sells it before the rent is due, he is not liable to account to the landlord for rent accruing subsequent to the levy and sale, although he have given notice, and though the corn be not removed from the premises until long afterwards.   Gwilliam *v.* Barker, 1 Price, 274.   And where the sheriff knows the fact of the arrear of rent, no other specific notice is needful to bind him, (Andrews *v.* Dixon, 3 B. & A. 645;) and, *semble*, he need not set about finding out what rent is due.   Smith *v.* Russel, 3 Taunt. 400.   And the sheriff is bound only as to the rent actually due at the time of the taking, and not such rent as shall have accrued due whilst he is in possession. Hoskins *v.* Knight, and Bassett *v.* Same, 1 M. & S. 245.—CHITTY.

(35) By stat. 1 & 2 Vict. c. 110, s. 12, the effect of a writ of *fieri facias* is also much extended.   The sheriff may now seize and take any money or bank-notes, cheques, bills of exchange, promissory-notes, bonds, specialties, or other securities for money belong-ing to the person against whose effects such *fieri facias* is sued out, and may pay the money or bank-notes to the execution-creditor, and sue for the amount secured by the bills of exchange and other securities.   The same statute, extended by stat. 3 & 4 Vict. c. 82, it may here be mentioned, provided a means by which stock in the public funds and stock or shares in public companies, standing in the name of the debtor or of any person in trust for him, or in which the debtor has an interest, whether in possession, reversion, or remainder, vested or contingent, may be charged with the payment of the amount for which judgment shall have been recovered.   Such stock or shares may be charged by order of a judge, which order may be made in the first instance *ex parte*, and, on notice to the bank or company, shall operate as a *distringas.*—STEWART.

(36) [That you cause to be levied.]
(37) Lloyd *v.* Wyckoff, 6 Hals. (N. J. Law) 218, 220 (1830).   1 Freeman on Execu-tions, § 6 (2 ed.).
(38) *Vide supra*, p. 417.
(39) [Of ecclesiastical goods.]
(40) [He hath chosen.]   Leake's Law of Contracts, 135 (3 ed.).

judgment for a debt, or damages, or upon the forfeiture of a recognizance taken in the king's court.(41)　By the common law a man could only have satisfaction of goods, chattels, and the present profits of lands, by the two last-mentioned writs of *fieri facias*, or *levari facias;* bu: not the possession of the lands themselves; which was a natural consequence of the feodal principles, which prohibited the alienation, and of course the encumbering, of the fief with the debts of the owner.(42)　And, when the restriction of alienation began to wear away, the consequence still continued; and no creditor could take the possession of lands, but only levy the growing profits: so that, if the defendant aliened his lands, the plaintiff was ousted of his remedy.　The statute therefore granted this writ, (called an *elegit*, because it is in the choice or election of the plaintiff whether he will sue out this writ or one of the former,) by which the defendant's goods and chattels are not sold, but only appraised; and all of them (except oxen and beasts of the plough) are delivered to the plaintiff, at such reasonable appraisement and price, in part of satisfaction of his debt.　If the goods are not sufficient, then the moiety or *one half of his freehold lands, which he　[*419 had at the time of the judgment given,(*f*) whether held in his own name, or by any other in trust for him,(*g*)(43) are also to be delivered to the plaintiff; to hold, till out of the rents and profits thereof the debt be levied, or till the defendant's interest be expired; as till the death of the defendant, if he be tenant for life or in tail.(44)　During this period the plaintiff is called tenant by *elegit*, of whom we spoke in a former part of these commentaries.(*h*)

(*f*) 2 Inst. 395.
(*g*) Stat. 29 Car. II. c. 3.

(*h*) Book ii. ch. 10.

---

(41) State *v.* Stout, 6 Hals. (N. J. Law) 362, 368 (1830).

(42) People *v.* Haskins, 7 Wend. 463, 466 (N. Y. 1831). Cox's Adm'r *v.* Wood, 20 Ind. 54, 62 (1863).

(43) The words in the statute referred to (29 Car. II. c. 3) are *at the time of the said execution sued*, and refer to the seisin of the trustee; therefore, if the trustee has conveyed the lands before execution sued, though he was seised in trust for the defendant at the time of the judgment, the lands cannot be taken in execution. Com. Rep. 227.—CHITTY.

(44) Calhoun *v.* Snider, 6 Binn. 135, 141 (Pa. 1813). Ridge *v.* Prather, 1 Blackf. 401, 402 (Ind. 1825). McAusland *v.* Pundt, 1 Neb. 211, 248 (1871). Tyler on Ejectment and Adverse Possession, 176 (1871). Newell on Ejectment, § 36, p. 84 (1892).

And the sheriff is not bound to deliver a moiety of each particular tenement and farm, but only certain tenements, etc. making in value a moiety of the whole. Doe d. Taylor *v.* Earl of Abingdon, 2 Doug. 473. He should return that he had delivered an equal moiety of the premises, and should set it out by metes and bounds, or the return is void. Fenny d. Masters *v.* Durrent, 1 B. & A. 40. And where the sheriff delivered one moiety, upon a second *elegit*, the other was held to be wholly void. Morris *v.* Jones, 3 D. & R. 603. 2 B. & C. 232, S. C.

It has been considered in practice that although the sheriff might deliver the moiety to the plaintiff in *elegit*, yet that ejectment was necessary to complete his title; but, *semble*, that entry is good under the writ. Rogers *v.* Pitcher, 6 Taunt. 202.

An examined copy of the judgment-roll, containing the award of the *elegit*, is evidence of the plaintiff's title; and, in action for use and occupation against the tenant, the production of a copy of the *elegit* and of the inquisition thereunder is unnecessary. Ramsbottom *v.* Buckhurst, 2 M. & S. 565.

The defendant, in the writ of *elegit*, may, on motion, obtain a reference to the master to take an account of rents, etc. received by the plaintiff; and if it appears that the debt and costs have been satisfied, possession will be restored. Price *v.* Varney, 5 D. & R. 612. 3 B. & C. 733, S. C.—CHITTY.

The effect of the proceeding under the writ is to give the creditor a legal title which he may enforce at law by ejectment. Robert *v.* Hodges, 1 C. E. Green (N. J. Eq.) 299, 304 (1863). In a creditor's suit, by a bond creditor, independently of any statutory provision, the personal estate was always first applied, as far as it would go, to save the realty; and the statute making lands liable to be taken in execution and sold for the payment of debts, has made no alteration as to any creditor in that respect. Tessier *v.* Wise, 3 Bland, 28 (Md. 1830).

We there observed that till this statute, by the ancient common law, lands were not liable to be charged with, or seised for, debts; because by these means the connection between lord and tenant might be destroyed, fraudulent alienations might be made, and the services be transferred to be performed by a stranger; provided the tenant incurred a large debt, sufficient to cover the land. And therefore, even by this statute, only one half was, and now is, subject to execution; that out of the remainder sufficient might be left for the lord to distrain upon for his services. And upon the same feodal principle, copyhold lands are at this day not liable to be taken in execution upon a judgment.(*i*)(45) But, in case of a debt to the king, it appears by *magna carta*, c. 8, that it was allowed by the common law for him to take possession of the lands till the debt was paid. For he, being the grand superior and ultimate proprietor of all landed estates, might seise the lands into his own hands, if any thing was owing from the vassal; and could not be said to be defrauded of his services, when the ouster of the vassal proceeded from his own command. This execution, or seising of lands by *elegit*, is of so high a nature, that after it the body of the defendant cannot be taken: but if execution can only be had of the goods, because there are no lands, and such goods are not sufficient to pay the debt, a *capias ad satisfaciendum*(46) may then be had after the *elegit;* for such *elegit* is in this case no more in effect than a *fieri facias.*(*j*)(47) So that body and goods may be taken in execution, or land and goods; but not body and land too, upon any judgment between subject and subject in the course of the common law. But,

5. Upon some prosecutions given by statute; as in the case of recog-
*420]   nizances or debts acknowledged on statutes merchant, or *statutes staple, (pursuant to the statutes 13 Edw. I. *de mercatoribus*, and 27 Edw. III. c. 9;) upon forfeiture of these, the body, lands, and goods may all be taken at once in execution to compel the payment of the debt. The process hereon is usually called an *extent*, or *extendi facias*, because the sheriff is to cause the lands, etc., to be appraised to their full extended value before he delivers them to the plaintiff, that it may be certainly known how soon the debt will be satisfied.(*k*) And by statute 33 Hen. VIII. c. 39, all obligations made to the king shall have the same force and of consequence the same remedy to recover them as a statute staple; though, indeed, before this statute the king was entitled to sue out execution against the body, lands, and goods of his accountant or debtor.(*l*)(48) And his debt shall, in

---

(*i*) 1 Roll. Abr. 888.   (*k*) F. N. B. 131.
(*j*) Hob. 58.   (*l*) 3 Rep. 12.

---

(45) By the statute 1 & 2 Vict. c. 110, a great alteration has been made in the law in this respect. By s. 11, the sheriff is empowered to deliver unto the judgment-creditor *all* lands, tenements, and hereditaments, including those of *copyhold* or customary tenure, which the person against whom execution is so sued out, or any person in trust for him, shall have been seised or possessed of at the time of entering up the judgment, or over which the judgment-debtor at the time has, or at any time afterwards shall have, a disposing power capable of being exercised for his own benefit.—STEWART.

In this country lands have always been subject to sale on execution for the payment of the debts of the owner. Dewit *v.* Osborn, 5 Ohio, 480, 483 (1832). And lands descended to the heirs are liable for the debts of the ancestor. Boone's Law of Real Property, § 275, pp. 311, 312 (1883). As to this liability in Rhode Island, see Hopkins *v.* Ladd, 12 R. I. 279 (1879). The homestead exemption in this country generally is not in derogation of the common law, but it is rather the limitation and exclusion of that exemption which is not in accordance with the common law. Riggs *v.* Sterling, 60 Mich. 643, 648 (1886).

(46) *Vide supra*, p. 414.
(47) *Vide supra*, p. 417.
(48) The writ in aid was formerly grossly abused; the king's name often became an engine of great fraud or oppression,—to remedy which stat. 57 Geo. III. c. 117 was passed. The abuse to which I have adverted was this: not only any person indebted or likely to be indebted to the crown on specialty or record, but any one so indebted in part, or by

suing out execution, be preferred to that of any other creditor who hath not obtained judgment before the king commenced his suit.(m) The king's judgment also affects all lands which the king's debtor hath at or after the time of contracting his debt, or which any of his officers mentioned in the statute 13 Eliz. c. 4 hath at or after the time of his entering on the office; so that, if such officer of the crown aliens for a valuable consideration, the land shall be liable to the king's debt even in the hands of a *bona fide* purchaser; though the debt due to the king was contracted by the vendor many years after the alienation.(n) Whereas, judgment between subject and subject related, even at common law, no further back than the first day of the term in which they were recovered, in respect of the lands of the debtor, and did not bind his goods and chattels but from the date of the writ of execution; and now, by the statute of frauds, 29 Car. II. c. 3, the judgment shall not bind the land in the hands of a *bona *fide* purchaser, but   [*421 only from the day of actually signing the same; which is directed by the statute to be punctually entered on the record: nor shall the writ of execution bind the goods in the hands of a stranger or the purchaser,(o) but only from the actual delivery of the writ to the sheriff or other officer, who is therefore ordered to endorse on the back of it the day of his receiving the same.

These are the methods which the law of England has pointed out for the execution of judgments: and when the plaintiff's demand is satisfied, either by the voluntary payment of the defendant or by this compulsory process or otherwise, satisfaction ought to be entered on the record, that the defendant may not be liable to be hereafter harassed a second time on the same account. But all these writs of execution must be sued out within a year and a day after the judgment is entered; otherwise the court concludes *prima facie* that the judgment is satisfied and extinct: yet, however, it will grant a writ of *scire facias*, in pursuance of statute Westm. 2, 13 Edw. I. c. 45, for the defendant to show cause why the judgment should not be revived, and execution had against him; to which the defendant may plead such matter as he has to allege in order to show why process of execution should not be issued;(49) or the plaintiff may still bring an action of debt, founded on this dormant judgment, which was the only method of revival allowed by the common law.(p)(50)

(m) Stat. 33 Hen. VII. c. 39, § 74.
(n) 10 Rep. 55, 56.

(o) Skin. 257.
(p) Co. Litt. 290.

simple contract only, might obtain the extent in aid to be issued in his favor. The instant that the writ issued, all the property of the debtor became liable to the extent at the suit of the crown; and thus his creditors were deprived of participation in such property, the whole perhaps being absorbed by the alleged crown-debtor. But the statute mentioned above limits the issuing of this writ to cases where a debt shall be actually due to and previously demanded on the part of the crown. Before the statute, it was sufficient that the party suggested the existence of the debt to entitle him to sue out the writ and to the money levied thereon; but now the writ cannot be issued unless the sum actually due to his majesty be stated and specified in the fiat endorsed thereon; and, when levied, the sheriff is to pay the amount over to his majesty's use. Any overplus is to be paid into court, subject to its disposition on summary application. The expectation of preference formerly capable of being realized is by the statute, therefore, in a great degree defeated.—CHITTY.

(49) Hannon *v.* Dedrick, 3 Barb. 122, 194, 195 (N. Y. 1848).

(50) But the writ of *scire facias* for the ordinary purpose of reviving a judgment, now called a "writ of reviver," is retained. During the lives of the parties to a judgment; or those of them, during whose lives execution may at present issue within a year and a day without a *scire facias;* and within six years from the recovery of the judgment, execution may now, however, issue without revival of the judgment. Com. Law Proc. Act, 1852, s. 128.—STEWART. The common law rules on this subject have been changed by statutory enactments in a majority of the United States. See Little *v.* Little, 5 Mo. 227, 228 (1838). Gilbert *v.* Stockman, 81 Wis. 602, 609 (1892).

In this manner are the several remedies given by the English law for all sorts of injuries, either real or personal, administered by the several courts of justice, and their respective officers. In the course therefore of the present book, we have, first, seen and considered the nature of remedies, by the mere act of the parties, or mere operation of law, without any suit in courts. We have next taken a review of remedies by suit or action in courts; and therein have contemplated, first, the nature and species of courts, instituted for the redress of injuries in general; and then have shown in what particular courts *422] application must be made for the redress of particular injuries, or the doctrine of jurisdictions and *cognizance. We afterwards proceeded to consider the nature and distribution of wrongs and injuries affecting every species of personal and real rights, with the respective remedies by suit, which the law of the land has afforded for every possible injury. And, lastly, we have deduced and pointed out the method and progress of obtaining such remedies in the courts of justice: proceeding from the first general complaint or *original* writ, through all the stages of *process*, to compel the defendant's appearance; and of *pleading*, or formal allegation on the one side, and excuse or denial on the other; with the examination of the validity of such complaint or excuse, upon *demurrer;* or the truth of the facts alleged and denied, upon *issue* joined, and its several *trials;* to the *judgment* or sentence of the law, with respect to the nature and amount of the redress to be specifically given: till, after considering the suspension of that judgment by writs in the nature of *appeals*, we have arrived at its final *execution;* which puts the party in specific possession of his right by the intervention of ministerial officers, or else gives him an ample satisfaction, either by equivalent damages, or by the confinement of his body who is guilty of the injury complained of.

This care and circumspection in the law,—in providing that no man's right shall be affected by any legal proceeding without giving him previous notice, and yet that the debtor shall not by receiving such notice take occasion to escape from justice; in requiring that every complaint be accurately and precisely ascertained in writing, and be as pointedly and exactly answered; in clearly stating the question either of law or of fact; in deliberately resolving the former after full argumentative discussion, and indisputably fixing the latter by a diligent and impartial trial; in correcting such errors as may have arisen in either of those modes of decision, from accident, mistake, or surprise; and in finally enforcing the judgment, when nothing can be alleged to impeach it;—this anxiety to maintain and restore to every individual the enjoyment of his civil rights, without intrenching upon those of any other indi- *423] vidual in the nation, this parental solicitude *which pervades our whole legal constitution, is the genuine offspring of that spirit of equal liberty which is the singular felicity of Englishmen. At the same time it must be owned to have given a handle, in some degree, to those complaints of delay in the practice of the law, which are not wholly without foundation, but are greatly exaggerated beyond the truth. There may be, it is true, in this, as in all other departments of knowledge, a few unworthy professors; who study the science of chicane and sophistry rather than of truth and justice; and who, to gratify the spleen, the dishonesty and wilfulness of their clients, may endeavor to screen the guilty, by an unwarrantable use of those means which were intended to protect the innocent. But the frequent disappointments, and the constant discountenance, that they meet with in the courts of justice, have confined these men (to the honor of this age be it spoken) both in number and reputation to indeed a very despicable compass.

Yet some delays there certainly are, and must unavoidably be, in the conduct of a suit, however desirous the parties and their agents may be to come to a speedy determination. These arise from the same original causes as were mentioned in examining a former complaint;(q) from liberty, property, civility, commerce, and an extent of populous territory: which, whenever we are willing to exchange for tyranny, poverty, barbarism, idleness, and a barren desert, we may then enjoy the same despatch of causes that is so highly extolled in some foreign countries.   But common sense and a little experience will convince us, that more time and circumspection are requisite in causes where the suitors have valuable and permanent rights to lose, than where their property is trivial and precarious, and what the law gives them to-day may be seized by their prince to-morrow.   In Turkey, says Montesquieu,(r) where little regard is shown to the lives or fortunes of the subject, all causes are quickly decided: the basha on a summary hearing, orders which party he pleases to be bastinadoed, and then sends them about their business.   But in *free states the trouble, expense, and delays of   [*424 judicial proceedings are the price that every subject pays for his liberty: and in all governments, he adds, the formalities of law increase, in proportion to the value which is set on the honor, the fortune, the liberty and life of the subject.

From these principles it might reasonably follow, that the English courts should be more subject to delays than those of other nations; as they set a greater value on life, on liberty, and on property.   But it is our peculiar felicity to enjoy the advantage, and yet to be exempted from a proportionable share of the burden.   For the course of the civil law, to which most other nations conform their practice, is much more tedious than ours; for proof of which I need only appeal to the suitors of those courts in England, where the practice of the Roman law is allowed in its full extent.   And particularly in France, not only our Fortescue(s) accuses (on his own knowledge) their courts of most unexampled delays in administering justice; but even a writer of their own(t) has not scrupled to testify, that there were in his time more causes there depending than in all Europe besides, and some of them a hundred years old.   But (not to enlarge on the prodigious improvements which have been made in the celerity of justice by the disuse of real actions, by the statutes of amendment and jeofails,(u) and by other more modern regulations, which it now might be indelicate to remember, but which posterity will never forget) the time and attendance afforded by the judges in our English courts are also greater than those of many other countries.   In the Roman calendar there were in the whole year but twenty-eight judicial or triverbial(w) days allowed to the prætor for deciding causes:(x) whereas, with us, one-fourth of the year is term-time, in which three courts constantly sit for the despatch of matters of law; besides the very close attendance of the court of chancery for determining *suits in equity, and   [*425 the numerous courts of assize and *nisi prius* that sit in vacation for the trial of matters of fact.   Indeed, there is no other country in the known world, that hath an institution so commodious and so adapted to the despatch of causes, as our trial by jury in those courts for the decision of facts; in no other nation under heaven does justice make her progress twice in each year into almost every part of the kingdom, to decide upon the spot by the voice of the people themselves the disputes of the remotest provinces.

And here this part of our commentaries, which regularly treats only of redress at the common law, would naturally draw to a conclusion.   But, as the proceedings in the courts of equity are very different from those at common law, and as those courts are of a very general and extensive jurisdic-

(q) See page 327.
(r) Sp. L. b. 6, c. 2.
(s) De Laud. LL. c. 53
(t) Bodin. de republ. l. 6, c. 6.
(u) See page 407.
(w) Otherwise called dies fasti in quibus licebat

prætori fari tria verba, do, dico, addico. [Lawful days, in which the prætor was permitted the use of three words, do, dico, addico, I give judgment, I expound the law, I execute the law.] Calv. Lex. 285.
(x) Spelman of the Terms, § 4, c. 2.

tion, it is in some measure a branch of the task I have undertaken, to give the student some general idea of the forms of practice adopted by those courts. These will therefore be the subject of the ensuing chapter.

CHAPTER XXVII.

OF PROCEEDINGS IN THE COURTS OF EQUITY.

*426]   *BEFORE we enter on the proposed subject of the ensuing chapter, viz., the nature and method of proceedings in the courts of equity, it will be proper to recollect the observations which were made in the beginning of this book(a) on the principal tribunals of that kind, acknowledged by the constitution of England; and to premise a few remarks upon those particular causes, wherein any of them claims and exercises a sole jurisdiction, distinct from and exclusive of the other.(1)

(a) Pages 45, 50, 78.

---

(1) That the courts of equity and courts of law are not opposed to each other, and often concur in the exercise of their powers, to promote the ends of substantial justice, is not now disputed. It is said that matters of fact should be left to courts of law for the decision of a jury, (1 Ridgway's Parl. Car. 9;) and issues are oftentimes directed for that purpose; yet "there is no doubt," says lord Eldon, "that according to the constitution of this court it may take upon itself the decision of every fact put in issue upon the record." And again, "This court has a right (to be exercised very tenderly and sparingly) of deciding without issues." 9 Ves. 168. The general rule is that a court of equity will never exercise jurisdiction over criminal proceedings. Yet in a case where the plaintiffs indicted defendant's agent at the sessions, where the plaintiffs themselves were judges, for a breach of the peace, lord Hardwicke made an order to restrain the prosecution till after hearing of the cause and further order; and where a bill is brought to quiet possession, if the plaintiff afterwards prefer an indictment for forcible entry, this court will stop the proceedings upon such indictment. 2 Atk. 302. The court of chancery has no jurisdiction to prevent a crime, except in the protection of infants. Therefore it is said that the publication of a libel cannot be restrained. 2 Swan. 413. Nor will the court compel a discovery in aid of criminal proceedings. 2 Ves. 398. The court of chancery has a concurrent jurisdiction with the admiralty, (Gilb. Eq. Rep. 228,) and may repeal letters of reprisal after a peace, though there is a clause in the patent that no treaty of peace shall prejudice it. 1 Vern. 54. So equity may relieve after verdict in King's Bench or Common Pleas, and even grant a perpetual injunction after five trials at law on the same point, and verdicts the same way; but equity is very tender in the exercise of this power. 2 P. W. 425. 10 Mod. 1. And a court of equity will not review the orders of the Exchequer as a court of revenue; nor interfere where that court, as a court of revenue, is competent to decide the subject-matter. 3 Ridgw. P. C. 80.

Matters arising out of England.—A question concerning the right and title to the Isle of Man may be determined in a court of chancery. 1 Ves. 202. Where the defendant is in England, though the cause of suit arose in the plantations, if the bill be brought here, the court *agens in personam* [Acting against the person] may, by compulsion of the person, force him to do justice; for the jurisdiction of the chancellor is not ousted, (3 Atk. 589. See 1 Jac. & W. 27;) and this although in general all questions respecting real estates belong to the country where they are situate. Elliott *v.* Lord Minto, 6 Mod. 16.

1st. It is assistant to the common law by removing legal impediments to a fair decision of a question depending in those courts; as preventing the setting up of outstanding terms, etc. 5 Mad. 428. 2 J. & W. 391.

2d. It acts concurrently with the common law by compelling a discovery which may enable those courts to decide according to the real facts and justice of the case; as where the discovery is to ascertain whether the defendant did not promise to marry, (Forrest, Rep. 42;) or to disprove the defendant's plea, that he had made no promise within six years, and to compel him to state whether he has not promised within that time, (5 Mad. 331;) but he has a right to protect himself in equity by the statute of limitations from a discovery as to the original constitution of the debt, or whether it has since been paid. 5 Mad. 331. So he may be required to disclose whether he is an alien or not, (2 Ves. Sen.

I have already(*b*) attempted to trace (though very concisely) the history, rise, and progress of the extraordinary court, or court of equity, in chancery.

(*b*) Page 50, etc.

287, 494;) but where a discovery would subject a party to penalty or forfeiture it is not to be obtained, (1 Ves. 56. 2 Ch. Rep. 68. 2 Atk. 392. 2 Ves. 265. 1 Eq. Abr. 131, p. 10;) except in cases under the stock-jobbing act, (7 Geo. II. c. 8, s. 1, 2 Marsh Rep. 125,) and some other particular provisions. Nor will the court compel a discovery in aid of criminal proceedings. 2 Ves. 398. *Vide* Mitf. Pl. 150. It exercises concurrent jurisdiction in perpetuating testimony in danger of being lost before it can be used; by preserving property during litigation; by counteracting fraudulent judgments; by setting bounds to oppressive litigation; and in cases of fraud, accident, mistake, account, partition, and dower.

3d. It claims *exclusive jurisdiction* in matters of trust and confidence, and whenever, upon the principles of universal justice, the interference of a court of judicature is necessary to prevent a wrong, and the positive law is silent. 1 Fonb. Eq. p. 9, n. (f.)

The matters over which the court of chancery maintains an equitable jurisdiction have been arranged in the following alphabetical order; and, as this analysis has the recommendation of practical utility, we shall proceed to embody the principal rules and decisions under each head respectively.

1st. ACCIDENT AND MISTAKE.
2d. ACCOUNT.
3d. FRAUD.
4th. INFANTS.
5th. SPECIFIC PERFORMANCE OF AGREEMENTS.
6th. TRUSTS.

1st. ACCIDENT AND MISTAKE.—By accident is meant, where a case is distinguished from others of the like nature by unusual circumstances; for the court of chancery cannot control the maxims of the common law, because of general inconvenience; but only where the observation of a rule is attended with some unusual and particular inconvenience. 10 Mod. 1.

1. *Bonds, etc.*—Equity will relieve against the loss of deeds (3 V. & B. 54) or bonds, (5 Ves. 235. 6 Ves. 812,) but not if the bond be voluntary. 1 Ch. Ca. 77. It will also set up a bond so lost, or destroyed, against sureties, though the principal be out of the jurisdiction. 3 Atk. 93. 1 Ch. Ca. 77. 9 Ves. 464. Bonds made *joint*, instead of several, may be modified according to intent in some cases. 2 Atk. 33. 9 Ves. 118. 17 Ves. 514. 1 Meriv. 564.

Boundaries, etc.—Equity will ascertain the boundaries, or fix the value, where lands have been intermixed by unity of possession. 2 Meriv. 507. 1 Swanst. 9. So to distinguish copyhold from freehold lands within the manor. 4 Ves. 180. Nels. 14.

Penalties, Forfeitures, etc., incurred by accident, are relieved against, (2 Vern. 594. 1 Stra. 453. 1 Bro. C. C. 418. 2 Sch. & Lef. 685,) where the thing may be done afterwards, or a compensation made for it. 1 Ch. Ca. 24. 2 Ventr. 352. 9 Mod. 22. 18 Ves. 63. But no relief is given in the case of a voluntary composition payable at a fixed period. Ambl. 332. See 1 Vern. 210. 2 Atk. 527. 3 Atk. 585. 16 Ves. 372. Equity will not relieve against the payment of stipulated, or, as they are sometimes called, liquidated, damages, (2 Atk. 194. Finch. 117. 2 Cha. Ca. 198. 6 Bro. P. C. 470. 1 Cox. 27. 2 Bos. & P. 346. 3 Atk. 395;) and forfeitures under acts of parliament, or conditions in law, which do not admit of compensation, or a forfeiture which may be considered as a limitation of an estate, which determines it when it happens, cannot be relieved against. 1 Ball & Bat. 373, 478. 1 Stra. 447, 452. Prec. Ch. 574.

Mistake.—A defective conveyance *to charitable uses* is always aided, (1 Eden, 14. 2 Vern. 755. Prec. Ch. 16. 2 Vern. 453. Hob. 136;) but neither a mistake in a fine (if after death of conusor) or in the names in a recovery is supplied, especially against a purchaser, (2 Vern. 3 Ambl. 102,) nor an erroneous recovery in the manorial court. 1 Vern. 367. Mistakes in a deed or contract, founded on *good consideration*, may be rectified. 1 Ves. 317. 2 Atk. 203. And if a bargain and sale be made and not enrolled within six months, equity will compel the vendor to make a good title by executing another bargain and sale which may be enrolled. 6 Ves. 745. A conveyance defective in form may be rectified, (1 Eq. Abr. 320. 1 P. W. 279,) even against assignees (2 Vern. 564. 1 Atk. 162. 4 Bro. C. C. 472) or against representatives. 1 Anst. 14. So defects in surrenders of copyhold, (2 Vern. 564. Salk. 449. 2 Vern. 151,) but not the omission of formalities required by act of parliament in conveyances. 5 Ves. 240. 3 Bro. C. C. 571. 13 Ves. 588. 15 Ves. 60. 6 Ves. 745. 11 Ves. 626. Defects in the mode of conveyance may be remedied. 4 Bro. C. C. 382. So the execution of powers. 2 P. Wms. 623.

2d. ACCOUNT.—*Mutual* dealings and demands between parties, which are too complex to be accurately taken by trial at law, may be adjusted in equity, (1 Sch. & Lefroy, 309.

The same jurisdiction is exercised, and the same system of redress pursued, in the equity court of the exchequer, with a distinction, however, as to some

13 Ves. 278, 279. 1 Mad. Ch. 86, and note (i.);) but if the subject be matter of set-off at law, and capable of proof, a bill will not lie, (6 Ves. 136;) and the difficulty in adjusting the account constitutes no legal objection to an action. 5 Taunt. 481. 1 Marsh. 115. 2 Camp. 238.

3d. FRAUD.—Equity has so great an abhorrence of fraud that it will set aside its own decrees if founded thereupon; and a bill lies to vacate letters-patent obtained by fraud. 13 Vin. Abr. 543, pl. 9. 1 Vern. 277. All deceitful practices and artful devices contrary to the plain rules of common honesty are frauds at common law, and punishable there, but for some frauds or deceits there is no remedy at law, in which cases they are cognizable in equity as one of the chief branches of its original jurisdiction. 2 Ch. Ca. 103. Finch, 161. 2 P. Wms. 270. 2 Vern. 189. 2 Atk. 324. 3 P. Wms. 130. Bridg. Ind. tit. Fraud, pl. 1. Where a person is prevented by fraud from executing a deed, equity will regard it as already done. 1 Jac. & W. 99

1. *Trustees* are in no case permitted to purchase from themselves the trust estate, (1 Vern. 465.) nor their solicitor, (3 Mer. 200;) nor in bankruptcy are the commissioners (6 Ves. 617) or assignees, (6 Ves. 627,) nor their solicitors, (10 Ves. 381;) nor committee or keeper of a lunatic, (13 Ves. 156,) nor an executor, (1 Ves. & B. 170. 1 Cox, 134,) nor governors of charities. 17 Ves. 500.

2dly. *Attorney and Client.*—Fraud in transactions between attorneys and client is guarded against most watchfully. 2 Ves. Jr. 201. 1 Mad. Ch. 114, 115, 116.

3dly. *Heirs, Sailors, etc.*—Equity will protect improvident heirs against agreements binding on their future expectancies negotiated during some temporary embarrassment, provided such agreement manifest great inadequacy of consideration. 1 Vern. 169. 2 Vern. 27. 1 P. Wms. 310. 1 Bro. C. C. 1. 2 Ves 157. It will also set aside unequal contracts obtained from sailors respecting their prize-money, (Newl. Cont. 443. 1 Wils. 229. 2 Ves. 281, 516;) and the fourth section of 20 Geo. III. c. 24 declares all bargains, etc. concerning any share of a prize taken from any of his majesty's enemies, etc. void. *Vide* Newl. Cont. 444.

4thly. *Guardian.*—Fraud between guardian and ward is also the subject of strict cognizance in the court of chancery. For the details under this head, see 1 book, ch. xvii. and notes

5thly *Injunctions.*—In a modern work the subject of injunctions is considered under the head of fraud, (see 1 Mad. Ch. 125;) but it seems to deserve a distinct consideration. An injunction is a method by which the court of chancery interferes to prevent the commission of fraud and mischief. The exercise of this authority may be obtained,—1st. To stay proceedings in other courts. 2d. To restrain infringements of patent. 3d. To stay waste. 4th. To preserve copyright. 5th. To restrain negotiation of bills, etc. or the transfer of stock. 6th. To prevent nuisances, and in most cases where the rights of others are invaded and the remedy by action at law is too remote to prevent increasing damage. See 1 Mad. Ch. 157 to 165. An injunction to stay proceedings at law does not extend to a distress for rent, (1 Jac. & W. 392;) nor has equity any jurisdiction to stop goods in transitu in any case; nor will the court restrain the sailing of a vessel for such purpose by injunction. 2 Jac. & W. 349.

6thly. *Bills of Peace*, which form an essential check on litigation. 1 Bro. P. C. 266. 2 Bro. P. C. 217. Bunb. 158. 1 P. Wms. 671. Prec. Cha. 262. 1 Stra. 404. For this purpose a perpetual injunction will be granted. See 10 Mod. 1. 1 Bro. P. C. 268. This bill cannot hold in disputes between two persons only. 2 Atk. 483, 391. 4 Bro. C. C. 157. Vin. tit. Ch. 425, pl. 35. 3 P. Wms. 156.

7thly. *Bill of Interpleader* will lie to prevent fraud or injustice, where two or more parties claim adversely to each other, from him in possession; otherwise it will not lie, (1 Mer. 405;) for in such case it is necessary the two claimants should settle their rights before the person holding possession be required to give up to either. 2 Ves. Jr. 310. Mitf. Pl. 39. 1 Mad. Ch. 173. And, on the same principle,

8thly. *Bills or Writs of Certiorari*, to remove a cause from an inferior or incompetent jurisdiction.

9thly. *Bills to perpetuate testimony* in danger of being lost before the right can be ascertained.

10thly. *Bills to discover evidence* in possession of defendant, whereof plaintiff would be otherwise wholly deprived, or of deeds, etc. in defendant's custody.

11thly. *Bills of Quia Timet*, for the purpose of preventing a possible future inquiry, and thereby quieting men's minds and estates, etc. 1 Mad. Ch. 224. Newl. on Contr. 93, 493.

12thly. *Bills for the delivering up of Deeds.*—As where an instrument is void at common law, as being against the policy of the law, it belongs to the jurisdiction of equity to order it to be delivered up. 11 Ves. 535. In Mayor, etc. of Colchester *v.* Lowton, lord

few matters, peculiar to each tribunal, and in which the other cannot interfere. And, first, of those peculiar to the chancery.

Eldon says, "My opinion has always been (differing from others) that a court of equity has jurisdiction and duty to order a void deed to be delivered up and placed with those whose property may be affected by it, if it remains in other hands." 1 Ves. & B. 244.

13th. Bills for *apportionment* or *contribution* between persons standing in particular relations one to another. 5 Ves. 792. 2 Freem. 97.

14th. For *dower* and *partition*.

15th. To establish *moduses*.

16th. Bills to *marshal securities*.

17th. Bills to secure property in litigation in *other courts*. And

18th and lastly. Bills to compel lords of manors to hold courts, or to admit copyholders and bills to reverse erroneous judgments in copyhold courts. *Vide* 1 Madd. Ch. 242 to 253.

4th. INFANTS.—The protection and care which the court of chancery exercises over infants have already been incidentally noticed. *Vide* 1 book, chs. xvi. xvii. and notes.

Wards of Court.—To make a child a ward of court, it is sufficient to file a bill; and it is a contempt to marry a ward of court, though the infant's father be living. Ambl. 301. The court of chancery, representing the king as *parens patriæ* [Parent of his country], has jurisdiction to control the right of the father to the possession of his infant; but the court of King's Bench has not any portion of that delegated authority. The court of chancery will restrain the father from removing his child, or doing any act towards removing it, out of the jurisdiction. So will the court refuse the possession of the child to its mother if she has withdrawn herself from her husband. 10 Ves. 52. Co. Litt. 89, (a.) n. 70. 2 Fonb. Tr. Eq. 224, n. (a.) 2 Bro. C. C. 499. 1 P. Wms. 705. 4 Bro. C. C. 101. 2 P. Wms. 102. The court retains its jurisdiction over the property of a ward of court after twenty-one, if it remains in court, and, if the ward marries, will order a proper settlement to be made, or reform an improper one, unless the ward consents to the settlement either in court or under a commission. 2 Sim. & Stu. 123, n. (a.) In case the husband assign the property of the wife, who is a ward of court, it shall not prevail, but the court will direct even the whole of the property in question to be settled on the wife and her children, and the assignee will not be entitled even to the arrear of interest accrued since the marriage. 3 Ves. 506.

5th. SPECIFIC PERFORMANCE OF AGREEMENTS.—The jurisdiction of the courts of equity in matters of this kind, though certainly as ancient as the reign of Edward IV., did not obtain an unresisting and uniform acquiescence on the part of the public till many years afterwards. See 1 Roll. Rep. 354. 2 ib. 443. Latch. 172.

Realty.—Thus equity enforces agreements for the purchase of lands or things which relate to realties, but not (generally) those which relate to personal chattels, as the sale of stock, corn, hops, etc.; in such cases the remedy is at law. 3 Atk. 383. Newl. Contr. 87.

That which is agreed to be done is in equity considered as already done, (2 P. Wms. 222;) and therefore when a husband covenants on his marriage to make a settlement charged upon his lands, which he is afterwards prevented from completing by sudden death, the heir shall make satisfaction of the settlement out of the estate. Ib. 233.

Personalty.—In agreements, with penalties for the breach of them, it is necessary to distinguish the cases of a penalty intended as a security for a collateral object from those where the contract itself has *assessed the damages* which the party is to pay upon his doing or omitting to do the particular act. In these latter cases equity will not interfere either to prevent or to enforce the act in question, or to restrain the recovery of damages after they have become due; but in the former, where it plainly appears that the specific performance of that act was the primary object of the agreement, and the penalty intended merely to operate as a collateral security for its being done, though at law the party might make his election either to do the particular act or to pay the penalty, a court of equity will not permit him to exercise such right, but will compel him to perform the object of the agreement. Newl. Contr. cap. 17. Thus, as the principle whereon a specific performance of agreement relating to personals is refused is that there is as complete a remedy to be obtained at law, therefore, where a party sues merely on a memorandum of agreement, (a mere memorandum not being regarded as valid at law,) a court of equity will give relief; for equity suffers not a right to be without a remedy. 3 Atk. 382, 385. But it is only where the legal remedy is inadequate or defective that courts of equity interfere. 8 Ves. 163. Equity will enforce an agreement for the transfer of stock, (10 Ves. 161;) but it has been held that a bill will lie for performance of agreement for purchase of government-stock where its prays for the delivery of the *certificates* which give the legal title to stock. 1 Sim. & Stu. 590. And it seems the court will entertain a suit for the specific performance of a contract for the purchase of a debt. 5 Price. 325. So to sell the good will of a trade and the exclusive use of a secret in dyeing, (1 Sim. & Stu. 74;) but not without great caution. See 1 P. Wms. 181.

1. Upon the abolition of the court of wards, the care, which the crown was bound to take as guardian of its infant tenants, was totally extin-

---

6th. TRUSTS.—Trusts may be created of real or personal estate, and are either, 1st, *Express;* or, 2d, *Implied.* Under the head of implied trusts may be included all resulting trusts, and all such trusts as are not express. Express trusts are created by deed or will. Implied trusts arise in general by construction of law upon the acts or situation of parties. 1 Mad. Cha. 446.

Lunatics.—The custody of the persons and estates of lunatics was a power not originally in the crown, but was given to it by statute for the benefit of the subject. 1 Ridgw. P. C. 224; *et vid.* 2 Inst. 14. And now, by the statute *de prerogativâ regis* [Concerning the prerogative of the king], (17 Edw. II. c. 9 & 10,) the king shall have the real estates of idiots to his own use, and he shall provide for the safe keeping of the real estates of lunatics, so that they shall have a competent maintenance, and the residue is to be kept for their use. 1 Ridgw. P. C. 519, 535. A liberal application of the property of a lunatic is made to secure every comfort his situation will admit, (6 Ves. 8,) without regard to expectants on estate. 1 Ves. Jr. 297. The power of the chancellor extends to making grants from time to time of the lunatic's estate, and, as this power is derived under the sign-manual, in virtue of the prerogative of the crown, the chancellor, who is usually invested with it, is responsible to the crown alone for the right exercise of it. Per Ld. Hardw., 3 Atk. 635. It is said that since the revolution the king has always granted the surplus profits of the estate of an idiot to some of his family. Ridgw. P. C. 510, App. note, (1).

Charities.—The general controlling power of the court over charities does not extend to a charity regulated by governors under a charter, unless they have also the management of the revenues and abuse their trust; which will not be presumed, but must be apparent and made out by evidence. 2 Ves. Jr. 42. The internal management of a charity is the exclusive subject of visitorial jurisdiction; but under a trust as to the revenue, abuse by misapplication is controlled in chancery. 2 Ves. & B. 134.

Executors.—Where an executor has an express legacy, the court of chancery looks upon him as a trustee with regard to the surplus, and will make him account, though the spiritual court has no such power. 1 P. Wms. 7. And where an executor, who was directed to lay out the testator's personalty in the funds, unnecessarily sold out stock, kept large balances in his hand, and resisted payment of debts by false pretences of outstanding demands, he was charged with five per cent. interest and costs, but the court refused to make rests in the account. 1 Jac. & W. 586. And see, on this subject, *ante,* 2 book, ch. 32.

Marshaling Assets.—The testator's whole personal property, whether devised or not, is assets both in law and equity, to which creditors by simple contract, or of any higher order, may have recourse for the satisfaction of their demands. But the testator may, by clear and explicit words, exempt his personalty from payment of debts as against the devisee of his realty, though not as against creditors. The rule in equity is, that in case even of a specialty debt the personal assets shall be first applied, and if deficient, and there be no devise for payment of debts, the heir shall then be charged for assets descended. 2 Atk. 426, 434. For lands are in equity a favored fund, insomuch that the heir at law or devisee of a mortgagor may demand to have the estate mortgaged by such devisor himself, cleared out of the personalty. Vin. Abr. tit. Heir, U. pl. 35. 1 Atk. 487. And a specific devisee of a mortgaged estate is entitled to have it exonerated out of real assets descended. 3 Atk. 430, 439. But at law there is no such distinction of favor shown to lands: a bond-creditor may if he please proceed immediately against the heir without suing the personal representative of his deceased debtor. As to the order in which real assets shall be applied in equity for payment of debts, (after exhausting the personal effects, supposing them not exempted,) the general rule is, first to take lands devised simply for that purpose, then lands descended, and lastly estates specifically devised, even though they are *generally charged with the payment of debts.* 2 Bro. 263.

Equitable assets are such as at law cannot be reached by a creditor as a devise in trust to pay debts of an equity of redemption subject to a mortgage *in fee,* or where the descent is broken by a devise to sell for the payment of debts. 1 Vern. 411. 1 Ch. Ca. 128, n. 2 Atk. 290. But land so devised, subject to a mortgage *for years,* are *legal* assets.

Bankruptcy.—See the consolidation act, (6 Geo. IV. c. 16,) commencing its operation with the present year, and the decisions applicable to its several enactments, *ante,* 2 book, ch. 31.—CHITTY.

In the United States, courts of equity exist in New Jersey, Kentucky, Alabama, Mississippi and Tennessee; in the states of Maine, New Hampshire, Vermont, Massachusetts, Rhode Island, Connecticut, Pennsylvania, Maryland, Virginia, West Virginia, North Carolina, Georgia, Florida, Texas, Arkansas, Michigan, Illinois, Iowa, North and South Dakota, Oregon and Washington, courts of equity as such do not exist, but the principles of equity are administered by the courts of law, under equitable forms and practices; in

guished in every feodal view; but *resulted to the king in his court of　[*427 chancery, together with the general protection(c) of all other *infants*
in the kingdom.　When therefore a fatherless child has no other guardian, the court of chancery has a right to appoint one; and from all proceedings relative thereto, an appeal lies to the house of lords.　The court of exchequer can only appoint a guardian *ad litem*, to manage the defence of the infant if a suit be commenced against him; a power which is incident to the jurisdiction of every court of justice:(d)(2) but when the interest of a minor comes before the court judicially, in the progress of a cause, or upon a bill for that purpose filed, either tribunal indiscriminately will take care of the property of the infant.

2. As to *idiots* and *lunatics:* the king himself used formerly to commit the custody of them to proper committees, in every particular case; but now, to avoid solicitations and the very shadow of undue partiality, a warrant is issued by the king(e) under his royal sign-manual to the chancellor or keeper of his seal to perform this office for him; and, if he acts improperly in granting such custodies, the complaint must be made to the king himself in council.(f)　But the previous proceedings on the commission, to inquire whether or no the party be an idiot or a lunatic, are on the law side of the court of chancery, and can only be redressed (if erroneous) by writ of error in the regular course of law.(3)

3. The king, as *parens patriæ*,(4) has the general superintendence of all *charities;* which he exercises by the keeper of his conscience, the chancellor.(5)　And therefore whenever it is necessary, the attorney-general, at the relation of some informant, (who is usually called the *relator,*) files *ex officio*(6) an information in the court of chancery to have the charity properly established.　By statute also 43 Eliz. c. 4, authority is given to the lord chancellor or lord keeper, and to the chancellor of the duchy of Lancaster, respectively, to grant *commissions under their several　[*428 seals, to inquire into any abuses of charitable donations, and rectify

(c) F. N. B. 27.
(d) Cro. Jac. 641.　2 Lev. 163.　T. Jones, 90.

(e) See book i. ch. 8.
(f) 3 P. Wms. 108.　See Reg. Br. 267.

New York, South Carolina, Ohio, Indiana, Minnesota, Nebraska, Wisconsin and California, the distinction between these two kinds of courts is totally abolished.

(2) Clark *v.* Gilmantien, 12 N. H. 515, 517 (1845).

(3) By stat. 9 Geo. IV. c 41, s. 41, all persons wheresoever in England (not keeping licensed houses, and not being relatives, or a committee appointed by the lord chancellor) receiving into their exclusive care and maintenance any insane person or persons, or represented or alleged to be insane, are required, under pain of misdemeanor, to have a certificate of insanity, an order for reception of every such person so received after 1st of August, 1828, and to transmit copies thereof within five days to the office of metropolitan commissioners in lunacy, to be marked "private return," and also forthwith to give notice of the death or removal of any such person.

And by s. 36 of the same statute, the persons by whose authority any patient shall be delivered into the care of the keeper of any licensed house for the reception of the insane, are, under like pain, required in person, or by some other person appointed in writing, under hand and seal, to visit such person once at least every six months during his confinement, and to enter, in the journal kept at such houses for registering the visits of the commissioners, the date of such visit.—CHITTY.

The proceedings of the court of chancery in the exercise of this branch of its jurisdiction are now regulated by the statute 16 & 17 Vict. c. 70, called "The Lunacy Regulation Act, 1853."—KERR.

(4) [Parent of his country.]

(5) "Here, the commonwealth being substituted for the king, as *parens patriæ*, should exercise the like superintendence and control." Chambers *v.* Educational Soc., 1 B. Mon. 215, 219 (Ky.) 1841.　In England, the sovereign may sustain the character of a trustee; and in this country a state may be a trustee.　Boone's Law of Real Property, § 164, p. 199 (1883).

(6) [Officially.]

the same by decree;(7) which may be reviewed in the respective courts of the several chancellors, upon exceptions taken thereto. But, though this is done in the petty-bag office in the court of chancery, because the commission is there returned, it is not a proceeding at common law, but treated as an original cause in the court of equity. The evidence below is not taken down in writing, and the respondent in his answer to the exceptions may allege what new matter he pleases; upon which they go to proof, and examine witnesses in writing upon all the matters in issue: and the court may decree the respondent to pay all the costs, though no such authority is given by the statute. And as it is thus considered as an original cause throughout, an appeal lies of course from the chancellor's decree to the house of peers, (g) notwithstanding any loose opinions to the contrary. (h)(8)

4. By the several statutes relating to *bankrupts*, a summary jurisdiction is given to the chancellor in many matters consequential or previous to the commissions thereby directed to be issued; from which the statutes give no appeal.(9)

On the other hand, the jurisdiction of the court of chancery doth not extend to some causes wherein relief may be had in the exchequer. No information can be brought, in chancery, for such mistaken charities as are given to the king by the statutes for suppressing superstitious uses. Nor can chancery give any relief against the king, or direct any act to be done by him, or make any decree disposing of or affecting his property; not even in cases where he is a royal trustee.(i)(10) Such causes must be determined in

the court of exchequer, as a court of revenue; which alone has
*429] power *over the king's treasury, and the officers employed in its management: unless where it properly belongs to the duchy court of

---

(g) Duke's Char. Uses, 62, 128. Corporation of Burford *v.* Lenthal, *Canc.* 9 May, 1743.
(h) 2 Vern. 118.
(i) Huggins *v.* York Buildings' Company, *Canc.*

24 Oct. 1740. Reeve *v.* Attorney-General, *Canc.* 27 Nov. 1741. Lightboun *v.* Attorney-General, *Canc.* 2 May, 1743.

---

(7) This jurisdiction exercised by the chancellor is personal in him, and not exercised in virtue of his ordinary or extraordinary jurisdiction in chancery. Green *v.* Allen, 5 Humph. 170, 202 (Tenn. 1844).

(8) See McCord *v.* Ochiltree, 8 Blackf. 15, 17 (Ind. 1846). When the court of wards was abolished (first by Cromwell's parliament and afterwards by the 12 Car. II.) that portion of its jurisdiction which was founded on the prerogative of the king in the supervision of charities, the care of lunatics, infants and idiots, returned to the chancellor as an original jurisdiction which had been merely suspended. Magill *v.* Brown, 1 Bright, 403 (Pa. 1851).

The latest and most important piece of legislation on this subject is "The Charitable Trusts Act, 1853," of which the professed object is to secure the due administration of charitable trusts, and in certain cases a more beneficial application of charitable funds than that previously in operation.—KERR.

"We can perceive no good reason why the same proceedings may not be instituted here for the enforcement of trusts or the judicial contract of charitable corporations, in their management of trust funds." Chambers *v.* Educational Soc. 1 B. Mon. 215, 219, 220 (Ky. 1841).

(9) The summary jurisdiction of the court of equity in cases of bankruptcy must be personally exercised by the chancellor, lord keeper, or the lords commissioners of the great seal. 2 Woodd. 400.—CHRISTIAN.

But, by stat. 1 & 2 W. IV. c. 56, this jurisdiction was transferred to the court of bankruptcy.—STEWART.

(10) Where the rights of the crown are concerned, if they extend only to the superintendence of a public trust, as in the case of a charity, the king's attorney-general may be made a party to sustain those rights; and, in other cases where the crown is not in possession, a title vested in it is not impeached, and its rights only incidentally concerned. It has generally been considered that the king's attorney-general may be made a party in respect of those rights; and the practice has been accordingly. 1 P. Wms. 445. But where the crown is in possession, or any title is vested in it which the suit seeks to divest, or its rights are the immediate and sole object of the suit, the application must be to the

Lancaster, which hath also a similar jurisdiction as a court of revenue, and, like the other, consists of both a court of law and a court of equity.

In all other matters, what is said of the court of equity in chancery will be equally applicable to the other courts of equity. Whatever difference there may be in the forms of practice, it arises from the different constitution of their officers: or, if they differ in any thing more essential, one of them must certainly be wrong; for truth and justice are always uniform, and ought equally to be adopted by them all.

Let us next take a brief, but comprehensive, view of the general nature of *equity*, as now understood and practiced in our several courts of judicature. I have formerly touched upon it,(*k*) but imperfectly: it deserves a most complete explication. Yet as nothing is hitherto extant, that can give a stranger a tolerable idea of the courts of equity subsisting in England, as distinguished from the courts of law, the compiler of these observations cannot but attempt it with diffidence: those who know them best are too much employed to find time to write; and those who have attended but little in those courts must be often at a loss for materials.

Equity, then, in its true and genuine meaning, is the soul and spirit of all law: *positive* law is construed, and *rational* law is made, by it. In this, equity is synonymous to justice; in that, to the true sense and sound interpretation of the rule.(11) But the very terms of a court of *equity*, and a court of *law*, as contrasted to each other, are apt to confound and mislead us: as if the one judged without equity, and the other was not bound by any law. Whereas every definition or illustration to be met with, which now draws a line between the two jurisdictions, by setting law and equity *in opposition to each other, will be found either totally erroneous, or   [*430 erroneous to a certain degree.

1. Thus in the first place it is said,(*l*) that it is the business of a court of equity in England to abate the rigor of the common law. But no such power is contended for. Hard was the case of bond-creditors whose debtor devised away his real estate; rigorous and unjust the rule which put the devisee in a better condition than the heir;(*m*) yet a court of equity had no power to interpose. Hard is the common law still subsisting, that land devised, or descending to the heir, shall not be liable to simple contract debts of the ancestor or devisor;(*n*)(12) although the money was laid out in purchasing the very land; and that the father shall never immediately succeed as heir to the real estate of the son;(*o*) but a court of equity can give no relief; though in both these instances the artificial reason of the law, arising from feudal principles, has long ago entirely ceased. The like may be observed of the descent of lands to a remote relation of the whole blood, or even their escheat to the lord, in preference to the owner's half-brother;(*p*) and of the total stop to all justice, by causing the *parol* to *demur*(*q*)(13) whenever an infant is sued as heir, or

(*k*) Book I. introd. §§ 2, 3, *ad calc.*
(*l*) Lord Kaims, Princ. of Equity, 44.
(*m*) See book ii. ch. 23, p. 378.
(*n*) Ibid. ch. 15, pages 243, 244; ch. 23, p. 377.

(*o*) Ibid. ch. 14, p. 208.
(*p*) Ibid. p. 227.
(*q*) See page 300.

---

king, by petition of right, (Reeve *v.* Attorney-General, mentioned in Penn *v.* Lord Baltimore, 1 Ves. 445, 446,) upon which, however, the crown may refer it to the chancellor to do right, and may direct that the attorney-general shall be made a party to a suit for that purpose. The queen has also the same prerogative. 2 Roll. Abr. 213. Mitf. Treat. on Pleadings in Chancery.—CHRISTIAN.

(11) 1 Barbour's Rights of Pers. and Prop. 51. Bowyer's Comm. on Eng. Const. 20. Edwards on Bailments. This rule is not now in use.

(12) In New York, a statute made the real estate of a decedent liable for his debts and gave the probate court power to direct the sale thereof for their payment. (L. 1786, c. 27). Read *v.* Patterson, 134 N. Y. (89 Sickels) 128, 131 (1892).

(13) Now abolished.

is party to a real action.(14) In all such cases of positive law, the courts of equity, as well as the courts of law, must say, with Ulpian,(r) " *hoc quidem perquam durum est, sed ita lex scripta est.*"(15)

2. It is said,(s) that a court of equity determines according to the spirit of the rule, and not according to the strictness of the letter. But so also does a court of law. Both, for instance, are equally bound, and equally profess, to interpret statutes according to the true intent of the legislature.(16) In general law all cases cannot be foreseen, or, if foreseen, cannot be

*431]   expressed: some will arise that will fall within the *meaning, though not within the words, of the legislator; and others, which may fall within the letter, may be contrary to his meaning, though not expressly excepted. These cases, thus out of the letter, are often said to be within the equity, of an act of parliament; and so cases within the letter are frequently out of the equity. Here by *equity* we mean nothing but the sound interpretation of the law;(17) though the words of the law itself may be too general, too special, or otherwise inaccurate or defective. These then are the cases which, as Grotius(t) says, " *lex non exacte definit, sed arbitrio boni viri permittit;*"(18) in order to find out the true sense and meaning of the lawgiver, from every other topic of construction. But there is not a single rule of interpreting laws, whether equitably or strictly, that is not equally used by the judges in the courts both of law and equity:(19) the construction must in both be the same: or, if they differ, it is only as one court of law may also happen to differ from another. Each endeavors to fix and adopt the true sense of the law in question; neither can enlarge, diminish, or alter that sense in a single tittle.(20)

3. Again, it hath been said(u) that *fraud, accident,* and *trust* are the proper and peculiar objects of a court of equity. But every kind of *fraud* is equally cognizable, and equally adverted to, in a court of law; and some frauds are cognizable only there:(21) as fraud in obtaining a devise of lands, which is always sent out of the equity courts to be there determined. Many *accidents* are also supplied in a court of law; as, loss of deeds, mistakes in receipts or accounts, wrong payments, deaths which make it impossible to perform a condition literally, and a multitude of other contingencies: and many cannot be relieved even in a court of equity; as, if by accident a recovery is ill suffered, a devise ill executed, a contingent remainder destroyed, or a power of

*432]   leasing omitted in a family settlement. A technical *trust*, indeed, created by the limitation of a second use, was forced into *the courts of equity in the manner formerly mentioned;(w)(22) and this species of trust, extended by inference and construction, have ever since remained as a kind of *peculium* in those courts. But there are other trusts which are cognizable in a court of law; as deposits, and all manner of bailments:(23)

(r) *Ff.* 40, 9, 12.
(s) Lord Kaims, Princ. of Equity, 177.
(t) *De aequitate,* § 3.

(u) 1 Roll. Abr. 374. 4 Inst. 84, 10. Mod. 1.
(w) Book ii. ch. 20.

(14) Tessier *v.* Wyse, 3 Bland Ch. 28, 51 (Md. 1830).
(15) [" This indeed is very hard, but such is the written law."]
(16) Where a statute has made provision for all the circumstances of a particular case, no relief in equity can be afforded in such case, although the provisions of the statute may conflict with the notions of natural justice and equity entertained by a court of chancery. Glenn *v.* Fowler, 8 G. & J. 340, 347 (1 Md. 1836).
(17) Beall *v.* Surv'g Ex'rs of Fox, 4 Ga. 404, 425 (1848).
(18) ["The law does not exactly define (this), but leaves it to the judgment of an honest man."]
(19) Metcalf on Contracts, 316 (Heard's ed.).
(20) Bishop on Stat. Crimes, § 190, p. 180, note 4 (2 ed. 1883).
(21) Phillips *v.* Potter, 7 R. I. 289, 296, 297 (1862).
(22) 1 Barbour's Rights Pers. and Prop. 364.
(23) Aycinena *v.* Peries, 6 W. & S. 243, 257 (Pa. 1843). Halle *v.* Nat. Park Bank of New York, 140 Ill. 413, 422 (1892). See Story on Bailments (8 note to p. 5, 9 ed. 1878).

and especially that implied contract, so highly beneficial and useful, of having undertaken to account for money received to another's use,(x) which is the ground of an action on the case almost as universally remedial as a bill in equity.

4. Once more: it has been said that a court of equity is not bound by rules or precedents, but acts from the opinion of the judge,(y)(24) founded on the circumstance of every particular case. Whereas the system of our courts of equity is a labored, connected system, governed by established rules, and bound down by precedents from which they do not depart, although the reason of some of them may perhaps be liable to objection.(25) Thus, the refusing a wife her dower in a trust-estate,(z)(26) yet allowing the husband his curtesy; the holding the penalty of a bond to be merely a security for the debt and interest, yet considering it sometimes as the debt itself, so that the interest shall not exceed that penalty;(a) the distinguishing between a mortgage at *five per cent.* with a clause of a reduction to *four* if the interest be regularly paid, and a mortgage at *four per cent.* with a clause of enlargement to *five* if the payment of the interest be deferred; so that the former shall be deemed a conscientious, the latter an unrighteous, bargain:(b) all these, and other cases that might be instanced, are plainly rules of positive law, supported only by *the reverence that is shown, and generally very   [*433 properly shown, to a series of former determinations, that the rule of property may be uniform and steady. Nay, sometimes a precedent is so strictly followed that a particular judgment founded upon special circumstances(c) gives rise to a general rule.

In short, if a court of equity in England did really act as many ingenious writers have supposed it (from theory) to do, it would rise above all law, either common or statute, and be a most arbitrary legislator in every particular case. No wonder they are so often mistaken. Grotius, or Puffendorf, or any other of the great masters of jurisprudence, would have been as little able to discover by their own light the system of a court of equity in England as the system of a court of law; especially as the notions before mentioned of the character, power, and practice of a court of equity were formerly adopted and propagated (though not with approbation of the thing) by our principal antiquaries and lawyers, Spelman,(d) Coke, (e) Lambard, (f) and Selden,(g) and even the great Bacon(h) himself. But this was in the infancy of our

---

(x) See page 163.

(y) This is stated by Mr. Selden (Table-Talk, tit. Equity) with more pleasantry than truth. "For *law* we have a measure, and know what to trust to: *equity* is according to the conscience of him that is chancellor; and as that is larger and narrower, so is equity. 'Tis all one as if they should make the standard for the measure a chancellor's foot. What an uncertain measure would this be! One chancellor has a long foot, another a short foot, a third an indifferent foot. It is the same thing with the chancellor's conscience."

(z) 2 P. Wms. 640. See book ii. page 337.

(a) Salk. 154.

(b) 2 Vern. 289, 316. 3 Atk. 520.

(c) See the case of Foster and Munt (1 Vern. 473) with regard to the undisposed *residuum* of personal estates.

(d) *Quæ in summis tribunalibus multi a legum canone decernunt judices, solus (si res exigerit) cohibet cancellarius ex arbitrio; nec aliter decretis tenetur suæ curiæ vel sui ipsius, quin, elucente nova ratione, recognoscat quæ voluerit, mutet et deleat prout suæ videbitur prudentiæ.* [Those decisions which many judges in the highest tribunals make according to the rules of law, the chancellor alone (if the case require it) can restrain according to his pleasure; nor is he so bound by the decrees of his court, or those of himself, but, a new reason appearing, he may revise whatever he pleases, may alter and reverse as he shall think fit.] Gloss. 108.

(e) See pages 54, 55.

(f) *Archeion,* 71, 72, 73.

(g) *Ubi supra.*

(h) *De Augm. Scien. l.* 8, c. 3.

---

(24) State *v.* Aiken, 42 S. C. 222, 246 (1894).

(25) Dickerman *v.* Burgess, 20 Ill. 267, 276 (1858). Even those rules of law which, in their nature, are technical and positive cannot be disregarded by a court of equity. Marshall *v.* Craig, 1 Bibb. 394, 395 (Ky. 1812). There are two cases in which equity has, in the construction of trust estates, deviated from the rules of law; that of dower, which is universally allowed to be wrong; and that of escheat, which has not met with any approbation. 2 Greenleaf's Cruise on Real Property, 272 n. (2 ed. 1856).

(26) By statute 3 & 4 Wm. 4, c. 105, a widow is entitled to dower in the equitable estate of her deceased husband.

courts of equity, before their jurisdiction was settled, and when the chancellors themselves, partly from their ignorance of law, (being frequently bishops or statesmen,) partly from ambition or lust of power, (encouraged by the arbitrary principles of the age they lived in,) but principally from the narrow and unjust decisions of the courts of law, had arrogated to themselves such unlimited authority as hath totally been disclaimed by their successors for now above a century past. The decrees of a court of equity were then rather in the nature of awards formed on the sudden *pro re nata*(27) with more probity of intention than knowledge of the subject, *founded

*434]   on no settled principles, as being never designed, and therefore never used, for precedents. But the systems of jurisprudence in our courts, both of law and equity, are now equally artificial systems, founded on the same principles of justice and positive law, but varied by different usages in the forms and mode of their proceedings; the one being originally derived (though much reformed and improved) from the feodal customs as they prevailed in different ages in the Saxon and Norman judicatures; the other (but with equal improvements) from the imperial and pontifical formularies introduced by their clerical chancellors.(28)

The suggestion, indeed, of every bill to give jurisdiction to the courts of equity (copied from those early times) is, that the complainant hath no remedy at the common law. But he who should from thence conclude that no case is judged of in equity where there might have been relief at law, and at the same time casts his eye on the extent and variety of the cases in our equity reports, must think the law a dead letter indeed. The rules of property, rules of evidence, and rules of interpretation in both courts are, or should be, exactly the same;(29) both ought to adopt the best, or must cease to be courts of justice. Formerly some causes, which now no longer exist, might occasion a different rule to be followed in one court from what was afterwards adopted in the other, as founded in the nature and reason of the thing; but the instant those causes ceased, the measure of substantial justice ought to have been the same in both. Thus, the penalty of a bond, originally contrived to evade the absurdity of those monkish constitutions which prohibited taking interest for money, was therefore very pardonably considered as the real debt in the courts of law, when the debtor neglected to perform his agreement for the return of the loan with interest; for the judges could not, as the law then stood, give judgment that the interest should be specifically paid.(30) But when afterwards the taking of interest became legal, as the necessary companion of commerce,(*i*) nay, after the statute of 37 Hen. VIII. c. 9,

*435]   had declared the *debt or loan itself to be "the just and true intent" for which the obligation was given, their narrow-minded successors still adhered wilfully and technically to the letter of the ancient precedents, and refused to consider the payment of principal, interest, and costs as a full satisfaction of the bond. At the same time, more liberal men, who sat in the courts of equity, construed the instrument according to its "just and true intent," as merely a security for the loan, in which light it was certainly

(*i*) See book ii. page 456.

---

(27) [From the circumstances of the case.]
(28) Bowyer's Commentaries on the Eng. Const. 26.
(29) Roberts *v.* Beatty, 2 P. & W. 63, 65 (Pa. 1830). McKim *v.* Odom, 12 Me. (3 Fairfield) 94, 100 (1835). 2 Parsons on Contracts (8 ed.) 494. 1 Hilliard on Mortgages, 43. Hughes *v.* Dundee M. & T. I. Co., 21 Fed. Rep. 169, 174 (U. S. c. c. 1884).
(30) Penalty is also annexed to secure the performance of certain covenants in a deed, articles of agreement, etc. In a bond also for payment of money, it is usual to annex the penalty in double the amount of the obligation. Binns' Justice (10 ed.) 79.

understood by the parties, at least after these determinations, and therefore this construction should have been universally received. So in mortgages, being only a landed as the other is a personal security for the money lent, the payment of principal, interest, and costs ought at any time before judgment executed to have saved the forfeiture in a court of law as well as in a court of equity. And the inconvenience as well as injustice of putting different constructions in different courts upon one and the same transaction obliged the parliament at length to interfere, and to direct, by the statutes 4 & 5 Anne, c. 16, and 7 Geo. II. c. 20, that, in the cases of bonds and mortgages, what had long been the practice of the courts of equity should also for the future be universally followed in the courts of law; wherein it had before these statutes in some degree obtained a footing.(*j*)(31)

Again: neither a court of equity nor of law can vary men's wills or agreements, or (in other words) make wills or agreements for them. Both are to understand them truly, and therefore both of them uniformly. One court ought not to extend, nor the other abridge, a lawful provision deliberately settled by the parties, contrary to its just intent. A court of equity, no more than a court of law, can relieve against a penalty in the nature of stated damages; as a rent of 5*l*. an acre for ploughing up ancient meadow:(*k*) nor against a lapse of time, where the time is material to the contract; as in covenants for renewal of leases. Both courts will equitably construe, but neither pretends to control or change, a lawful stipulation or engagement.(32)

*The rules of decision are in both courts equally apposite to the　　[*436 subjects of which they take cognizance. Where the subject-matter is such as requires to be determined *secundum æquum et bonum*,(33) as generally upon actions on the case, the judgments of the courts of law are guided by the most liberal equity. In matters of positive right, both courts must submit to and follow those ancient and invariable maxims "*quæ relicta sunt et tradita.*"(*l*)(34) Both follow the law of nations, and collect it from history and the most approved authors of all countries, where the question is the object of that law; as in the case of the privileges of embassadors,(*m*) hostages, or ransom-bills.(*n*) In mercantile transactions they follow the marine law,(*o*) and argue from the usages and authorities received in all maritime countries. Where they exercise a concurrent jurisdiction, they both follow the law of the proper *forum:*(*p*) in matters originally of ecclesiastical cognizance, they both equally adopt the canon or imperial law, according to the nature of the subject;(*q*) and, if a question came before either, which was properly the object of a foreign municipal law, they would both receive information what is the rule of the country,(*r*) and would both decide accordingly.

Such then being the parity of law and reason which governs both species of courts, wherein (it may be asked) does their essential difference consist? It principally consists in the different modes of administering justice in each; in the mode of proof, the mode of trial, and the mode of relief. Upon these,

(*j*) 2 Keb. 553, 555. Salk. 597. 6 Mod. 11, 60, 101.
(*k*) 2 Atk. 239.
(*l*) *De jure naturæ cogitare per nos atque dicere debemus; de jure populi Romani, quæ relicta sunt et tradita.* [We ought to think and decide for ourselves concerning our natural rights; but the rights of the Roman people should be determined by the laws which are left and handed down to us.] *Cic. de leg.*

l. 3, *ad calc.*
(*m*) See book i. page 253.
(*n*) Ricord *v.* Bettenham, Tr. 5 Geo. III. B. R.
(*o*) See book i. page 75. Book ii. pages 459, 461, 467.
(*p*) See book ii. page 513.
(*q*) Ibid. 504.
(*r*) Ibid. 463.

(31) Rosenkrantz *v.* Durling, 5 Dutch. 191, 192 (N. J. 1861).
(32) 1 Hilliard on Mortgages, 43.
(33) [According to right and justice.]
(34) ["Which are left and handed down to us."]

and upon two other accidental grounds of jurisdiction, which were formerly driven into those courts by narrow decisions of the courts of law, viz., the
*437]   true construction of securities for money lent, and the form and effect
*of a trust or second use; upon these main pillars hath been gradually erected that structure of jurisprudence which prevails in our courts of equity, and is inwardly bottomed upon the same substantial foundations as the legal system which hath hitherto been delineated in these commentaries; however different they may appear in their outward form, from the different taste of their architects.(35)

1. And, first, as to the mode of *proof*. When facts, or their leading circumstances, rest only in the knowledge of the party, a court of equity applies itself to his conscience, and purges him upon oath with regard to the truth of the transaction,(36) and, that being once discovered, the judgment is the same in equity as it would have been at law.(37)   But, for want of this discovery at law, the courts of equity have acquired a concurrent jurisdiction with every court in all matters of account.(*s*)(38) As incident to accounts, they take a concurrent cognizance of the administration of personal assets,(*t*) consequently of debts, legacies, the distribution of the residue, and the conduct of executors and administrators.(*u*)(39) As incident to accounts, they also take the concurrent jurisdiction of tithes, and all questions relating thereto;(*w*) of all dealings in partnership,(*x*) and many other mercantile transactions; and so of bailiffs, receivers, factors, and agents.(*y*)(40) It would be endless to point out all the several avenues in human affairs, and in this commercial age, which lead to or end in accounts.

From the same fruitful source, the compulsive discovery upon oath, the courts of equity have acquired a jurisdiction over almost all matters of fraud;(*z*) all matters in the private knowledge of the party, which, though concealed, are binding in conscience; and all judgments at law,
*438]   obtained through such fraud or concealment.   And this, not by *impeaching or reversing the judgment itself, but by prohibiting the plaintiff from taking any advantage of a judgment obtained by suppressing

(*s*) 1 Cha. Ca. 57.
(*t*) 2 P. Wms. 145.
(*u*) 2 Cha. Ca. 152.
(*w*) 1 Eq. Ca. Abr. 367.

(*x*) 2 Vern. 277.
(*y*) Ibid. 638.
(*z*) 2 Cha. Ca. 46.

(35) Equity does not control the principles of the common law, but compels the parties to put the transaction as will bring it under the operation of the rule of law originally intended to govern it; and in thus compelling them to give entire effect to their agreement, according to the true meaning, it performs the office of a handmaid to the law, but without power even to abate its rigor.   Whitehill *v.* Wilson, 3 P. & W. 405, 413 (1832).

(36) Skinner *v.* Judson, 8 Conn. 527, 533 (1831).   Supervisors etc. *v.* M. & W. R. R. Co., 21 Ill. 338, 368 (1859).

(37) 1 Hilliard on Mortgages, 43.

(38) Ludlow *v.* Simond, 2 Caines, 1, 38, 52 (N. Y. 1805).   Allen *v.* Smith, 16 N. Y. (2 Smith) 415, 418 (1857).   Johnson *v.* Campbell, 13 Bradw. 120, 124 (Ill. 1883).   Yates *v.* Stuart's Adm'r, 39 W. Va. 124, 132 (1894).   1 Wait's Actions and Defences, 174 (1877). In cases of account, there seems a distinct ground upon which the jurisdiction for discovery should incidentally carry the jurisdiction for relief.   In the first place, the remedy at law in most cases of this sort is imperfect or inadequate.   In the next place, where this objection does not occur, the discovery sought must often be obtained through the instrumentality of a master, or of some interlocutory order of the court; in which case it would seem strange that the court would grant some, and not proceed to full relief.   Beecher *v.* Lewis, 84 Va. 630, 633 (1888).   Both the old action of account, and a bill in equity to account, are founded upon a relation in the nature of a trust, or debtor and creditor. Whitwell *v.* Willard, 1 Metc. 216, 218 (Mass. 1840).

(39) Bate *v.* Graham, 1 Kern. 237, 238 (N. Y. 1854).   Cass *v.* Cass, 68 N. Y. (61 Hun.) 460, 465 (1892).

(40) McKim *v.* Odom, 12 Me. (3 Fairfield) 94, 107 (1835).

the truth;(*a*) and which, had the same facts appeared on the trial as now are discovered, he would never have attained at all.(41)

2. As to the mode of *trial.* This is by interrogatories administered to the witnesses, upon which their depositions are taken in writing, wherever they happen to reside. If therefore the cause arises in a foreign country, and the witnesses reside upon the spot; if, in causes arising in England, the witnesses are abroad, or shortly to leave the kingdom; or if witnesses residing at home are aged or infirm; any of these cases lays a ground for a court of equity to grant a commission to examine them, and (in consequence)(42) to exercise the same jurisdiction, which might have been exercised at law, if the witnesses could probably attend.

3. With respect to the mode of *relief.* The want of a more specific remedy, than can be obtained in the courts of law, gives a concurrent jurisdiction to a court of equity in a great variety of cases. To instance in executory agreements. A court of equity will compel them to be carried into strict execution,(*b*) unless where it is improper or impossible: instead of giving damages for their non-performance. And hence a fiction is established, that what ought to be done shall be considered as being actually done,(*c*) and shall relate back to the time when it ought to have been done originally: and this fiction is so closely pursued through all its consequences, that it necessarily branches out into many rules of jurisprudence, which form a certain regular system. So of waste, and other similar injuries, a court of equity takes a concurrent cognizance, in order to prevent them by injunction.(*d*) Over questions that may be tried at law, in a great multiplicity of actions, a court of equity assumes a *jurisdiction, to prevent the expense and   [*439 vexation of endless litigations and suits.(*e*) In various kinds of frauds it assumes a concurrent(*f*) jurisdiction, not only for the sake of a discovery, but of a more extensive and specific relief :(43) as by setting aside fraudulent deeds,(*g*) decreeing reconveyances,(*h*) or directing an absolute conveyance merely to stand as a security.(*i*)(44) And thus, lastly, for the sake of a more beneficial and complete relief by decreeing a sale of lands,(*j*) a court of equity holds plea of all debts, encumbrances, and charges that may affect it or issue thereout.

(*a*) 3 P. Wms. 148. Year-Book, 22 Edw. IV. 37, pl. 21.
(*b*) Eq. Ca. Abr. 16.
(*c*) 3 P. Wms. 215.
(*d*) 1 Cha. Rep. 14. 2 Cha. Ca. 32.
(*e*) 1 Vern. 308. Prec. Cha. 261. 1 P. Wms. 672.

(*f*) 2 P. Wms. 156.
(*g*) 1 Vern. 32. 1 P. Wms. 289.
(*h*) 1 Vern. 237.
(*i*) 2 Vern. 84.
(*j*) 1 Eq. Ca. Abr. 337.

Stra. 404.

---

(41) One material difference between a court of equity and a court of law as to the mode of proof is thus described by lord chancellor Eldon:—"A defendant in a court of equity has the protection arising from his own conscience in a degree in which the law does not affect to give him protection. If he positively, plainly, and precisely denies the assertion, and one witness only proves it as positively, clearly, and precisely as it is denied, and there is no circumstance attaching credit to the assertion, overbalancing the credit due to the denial as a positive denial, a court of equity will not act upon the testimony of that witness. Not so at law. There the defendant is not heard. One witness proves the case; and, however strongly the defendant may be inclined to deny it upon oath, there must be a recovery against him." 6 Ves. Jr. 184.—CHRISTIAN.

(42) It is not correct that where a court of equity will grant a commission to examine witnesses, whose attendance cannot be procured to give testimony in a court of common law, it will in such case also grant relief. For though it is very usual to file a bill praying a discovery, and that a commission may be issued to examine witnesses who live abroad, no doubt can be entertained that if the bill proceeded to pray relief, and that relief was such as a court of law was fully competent to administer, a demurrer to the bill would hold, unless it was a case where the courts exercise a concurrent jurisdiction. —CHRISTIAN.

(43) Arnold *v*. Grimes, 2 G. Green (Iowa) 77, 81 (1849).

(44) Roberts on Fraud. Convey. 526.

4. The true construction of *securities* for money lent is another fountain of jurisdiction in courts of equity. When they held the penalty of a bond to be the form, and that in substance it was only as a pledge to secure the repayment of the sum *bona fide* advanced, with a proper compensation for the use, they laid the foundation of a regular series of determinations, which have settled the doctrine of personal pledges or securities, and are equally applicable to mortgages of real property. The mortgagor continues owner of the land, the mortgagee of the money lent upon it; but this ownership is mutually transferred, and the mortgagor is barred from redemption if, when called upon by the mortgagee, he does not redeem within a time limited by the court; or he may when out of possession be barred by length of time, by analogy to the statute of limitations.(45)

5. The form of a *trust*, or second use, gives the courts of equity an exclusive jurisdiction as to the subject-matter of all settlements and devises in that form, and of all the long terms created in the present complicated mode of conveyancing. This is a very ample source of jurisdiction: but the trust is governed by very nearly the same rules, as would govern the estate *440] in a court of law,(k) if no trustee was interposed: and *by a regular positive system established in the courts of equity, the doctrine of trusts is now reduced to as great a certainty as that of legal estates in the courts of the common law.

These are the principal (for I omit the minuter) grounds of the jurisdiction at present exercised in our courts of equity: which differ, we see, very considerably from the notions entertained by strangers, and even by those courts themselves before they arrived to maturity; as appears from the principles laid down, and the jealousies entertained of their abuse, by our early juridical writers cited in a former page;(l) and which have been implicitly received and handed down by subsequent compilers, without attending to those gradual accessions and derelictions, by which in the course of a century this mighty river hath imperceptibly shifted its channel. Lambard in particular, in the reign of queen Elizabeth, lays it down,(m) that "equity should not be appealed unto, but only in rare and extraordinary matters: and that a good chancellor will not arrogate authority in every complaint that shall be brought before him upon whatsoever suggestion: and thereby both overthrow the authority of the courts of common law, and bring upon men such a confusion and uncertainty, as hardly any man should know how or how long to hold his own assured to him." And certainly, if a court of equity were still at sea, and floated upon the occasional opinion which the judge who happened to preside might entertain of conscience in every particular case, the inconvenience that would arise from this uncertainty would be a worse evil than any hardship that could follow from rules too strict and inflexible. Its powers would have become too arbitrary to have been endured in a country like this,(n) which boasts of being governed in all respects by law and not by will. But since the time when Lambard wrote, a set of great and eminent lawyers,(o) who have successively held the great seal, have by degrees erected the system of relief administered by a court of equity into a *441] regular *science, which cannot be attained without study and experience, any more than the science of law: but from which, when understood, it may be known what remedy a suitor is entitled to expect, and by what mode of suit, as readily and with as much precision in a court of equity as in a court of law.

(k) 2 P. Wms. 643, 668, 669.
(l) See page 433.
(m) *Archeion*, 71, 78.

(n) 2 P. Wms. 685, 688.
(o) See pages 54, 55, 56.

(45) The Real Property Limitation Act of 1874, § 7, provides an express bar in such case.

It were much to be wished, for the sake of certainty, peace, and justice, that each court would as far as possible follow the other, in the best and most effectual rules for attaining those desirable ends. It is a maxim that equity follows the law; and in former days the law had not scrupled to follow even that equity which was laid down by the clerical chancellors. Every one who is conversant in our ancient books, knows that many valuable improvements in the state of our tenures (especially in leaseholds(p) and copyholds(q) and the forms of administering justice,(r) have arisen from this single reason, that the same thing was constantly effected by means of a *subpœna* in the chancery. And sure there cannot be a greater solecism, than that in two sovereign independent courts established in the same country, exercising concurrent jurisdiction, and over the same subject-matter, there should exist in a single instance two different rules of property, clashing with or contradicting each other.

It would carry me beyond the bounds of my present purpose to go further into this matter. I have been tempted to go so far, because strangers are apt to be confounded by nominal distinctions, and the loose unguarded expressions to be met with in the best of our writers; and thence to form erroneous ideas of the separate jurisdictions now existing in England, but which never were separated in any other country in the universe. It hath also afforded me an opportunity to vindicate, on the one hand, the justice of our *courts of law from being that harsh and illiberal rule, which many   [*442 are too ready to suppose it; and, on the other, the justice of our courts of equity from being the result of mere arbitrary opinion, or an exercise of dictatorial power, which rides over the law of the land, and corrects, amends, and controls it by the loose and fluctuating dictates of the conscience of a single judge. It is now high time to proceed to the practice of our courts of equity, thus explained, and thus understood.(46)

The first commencement of a suit in chancery is by preferring a bill to the lord chancellor, in the style of a petition; "humbly complaining showeth to your lordship your orator A B, that," etc. This is in the nature of a declaration at common law, or a libel and allegation in the spiritual courts: setting forth the circumstances of the case at length, as, some fraud, trust, or hardship; "in tender consideration whereof," (which is the usual language of the bill,) "and for that your orator is wholly without remedy at the common law," relief is therefore prayed at the chancellor's hands, and also process of *subpœna* against the defendant, to compel him to answer upon oath to all the matter charged in the bill. And, if it be to quiet the possession of lands, to stay waste, or to stop proceedings at law, an injunction is also prayed, in the nature of an *interdictum* by the civil law, commanding the defendant to cease.(47)

This bill must call all necessary parties, however remotely concerned in interest, before the court; otherwise no decree can be made to bind them; and must be signed by counsel, as a certificate of its decency and propriety. For it must not contain matter either scandalous or impertinent: if it does, the defendant may refuse to answer it, till such scandal or impertinence is expunged,(48) which is done upon an order to refer it to one of the officers of the court, called a master in chancery; of whom there are in number

---

(p) Gilb. of Ejectment. 2. 2 Bac. Abr. 160.   (r) See page 200.
(q) Bro. Abr. tit. *tenant per copie.* 10 Litt. § 77.

---

(46) Very important alterations have been made in the whole process and proceedings in chancery by the statute 15 & 16 Vic. c. 86.—SHARSWOOD.
(47) 2 Barb. Rights of Pers. and Prop. 833.
(48) Sumner *v.* Lyman, Kirby, 241, 246 (Conn. 1787).

twelve, including the master of the rolls, all of whom, so late as the
*443]   reign of queen Elizabeth, were commonly doctors of the civil †law.(s)

The master is to examine the propriety of the bill: and if he reports
it scandalous or impertinent, such matter must be struck out, and the defendant shall have his costs; which ought of right to be paid by the counsel who
signed the bill.

When the bill is filed in the office of the six clerks, (who originally were
all in orders; and therefore, when the constitution of the court began to alter,
a law(t) was made to permit them to marry,) when, I say, the bill is thus
filed, if an injunction be prayed therein, it may be had at various stages of
the cause, according to the circumstances of the case.(49)   If the bill be to
stay execution upon an oppressive judgment, and the defendant does not put
in his answer within the stated time allowed by the rules of the court, an
injunction will issue of course; and, when the answer comes in, the injunction can only be continued upon a sufficient ground appearing from the
answer itself.   But if an injunction be wanted to stay waste, or other injuries of an equally urgent nature, then upon the filing of the bill, and a proper case supported by *affidavits*, the court will grant an injunction
immediately, to continue till the defendant has put in his answer, and till the
court shall make some further order concerning it, and when the answer
comes in, whether it shall then be dissolved or continued till the hearing of
the cause, is determined by the court upon argument, drawn from considering the answer and affidavit together.

But, upon common bills, as soon as they are filed, process of *subpœna* is
taken out: which is a writ commanding the defendant to appear and answer
to the bill, on pain of 100*l.*   But this is not all; for if the defendant, on
service of the *subpœna*, does not appear within the time limited by the rules
of the court, and plead, demur, or answer to the bill, he is then said to be in
contempt; and the respective processes of contempt are in successive order
awarded against him.   The first of which is an *attachment*, which is
*444]   a writ *in the nature of a *capias*, directed to the sheriff, and commanding him to attach, or take up, the defendant, and bring him
into court.   If the sheriff returns that the defendant is *non est inventus*,(50)
then an *attachment with proclamations* issues; which, besides the ordinary
form of attachment, directs the sheriff, that he cause public proclamations to
be made, throughout the county, to summon the defendant, upon his
allegiance, personally to appear and answer.   If this be also returned with a
non est inventus, and he still stands out in contempt, a *commission of rebellion*
is awarded against him, for not obeying the king's proclamations according
to his allegiance; and four commissioners therein named, or any of them, are
ordered to attach him wheresoever he may be found in Great Britain, as a
rebel and contemner of the king's laws and government, by refusing to
attend his sovereign when thereunto required: since, as was before
observed,(u) matters of equity were originally determined by the king in
person, assisted by his council; though that business is now devolved upon
his chancellor.   If upon this commission of rebellion a *non est inventus* is
returned, the court then sends a *sergeant-at-arms* in quest of him; and if he

---

(s) Smith's Commonw. b. ii. c. 12.   (u) Page 50.
(t) Stat. 14 & 15 Hen. VIII. c. 8.

---

(49) An injunction in the court of exchequer stays all further proceedings, in whatever
stage the cause may be; but in chancery, if a declaration be delivered, the party may
proceed to judgment notwithstanding an injunction, and execution is only stayed; but
if no declaration has been delivered, all proceedings at law are restrained.   3 Woodd.
411.—CHRISTIAN.

(50) [He is not forthcoming.]

eludes the search of the sergeant also, then a *sequestration* issues to seize all his personal estate, and the profits of his real, and to detain them, subject to the order of the court. Sequestrations were first introduced by Sir Nicholas Bacon, lord keeper in the reign of queen Elizabeth; before which the court found some difficulty in enforcing its process and decrees.(*v*)(51) After an order for a sequestration issued, the plaintiff's bill is to be taken *pro confesso*,(52) and a decree to be made accordingly.(53) So that the sequestration does not seem to be in the nature of process to bring in the defendant, but only intended to enforce the performance of the decree. Thus much if the defendant absconds.

If the defendant is taken upon any of this process, he is to be committed to the Fleet or other prison till he puts in his appearance or answer, or performs whatever else this *process is issued to enforce, and also [*445 clears his contempts by paying the costs which the plaintiff has incurred thereby. For the same kind of process (which was also the process of the court of star-chamber till its dissolution)(*w*) is issued out in all sorts of contempts during the progress of the cause if the parties in any point refuse or neglect to obey the order of the court.

The process against a body corporate is by *distringas*, to distrain them by their goods and chattels, rents and profits, till they shall obey the summons or directions of the court. And if a peer is a defendant, the lord chancellor sends a *letter missive* to him to request his appearance, together with a copy of the bill; and if he neglects to appear, then he may be served with a *subpœna*; and if he continues still in contempt, a sequestration issues out immediately against his lands and goods, without any of the mesne process of attachments, etc., which are directed only against the person, and therefore cannot affect a lord of parliament. The same process issues against a member of the house of commons, except only that the lord chancellor sends him no letter missive.

The ordinary process before mentioned cannot be sued out till after the service of the *subpœna*, for then the contempt begins; otherwise he is not presumed to have notice of the bill; and therefore by absconding to avoid the *subpœna* a defendant might have eluded justice, till the statute 5 Geo. II. c. 25, which enacts that where the defendant cannot be found to be served with process of *subpœna*, and absconds (as is believed) to avoid being served therewith, a day shall be appointed him to appear to the bill of the plaintiff, which is to be inserted in the London gazette, read in the parish church where the defendant last lived, and fixed up at the royal exchange; and, if the defendant doth not appear upon that day, the bill shall be taken *pro confesso*.

But if the defendant appears regularly, and takes a copy of the bill, he is next to *demur*, *plead*, or *answer*.

*A demurrer in equity is nearly of the same nature as a demurrer [*446 in law, being an appeal to the judgment of the court, whether the defendant shall be bound to answer the plaintiff's bill; as for want of sufficient matter of equity therein contained; or where the plaintiff, upon his own showing, appears to have no right; or where the bill seeks a discovery of a thing which may cause a forfeiture of any kind, or may convict a man of any criminal misbehavior. For any of these causes a defendant may demur to the bill. And if, on demurrer, the defendant prevails, the plaintiff's

---

(*v*) 1 Vern. 421.   (*w*) 18 Rym. *Fœd.* 195.

(51) Christy *v.* Flanagan, 14 Mo. App. 250, 253 (1883).
(52) [As acknowledged.]
(53) Hahn *v.* Kelly, 34 Cal. 391, 418, 419.

bill shall be dismissed: if the demurrer be overruled, the defendant is ordered to answer.(54)

A plea may be either to the *jurisdiction*, showing that the court has no cognizance of the cause, or to the *person*, showing some disability in the plaintiff, as by outlawry, excommunication, and the like: or it is in *bar;* showing some matter wherefore the plaintiff can demand no relief, as an act of parliament, a fine, a release, or a former decree. And the truth of this plea the defendant is bound to prove, if put upon it by the plaintiff. But as bills are often of a complicated nature, and contain various matter, a man may plead as to part, demur as to part, and answer to the residue. But no exceptions to formal *minutiæ* in the pleadings will be here allowed; for the parties are at liberty, on the discovery of any errors in form, to amend them.(*r*)

An *answer* is the most usual defence that is made to a plaintiff's bill. It is given in upon oath, or the honor of a peer or peeress: but where there are amicable defendants, their answer is usually taken without oath, by consent of the plaintiff. This method of proceeding is taken from the ecclesiastical courts, like the rest of the practice in chancery; for there, in almost *447] every case, the plaintiff may demand the *oath of his adversary in supply of proof. Formerly this was done in those courts with compurgators, in the manner of our waging of law; but this has been long disused; and instead of it the present kind of purgation, by the single oath of the party himself, was introduced. This oath was made use of in spiritual courts, as well in criminal cases of ecclesiastical cognizance as in matters of civil right; and it was then usually denominated the oath *ex officio*.(55) whereof the high commission court in particular made a most extravagant and illegal use; forming a court of inquisition, in which all persons were obliged to answer in cases of bare suspicion, if the commissioners thought proper to proceed against them *ex officio* for any supposed ecclesiastical enormities. But when the high commission court was abolished by statute 16 Car. I. c. 11, this oath *ex officio* was abolished with it; and it is also enacted, by statute 13 Car. II. st. 1, c. 12, "that it shall not be lawful for any bishop or ecclesiastical judge to tender to any person the oath *ex officio*, or any other oath, whereby the party may be charged or compelled to confess, accuse, or purge himself of any criminal matter." But this does not extend to oaths in a civil suit; and therefore it is still the practice, both in the spiritual courts and in equity, to demand the personal answer of the party himself upon oath. Yet if in the bill any question be put that tends to the discovery of any crime, the defendant may thereupon demur, as was before observed, and may refuse to answer.(56)

If the defendant lives within twenty miles of London, he must be sworn before one of the masters of the court: if farther off, there may be a *dedimus potestatem*,(57) or commission to take his answer in the country, where the commissioners administer him the usual oath; and then, the answer being sealed up, either one of the commissioners carries it up to the court, or it is

---

(*r*) *En cest court de chauncerie, home ne serra prejudice par son mispleiding ou pur defaut de ferme, mes solonque le reigle del mater, car il doit agarder solonque conscience, et nemi ex rigore juris.* [In this court of chancery a man shall not be prejudiced by his mis-pleading, or defect of form, but according to the truth of the matter; for the decision should be made according to conscience and not according to the rigor of law.] *Dyversyte des courtes,* edit. 1534, fol. 296, 297. Bro. Abr. tit. *Jurisdiction,* 50.

---

(54) Bottorf *v.* Conner, 1 Blackford (Ind.) 287, 288 (1823). If a demurrer be overruled, the defendant may at the hearing demur *ore tenus*[Verbally], though not where he pleads to the bill. 1 Sim. & Stu. 227; *et vid.* Mitf. Pl. 178, *et seq.*—CHITTY.

(55) [Officially.]

(56) Bow. Eng. Const. (2 ed.) 25.

(57) [We have given the power.]

sent by a messenger, who swears he received it from one of the commissioners, and that the same has not been opened or altered since he received it. An answer must be signed by counsel, and must either deny or confess all the *material parts of the bill; or it may confess and avoid, that   [*448 is, justify or palliate the facts. If one of these is not done, the answer may be excepted to for insufficiency, and the defendant be compelled to put in a more sufficient answer. A defendant cannot pray any thing in this his answer but to be dismissed the court; if he has any relief to pray against the plaintiff, he must do it by an original bill of his own, which is called a *cross-bill.*

After answer put in, the plaintiff upon payment of costs may amend his bill, either by adding new parties, or new matter, or both, upon the new lights given him by the defendant;(58) and the defendant is obliged to answer afresh to such amended bill. But this must be before the plaintiff has replied to the defendant's answer, whereby the cause is at issue; for afterwards, if new matter arises, which did not exist before, he must set it forth by a *supplemental-bill.* There may be also a bill of *revivor* when the suit is abated by the death of any of the parties; in order to set the proceedings again in motion, without which they remain at a stand. And there is likewise a bill of *interpleader;* where a person who owes a debt or rent to one of the parties in suit, but, till the determination of it, he knows not to which, desires that they may interplead, that he may be safe in the payment. In this last case it is usual to order the money to be paid into court for the benefit of such of the parties to whom upon hearing the court shall decree it to be due. But this depends upon circumstances; and the plaintiff must also annex an *affidavit* to his bill, swearing that he does not collude with either of the parties.(59)

If the plaintiff finds sufficient matter confessed in the defendant's answer to ground a decree upon, he may proceed to the hearing of the cause upon bill and answer only. But in that case he must take the defendant's answer to be true, in every point.(60) Otherwise the course is for the plaintiff to reply generally to the answer, averring his bill to be true, certain, and sufficient, and the defendant's answer to be *directly the reverse;   [*449 which he is ready to prove as the court shall award; upon which the defendant rejoins, averring the like on his side: which is joining issue upon the facts in dispute. To prove which facts is the next concern.

This is done by examination of witnesses, and taking their *depositions* in writing, according to the manner of the civil law. And for that purpose *interrogatories* are framed, or questions in writing; which, and which only, are to be proposed to, and asked of, the witnesses in the cause. These interrogatories must be short and pertinent: not leading ones; (as, "did not you see this? or, did not you hear that?") for if they be such, the depositions taken thereof will be suppressed and not suffered to be read. For the purpose of examining witnesses in or near London, there is an examiner's office appointed; but for such as live in the country, a commission to examine witnesses is usually granted to four commissioners, two named of each side, or any three or two of them, to take the depositions there. And if the witnesses reside beyond sea, a commission may be had to examine them there upon their own oaths, and (if foreigners) upon the oaths of skilful interpreters.

---

(58) Amendment implies that there is something defective, which needs correction before the plaintiff can legally proceed. Bachus *v.* Mickle, 45 Ala. 445, 446 (1871).

(59) And must bring the money (if any is due) into court, or at least offer to do so by his bill. Prac. Reg. 39. Bunb. 303. Bargard. Ch. 250. Mitf. Pl. 40.—CHITTY.

(60) Estep *v.* Watkins, 1 Bland, Ch. Rep. (Md.) 486, 488 (1857).

And it hath been established(*y*) that the deposition of a heathen who believes in the Supreme Being, taken by commission in the most solemn manner according to the custom of his own country, may be read in evidence.(61)

The commissioners are sworn to take the examinations truly and without partiality, and not to divulge them till published in the court of chancery; and their clerks are also sworn to secrecy. The witnesses are compellable by process of *subpœna*, as in the courts of common law, to appear and submit to examination. And when their depositions are taken, they are transmitted to the court with the same care that the answer of a defendant is sent.(62)

*450]   *If witnesses to a disputable fact are old and infirm, it is very usual to file a bill to perpetuate the testimony of those witnesses, although no suit is depending; for, it may be, a man's antagonist only waits for the death of some of them to begin his suit. This is most frequent when lands are devised by will away from the heir at law, and the devisee, in order to perpetuate the testimony of the witnesses to such will, exhibits a bill in chancery against the heir, and sets forth the will *verbatim*(63) therein, suggesting that the heir is inclined to dispute its validity: and then, the defendant having answered, they proceed to issue as in other cases, and examine the witnesses to the will; after which the cause is at an end, without proceeding to any decree, no relief being prayed by the bill: but the heir is entitled to his costs, even though he contests the will. This is what is usually meant by proving a will in chancery.

When all the witnesses are examined, then, and not before, the depositions may be published, by a rule to pass publication; after which they are open for the inspection of all the parties, and copies may be taken of them. The cause is then ripe to be set down for hearing, which may be done at the procurement of the plaintiff, or defendant, before either the lord chancellor or the master of the rolls, according to the discretion of the clerk in court, regulated by the nature and importance of the suit, and the arrear of causes depending before each of them respectively. Concerning the authority of the master of the rolls, to hear and determine causes, and his general power in the court of chancery, there were (not many years since) divers questions, and disputes very warmly agitated; to quiet which it was declared, by statute 3 Geo. II. c. 30, that all orders and decrees by him made, except such as by the course of the court were appropriated to the great seal alone, should be deemed to be valid; subject nevertheless to be discharged or altered by the lord chancellor, and so as they shall not be enrolled, till the same are signed by his lordship. Either party may be *subpœnaed* to hear judgment

*451]   *on the day so fixed for the hearing; and then, if the plaintiff does not attend, his bill is dismissed with costs; or, if the defendant makes default, a decree will be made against him, which will be final, unless he pays the plaintiff's cost of attendance, and shows good cause to the contrary on a day appointed by the court. A plaintiff's bill may also at any time be dismissed for want of prosecution, which is in the nature of a non-suit at law, if he suffers three terms to elapse without moving forward in the cause.

When there are cross-causes, on a cross-bill filled by the defendant against the plaintiff in the original cause, they are generally contrived to be brought on together, that the same hearing and the same decree may serve for both of them. The method of hearing causes in court is usually this. The parties on both sides appearing by their counsel, the plaintiff's bill is first opened,

(*y*) Ormichund *v.* Barker, 1 Atk. 21.

---

(61) Hale *v.* Everett, 53 N. H. 9, 214 (1868).
(62) Winder *v.* Diffenderffer, 2 Bland, Ch. Rep. (Md.) 166, 185 (1840).
(63) [Literally.]

or briefly abridged, and the defendant's answer also, by the junior counsel on each side: after which the plaintiff's leading counsel states the case and the matters in issue, and the points of equity arising therefrom: and then such depositions as are called for by the plaintiff are read by one of the six clerks, and the plaintiff may also read such part of the defendant's answer as he thinks material or convenient:(z) and after this the rest of the counsel for the plaintiff make their observations and arguments. Then the defendant's counsel go through the same process for him, except that they may not read any part of his answer; and the counsel for the plaintiff are heard in reply. When all are heard, the court pronounces the *decree*, adjusting every point in debate according to equity and good conscience; which decree being usually very long, the minutes of it are taken down, and read openly in court by the registrar.(64) The matter of costs to be given to either party is not here held to be a point of right, but merely discretionary (by the statute 17 Ric. II. c. 6) according to the circumstances of the case, as they *appear more or less favorable to the party vanquished. [*452 And yet the statute 15 Hen. VI. c. 4 seems expressly to direct, that as well damages as costs shall be given to the defendant, if wrongfully vexed in this court.

The chancellor's decree is either *interlocutory* or *final*. It very seldom happens that the first decree can be final, or conclude the cause; for, if any matter of fact is strongly controverted, this court is so sensible of the deficiency of trial by written depositions, that it will not bind the parties thereby, but usually directs the matter to be tried by jury; especially such important facts as the validity of a will, or whether A. is the heir at law to B., or the existence of a *modus decimandi*,(65) or real and immemorial composition for tithes. But, as no jury can be summoned to attend this court, the fact is usually directed to be tried at the bar of the court of king's bench, or at the assizes, upon a *feigned issue*. For (in order to bring it there, and have the point in dispute, and that only, put in issue) an action is brought, wherein the plaintiff by a fiction declares that he laid a wager of 5l. with the defendant that A. was heir at law to B.; and then avers that he is so; and therefore demands the 5l. The defendant admits the feigned wager, but avers that A. is not the heir to B.; and thereupon that issue is joined, which is directed out of chancery to be tried; and thus the verdict of the jurors at law determines the fact in the court of equity. These feigned issues seem borrowed from the *sponsio judicialis* of the Romans;(a) and are also frequently used in the courts of law, by consent of the parties, to determine some disputed rights without the formality of pleading, and thereby to save much time and expense in the decision of a cause.(66)

(z) On a trial at law, if the plaintiff reads any part of the defendant's answer, he must read the whole of it; for by reading any of it he shows a reliance on the truth of the defendant's testimony, and makes the whole of his answer evidence.

(a) *Nota est sponsio judicialis: "spondesne quingentos si meus sit? spondeo si tuus sit. Et tu quoque spondesne quingentos, ni tuus sit? spondeo, ni meus sit."*

[The judicial wager is known: "Do you engage to give me five hundred pounds, if it be mine? I promise it, if it be thine. And you also, Do you promise me five hundred pounds if it be not thine? I promise it, if it be not mine." [*Vide* Heinec. *Antiquitat. l. 3, t. 16, § 3*, and Sigon. *de judiciis, l. 21*, p. 466, *citat*. ibid.

(64) It is not now the practice for the registrar to read the minutes of the decree openly in court; but any party to the suit may procure a copy of them, and, if there is any mistake, may move to have them amended. But after a decree has been drawn up and entered, no errors in it can be rectified on motion, or by any other proceeding than by rehearing the cause.—CHRISTIAN.

(65) [Custom of tithing.]

(66) Harris *v.* Hopson, 5 Texas Rep. 529, 533 (1853). The consent of the court ought also to be previously obtained; for a trial of a feigned issue without such consent is a contempt, which will authorize the court to order the proceedings to be stayed. 4 T. R. 402. —CHITTY.

So, likewise, if a question of mere law arises in the course of a
*453]   cause, as whether by the words of a will an estate for life or *in tail
is created, or whether a future interest devised by a testator shall
operate as a remainder or any executory devise, it is the practice of this
court to refer it to the opinion of the judges of the court of king's bench or
common pleas, upon a case stated for that purpose,(67) wherein all the
material facts are admitted, and the point of law is submitted to their decision;
who thereupon hear it solemnly argued by counsel on both sides, and certify
their opinion to the chancellor. And upon such certificate the decree is
usually founded.

Another thing also retards the completion of decrees. Frequently long
accounts are to be settled, encumbrances and debts to be inquired into, and
a hundred little facts to be cleared up, before a decree can do full and sufficient justice. These matters are always, by the decree on the first hearing,
referred to a master in chancery to examine, which examinations frequently
last for years; and then he is to report the fact, as it appears to him, to the
court. This report may be excepted to, disproved, and overruled; or otherwise is confirmed, and made absolute, by order of the court.(68)

When all issues are tried and settled, and all references to the master
ended, the cause is again brought to hearing upon the matters of equity
reserved, and a final decree is made; the performance of which is enforced
(if necessary) by commitment of the person, or sequestration of the party's
estate. And if by this decree either party thinks himself aggrieved, he may
petition the chancellor for a *rehearing;* whether it was heard before his lordship, or any of the judges sitting for him, or before the master of the rolls.
For, whoever may have heard the cause, it is the chancellor's decree, and
must be signed by him before it is enrolled;(b) which is done of course unless
a rehearing be desired. Every petition for a rehearing must be signed by two
counsel of character, usually such as have been concerned in the cause, certifying that they apprehend the cause is proper to be reheard. And
*454]   upon the *rehearing, all the evidence taken in the cause, whether
read before or not, is now admitted to be read; because it is the
decree of the chancellor himself, who only now sits to hear reasons why it
should not be enrolled and perfected; at which time all omissions of either
evidence or argument may be supplied.(c)   But, after the decree is once
signed and enrolled, it cannot be reheard or rectified but by bill of review,
or by appeal to the house of lords.

A bill of *review*(69) may be had upon apparent error in judgment appearing
on the face of the decree; or, by special leave of the court, upon oath made
of the discovery of new matter or evidence, which could not possibly be had
or used at the time when the decree passed.(70)   But no new evidence or

(b) Stat. 3 Geo. III. c. 39. See p. 450.   (c) Gilb. Rep. 151, 152.

(67) Formerly, when a case was heard before the master of the rolls sitting in his own
court, on which he wished to have the opinion of a court of law, he directed an action
to be commenced by the parties in a court of law, in such a form that the question on
which he had a doubt might be decided in that suit, and he suspended his decree till the
court of law had given its judgment. It appears that the first case sent from the rolls to
the King's Bench is in 6 T. R. 313, where lord Kenyon says, " I believe that there is no
instance in which this court ever certified their opinion on a case sent here from the
master of the rolls. In Colson v. Colson it was refused; but I think it was an idle
formality, and I shall feel no reluctance in certifying in such cases, because I think it is
convenient to the suitors of that court."—CHRISTIAN.
(68) Berryhill v. McKee, 3 Yerg. (Tenn.) 157, 159 (1832).
(69) A bill of review is only necessary where a decree is signed and enrolled. Mitf.
Pl. 71. It cannot be brought after twenty years. Id. 69. 1 Bro. P. C. 95. 5 Bro. P. C.
460. 6 Bro. P. C. 395.—CHITTY.
(70) Sumner v. Lyman, Kirby, 241, 244 (Conn. 1787).

matter then in the knowledge of the parties, and which might have been used before, shall be a sufficient ground for a bill of review.

An *appeal* to parliament, that is, to the house of lords, is the dernier resort of the subject who thinks himself aggrieved by an interlocutory order or final determination in this court; and it is effected by *petition* to the house of peers, and not by *writ of error*, as upon judgments at common law. This jurisdiction is said(*d*) to have begun in 18 Jac. I., and it is certain that the first petition, which appears in the records of parliament, was preferred in that year;(*e*) and that the first which was heard and determined (though the name of appeal was then a novelty(was presented in a few months after;(*f*) both levelled against the lord chancellor Bacon for corruption and other misbehavior. It was afterwards warmly controverted by the house of commons in the reign of Charles the Second.(*g*) But this dispute is now at rest:(*h*) it being obvious to the reason of all mankind, that, when the courts of equity became principal tribunals for deciding causes of property, a revision of their *decrees (by way of appeal) became equally necessary as a   [*455 writ of error from the judgment of a court of law. And, upon the same principle, from decrees of the chancellor relating to the commissioners for the dissolution of chauntries, etc., under the statute 37 Hen. VIII. c. 4, (as well as for charitable uses under the statute 43 Eliz. c. 4,) an appeal to the king in parliament was always unquestionably allowed.(*i*) But no new evidence is admitted in the house of lords upon any account; this being a distinct jurisdiction:(*k*) which differs it very considerably from those instances, wherein the same jurisdiction revises and corrects its own acts, as in rehearings and bills of review. For it is a practice unknown to our law, (though constantly followed in the spiritual courts,) when a superior court is reviewing the sentence of an inferior, to examine the justice of the former decree by evidence that was never produced below. And thus much for the general method of proceeding in the courts of equity.(71)

(*d*) Com. Jour. 13 Mar. 1704.
(*e*) Lords' Jour. 23 Mar. 1620.
(*f*) Ibid. 3, 11, 12 Dec. 1621.
(*g*) Com. Jour. 19 Nov. 1675, etc.

(*h*) Show. Parl. C. 81.
(*i*) Duke's Charitable Uses, 62.
(*k*) Gilb. Rep. 155, 156.

---

(71) By the General Judicature Acts of 1873 and 1875, the proceedings in courts of equity have been made to conform as near as possible to those of the courts of law.

THE END OF THE THIRD BOOK.

APPENDIX.

No. I.

PROCEEDINGS ON A WRIT OF RIGHT PATENT.

SECT. 1. WRIT OF RIGHT PATENT IN THE COURT BARON.

GEORGE the Second, by the grace of God, of Great Britain, France, and Ireland King, Defender of the Faith, and so forth, to Willoughby, earl of Abingdon, greeting. We command you that without delay you hold full right to William Kent, Esquire, of one messuage and twenty acres of land, with the appurtenances, in Dorchester, which he claims to hold of you by the free service of one penny yearly in lieu of all services, of which Richard Allen deforces him. And unless you do so, let the sheriff of Oxfordshire do it, that we no longer hear complaint thereof for defect of right. WITNESS ourself at Westminster, the twentieth day of August, in the thirtieth year of our reign.

Pledges of prosecution. { JOHN DOE. { RICHARD ROE.

SECT. 2. WRIT OF TOLT, TO REMOVE IT INTO THE COUNTY COURT.

CHARLES MORTON, Esquire, sheriff of Oxfordshire, to John Long, bailiff-errant of our Lord the king and of myself, greeting. BECAUSE by the complaint of William Kent, Esquire, personally present at my county court, to wit, on Monday, the sixth day of September, in the thirtieth year of the reign of our Lord GEORGE the Second, by the grace of God, of Great Britain, France, and Ireland King, Defender of the Faith, and so forth, at Oxford, in the shirehouse there holden, I am informed, that although he himself the writ of our said Lord the King of right patent directed to Willoughby, earl of Abingdon, for this that *he should hold full right to the said William Kent, of one messuage and twenty acres of land, with the appurtenances, in Dorchester, within my said county, of which Richard Allen deforces him, hath brought to the said Willoughby, earl of Abingdon; yet for that the said Willoughby, earl of Abingdon, favoreth the said Richard Allen in this part, and hath hitherto delayed to do full right according to the exigence of the said writ, I command you on the part of our said Lord the King, firmly enjoining that in your proper person you go to the court-baron of the said Willoughby, earl of Abingdon, at Dorchester aforesaid, and take away the plaint which there is between the said William Kent and Richard Allen by the said writ into my county court to be next holden; and summon by good summoners the said Richard Allen that he be at my county court, on Monday, the fourth day of October next coming, at Oxford, in the shirehouse there to be holden to answer to the said William Kent thereof. And have you there then the said plaint, the summoners, and this precept. GIVEN in my county court, at Oxford, in the shirehouse, the sixth day of September, in the year aforesaid.

[*ii.

SECT. 3. WRIT OF PONE, TO REMOVE IT INTO THE COURT OF COMMON PLEAS.

GEORGE the Second, by the grace of God, of Great Britain, France, and Ireland King, Defender of the Faith, and so forth, to the sheriff of Oxfordshire, greeting. PUT at the request of William Kent, before our justices at Westminster, on the morrow of All Souls, the plaint which is in your county court, by our writ of right, between the said William Kent, demandant, and Richard Allen, tenant, of one messuage and twenty acres of land, with the appurtenances, in Dorchester; and summon by good summoners

No. 1.

the said Richard Allen, that he be then there to answer to the said William Kent thereof. And have you there the summoners and this writ. WITNESS ourself at Westminster, the tenth day of September, in the thirtieth year of our reign.

SEC. 4. WRIT OF RIGHT, *quia Dominus remisit Curiam.*

GEORGE the Second, by the grace of God, of Great Britain, France and Ireland King, Defender of the Faith, and so forth, to the sheriff of Oxfordshire, greeting. COMMAND Richard Allen, that he justly and without delay render unto William Kent one messuage and twenty acres of land, with the appurtenances, in Dorchester, which he claims to be his right and inheritance, and whereupon he complains that the aforesaid Richard unjustly deforces him. And unless he shall do so, and *if the said William shall give you security of prosecuting his claim, then summon by good summoners the said Richard, that he appear before our justices at Westminster, on the morrow of All Souls, to show wherefore he hath not done it. And have you there the summoners and this writ. WITNESS ourself at Westminster, the twentieth day of August, in the thirtieth year of our reign. Because Willoughby, earl of Abingdon, the chief lord of that fee, hath thereupon remised unto us his court.

*iii.]

Sheriff's return.

Pledges of } JOHN DOE. Summoners of the } JOHN DEN.
prosecution. } RICHARD ROE. within named Richard. } RICHARD FEN.

SECT. 5. THE RECORD, WITH THE AWARD OF BATTEL.(*a*)

PLEAS at Westminster before Sir John Willes, Knight, and his brethren, Justices of the Bench of the Lord the King at Westminster, of the term of Saint Michael, in the thirtieth year of the reign of the Lord GEORGE the Second, by the grace of God, of Great Britain, France, and Ireland King, Defender of the Faith, &c.

Writ.

Oxon, } WILLIAM KENT, Esquire, by James Parker, his attorney, de-
to wit. } mands against Richard Allen, gentleman, one messuage and twenty acres of land, with the appurtenances, in Dorchester, as his right

Dominus remisit curiam.

and inheritance, by writ of the Lord the King of right, because Willoughby, earl of Abingdon, the chief lord of that fee, hath now thereupon remised to the Lord the King his court. AND WHEREUPON he saith that he himself

Count.

was seised of the tenements aforesaid, with the appurtenances, in his demesne as of fee and right, in the time of peace, in the time of the Lord GEORGE

Esplees.

the First, late King of Great Britain, by taking the esplees thereof to the value (*b*) [of ten shillings, and more, in rents, corn, and grass.] And that

Defence.

such is his right he offers [suit and good proof.] AND the said Richard Allen, by Peter Jones his attorney, comes and defends the right of the said William Kent and his seisin, when [and where it shall behoove him,] and all [that concerns it,] and whatsoever [he ought to defend] and chiefly the tenements aforesaid, with the appurtenances, as of fee and right, [namely, one messuage and twenty acres of land, with appurtenances in Dorchester].

Wager of battel.

AND this he is ready to defend by the body of his freeman, George Rumbold by name, who is present here in court, ready to defend the same by his body, or in what manner soever the court of the Lord the King shall consider that

*iv]

he ought to defend. *And if any mischance should befall the said George, (which God defend,) he is ready to defend the same by another man, who

Replication.

[is bounden and able to defend it.] AND the said William Kent saith, that the said Richard Allen unjustly defends the right of him the said William, and his seisin, &c., and all, &c., and whatsoever, &c., and chiefly of the tenements aforesaid, with the appurtenances, as of fee and right, &c.: because he saith that he himself was seised of the tenements aforesaid, with the appurtenances, in his demesne as of fee and right, in the time of peace, in the time of the said Lord GEORGE the First, late King of Great Britain,

Joinder of battel.

by taking the esplees thereof to the value, &c. AND that such is his right he is prepared to prove by the body of his freeman, Henry Broughton by name, who is present here in court, ready to prove the same by his body, or in what manner soever the court of the Lord the King shall consider that he ought to prove; and if any mischance should befall the said Henry, (which God defend,) he is ready to prove the same by another man, who, &c. AND

(*a*) As to battel, see page 337, n. 7.
(*b*) N. B.—The clauses between hooks in this and the subsequent numbers of the Appendix are usually not otherwise expressed in the records than by an "&c."

hereupon it is demanded of the said George and Henry whether they are **No. I.**
ready to make battel as they before have waged it; who say that they are.
AND the same George Rumbold giveth gage of defending, and the said Gages given.
Henry Broughton giveth gage of proving; and such engagement being given
as the manner is, it is demanded of the said William Kent and Richard Allen
if they can say any thing wherefore battel ought not to be awarded in this
case; who say that they cannot. THEREFORE IT IS CONSIDERED, that battel Award of bat-
be made thereon, &c. AND the said George Rumbold findeth pledges of tel.
battel, to wit, Paul Jenkins and Charles Carter; and the said Henry Brough- Pledges.
ton findeth also pledges of battel, to wit, Reginald Read and Simon Tayler.
AND THEREUPON day is here given as well to the said William Kent as to Continuance.
the said Richard Allen, to wit, on the morrow of Saint Martin next coming,
by the assent as well of the said William Kent as of the said Richard Allen.
And it is commanded that each of them then have here his champion, sufficiently furnished with competent armor as becomes him, and ready to make
the battel aforesaid; and that the bodies of them in the mean time be safely
kept, on peril that shall fall thereon. AT which day here come as well the Champions ap-
said William Kent as the said Richard Allen by their attorneys aforesaid, pear.
and the said George Rumbold and Henry Broughton in their proper persons
likewise come, sufficiently furnished with competent armor as becomes
them, ready to make the battel aforesaid as they had before waged it. AND Adjournment
hereupon day is further given by the court here, as well to the said William to Tothill
Kent as to the said Richard Allen, at Tothill, near the city of Westminster, Field.
in the county of Middlesex, to wit, on the morrow of the Purification of the
Blessed Virgin Mary next coming, by the assent as well of the said *William [*v
as of the aforesaid Richard. And it is commanded that each of them have
then there his champion, armed in the form aforesaid, ready to make the
battel aforesaid, and that their bodies in the mean time, &c. At which day
here, to wit, at Tothill aforesaid, comes the said Richard Allen by his attorney aforesaid, and the said George Rumbold and Henry Broughton in their
proper persons likewise come, sufficiently furnished with competent armor
as becomes them, ready to make the battel aforesaid as they before had waged
it. And the said William Kent being solemnly called doth not come, nor
hath prosecuted his writ aforesaid. THEREFORE IT IS CONSIDERED, that Demandant
the same William, and his pledges of prosecuting, to wit, John Doe and non-suit.
Richard Roe, be in mercy for his false complaint, and that the same Richard
go thereof without a day, &c., and also that the said Richard do hold the Final judgment
tenements aforesaid with the appurtenances to him and his heirs, quit of the for the tenant.
said William and his heirs, forever, &c.

SECT. 6. TRIAL BY THE GRAND ASSIZE.

——And the said Richard Allen, by Peter Jones, his attorney, comes and Defence.
defends the right of the said William Kent, and his seisin, when, &c., and
all, &c., and whatsoever, &c., and chiefly of the tenements aforesaid with
the appurtenances, as of fee and right, &c., and puts himself upon the grand Mise.
assize of the Lord the King, and prays recognition to be made, whether he
himself hath greater right to hold the tenements aforesaid, with the appurtenances, to him and his heirs as tenants thereof, as he now holdeth them,
or the said William to have the said tenements with the appurtenances, as
he above demandeth them. AND he tenders here in court six shillings and Tender of
eight-pence to the use of the Lord the now King, &c., for that, to wit, it demi-mark.
may be inquired of the time [of the seisin alleged by the said William.]
And he therefore prays that it may be inquired by the assize, whether the
said William Kent was seised of the tenements aforesaid, with the appurtenances in his demesne, as of fee, in the time of the said Lord the King
GEORGE the First, as the said William in his demand before hath alleged.
THEREFORE it is commanded the sheriff, that he summon by good summon- Summons of
ers four lawful knights of his county, girt with swords, that they be here on the knights.
the octaves of Saint Hilary next coming, to make election of the assize aforesaid. The same day is given as well to the said William Kent as to the said Return.
Richard Allen, here, &c. At which day here come as well the said William
Kent as the said Richard Allen; and the sheriff, to wit, Sir Adam Alstone,
Knight, now returns, that he had caused to be summoned Charles Stephens, [*vi.
Randel Wheler, Toby Cox, and Thomas Munday, four lawful knights of *his
county, girt with swords, by John Doe and Richard Roe, his bailiffs, to be
here at the said octaves of Saint Hilary, to do as the said writ thereof commands and requires; and that the said summoners, and each of them, are
mainprized by John Day and James Fletcher. Whereupon the said Charles

No. II.

Stephens, Randel Wheler, Toby Cox, and Thomas Munday, four lawful knights of the county aforesaid, girt with swords, being called, in their proper persons come, and being sworn upon their oath in the presence of the

Election of the recognitors.
parties aforesaid, chose of themselves and others twenty-four, to wit, Charles Stephens, Randel Wheler, Toby Cox, Thomas Munday, Oliver Greenway, John Boys, Charles Price, knights; Daniel Prince, William Day, Roger Lucas, Patrick Fleming, James Harris, John Richardson, Alexander Moore, Peter Payne, Robert Quin, Archibald Stewart, Bartholomew Norton, and Henry Davis, Esquires; John Porter, Christopher Ball, Benjamin Robinson, Lewis Long, William Kirby, gentlemen, good and lawful men of the county aforesaid, who neither are of kin to the said William Kent nor to the said

Venire facias.
Richard Allen, to make recognition of the grand assize aforesaid. THEREFORE it is commanded the sheriff, that he cause them to come here from the day of Easter in fifteen days, to make the recognition aforesaid. The same day is there given to the parties aforesaid. At which day here come as well the said William Kent as the said Richard Allen, by their attorneys aforesaid, and the recognitors of the assize, whereof mention is made above, being

Recognitors sworn.
called, come, and certain of them, to wit, Charles Stephens, Randel Wheler, Toby Cox, Thomas Munday, Charles Price, knights; Daniel Prince, Roger Lucas, William Day, James Harris, Peter Payne, Robert Quin, Henry Davis, John Porter, Christopher Ball, Lewis Long, and William Kirby, being elected,

Verdict for the demandant.
tried, and sworn upon their oath, say that the said William Kent hath more right to have the tenements aforesaid, with the appurtenances, to him and his heirs, as he demandeth the same, than the said Richard Allen to hold the same as he now holdeth them, according as the said William Kent by

Judgment.
his writ aforesaid hath supposed. THEREFORE IT IS CONSIDERED, that the said William Kent do recover his seisin against the said Richard Allen of the tenements aforesaid, with the appurtenances, to him and his heirs, quit of the said Richard Allen and his heirs forever: and the said Richard Allen in mercy, &c.

*vii.]

*No. II.

PROCEEDINGS ON AN ACTION OF TRESPASS IN EJECTMENT, BY ORIGINAL, IN THE KING'S BENCH.

SECT. 1. THE ORIGINAL WRIT.

Si fecerit te se curum.
GEORGE the Second, by the grace of God, of Great Britain, France, and Ireland King, defender of the Faith, and so forth, to the sheriff of Berkshire, greeting. IF Richard Smith shall give you security of prosecuting his claim, then put by gage and safe pledges William Stiles, late of Newbury, gentleman, so that he be before us on the morrow of All Souls, wheresoever we shall then be in England, to show wherefore with force and arms he entered into one messuage, with the appurtenances, in Sutton, which John Rogers, Esquire, hath demised to the aforesaid Richard, for a term which is not yet expired, and ejected him from his said farm, and other enormities to him did, to the great damage of the said Richard, and against our peace. And have you there the names of the pledges and this writ. WITNESS ourself at Westminster, the twelfth day of October, in the twenty-ninth year of our reign.

Sheriff's return.
Pledges of   } JOHN DOE.   The within-named William } JOHN DEN.
prosecution. } RICHARD ROE.   Stiles is attached by pledges. } RICHARD FEN.

SECT. 2. COPY OF THE DECLARATION AGAINST THE CASUAL EJECTOR, WHO GIVES NOTICE THEREUPON TO THE TENANT IN POSSESSION.

Michaelmas, the 29th of King George the Second.

Declaration.
Berks, } WILLIAM STILES, late of Newbury in the said county, gentleman, *to wit.* was attached to answer Richard Smith, of a plea, wherefore with force and arms he entered into one messuage, with the appurtenances, in Sutton in the county aforesaid, which John Rogers, Esquire, demised to the said Richard Smith for a term which is not yet expired, and ejected him from his said farm, and other wrongs to him did, to the great damage of the said Richard, and against the peace of the Lord the King, &c. And where-

*viii.]
upon the said Richard by *Robert Martin his attorney complains, that whereas the said John Rogers, on the first day of October, in the twenty-ninth year

of the reign of the Lord the King that now is, at Sutton aforesaid, had demised to the same Richard the tenement aforesaid, with the appurtenances, to have and to hold the said tenement, with the appurtenances, to the said Richard and his assigns, from the Feast of Saint Michael the Archangel then last past, to the end and term of five years from thence next following and fully to be complete and ended, by virtue of which demise the said Richard entered into the said tenement, with the appurtenances, and was thereof possessed; and the said Richard being so possessed thereof, the said William afterwards, that is to say, on the said first day of October in the said twenty-ninth year, with force and arms, that is to say, with swords, staves, and knives, entered into the said tenement, with the appurtenances, which the said John Rogers demised to the said Richard in form aforesaid for the term aforesaid, which is not yet expired, and ejected the said Richard out of his said farm, and other wrongs to him did, to the great damage of the said Richard, and against the peace of the said Lord the King; whereby the said Richard saith, that he is injured and damaged to the value of twenty pounds. And thereupon he brings suit, &c.

MARTIN, for the plaintiff. }
PETERS, for the defendant. }

Pledges of } JOHN DOE.
prosecution. } RICHARD ROE.

MR. GEORGE SAUNDERS,

I am informed that you are in possession of, or claim title to, the premises mentioned in this declaration of ejectment, or to some part thereof; and I, being sued in this action as a casual ejector, and having no claim or title to the same, do advise you to appear next Hilary Term in his Majesty's court of King's Bench at Westminster, by some attorney of that court, and then and there, by a rule to be made of the same court, to cause yourself to be made defendant in my stead; otherwise I shall suffer judgment to be entered against me, and you will be turned out of possession.

Your loving friend,

5th January, 1756.   WILLIAM STILES.

*SECT. 3. THE RULE OF COURT.   [*ix.

Hilary Term, in the twenty-ninth Year of King George the Second.

Berks, } IT IS ORDERED by the court, by the assent of both parties, and their *to wit.* } attorneys, that George Saunders, gentleman, may be made defendant, in the place of the now defendant, William Stiles, and shall immediately appear to the plaintiff's action, and shall receive a declaration in a plea of trespass and ejectment of the tenements in question, and shall immediately plead thereto Not Guilty; and, upon the trial of the issue, shall confess lease, entry, and ouster, and insist upon his title only. And if upon the trial of the issue, the said George do not confess lease, entry, and ouster, and by reason thereof the plaintiff cannot prosecute his writ, then the taxation of costs upon such *non pros.* shall cease, and the said George shall pay such costs to the plaintiff, as by the court of our Lord the King here shall be taxed and adjudged, for such his default in non-performance of this rule; and judgment shall be entered against the said William Stiles, now the casual ejector, by default. And it is further ordered, that if upon the trial of the said issue a verdict shall be given for the defendant, or if the plaintiff shall not prosecute his writ upon any other cause than for the not confessing lease, entry, and ouster as aforesaid, then the lessor of the plaintiff shall pay costs, if the plaintiff himself doth not pay them.

By the Court.

MARTIN, for the plaintiff. }
NEWMAN, for the defendant. }

SECT. 4. THE RECORD.

PLEAS before the Lord the King at Westminster, of the Term of Saint Hilary, in the twenty-ninth Year of the Reign of the Lord GEORGE the Second, by the grace of God, of Great Britain, France, and Ireland King, Defender of the Faith, &c.

Berks, } GEORGE SAUNDERS, late of Sutton, in the county aforesaid, gentle-*to wit.* } man, was attached to answer Richard Smith, of a plea, wherefore with force and arms he entered into one messuage, with the appurtenances, in Sutton, which John Rogers, Esq. hath demised to the said Richard for a term which is not yet expired, and ejected him from his said farm, and other

No. II.

*x.]
Declaration, or count.

Defence.

Plea, not guilty.
Issue.

Venire
awarded.

Respite, for default of jurors.
Nisi prius.

*xi.]
Postea.

Tales de circumstantibus.

Verdict for the plaintiff.

wrongs to him did, to the great damage of the said Richard, and against the peace of the Lord the King that *now is. AND WHEREUPON the said Richard by Robert Martin, his attorney, complains, that whereas the said John Rogers on the first day of October in the twenty-ninth year of the reign of the Lord the King that now is, at Sutton aforesaid, had demised to the same Richard the tenement aforesaid, with the appurtenances, to have and to hold the said tenement, with the appurtenances, to the said Richard and his assigns, from the feast of Saint Michael the Archangel then last past, to the end and term of five years from thence next following and fully to be complete and ended; by virtue of which demise the said Richard entered into the said tenement, with the appurtenances, and was thereof possessed: and, the said Richard being so possessed thereof, the said George afterwards, that is to say, on the first day of October in the said twenty-ninth year, with force and arms, that is to say, with swords, staves, and knives, entered into the said tenement, with the appurtenances, which the said John Rogers demised to the said Richard in form aforesaid for the term aforesaid, which is not yet expired, and ejected the said Richard out of his said farm, and other wrongs to him did, to the great damage of the said Richard, and against the peace of the said Lord the King; whereby the said Richard saith that he is injured and endamaged to the value of twenty pounds: and thereupon he brings suit, [and good proof.] AND the aforesaid George Saunders, by Charles Newman, his attorney, comes and defends the force and injury, when [and where it shall behoove him;] and saith that he is in no wise guilty of the trespass and ejectment aforesaid, as the said Richard above complains against him; and thereof he puts himself upon the country; and the said Richard doth likewise the same; THEREFORE let a jury come thereupon before the Lord the King, on the octave of the Purification of the Blessed Virgin Mary, wheresoever he shall then be in England, who neither [are of kin to the said Richard, nor to the said George,] to recognise [whether the said George be guilty of the trespass and ejectment aforesaid;] because as well [the said George as the said Richard, between whom the difference is, have put themselves on the said jury.] The same day is there given to the parties aforesaid. AFTERWARDS the process therein, being continued between the said parties of the plea aforesaid by the jury, is put between them in respite, before the Lord the King, until the day of Easter in fifteen days, wheresoever the said Lord the King shall then be in England; unless the justices of the Lord the King assigned to take assizes in the county aforesaid, shall have come before that time, to wit, on Monday the eighth day of March, at Reading in the said county, by the form of the statute [in that case provided,] by reason of the default of the jurors, [summoned to appear as aforesaid.] At which day before the Lord the King, at Westminster, come the parties aforesaid by their attorneys; and the aforesaid justices of *assize, before whom [the jury aforesaid came,] sent here their record before them, had in these words, to wit, AFTERWARDS, at the day and place within contained, before Heneage Legger, Esquire, one of the Barons of the Exchequer of the Lord the King, and Sir John Eardley Wilmot, Knight, one of the justices of the said Lord the King, assigned to hold pleas before the King himself, justices of the said Lord the King, assigned to take assizes in the county of Berks by the form of the statute [in that case provided,] come as well the within-named Richard Smith, as the within-written George Saunders, by their attorneys within contained; and the jurors of the jury whereof mention is within made being called, certain of them, to wit, Charles Holloway, John Hooke, Peter Graham, Henry Cox, William Brown, and Francis Oakley, come, and are sworn upon that jury; and because the rest of the jurors of the same jury did not appear, therefore others of the bystanders being chosen by the sheriff, at the request of the said Richard Smith, and by the command of the justices aforesaid, are appointed anew, whose names are affixed to the panel within written, according to the form of the statute in such case made and provided; which said jurors so appointed anew, to wit, Roger Bacon, Thomas Small, Charles Pye, Edward Hawkins, Samuel Roberts, and Daniel Parker, being likewise called, come; and together with the other jurors aforesaid before impanelled and sworn, being elected, tried, and sworn, to speak the truth of the matter within contained, upon their oath say, that the aforesaid George Saunders is guilty of the trespass and ejectment within written, in manner and form as the aforesaid Richard Smith within complains against him; and assess the damages of the said Richard Smith, on occasion of that trespass and ejectment, besides his costs and charges which he hath been put unto about his suit in that behalf, to twelve pence; and, for those costs and charges, to forty shillings. WHEREUPON the said Richard Smith, by his attorney aforesaid, prayeth judgment against the said George Saunders, in and upon the verdict aforesaid by the jurors aforesaid given in the form aforesaid; and the said George Saunders, by his attorney aforesaid, saith, that the court here ought not to proceed to give judgment upon the said verdict, and prayeth Motion in arthat judgment against him the said George Saunders, in and upon the ver- rest of judgdict aforesaid by the jurors aforesaid given in the form aforesaid, may be ment. stayed, by reason that the said verdict is insufficient and erroneous, and that the same verdict may be quashed, and that the issue aforesaid may be tried anew by other jurors to be afresh impanelled. And, because the court of the Lord the King here is not yet advised of giving their judgment of Continuance. and upon the premises, therefore day thereof is given as well to the said Richard Smith as the said George Saunders, before the Lord the King, until [*xii. the morrow of the Ascension of our Lord, wheresoever the said Lord *the King shall then be in England, to hear their judgment of and upon the premises, for that the court of the Lord the King is not yet advised thereof. At which day before the Lord the King, at Westminster, come the parties aforesaid by their attorneys aforesaid; upon which, the record and matters aforesaid having been seen, and by the court of the Lord the King now here fully understood, and all and singular the premises having been examined, and mature deliberation being had thereupon, for that it seems to the court Opinion of the of the Lord the King now here that the verdict aforesaid is in no wise insuf- court. ficient or erroneous, and that the same ought not to be quashed, and that no new trial ought to be had of the issue aforesaid, THEREFORE IT IS CONSID- Judgment for ERED, that the said Richard do recover against the said George his term yet the plaintiff. to come, of and in the said tenements, with the appurtenances, and the said damages assessed by the said jury in form aforesaid, and also twenty-seven pounds six shillings and eight-pence for his costs and charges aforesaid, by Costs. the court of the Lord the King here awarded to the said Richard, with his assent, by way of increase; which said damages in the whole amount to twenty-nine pounds, seven shillings and eight-pence. "And let the said George be taken, [until he maketh fine to the Lord the King."](c) AND Capiatur pro HEREUPON the said Richard, by his attorney aforesaid, prayeth a writ to the fine. Lord the King, to be directed to the sheriff of the county aforesaid, to cause him to have possession of his term aforesaid yet to come, of and in the tene- Writ of possesments aforesaid, with the appurtenances; and it is granted unto him, return- sion able before the Lord the King on the morrow of the Holy Trinity, wheresoever he shall then be in England. At which day before the Lord the King, at and return. Westminster, cometh the said Richard, by his attorney aforesaid; and the sheriff, that is to say, Sir Thomas Reeve, Knight, now sendeth, that he by virtue of the writ aforesaid to him directed, on the ninth day of June last past, did cause the said Richard to have his possession of his term aforesaid yet to come, of and in the tenements aforesaid, with the appurtenances, as he was commanded.

*No. III. [*xiii.

PROCEEDINGS OF AN ACTION OF DEBT IN THE COURT OF COM-MON PLEAS; REMOVED INTO THE KING'S BENCH BY WRIT OF ERROR.

SECT. I. ORIGINAL.

GEORGE the Second, by the grace of God, of Great Britain, France, and Præcipe. Ireland King, Defender of the Faith, and so forth; to the sheriff of Oxfordshire, greeting. COMMAND Charles Long, late of Burford, gentleman, that justly and without delay he render to William Burton two hundred pounds, which he owes him and unjustly detains, as he saith. And unless he shall so do, and if the said William shall make you secure of prosecuting his claim, then summon by good summoners the aforesaid Charles, that he be before our justices, at Westminster, on the octave of Saint Hilary, to show wherefore he hath not done it. And have you there then the summoners, and this writ. WITNESS ourself at Westminster, the twenty-fourth day of December, in the twenty-eighth year of our reign.

Pledges of {JOHN DOE. Summoners of the within-{ROGER MORRIS. Sheriff's return. prosecution. {RICHARD ROE. named Charles Long. HENRY JOHNSON.

(c) Now omitted. See page 398.

SECT 2. PROCESS.

Attachment.

Pone.

GEORGE the Second, by the grace of God, of Great Britain, France, and Ireland King, Defender of the Faith, and so forth; to the sheriff of Oxfordshire, greeting. PUT by gage and safe pledges Charles Long, late of Burford, gentleman, that he be before our justices, at Westminster, on the octave of the Purification of the Blessed Mary, to answer to William Burton of a plea, that he render to him two hundred pounds which he owes him and unjustly detains, as he saith; and to show wherefore he was not before our justices at Westminster on the octave of Saint Hilary, as he was summoned. And have there then the names of the pledges and this writ. WITNESS, Sir John Willes, Knight, at Westminster, the twenty-third day of January, in the twenty-eighth year of our reign.

Sheriff's return.

The within-named Charles Long } EDWARD LEIGH.
is attached by Pledges. } ROBERT TANNER.

Distringas.
*xiv.]

*GEORGE the Second, by the grace of God, of Great Britain, France, and Ireland King, Defender of the Faith, and so forth; to the sheriff of Oxfordshire, greeting. WE command you, that you distrein Charles Long, late of Burford, gentleman, by all his lands and chattels within your bailiwick, so that neither he nor any one through him may lay hands on the same, until you shall receive from us another command thereupon; and that you answer to us of the issues of the same; and that you have his body before our justices at Westminster, from the day of Easter, in fifteen days, to answer to William Burton of a plea that he render to him two hundred pounds which he owes him and unjustly detains, as he saith, and to hear his judgment of his many defaults. WITNESS, Sir John Willes, Knight, at Westminster, the twelfth day of February, in the twenty-eighth year of our reign.

Sheriff's return.
Nihil.

The within-named Charles Long hath nothing in my bailiwick whereby he may be distreined.

Capias ad respondendum.

GEORGE the Second, by the grace of God, of Great Britain, France, and Ireland King, Defender of the Faith, and so forth; to the sheriff of Oxfordshire, greeting. WE command you that you take Charles Long, late of Burford, gentleman, if he may be found in your bailiwick, and him safely keep, so that you may have his body before our justices at Westminster, from the day of Easter, in five weeks, to answer to William Burton, gentleman, of a plea that he render to him two hundred pounds which he owes him and unjustly detains, as he saith; and whereupon you have returned to our justices at Westminster that the said Charles hath nothing in your bailiwick whereby he may be distreined. And have you there then this writ. WITNESS, Sir John Willes, Knight, at Westminster, the sixteenth day of April, in the twenty-eighth year of our reign.

Sheriff's return.
Non est inventus.

The within-named Charles Long is not found in my bailiwick.

Testatum capias.

GEORGE the Second, by the grace of God, of Great Britain, France, and Ireland King, Defender of the Faith, and so forth; to the sheriff of Berkshire, greeting. WE command you that you take Charles Long, late of Burford, gentleman, if he may be found in your bailiwick, and him safely keep, so that you may have his body before our justices at Westminster, on the morrow of the Holy Trinity, to answer to William Burton, gentleman, of a plea that he render to him two hundred pounds which he owes him and unjustly detains, as he saith; and whereupon our sheriff at Oxfordshire hath made a return to our justices at Westminster at a certain day now past, that

*xv.]

the *aforesaid Charles is not found in his bailiwick; and thereupon it is testified in our said court that the aforesaid Charles lurks, wanders, and runs about in your county. And have you there then this writ. WITNESS, Sir John Willes, Knight, at Westminster, the seventh day of May, in the twenty-eighth year of our reign.

Sheriff's return.
Cepi Corpus.

By virtue of this writ to me directed, I have taken the body of the within-named Charles Long; which I have ready at the day and place within contained, according as by this writ it is commanded me.

Or upon the Return of Non est inventus *upon the first* Capias, *the Plaintiff may sue out an* Alias *and a* Pluries, *and thence proceed to Outlawry; thus:*

No. III

GEORGE the Second, by the grace of God, of Great Britain, France, and Ireland King, Defender of the Faith, and so forth; to the sheriff of Oxfordshire, greeting. WE command you, as formerly we commanded you, that you take Charles Long, late of Burford, gentleman, if he may be found in your bailiwick, and him safely keep, so that you may have his body before our justices at Westminster, on the morrow of the Holy Trinity, to answer to William Burton, gentleman, of a plea that he render to him two hundred pounds which he owes him and unjustly detains, as he saith. And have you there then this writ. WITNESS, Sir John Willes, Knight, at Westminster, the seventh day of May, in the twenty-eighth year of our reign.

Alias capias.

The within-named Charles Long is not found in my bailiwick.

Sheriff's return.
Non est inventus.

GEORGE the Second, by the grace of God, of Great Britain, France, and Ireland King, Defender of the Faith, and so forth; to the sheriff of Oxfordshire, greeting. WE command you, as we have more than once commanded you, that you take Charles Long, late of Burford, gentleman, if he may be found in your bailiwick, and him safely keep, so that you may have his body before our justices at Westminster, from the day of the Holy Trinity, in three weeks, to answer to William Burton, gentleman, of a plea that he render to him two hundred pounds which he owes him and unjustly detains, as he saith. And have you there then this writ. WITNESS, Sir John Willes, Knight, at Westminster, the thirtieth day of May, in the twenty-eighth year of our reign.

Pluries capias.

The within-named Charles Long is not found in my bailiwick.

Sheriff's return.
Non est inventus.

*GEORGE the Second, by the grace of God, of Great Britain, France, and Ireland King, Defender of the Faith, and so forth; to the sheriff of Oxfordshire, greeting. WE command you that you cause Charles Long, late of Burford, gentleman, to be required from county court to county court, until, according to the law and custom of our realm of England, he be outlawed if he doth not appear; and if he doth appear, then take him and cause him to be safely kept, so that you may have his body before our justices at Westminster, on the morrow of All Souls, to answer to William Burton, gentleman, of a plea that he render to him two hundred pounds which he owes him and unjustly detains, as he saith; and whereupon you have returned to our justices at Westminster, from the day of the Holy Trinity, in three weeks, that he is not found in your bailiwick. And have you there then this writ. WITNESS, Sir John Willes, Knight, at Westminster, the eighteenth day of June, in the twenty-eighth year of our reign.

[*xvi.
Exigi facias.

By virtue of this writ to me directed at my county court, held at Oxford, in the county of Oxford, on Thursday the twenty-first day of June, in the twenty-ninth year of the reign of the Lord the King within written, the within-named Charles Long was required the first time and did not appear; and at my county court, held at Oxford aforesaid, on Thursday the twenty-fourth day of July, in the year aforesaid, the said Charles Long was required the second time and did not appear; and at my county court, held at Oxford aforesaid, on Thursday the twenty-first day of August, in the year aforesaid, the said Charles Long was required the third time and did not appear; and at my county court, held at Oxford aforesaid, on Thursday the eighteenth day of September, in the year aforesaid, the said Charles Long was required the fourth time and did not appear; and at my county court, held at Oxford aforesaid, on Thursday the sixteenth day of October, in the year aforesaid, the said Charles Long was required the fifth time and did not appear; therefore the said Charles Long, by the judgment of the coroners of the said Lord the King, of the county aforesaid, according to the law and custom of the kingdom of England, is outlawed.

Sheriff's return.
Primo exactus.

Secundo exactus.

Tertio exactus.

Quarto exactus.

Quinto exactus.

Ideo utlagatus.

GEORGE the Second, by the grace of God, of Great Britain, France, and Ireland King, Defender of the Faith, and so forth; to the sheriff of Oxfordshire, greeting. WHEREAS, by our writ, we have lately commanded you that you should cause Charles Long, late of Burford, gentleman, to be required from county court to county court, until, according to *the law and custom of our realm of England, he should be outlawed if he did not appear; and if he did appear, then that you should take him and cause him to be

Writ of proclamation.

[*xvii.

No. III.

safely kept, so that you might have his body before our justices at Westminster, on the morrow of All Souls, to answer to William Burton, gentleman, of a plea that he render to him two hundred pounds which he owes him and unjustly detains, as he saith: THEREFORE, we command you, by virtue of the statute in the thirty-first year of the Lady Elizabeth, late Queen of England, made and provided, that you cause the said Charles Long to be proclaimed, upon three several days, according to the form of that statute, (whereof one proclamation shall be made at or near the most usual door of the church of the parish wherein he inhabits,) that he render himself unto you; so that you may have his body before our justices at Westminster, at the day aforesaid, to answer the said William Burton of the plea aforesaid. And have you there then this writ. WITNESS, Sir John Willes, Knight, at Westminster, the eighteenth day of June, in the twenty-eighth year of our reign.

Sheriff's return.
Proclamari feci.

By virtue of this writ to me directed, at my county court held at Oxford, in the county of Oxford, on Thursday, the twenty-sixth day of June, in the twenty-ninth year of the reign of the Lord the King within written, I caused to be proclaimed the first time; and at the general quarter sessions of the peace, held at Oxford aforesaid, on Tuesday the fifteenth day of July in the year aforesaid, I caused to be proclaimed the second time; and at the most usual door of the church of Burford within written, on Sunday the third day of August in the year aforesaid, immediately after divine service, one month at the least before the within-named Charles Long was required the fifth time, I caused to be proclaimed the third time, that the said Charles Long should render himself unto me, as within it is commanded me.

Capias utlagatum.

GEORGE the Second, by the grace of God, of Great Britain, France, and Ireland King, Defender of the Faith, and so forth, to the sheriff of Berkshire, greeting. WE command you, that you omit not by reason of any liberty of your county, but that you take Charles Long, late of Burford, in the county of Oxford, gentleman, (being outlawed in the said county of Oxford, on Thursday the sixteenth day of October last past, at the suit of William Burton, gentleman, of a plea of debt, as the sheriff of Oxfordshire aforesaid returned to our justices at Westminster on the morrow of All Souls then next ensuing,) if the said Charles Long may be found in your bailiwick; and him safely keep, so that you may *have his body before our justices at Westminster from the day of St. Martin in fifteen days, to do and receive what our court shall consider concerning him in this behalf. WITNESS, Sir John Willes, Knight, at Westminster, the sixth day of November, in the twenty-ninth year of our reign.

*xviii.]

Sheriff's return.
Cepi corpus.

By virtue of this writ to me directed, I have taken the body of the within-named Charles Long; which I have ready at the day and place within contained, according as by this writ it is commanded me.

SECT. 3. (*d*) BILL OF MIDDLESEX, AND LATITAT THEREUPON IN THE COURT OF KING'S BENCH.

Bill of Middlesex for trespass.

Middlesex,
to wit.

THE SHERIFF is commanded that he take Charles Long, late of Burford, in the county of Oxford, if he may be found in his bailiwick, and him safely keep, so that he may have his body before the Lord the King at Westminster, on Wednesday next after fifteen days of Easter, to answer William Burton, gentleman, of a plea of trespass; [AND ALSO to a bill of the said William against the aforesaid Charles, for two hundred pounds of debt, according to the custom of the court of the said Lord the King, before the King himself to be exhibited;] and that he have there then this precept.

ac etiam in debt.

Sheriff's return.
Non est inventus.

The within-named Charles Long is not found in my bailiwick.

Latitat.

GEORGE the Second, by the grace of God, of Great Britain, France, and Ireland King, Defender of the Faith, and so forth; to the sheriff of Berkshire, greeting. WHEREAS we lately commanded our sheriff of Middlesex that he should take Charles Long, late of Burford, in the county of Oxford, if he might be found in his bailiwick, and him safely keep, so that he might

(*d*) Note, that sections 3 and 4 are the usual method of process to compel an appearance in the courts of King's Bench and Exchequer, in which the practice of those courts does principally differ from that of the court of Common Pleas, the subsequent stages of proceeding being nearly alike in them all.

be before us at Westminster, at a certain day now past, to answer unto No. III.
William Burton, gentleman, of a plea of trespass; [AND ALSO to a bill of the
said William against the aforesaid Charles, for two hundred pounds of debt, *Ac etiam.*
according to the custom of our court, before us to be exhibited;] and our said
sheriff of Middlesex at that day returned to us that the aforesaid Charles
was not found in his bailiwick; whereupon on the behalf of the aforesaid
William, in our court before us, it is sufficiently attested that the aforesaid
Charles lurks and runs about in your county: THEREFORE we command you
that you take him, if he may be found in *your bailiwick, and him safely [*xix.
keep, so that you may have his body before us at Westminster on Tuesday
next after five weeks of Easter, to answer the aforesaid William of the plea
[and bill] aforesaid; and have you there then this writ. WITNESS, Sir
Dudley Ryder, Knight, at Westminster, the eighteenth day of April, in the
twenty-eighth year of our reign.

By virtue of this writ to me directed, I have taken the body of the within- Sheriff's return.
named Charles Long, which I have ready at the day and place within con- *Cepi corpus.*
tained, according as by this writ it is commanded me.

SECT. 4. WRIT OF QUO MINUS IN THE EXCHEQUER.

GEORGE the Second, by the grace of God, of Great Britain, France, and
Ireland King, Defender of the Faith, and so forth; to the sheriff of Berkshire, greeting. WE command you that you omit not by reason of any
liberty of your county, but that you enter the same, and take Charles Long,
late of Burford, in the county of Oxford, gentleman, wheresoever he shall
be found in your bailiwick, and him safely keep, so that you may have his
body before the Barons of our Exchequer at Westminster on the morrow
of the Holy Trinity, to answer William Burton, our debtor of a plea, that
he render to him two hundred pounds which he owes him and unjustly detains, whereby he is the less able to satisfy us the debts which he owes us at
our said Exchequer, as he saith that he can reasonably show that the same
he ought to render: and have you there this writ. WITNESS, Sir Thomas
Parker, Knight, at Westminster, the sixth day of May, in the twenty-eighth
year of our reign.

By virtue of this writ to me directed, I have taken the body of the within- Sheriff's return
named Charles Long, which I have ready before the barons within written, *Cepi corpus.*
according as within it is commanded me.

SECT. 5. SPECIAL BAIL, ON THE ARREST OF THE DEFENDANT, PURSUANT TO THE TESTATUM CAPIAS, in page xiv.

KNOW ALL MEN, by these presents, that we, Charles Long, of Burford, in Bail-bond to the
the county of Oxford, gentleman, Peter Hamond, of Bix, in the said county, sheriff.
yeoman, and Edward Thomlinson, of Woodstock, in the said county, inn-
holder, are held and firmly bound to Christopher Jones, esquire, sheriff of
the county of Berks, in four hundred pounds of lawful money of Great
Britain, to be paid to the said sheriff, or his certain attorney, executors,
administrators, or assigns; for which payment well and truly to be made
we bind ourselves, and each of us by himself *for the whole and in gross, [*xx.
our and every of our heirs, executors, and administrators, firmly by these
presents, sealed with our seals. Dated the fifteenth day of May, in the
twenty-eighth year of the reign of our sovereign Lord GEORGE the Second,
by the grace of God King of Great Britain, France, and Ireland, Defender
of the Faith, and so forth, and in the year of our Lord one thousand seven
hundred and fifty-five.

THE CONDITION of this obligation is such, that if the above-bounden
Charles Long do appear before the justices of our sovereign Lord the King,
at Westminster, on the morrow of the Holy Trinity, to answer William
Burton, gentleman, of a plea of debt of two hundred pounds, then this obligation shall be void and of none effect, or else shall be and remain in full
force and virtue.

Sealed and delivered, being first duly   CHARLES LONG.   (L.S.)
    stamped, in the presence of   PETER HAMOND.   (L.S.)
            HENRY SHAW.   EDWARD THOMLINSON.   (L.S.)
        TIMOTHY GRIFFITH.

No. III.

Recognizance of bail before the commissioner.

You Charles Long do acknowledge to owe unto the plaintiff four hundred pounds, and you John Rose and Peter Hamond do severally acknowledge to owe unto the same person the sum of two hundred pounds apiece, to be levied upon your several goods and chattels, lands and tenements, UPON CONDITION that, if the defendant be condemned in the action, he shall pay the condemnation, or render himself a prisoner in the Fleet for the same; and, if he fail so to do, you John Rose and Peter Hamond do undertake to do it for him.

Trinity Term, 28 Geo. II.

Bail piece.

Berks, } ON a *Testatum Capias* from Oxfordshire against Charles Long, *to wit*. } late of Burford, in the county of Oxford, gentleman, returnable on the morrow of the Holy Trinity, at the suit of William Burton, of a plea of debt of two hundred pounds:

THE BAIL are, John Rose, of Witney, in the county of Oxford, esquire Peter Hamond, of Bix, in the said county, yeoman.

RICHARD PRICE, attorney }
for the defendant, }

The party himself in 400*l.*
Each of the bail in 200*l.*
Taken and acknowledged the twenty-eighth day of May, in the year of our Lord one thousand seven hundred and fifty-five, *de bene esse*, before me,
ROBERT GROVE,
one of the commissioners.

*xxi.]   *SECT. 6. THE RECORD AS REMOVED BY WRIT OF ERROR.

Writ of error.

THE LORD the King hath given in charge to his trusty and beloved Sir John Willes, Knight, his writ closed in these words:—GEORGE the Second, by the grace of God, of Great Britain, France, and Ireland King, Defender of the Faith, and so forth: to our trusty and beloved Sir John Willes, Knight, greeting. BECAUSE in the record and process, and also in the giving of judgment of the plaint, which was in our court before you and your fellows, our justices of the bench, by our writ between William Burton, gentleman, and Charles Long, late of Burford, in the county of Oxford, gentleman, of a certain debt of two hundred pounds, which the said William demands of the said Charles, manifest error hath intervened, to the great damage of him the said William, as we from his complaint are informed; we being willing that the error, if any there be, should be corrected in due manner, and that full and speedy justice should be done to the parties aforesaid in this behalf, do command you, that if judgment thereof be given, then under your seal you do distinctly and openly send the record and process of the plaint aforesaid, with all things concerning them, and this writ; so that we may have them from the day of Easter in fifteen days, wheresoever we shall then be in England; that the record and process aforesaid being inspected, we may cause to be done thereupon, for correcting that error, what of right and according to the law and custom of our realm of England ought to be done. WITNESS ourself at Westminster, the twelfth day of February, in the twenty-ninth year of our reign.

Chief-justice's return.

THE record and process whereof in the said writ mention above is made, follow in these words, to wit:—

The record.

PLEAS at Westminster before Sir John Willes, Knight, and his brethren, justices of the bench of the Lord the King at Westminster, of the term of the Holy Trinity, in the twenty-eighth year of the reign of the Lord GEORGE the Second, by the grace of God, of Great Britain, France, and Ireland King, Defender of the Faith, etc.

Writ.

Declaration, or count, on a bond.

Oxon, } CHARLES LONG, late of Burford, in the county aforesaid, gentle-
to wit. } man, was summoned to answer William Burton, of Yarnton in the said county, gentleman, of a plea that he render unto him two hundred pounds, which he owes him and unjustly detains, [as he saith.] AND WHEREUPON the said William, by Thomas Gough, his attorney, complains,

that whereas on the first day of December, in the year of our Lord *one thousand seven hundred and fifty-four, at Banbury in this county, the said Charles by his writing obligatory did acknowledge himself to be bound to the said William in the said sum of two hundred pounds of lawful money of Great Britain, to be paid to the said William whenever after the said Charles should be thereto required; nevertheless the said Charles (although often required) hath not paid to the said William the said sum of two hundred pounds, nor any part thereof, but hitherto altogether hath refused, and doth still refuse, to render the same; wherefore he saith that he is injured and hath damage to the value of ten pounds: and thereupon he brings suit, [and good proof.] AND he brings here into court the writing obligatory aforesaid; which testifies the debt aforesaid in form aforesaid; the date whereof is the day and year before mentioned. AND the aforesaid Charles, by Richard Price his attorney, comes and defends the force and injury when [and where it shall behoove him,] and craves oyer of the said writing obligatory, and it is read unto him [in the form aforesaid:] he likewise craves oyer of the condition of the said writing, and it is read unto him in these words: "The condition of this obligation is such, that if the above-bounden Charles Long, his heirs, executors, and administrators and every of them, shall and do from time to time, and at all times hereafter, well and truly stand to, obey, observe, fulfil, and keep the award, arbitrament, order, rule, judgment, final end, and determination of David Stiles, of Woodstock, in the said county, clerk, and Henry Bacon, of Woodstock aforesaid, gentleman, (arbitrators indifferently nominated and chosen by and between the said Charles Long and the above-named William Burton, to arbitrate, award, order, rule, judge, and determine of all and all manner of actions, cause or causes of action, suits, plaints, debts, duties, reckonings, accounts, controversies, trespasses, and demands whatsoever had, moved, or depending, or which might have been had, moved, or depending, by and between the said parties, for any matter, cause, or thing, from the beginning of the world until the day of the date hereof,) which the said arbitrators shall make and publish, of or in the premises, in writing under their hands and seals, or otherwise by word of mouth in the presence of two credible witnesses, on or before the first day of January next ensuing the date hereof; then this obligation to be void and of none effect, or else to be and remain in full force and virtue." WHICH being read and heard, the said Charles prays leave to imparl therein here until the octave of the Holy Trinity; and it is granted unto him. The same day is given to the said William Burton, here, &c. At which day, to wit, on the octave of the Holy Trinity, here come as well the said William Burton as the said Charles Long, by their attorneys aforesaid; and hereupon the said William *prays that the said Charles may answer to his writ and count aforesaid. And the aforesaid Charles defends the force and injury, when, &c., and saith that the said William ought not to have or maintain his said action against him; because he saith, that the said David Stiles and Henry Bacon, the arbitrators before named in the said condition, did not make any such award, arbitrament, order, rule, judgment, final end, or determination, of or in the premises above specified in the said condition, on or before the first day of January, in the condition aforesaid above mentioned, according to the form and effect of the said condition: and this he is ready to verify. Wherefore he prays judgment, whether the said William ought to have or maintain his said action thereof against him [and that he may go thereof without a day]. AND the aforesaid William saith that for any thing above alleged by the said Charles in pleadings he ought not to be precluded from having his said action thereof against him; because he saith, that after the making of the said writing obligatory, and before the said first day of January, to wit, on the twenty-sixth day of December, in the year aforesaid, at Banbury aforesaid, in the presence of two credible witnesses, namely, John Dew, of Chalbury, in the county aforesaid, and Richard Morris, of Wytham, in the county of Berks, the said arbitrators undertook the charge of the award, arbitrament, order, rule, judgment, final end, and determination aforesaid, of and in the premises specified in the condition aforesaid; and then and there made and published their award by word of mouth in manner and form following: that is to say, the said arbitrators did award, order, and adjudge that he the said Charles Long should forthwith pay to the said William Burton the sum of seventy-five pounds, and that thereupon all differences between them at the time of the making the said writing obligatory should finally cease and determine. And the said William further saith that although he afterwards, to

Side notes:

No. III.

[*xxii.

Profert in curas.

Defence.

Oyer prayed of the bond and condition,— viz., to perform an award.

Imparlance.

Continuance.

[*xxiii.

Plea: No such award.

Replication, setting forth award.

No. III

Protestando.

Demurrer.

*xxiv.]

Causes of demurrer.

Joinder in demurrer.

Continuances.

Opinion of the court.

Replication insufficient.

*xxv.]
Judgment for the defendant.
Querens nihil capiat per breve.
Amercement.
Costs.

Execution.
General error assigned.

wit, on the sixth day of January, in the year of our Lord one thousand seven hundred and fifty-five, at Banbury aforesaid, requested the said Charles to pay to him the said William the said seventy-five pounds, yet (by protestation that the said Charles hath not stood to, obeyed, observed, fulfilled, or kept any part of the said award, which by him the said Charles ought to have been stood to, obeyed, observed, fulfilled, and kept) for further plea therein he saith, that the said Charles the said seventy-five pounds to the said William hath not hitherto paid; and this he is ready to verify. Wherefore he prays judgment, and his debt aforesaid, together with his damages occasioned by the detention of the said debt, to be adjudged unto him, &c. AND the aforesaid Charles saith, that the plea aforesaid by him the said William in manner and form aforesaid above in his replication pleaded, and the matter in the same contained, are in no wise sufficient in *law for the said William to have or maintain his action aforesaid thereupon against him the said Charles; to which the said Charles hath no necessity, neither is he obliged, by the law of the land, in any manner to answer; and this he is ready to verify. Wherefore, for want of a sufficient replication in this behalf, the said Charles, as aforesaid, prays judgment, and that the aforesaid William may be precluded from having his action aforesaid thereupon against him, &c. AND the said Charles according to the form of the statute in that case made and provided, shows to the court here the causes of demurrer following, to wit: that it doth not appear, by the replication aforesaid, that the said arbitrators made the same award in the presence of two credible witnesses on or before the said first day of January, as they ought to have done, according to the form and effect of the condition aforesaid; and that the replication aforesaid is uncertain, insufficient, and wants form. AND the aforesaid William saith, that the plea aforesaid by him the said William in manner and form aforesaid above in his replication pleaded, and the matter in the same contained, are good and sufficient in law for the said William to have and maintain the said action of him the said William thereupon against the said Charles; which said plea, and the matter therein contained, the said William is ready to verify and prove as the court shall award: and because the aforesaid Charles hath not answered to that plea, nor hath he hitherto in any manner denied the same, the said William as before prays judgment, and his debt aforesaid, together with his damages occasioned by the detention of that debt, to be adjudged unto him, &c. AND BECAUSE the justices here will advise themselves of and upon the premises before they give judgment thereupon, a day is thereupon given to the parties aforesaid here, until the morrow of All Souls, to hear their judgment thereupon, for that the said justices here are not yet advised thereof. At which day here come as well the said Charles as the said William, by their said attorneys; and because the said justices here will farther advise themselves of and upon the premises before they give judgment thereupon, a day is farther given to the parties aforesaid here until the octave of Saint Hilary, to hear their judgment thereupon, for that the said justices here are not yet advised thereof. At which day here come as well the said William Burton as the said Charles Long, by their said attorneys. WHEREFORE, the record and matters aforesaid having been seen, and by the justices here fully understood, and all and singular the premises being examined, and mature deliberation being had thereupon; for that it seems to the said justices here that the said plea of the said William Burton before in his replication pleaded, and the matter therein contained, are not sufficient in law to have and maintain the action of the aforesaid William against the aforesaid Charles; THEREFORE IT IS CONSIDERED, that the aforesaid William *take nothing by his writ aforesaid, but that he and his pledges of prosecuting, to wit, John Doe and Richard Roe, be in mercy for his false complaint; and that the aforesaid Charles go thereof without a day, &c. AND IT IS FARTHER CONSIDERED, that the aforesaid Charles do recover against the aforesaid William eleven pounds and seven shillings, for his costs and charges by him about his defence in this behalf sustained, adjudged by the court here to the said Charles with his consent, according to the form of the statute in that case made and provided: and that the aforesaid Charles may have execution thereof, &c.

AFTERWARDS, to wit, on Wednesday next after fifteen days of Easter in this same term, before the Lord the King, at Westminster, comes the aforesaid William Burton, by Peter Manwaring, his attorney, and saith, that in the record and process aforesaid, and also in the giving of the judgment in the plaint aforesaid, it is manifestly erred in this, to wit, that the judgment aforesaid was given in form aforesaid for the said Charles Long against the aforesaid William Burton, where, by the law of the land, judgment should have been given for the said William Burton against the said Charles Long; and this he is ready to verify. AND the said William prays the writ of the said Lord the King, to warn the said Charles Long to be before the said Lord the King, to hear the record and process aforesaid; and it is granted unto him; by which the sheriff aforesaid is commanded that by good [and lawful men of his bailiwick] he cause the aforesaid Charles Long to know that he be before the Lord the King from the day of Easter in five weeks, wheresoever [he shall then be in England,] to hear the record and process aforesaid, if [it shall have happened that in the same any error shall have intervened;] and further [to do and receive what the court of the Lord the King shall consider in this behalf.] The same day is given to the aforesaid William Burton. AT WHICH DAY before the Lord the King, at Westminster, comes the aforesaid William Burton, by his attorney aforesaid; and the sheriff returns, that by virtue of the writ aforesaid to him directed he had caused the said Charles Long to know that he be before the Lord the King at the time aforesaid in the said writ contained, by John Den and Richard Fen, good, &c., as by the same writ was commanded him; which said Charles Long, according to the warning given him in this behalf, here cometh by Thomas Webb, his attorney. WHEREUPON the said William saith, that in the record and process aforesaid, and also in the giving of the judgment aforesaid, it is manifestly erred, alleging the error aforesaid by him in the form aforesaid alleged, and prays that the judgment aforesaid for the error aforesaid, and others, in the record and process aforesaid being may be reversed, annulled, and entirely for nothing esteemed, and that the said Charles *may rejoin to the errors aforesaid, and that the court of the said Lord the King here may proceed to the examination as well of the record and process aforesaid as of the matter aforesaid above for error assigned. AND the said Charles saith, that neither in the record and process aforesaid, nor in the giving of the judgment aforesaid, in any thing is there erred; and he prays in like manner that the court of the said Lord the King here may proceed to the examination as well of the record and process aforesaid as of the matters aforesaid above for error assigned. AND BECAUSE the court of the Lord the King here is not yet advised what judgment to give of and upon the premises, a day is thereof given to the parties aforesaid until the morrow of the Holy Trinity, before the Lord the King, wheresoever he shall then be in England, to hear their judgment of and upon the premises, for that the court of the Lord the King here is not yet advised thereof. At which day before the Lord the King, at Westminster, come the parties aforesaid by their attorneys aforesaid. WHEREUPON, as well the record and process aforesaid, and the judgment thereupon given, as the matters aforesaid by the said William above for error assigned, being seen, and by the court of the Lord the King here being fully understood, and mature deliberation being thereupon had, for that it appears to the court of the Lord the King here, that in the record and process aforesaid, and also in the giving of the judgment aforesaid, it is manifestly erred, THEREFORE IT IS CONSIDERED that the judgment aforesaid, for the error aforesaid, and others, in the record and process aforesaid, be reversed, annulled, and entirely for nothing esteemed; and that the aforesaid William recover against the aforesaid Charles his debt aforesaid, and also fifty pounds for his damages which he hath sustained, as well on occasion of the detention of the said debt, as for his costs and charges unto which he hath been put about his suit in this behalf, to the said William with his consent by the court of the Lord the King here adjudged. And the said Charles in mercy.

Marginalia:
No. III.

Writ of *scire facias*, to hear errors.

Sheriff's return. *Scire feci.*

Error as signed afresh.

[*xxvi.

Rejoinder. *In nullo est erratum.*

Continuance.

Opinion of the court.

Judgment of the Common Pleas reversed. Judgment for the plaintiff.

Costs.

Defendant amerced.

SECT. 7. PROCESS OF EXECUTION.

GEORGE the Second, by the grace of God, of Great Britain, France, and Ireland King, Defender of the Faith, and so forth, to the sheriff of Oxfordshire, greeting. WE command you that you take Charles Long, late of Burford, gentleman, if he may be found in your bailiwick, and him safely keep, so that you may have his body before us in three weeks from the day of the Holy Trinity, wheresoever we shall then be in England, to satisfy William Burton for two hundred pounds debt, which the said William Burton hath lately recovered against him in our court before us, and also fifty pounds, which were *adjudged in our said court before us to the said William Burton for his damages which he hath sustained, as well by occasion of the detention of the said debt as for his costs and charges to which he hath been put about his suit in this behalf, whereof the said Charles Long is convicted,

Marginalia:
Writ of *capias ad satisfaciendum.*

[*xxvii.

No. III.

as it appears to us of record; and have you there then this writ. WITNESS Sir Thomas Denison, (e) Knight, at Westminster, the nineteenth day of June, in the twenty-ninth year of our reign.

Sheriff's return.
Cepi corpus.

By virtue of this writ to me directed, I have taken the body of the within-named Charles Long, which I have ready before the Lord the King at Westminster, at the day within written, as within it is commanded me.

Writ of *fieri facias.*

GEORGE the Second, by the grace of God, of Great Britain, France, and Ireland King, Defender of the Faith, and so forth, to the sheriff of Oxfordshire, greeting. WE command you that of the goods and chattels within your bailiwick of Charles Long, late of Burford, gentleman, you cause to be made two hundred pounds debt, which William Burton lately in our court before us at Westminster hath recovered against him, and also fifty pounds, which were adjudged in our court before us to the said William for his damages which he hath sustained, as well by occasion of the detention of his said debt as for his costs and charges to which he hath been put about his suit in this behalf, whereof the said Charles Long is convicted, as it appears to us of record; and have that money before us in three weeks from the day of the Holy Trinity, wheresoever we shall then be in England, to render to the said William of his debt and damages aforesaid; and have there then this writ. WITNESS Sir Thomas Denison, Knight, at Westminster, the nineteenth day of June, in the twenty-ninth year of our reign.

Sheriff's return.
Fieri feci.

By virtue of this writ to me directed, I have caused to be made of the goods and chattels of the within-written Charles Long two hundred and fifty pounds, which I have ready before the Lord the King at Westminster, at the day within written, as it is within commanded me.

(e) The senior puisne justice, there being no chief-justice that term.

www.bookjungle.com *email: sales@bookjungle.com fax: 630-214-0564 mail: Book Jungle PO Box 2226 Champaign, IL 61825*

The Two Babylons
Alexander Hislop

You may be surprised to learn that many traditions of Roman Catholicism in fact don't come from Christ's teachings but from an ancient Babylonian "Mystery" religion that was centered on Nimrod, his wife Semiramis, and a child Tammuz. This book shows how this ancient religion transformed itself as it incorporated Christ into its teachings....

Religion/History   Pages:358

ISBN: *1-59462-010-5*   MSRP *$22.95*

The Power Of Concentration
Theron Q. Dumont

It is of the utmost value to learn how to concentrate. To make the greatest success of anything you must be able to concentrate your entire thought upon the idea you are working on. The person that is able to concentrate utilizes all constructive thoughts and shuts out all destructive ones...

Self Help/Inspirational   Pages:196

ISBN: *1-59462-141-1*   MSRP *$14.95*

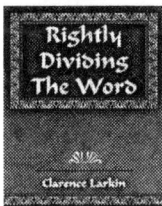

Rightly Dividing The Word
Clarence Larkin

The "Fundamental Doctrines" of the Christian Faith are clearly outlined in numerous books on Theology, but they are not available to the average reader and were mainly written for students. The Author has made it the work of his ministry to preach the "Fundamental Doctrines." To this end he has aimed to express them in the simplest and clearest manner..

Religion   Pages:352

ISBN: *1-59462-334-1*   MSRP *$23.45*

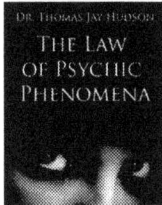

The Law of Psychic Phenomena
Thomson Jay Hudson

"I do not expect this book to stand upon its literary merits; for if it is unsound in principle, felicity of diction cannot save it, and if sound, homeliness of expression cannot destroy it. My primary object in offering it to the public is to assist in bringing Psychology within the domain of the exact sciences. That this has never been accomplished..."

New Age   Pages:420

ISBN: *1-59462-124-1*   MSRP *$29.95*

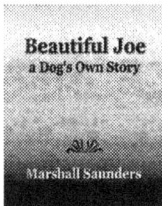

Beautiful Joe
Marshall Saunders

When Marshall visited the Moore family in 1892, she discovered Joe, a dog they had nursed back to health from his previous abusive home to live a happy life. So moved was she, that she wrote this classic masterpiece which won accolades and was recognized as a heartwarming symbol for humane animal treatment...

Fiction   Pages:256

ISBN: *1-59462-261-2*   MSRP *$18.45*

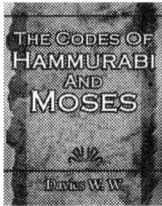

The Codes Of Hammurabi And
Moses - W. W. Davies

The discovery of the Hammurabi Code is one of the greatest achievements of archaeology, and is of paramount interest, not only to the student of the Bible, but also to all those interested in ancient history...

Religion   Pages:132

ISBN: *1-59462-338-4*   MSRP *$12.95*

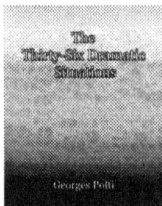

The Thirty-Six Dramatic Situations
Georges Polti

An incredibly useful guide for aspiring authors and playwrights. This volume categorizes every dramatic situation which could occur in a story and describes them in a list of 36 situations. A great aid to help inspire or formalize the creative writing process...

Self Help/Reference   Pages:204

ISBN: *1-59462-134-9*   MSRP *$15.95*

QTY

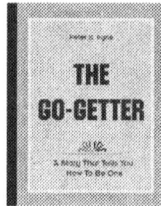

The Go-Getter
Kyne B. Peter

The Go Getter is the story of William Peck. He was a war veteran and amputee who will not be refused what he wants. Peck not only fights to find employment but continually proves himself more than competent at the many difficult test that are throw his way in the course of his early days with the Ricks Lumber Company...

Business/Self Help/Inspirational   Pages:68

ISBN: *1-59462-186-1*   MSRP *$8.95*

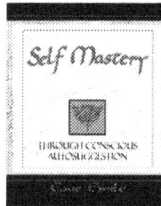

Self Mastery
Emile Coue

Emile Coue came up with novel way to improve the lives of people. He was a pharmacist by trade and often often saw ailing people. This lead him to develop autosuggestion, a form of self-hypnosis. At the time his theories weren't popular but over the years evidence is mounting that he was indeed right all along...

New Age/Self Help   Pages:98

ISBN: *1-59462-189-6*   MSRP *$7.95*

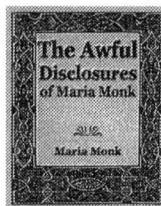

The Awful Disclosures Of
Maria Monk

"I cannot banish the scenes and characters of this book from my memory. To me it can never appear like an amusing fable, or lose its interest and importance. The story is one which is continually before me, and must return fresh to my mind with painful emotions as long as I live..."

Religion   Pages:232

ISBN: *1-59462-160-8*   MSRP *$17.95*

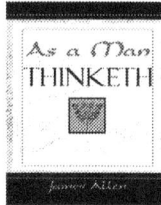

As a Man Thinketh
James Allen

"This little volume (the result of meditation and experience) is not intended as an exhaustive treatise on the much-written-upon subject of the power of thought. It is suggestive rather than explanatory, its object being to stimulate men and women to the discovery and perception of the truth that by virtue of the thoughts which they choose and encourage..."

Inspirational/Self Help   Pages:80

ISBN: *1-59462-231-0*   MSRP *$9.45*

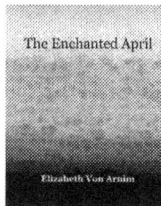

The Enchanted April
Elizabeth Von Arnim

It began in a woman's club in London on a February afternoon, an uncomfortable club, and a miserable afternoon when Mrs. Wilkins, who had come down from Hampstead to shop and had lunched at her club, took up The Times from the table in the smoking-room...

Fiction   Pages:368

ISBN: *1-59462-150-0*   MSRP *$23.45*

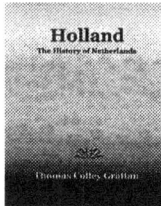

Holland - The History Of Netherlands
Thomas Colley Grattan

Thomas Grattan was a prestigious writer from Dublin who served as British Consul to the US. Among his works is an authoritative look at the history of Holland. A colorful and interesting look at history....

History/Politics   Pages:408

ISBN: *1-59462-137-3*   MSRP *$26.95*

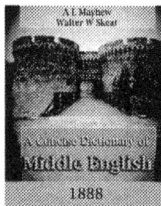

A Concise Dictionary of Middle English
A. L. Mayhew
Walter W. Skeat

The present work is intended to meet, in some measure, the requirements of those who wish to make some study of Middle-English, and who find a difficulty in obtaining such assistance as will enable them to find out the meanings and etymologies of the words most essential to their purpose...

Reference/History   Pages:332

ISBN: *1-59462-119-5*   MSRP *$29.95*

QTY

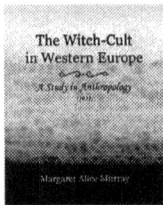

The Witch-Cult in Western Europe
Margaret Murray
QTY

The mass of existing material on this subject is so great that I have not attempted to make a survey of the whole of European "Witchcraft" but have confined myself to an intensive study of the cult in Great Britain. In order, however, to obtain a clearer understanding of the ritual and beliefs I have had recourse to French and Flemish sources...

Occult   Pages:308

ISBN: *1-59462-126-8*   **MSRP** *$22.45*

The Science Of Psychic Healing
Yogi Ramacharaka

This book is not a book of theories it deals with facts. Its author regards the best of theories as but working hypotheses to be used only until better ones present themselves. The "fact" is the principal thing the essential thing to uncover which the tool, theory, is used...

New Age/Health   Pages:180

ISBN: *1-59462-140-3*   **MSRP** *$13.95*

Bible Myths
Thomas Doane

In pursuing the study of the Bible Myths, facts pertaining thereto, in a condensed form, seemed to be greatly needed, and nowhere to be found. Widely scattered through hundreds of ancient and modern volumes, most of the contents of this book may indeed be found; but any previous attempt to trace exclusively the myths and legends...

Religion/History   Pages:644

ISBN: *1-59462-163-2*   **MSRP** *$38.95*

Tertium Organum
P. D. Ouspensky

A truly mind expanding writing that combines science with mysticism with unprecedented elegance. He presents the world we live in as a multi dimensional world and time as a motion through this world. But this isn't a cold and purely analytical explanation but a masterful presentation filled with similes and analogies...

New Age   Pages:356

ISBN: *1-59462-205-1*   **MSRP** *$23.95*

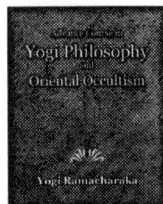

Advance Course in Yogi Philosophy
Yogi Ramacharaka

"The twelve lessons forming this volume were originally issued in the shape of monthly lessons, known as "The Advanced Course in Yogi Philosophy and Oriental Occultism" during a period of twelve months beginning with October, 1904, and ending September, 1905."

Philosophy/Inspirational/Self Help   Pages:340

ISBN: *1-59462-229-9*   **MSRP** *$22.95*

Ambassador Morgenthau's Story
Henry Morgenthau

"By this time the American people have probably become convinced that the Germans deliberately planned the conquest of the world. Yet they hesitate to convict on circumstantial evidence and for this reason all eye witnesses to this, the greatest crime in modern history, should volunteer their testimony..."

History   Pages:472

ISBN: *1-59462-244-2*   **MSRP** *$29.95*

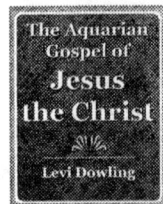

The Aquarian Gospel of Jesus the Christ
Levi Dowling

A retelling of Jesus' story which tells us what happened during the twenty year gap left by the Bible's New Testament. It tells of his travels to the far-east where he studied with the masters and fought against the rigid caste system. This book has enjoyed a resurgence in modern America and provides spiritual insight with charm. Its influences can be seen throughout the Age of Aquarius.

Religion   Pages:264

ISBN: *1-59462-321-X*   **MSRP** *$18.95*

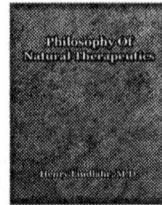

Philosophy Of Natural Therapeutics
Henry Lindlahr
QTY

We invite the earnest cooperation in this great work of all those who have awakened to the necessity for more rational living and for radical reform in healing methods...

Health/Philosophy/Self Help   Pages:552

ISBN: *1-59462-132-2*   **MSRP** *$34.95*

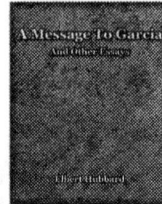

A Message to Garcia
Elbert Hubbard

This literary trifle, A Message to Garcia, was written one evening after supper, in a single hour. It was on the Twenty-second of February, Eighteen Hundred Ninety-nine, Washington's Birthday, and we were just going to press with the March Philistine...

New Age/Fiction   Pages:92

ISBN: *1-59462-144-6*   **MSRP** *$9.95*

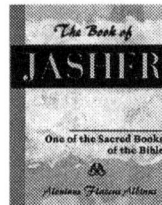

The Book of Jasher
Alcuinus Flaccus Albinus

The Book of Jasher is an historical religious volume that many consider as a missing holy book from the Old Testament. Particularly studied by the Church of Later Day Saints and historians, it covers the history of the world from creation until the period of Judges in Israel. It's authenticity is bolstered due to a reference to the Book of Jasher in the Bible in Joshua 10:13

Religion/History   Pages:276

ISBN: *1-59462-197-7*   **MSRP** *$18.95*

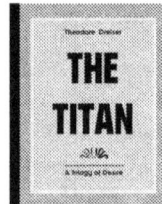

The Titan
Theodore Dreiser

"When Frank Algernon Cowperwood emerged from the Eastern District Penitentiary, in Philadelphia he realized that the old life he had lived in that city since boyhood was ended. His youth was gone, and with it had been lost the great business prospects of his earlier manhood. He must begin again..."

Fiction   Pages:564

ISBN: *1-59462-220-5*   **MSRP** *$33.95*

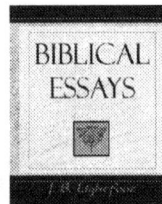

Biblical Essays
J. B. Lightfoot

About one-third of the present volume has already seen the light. The opening essay "On the Internal Evidence for the Authenticity and Genuineness of St John's Gospel" was published in the "Expositor" in the early months of 1890, and has been reprinted since...

Religion/History   Pages:480

ISBN: *1-59462-238-8*   **MSRP** *$30.95*

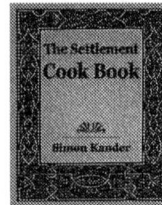

The Settlement Cook Book
Simon Kander

A legacy from the civil war, this book is a classic "American charity cookbook," which was used for fundraisers starting in Milwaukee. While it has transformed over the years, this printing provides great recipes from American history. Over two million copies have been sold. This volume contains a rich collection of recipes from noted chefs and hostesses of the turn of the century...

How-to   Pages:472

ISBN: *1-59462-256-6*   **MSRP** *$29.95*

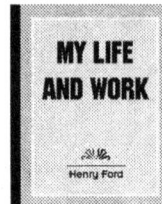

My Life and Work
Henry Ford

Henry Ford revolutionized the world with his implementation of mass production for the Model T automobile. Gain valuable business insight into his life and work with his own auto-biography... "We have only started on our development of our country we have not as yet, with all our talk of wonderful progress, done more than scratch the surface. The progress has been wonderful enough but..."

Biographies/History/Business   Pages:300

ISBN: *1-59462-198-5*   **MSRP** *$21.95*

Bringing Classics to Life

BOOK JUNGLE

www.bookjungle.com *email: sales@bookjungle.com fax: 630-214-0564 mail: Book Jungle PO Box 2226 Champaign, IL 61825*

QTY

☐	**The Rosicrucian Cosmo-Conception Mystic Christianity** by *Max Heindel* ISBN: *1-59462-188-8* **$38.95**
	The Rosicrucian Cosmo-conception is not dogmatic, neither does it appeal to any other authority than the reason of the student. It is not controversial, but is sent forth in the hope that it may help to clear... New Age Religion Pages 646
☐	**Abandonment To Divine Providence** by *Jean-Pierre de Caussade* ISBN: *1-59462-228-0* **$25.95**
	"The Rev. Jean Pierre de Caussade was one of the most remarkable spiritual writers of the Society of Jesus in France in the 18th Century. His death took place at Toulouse in 1751. His works have gone through many editions and have been republished... Inspirational/Religion Pages 400
☐	**Mental Chemistry** by *Charles Haanel* ISBN: *1-59462-192-6* **$23.95**
	Mental Chemistry allows the change of material conditions by combining and appropriately utilizing the power of the mind. Much like applied chemistry creates something new and unique out of careful combinations of chemicals the mastery of mental chemistry... New Age Pages 354
☐	**The Letters of Robert Browning and Elizabeth Barret Barrett 1845-1846 vol II** ISBN: *1-59462-193-4* **$35.95**
	by *Robert Browning* and *Elizabeth Barrett* Biographies Pages 596
☐	**Gleanings In Genesis (volume I)** by *Arthur W. Pink* ISBN: *1-59462-130-6* **$27.45**
	Appropriately has Genesis been termed "the seed plot of the Bible" for in it we have, in germ form, almost all of the great doctrines which are afterwards fully developed in the books of Scripture which follow... Religion Inspirational Pages 420
☐	**The Master Key** by *L. W. de Laurence* ISBN: *1-59462-001-6* **$30.95**
	In no branch of human knowledge has there been a more lively increase of the spirit of research during the past few years than in the study of Psychology, Concentration and Mental Discipline. The requests for authentic lessons in Thought Control, Mental Discipline and... New Age/Business Pages 422
☐	**The Lesser Key Of Solomon Goetia** by *L. W. de Laurence* ISBN: *1-59462-092-X* **$9.95**
	This translation of the first book of the "Lemegton" which is now for the first time made accessible to students of Talismanic Magic was done, after careful collation and edition, from numerous Ancient Manuscripts in Hebrew, Latin, and French... New Age Occult Pages 92
☐	**Rubaiyat Of Omar Khayyam** by *Edward Fitzgerald* ISBN: *1-59462-332-5* **$13.95**
	Edward Fitzgerald, whom the world has already learned, in spite of his own efforts to remain within the shadow of anonymity, to look upon as one of the rarest poets of the century, was born at Bredfield, in Suffolk, on the 31st of March, 1809. He was the third son of John Purcell... Music Pages 172
☐	**Ancient Law** by *Henry Maine* ISBN: *1-59462-128-4* **$29.95**
	The chief object of the following pages is to indicate some of the earliest ideas of mankind, as they are reflected in Ancient Law, and to point out the relation of those ideas to modern thought. Religion/History Pages 452
☐	**Far-Away Stories** by *William J. Locke* ISBN: *1-59462-129-2* **$19.45**
	"Good wine needs no bush, but a collection of mixed vintages does. And this book is just such a collection. Some of the stories I do not want to remain buried for ever in the museum files of dead magazine-numbers an author's not unpardonable vanity..." Fiction Pages 272
☐	**Life of David Crockett** by *David Crockett* ISBN: *1-59462-250-7* **$27.45**
	"Colonel David Crockett was one of the most remarkable men of the times in which he lived. Born in humble life, but gifted with a strong will, an indomitable courage, and unremitting perseverance... Biographies/New Age Pages 424
☐	**Lip-Reading** by *Edward Nitchie* ISBN: *1-59462-206-X* **$25.95**
	Edward B. Nitchie, founder of the New York School for the Hard of Hearing, now the Nitchie School of Lip-Reading, Inc, wrote "LIP-READING Principles and Practice". The development and perfecting of this meritorious work on lip-reading was an undertaking... How-to Pages 400
☐	**A Handbook of Suggestive Therapeutics, Applied Hypnotism, Psychic Science** ISBN: *1-59462-214-0* **$24.95**
	by *Henry Munro* Health New Age/Health Self-help Pages 376
☐	**A Doll's House: and Two Other Plays** by *Henrik Ibsen* ISBN: *1-59462-112-8* **$19.95**
	Henrik Ibsen created this classic when in revolutionary 1848 Rome. Introducing some striking concepts in playwriting for the realist genre, this play has been studied the world over. Fiction/Classics/Plays 308
☐	**The Light of Asia** by *sir Edwin Arnold* ISBN: *1-59462-204-3* **$13.95**
	In this poetic masterpiece, Edwin Arnold describes the life and teachings of Buddha. The man who was to become known as Buddha to the world was born as Prince Gautama of India but he rejected the worldly riches and abandoned the reigns of power when... Religion/History/Biographies Pages 170
☐	**The Complete Works of Guy de Maupassant** by *Guy de Maupassant* ISBN: *1-59462-157-8* **$16.95**
	"For days and days, nights and nights, I had dreamed of that first kiss which was to consecrate our engagement, and I knew not on what spot I should put my lips..." Fiction/Classics Pages 240
☐	**The Art of Cross-Examination** by *Francis L. Wellman* ISBN: *1-59462-309-0* **$26.95**
	Written by a renowned trial lawyer, Wellman imparts his experience and uses case studies to explain how to use psychology to extract desired information through questioning. How-to/Science/Reference Pages 408
☐	**Answered or Unanswered?** by *Louisa Vaughan* ISBN: *1-59462-248-5* **$10.95**
	Miracles of Faith in China Religion Pages 112
☐	**The Edinburgh Lectures on Mental Science (1909)** by *Thomas* ISBN: *1-59462-008-3* **$11.95**
	This book contains the substance of a course of lectures recently given by the writer in the Queen Street Hall, Edinburgh. Its purpose is to indicate the Natural Principles governing the relation between Mental Action and Material Conditions... New Age Psychology Pages 148
☐	**Ayesha** by *H. Rider Haggard* ISBN: *1-59462-301-5* **$24.95**
	Verily and indeed it is the unexpected that happens! Probably if there was one person upon the earth from whom the Editor of this, and of a certain previous history, did not expect to hear again... Classics Pages 380
☐	**Ayala's Angel** by *Anthony Trollope* ISBN: *1-59462-352-X* **$29.95**
	The two girls were both pretty, but Lucy who was twenty-one who supposed to be simple and comparatively unattractive, whereas Ayala was credited, as her Bombwhat romantic name might show, with poetic charm and a taste for romance. Ayala when her father died was nineteen... Fiction Pages 484
☐	**The American Commonwealth** by *James Bryce* ISBN: *1-59462-286-8* **$34.45**
	An interpretation of American democratic political theory. It examines political mechanics and society from the perspective of Scotsman James Bryce Politics Pages 572
☐	**Stories of the Pilgrims** by *Margaret P. Pumphrey* ISBN: *1-59462-116-0* **$17.95**
	This book explores pilgrims religious oppression in England as well as their escape to Holland and eventual crossing to America on the Mayflower, and their early days in New England... History Pages 268

BOOK JUNGLE

Bringing Classics to Life

www.bookjungle.com *email: sales@bookjungle.com fax: 630-214-0564 mail: Book Jungle PO Box 2226 Champaign, IL 61825*

QTY

The Fasting Cure *by Sinclair Upton*   ISBN: *1-59462-222-1*   **$13.95**
In the Cosmopolitan Magazine for May, 1910, and in the Contemporary Review (London) for April, 1910, I published an article dealing with my experiences in fasting. I have written a great many magazine articles, but never one which attracted so much attention... New Age/Self Help/Health Pages 164

Hebrew Astrology *by Sepharial*   ISBN: *1-59462-308-2*   **$13.45**
In these days of advanced thinking it is a matter of common observation that we have left many of the old landmarks behind and that we are now pressing forward to greater heights and to a wider horizon than that which represented the mind-content of our progenitors... Astrology Pages 144

Thought Vibration or The Law of Attraction in the Thought World   ISBN: *1-59462-127-6*   **$12.95**
by William Walker Atkinson   *Psychology/Religion Pages 144*

Optimism *by Helen Keller*   ISBN: *1-59462-108-X*   **$15.95**
Helen Keller was blind, deaf, and mute since 19 months old, yet famously learned how to overcome these handicaps, communicate with the world, and spread her lectures promoting optimism. An inspiring read for everyone... Biographies/Inspirational Pages 84

Sara Crewe *by Frances Burnett*   ISBN: *1-59462-360-0*   **$9.45**
In the first place, Miss Minchin lived in London. Her home was a large, dull, tall one, in a large, dull square, where all the houses were alike, and all the sparrows were alike, and where all the door-knockers made the same heavy sound... Childrens Classic Pages 88

The Autobiography of Benjamin Franklin *by Benjamin Franklin*   ISBN: *1-59462-135-7*   **$24.95**
The Autobiography of Benjamin Franklin has probably been more extensively read than any other American historical work, and no other book of its kind has had such ups and downs of fortune. Franklin lived for many years in England, where he was agent... Biographies/History Pages 332

Name	
Email	
Telephone	
Address	
City, State ZIP	

☐ **Credit Card**   ☐ **Check / Money Order**

Credit Card Number	
Expiration Date	
Signature	

Please Mail to: Book Jungle
PO Box 2226
Champaign, IL 61825
or Fax to: 630-214-0564

ORDERING INFORMATION

web: *www.bookjungle.com*
email: *sales@bookjungle.com*
fax: *630-214-0564*
mail: *Book Jungle PO Box 2226 Champaign, IL 61825*
or PayPal *to sales@bookjungle.com*

Please contact us for bulk discounts

DIRECT-ORDER TERMS

20% Discount if You Order Two or More Books
Free Domestic Shipping!
Accepted: Master Card, Visa, Discover, American Express

www.bookjungle.com *email: sales@bookjungle.com fax: 630-214-0564 mail: Book Jungle PO Box 2226 Champaign, IL 61825*

www.ingramcontent.com/pod-product-compliance
Lightning Source LLC
Chambersburg PA
CBHW082125210326
41599CB00031B/5878